W9-BSI-812

"Berg's whole narrative is first-rate—filled with humor and feeling. Max would have published it in a minute."

—*Newsweek*

"A labor of love, one pursued by Berg with a single-minded devotion . . . The result, a long and comprehensive but never tedious book, completely justifies all the effort . . . A very large accomplishment."

—Jonathan Yardley, *The Miami Herald*

"A fully achieved biography of a man whose career and life were marvels of self-effacement. It gives a wealth of insight into the creative process."

—Peter Davison, *The New York Times Book Review*

"A welcome biography . . . a definitive work."

—*St. Louis Globe-Democrat*

"A. Scott Berg's biography is, surprisingly, the first major study of this legendary figure, and it would thus be welcome for that reason alone. But this superb book is so meticulously researched, so richly detailed, so beautifully 'cultured,' that it will undoubtedly become an indispensable account of modern literary life in America, as well as a highly rewarding portrait of a man previously hidden behind the scenes . . . While lamenting a lack of space to describe fully the incredibly fascinating detail that marks so much of this outstanding book, we must recommend A. Scott Berg's biography of Max Perkins as one of the most important, most readable books of the year."

—*The Dallas Morning News*

"Beautifully written . . . an exciting portrait of an era."

—Howard Kissell, *Women's Wear Daily*

"A delightful biography, rich in literary anecdotes, and a mine of advice for writers and editors."

—*Publishers Weekly*

"It is a pity that Perkins could not see the manuscript of his biography. He enjoyed finding promising young writers, and Berg, 28, is one of that small group . . . Although Perkins would have been embarrassed by the attention, Berg's tribute would have touched him."

—*Time*

"A. Scott Berg's *Max Perkins: Editor of Genius* seems such a natural that it makes you wonder why no one ever thought of writing such a book before. [Among] the virtues of this biography is that Perkins emerges from the shadows . . . The details enrich the legend."

—Christopher Lehmann-Haupt, *The New York Times*

"Max Perkins was the best of the best. This book brings him back alive."

—Erskine Caldwell

continued on next page...

"A book about Maxwell Perkins? Of course! Why didn't someone think of it before? . . . Berg has done very well . . . It's a fascinating and illuminating story."
—*Chicago Sun-Times*

"As complete a Max Perkins as we will ever need. It's an extraordinary vivid portrait . . . Berg documents the Perkins-Wolfe season in hell as no one else ever has."
—Webster Schott, *The Washington Post Book World*

"All his life and since his death, Max Perkins has remained a kind of shadow figure . . . but now, with A. Scott Berg's comprehensive and readable biography, he's sure to come into his own . . . There's not a speck of pedantry in Berg's book and I for one thank him for it."
—Judson Hand, *New York Daily News*

"Berg has done a fine job of assembling and organizing a vast amount of fascinating material."
—*St. Louis Post-Dispatch*

"Though he is not of Perkins's generation, Berg has a real feel for it and for Perkins, and does justice to him and his geniuses."
—*Wilmington Sunday News Journal*

"Berg makes the major revelation of a long, discreet, and (perhaps regretfully) platonic love affair between Max and Elizabeth Lemmon . . . Their correspondence enriches the biography immeasurably . . . This is a significant book."
—Larry Swindell, *The Philadelphia Inquirer*

"Extraordinary . . . Berg brings Perkins and his writers to life . . . With access to the most intimate and detailed files from the publishers, Berg has drawn together a massive book that Perkins would have been proud to edit. There is a good story about someone on nearly every page."
—*The Houston Post*

"Berg displays immense talent in his writing, keeping it dramatic, suspenseful and lively, yet never losing sight of the fact that this is a serious work. For those who are avid readers of biographies, this book will come as a delightful and rewarding surprise. For those students of literature and those who labor in it, the comments and writings of Perkins will stand out as beacons of light in a sometimes darkened world . . . With this book alone Berg now appears to be one of the major new literary talents of the last quarter of the 20th century."
—*San Diego Union*

"Wolfe, Fitzgerald and Hemingway scholars will find this book a valued source of new information and a highly readable, warm and enjoyable biography. Those who are not scholars will find this biography flows like a novel." —*The Charlotte Observer*

"One reads these pages with awe and admiration for both their subject and for the remarkable young biographer." —*Baltimore Evening Sun*

"Perkins turns out to have been as fascinating, dark, complex, and sad as any of his golden boys. A lovely book about the age of giants and the extraordinary man in the shadows behind them." —Russell Baker

"A. Scott Berg, who came to Perkins through an early enthusiasm for Fitzgerald, has gone deeply into his subject, and done so with attention to detail and something like love . . . Superb biography . . . Perkins's fruitful and tortuous relationship with Wolfe is brilliantly described." —*Washington Star*

"This is the first major study of Perkins, and Berg has done a masterful job . . . both a fascinating chronicle of Perkins's contribution to American literature and a collection of wonderful anecdotes . . . a fine book." —*Newsday*

"A sympathetic, full-bodied treatment of Perkins." —*Richmond News Leader*

"Nothing previously published will prepare the reader for this stunning new biography. Berg's depth of research is simply astounding. He not only brings Perkins vividly on stage, but also all the major figures in an exciting and pivotal era of American letters . . . a sweeping, landmark biography . . . superb." —*Fort Worth Star-Telegram*

"Magnificent . . . Berg vividly demonstrates how Perkins changed the conception of an editor's function and how he thereby came to influence American literary taste as no other man for 30 years." —*Boston Herald American*

"Packed with diverting anecdotes." —*The New Yorker*

"Splendid . . . fills a gaping void in the history of American literature in the first half of this century . . . His greatest achievement, aside from showing us exactly how a truly great editor functioned, is to remind those of us who love books even remotely as much as Perkins, what we owe him." —*Kansas City Star*

"[Berg] has marshalled much material to bring the editor to life, to prove that lonely, hard-drinking, eccentric Perkins was, as the book's subtitle says, 'an editor of genius.'" —Doris Grumbach, *Saturday Review*

Maxwell E. Perkins

MAX PERKINS

Editor of Genius / A. Scott Berg

RIVERHEAD BOOKS, NEW YORK

Most Riverhead Books are available at special quantity discounts for bulk purchases for sales promotions, premiums, fund-raising, or educational use. Special books, or book excerpts, can also be created to fit specific needs.

For details, write: Special Markets, The Berkley Publishing Group, 375 Hudson Street, New York, New York 10014.

Riverhead Books
Published by The Berkley Publishing Group
A division of Penguin Putnam Inc.
375 Hudson Street
New York, New York 10014

Copyright © A. Scott Berg, 1978.
Reprinted by arrangement with Dutton Signet, a division of Penguin Books USA, Inc.
A continuation of copyright credits appears on page 499.
Cover illustration by A. Birnbaum © 1944 The New Yorker Magazine Inc. All rights reserved.

All rights reserved. This book, or parts thereof, may not be reproduced
in any form without permission.

E. P. Dutton edition published 1978
First Riverhead trade paperback edition: June 1997

The Penguin Putnam Inc. World Wide Web site address is
http://www.penguinputnam.com

Library of Congress Cataloging-in-Publication Data

Berg, A. Scott (Andrew Scott)
     Max Perkins, editor of genius / A. Scott Berg.—1st Riverhead
trade pbk. ed.
         p.   cm.
     Originally published: New York : Dutton, ©1978.
     Includes bibliographical references and index.
     ISBN 1-57322-621-1
     1. Perkins, Maxwell E. (Maxwell Evarts), 1884–1947.   2. Editors—
United States—Biography.   3. Book editors—United States—
Biography.   I. Title.
PN149.9.P4B4   1997
070.4'1'092—dc21
     [B]   96-52584
                                                            CIP

Printed in the United States of America

10   9   8   7   6   5   4

To my friend
Carlos Baker
and
my parents
Barbara and Richard Berg

Contents

CONTENTS

PART THREE

PART FOUR

Through the unheeding many he did move,
A splendour among shadows, a bright blot
Upon this gloomy scene, a Spirit that strove
For truth, and like the Preacher found it not.

—SHELLEY, "Sonnet"

PART ONE

I

The Real Thing

Shortly after six o'clock on a rainy March evening in 1946, a slender, gray-haired man sat in his favorite bar, the Ritz, finishing the last of several martinis. Finding himself adequately fortified for the ordeal ahead, he paid the check, got up, and pulled on his coat and hat. A well-stuffed briefcase in one hand and an umbrella in the other, he left the bar and ventured into the downpour drenching mid-Manhattan. He headed west toward a small storefront on Forty-third Street, several blocks away.

Inside the storefront, thirty young men and women were awaiting him. They were students in an extension course on book publishing which New York University had asked Kenneth D. McCormick, editor-in-chief of Doubleday & Company, to conduct. All were eager to find a foothold in publishing and were attending the weekly seminars to increase their chances. On most evenings there were a few latecomers, but tonight, McCormick noted, every student was on hand and seated by the stroke of six. McCormick knew why. This evening's lecture was on book editing, and he had persuaded the most respected, most influential book editor in America to "give a few words on the subject."

Maxwell Evarts Perkins was unknown to the general public, but to people in the world of books he was a major figure, a kind of hero. For he was the consummate editor. As a young man he had discovered great new talents—such as F. Scott Fitzgerald, Ernest Hemingway, and

3

Thomas Wolfe—and had staked his career on them, defying the established tastes of the earlier generation and revolutionizing American literature. He had been associated with one firm, Charles Scribner's Sons, for thirty-six years, and during this time, no editor at any house even approached his record for finding gifted authors and getting them into print. Several of McCormick's students had confessed to him that it was the brilliant example of Perkins that had attracted them to publishing.

McCormick called the class to order, thumping the collapsible card table in front of him with the palm of his hand, and began the session by describing the job of editor. It was not, he said, as it once had been, confined mainly to correcting spelling and punctuation. Rather, it was to know what to publish, how to get it, and what to do to help it achieve the largest readership. At all this, said McCormick, Max Perkins was unsurpassed. His literary judgment was original and exceedingly astute, and he was famous for his ability to inspire an author to produce the best that was in him or her. More a friend to his authors than a taskmaster, he aided them in every way. He helped them structure their books, if help was needed; thought up titles, invented plots; he served as psychoanalyst, lovelorn adviser, marriage counselor, career manager, money-lender. Few editors before him had done so much work on manuscripts, yet he was always faithful to his credo, "The book belongs to the author."

In some ways, McCormick suggested, Perkins was unlikely for his profession: He was a terrible speller, his punctuation was idiosyncratic, and when it came to reading, he was by his own admission "slow as an ox." But he treated literature as a matter of life and death. He once wrote Thomas Wolfe: "There could be nothing so important as a book can be."

Partly because Perkins was the preeminent editor of his day, partly because many of his authors were celebrities, and partly because Perkins himself was somewhat eccentric, innumerable legends had sprung up about him, most of them rooted in truth. Everyone in Kenneth McCormick's class had heard at least one breathless version of how Perkins had discovered F. Scott Fitzgerald; or of how Scott's wife, Zelda, at the wheel of Scott's automobile, had once driven the editor into Long Island Sound; or of how Perkins had made Scribners lend Fitzgerald many thousands of dollars and had rescued him from his breakdown. It was said that Perkins had agreed to publish Ernest Hemingway's first novel, *The Sun Also Rises*, sight unseen, then had to fight to keep his job when the manuscript arrived because it contained off-color language. Another favorite Perkins story concerned his confrontation with his ultraconservative publisher,

Charles Scribner, over the four-letter words in Hemingway's second novel, *A Farewell to Arms.* Perkins was said to have jotted the troublesome words he wanted to discuss—*shit, fuck,* and *piss*—on his desk calendar, without regard to the calendar's heading: "Things to Do Today." Old Scribner purportedly noticed the list and remarked to Perkins that he was in great trouble if he needed to remind himself to do those things.

Many stories about Perkins dealt with the untamed writing and temperament of Thomas Wolfe. It was said that as Wolfe wrote *Of Time and the River* he leaned his six-and-a-half-foot frame against his refrigerator and used the appliance's top for a desk, casting each completed page into a wooden crate without even rereading it. Eventually, it was said, three husky men carted the heavily laden box to Perkins, who somehow shaped the outpouring into books. Everyone in McCormick's class had also heard about Maxwell Perkins's hat, a battered fedora, which he was reputed to wear all day long, indoors and out, removing it from his head only before going to bed.

As McCormick talked, the legend himself approached the shop on Forty-third Street and quietly entered. McCormick looked up, and seeing a stooped figure in the door at the rear, cut himself off in mid-sentence to welcome the visitor. The class turned to get their first glimpse of America's greatest editor.

He was sixty-one years old, stood five feet ten inches, and weighed 150 pounds. The umbrella he carried seemed to have offered him little protection—he was dripping wet, and his hat drooped over his ears. A pinkish glow suffused Perkins's long, narrow face, softening the prominences. The face was aligned upon a strong, rubicund nose, straight almost to the end, where it curved down like a beak. His eyes were a blue pastel. Wolfe had once written that they were "full of a strange misty light, a kind of far weather of the sea in them, eyes of a New England sailor long months outbound for China on a clipper ship, with something drowned, seasunken in them."

Perkins took off his sopping raincoat and revealed an unpressed, pepper-and-salt, three-piece suit. Then his eyes shot upward and he removed his hat, under which a full head of metallic-gray hair was combed straight back from a V in the center of his forehead. Max Perkins did not care much about the impression he gave, which was just as well, for the first one he made on this particular evening was of some Vermont feed-and-grain merchant who had come to the city in his Sunday clothes and got caught in the rain. As he walked to the front of the room, he seemed slightly bewildered, and more so as Kenneth McCormick introduced him as "the dean of American editors."

Perkins had never spoken to a group like this before. Every year he received dozens of invitations, but he turned them all down. For one thing, he had become somewhat deaf and tended to avoid groups. For another, he believed that book editors should remain invisible; public recognition of them, he felt, might undermine readers' faith in writers, and writers' confidence in themselves. Moreover, Perkins had never seen any point in discussing his career—until McCormick's invitation. Kenneth McCormick, one of the most able and best-liked people in publishing, who himself practiced Perkins's philosophy of editorial self-effacement, was a hard man to refuse. Or perhaps Perkins sensed how much fatigue and sorrow had subtracted from his own longevity and felt he had better pass along what he knew before it was too late.

Hooking his thumbs comfortably into the armholes of his waistcoat, speaking in his slightly rasping, well-bred voice, Perkins began. "The first thing you must remember," he said, without quite facing his audience: "An editor does not add to a book. At best he serves as a handmaiden to an author. Don't ever get to feeling important about yourself, because an editor at most releases energy. He creates nothing." Perkins admitted that he had suggested books to authors who had no ideas of their own at the moment, but he maintained that such works were usually below their best, though they were sometimes financially and even critically successful. "A writer's best work," he said, "comes entirely from himself." He warned the students against any effort by an editor to inject his own point of view into a writer's work or to try to make him something other than what he is. "The process is so simple," he said. "If you have a Mark Twain, don't try to make him into a Shakespeare or make a Shakespeare into a Mark Twain. Because in the end an editor can get only as much out of an author as the author has in him."

Perkins spoke carefully, with that hollow timbre of the hard-of-hearing, as if he were surprised at the sound of his own voice. At first the audience had to strain to hear him, but within minutes they had become so still that his every syllable was quite audible. They sat listening intently to the diffident editor talking about the electrifying challenges of his work—the search for what he kept calling "the real thing."

Once Perkins had concluded his prepared remarks, Kenneth Mc-Cormick asked the class for questions. "What was it like to work with F. Scott Fitzgerald?" was the first.

A fragile smile floated across Perkins's face as he thought for a moment. Then he replied, "Scott was always the gentleman. Sometimes he needed extra support—and sobering up—but the writing was so rich it was worth it." Perkins went on to say that Fitzgerald was comparatively simple to edit because he was a perfectionist about his work and wanted it to be right. However, Perkins added, "Scott was especially sensitive to criticism. He could accept it, but as his editor you had to be sure of everything you suggested."

The discussion turned to Ernest Hemingway. Perkins said Hemingway needed backing in the beginning of his career, and even more later, "because he wrote as daringly as he lived." Perkins believed Hemingway's writing displayed that virtue of his heroes, "grace under pressure." Hemingway, he said, was susceptible to overcorrecting himself. "He once told me that he had written parts of *A Farewell to Arms* fifty times," Perkins said. "Before an author destroys the natural qualities of his writing—that's when an editor has to step in. But not a moment sooner."

Perkins shared stories about working with Erskine Caldwell, then commented on several of his best-selling women novelists, including Taylor Caldwell, Marcia Davenport, and Marjorie Kinnan Rawlings. At last, as though the class had been reluctant to raise a tender subject, came questions about the late Thomas Wolfe, from whom Perkins had become estranged. Most of the inquiries for the rest of the evening concerned Perkins's intense involvement with Wolfe, the most arduous endeavor of his career. For years it had been widely rumored that Wolfe and Perkins had been equal partners in producing Wolfe's sprawling novels. "Tom," he said, "was a man of enormous talent, genius. That talent, like his view of America, was so vast that neither one book nor a single lifetime could contain all that he had to say." As Wolfe transposed his world into fiction, Perkins had felt it was his responsibility to create certain boundaries—of length and form. He said, "These were practical conventions that Wolfe couldn't stop to think about for himself."

"But did Wolfe take your suggestions gracefully?" someone asked.

Perkins laughed for the first time that evening. He told of the time, at the midpoint of their relationship, when he had tried to get Wolfe to delete a big section of *Of Time and the River*. "It was late on a hot night, and we were working at the office. I put my case to him and then sat in silence, reading on in the manuscript." Perkins had known Wolfe would eventually agree to the deletion because the reasons for it were artistically sound. But Wolfe would not give in easily. He tossed his head about and swayed in his chair, while his eyes roved over Perkins's sparsely furnished office. "I went on reading in the manuscript for not less than fifteen minutes," Max continued, "but I was aware of Tom's movements—aware at last that he was looking fixedly at one corner of the office. In that corner hung my hat and overcoat, and down from under the hat, along the coat, hung a sinister rattlesnake skin with seven rattles." It was a present from Marjorie Kinnan Rawlings. Max looked at Tom, who was glaring at the hat, coat, and serpent. "Aha!" Wolfe exclaimed. "The portrait of an editor!" Having had his little joke, Wolfe then agreed to the deletion.

A few of the questions from the would-be publishers that evening had to be repeated so that Perkins could hear them. There were long, puzzling silences in his speech. He answered the questions eloquently, but in between them his mind seemed to wander among a thousand different remembrances. "Max seemed to be going into a private world of his own thoughts," McCormick said years later, "making interior, private associations, as though he had entered a little room and closed the door behind him." All in all it was a memorable performance, and the class sat mesmerized. The rural Yankee who had stumbled in out of the rain hours earlier had transformed himself before them into the very legend of their imaginings.

Shortly after nine o'clock, McCormick notified Perkins of the time so that Max could catch his train. It seemed a shame to stop. He had not even mentioned his experiences with novelists Sherwood Anderson, J. P. Marquand, Morley Callaghan, Hamilton Basso; he had not spoken of biographer Douglas Southall Freeman, or Edmund Wilson, or Allen Tate, or Alice Roosevelt Longworth or Nancy Hale. It was too late to talk about Joseph Stanley Pennell, whose *Rome Hanks* Perkins considered the most exciting novel he had edited in recent years. There was no time to talk about new writers—Alan Paton and James Jones, for example, two authors whose promising manuscripts he was presently editing. Perkins, however, undoubtedly felt he had said more than enough. He picked up his hat and tugged it down over his head, put on his raincoat, turned his back on the standing ovation of his audience, and slipped out as unobtrusively as he had entered.

It was still raining hard. Under his black umbrella he trudged to Grand Central Station. He had never talked so much about himself so publicly in his life.

When he arrived at his home in New Canaan, Connecticut, late that night, Perkins found that the eldest of his five daughters had come over for the evening and was waiting up for him. She noticed that her father seemed melancholy, and she asked why.

"I gave a speech tonight and they called me 'the dean of American editors,' " he explained. "When they call you the dean, that means you're through."

"Oh, Daddy, that doesn't mean you're through," she objected. "It just means you've reached the top."

"No," Perkins said flatly. "It means you're through."

It was the twenty-sixth of March. On March 26, twenty-six years earlier, there had been a great beginning for Maxwell Perkins—the publication of a book that changed his life, and a great deal more.

II

Paradise

In 1919 the rites of spring in Manhattan were extraordinary demonstrations of patriotism. Week after week, battalions marched triumphantly up Fifth Avenue. The "war to end all wars" had been fought and won.

At Forty-eighth Street the parades passed before the offices of Charles Scribner's Sons—Publishers and Booksellers. The Scribner Building was a ten-story structure of classical design, crowned with two obelisks and graced with stately pilasters. The ground floor was faced in shiny brass— the elegant storefront of the Scribner bookshop, a spacious, oblong room with a high vaulted ceiling and narrow metal staircases which spiraled to upper galleries. John Hall Wheelock, who managed the store before becoming a Scribner editor, called it "a Byzantine cathedral of books."

Adjacent to the bookstore was an unobtrusive entrance. Behind it, a vestibule led to an elevator that clattered its way into the upper realms of the Scribner enterprise. The second and third floors housed financial and business departments. Advertising was on the fourth floor. And on the fifth were the editorial rooms—bare white ceilings and walls; uncarpeted concrete floors; rolltop desks and bookcases. In this austere style, Scribners, a family business in its second generation, maintained itself as the most genteel and tradition-encrusted of all the American publishing houses. There was still a Dickensian atmosphere about the place. The accounting office, for example, was run by a man in his seventies who spent his days perched on a high stool, poring over leather-bound ledgers. Typewriters had by then become standard equipment, and because women had to be hired to operate the contraptions, gentlemen were expected not to smoke in the offices.

From the fifth floor, the company was governed like a nineteenth-century monarchy. Charles Scribner II, "old CS," was the undisputed ruler. His face usually wore a severe expression, and he had a sharp nose and white close-cropped hair and mustache. At age sixty-six, he had reigned forty years. Next in succession was his amiable brother Arthur, nine years younger, with softer features, who Wheelock said "was always a little paralyzed by his brother's vitality." William Crary Brownell, the editor-in-chief, white-bearded and walrus-mustached, had a brass spittoon and a leather couch in his office. Every afternoon he would read a newly sub-mitted manuscript and then "sleep on it" for an hour. Afterward he would take a walk around the block, puffing a cigar, and by the time he had returned to his desk and spat, he was ready to announce his opinion of the book.

There were also younger men at Scribners. One of them, Maxwell Evarts Perkins, had arrived in 1910. He had spent four and a half years as advertising manager before ascending to the editorial floor to be appren-ticed under the venerable Brownell. By 1919, Perkins had already estab-lished himself as a promising young editor. Yet as he observed the parades outside his office window, he felt twinges of disappointment about his career. In his thirties, he had considered himself too old and overburdened with responsibilities to enlist for action overseas. Watching the colorful homecoming, he felt sorry that he had not witnessed the war firsthand.

Scribners itself had scarcely experienced the war and its upheavals. The Scribner list was a backwater of literary tastes and values. Its books never transgressed the bounds of "decency." Indeed, they seldom went beyond merely diverting the reader. There were none of the newer writers who were attracting attention—Theodore Dreiser, Sinclair Lewis, Sher-wood Anderson. The three pillars of the House of Scribner were long-established writers steeped in the English tradition. The firm published John Galsworthy's *Forsyte Saga* and the complete works of Henry James and Edith Wharton. Indeed, most of Scribners' important books were by writers they had been publishing for years, whose manuscripts required no editing. William C. Brownell stated the company's editorial policy in responding to one of Mrs. Wharton's manuscripts: "I don't believe much in tinkering, and I am not *suffisant* enough to think the publisher can con-tribute much by counselling modifications."

For the most part, Maxwell Perkins's duties as an editor were limited to proofreading galleys—long printed sheets, each containing the equivalent of three book pages—and to other perfunctory chores. Occasionally he was called upon to correct the grammar in a gardening book or arrange the selections in school anthologies of classic short stories and translations of Chekhov. The work demanded little creativity.

One regular Scribner author was Shane Leslie, an Irish journalist, poet, and lecturer who spent years at a time in America. On one of his extended tours he was introduced to a teen-aged boy by the headmaster of the Newman School in New Jersey. Leslie and the handsome youth—an aspiring writer from Minnesota—became friends. Eventually the young man entered Princeton University but enlisted in the army before graduating. He was commissioned and sent to Fort Leavenworth, Kansas. "Every Saturday at one o'clock when the week's work was over," he recalled years later, "I hurried up to the Officer's Club and there in a corner of a room full of smoke, conversation and rattling newspapers, I wrote a one hundred and twenty thousand word novel on the consecutive weekends of three months." In the spring of 1918 he believed the army was about to send him overseas. Unsure of his future, the young officer—F. Scott Fitzgerald—entrusted the manuscript to Leslie.

The work, entitled *The Romantic Egotist*, was little more than a grab bag of stories, poems, and sketches recounting the author's coming of age. Leslie sent it to Charles Scribner, suggesting that he give a "judgment" upon it. By way of introduction he wrote,

> In spite of its disguises, it has given me a vivid picture of the American generation that is hastening to war. I marvel at its crudity and its cleverness. It is naive in places, shocking in others, painful to the conventional and not without a touch of ironic sublimity especially toward the end. About a third of the book could be omitted without losing the impression that it is written by an American Rupert Brooke. . . . It interests me as a boy's book and I think gives expression to that real American youth that the sentimentalists are so anxious to drape behind the canvas of the YMCA tent.

The manuscript went from editor to editor during the next three months. Brownell "could not stomach it at all." Edward L. Burlingame, another senior editor, found it "hard sledding." The material was passed down until it reached Maxwell Perkins. "We have been reading 'The Romantic Egoist' * with a very unusual degree of interest," Perkins wrote

* Perkins misspelled the title. All spellings and punctuation are preserved in the directly quoted material in this book, except where the error might cause confusion.

Fitzgerald that August; "in fact no ms. novel has come to us for a long time that seemed to display so much vitality." But Perkins was extrapolating from a single response. Only *he* had liked the book, and his letter went on reluctantly to decline it. He cited governmental restrictions on printing supplies, high manufacturing costs, and "certain characteristics of the novel itself."

Editors at Scribners considered criticism of works they turned down as beyond their function and likely to be resented by an author. But Perkins's enthusiasm for Fitzgerald's manuscript impelled him to comment further. Commandeering the editorial "we," he risked offering some general remarks, because, he said, "we should welcome a chance to reconsider its publication."

His main complaint with *The Romantic Egotist* was that it did not advance to a conclusion. The protagonist drifted, hardly changing over the course of the novel.

> This may be intentional on your part for it is certainly not untrue to life [Perkins wrote]; but it leaves the reader distinctly disappointed and dissatisfied since he has expected him to arrive somewhere either in an actual sense by his response to the war perhaps, or in a psychological one by "finding himself" as for instance Pendennis is brought to do. He does go to the war, but in almost the same spirit that he went to college and school— because it is simply the thing to do.

"It seems to us in short," Perkins asserted, "that the story does not culminate in anything as it must to justify the reader's interest as he follows it; and that it might be made to do so quite consistently with the characters and with its earlier stages." Perkins did not want Fitzgerald to "conventionalize" the book so much as intensify it. "We hope we shall see it again," he wrote in closing, "and we shall then reread it immediately."

Perkins's letter encouraged Lieutenant Fitzgerald to spend the next six weeks revising his novel. By mid-October he sent the reworked manuscript to Scribners. Perkins read it immediately, as promised, and was delighted to find it much improved. Rather than approaching old CS directly, he sought an ally in Scribner's son. Charles III liked the book too, but his support was not enough. The older editors again voted Perkins down. With that, as Perkins later admitted to Fitzgerald, "I was afraid that . . . you might be done with us conservatives."

Max was nonetheless determined to see the book published. He brought it to the attention of two rival publishers. One Scribner colleague remembered Perkins was "terrified that they would accept it, for all the time he saw how vitally it might still be improved. The other publishers, however, sent it back without comment."

Undeterred, Perkins continued to harbor a private hope that he could still get it published. He believed that Fitzgerald might revise the novel further after he got out of the army, then allow Perkins to take it before his editorial board a third time.

Fitzgerald, however, was not as indomitable as his champion in New York. When *The Romantic Egotist* was turned down for the second time, he was at Camp Sheridan in Montgomery, Alabama. He lost confidence in the book, but his disappointment was softened by a distraction—Zelda Sayre, an Alabama supreme court justice's daughter whose graduating high school class had just voted her the "prettiest and most attractive." Lieutenant Fitzgerald was introduced to her at a country club dance in July and was one of the admirers who called on her that August. Fitzgerald later confided to his Ledger that on the seventh of September he "fell in love." Zelda loved him too, but kept him at bay. She was waiting to see whether his talents were strong enough to earn them the luxuries they both dreamed of. The army discharged Fitzgerald in February, 1919, and he headed for New York and a job at the Barron Collier advertising agency. Upon his arrival he wired Zelda: I AM IN THE LAND OF AMBITION AND SUCCESS AND MY ONLY HOPE AND FAITH IS THAT MY DARLING HEART WILL BE WITH ME SOON.

Fitzgerald, of course, went to see Max Perkins. It is not known what they said to each other, except that Perkins suggested, off the record, that Scott rewrite his novel, changing the narrative from first to third person. "Max's idea was to give the author some distance from the material," John Hall Wheelock said years later of Perkins's advice. "He admired the exuberance of Fitzgerald's writing and personality but believed no publisher, certainly not Scribners, would accept an author's work so brash and self-indulgent as it was."

In midsummer, 1919, Fitzgerald wrote Perkins from St. Paul. "After four months attempt to write commercial copy by day and painful half-hearted imitations of popular literature at night," he said, "I decided that it was one thing or another. So I gave up getting married and went home." By the end of July he finished a draft of a novel called *The Education of a Personage*. "It is in no sense a revision of the ill-fated *Romantic Egotist*," he assured Perkins, "but it contains some of the former material improved and worked over and bears a strong family resemblance besides." Fitzgerald added, "While the other was a tedius disconnected casserole this is a definite attempt at a big novel and I really believe I have hit it."

Once again sanguine about his novel, Fitzgerald asked if an August 20 submission might result in an October publication. "This is an odd question I realize since you haven't even seen the book," he wrote Perkins, "but you have been so kind about my stuff that I venture to intrude once more upon your patience." Fitzgerald gave Perkins two reasons for rushing the book out: "because I want to get started both in a literary and financial way; second—because it is to some extent a timely book and it seems to me that the public are wild for decent reading matter."

The Education of a Personage struck Max as an excellent title and aroused his curiosity about the work. "Ever since the first reading of your first manuscript we have felt that you would succeed," he wrote back immediately. Regarding publication, he said, he was certain of one thing: Nobody could bring this book out in two months without greatly injuring its chances. To shorten the deliberation period, however, Perkins offered to read chapters as they were finished.

Fitzgerald sent no chapters, but in the first week of September, 1919, a complete revision arrived on Perkins's desk. Fitzgerald had changed the book considerably, taking, in fact, every one of Perkins's suggestions. He had transposed the story to the third person and put the material he had salvaged to much better use. He had also given the work a new title: *This Side of Paradise.*

Perkins prepared for his third assault on the monthly meeting of the editorial board, dutifully circulating the new manuscript among his colleagues. In mid-September the editors met. Charles Scribner sat at the head of the table, glowering. His brother Arthur sat by his side. Brownell was there too, a formidable figure, for he was not just editor-in-chief but one of the most eminent literary critics in America. He had "slept on the book," and he looked eager to argue against any of the half-dozen other men sitting around the table who might want to accept it.

Old CS held forth. According to Wheelock, "He was a born publisher with great flair, who truly loved getting books into print. But Mr. Scribner said, 'I'm proud of my imprint. I cannot publish fiction that is without literary value.' Then Brownell spoke for him when he pronounced the book 'frivolous.' " The discussion seemed over—until old CS, with his forbidding eyes, peered down the conference table and said, "Max, you're very silent."

Perkins stood and began to pace the room. "My feeling," he explained, "is that a publisher's first allegiance is to talent. And if we aren't going to publish a talent like this, it is a very serious thing." He contended that the ambitious Fitzgerald would be able to find another publisher for this novel and young authors would follow him: "Then we might as well go out of business." Perkins returned to his original place at the meeting table and, confronting Scribner head on, said, "If we're going to turn down the likes of Fitzgerald, I will lose all interest in publishing books." The vote of hands was taken. The young editors tied the old. There was a silence. Then Scribner said he wanted more time to think it over.

Fitzgerald was earning some money at a temporary job of repairing the roofs of railroad cars. On the eighteenth of September, just before his twenty-third birthday, he received a special delivery letter from Maxwell Perkins.

> I am very glad, personally, to be able to write to you that we are all for publishing your book *This Side of Paradise*. Viewing it as the same book that was here before, which in a sense it is, though translated into somewhat different terms and extended farther, I think that you have improved it enormously. As the first manuscript did, it abounds in energy and life and it seems to me to be in much better proportion. . . . The book is so different that it is hard to prophesy how it will sell but we are all for taking a chance and supporting it with vigor.

Scribners' expectation was to publish that spring.

No money was to be paid Fitzgerald as an advance against future earnings—advances, customary today, were not always offered in that time. But Fitzgerald already envisioned a prosperous future. In his essay "Early Success" (1937) he wrote, "That day I quit work and ran along the streets, stopping automobiles to tell friends and acquaintances about it— my novel *This Side of Paradise* was accepted for publication. . . . I paid off my terrible small debts, bought a suit, and woke up every morning with a world of ineffable toploftiness and promise." Fitzgerald left all the terms of the contract to Perkins, but there was one condition which he did not relinquish without a slight struggle. He was obsessed with the idea of being a published writer by Christmas, February at the latest. He finally told Perkins why: Zelda Sayre was within his grasp. Beyond that, Fitzgerald wrote Perkins, "It will have a psychological effect on me and all my surroundings and besides open up new fields. I'm in that stage where every month counts frantically and seems a cudgel in a fight for happiness against time."

Perkins explained that there were two seasons in the publishing year and that Scribners prepared for each long before it began. For example, each July and August, Scribner salesmen canvassed the country, carrying trunks filled with sample chapters and dust jackets of books meant to enjoy their greatest sale during the Christmas season. A book put on the fall list after the "travelers" had visited their stores would have to make it entirely on its own. It would come without introduction to the bookseller, who, said Perkins, was already going "nearly mad with the number of books in his store and had invested all the money he could in them"; it would come, he said, "as a most unwelcome and troublesome thing which would suffer accordingly." Perkins recommended the second publishing season, preparations for which began the month after the Christmas rush. By then the booksellers had made their year's biggest profits and were ready to stock up again, this time on the new spring books, including, one hoped, *This Side of Paradise*.

Fitzgerald understood and acquiesced. "While I waited for the novel to appear," he wrote further in his 1937 essay, "the metamorphosing of amateur into professional began to take place—a sort of stitching together of your whole life into a pattern of work, so that the end of one job is automatically the beginning of another." He broke ground on a number of projects. Of greatest interest to Perkins was a novel called *The Demon Lover*, which Fitzgerald estimated would take a year to complete. When his enthusiasm on that flagged, he wrote short stories and submitted them to *Scribner's*, a monthly magazine published by the firm. It accepted only one of his first four submissions.

Fitzgerald wanted some word of encouragement to offset the rejection slips. Perkins read the pieces that had been declined and told Scott he was sure there would be no difficulty in placing them elsewhere. "The great beauty of them," Perkins wrote, "is that they are alive. Ninety percent of the stories that appear are derived from life through the rarefying medium of literature. Yours are direct from life it seems to me. This is true also of the language and style; it is that of the day. It is free of the conventions of the past which most writers love . . . to their great inconvenience." The pieces, Perkins wrote, "indicate to me that you are pretty definitely lodged as a writer of short stories."

Later, in the final weeks of the year, Fitzgerald wrote Perkins: "I feel I've certainly been lucky to find a publisher who seems so generally interested in his authors. Lord knows this literary game has been discouraging enough at times." What Fitzgerald did not realize was that

Maxwell Perkins was just as jubilant about having Scribners' brightest young author as his first literary discovery.

When Fitzgerald was a student at Princeton he told the visiting poet-in-residence Alfred Noyes that he thought it in his power "to write either books that would sell or books of permanent value" and he was not sure which he should do. It became a conflict with which Scott would wrestle for the remainder of his life. Perkins quickly realized that while both objectives mattered to Fitzgerald, money mattered a very great deal. As *This Side of Paradise* was being set into galleys, Fitzgerald wrote Perkins that he had a notion for still another novel. "I want to start it," he said, "but I don't want to get broke in the middle and start in and have to write short stories again—because I don't enjoy [writing stories] and just do it for money." Thinking of cash on hand more than future literary credit, he asked, "There's nothing in collections of short stories is there?"

Perkins confirmed Fitzgerald's hunch that as a rule anthologies did not make best-selling books. "The truth is," Perkins explained, "it has seemed to me that your stories were likely to constitute an exception, after a good many of them had been printed and your name was widely known. It seems to me that they have the popular note which would be likely to make them sell in book form. I wish you did care more about writing them . . . because they have great value in making you a reputation and because they are quite worthwhile in themselves."

Fitzgerald remained anxious all winter. Zelda Sayre agreed to marry him, but the wedding still hinged on his success as an author. He saw the short stories as a shortcut to his goal. He broke up the work he had done on *The Demon Lover* into several character sketches and sold them for forty dollars apiece to *The Smart Set*, the popular literary magazine published by George Jean Nathan and H. L. Mencken. More than anyone else in 1920, editor and critic Mencken encouraged writers to buck the "genteel tradition" and record the living language of the day. By winter's end, after *The Smart Set* had published six of Fitzgerald's slick pieces about idle dandies and cheeky debutantes, the young writer's reputation was spreading rapidly.

As publication of *This Side of Paradise* drew near, many people at Charles Scribner's Sons caught the fever of excitement that had infected Maxwell Perkins months earlier. Some, however, were not so much excited as appalled. Malcolm Cowley, a literary critic, wrote that even before its publication the book was recognized as "the terrifying voice of a new age, and it made some of the older employees of Scribners cringe." Roger Burlingame, son of senior editor Edward L. Burlingame and later a Scribners editor himself, gave an example of this reaction in his *Of Making Many Books*, an informal history of Scribners. The bellwether at Scribners in those days, Burlingame noted, was an important member of the sales department. Often mistrusting his own literary judgment he spoke "advisedly" about many books, and used to take them home for an erudite sister to read. His sister was supposed to be infallible and it was true that many of the novels she had "cried over" sold prodigiously. So when it was known that he had taken *This Side of Paradise* home for the weekend, his colleagues were agog on Monday morning. "And what did your sister say?" they asked in chorus. "She picked it up with the tongs," he replied, "because she wouldn't touch it with her hands after reading it, and put it into the fire."

On March 26, 1920, *This Side of Paradise* appeared at last, and Fitzgerald was proudly advertised as "the youngest writer for whom Scribners have ever published a novel." Perkins wandered down into the store that day and saw two copies sold right before him, which he thought augured well. A week later, in the rectory of St. Patrick's Cathedral, just blocks from the Scribner Building, Zelda Sayre and Scott Fitzgerald were married. They always considered their wedding to have occurred under Perkins's auspices.

This Side of Paradise unfurled like a banner over an entire age. It commanded attention in literary columns and sales charts. H. L. Mencken in his *Smart Set* review wrote that Fitzgerald had produced "a truly amazing first novel—original in structure, extremely sophisticated in manner, and adorned with brilliancy that is as rare in American writing as honesty is in American statecraft." Mark Sullivan, in his social history of America, *Our Times*, which was published by Scribners, wrote that Fitzgerald's first book "has the distinction, if not of creating a generation, certainly of calling the world's attention to a generation."

Fitzgerald himself had made just that point in the book's final pages. "Here was a new generation," he wrote, "shouting the old cries, learning the old creeds, through a revery of long days and nights; destined finally to go out into that dirty gray turmoil to follow love and pride; a new generation dedicated more than the last to the fear of poverty and the worship of success; grown up to find all Gods dead, all wars fought, all faiths in man shaken."

Of the book's popular appeal, the author himself recalled in "Early Success":

> In a daze I told the Scribner Company that I didn't expect my novel to sell more than twenty thousand copies and when the laughter died away I was told that a sale of five thousand was excellent for a first novel. I think it was a week after publication that it passed the twenty thousand mark, but I took myself so seriously that I didn't even think it was funny.

The book did not make Fitzgerald rich so much as it made him famous. He was only twenty-four and seemingly destined to succeed. Charles Scribner wrote Shane Leslie later in the year: "Your introduction of Scott Fitzgerald proved to be an important one for us; *This Side of Paradise* has been our best seller this season and is still going strong."

In the first rush of the book's celebrity many serious misprints went overlooked. Perkins took all the blame for them. He had been so frightened of the reaction to the book from the other employees at Scribners that he had hardly let it out of his hands during any stage of its preparation—not even to proofreaders. In *Of Making Many Books*, Roger Burlingame noted that if it had not been for the stern supervision of Irma Wyckoff, Perkins's devoted secretary, Max "would probably be something of an orthographic phenomenon himself." Soon the misspellings Perkins never spotted became a major topic of literary conversation. By summer, the witty New York *Tribune* book columnist Franklin P. Adams had turned the search for errors into a parlor game. Finally, a Harvard scholar sent Scribners a list of over 100 mistakes. This was humiliating for Perkins; but even more humiliating was that the author, himself an atrocious speller, was pointing out errors too. Scott was excited that his book was running through entire printings each week but disgruntled that many of those errors on Franklin Adams's growing list remained uncorrected as late as the sixth printing.

The misprints seemed not to matter to the reading public. The writing especially excited the uncertain youth of the nation. Mark Sullivan later said of Fitzgerald's hero: "Young people found in Amory's behavior a model for their conduct—and alarmed parents found their worst apprehensions realized." Roger Burlingame noted further that the novel "waked all the comfortable parents of the war's fighting generation out of the hangover of their security into the consciousness that something definite, terrible and, possibly, final, had happened to their chidren. And it gave their children their first proud sense of being 'lost.' " "America was going on the greatest, gaudiest spree in history and there was going to be plenty to tell about it," Fitzgerald later wrote.

Within a month of his novel's publication, Fitzgerald mailed to his editor eleven stories, six poems—three of which had drawn "quite a bit of notice in the *Second Book of Princeton Verse*"—and a hatful of possible titles for an anthology. Max read all the material, selected eight stories, and chose *Flappers and Philosophers* as the strongest of Fitzgerald's lighthearted titles. Charles Scribner thought the choice was "horrid" but was inclined to let Perkins parlay his first success into another.

Fitzgerald's income from writing zoomed from $879 in 1919 to $18,850 in 1920, and he frittered it all away. So far as Scribner could see, Fitzgerald was not much concerned with thrift and seemed little interested in the future. He wrote Shane Leslie that Fitzgerald "is very fond of the good things of life and is disposed to enjoy it to the full while the going is good. Economy is not one of his virtues."

Beginning with Fitzgerald, Perkins developed the habit of sending books to his laboring authors. "Max was like an old-time druggist," remarked one of them, James Jones. "Whenever he saw you getting sluggish, he prescribed a book that he thought would pep you up. They were always specially selected for your condition, perfectly matched to your particular tastes and temperament, but with enough of a kick to get you thinking in a new direction." In June, 1920, Max sent Fitzgerald a copy of *The Ordeal of Mark Twain* by Van Wyck Brooks. Brooks, Max wrote Scott, "is a brilliant chap and very attractive and if you do care for the book I would like to have you meet him at lunch some day." Van Wyck Brooks was Max Perkins's closest friend. They had known each other since kindergarten in Plainfield, New Jersey, and had been at Harvard together. Now, twelve years after graduation, Brooks was on his way to becoming the era's foremost surveyor of American literature.

"It's one of the most inspirational books I've read and has seemed to put the breath of life back in me," Fitzgerald wrote back a few days after receiving the book. "Just finished the best story I've done yet & my novel is going to be my life masterpiece." Fitzgerald's heavily underlined copy of *The Ordeal of Mark Twain* is evidence of the deeper effect Brooks's work had on his next group of stories. Scott read in Brooks about a Clemens novel called *The Gilded Age*, in which a man goes west in search of a mountain of coal and strikes it rich enough to marry the woman he loves. Scott then wrote a novella in which FitzNorman Culpepper Washington stumbled upon a mineral treasure, at about the same time, in Montana. Fitzgerald called his story "The Diamond as Big as the Ritz."

The author worked on through the summer, but Perkins did not. He was never content on a vacation unless he felt he had earned it, and that summer, for the first time in his career as an editor, he believed he had. Before leaving for his respite, Perkins sent Fitzgerald his address, to be used should he need him for anything. It was simply the name of the small town he had gone to practically every summer of his life.

Windsor, Vermont rests a third of the way up the Vermont-New Hampshire border, on the western bank of the Connecticut River. It was for Max Perkins the most glorious place on earth. Some seventy years earlier, just beyond the shadow of Mount Ascutney, his maternal grandfather had built a compound of houses in which to assemble his family around him. "Windsor was the personal heaven of my grandfather's grandchildren," Max's sister Fanny Cox wrote in *Vermonter*. "In the winter we lived in different settings . . . but in the summer we gathered together in the big place behind the picket fence where six houses faced the village street and the grounds stretched back across green lawns with clipped hemlock hedges and round begonia-filled flower beds to slope down the hill to the pond." Rising behind the pond was a particularly lovely part of the acreage, where streams raced down hills and footpaths wove through stands of pine and birch. The family called these special woods "Paradise."

In Paradise a youth could run as wild and free as his imagination. Young Max Perkins had spent innumerable hours there with his brothers and sisters and cousins. Later, as a father, he took his own children. All the pleasures at the other end of the seven-hour ride from New York on the White Mountain Express, a wonderfully comfortable summer train, were passed on to them.

Perkins told one of his daughters, "The greatest feeling is to go to bed tired." Bedtime had always been Perkins's favorite time of day, those few minutes just before falling asleep when he could "steer his dreams." In those final moments of wakefulness Maxwell Perkins recurringly transported himself back to Russia in 1812—the scene of his favorite book, *War and Peace*. Night after night his mind filled with visions of Napoleon's army retreating from Moscow in the frost and early winter snow. On mornings in Vermont after Tolstoi's characters had paraded before him, he insisted that his dreams were more vivid and that he slept more soundly in Windsor than anywhere else.

Once every summer Max took his daughters for a hike up Mount Ascutney, marching them for thirty minutes and then resting for ten, just as Prince Andrei in *War and Peace* might have marched his soldiers. But Perkins's greatest pleasure in Windsor was in losing himself on a long solitary stroll. A "real walk" he used to call it. Alone, he would stride across the same ground his ancestors had before him.

III

Provenance

N̲o one could have known Max who did not understand what Windsor, or Vermont in general, meant for him, the deep stake in the old rural America from which the foreground of his life was in many of its elements so far removed," Van Wyck Brooks wrote in *Scenes and Portraits*. Practically all of Perkins's life was spent in New York City or its suburbs, but the tart values of New England were the essence of his character. He was full of Yankee quirks and biases. He could be crotchety in his behavior and literary taste, obtuse and old-fashioned. And yet, Brooks believed, Windsor and all it stood for had kept him at heart "so direct, so uninfluenced by prejudice, so unclouded by secondary feelings, so immediate, so fresh." Max's was a New England mind, filled with dichotomies.

He was born on September 20, 1884, in Manhattan, at the corner of Second Avenue and Fourteenth Street, and named William Maxwell Evarts Perkins, thus becoming the nominative heir of two distinguished families. Brooks said he had known "few other Americans in whom so much history was palpably and visibly embodied, so that one saw it working in him, sometimes not too happily, for his mind was always in a state of civil war."

It was the English battle between Roundheads and Cavaliers in 1642, Brooks said, that Max never quite fought through. That war had crossed the ocean and found its way to Perkins eight generations later. While the Perkins side of the family made him "the romantic, adventurous boy, indolent, graceful and frank, all gaiety, sweetness and animal charm," the Evartses made him believe in doing things the hard way—"living against the grain." Brooks said, "One or the other side . . . of [the battle] constantly came to the front at crises in his life."

John Evarts, a Welshman, was the first of Maxwell Perkins's forebears to emigrate to the New World. As an indentured servant he sailed in 1635, settled in Concord, Massachusetts, and was made a freeman in 1638. A century and a half later he had only one direct descendant—Jeremiah Evarts. Born in 1782 and educated at Yale College, Evarts practiced law in New Haven. He was a stern, puritanical, religious man. A contemporary alleged that Evarts "had too much unbending integrity to be a popular lawyer." He married Mehitabel Barnes, a widowed daughter of Roger Sherman, one of Connecticut's signers of the Declaration of Independence. They settled in Charlestown, Massachusetts, where he assumed the editorship of the *Panoplist*, an organ of the orthodox Congregationalists. He began devoting his life entirely to pamphleteering and missionary enterprises, but did not restrict his proselytizing to religious concerns. For preaching abolition during one of his missions, he spent a year in a Georgia jail. In early March, 1818, traveling from Savannah, he was informed of the birth of a son—William Maxwell Evarts.

William entered Yale in 1833, where he was one of the founders of the *Yale Literary Magazine*. He graduated with honors, then attended law school at Harvard. Richard Henry Dana, who was writing up his maritime adventures in *Two Years Before the Mast* while matriculating at Harvard, later remembered: "The most successful speech made at the school during the whole time I was there, was made before a jury of undergraduates . . . by Wm. M. Evarts. . . . If he does not become distinguished he will disappoint more persons than any other young man whom I have ever met with." In 1843, Evarts married Helen Minerva Wardner in her hometown of Windsor. During the next twenty years, they produced seven sons and five daughters.

Evarts lived up to Dana's expectations. His law career in New York City drew national attention in 1855 when he gave $1,000—one fourth of his entire fortune—to the Abolitionist cause. By 1889, when he made his last court appearance, he had taken part in a number of trials that tested basic principles of the Constitution. The *Dictionary of American Biography* dubbed him the "hero of the three great cases" of his generation—the Geneva arbitration case, the Tilden-Hayes election case of 1876, and the Andrew Johnson impeachment. In each trial he was victorious: He secured remuneration from foreign nations that fought against the Union during the Civil War, obtained the presidency for one man who did not win the popular vote of the nation, and defended another man's right to continue serving as president.

When Evarts prepared his cases he invariably sought the counsel of learned friends. He often turned to Henry Adams, who wrote in his third-person autobiography: "In doubt, the quickest way to clear one's mind is to discuss, and Evarts deliberately forced discussion. Day after day, driving, dining, walking he provoked Adams to dispute his positions. He needed an anvil, he said, to hammer his ideas on." In 1877, President Hayes named Evarts Secretary of State. The New York legislature twice elected him to the United States Senate.

Upon his retirement from Washington, Evarts returned to Vermont, where he imperiously presided over family activities. His "White House" in Windsor was dark inside and full of Victorian clutter, including gold-framed portraits of Evarts ancestors and a white marble bust of himself wearing a toga.

The colorful Perkinses fill almost as many columns in the *Dictionary of American Biography* as the dour Evartses, but most of the Evartses failed to appreciate them. One Evarts cousin, ninety years after Max's birth, still maintained, "The Perkinses had the wrong politics, sat on the wrong side of the church, and were all buried on the wrong side of the cemetery."

Charles Callahan Perkins, Max's paternal grandfather, inherited from his parents both the money and the temperament that naturally made him an influential friend of the arts in his native city of Boston. He was descended from Edmund Perkins, who emigrated to New England in 1650 and became a wealthy and philanthropic merchant—an East India magnate, who spawned several children who were Loyalists in the Revolution. Charles graduated from Harvard in 1843, having shown an interest in drawing and painting. He declined the customary opportunities to enter business and went abroad, determined to turn his enthusiasm for art into serious study. In Rome he mingled with several important artists of the day, but the limitations of his own talent kept him an amateur. He realized he could at least devote his life to the interpretation of art, and he became the first American art critic. In 1855 he married Frances D. Bruen of New York. Perkins kept close company with the Brownings in Europe and Longfellow in Boston. He wrote a half-dozen major studies of European sculpture.

By the time Charles Perkins's three children came of age, most of his fortune had been exhausted. He resettled his family in New England and became friendly with Senator Evarts. Charles's middle child, Edward Clifford—an alumnus of Harvard and Harvard Law School—met and fell in love with the senator's daughter Elizabeth. In 1882, when they were each twenty-four, they married in Windsor.

Elizabeth was a dignified and gracious woman who, it was said, always walked at the same pace—not so slowly as to seem to have no purpose, but not so fast as to be unladylike—with her hands folded at her waist. She had often served as her father's hostess in Washington. Her husband was dapper and possessed a freer spirit. They went to live in Plainfield, New Jersey, and Edward commuted to his law practice in New York, bicycling to and from the train station on a highwheeler, the first such vehicle in the town. Over thirteen years they had six children. She was a mother who never demanded good behavior but rather expected it; he was a gentle father.

The divergent traits of the two families came together in their second child, William Maxwell Evarts Perkins. Within him the two spirits— Perkins aestheticism and Evarts discipline—were blended. Even as a boy, Max had an artistic flair but New England common sense.

Every Sunday night, Edward Perkins read to his young family. "We all sat before our father and listened to *Ivanhoe* and *The Rose and the Ring*," Max's youngest sister, Fanny, remembered, "and we'd all laugh out loud, because the romance even then was so melodramatic." For Max and his older brother, Edward, their father gave special readings of French books, which he translated as he went along to keep up his knowledge of the language. Spellbound, the two boys listened to the fabulous adventures of *The Three Musketeers*, General Marbot's *Memoirs*, and Erckmann-Chatrian's *Conscript of 1813*. Max grew infatuated with the military, especially the heroic accounts of Napoleon.

When he was sixteen, Max went to St. Paul's Academy in Concord, New Hampshire, but was called home the following year to ease the pull on the family pursestrings. Then, in late October, 1902, Max's father, who stubbornly disapproved of ever wearing topcoats, caught pneumonia. He died three days later at the age of forty-four. Edward C. Perkins had not saved any money, but his widow and six children were able to live comfortably on various family trust funds. Max completed his secondary education at the Leal School in Plainfield.

Edward, the eldest Perkins son, was away at Harvard, so Max took the chair at the head of the dinner table. Yankee instinct drove him to veil his grief and assume as many of his father's roles as possible. He felt he must stand before his family as a monument of fortitude in adversity. He tended his younger siblings firmly but fondly, and they revered him. One morning after prayers, when his mother broke down in tears, he patted her on the shoulder until she stopped. A generation later, he told one of his own children, "Every good deed a man does is to please his father."

As a teen-ager, Max passed through puppy love normally. "I kissed the dickens out of a pretty girl this afternoon," he wrote Van Wyck Brooks in 1900. "It took about three hours of steady arguing to get it out of her, but finally she gave me permission." Several summers he tutored children in Southampton, Long Island, and at age sixteen he worked as a counselor at Camp Chesterfield in New Hampshire. Out in the woods one day with several young hikers, Max heard terrible cries. He sent the boys back to camp and set off to find where the screams were coming from. He came to a barn and saw a woman standing in the doorway, struggling with two men who were holding her arms. One of the men said: "What do you want?" Max replied, "I've come to rescue the lady." Years later Max would shake with laughter as he told that story, for it turned out that the woman had delirium tremens and the men were simply trying to get her indoors.

The following summer one small event occurred which was to affect Max for the rest of his life. He went swimming one afternoon with a younger boy named Tom McClary in a deep pond in Windsor. Tom was a poor swimmer, and halfway across the pond he lost his nerve and clamped his arms around Max's neck. They both sank. Max fought free and swam toward shore. Then he thought of Tom. He looked over his shoulder and saw the boy floating face down. Max swam back, grabbed Tom's wrist and towed him ashore. To pull him up the bank he clasped his hands under Tom's stomach, which had the happy effect of making water gush out of Tom's mouth, and in a moment he was breathing again. The boys agreed to say nothing of the accident, but it was not forgotten.

In that moment of Tom McClary's near drowning, he confided but once, years later, to a friend, he saw that he was "by nature careless, irresponsible and timid." He admitted: "When I was seventeen I realized this by one little incident not worth recounting when I was ineffectual, and I then made the only resolution that I ever kept. And it was, never to refuse a responsibility." The oath was so solemn that selflessness and duty soon dominated Perkins's judgment.

As generations of Perkinses had before him, Max went to Harvard. There he dropped his unused first name, his way of shucking his ancestors. When a senior in the class of 1907 he wrote,

> To my mind, college is the place to expand, to overcome prejudices, to look at things through one's own eyes. Here the boy first stands upon his own feet. Hitherto he has been in the hands of others to mould, now he must mould himself. He must cut loose from old ideas.

When he arrived at Harvard only the social side really appealed to Max. "I admired the 'sport,' the social butterfly," he wrote in his college essay "Varied Outlooks." "I too wished to dress well, to have many friends, to smoke and drink in cafés, to occupy a front row seat at light operas." He had thick blond hair and from some angles a delicate beauty; from others he appeared striking rather than handsome. In yearbook photographs the literary critic Malcolm Cowley saw a close resemblance to Napoleon, one of Perkins's childhood heroes, when the Corsican had been a young lieutenant of artillery—the "same wide, sensitive mouth, the same Roman nose under a high forehead, and the same big ears close to the skull."

In November of his freshman year Perkins was arrested after the Yale game for being in the company of a drunk and disorderly classmate and locked up in jail. In December his grades entitled him to become the first member of his class to be placed on probation. It was a distinction "the sport" always remembered with pride.

Perkins carried a chip on his shoulder in Cambridge. Unlike the wealthy "Gold Coast" men, he was at Harvard on limited funds. Max worked in the summers and felt shabby. He was proud of the Evartses and Perkinses, and he was fond of saying that "some of them were very wealthy and some of them were very poor, but it is impossible to tell which were which." In college, he felt as though his family's dignity had been worn to its barest threads. That hardly affected the way others regarded him, but Max developed the New Englander's horror of accepting anything he did not work for. "When a man does you a favor, he owns a little piece of you," he once explained to his third daughter, who recalled further: "One of his best friends, who lived on Long Island, in a luxurious house, used to beg him to come on weekends. My father longed to go, but wouldn't because he couldn't afford to tip the butler."

Instead, almost weekly, Perkins, in frayed shirt cuffs, walked to the home of one of his uncles, the Reverend Prescott Evarts, rector of Christ's Church in Cambridge. "Max always seemed to enjoy the family get-togethers," the clergyman's son Richard remembered. "We played checkers, ate dinner, and often got into loud arguments, usually social questions, about the importance of heredity versus environment. But we all knew Sunday night with us was his way to save money."

"Men measure social success by what clubs they belong to," Perkins wrote as an upperclassman. When his Uncle Prescott, a Harvard alumnus, learned that Max had been invited to join Fox Club but couldn't afford it, he wrote a check to cover the expenses. Max was reluctant to accept it but joined because, he observed, at Harvard the "importance of clubs simply could not be denied."

Perkins was also on the staff of the *Harvard Advocate*, the campus literary magazine, and rose to its board of editors. For the most part his contributions satirized the gentlemanly practices and pursuits of Harvard students. In one essay, "On Girls and Gallantry," he wrote: "Authorities affirm that man's reverence for woman is the scale by which civilization is measured. . . . Of this much at least I am sure: not only are no two girls alike but no single girl is the same, save by the purest coincidence, at two different times."

Three of Max's Harvard friends were also making regular contributions to the *Advocate*: the poet John Hall Wheelock; Edward Sheldon, whose play *Salvation Nell* was a Broadway hit while he was still an undergraduate; and Van Wyck Brooks.

Brooks said he followed Perkins to Harvard from Plainfield because "I was a writer born,—I seemed always to have known this—and I supposed that Harvard was the college for writers." Max had been there for a year before Van Wyck arrived, and he gave his hometown friend every chance to meet the right people. The two of them spent most of their time at the Stylus, the literary club Perkins enjoyed most in Cambridge. They lived together in its straw-yellow wooden house at 41 Winthrop Street. Brooks observed that a Puritanical "Cromwell" spirit in Max was uppermost then. For a while Max awakened Van Wyck regularly at six A.M. and read Herbert Spencer and other philosophers aloud to him. He occasionally wore a jaunty Norfolk jacket—as did Professor William James —but usually dressed in funereal grays and black.

Max chose to study economics. He did so, Brooks believed, because Max "did *not* like to know about railway rates and fire-insurance statistics." The choice was an extension of one of his grandfather Evarts's aphorisms: "I pride myself on my success in doing not the things I like to do, but the things I don't like to do." That kind of Yankee thinking, which found virtue in hardship, enabled Max to move upstairs at the Stylus, into a tiny attic with a table and a cot, and often to study through the night. Years later Perkins realized, "I threw away my education though by majoring in political economy which I hated, on some theory that for that very reason it was good discipline and that whatever courses in literature which I would have loved could give me, I would get in the natural course of things." Max never read all he would have liked. Throughout his career, for example, he was embarrassed about his shallow knowledge of Shakespeare's works.

Outside the Stylus Club, Max found most of his literary inspiration in "Copey's" circle. Whether or not they had been among his students, most men who were at Harvard during his forty years of residence in the Yard remembered Professor Charles Townsend Copeland. Copey was the little man from Calais, Maine, with wire-rim spectacles and a bulbous head—topped in the cooler months by a derby and in the summer by a straw boater. By the time he had become a member of the English Department at Harvard he had turned his back on an acting career, dropped out of Harvard Law School, and worked seven years on the staff of the Boston *Post*. He was neither an intellectual nor a scholar, but he had the ability to teach with almost mystical enthusiasm. Scanning sonnets meant less to Copey than performing them; a curmudgeonly iconoclast who turned ham before an audience of any size, he took Harvard by storm. Students flocked to his recitations of the English masterpieces and joined his indulgent literary discussions. But Copey's reputation was deserved: He could breathe life into the dustiest classics.

Copeland was Perkins's instructor when he took freshman English, and the young professor's approach to literature roused Max. When Copey took over the expository writing course, English 12, Perkins immediately petitioned to be among the thirty persons admitted. "Copey was not a professor teaching a crowd in a classroom," Walter Lippmann remembered in a tribute to Copeland. "He was a very distinct person in a unique relationship with each individual who interested him."

The method of his teaching, as it lives in my own memory [Lippmann elaborated], seems to me to have been more like a catch-as-catch-can wrestling match than like ordinary instruction. What happened was that you were summoned to his chambers in Hollis and told to bring with you your manuscript. You were told how to read what you had written. Soon you began to feel that out of the darkness all around you long fingers were searching through the layers of fat and fluff to find your bones and muscles underneath. You could fight back but eventually he stripped you to your essential self. Then he cuffed the battered remains and challenged them into their own authentic activity.

Almost from the moment he and Professor Copeland became friends, Max applied himself to his studies. Copey's influence on Perkins grew steadily. Certainly he developed Max's editorial instincts. By his fourth year at Harvard, Max was earning honors grades. More important, he acquired Copeland's love for writing. "So far as I am concerned," Max wrote Copey years later, "you did more good than all the rest of Harvard put together."

During Max's senior year, a Miss Mary Church, who ran a girls' finishing school on Beacon Street in Boston, asked Copeland to recommend a student to instruct her senior pupils in English composition. Copey picked Perkins. One of the dozen schoolgirls, Marjorie Morton Prince, clearly remembered this young man of twenty-two, just a few years older than his audience. "Every time he arrived we sat there hypnotized. We must have seemed absolutely dumb to him. He talked about writing as though it were the most important subject in the world. And we all worked like slaves for him. After a few weeks, Max started to wear dark glasses in class. We knew it was to keep from looking at us and getting embarrassed, because we all stared at him with a kind of dreamy glaze over our eyes."

Max graduated from Harvard in June of 1907 with an Honorable Mention for his work in Economics. The only one of his circle of friends who did not celebrate his commencement with a grand tour of Europe, he went right to work. He did not even consider preparing for the bar (though his three brothers became lawyers). Instead, he took a job at the Civic Service House in the Boston slums. It called for teaching Russian and Polish immigrants at night and district visiting by day, but it allowed Max free time for reading and learning to type. At summer's end he took a short vacation in Windsor, then went to New York to work on a newspaper. Van Wyck Brooks said, "Copey, no doubt, the old newspaperman, had worked on Max's imagination."

Getting a good newspaper job in those days usually depended on one's connections. Perkins knew the son of the managing editor of the

New York Times, but that proved to be almost as much of a liability as an asset. The *Times* hired Max, but it was the city editor—not the managing editor—who handed out assignments. This particular city editor liked to choose his own reporters. Max was put on "emergency work"— he was one of the reporters who hung around the office from six P.M. to three A.M. waiting for suicides, fires, and other nocturnal catastrophes. For three months Perkins sat through the night, staring at the city editor and wondering, "Does this man know the paper is paying me $15 a week?"

Then Max was moved up to police reporting, covering everything from murders in Chinatown to rent strikes on the Lower East Side. In due course he was promoted to the *Times*'s general staff. He scooped the city with his story on the collision of the S.S. *Republic* off Nantucket Light and covered William Jennings Bryan's final campaign speech at Madison Square Garden.

Max volunteered for any risky assignment. Covering one story, he got strapped in the electric chair at Sing Sing; another time he accompanied champion race-car driver George Robertson in a record-breaking, sixty-miles-per-hour test ride in a Locomobile car No. 16. But few of Perkins's articles got closer to the front page than the society news.

He enjoyed his independence and forever thereafter joked about his "roughing it" in his cold-water flat, saying, "I had to go to the Harvard Club for hot baths." A few years later, Perkins spoke to one of Copey's classes and said that a time comes when a man "assimilates the mental habits of a newspaperman and this will hurt him. It is obvious that the rapidity and carelessness with which the newspaperman must write will be fatal to any higher form of writing in the end; but I am thinking rather of the interest the reporter takes in events as such, quite apart from any true significance. He is a recorder and nothing more. He does not look below the surface of things." Max was still interested in what he called "one of those professions whose practitioners deal in the most powerful of all commodities—words." But he was tiring of the journalist's erratic hours and constant deadlines.

During his years at the *Times* he had been calling on Louise Saunders, a girl with whom he had attended dancing class in Plainfield years earlier. Louise came from a prominent Plainfield family. Her mother, she once wrote, "was very beautiful—much more beautiful than were the other mothers in the little suburban town in which we lived." Louise's father, William Lawrence Saunders, pursued politics, engineering, and business.

A friend of Woodrow Wilson, he was twice elected mayor of Plainfield. After patenting more than a dozen major inventions based on his experiments with compressed air, he became the first president of the Ingersoll-Rand corporation. He constantly entreated his two children to "learn the value of money" and he wanted everything to be "practical."

Every Easter Sunday the Saunders family kept their team of horses stabled and walked to church. Louise adored the ritual, particularly one Easter in the 1890s when her hat was especially pretty; it was made of dark-green straw with a wreath of leaves and tiny red button roses. That Easter, for the first time, she became aware of the church itself; she noticed the blue ceiling sprinkled with bright silver stars. Under heaven's blue dome she rested her hand on the pew in front of her and thought about her Easter hat. Three rows in front of the Saunderses sat the Perkins family. Louise's eyes were drawn to Max, as she later confessed, "because he looked up at the blue ceiling and the stars. He seemed to wonder what could be understood."

A few years later, when the Saunders daughters were in their early teens, their mother died of cancer. Mr. Saunders adored his girls but his overriding passion was for travel. His children sometimes accompanied him for months of living abroad, but more and more often he embarked alone on long voyages. Left at home, the girls were raised by a governess who persistently remarked to Louise, "Isn't it a pity you're not pretty like your sister."

For a time Louise withdrew into herself. Years later, when Max Perkins began paying serious attention to her, she had grown out of her shell and had developed the talent and passion to become an actress. And by then Louise was beautiful. She was petite, with a fine, slim figure. She had long almond-shaped eyes, light-brown hair, a winning smile, and a small straight nose. Her father had converted a stable into a kind of theater for her. She became well known in Plainfield for her amateur performances as well as for several plays she had written.

Max found Louise Saunders delightfully feminine. She had intelligence, humor, and a volatile personality that contrasted with his steady one. Full of vitality, she could be temperamental and vain and unpredictable with her clever remarks. She depended on her intuition, what one daughter called her "uncanny knack for arriving at solutions for things without reasoning."

Max first thought seriously about Louise in the summer of 1909, after she had invited him to a swimming party and picnic at her family's place in Sea Girt, New Jersey. When he returned to New York he wrote her that he had left behind a pair of pajamas. Louise could not find them but came across somebody else's bathing suit. "Here are your pajamas," she explained. "I'm afraid they have suffered a sea change into something rich and strange."

Max began inviting Louise to Windsor for weekends. On one occasion his younger sister Fanny spied on the two of them sitting in the parlor. They were holding a pincushion between them, trying to push out the needles stuck inside. "I don't think they looked down at their hands once," Fanny remembered. "They just gazed into each other's eyes and seemed very much in love."

Max Perkins was full of notions about women, pro and con. One of his favorite saws was that a man who didn't marry was a coward, as was a woman who did. After a certain age, he believed, bachelors were just shirking responsibilities and women started looking for husbands only to avoid gossip or pity. But the warring factions in Max's personality seemed balanced by Louise. In her he found every quality he deemed desirable in a wife. His romantic side responded to her beauty and her need to be protected; his cerebral side foresaw and welcomed a lifelong battle of wits. On her part, Louise spoke of Max as "my Greek God."

By the winter of 1909, Max was looking for a job with regular hours. He heard about an opening in the advertising department at Charles Scribner's Sons and got an appointment with the head of the company. Max had learned that one of his professors from Harvard was an old friend of Charles Scribner and so, before the interview, he solicited a letter from him. Barrett Wendell obliged.

> *Dear Charles:*
>   *May I have the pleasure of giving Maxwell Perkins this personal word of introduction to you. Old fellows like me don't know young ones so well as we should like to. But I knew Perkins's father well; and you as well, if I am not mistaken, knew his mother yrs. ago—a daughter of Mr. Evarts. And I have known and admired all four of his grandparents. So when he came to college, he had a rather hard record to hold in my esteem; and he held it, happily and pleasantly. He has in him the right stuff. He is really the sort one can depend on.*

"Of course, those who could most competently recommend me are my superiors on the *Times*," Perkins wrote Mr. Scribner, after they had discussed the post of advertising manager, and without their recommendation I could hardly hope for the position of which you spoke to me. Yet I cannot afford to set my bridge afire while I am crossing it. So far, I have said nothing here of my intention to leave the newspaper business. But if things so work out that the want of recommendation from my editors alone stands in my way with regard to this position, I shall ask instantly for it.

Max continued working at the *Times*, waiting for Scribner to make his decision. One night in the early spring of 1910, he was sent to the Bowery to cover a story. An enterprising burglar had rented a vacant store across the street from the Bowery Savings Bank and had dug a tunnel most of the way to the bank's vault when his passageway collapsed. The thief was trapped underground. Perkins's assignment was to report to his office every half-hour on the progress of the rescue mission. The nearest telephone to the scene was a private line in a saloon across the street. As policemen worked deep into the night, Perkins felt embarrassed about making repeated calls on the house, so he ordered a drink with each call. It was almost dawn when the robber was brought to the surface and arrested. Max went home to collapse from intoxication as much as exhaustion. Just a few hours later his roommate, Barry Benefield, awakened him with the message that Mr. Scribner wanted to see him that morning at nine.

Max was tired and hung over throughout the interview, but Scribner was nonetheless impressed by the young man's earnestness. Perkins had explained his motives to him previously in a letter:

> I know that people generally, and with considerable reason, suspect a newspaperman of wanting the quality of steadiness. They do not think him capable of settling down to a regular and unexciting life. In case you share in that idea, I want to tell you that aside from my natural interest in books and all connected with them, I am anxious to make this change because of my desire for a regular life; and I have the strongest reasons a young man can have for desiring such a life, and for liking it once I have it.

Perkins was hired as advertising manager and promptly got engaged.

At noon on December 31, 1910, he and Louise Saunders were married in Plainfield's Holy Cross Episcopal Church, under the silver stars. William Saunders gave his new son-in-law a gold watch as a wedding present, which Max carried from that day on. As a minor hearing deficiency worsened each year, it became Perkins's habit to put the watch up to his weak left ear, then slowly move it away to measure his auditory powers by the distance at which he could still discern the ticking.

Max and Louise honeymooned in Cornish, New Hampshire—just across the river from Windsor—in a small cottage belonging to one of the Evarts cousins. Louise's father had told his daughters that when each started out in marriage he would present her with a home. The Perkinses accepted his offer—though Max felt uneasy about it—and when they returned to New Jersey they crossed the threshold of a small, plain house at 95 Mercer Avenue in North Plainfield. Shortly after settling in, they took back all the duplicate silver trays and bread baskets they received as wedding presents and bought a thirty-inch marble statue of the Venus de Milo. It became a favorite possession.

Perkins was happy with his new job and its more normal hours. The position of advertising manager at Scribners required imagination (though not daring), an instinctive appreciation for the literary product, and a feel for what the public would buy. Forgetting his college training in economics, Max sometimes spent well over his budget on books he liked. In 1914 one of the editors of the Scribner staff left to become a partner in another firm. Charles Scribner had been so impressed with Perkins's work that he moved him up to the fifth floor. Max's brother Edward recalled, "He used to say they made an editor out of him to keep the company from going bankrupt."

In almost the same time it took Max to become an editor at Scribners, he and Louise had produced three children—all daughters. Bertha, born in 1911, was named for Louise's mother. When the second girl arrived two years later, Max wanted to name her Ascutney, after his beloved mountain in Vermont. Upon Louise's protest she was named Elisabeth, after Max's mother, and later nicknamed "Zippy," the attempt of a younger sister to pronounce her real name. Two years after Zippy came Louise Elvire—called Peggy and a number of variations.

In the summer of 1916, Max volunteered for reserve duty in the United States Cavalry and was sent to the Mexican border with a company composed of men from the Plainfield area. While he was away, Louise's sister insisted that she and her husband could not afford the large house her father had given them, and she proposed swapping homes with the Perkinses. Shortly after Max returned to New Jersey, the Perkinses packed up and moved the Venus to the front hall at 112 Rockview Avenue. Across the living room mantel Louise painted in blue and gold Gothic script an aphorism her husband had composed: "The more a man is, the less he wants."

Two years later the Perkinses' fourth child was born. Max was on the stairs in the house in Plainfield early that August morning when he heard a baby's cry. He wrote of the event years later: "I said to myself, 'That's the cry of a boy baby. God sent me a boy to make up for my not going to war.'" When he learned the facts he dispatched a one-word telegram to his mother: GIRL. She was named Jane.

Among his five women, Max enjoyed posing as a hardhearted misogynist. To the repetitious questions about his not having any sons, he replied flintily, "Oh yeah, we had sons, but we always drowned them." Whenever he heard of a married man dying, he remarked, "She killed him." It was more the humor of the period than an animosity toward women.

Perkins found his own wife formidable. Louise was a woman of unending energy, every bit as strong-willed and determined as her husband. Their love match, according to Andrew Turnbull, the literary historian, was a little like the "union of a Scotch professor and a midinette." It was a battle of the sexes made unique by the eccentricities of both their characters. At the start, relatives whispered of their arguments as "getting adjusted," but soon it was clear that they were more serious than that. The romance in their marriage disappeared. Max's emotions went behind a stone wall of Yankee reserve, while Louise's were always on display. She wanted him to respect the acting career she desired, but he believed that women should not be seen on stage. Before their wedding, Max had extracted one simple promise from Louise: She would give up her theatrical aspirations.

There were other injustices Louise had to put up with. While Evartses were often scornful of Perkinses, they looked with absolute disdain upon Louise Saunders. "She was the actress type to us, all made up with cheek rouge—a real scalp-hunter who liked her men," one of them once said. "She was the last kind of woman we expected Max to marry." Men liked her, but for years afterward, all the strait-laced women watched Louise's every move, as though expecting some wicked act.

In fact, Louise was more worldly than any of the Evartses, and considerably more kindhearted. The clan in Windsor interpreted her behavior as haughty. They resented the fact that she had a wealthy father who allowed her to fling money around. Max, like them, had been taught that something earned was worth more than a gift. Louise could be frivolous, and Max had always been a pillar of prudence. But the instant Max's mother expressed something less than approval of Louise's domestic abilities, he hastened to insist, "Mamma, I didn't marry Louise for a house-keeper. I married for companionship."

Louise cared for their daughters, though she was sometimes a distracted parent. She still had loftier ambitions than merely sitting at home to raise four children. When she was not writing children's plays, she busied herself directing amateur productions, or redecorating her house. Early in his marriage Max wrote Van Wyck Brooks, "Louise could make a hovel more attractive than a palace."

No love was stronger than that which Max felt for his daughters, and they clung very close to him. Every evening he read to them, starting with simple poems and working up to more complicated nineteenth-century novels as they grew older. Max instilled romantic values into his eldest daughter Bertha to such an extent that for years she wanted to grow up to become a knight—Max had bought her a toy sword and armor to train for it. When Zippy said she'd love to see a burning house, he took one of the old family dollhouses, stuffed it with paper, and set it afire, delighting her as flames came out of the windows and the roof caved in. In the winter he put on a balaclava helmet, a knitted cap that covered most of his face, and coasted down long, snow-covered hills on the same sled with Peg. "Uncle Max imposed all sorts of strict rules on his girls," one niece said, "but none of them was ever enforced."

Whenever he was separated from his family, even when he was no farther than his office, Max felt low and stayed close by writing letters to them. He insisted that his secretary, the dedicated Irma Wyckoff, come to work every Lincoln's Birthday holiday to type up the elaborate valentines he wrote and illustrated. When the family was away in Windsor he tried writing to at least one daughter every night. Sometimes the letters were splendid works, full of original fairy tales. They were always expressions of his love that any child could understand. He once wrote Zippy: "A daddy can't have any fun without his children. There is no use his trying. Everywhere he goes he thinks, 'Yes, this would be fun if only my little girls were here, but what good is it without them.' He can't get them out of his head. He may go to see statues of something, but they are not what he really sees;—he sees his little girls, playing, far away. But when he gets their letters, then he is happy." During summers Perkins joined his vacationing family in Windsor as often as he could. He always returned from Paradise rejuvenated, ready to face the accumulated papers on his untidy desk.

IV

Branching Out

Not long after Maxwell Perkins introduced F. Scott Fitzgerald to Van Wyck Brooks in the summer of 1920, Edmund Wilson, one of Fitzgerald's Princeton companions, wrote an imaginary conversation for the *New Republic* between Perkins's newest friend and his oldest, a meeting of two of the most celebrated literary minds of the day. Wilson supposed Fitzgerald would acknowledge that Brooks was "the greatest writer on the subject [of American literature]" and then tell him: "Of course, there were a lot of people writing before *This Side of Paradise*—but the Younger Generation never really became self-conscious before then nor did the public at large become conscious of it. I am the man, as they say in the ads, who made America Younger Generation-conscious." Brooks later remarks, "Scarcely had the first crop of young writers arrived and achieved, like you, some impressive success than a host of publishers, editors and journalists appeared ready to exploit and commercialize them—with the result that there is now more demand for 'younger' writers than there are younger writers to supply it."

Scribners resisted the trend. Old CS had no intention of converting his publishing house into a pulp factory, grinding out trashy fiction that failed to live up to his company's seventy-five-year reputation for responsible publishing. Maxwell Perkins respected the company's standards but was inclined to take risks. More actively than any of his colleagues, he scouted the work of new authors from all corners of the country. In what seemed a personal crusade, he gradually replaced the hackneyed works in the Scribners catalog with new books he hoped might be more enduring. Beginning with Fitzgerald and continuing with each new writer he took on, he slowly altered the traditional notion of the editor's role. He sought out authors who were not just "safe," conventional in style and bland in content, but who spoke in a new voice about the new values of the postwar world. In this way, as an editor he did more than reflect the standards of his age; he consciously influenced and changed them by the new talents he published.

Of his first year as a published author, Fitzgerald jotted in his Ledger: "Revelry and Marriage. The rewards of the year before. The happiest year since I was 18." By August, 1920, his second novel, then called *The Flight of the Rocket*, was under way. It narrated the life of one Anthony Patch between his twenty-fifth and thirty-third years—1913–1921. "He is one of those many with the tastes and weakness of an artist," Scott explained to Charles Scribner, "but with no actual creative inspiration. How he and his beautiful young wife are wrecked on the shoals of dissipation is told in the story. This sounds sordid but it's really a most sensational book, and I hope won't disappoint the critics who liked my first one."

Six months after the publication of *This Side of Paradise*, Fitzgerald had not yet received any royalties from its sales. He had little patience with Scribners' payment procedure, normal in the industry, by which a statement was sent to the author every six months and a check four months after that. Scott remembered Perkins's invitation to ask for money whenever he needed it and requested $1,500, noting that his bride needed a new fur coat. Perkins sent the money promptly, along with the news that *This Side of Paradise* had sold almost 35,000 copies in its first seven months. Fitzgerald, who had expected his sales to have reached 40,000 copies, spent the money before it arrived. By the end of the year he had received some $5,000 against his earnings. Soon he had lost count of his requests, and the next time he needed money he simply asked, "Can this nth advance be arranged?" He went through his cash and credit so fast that he was to spend the rest of his life trying to catch up. He never succeeded.

On December 31, 1920, Fitzgerald wrote Perkins that his bank had resolved no longer to lend him anything against the security of stock he held. He also had $6,000 worth of bills and owed his literary agent, Paul Reynolds and Company, over $600 more for an advance on a story that he was unable to write. He told Max, "I've made half a dozen starts yesterday and today, and I'll go mad if I have to do another debutante," which is what they wanted him to write about. Then he asked if there was some way that his editor could arrange a loan as an advance on his new novel. Perkins successfully pleaded Scott's case for $1,600 before the company bursar. A month later Fitzgerald was able to write the editor, "Working like the deuce." The launching of *The Flight of the Rocket* was postponed several times. By February, however, Part One of Fitzgerald's novel was being typed, Part Two was being read by Edmund Wilson, and Part Three was receiving its final polish by the author. Income taxes brought Fitzgerald up another $1,000 short, but Perkins reminded the "Inevitable Beggar," as Fitzgerald had signed his latest letter, that he still had a couple of thousand dollars coming to him from *This Side of Paradise*.

Fitzgerald completed his novel at the end of April, by which time he had changed the title to *The Beautiful and Damned*. He delivered the book to Perkins in person and announced that he needed $600 to pay for a pair of steamship tickets to Europe. Soon editor and author had put Scott's account in order. Fitzgerald absentmindedly left behind his copy of the contract, so Perkins put on paper their verbal agreement:

> The only reason why we are not making you a very handsome advance is that the figure is perhaps a little difficult to fix upon, but chiefly because we thought that in view of our previous association, an arrangement by which you were free to draw against your account here and reasonably in excess of it, would be more convenient and satisfactory.

That policy made Perkins Fitzgerald's financial overseer for many years to come.

The Fitzgeralds did not especially enjoy their romp across Europe. Zelda was sick most of the time they were abroad. Scott carried Max's letter of introduction to John Galsworthy (Perkins wrote much of the advertising copy for Galsworthy's books in America, and thought *The Forsyte Saga* was "a really astonishing accomplishment in fiction"). Galsworthy received the Fitzgeralds but pontificated about the new writing coming out of the United States, disparaging its practitioners as inexperienced youngsters. Perkins knew nothing of Galsworthy's snippy remarks. In thanking him for inviting the Fitzgeralds to dinner, Max wrote, "I think it may turn out to have done him a great deal of good, for he needs steering." Fitzgerald felt privileged to have had an audience with Galsworthy but wrote Shane Leslie afterward, "I was rather disappointed in him. I can't stand pessimism with neither irony nor bitterness."

After a few weeks in France and Italy—and several pleas for "gold"—the Fitzgeralds roamed back to Minnesota. There Scott's drinking soon began to rival that of his novel's protagonist, Anthony Patch, and he settled in for a long unproductive summer at White Bear Lake. After a "hell of a time" trying to rally his creative forces, he wrote Perkins, "Loafing puts me in this particularly obnoxious and abominable gloom. My 3d novel, if I ever write another, will I am sure be black as death with gloom." During this first serious depression of their relationship, he revealed to Max:

> I should like to sit down with $\frac{1}{2}$ dozen chosen companions and drink myself to death but I am sick alike of life, liquor and literature. If it wasn't for Zelda I think I'd disappear out of sight for three years. Ship as a sailor or something & get hard—I'm sick of the flabby semi-intellectual softness in which I flounder with my generation.

Perkins's reply burst with optimism in every line, including sunny comments on the positive aspects of St. Paul weather for writing. As for life, liquor, and literature, Perkins wrote, "Everybody that practices the last is at uncertain intervals weary of the first, but that is the very time they are likely to take strongly to the second." By the end of the summer Fitzgerald was writing again.

In October, 1921, the Fitzgeralds awaited the arrival of their first child and the publication of *The Beautiful and Damned*. The child—named Frances Scott Fitzgerald and called "Scottie"—came easily, near the end of the month. Perkins sent hearty congratulations, guessing that Zelda would be delighted with a daughter. "But if you are like me," Max wrote Scott, "you will need some slight consolation and having had great experience with daughters—four of them, I can forecast that you will be satisfied later on."

By the end of the month Perkins had sent Fitzgerald the first batch of page proofs.* Scott was correcting the smallest details—he had some technical questions about student life at the Harvard of his hero, which Max easily fielded—and the novel looked "awfully good" to him. At

---

* The next stage after galleys, long printed sheets with errors corrected and the pages numbered.

Scribners the feeling about the book was equally high. Even the editors who still did not much approve of Fitzgerald's writing at least recognized that they had a hot property on their list. "The galleys are demoralizing the stenographers on the fourth floor, I mean as to work," Perkins wrote the author. "I even saw one taking some proofs out to lunch with her . . . because she could not stop reading it. That is the way with all of them who are near enough to get their hands on the proofs—not only the stenographers."

One editorial problem in Fitzgerald's text remained unresolved: a passage centering on one of Anthony Patch's friends, Maury Noble, who made some bold statements about the Bible, calling it the work of ancient skeptics whose primary goal was their own literary immortality. It is safe to assume that no Scribners editor had ever encountered such sacrilege in one of his authors' manuscripts. Perkins himself was not in the least offended by the substance of the passage. Maury's drunken oratory seemed consistent with his character. But Max feared that some readers would accuse Fitzgerald of sharing Maury's point of view and would vehemently object. "I think I know exactly what you mean to express," Perkins said, "but I don't think it will go. Even when people are altogether wrong, you cannot but respect those who speak with such passionate sincerity."

Fitzgerald took the offensive. He said he could not help imagining that remark being made to Galileo or Mencken, Samuel Butler, Anatole France, Voltaire, or Shaw—all Scott's brethren in reform. "*In fact*," he added, "*Van Wyke Brooks* in *The Ordeal* criticizes Clemens for allowing many of his statements to be toned down at the request of Wm. Dean Howells." He asked Perkins, "Don't you think all changes in the minds of people are brought about by the assertion of things—startling perhaps at first but later often becoming with the changes of the years, bromidic?" If this particular incident was without any literary merit, Scott said, "I should defer to your judgment without question but that passage belongs beautifully to that scene and is exactly what was needed to make it more than a beautiful setting for ideas that fail to appear." Fitzgerald stood fast until he heard again from Perkins.

Perkins's response to Fitzgerald became the watchword by which he edited every writer thereafter: "Don't ever *defer* to my judgment. You won't on any vital point, I know, and I should be ashamed if it were possible to have made you, for a writer of any account must speak solely for himself. I should hate to play (assuming V. W. B.'s position to be sound) the W. D. Howells to your Mark Twain." Perkins wanted Fitzgerald to realize that his objection was not on literary grounds.

> It is here that the question of the public comes in [he wrote]. They will not make allowances for the fact that a character is talking extemporaneously. They will think F. Scott Fitzgerald is writing deliberately. Tolstoi did that even, and Shakespeare. Now you are, through Maury, expressing your views, of course; but you would do so differently if you were deliberately stating them as your views.

He wished Fitzgerald would so revise it "as not to antagonize even the very people who agree with the substance of it."

Fitzgerald realized that the material had been flippant. He refined Maury's speech by substituting the word *deity* for *Godalmighty*, cutting the word *bawdy*, and transforming "Oh, Christ" into "Oh, my God."

While the dust jacket was being printed and the page proofs were at the foundry for the manufacturing of the printing plates, Fitzgerald came up with a new final paragraph for the novel which he thought would "leave the 'taste' of the whole book in the reader's mouth as it didn't before." The climax of *The Beautiful and Damned* comes as the hero and heroine, Anthony and Gloria Patch, win their long struggle to obtain a huge inheritance. But they have also been ravaged by alcohol. To celebrate their new wealth they take a cruise to Europe, and aboard ship Anthony declares that he has come through; he has made it. The ending of the book that Scott was now proposing read:

> That exquisite heavenly irony which has tabulated the demise of many generations of sparrows doubtless recorded the subtlest verbal inflection made upon such a ship as the Imperator. And unquestionably the allseeing Eyes must have been present at a certain place in Paradise something over a year before—when Beauty, who was born anew every hundred years, came back from earth into a sort of outdoor waiting room through which blew gusts of white wind and occasionally a breathless hurried star. The stars greeted her intimately as they went by and the winds made a soft welcoming flurry in her hair. Sighing, she began a conversation with a voice that was in the white wind.
>
> "Back again," the voice whispered.
>
> "Yes."
>
> "After fifteen years."

"Yes."

The voice hesitated.

"How remote you are," it said. "Unstirred . . . you seem to have no heart. How about the little girl? The glory of her eyes is gone—"

But beauty had forgotten long ago.

Zelda Fitzgerald detested this lyrical coda, and she denounced it so strongly that the author cabled Perkins for an objective opinion: ZELDA THINKS BOOK SHOULD END 'ITH ANTHONY'S LAST SPEECH ON SHIP— SHE THINKS NEW ENDING IS A PIECE OF MORALITY. LET ME KNOW YOUR ADVICE IF YOU AGREE LAST WORD OF BOOK SHOULD BE I HAVE COME THROUGH OR DO YOU PREFER PRESENT ENDING I AM UNDECIDED JACKET IS EXCELLENT.

Perkins did not balk. I AGREE WITH ZELDA, he wired Scott. Then he wrote him: "I think she is dead right about that. Anthony's final reflection is exactly the right note to end upon."

Fitzgerald's writing in *The Beautiful and Damned*—the smart dialogue, plot twists, and action by implication—still did not conform to stylistic conventions of the novel. And so Max thought for a while that it might be good for the ending to point out a moral. The satire, he told Scott, "will not of itself be understood by the great simple-minded public without a little help. For instance, in talking to one man about the book I received the comment that Anthony was unscathed; that he came through with his millions, and thinking well of himself. This man completely missed the extraordinarily effective irony of the last few paragraphs." Still Max did not think the advantages of making the meaning more explicit were such as to overcome the artistic losses. He put aside Scott's new half-page and revised the copy for the dust jacket so that it would insure the understanding of Fitzgerald's irony.

Perkins believed the general reading public had been entertained by Fitzgerald's writings but had not accorded them their due literary significance, mainly because of the frivolity of his characters. Max was greatly impressed with the depths Fitzgerald plumbed in this second novel. "There is especially in this country a rootless class of society," he wrote Scott, "into which Gloria and Anthony drifted—a large class and one which has an important effect on society in general. It is certainly worth presenting in a novel. I know that you did not deliberately undertake to do this, but I think *The Beautiful and Damned* has in effect done this; and that this makes it a valuable as well as brilliant commentary upon American society."

The Beautiful and Damned—dedicated to Shane Leslie, George Jean Nathan, and Maxwell Perkins "in appreciation of much literary help and encouragement"—was published on March 3, 1922. Six weeks after publication, Perkins reported to Fitzgerald that Scribners was not getting reorders on the book as large as he would like, though it had run through its third edition of 10,000 copies by mid-April. (The same week Scribners printed the thirteenth edition of *This Side of Paradise*.) His hopes of its being an overwhelming success were deflated, but, Max wrote, he was sorry Fitzgerald's letters already spoke of its being a disappointment. "Of course I wanted it to sell a hundred thousand or more," Perkins said, "and I hoped that the extraordinary exhilaration of your style from paragraph to paragraph might make it do so in spite of the fact that it was a tragedy and necessarily unpleasant because of its nature, so that its principal elements were not of such a kind as in themselves to recommend it to the very great mass of readers who read purely for entertainment and nothing else. Now, at least this book is going to have a pretty large sale. The trade * are going to get rid of it easily. It has made a stir among the discriminating and has therefore been all to the good except from the most purely commercial viewpoints. I know that that is an important viewpoint to you as well as to us; but for our part we are backing you for a long race and are more than ever convinced that you will win it."

Perkins was already thinking of the next project in Fitzgerald's career. He thought it should be a collection of short stories. He liked to follow a novel with a collection, for he found the sales of one generally stimulated the other. Fitzgerald picked a dozen magazine pieces and offered a title for the anthology: *Tales of the Jazz Age.* After the next meeting of the Scribners salesmen, Max reported back: "There were loud and precipitous criticisms of the title. . . . They feel there is an intense reaction against all jazz, and that the word whatever implication it actually has, will itself injure the book."

Scott polled his wife, two booksellers, and several friends, all of whom liked his title. He would not budge. "It will be bought by *my own personal public*," he wrote Max, "that is, by the countless flappers and college kids who think I am a sort of oracle." Scott offered to sacrifice

---

* Trade books are books of fiction and nonfiction that are sold through the trade—bookstores and other commercial outlets—as distinct from textbooks and other technical books, which are sold differently.

Jazz Age only if Perkins himself were dead set against it and would blazon another, more arresting title over half the cover. Perkins did not spell out his own objections to the title, and so it stuck.

But for several months Perkins had been attempting to influence Fitzgerald on a more important matter. With *The Beautiful and Damned*, he believed, Fitzgerald had taken the character of the flapper its full distance. ("Don't you ever be one," he warned his nine-year-old daughter Zippy that summer. "They're so silly.") Scott's short-skirted, bob-haired heroines were attractive, but, as Perkins told him when they discussed advertising the novel, "We ought to . . . get away altogether from the flapper idea." Scott was unsure about giving up what he did best. He could not forget how good those jazz babies had been to him. Upon Max's suggestion, however, he entered a new phase in his short stories: His characters began growing up. Most of his pieces in the next few years were not about finding love so much as losing romance. Money, formerly an object of awe, became an instrument of power. Fantasies were abandoned for unfulfilled dreams.

When Max asked Scott in May, 1922, if he had thought any more about a new novel, Fitzgerald had not yet developed a story in the rounded way Perkins had hoped, but he was at least on the right track. Scott replied, "Its locale will be the middle west and New York of 1885 I think. It will concern less superlative beauties than I run to usually & will be centered on a small period of time. It will have a catholic element. I'm not quite sure whether I'm ready to start it quite yet or not." Perkins hoped the idea of the novel would grow on Scott until he would feel compelled to write it, but for months Fitzgerald bounced between projects, ultimately deciding to complete a play that he had started early in the year.

Gabriel's Trombone was a romantic farce about a henpecked postman, Jerry Frost, who dreamed of becoming President of the United States. Scott announced that the work was "the best American comedy to date, and undoubtedly the best thing I have ever written." By Christmas, 1922, Max had a copy of the play before him.

Editing drama was not exactly Perkins's métier, but after reading Scott's work of absurdist theater, he was convinced that the play failed to lift the audience onto its wacky plane, and wrote a 1,000-word critique. Perkins spotlighted the play's trouble and set down suggestions he thought would keep it from pratfalling into burlesque nonsense. Each part of the second act, he said, should do three things: "add to the quality of a fantastic dream, satirize Jerry and his family as representing a large class of Americans, and satirize the government or army or whatever institution is at the moment in use." Perkins told Fitzgerald, "Satirize as much as you can . . . but keep one eye always on your chief motive. Throughout the entire wild second act there should still be a kind of 'wild logic.' "

While Scott had been writing *Gabriel's Trombone*, he and Zelda had moved to Long Island, where they rented a magnificent house in the newly incorporated village of Great Neck. He was again drinking too much. Later he wrote in his Ledger that 1923 was a "comfortable but dangerous and deteriorating year." A few stories, a motion-picture option, and various advances brought him almost $30,000 in 1923, $5,000 more than he had earned the year before. But after months of careless living, Fitzgerald admitted to Max Perkins that he had spent himself into a "terrible mess." He had brought the play, now called *The Vegetable*, to the point where it could be put on—he found a producer—but at considerable cost to his main career. He rewrote it from top to bottom four times—without doing much to meet Max's criticisms—and then he lost many weeks attending rehearsals in the city every day and doctoring the script every night. "I'm at the end of my rope," he wrote Perkins in late 1923. Even after deducting his earnings from *The Beautiful and Damned*, he owed Scribners several thousand dollars. He anxiously asked if he could assign them the first royalty payments of his play, which all the people backstage assured him would be a great hit, to be paid until the full amount was cleared up. "If I don't in some way get $650 in the bank by Wednesday morning, I'll have to pawn the furniture," he told Perkins in horror. "I don't even dare come up there personally but for God's sake try to fix it." Max got the money deposited without the assignment that Fitzgerald had proposed.

Nineteen twenty-three was one of Broadway's brightest years. John Barrymore played *Hamlet* just a few blocks away from where his sister Ethel was appearing in *Romeo and Juliet*. Elmer Rice's *The Adding Machine* and Pirandello's *Six Characters in Search of an Author* also opened. Most critics cited Galsworthy's *Loyalties* as the best play of the season. F. Scott Fitzgerald's *The Vegetable* never got into town. In fact, a good number of people who saw the curtain raised in Atlantic City didn't stay in the theater long enought to see it drop.

"Did you hear that Scott's play fell absolutely flat?" Perkins wrote Charles Scribner. "The second act seemed altogether to bewilder the audience. And Scott was a great sport. The moment he got back he called me up and described the failure in the most uncompromising way. He said, 'I said to Zelda, here we are after all these books with nothing. Not a cent to show. We'll have to begin all over.' "

The successful editor is one who is constantly finding new writers, nurturing their talents, and publishing them with critical and financial success. The thrill of developing fresh writing makes the search worthwhile, even when the waiting and working becomes months, sometimes years, of drudgery and frequent disappointment. William C. Brownell once heard that Roger Burlingame, one of Max's young colleagues, was discouraged by the labor. He went to him and suggested that 90 percent of the time editors perform duties any office boy could do as well. "But once a month, or once every six months," said Brownell, "there comes a moment which no one but you could cope with. Into that single moment of work goes all your education, all your background, all the thinking of your life."

In the summer of 1923 Scott Fitzgerald drew Perkins's attention to his Long Island neighbor and friend Ringgold Wilmer Lardner, the popular sportswriter and humorous newspaper columnist. Lardner and Fitzgerald were different in several ways. At thirty-eight Lardner was tall and dark, with deep moody eyes; he worked steadily at his writing and never considered it especially indelible. Fitzgerald was short and fair and fresh; he was sporadic in his work habits and wrote for posterity. But the two men had one strong thing in common: Both loved to revel and could drink from dusk until the sun rose over Long Island Sound.

Lardner had published several volumes of first-person sketches with other houses, but they had never been given any serious critical attention. One of them, *You Know Me Al,* was a collection of short stories in the form of letters written by a semiliterate baseball rookie. His other heroes included Tin Pan Alley songwriters, chorus girls, and stenographers, whose slangy speech identified him with the less sophisticated segments of the population. Reading Lardner's long story "The Golden Honeymoon," Perkins thought of collecting several of his pieces into one volume. "I am therefore writing to tell you how very much interested we should be to consider this possibility," Perkins suggested that July. "I would hardly have ventured to do this if Scott had not spoken of the possibility because your position in the literary world is such that you must be besieged by publishers, and to people in that situation their letters of interest are rather a nuisance."

Perkins and Lardner met that summer in Great Neck. Fitzgerald joined them for dinner at René Durand's restaurant and speakeasy. Ring mentioned a number of his stories he thought would interest the editor, and Scott babbled about all his friends—"the good eggs," he called them. As the evening got less sober, Ring went home and Scott insisted on driving Max around Long Island. They got to the car without incident, but not much farther. "There was no reason on this occasion why [Fitzgerald] should not have turned the car to the right as most people did and as the publicity man comfortably expected," *The New Yorker* wrote of the subsequent mishap, mistaking Perkins's position, "but having had perhaps a cocktail or two, it seemed more amusing to turn to the left off the road." In the dark, Scott drove Max down a steep hill into a lily pond. The next weekend Perkins went to Windsor and told Louise, "Scott Fitzgerald was saying what a good egg I was, and what a good egg Ring was, and what a good egg he was, and then, without thinking, as though it was something one good egg did to another good egg, he just drove me into the damned lake." Perkins laughed about it for years, and the body of water got larger with each retelling of the story.

With Fitzgerald's help Max set about gathering the stories Lardner had spoken of that early summer evening. It was no small task, because Ring thought so little of them he did not even keep copies for himself. Once a story was written, he was finished with it. For the most part Max had to rely on Lardner's faulty memory to discover where his efforts had been published. Even when he remembered, they had to search library vaults and magazine morgues, and it was not until December that Perkins found them all. By then he was so enthusiastic about the collection, called *How to Write Short Stories,* that he steamrollered its acceptance past his dissenting older colleagues and onto the spring list. The procedure was most irregular because the author had never gotten around to giving the enterprise his official sanction.

Ring Lardner, Jr., commented that his father might never have written another short story after "The Golden Honeymoon" if it had not been for Scott Fitzgerald and Max Perkins. "The publication of *How to Write Short Stories* made him feel for the first time that he existed in the literary world, that he was more than a newspaperman. That support didn't affect *how* he wrote, but *what* he wrote," young Lardner said. Ring sent Max his apologies for the months of trouble involved in "gathering the stuff" and extended an invitation to visit Great Neck again. "It's safer now," he assured Perkins, thinking of Scott, "as Durand's pond is frozen over."

While Perkins arranged the contents of the book, Lardner left for Nassau. Reading the stories over for the fourth and fifth times, Perkins felt there was a problem in the title *How to Write Short Stories*—it promised instruction the book did not supply. Max suggested that Lardner could easily solve the problem by writing a brief comment for each story, a satirical foreword affecting to present it as an illustration of short story writing. Lardner liked the idea, and Perkins had the captions for each story from him within days. The swiftness of delivery surprised him. "I had pictured you as chiefly occupied with golf or Mah Jongg," he told Ring, "from what Scott said."

Several of the introductions in *How to Write Short Stories* display the derisive attitude toward his fiction that Lardner never quite got over. He knew his work was funny but did not take it very seriously. Edmund Wilson wrote in his journals about one party at the Fitzgeralds' around that time.

> Lardner and I started talking about the oil scandal, and Fitz fell asleep in his chair. . . . When we were talking about his own work, Lardner said that the trouble was he couldn't write straight English. I asked him what he meant, and he said: "I can't write a sentence like 'We were sitting in the Fitzgeralds' house, and the fire was burning brightly.' "

Lardner had approached with vigor the assignment of writing the forewords, though he always resorted to a self-deprecating joke. Introducing "The Facts" he wrote:

> A sample story of life in the Kentucky mountains. An English girl leaves her husband, an Omaha policeman, but neglects to obtain a divorce. She later meets the man she loves, a garbage inspector from Bordeaux, and goes with him "without the benefit of clergy." This story was written on top of a Fifth Avenue bus, and some of the sheets blew away, which may account for the apparent scarcity of interesting situations.

By the end of the book he seemed to have petered out and was writing one-liners. His introduction to "Champion":

> An example of the mystery story. The mystery is how it came to get printed.

How to Write Short Stories (with Samples) enjoyed every kind of success. Its sales were brisk, and the reviews were excellent, almost all referring to the clever introductions and treating the veteran writer as though he were an up-and-coming new talent. The stories amused even old Charles Scribner.

Through Roger Burlingame and John Biggs, Jr., a friend of Fitzgerald's, Perkins came to meet a determined young writer from Wilmington, Delaware. John Phillips Marquand had graduated from Harvard in 1915, a classmate of Burlingame. He served on the staff of the *Boston Transcript,* the *New York Times,* and the American Expeditionary Force before joining the J. Walter Thompson advertising agency. He wrote slogans for several months, then took stock of his economic resources—$400—and decided to make a serious attempt at some of the longer forms of fiction. He moved to Newburyport, Massachusetts, and finished a romantic novel that he had been working on only in his spare time. When the novel was completed and his money nearly gone, he went to New York to find either a publisher or another job.

The sole copy of Marquand's manuscript of *The Unspeakable Gentleman* then fell victim to circumstances almost as melodramatic as its nineteenth-century hero. The suitcase containing the manuscript fell off the luggage rack of a Manhattan taxicab, and its loss was not discovered for blocks. Marquand had come to believe his manuscript—a tale about a colorful fellow who cavorted about, setting his son as bad an example as possible—was a very important work indeed, "if not the very greatest book in the English language," he later wrote, "at least the second." He placed an urgent want ad in the papers and, ten days later, miraculously the manuscript turned up. He immediately riffled through its pages as though inspecting the prose for bruises and discovered that it was not the second-greatest book in the English language or even the third. "In fact," he wrote, "I hardly believe that it is even fourth on the list." Marquand finally decided it was a very bad costume novel. Still, he said, "It was fun to write and perhaps it will be fun to read." His agent, Carl Brandt, submitted a copy of it to the *Ladies' Home Journal* and another to Roger Burlingame.

Like the other young editors at Scribners, Burlingame knew the most effective way to get an unpublished novelist on the house's list: give the manuscript to Perkins. Max took an instant liking to it and became its advocate. The writing was often florid, overdone in a Victorian manner, but its plot full of duels, midnight attacks, complicated intrigues, and escapes on horseback and by sea, all set in Napoleonic times, carried him away. Perkins and Marquand, whom Max once privately described as "an eager young man with the insecure sneer of a poor relation," met in the spring of 1921. Despite some reservations about the ultimate handling of the overstuffed plot, Max saw to it that Scribners accepted the book, because at the heart of the story, the unspeakable gentleman himself was a winning character. Perkins told Carl Brandt that the story was "promising of the author's future."

Even before *The Unspeakable Gentleman* was published, signs led Perkins to believe that that promising future was not so distant. Marquand sold three short stories and a novelette to the *Saturday Evening Post* and the *Ladies' Home Journal,* and received as much money and space as their best-known writers. At Perkins's suggestion, Scribners promptly collected and published them under the title *Four of a Kind*.

Neither of Marquand's first two books had enough of a sale to turn a profit, but the author's name was fast becoming familiar to the vast magazine-reading audience. Burlingame served as his liaison at Scribners, but whenever Marquand had any literary problems or needed serious advice about writing, he shuttled from Boston, where he had decided to make his home, to New York to meet with Max Perkins.

Like most of the other young writers at Scribners, Marquand discovered even at this early stage of Perkins's career that the "greatest thing about Max was that none of our affairs or difficulties ever seemed small to him. Without being a writer himself, he could speak the language of writers better than any editor or publisher" one would ever meet. Despite this attention from Perkins, Marquand felt insecure. His next novel, another elaborately plotted work called *The Black Cargo,* had done no better than his first two books. Max still regarded him as a potential big seller and wrote consolingly: "The fact is, the best writers are not the ones who make a great immediate success as a rule." But Marquand remained apprehensive and became convinced that his arrangement with Scribners was little more than a marriage of convenience. On one of his visits to New York he went to see Earl Balch, part owner of a small publishing house called Minton-Balch. Balch told Marquand that he was looking for books about early Americans. The author got to talking about an eccentric character named Timothy Dexter, a resident of Newburyport over a century earlier who had made several fortunes— by marrying a widow of means, shrewdly investing in continental currency, cornering the whalebone market, and selling secondhand Bibles; he then knighted himself Lord Dexter, America's first nobleman. Marquand thought a short life of Dexter would be "amusing" to write and once he had returned to Newburyport, he put his mind to the book. In light of his dismal sales record, he went so far as to tell Balch that he did not believe Scribners would be interested in such a "tenuous and doubtful venture."

But the moment the Scribners editors heard of the Dexter biography, they saw how admirably suited Marquand's writing was to such material. Furthermore, one of them explained, "Our greatest interest is the development of an author. . . . We do not, therefore, like many publishers, simply seize upon a single individual book which seems to have selling possibilities while neglecting his others, or letting them go elsewhere." But Balch had already said he would publish the book and Scribners would not ignore his claim. They released Marquand to do the book, and Burlingame assured him that "however it may turn out, it will not in any way interfere with our publishing of your books in the future and I can assure you that it will have no effect on our relations."

After Minton-Balch published Marquand's book, Perkins did his best to shepherd the author back into his fold. To demonstrate Scribners' interest in his writing other biographies on the order of Timothy Dexter, Max sent Marquand the names of several of his favorite Yankee heroes— Ethan Allan of Vermont was one—and material about them. Marquand liked the suggestions but said he didn't think there was enough money in that genre. "At any rate it seems to me that the whole field of biography is now over-run by the hack writers," he wrote Perkins, "and that there isn't the credit there used to be in it for a bright young man."

Having strayed from his publishing vows once, Marquand found his next act of infidelity that much easier. When his third novel, *Warning Hill,* was finished, Scribners' proposed advance seemed stingy alongside Little, Brown's offer of $1,000. He left Scribners for good, going on to write his popular Mr. Moto detective series and many other novels, including *The Late George Apley,* which won the Pulitzer Prize. Through the forties and fifties he had the longest string of best sellers of any writer in America.

In 1923 *Scribner's Magazine* received an article on bucking horses, of all things, and it came to the attention of Max Perkins, who admired its authentic American vernacular. Its author was Will James, a bowlegged cowboy with a bony, aquiline face. James had been orphaned at the age of four and been taken in by an old trapper. "The trapper had teached me how to read and write a little and I'd picked up some more on that through some old magazines I'd found at different cow camps," James recalled years later. Max urged *Scribner's* to publish the article and asked James for more. Soon he had James writing books. During the next twenty years James produced

twenty books, most of them very successful, including *Smoky,* winner of
the Newbery Medal in 1927 as the best children's book written by an
American, and *Lone Cowboy.*

On one of James's visits to New York, Max took a fancy to his ten-
gallon hat. James sent one to Perkins, and it fit perfectly. "I happened to
be walking in it with a portrait painter," Max wrote in thanking him, "and
he begged me to let him paint me in it, and that never happened before
I got this hat." From that day forward, there was hardly a moment when
Perkins did not wear a hat, indoors and out. Eventually he traded off permanently to a soft gray-felt fedora, size seven, which he wore so low that
it folded his ears forward.

His habit of hat-wearing became Perkins's most famous eccentricity
and the subject of much speculation. "Why the hat?" people kept wondering. The answer seems to be that he found it useful as well as ornamental.
It gave the impression to unexpected office visitors that he was on his way
out, and this kept them from buttonholing him into idle conversation. The
hat also thrust his ears forward, which helped his hearing. Miss Wyckoff
suggested that Perkins wore his hat to keep customers in the Scribners bookstore from mistaking him for a clerk as he made his afternoon
promenade. Perkins himself revealed something of his attitude on the
matter in a column he wrote for the Plainfield newspaper. The slouch hat,
he apotheosized, was "the hat of independence and individuality, the
American hat."

Perkins's attachment to his hat was hardly greater than his attachment
to his clothing in general. At first glance he seemed to be an elegantly
dressed New Yorker, but under close scrutiny he looked rather ragged. His
daughters often pointed out his white shirt peeking through the thinning
fabric of his suit-jacket elbows. Louise once tried to shame him into buying
a new suit by telling him all his clothes looked secondhand, but that did not
bother Max. Only at her sternest insistence would he give in to her demand that he buy a new suit. He would allow her to pick one suit from his
closet, take it to the tailor, and have another made exactly like it.

This Yankee penchant for the sparse made Perkins the ideal editor
for President Calvin Coolidge. Max published a collection of his speeches;
it took months to talk "Silent Cal" down from 160,000 to 98,000 words.

In the early twenties Perkins brought out two first novels that not only
sold well but were much acclaimed—*Drums,* by James Boyd, and *Through
the Wheat,* by Thomas Boyd. (The authors were not related.) Perkins now
began to find he no longer had to speak up so loudly to be heard at the

monthly board meetings. Many of the better manuscripts that came to the house were now routed directly to him. Even writers who had worked with other editors at Scribners were being drawn to Perkins's growing reputation.

Arthur Train, a suave criminal lawyer with puffy circles under his eyes and hair parted in the middle, had been writing true stories of crime and mannered escape fiction since 1905. Robert Bridges, who had been at Scribners since the 1880s, received his manuscripts. Shortly after Max Perkins was moved to the editorial department, he and Train were introduced. It turned out that Max had been one of the "genial lot" of journalists Train enjoyed so much when each worked at the New York District Attorney's office—Max for the *Times,* Train for the DA. In 1914, when Bridges became editor of *Scribner's Magazine,* Train began working more closely with Perkins. The young editor hoped there might be some way to enliven Train's writing, which stressed atmosphere at the expense of plot and character. Not long after he met Perkins, they chatted about cranky New England lawyers each knew. Thereupon Train created a fictitious lawyer named Ephraim Tutt, an eccentric, dyed-in-the-wool Yankee who had come to New York, where he employed the tricks of the law in the interest of justice. Suddenly, Train freely acknowledged in an interview, "I felt differently about my writing. I felt much more intent about it. It took hold of me very strongly when I was writing about Ephraim Tutt. . . . I think those were possibly the first stories I had written which made me feel emotion."

By the fall of 1919 Arthur Train had submitted several stories about Ephraim Tutt (of the firm of Tutt and Tutt) to Perkins. "I have read [them] . . . with great enjoyment and considerable laughter," Max wrote the author. "Certainly there were never any stories nor any other kind of writing . . . that gave such a picture of the legal life in and about the criminal courts and the district attorney's office, and that of the lawyers connected with them." That first batch, totaling 44,000 words, was serialized by the *Saturday Evening Post* over several months. Perkins then suggested publishing them all together in a book because combined they were a vivid portrait of the sympathetic Mr. Tutt. At the same time, Perkins could not resist conjuring up new plots for Train. In October, 1919, Perkins wrote,

> I have two very general ideas that might result in something: the kind of a case Tutt would not handle might furnish a story—a case for which rich clients wanted to retain him and in which, because of the great fee, he be-

came involved up to a certain point, and then stuck upon the question of
right and wrong and dropped it. . . . The other, which would bring out
the sympathy and sentiment of Mr. Tutt, might be based on one of those
not uncommon incidents where a young man, or girl, comes to the city
from the country and gets into ways of crime, or semi-crime, mainly through
ignorance and greenness. I do not think you have referred to Tutt's origin,
and it might be that the element of reminiscence—which has been rather
overworked, it is true—by which a man's sympathy is engaged because he
recalls his own first contact with the city, could be effectively evoked. In
such a story, might not Mr. Tutt ethically free the victim from the techni-
calities of law because of his conviction that his fault was due not to his
nature but to his ignorance?

In time, with Perkins's encouragement, Train invented an entire history for Tutt. It included his being born but a short buggy ride from
Windsor, in Plymouth, Vermont, and a happy boyhood during which he
went fishing with his friend Calvin Coolidge. Perkins read each story with
an anthology in mind. When the second collection of Tutt stories which
he selected appeared, critics appreciated the difference from the first volume.
They lauded the emergence of the protagonist as a more developed character. During the next three years, twenty-five Tutt stories appeared in the
Post, making him the most popular feature in the magazine. For two decades Ephraim Tutt was a household name and a hero on law school cam-
puses, where his cases were often integrated into the curriculum. Many
readers wrote in to Scribners, which continued to publish the stories in book
form, insisting they recognized the actual prototype of the character, often
guessing that it was the former Senator Evarts of New York. That guess
was plausible to Perkins. Mr. Tutt resembled many of his relatives who
had become small-town New England attorneys.

Perkins enjoyed the Tutt series but found greater satisfaction working
on Train's other works of fiction. Methodical and intellectually curious,
Train seemed the ideal author to sort out a complicated plot Max had con-
cocted. It concerned the discovery by two archaeologists of the long-buried
manuscript of an imaginary "Fifth Gospel" in which someone, after having
interviewed Jesus as to His economic and political ideas, had committed
His actual sayings to papyrus. The scroll might be assumed to contain
teachings so revolutionary, or at least antagonistic to present economic and
social theories, that its finders would choose to destroy it rather than to
plunge civilization into chaos.

The idea fascinated Train and engaged him for two years. When "The
Lost Gospel" appeared in the *Post* it caused such a stir that Scribners re-

published it alone in a slender blue volume. One reviewer called it "one of the most striking short stories of all time." Scott Fitzgerald thought it was most "ingeniously worked out" and conceded, "I never could have handled such an intricate plot in a thousand years."

Other writers wanted to hear Maxwell Perkins's ideas too. Although he was still a junior staff member at Scribners, he was becoming the company's center of gravity, gathering power without quite understanding why. "I have been trying to tell a writer and his wife how he should write," Perkins had recently written his daughter Bertha. "Isn't that funny when I don't know how to do it myself? I even told him a story to write that I made up—and he was delighted with it. It's pretty hard to talk all evening about things you don't know anything about."

For Christmas, 1923, Perkins took his family and some manuscripts to Windsor. When he returned he spoke to Charles Scribner about a matter that he had been pondering for some time. The job of the present staff of editors had increased considerably in recent years, he remarked. In manuscript submissions alone, Scribners was averaging 500 more a year than in the period just before the war. Perkins said he needed help. He was being diverted from his main work—seeking out and developing new writers.

There were several other good young people on the staff who looked to Perkins as their leader. Beatrice Kenyon, a poet who worked for the magazine, told Byron Dexter when he arrived at the House of Scribner to become an editor, "We have a genius—Maxwell Perkins." There was also Roger Burlingame. And there was Max's closest colleague, John Hall Wheelock, whom Perkins had known since their days together on the *Harvard Advocate*. In 1913, at a chance meeting at a cheap lunch counter on Twenty-third Street, Max had informed the tall, lean poet with a brushy mustache of a job opening at his company's bookstore. Wheelock had been hired and subsequently had moved up to the fifth floor. Now Max told Mr. Scribner of a need for additional editors, to spread the work load. "I should be of more value," said Perkins gamely, "if I were more free." In due course Scribner complied with Max's request.

The job of an editor in a publishing house, John Hall Wheelock wrote toward the end of his career at Scribners, is the "dullest, hardest, most exciting, exasperating and rewarding of perhaps any job in the world." Indeed, literature took on a new vibrancy, a new excitement in the early twenties. Novelist Robert Nathan once said, "It was a flower show of budding authors; and to be an editor, I guess, was to be full of hope and excitement, and that feeling of not having enough hours in the day, because it sometimes seemed that everyone you met had a good book in him."

V

A New House

By April, 1924, F. Scott Fitzgerald had fallen away from his third novel a dozen times. Maxwell Perkins thought he should buckle down and get it finished. But he was tactful. Scribners was preparing its fall list, Max told him, and he wanted Scott's novel on it. That got the author absorbed in his book once again, a work that he was deliberately undertaking for the enrichment of his craft more than his bank account. It was called *Among the Ash-Heaps and Millionaires.* He replied that he had every hope of finishing it by June. But, he told Max, "You know how those things often come out. And even if it takes me 10 times that long I cannot let it go out unless it has the very best I'm capable of in it or even as I feel sometimes, something better than I'm capable of." Fitzgerald was pleased with much of what he had written the preceding summer, but the book had been interrupted so many times that it was jagged. He smoothed the uneven writing down and cut away whole sections of manuscript—in one case 18,000 words, from which he salvaged a short story, "Absolution."

Religious overtones darken this story of a poor young Midwestern boy who, confused by his first sexual stirrings and romantic desires, finds solace in an imaginary alter ego. Perkins read it in the *American Mercury* and wrote Fitzgerald, "It showed a more steady and complete mastery, it seemed to me. Greater maturity might be the word. At any rate, it gave me a more distinct sense of what you could do." Scott was glad Max liked the story because it set the scene for his new novel. In fact at one time, he said, it was to have been the prologue to the book, but now it interfered with the schema he was following.

Like young Rudolph Miller in "Absolution," Scott Fitzgerald had been mulling over his own Catholic roots. Within days of Easter, he talked with Perkins, after which he haltingly confessed in a letter, "It is only in the last 4 months that I've realized how much I've—well, almost *deteriorated* in the 3 years since I finished *The Beautiful and Damned*." He admitted to the meagerness of his output in the last two years: one play, a half-dozen short stories, and three or four articles—an overall average of 100 words a day. "If I'd spent this time reading or travelling or doing anything—even staying healthy—" he told Perkins, "it'd be different but I spent it uselessly —neither in study nor in contemplation but only in drinking and raising hell generally. If I had written the B & D at the rate of one hundred words a day, it would have taken me 4 years. So you can imagine the moral effect the whole chasm has had on me. I'll have to ask you to have patience about the book and trust me that at last or at least for the first time in years I'm doing the best I can."

Fitzgerald realized that he had acquired numerous bad habits:

1. Laziness
2. Referring everything to Zelda—a terrible habit, nothing ought to be referred to anyone until it is finished
3. Word consciousness—self doubt
   ect. ect. ect. ect.

and was trying to get rid of them all.

Scott's new self-understanding buoyed him up. He wrote Max, "I feel I have an enormous power in me now, more than I've ever had in a way but it works so fitfully and with so many bogeys because I've *talked so much* and not lived enough within myself to develop the necessary self reliance. Also I don't know anyone who has used up so much personal experience as I have at 27." Neither did Perkins.

"If I ever win the right to any leisure again," Scott vowed, "I will assuredly not waste it as I wasted the past time. . . . So in my new novel I'm thrown directly on purely creative work—not trashy imaginings as in my stories but the sustained imagination of a sincere and yet radiant world. So I tread slowly and carefully & at times in considerable distress. This book will be a consciously artistic achievement & must depend on that as the 1st books did not."

"I understand exactly what you have to do," Perkins replied, "and I know that all these superficial matters of exploitation and so on are not of the slightest consequence alongside of the importance of your doing the very best work the way you want to do it, that is according to the demands of the situations." So far as Scribners was concerned, he assured Fitzgerald, "you are to go ahead at just your own pace and if you should finish the book when you think you will, you will have performed a very considerable feat, even in the matter of time, it seems to me."

Perkins told Fitzgerald that he did not like the title *Among the Ash-Heaps and Millionaires* and that if he had another, Scribners could prepare a jacket and hold it in readiness, thereby gaining several weeks if the book should be written in time for the fall. "I do like the idea you have tried to express," Perkins explained. "The weakness is in the words 'Ash Heap' which do not seem to me to be a sufficiently definite and concrete expression of that part of the idea." Perkins had only the vaguest knowledge of the book and its protagonist, but one title Fitzgerald had thrown out some months earlier stuck with him. He told Scott, "I always thought that *The Great Gatsby* was a suggestive and effective title."

As had Fitzgerald's own life, the scene of his novel shifted from the Midwest at the turn of the century to what he called that "slender riotous island which extends itself due east of New York." Fictionalizing his glamorous neighbors' lives was not coming easily, however, and his remedy was typical of him. "I would take the Long Island atmosphere that I had familiarly breathed," Fitzgerald wrote years later in his essay "My Lost City," "and materialize it beneath unfamiliar skies." The Fitzgeralds sailed to France.

Perkins sent a copy of *War and Peace* to meet Scott there, with instructions not to feel compelled to read it. Max presented copies of Tolstoi's novel in the same spirit that Gideons dispense Bibles. He gave one to almost every friend and author, and there was always a copy close to him at work and at home which he read time and again from start to finish. "Every time I read it," Max once wrote Galsworthy, "its dimensions seem to grow larger and its details to have more meaning. I have always tried to get other people to read it, but they, most of them, trip on the crowd of characters with unrememberable names, at the beginning."

Between his reading and writing that summer Scott was so preoccupied that he hardly noticed his wife's involvement with a French aviator named Edouard Jozan. Shortly after their affair was discovered, the Fitzgeralds were reconciled and he sent his editor a sixteen-point checklist of the season's labor. Item six was an emphatic plea not to let any other book have the early dust jacket sketch that Max had casually shown him months earlier. It featured two gigantic eyes—supposedly those of the heroine, Daisy Fay Buchanan—brooding over New York City. That illustration had inspired Fitzgerald to create an image for the book—the billboard of an oculist named Dr. T. J. Eckelburg; the sign had two enormous eyes on it, which would stare from above onto the novel's proceedings. The other highlights of Fitzgerald's letter were:

1. The novel will be done next week. That doesn't mean however that it'll reach America before October 1st as Zelda and I are contemplating a careful revision after a weeks complete rest.
7. I think my novel is about the best American novel ever written. It is rough stuff in places, runs only to about 50,000 words & I hope you won't shy at it.
8. It's been a fair summer. I've been unhappy but my work hasn't suffered from it. I am grown at last.

In closing, after filling several pages with the names of books and authors that interested him that year, Scott wrote Max, "I miss seeing you like the devil."

In his position as a leader among young writers, Fitzgerald continued to recommend promising talents to Perkins. Max appreciated Scott's concern for the unpublished, but few of his prospects in the last few years had panned out. In early October, 1924, Scott sent Perkins still another name, that of a young American living in France who wrote for the *transatlantic review*. Scott said he "has a brilliant future. Ezra Pound published a collection of his short pieces in Paris at some place like the Egotist Press. I havent it hear [sic] now but its remarkable and I'd look him up right away. He's the real thing." Fitzgerald gave his name as "Ernest Hemmingway"—a misspelling he would not learn to correct for years. Grateful for the tip, Perkins sent to Paris for copies of his books.

It would take months for Hemingway's stories to arrive, but within three weeks Perkins received another package from France—Fitzgerald's third novel, *The Great Gatsby*. "I think that at last I've done something really my own," his covering letter read, "but how good 'my own' is remains to be seen." The book was only a little over 50,000 words long, but he believed that Whitney Darrow, Scribners' sales director, had the wrong psychology about prices and about what class constituted the book-buying public now that "the lowbrows" were queuing up at motion-picture theaters for their entertainment. Fitzgerald still wanted to charge the standard two dollars for his novel and publish it as a full-sized book. He did not want any signed blurbs on the jacket eulogizing his past. "I'm tired of being the author of *This Side of Paradise*," he told Max, "and I want to start over."

Almost simultaneously Perkins received another letter announcing the author's decision to stick to the title he had placed on the book at the last minute: *Trimalchio in West Egg.* He had several others that he was considering as well. Furthermore, he was not completely satisfied with the manuscript, especially the middle of the book, but he felt he had been with it alone long enough. "Naturally I won't get a night's sleep until I hear from you," he wrote Max, "but do tell me the absolute truth, *your first impression of the book,* & tell me anything that bothers you in it."

Perkins tore into the novel and read it in one sitting. Immediately he cabled, THINK NOVEL SPLENDID. He meant much more than that and wrote Fitzgerald the next day:

> I think the novel is a wonder. I'm taking it home to read again and shall then write my impressions in full; but it has vitality to an extraordinary degree and *glamour,* and a great deal of underlying thought of unusual quality. It has a kind of mystic atmosphere at times that you infused into parts of *Paradise* and have not since used. It is a marvelous fusion, into a unity of presentation, of the extraordinary incongruities of life today. And as for sheer writing, it is astonishing.

Nobody at Scribners liked *Trimalchio at West Egg* as a title except Max, he reported to Scott. "The strange incongruity of the words in it sound the note of the book. But the objectors are more practical men than I." He thought book buyers would not know that West Egg in the title referred to the locale of the novel, a community somewhat like Great Neck, or that Trimalchio referred to the ostentatious multimillionaire in Petronius Arbiter's *Satyricon,* who was famous for his colossal and extravagant banquets. "Consider as quickly as you can a change," Max wrote, urging him to "judge the value of the title when it stands alone."

The book was a tragic romance about a bourgeois Midwesterner named James Gatz, who had made a fortune in shady business dealings, changed his name to Jay Gatsby, and moved to Long Island to be near the woman he had long pined for—Daisy Fay, now married to Tom Buchanan. After another few days with the typescript, Perkins wrote Fitzgerald, "I think you have every kind of right to be proud of this book. It is an extraordinary book, suggestive of all sorts of thoughts and moods." He praised it at length but said he had several points of criticism, all of which stemmed from his dissatisfaction with the character of Gatsby himself.

Perkins pointed out "that among a set of characters marvelously palpable and vital—I would know Tom Buchanan if I met him on the street and would avoid him—Gatsby is somewhat vague. The reader's eyes can never quite focus upon him, his outlines are dim. Now everything about Gatsby is more or less a mystery, i.e. more or less vague, and this may be somewhat of an artistic intention, but I think it is mistaken." To correct that, Perkins suggested:

> Couldn't *he* be physically described as distinctly as the others, and couldn't you add one or two characteristics like the use of that phrase "old sport," not verbal, but physical ones, perhaps. I think that for some reason or other a reader—this was true of Mr. Scribner and of Louise—gets an idea that Gatsby is a much older man than he is, although you have the writer say that he is a little older than himself. But this would be avoided if on his first appearance he was seen as vividly as Daisy and Tom are, for instance;—and I do not think your scheme would be impaired if you made him so.

Perkins knew that Gatsby's career must also remain mysterious but he did not want Fitzgerald to shortchange the reader. "Now almost all readers numerically are going to be puzzled by his having all this wealth and are going to feel entitled to an explanation," he wrote Scott. "To give a distinct and definite one would be, of course, utterly absurd." Max went on:

> You might here and there interpolate some phrases, and possibly incidents, little touches of various kinds, that would suggest that he was in some active way mysteriously engaged. You do have him called on the telephone, but couldn't he be seen once or twice consulting at his parties with people of some sort of mysterious significance, from the political, the gambling, the sporting world, or whatever it may be. I know I am floundering, but that fact may help you to see what I mean. The *total* lack of an explanation through so large a part of the story does seem to me a defect;—or not of an explanation, but of the suggestion of an explanation. I wish you were here so I could talk about it to you for then I know I could at least make you understand what I mean. What Gatsby did ought never be definitely imparted, even if it could be. Whether he was an innocent tool in the hands of somebody else, or to what degree he was this, ought not be explained. But if some sort of business activity of his were simply adumbrated, it would lend probability to that part of the story.

The feeble explanation Fitzgerald had offered caused the sagging which both editor and author detected in Chapters Six and Seven. In those scenes Gatsby's love for Daisy is revealed, the principal characters meet, and they all drive to the Plaza Hotel. Their confrontation in New York is the novel's fulcrum, on which the lives of all the characters teeter. Tom Buchanan's crucial dialogue in which he calls Gatsby's bluff never was as effective as it should have been because Buchanan was fighting an always shadowy opponent. "I don't know how to suggest a remedy," Perkins wrote the author. "I hardly doubt that you will find one and I am only writing to say that I think it does need something to hold up to the pace set, and ensuing."

Perkins's final criticism of the book concerned the way Fitzgerald conveyed those bits of Gatsby's past that he did divulge: He lumped them. "In giving deliberately Gatsby's biography when he gives it to the narrator," Max wrote Scott, "you do depart from the method of the narrative in some degree, for otherwise almost everything is told, and beautifully told, in the regular flow of it,—in the succession of events in accompaniment with time." Max acknowledged that Scott would be obliged to recite a certain amount of Gatsby's background, but he suggested a subtler way to deal with some of it:

> I thought you might find ways to let the truth of some of his claims like "Oxford" and his army career come out bit by bit in the course of actual narrative. I mention the point anyway for consideration in this interval before I send the proofs.

Having done his duty as a critic, Perkins hastened to assuage his author. "The general brilliant quality of the book makes me ashamed to make even these criticisms," he wrote.

> The amount of meaning you get into a sentence, the dimensions and intensity of the impression you make a paragraph carry, are most extraordinary. The manuscript is full of phrases which make a scene blaze with life. If one enjoyed a rapid railroad journey I would compare the number and vividness of pictures your living words suggest to the living scenes disclosed in that way. It seems in reading a much shorter book than it is, but it carries the mind through a series of experiences that one would think would require a book of three times its length. . . . The presentation of Tom, his place, Daisy and Jordan, and the unfolding of their characters is unequalled so far as I know. The description of the valley of ashes ad-

jacent to the lovely country, the conversation and the action in Myrtle's apartment, the marvelous catalogue of those who came to Gatsby's house—these are such things as make a man famous. And all these things, the whole pathetic episode, you have given a place in time and space, for with the help of T. J. Eckleberg [sic] and by an occasional glance at the sky, or the sea, or the city, you have imparted a sort of sense of eternity.

Perkins could not help recalling Fitzgerald's once telling him he was not a "natural writer." "My God!" Max now exclaimed. "You have plainly mastered the craft, of course, but you needed far more than craftsmanship for this."

"Your wire and your letters made me feel like a million dollars," Scott replied from Rome. Fitzgerald said that he would rather have Max like his book than anyone he knew; and he thought that all the editor's criticisms were valid.

He began his revisions with the very first page, the title page. He now thought that maybe the book should be called *Trimalchio*. Or just *Gatsby*. Within weeks, however, Fitzgerald had brought the title back to the one Perkins first liked, *The Great Gatsby*.

Along with this news, Scott tendered a request: He wondered if Perkins could deposit several hundred dollars more into his account, making his advance on the book an even $5,000. Perkins agreed, but he confessed he was somewhat puzzled about another request of Fitzgerald's: The author had asked for royalty percentages on this book that were lower than those on his previous books. Scott explained that this was his way of paying Scribners interest on all the money he had been advanced over the last two years. Max made a counterproposal and they dickered in reverse until they struck a compromise—15 percent of the retail price (two dollars) on the first 40,000 copies and 20 percent thereafter. For the moment, money seemed secondary to Fitzgerald. He and Zelda moved into a small, unfashionable, but comfortable hotel in Rome, planning to stay there until he had finished revising the novel.

"With the aid you've given me," Scott wrote Max, "I can make 'Gatsby' perfect." But he excepted the crucial scene at the Plaza Hotel. He told Max he feared that it would "never quite be up to mark—I've worried about it too long and I can't quite place Daisy's reaction. But I can improve it a lot. It isn't imaginative energy that's lacking—its because I'm automatically prevented from thinking it over again." He had driven his characters along the road from Long Island to New York and up to the plot's climax so many times, he said, that there was "no chance of bringing the freshness to it that a free conception sometimes gives. The rest," Scott wrote Max, "is easy and I see my way so clear that I even see the mental quirks that queered it before." Perkins's letter of editorial comments made him realize he had played the reader false. He admitted to Max:

> *I myself didn't know what Gatsby looked like or was engaged in* & you felt it. If I'd known & kept it from you you'd have been *too impressed with my knowledge to protest.* This is a complicated idea but I'm sure you'll understand. But I know now—and as a penalty for not having known first, in other words to make sure[,] I'm going to tell more.

It seemed of almost mystical significance to Fitzgerald that Perkins envisioned Gatsby as an older man, because in fact the actual model whom Scott had half-consciously used, a man named Edward M. Fuller, was older. Fuller, one of Fitzgerald's neighbors in Great Neck, and his brokerage firm partner, William F. McGee, had been convicted, after four trials, of pocketing their customers' order money. One month after receiving Perkins's list of suggestions, Fitzgerald wrote him, "Anyhow after careful searching of the files (of a man's mind here) for the Fuller McGee case & after having had Zelda draw pictures until her fingers ache I know Gatsby better than I know my own child. My first instinct after your letter was to let him go & have Tom Buchanan dominate the book (I suppose he's the best character I've ever done—I think he and the brother in 'Salt' & Hurstwood in 'Sister Carrie' are the three best characters in American fiction in the last twenty years, perhaps and perhaps not) but Gatsby sticks in my heart. I had him for awhile then lost him & now I know I have him again."

F. Scott Fitzgerald is generally regarded as having been his own best editor, as having had the patience and objectivity to read his words over and over again, eliminating flaws and perfecting his prose. Most of the writing in the draft of *The Great Gatsby* was polished, but it was not until the final revision of the manuscript that it acquired its brilliance.

Fitzgerald did some cutting—he deleted a few scenes that were unimportant to the main story, Gatsby's love for Daisy—but the bulk of his work was in additions. Not counting Chapter Six, which Fitzgerald junked and completely rewrote in proofs, he spliced in some twenty fresh passages, which together accounted for about 15 percent of the new version. This amplification is evident in the work he did on the first close description of Gatsby. In the draft version, Fitzgerald, speaking through Nick Carraway, the narrator of the novel, had described Gatsby's face in one sentence: "He was undoubtedly one of the handsomest men I had ever seen—the dark blue eyes opening out into lashes of shiny jet were arresting and unforgettable.". This was merely a rewording of a description Fitzgerald had used before, that of his boy hero in his short story "Absolution." Now, revising the novel, Fitzgerald returned to the Gatsby portrait and developed it from a simple observation into a perception of character:

> He smiled understandingly—much more than understandingly. It was one of those rare smiles with a quality of eternal reassurance in it that you may come across four or five times in life. It faced—or seemed to face—the whole external world for an instant, and then concentrated on *you* with an irresistible prejudice in your favor. It understood you just so far as you would like to believe in yourself and assured you that it had precisely that impression that, at your best, you hoped to convey. Just at that point it vanished—and I was looking at an elegant young roughneck, a year or two over thirty, whose elaborate formality of speech just missed being absurd.

Fitzgerald inserted comments on Gatsby's smile several more times until it became the dominant feature of his appearance and a mark of his personality.

The author responded creatively to nearly all of Perkins's suggestions. As Perkins had urged him to, he broke up the block of information on Gatsby's past and sprinkled the pieces in earlier chapters. Picking up on a comment of Perkins's, he made Gatsby's purported career at Oxford University a recurring topic of conversation, so that each time Fitzgerald touched upon Gatsby's claims, he brought the entire mystery of Gatsby's origins closer to the truth. Again stimulated by something Perkins had said, Fitzgerald worked a small wonder with a certain habit of Gatsby's. In the original manuscript Gatsby had called people "old man," "old fellow," and a number of other affected appellations. Now Fitzgerald seized upon the one Perkins had liked so much, adding it a dozen times, making it into a leitmotiv. This phrase became so persistent a mannerism that in the Plaza Hotel scene it provoked Tom Buchanan into an outburst: "That's a great expression of yours, isn't it? All this 'old sport' business. Where'd you pick that up?"

Fitzgerald did major work on a matter Perkins had considered important, the clarification of the sources of Gatsby's wealth. Three conversations on the subject were added in Chapter Five, and later in the book, after Gatsby's death, there now was a phone call from a business associate of Gatsby's named Slagle, about some dealings in bad bonds.

One of the ways Fitzgerald intensified the somewhat limp confrontation scene at the Plaza was to strengthen an accusation Tom Buchanan had made against Gatsby concerning his money. Buchanan had learned, he said, from a private investigation of Gatsby's affairs, a shocking fact:

> "I found out what your 'drugstores' were." He turned to us and spoke rapidly. "He and this Wolfsheim [a gangster] bought up over a hundred side-street drugstores here and in Chicago and sold grain alcohol over the counters. That's one of his little stunts. I picked him for a bootlegger the first time I saw him and I wasn't far wrong."

Before Perkins nobody at Scribners had edited so boldly or closely as he did Fitzgerald, and some of the older editors considered the practice questionable. They liked Max and sensed his ability, but they did not always understand him. In small ways as well as large, Max was different. He raised eyebrows, for example, by having a special desk built for himself. It was a high, broad-surfaced lecternlike affair, at which he could work standing up, his theory being that if he could not be outdoors exercising, he could at least avoid sitting down so much. People passing his office door could look in and see him at his peculiar desk, immersed in a manuscript, one leg bent at the knee and resting against the other, like a flamingo.

It took some time for the older editors to appreciate what Max was accomplishing at that desk, or indeed to value the new writers Perkins had brought into their house. Fitzgerald, more than the rest, seemed brash and impetuous, and a few of the more dignified staff members resented his storming of their bastion of conservatism and good taste. It was a memorable occasion, then, when Brownell emerged from his office one day and called to his colleagues: "May I read you something beautiful?" And then, loudly and with savor, he recited two pages from *Gatsby*.

Fitzgerald himself never doubted the worth of Max's assistance. For the first time since the failure of *The Vegetable*, he wrote to his editor, he believed he was "a wonderful writer" . . . "& its your wonderful letters that help me go on believing in myself." Years later he remarked: "I had rewritten *Gatsby* three times before Max said something to me [that is, before Fitzgerald had submitted the draft to Perkins for criticism]. Then I sat down and wrote something I was proud of."

He made that admission to a friend of Perkins's, perhaps the most important friend Max made outside his work, a woman named Elizabeth Lemmon.

They were introduced in the spring of 1922. Elizabeth Lemmon was eight years younger than Max, and unlike any other woman he had met. She was the embodiment of his nineteenth-century romantic vision of womanhood. She was from a large old family rooted in Virginia and Baltimore, the youngest of eight daughters, but she was not effete or spoiled. A hearty laugh enlivened her gentility. She was equally comfortable among Baltimore society or on the family's country estate, Welbourne, in Middleburg, Virginia. She had always loved to read. As a schoolgirl she had come to know a girl named Wallis Warfield. "Wally always had 'crushes' on the older girls and used to follow us as closely as a shadow," Elizabeth remembered. "That was before she decided to marry a king." Elizabeth made her debut in Baltimore, where she was known as the "second-best dancer" in the city; studied voice—she had trained for an operatic career, but her mother had allowed her to take lessons on the condition that she never perform in public; taught singing and dance at the fashionable Foxcroft School in Middleburg; and, the year she met Max, managed the Upperville, Virginia, baseball team.

Miss Lemmon went north for six weeks every spring to visit family and friends in Plainfield, New Jersey, and to attend concerts in New York. During her trip in April, 1922, she met Max and Louise Perkins. Before returning south she went to their home one evening to say good-bye.

Max Perkins had always been attracted to blondes, finding them especially womanly. When Elizabeth Lemmon strode confidently through the Perkinses' front hall that night, her golden hair set off by a gray dress, Max was entranced. Their evening together was full of warm conversation, often about authors Max worked with. She was literate but not literary; engaging but not demanding. Louise believed Max had fallen in love again that night, but not in a way that threatened her at all. Max's ardor was like that of heroes in ancient mythology or romantic poetry: It was of the spirit, not of the flesh; he wanted to put Elizabeth on a pedestal.

Miss Lemmon left behind an almost empty, cream-colored box of Pera cigarettes, a mild Turkish blend she liked. When Max came across them he sat down to write a letter. "Dear Miss Lemon," he wrote, misspelling her name:

April 14th 1922

112 ROCKVIEW AVENUE,
PLAINFIELD, N.J.

Dear Miss Lemon :—

When I found these cigarettes you had
left I thought at first to keep them as
a remembrance. But I am far from
needing a remembrance to thank me. An
recalled that you had sa you gave me —
to stop smoking because
this brand were no long.   neighbourhood
I thought I must save you
dreadful heart-broken feel
when you don't smoke, at   I always greatly
only for the brief space   But I never real
                                  coming toward

Courtesy of the Maxwell E. Perkins Estate

cigarettes would last. If you have
stopped, & felt as I have felt, this
brief reprieve will make you think of one
with extraordinary gratitude. — Maybe
that's too much to hope; but short of
that I'll ... ... give one a
now thank you for all the pleasure   to say
f. I suppose . why one else in the   & just
ly being here this year   . think

                                     of .....
Sincerely Yours   ... .
    Maxwell E. Perkins   me :—

... the phrase "dea incessu patuit,"   ... ...
knew its meaning till I saw you
through our hall the other night.

When I found these cigarettes you had left I thought at first to keep them as a remembrance. But I am far from needing a remembrance. I then recalled that you had said you meant to stop smoking because cigarettes of this brand were no longer made & I thought I must save you from that dreadful heart-broken feeling you have when you don't smoke, at times, if only for the brief space these two cigarettes would last. If you have stopped, & feel as I have felt, this brief reprieve will make you think of me with extraordinary gratitude.—Maybe that's too much to hope; but short of that, these cigarettes have given me a chance to say something too trivial to say without an excuse. It is, that I had just the faintest fear you might really think me so pusilanimous as to have been offended that you "could not bear the sight of me." I guess not though.

Next year, please remember I sent these and thank me. And I now thank you for all the pleasure you gave me—& I suppose, everyone else in the neighborhood—by being here *this* year.

After closing the letter with his formal, high, angular signature, Perkins added a postscript. He had always, he wrote, greatly liked Virgil's phrase *dea incessu patuit* ("and she revealed herself to be a goddess," as Venus did before Aeneas). "But I never really knew its meaning till I saw you coming toward me through our hall the other night."

"You can't in all honesty say Max Perkins fell in love with me," Elizabeth Lemmon said fifty years later. "We were, after all, Victoria's children—we met at a time when a smile across a room meant as much as two kids in the back seat of a car today. I think Andrew Turnbull came closest when he said Max and I had a 'true friendship.' " The evaluations of both Miss Lemmon and biographer Turnbull are accurate to a point, but incomplete. Perkins had a deeper feeling—a golden love—that Elizabeth modestly refused to admit. He adored her. She became an oasis of warmth and understanding in an increasingly difficult marriage.

Max's atavistic yearnings were at odds again, and they led him into a unique love affair—a Yankee editor's romance. Perkins allowed himself to be drawn to Elizabeth Lemmon, but he felt compelled to make any relationship with her hard on himself. He was never so at peace as when she was near, but he did everything he could to make her unreachable. He restricted their contact largely to the mails.

For the next twenty-five years they wrote privately to each other. It was the longest sustained personal correspondence in his life. In times both of happiness and of tragedy—usually out of loneliness, when he felt unfulfilled—he poured lovely thoughts onto paper, constantly expressing gratitude to Elizabeth for being not merely an inspiration but a divine crea-ture. A year might pass between letters, or three might be bunched in a month, but the continuity was maintained. Elizabeth kept the letters, and they are the only diary he left. Except for a few pages her replies do not exist. "Thank God for that," Miss Lemmon remarked decades later. "I really had nothing to say worth saving."

Max neither expected nor required of her anything more than an oc-casional response to assure him that she was still there, unchanged and constant. When his homelife seemed empty or his work life hectic, writing to Elizabeth remained his outlet, the least complicated, most perfect plea-sure in his life. In the entire quarter-century of their friendship, Max visited her in Middleburg only twice.

Within weeks of their meeting in 1922, Miss Lemmon invited the Perkinses for an informal weekend at Welbourne. She wrote of mint juleps, polo, and amateur horse shows. Louise replied that "Max was al-most overcome at your invitation, especially as you said that he might wear his sneakers all the time." She thought her husband was "tempted to give up his position in Scribners to accept it." But faithful employees worked on Saturdays, and, Louise wrote, Max said he was sorry he could not go.

Louise went by herself. It was still cold in Plainfield on the twentieth of May, but she left for Virginia with suitcases packed with summer clothes, not realizing it was just as cold where she was going. She found the rolling green hills of northern Virginia the most sublime horse coun-try she had ever seen and the Lemmons' estate glorious. The long ser-pentine drive up to Welbourne made its way through an untended lawn past big trees up to the same front door that long ago had opened for guests such as Jeb Stuart. On a small scale the house resembled Mount Vernon, with its simple lines and tall pillars in front. Two graceful one-story wings flanked the stocky central box of the mansion. Welbourne was built in 1821 and pre-Revolution family portraits hung in the parlors. An airy verandah looked out onto the overgrown grounds in the back. A Yankee cannonball had gone through one of the windows in the greenhouse, and though the pane was replaced in 1865, it was still referred to as the "new window."

Louise Perkins, in her light clothing, was cold most of the time, but she felt comfortable with Miss Lemmon and her family in their mag-nificent house. When Elizabeth's mother asked her how Mr. Perkins was, she replied, "Very enamored of Elizabeth." Louise grew especially fond of her hostess. Elizabeth was just developing an interest in the occult, and she recommended a fortune teller for Louise to consult up north.

When Louise returned to Plainfield she filled Max's ears with stories of Welbourne. He was sorrier than ever that he had not gone, but in another sense he was just as glad. From his wife's descriptions, Welbourne seemed like a mythical kingdom to him, one better visited in dreams.

In late May, 1924, Louise joined friends for a cruise to the Caribbean. Max was again unable to accompany her because of work, this time with his newest writer, Douglas Southall Freeman. Freeman had a doctorate in history from Johns Hopkins University and was editor of the Richmond *News-Leader*. The history of the Confederacy was his passion, and he had edited the wartime correspondence between Robert E. Lee and Jefferson Davis. In 1914 Scribners had commissioned him to write a short biography of Lee, on which he worked under Edward L. Burlingame. Almost a decade later the book still had not appeared. Burlingame had died, and Perkins, with a lifelong interest in the Civil War, was assigned to assist the author. In 1924 Freeman wrote his new editor:

> The whole trouble about my Lee is that I have been waiting to have a view of the final cache of Lee papers in the Confederate Memorial Institute. I did not think it quite fair, nor in any sense desirable to publish a book on Lee until I was able to examine this material. It seemed quite stupid to go into print when the last remaining collection of Lee matter was almost in one's hands.

The papers were due to be turned over forthwith, but Freeman projected another long delay before he could meet the demands of his contract. The thought of compacting all the material into 100,000 words, as Scribners expected, was mind-boggling. During his nine years of waiting for the manuscript, Burlingame had always been patient in dealing with Freeman. "I hope a like mantle covers your shoulders," the author wrote Perkins. Max had more than patience. He had a new plan which would postpone the appearance of Dr. Freeman's work for another decade but might ensure its place for centuries. Perkins suggested that Freeman undertake a definitive biography of Robert E. Lee, without regard for time or length.

In May, 1924, Max went to Virginia to discuss the project with him. On the way down, he considered the idea of seeing Elizabeth Lemmon; in Richmond he made inquiries about how he could get to Middleburg. But, just a few hours' drive away, he could not bring himself to approach her. Max stuck to business instead, staying in Richmond with Freeman and trooping across the city that would be the backdrop for so much of Freeman's writing. It would be ten more years before Freeman would present Max with a completed manuscript of his monumental work.

A letter Max received from Elizabeth Lemmon after his return to New York made him wish he had seen her when he was in Virginia. She mentioned a haircut that had given her a new look, and said her deepening involvement in astrology had added to the "transformation." Just the thought that Elizabeth might somehow be different from the first vision he had of her disturbed him. He replied:

> I can imagine no substitute that would be even "just as good." Will the new Elizabeth lack that Goddesslike repose which was among the qualities that so distinguished her from all the others—eager, restless, striving women. And if she should I'd almost rather not see her, for to do so would be to impair the image of *The Elizabeth* who would otherwise, at least survive in my memory.

"You make me still more regret that I did not risk the digression from Richmond," he wrote, explaining, "I dreaded arriving in the midst of one of those Virginia parties where a block of New England granite would be only an obstacle." Louise had called Max "a block of New England granite" just nights earlier, because he had not wept over Lillian Gish in *The White Sister*.

Several times that summer Max went to Great Neck, Long Island, ostensibly to talk to Ring Lardner about his writing. They drank what would ordinarily have been a dangerous number of highballs, but, Perkins said, they felt no serious effects because of the heat.

Lardner was planning to go to Europe and to see the Fitzgeralds there, but he hardly looked well enough to make the trip. He was coughing a great deal, eating almost nothing, and chain-smoking when he did eat. He told Perkins that he was giving up alcohol and cigarettes so he could get enough ahead on a comic strip he wrote with cartoonist Dick Dorgan to go abroad.

With Lardner's approval, Max again searched through Ring's syndicated newspaper and magazine articles until he found enough material to fill a book. The collection would be brought out in 1925, and Max was happy to publish it, though he wished Ring would attempt something ambitious. "Ring," he said, "if it were a matter of money we would be willing to help toward a novel, you know. But I judge the $5,000 or so we'd gladly put up wouldn't count." Lardner said it was not at all a question of money. It was rather that his métier was the shorter forms.

By Christmas, 1924, Ring had gone to Europe and returned, and his anthology, *What of It?*, was set in type. A new article opened the book, a piece called "The Other Side," about his companions and recent adventures "acrost the old pond" in Europe. In it he wrote, "Mr. Fitzgerald is a novelist and Mrs. Fitzgerald a novelty."

Never before had Ring been so pleased with his literary work—he had previously been quite cynical about it—and he believed he owed his growing stature as a writer to his relationship with Perkins. *How to Write Short Stories* had passed the 16,000 mark in sales; and, as Max had predicted, the Scribners republication of his old works in new wrappers gave fresh life to all the other Lardner books on the market. Excellent reviews were being written about the new book everywhere, including one by Mencken.

Ring Lardner, Jr., wrote in his family memoir, *The Lardners*: "It took the unexpected success of *How to Write Short Stories,* the extent to which reviewers hailed him as a master of the form, and unremitting pressure from Perkins to bring him back to the work on which his reputation was ultimately to rest." In December, 1924, Ring wrote Perkins, "I think I am going to be able to sever connections with the daily cartoon. This ought to leave me with plenty of time and it is my intention to write at least ten short stories a year." Three months later, Perkins read Ring's story "Haircut," a small-town barber's account of how a practical joker was shot to death by the local half-wit. It was darker than most of his earlier tales. "I can't shake it out of my mind," Max wrote Ring; "in fact the impression it made has deepened with time. There's not a man alive who could have done better, that's certain." Lardner replied with a formally typed, one-word letter: "Thanks."

After another Lardner anthology, Scott Fitzgerald wrote Max to express his concern that Ring would stagnate if he kept on writing nothing but stories. "God, I wish he'd write a more or less personal novel," he told Perkins. "Couldn't you persuade him?" Fitzgerald's suggestion was timely. At that moment Max was about to come upon a big idea for Lardner. It all began when Max decided there ought to be a "sort of burlesque on those dictionaries of biography," satirizing those "most astonishing pieces of bunk, written in all solemnity." Perkins thought of asking celebrated wits such as Lardner, Robert Benchley, Donald Ogden Stewart, George Ade, and Scott Fitzgerald each to "do a number of fictional biographies which hit off various types of people. And then to illustrate, make and bind the book in imitation of these volumes." Perkins talked the idea around at the same time that he was urging Ring to compose some long work. Within the week Max found before him the first chapter of Ring Lardner's "autobiography."

"For Heaven's sake," Perkins pleaded, "keep it up to the length of twenty-five thousand words at least, and the more beyond, the better." Lardner said there was no chance of stretching it out that long because "it would get to be a terrible strain on both readers and writer," but Perkins persisted. He said the complete "autobiography" should be published by itself, fattened with illustrations, if necessary, and that it ought to be published quickly, "for ever so many of its hits are of the moment." Within weeks the installments amassed to 15,000 words, and Lardner called the work *The Story of a Wonder Man.*

Lardner's actual life provided only the barest structure for his parody of autobiographies. He recorded such events as: "It was at a petting party in the White House that I first met Jane Austen. The beautiful little Englishwoman had come to our shores in response to an attractive offer from the Metro-Goldwyn-Mayer people, one of whose officers had spelled out her novel *Pride and Prejudice* and considered it good material for a seven-reel comedy." Perkins selected the installments that he thought should be included in the book and tacked a title onto every chapter. "I am not under any illusions about myself as a humorist," he told Ring, but he went about writing titles anyway and was teeming with more ideas for Lardner: "Why don't you write about the boy who believed the 'ads' . . . read up on all the highbrow stuff and tried it on the gals!" "Some day you ought to take a shot at the 'Clean Desk' executive." "Did you ever discuss hay fever? . . . The wretched patient has to pretend he thinks it's funny too. If you consider the topic, I'll submit myself, in the interests of science, to scrutiny." Perkins never stopped urging Ring to write a novel, or at least one long story to lead off a book, but other projects kept catching Lardner's eye, including a collaboration on a musical with George M. Cohan.

That summer the Perkinses had taken a cottage on the outskirts of New Canaan, Connecticut. "You would hate it," Max wrote Fitzgerald, "but I like it." In due course Max and Louise began to think about living in New Canaan permanently. Max had lived in Plainfield all his life, and he believed once a man had put roots down somewhere, he should not dig them up. But he believed Plainfield had sprouted into "a damnable, flat, damp, dull, cheap place." As for Connecticut, he wrote to novelist Thomas Boyd, "The people thereabouts are the right sort, at least to one of New England descent. In fact, if we could only get rid of that house in Plainfield, we would buy one here in a minute, and if controversies between Louise and me end the way they usually do, we'll buy one anyway. But I hope not. I know it would be a risky business."

Louise had given Max a list of reasons for buying a new house, beginning with her hatred of the one they owned in Plainfield. She detested the place because she associated it with the slow death of her mother. It was also costly to keep up. Added to those reasons for moving, Max wrote, "is the charm of New Canaan, a New England village at the end of a single track railroad with almost wild country in three directions, i.e. wild to an Easterner. An ideal place for bringing up children in the way they should go, girls anyhow."

Louise was already eyeing the home she wanted, and they bought it that season. Max was most impressed with the exterior of the place. It had four fluted wooden columns—"one," he wrote Elizabeth Lemmon, "for each daughter to lean against when the young men drive up in their buggies."

On January 16, 1925, Louise made what Max called another "gallant attempt to become the mother of a manchild." "It ended in failure," he wrote Elizabeth Lemmon. "They tell me what strength, what a splendid physique the girl has. That if she had been a boy it would have been a fine boy—quarterback on a Harvard Eleven and leader of an army into Germany perhaps. But as it is, what use is strength?" One New Canaanite asked Max at the train station one day what he was going to name his fifth daughter. "Blaspheme," he said, but in a more reasonable moment he and Louise chose Nancy Galt Perkins instead. The day the fifth girl "materialized" Perkins again wired his mother just one word: ANOTHER.

The Perkinses enjoyed a more active social life in New Canaan than they had in Plainfield. There were several minor literary celebrities living nearby, and Max took an instant liking to the Colums, intimate friends of James Joyce, both authors and critics in their own right. Mary—Molly to all her friends—was a big, redheaded woman. She was not at all pretty, but Max found her a "wonder, quick as a cat." Padraic, he wrote Elizabeth, "trails clouds of Irish geniality and comfort, a most charming, amusing, kindly man, who though youngish, has a kind of tolerant wisdom and an air of learning that make him seem like sixty." William Rose Benét and his wife, the poet Elinor Wylie, also lived in the neighborhood, and Max was especially eager to know her better. He did not find her much of a beauty either—"her features are small and undistinguished of a blunt, squarish sort, and her figure is angular, and I thought awkward," he wrote Elizabeth

—"though Louise was scornful when I said so." But her personality was alluring: "It is that of a brave sensitive person, wholly herself . . . She holds her head back, rather her chin up, and all together says,—but not proudly or aggressively—'I represent myself.' "

"We had many good literary evenings, though it was by no means a literary neighborhood," Molly Colum recalled in her memoirs, *Life and the Dream*. The Perkinses, Benéts, and Colums often gathered for dinner, sometimes inviting the Van Wyck Brookses, who were living in Westport, and Hendrik Willem van Loon, an "enormous Dutchman with a kind of ill-natured sneer for almost everything," who wrote the popular *Story of Mankind*.

In a short time Perkins recognized Elinor Wylie as the real spark in New Canaan. "The true basis for friendships is a prejudice or two in common," Max liked to say. With each conversation between them, he grew fonder of Elinor, for she disliked many of the same things he did, including the sort of flashy, glib writing that had become popular. They both found little that was worthy in Michael Arlen's best-selling *The Green Hat,* which was the literary rage that year. Max was also aware of Elinor's vulnerability; when she was reflective she reminded him of a waif. He felt sorry for her at the same time that he admired her. "There's something tragic in her," Perkins mused in a letter to Elizabeth Lemmon, "as if she were one who, desiring the opposite, was destined to bring sorrow to those who loved her. An ill-beloved."

As though it were written into the deed of the new house, the Perkinses promptly joined the New Canaan Country Club, and Max became a regular in the New York, New Haven & Hartford club car. Molly Colum constantly accused him of being "highly conventional and genteel," but Max said it was just that "in a town like this it's regarded as a matter of patriotism to join everything joinable." He admitted, however, that his life in Connecticut had become gayer than he liked. Preferring to spend more time with his adolescent girls, he began turning down dinner invitations. "I only see my children two hours a day at best, and I'm not going to give that little up," he insisted. That did not stop Louise, who happily went to parties alone. Left in the evenings with his daughters, Max read aloud to them, most often from *War and Peace*. During crucial battle sequences he laid out matchsticks to show his devoted girls how the Russian and French troops had been arranged. He thought all his daughters should hear that story, "for in it," he once wrote Peggy, "is the best man that ever was written about, except Hamlet. He is Prince Andrei. I wish each of you, if you *must* marry, would find a Prince Andrei for a husband,—even if he is a little too scornful and impatient."

Max corresponded steadily with Elizabeth Lemmon that year. From any of his clubs—which grew to include the Harvard Club, the Century Association, and The Coffee House in New York—he sent newsy letters about his family and town and work. In the spring of 1925, he also sent her several books. One was Lardner's latest anthology, *What of It?* Another was Scott Fitzgerald's novel. Max told her *The Great Gatsby* was better than anything the author had done, "a combination of satire and romance that no one else can give. It comes from the fact that even while he sees things with a critical eye there still hangs over them the glamour of his youthful illusions. This gives the story a kind of wistful quality."

Perkins had examined Fitzgerald's revised proofs and then written the author, "I think the book is a wonder and Gatsby is now most appealing, effective and real, and yet altogether original." All of the editor's criticisms of several months earlier had been dealt with. He wrote Scott, "Gatsby ought to do much for his creator."

As publication neared, Fitzgerald lacked Perkins's confidence. He was shakiest about the title. In early March he wired Max, asking if it was too late to change it to *Gold-Hatted Gatsby.* Max cabled that such a change would cause not only a harmful delay but also considerable confusion. The author tried to live with *The Great Gatsby,* but he still believed in his heart that the title would forever stand as his book's one flaw.

Perkins went right on making the final preparations for *The Great Gatsby*'s April 10 publication; but on March 19 Fitzgerald could not refrain from sending him an exigent telegram from Capri: CRAZY ABOUT TITLE UNDER THE RED WHITE AND BLUE. WHAT WOULD DELAY BE? Perkins responded that there would be a delay of several weeks. Besides, he wired, THINK IRONY IS FAR MORE EFFECTIVE UNDER LESS LEADING TITLE. EVERYONE LIKES PRESENT TITLE URGE WE KEEP IT. Three days later Fitzgerald acceded. He wired: YOU'RE RIGHT. But his nervousness mounted.

By publication day Fitzgerald was so overcome with "fears and forebodings" that, in a letter to Max, he turned on *The Great Gatsby,* calling it a certain disappointment to the public, the reviewers, and himself. "Supposing women didn't like the book because it has no important female characters in it," he said, "and the critics didn't like it because it dealt with the rich." Worst of all, wrote Fitzgerald, "Suppose it didn't even wipe out my debt to you—why it will have to sell 20,000 copies even to do that! In fact all my confidence is gone . . . I'm sick of the book myself."

It was an entire week before Perkins had a trend to report, and then it was with great sorrow that he found Fitzgerald's worries were borne out. He cabled: SALES SITUATION DOUBTFUL EXCELLENT REVIEWS. This was more optimistic than was the case on both counts. Later that day he wrote the qualifying details to Fitzgerald, explaining that "the trade" had been skeptical. One reason seemed to be the small number of pages in the book, only 218. This was an old objection which Perkins had thought the book market had gotten past.

> To attempt to explain to them that the way of writing which you have chosen and which is bound to come more and more into practice is one where a vast amount is said by implication, and that therefore the book is as full as it would have been if written to much greater length by another method, is of course utterly futile.

Several major distributors had, in fact, drastically reduced their orders upon receiving the short book.

Knowing how trying this period must be for Scott to bear, Perkins promised to cable any significant developments, especially the appearance of more good reviews. "I like the book so much myself and see so much in it that its recognition and success mean more to me than anything else in sight at the present time," he told Scott, "—I mean in any department of interest, not only that of literature. But it does seem to me from the comments of many who yet feel its enchantment, that it is over the heads of more people than you would probably suppose." He assured Scott, "I shall watch [its progress] with the greatest anxiety imaginable in anyone but the author."

Just a week earlier Fitzgerald had hoped his book would sell over 75,000 copies. Now he wished for but a fraction of that—enough to clear his $6,000 advance from Scribners. If the final sales projection were as low as it threatened to be, Fitzgerald said, he would give himself just one more book to decide whether or not he would continue as a serious writer. "If it will support me with no more intervals of trash I'll go on as a novelist," he told Max. "If not I'm going to quit, come home, go to Hollywood and learn the movie business. I can't reduce our scale of living, and I can't stand this financial insecurity. Anyhow there's no point in trying to be an artist if you can't do your best. I had my chance back in 1920 to start my life on a sensible scale and I lost it and so I'll have to pay the penalty. Then perhaps at 40 I can start writing again without this constant worry and interruption."

Two weeks after publication Perkins still had little basis for optimism. DEVELOPMENTS FAVORABLE REVIEWS EXCELLENT MUST STILL WAIT, he wired, and then wrote to explain: "While most of the reviewers seem rather to fumble with the book, as if they did not fully understand it, they did praise it very highly, and better still, they all show a kind of excitement which they caught from its vitality." The people who remained to be heard from were those who fully grasped the book, as thus far nobody had done. Perkins remained confident that "when the tumult and shouting of the rabble of reviewers and gossipers dies, *The Great Gatsby* will stand out as a very extraordinary book."

To blot out Fitzgerald's debt to Scribners, Scott offered his collection of stories for the fall, once bullishly entitled *Dear Money,* now more re-flectively called *All the Sad Young Men.* Max thought the title was ex-cellent, and he was pleased that Fitzgerald had made no further mention of going to Hollywood. He well knew that Scott hated to linger in debt, but he did not want Scott's debt to prey on his mind. He must not think Scribners was anxious about it. "If we wanted to be utterly hard-boiled we could look upon it as a good investment," he told him.

Perkins himself took plenty of knocks because of *The Great Gatsby.* The sales and advertising departments had bet heavily on the book because of Perkins's previous record, and they made their anger known when the book did not pay off. Several critics he knew personally took shots at the book in their reviews, then told him point-blank that he was foolish to have published such a trivial mystery novel. Ruth Hale, in the *Brook-lyn Eagle,* wrote that she found "not one chemical trace of magic, life, irony, romance or mysticism in all *The Great Gatsby.*" At a party a few weeks later she told Perkins, "That new book by your *enfant terrible* is really *terrible.*"

"So many people have attacked me about [*The Great Gatsby*] that I feel bruised," Max wrote Elizabeth Lemmon, "but they don't know. They can't see that Fitzgerald is a satirist. The fact that he throws a glamour over vice—if it didn't have it there would be none—prevents them from seeing that he lays a lash upon the vicious." Perkins realized that Fitzgerald had outgrown his public. "His virtuosity has made a 'popular novelist' of one who is above the heads of the multitudes." Max believed they never looked deeply into *This Side of Paradise*. "It was a bag full of jewels, some, cheap imitations, some pretty pebbles," he wrote Elizabeth, "and mixed among them pure and priceless ones." *The Great Gatsby* was more like one exquisitely cut gem, with more brilliant facets than anyone in America had seen before.

"Perhaps it's not perfect!" Max wrote Scott on April 25, 1925. "It is one thing to ride a sleepy cob of a talent to perfection and quite another to master a wild young thoroughbred of a talent."

By late spring—after all hopes of *The Great Gatsby*'s success had faded—fine reviews did appear, and Willa Cather, Edith Wharton, and T. S. Eliot all sent Fitzgerald personal letters praising the book.

Fitzgerald himself realized how far he had advanced since the beginning of the Jazz Age, and he never failed to express his appreciation to those who helped him. "Max," he wrote his editor in July, 1925, "it amuses me when praise comes in on the 'structure' of the book—because it was you who fixed up the structure, not me. And don't think I'm not grateful for all that sane and helpful advice about it."

Along with the somber news of *Gatsby*'s sales, Fitzgerald heard from Perkins of a rumor circulating about his dissatisfaction with Charles Scribner's Sons and his plans to transfer to Boni & Liveright for his books. Max hesitantly mailed a longhand letter from New Canaan to Paris requesting the details of the story.

LIVERIGHT RUMOR ABSURD, Scott wired. In fact, Fitzgerald had heard from an editor at Boni & Liveright who asked for Scott's next book in the event that he was not satisfied with Scribners. Fitzgerald responded at once, affirming that Max Perkins was one of his closest friends and that his relations with Scribners had always been so cordial and pleasant that he could not even think of changing publishers. The rumor was apparently a thirdhand rendition of a misunderstanding, and Fitzgerald became depressed that Perkins should have believed it enough to mention it.

> Now Max, [Scott wrote] I have told you many times that you are my publisher, and permanently, as far as one can fling about the word in this too mutable world. If you like I will sign a contract with you immediately for my next three books. The idea of leaving you has never for *one single moment* entered my head.

Fitzgerald enumerated four reasons why he could not change publishers, ranging from corporate matters to personal allegiances. One was his strong feeling about having one house's support from book to book—if only to have uniform bindings on all his works; another was the "curious advantage to a rather radical writer in being published by what is now an ultra-conservative house." Thirdly, Fitzgerald felt that it would be awkward to sign with another publisher while he had a debt, which was "both actual and a matter of honor," of several thousand dollars. The foremost reason for Fitzgerald's loyalty had been swelling within him since their first correspondence. "Tho, as a younger man, I have not always been in sympathy with some of your publishing ideas (which were evolved under the pre-movie, pre-high-literacy-rate condition of twenty to forty years ago)," Scott wrote Max, "the personality of you and of Mr. Scribner, the tremendous squareness, courtesy, generosity, and open-mindedness I have always met there and, if I may say it, the special consideration you have all had for me and my work, much more than make up the difference."

Maxwell Perkins gave all his authors the feeling that he cared as much for their work as they did themselves. Even Scott Fitzgerald, the keystone of Scribners' revitalized success, needed that assurance. Max never asked Fitzgerald (or any writer) to sign a permanent contract for "the simple reason that it might be right for you sometime to change publishers, and while this would be a tragedy to me, I should not be so small as to stand in the way on personal grounds." Indeed, dozens of Perkins's agreements to publish were oral—and inviolate.

Perkins was still casting his lot with the up-and-coming and challenging those he already published to attempt the untried. In 1944, Malcolm Cowley commented on the effect that this policy had on Perkins's company. "Scribners, when he went to work there, was a fantastic publishing house, with an atmosphere like Queen Victoria's parlor," he said. Because of Perkins and his sweeping changes, that house "took a sudden leap from the age of innocence into the midst of the lost generation."

VI

Companions

In December, 1924, a package containing a collection of vignettes, published in France under the title *in our time,* arrived at the New York City customs house. The author was "that Hemingway" of whom Fitzgerald had spoken a few months earlier. It was not until late February that Perkins read the sketches. Several of them chronicled the life of Nick Adams, a young man from Michigan who had fought in the World War. Max reported to Scott that the book "accumulates a fearful effect through a series of brief episodes, presented with economy, strength and vitality. A remarkable, tight, complete expression of the *scene,* in our time, as it looks to Hemingway."

Hemingway's writing had a distinctive sound, the likes of which Perkins had never heard: hard-hammered words that reverberated long after the short, staccato sentences had been read. "I was greatly impressed by the power in the scenes and incidents pictured, and by the effectiveness of their relation to each other," Max wrote Hemingway, but added:

> I doubt if we could have seen a way to the publication of this book itself on account of material considerations: it is so small that it would give the booksellers no opportunity for substantial profit if issued at a price which custom would dictate. This is a pity, because your method is obviously one which enables you to express what you have to say in very small compass.

It occurred to Perkins that Hemingway might be writing something that would not raise such practical objections, and so he assured him, "Whatever you are writing, we should be most interested to consider."

Five days later Perkins followed up his letter to Hemingway with another. He had heard from John Peale Bishop—one of Fitzgerald's friends from Princeton, who collaborated with Edmund Wilson on a book of verse called *The Undertaker's Garland*—that Hemingway had been working on another book. "I hope this is so and that we may see it," Perkins wrote the author. "We would certainly read it with promptness and sympathetic interest if you gave us the opportunity."

Seven weeks passed with no response from Hemingway. It was Max's first exposure to Ernest Hemingway's habit of vanishing to some remote part of the world. On this occasion it was Schruns, Austria, where he was skiing. Hemingway read Perkins's letters upon his return to Paris and was excited by his interest. But he had committed himself just days before to another publisher who had connected with him in the Alps and he told Max he did not see how he could talk seriously with him until he had seen the contract for *In Our Time* (by now Hemingway had capitalized it) being offered by Boni & Liveright. To show Perkins his appreciation and his interest in Scribners, he offered some notions about writing. He said he found the novel "an awfully artificial and worked-out form" and that he hoped someday to write an exhaustive study of the Spanish bullring. Priding himself on such unconventional ideas, Hemingway tried to console Perkins by suggesting he was a bad prospect for a publisher anyway.

"What rotten luck—for me I mean," Perkins wrote back, sorry that he had not been able to locate Hemingway sooner. He asked him to remember that Scribners had been at least one of the first to try to publish him in America. "It is too bad about Hemingway," Max wrote Scott Fitzgerald.

The Fitzgeralds rented a fifth-floor walk-up in Paris that spring, and in May, 1925, he and Ernest Hemingway met. Hemingway found Fitzgerald "very good looking in a too pretty way." Scott was drinking hard that month and got so tight at their first meeting at the Dingo Bar that he started to pass out. Ernest observed that every time Fitzgerald took a drink his face changed, and after four shots the skin was so drawn that it resembled a death's head. Scott found Hemingway to be "a fine charming fellow" who liked Max's letters enormously. "If Liveright doesn't please him," Fitzgerald wrote Perkins, "he'll come to you, and he has a future. He's 27."

By summer Scott and Ernest were seeing more and more of each other, occasionally at the home of Gertrude Stein. The walls of her salon at 27 Rue de Fleurus were covered with paintings by young Picasso, Cézanne,

Matisse, and other modern artists whom she sponsored before they became famous. Perkins had never met Miss Stein but he admired her novel *The Making of Americans*. However, he wrote Fitzgerald, he doubted if many readers would have patience with her peculiarly repetitious and impressionistic method, "effective as it does become." Fitzgerald and Hemingway found her presence at least as commanding as her writing. They enjoyed mixing with the other literary expatriates who dropped in—among them John Dos Passos, Ford Madox Ford, Ezra Pound, and Robert McAlmon, who had published a slim book of Hemingway's work called *Three Stories and Ten Poems*.

Hemingway and Fitzgerald began going on expeditions together, which because of Scott's childish impracticality always brought untold complications. Hemingway was amused enough by one trip, driving Scott's car up from Lyons through the Côte-d'Or, to write Max Perkins about it. The journey started with Fitzgerald's missing his train from Paris, involved a lot of wine and a few wild-goose chases through the Mâconnais region, and ended with Hemingway's concluding, "Never . . . go on trips with anyone you do not love." Max replied, "My trips are only to Boston, Philadelphia and Washington and my companions then are those of the smoking compartment."

Ernest's earliest feelings for Fitzgerald were of great fondness and respect; he thought *The Great Gatsby* an "absolutely first-rate book." But from the start he was impatient with Scott's immaturity and he developed a paternalistic attitude toward him although he was three years Fitzgerald's junior. By 1960, when Hemingway wrote about the first year of their friendship in *A Moveable Feast,* his reminiscences of his early days as a writer in Paris, his tone had changed from paternalistic to patronizing. He remembered finishing Fitzgerald's novel and then feeling that "no matter what Scott did, nor how he behaved, I must know it was like a sickness and be of any help I could to him and try to be a good friend. He had many good, good friends, more than anyone I knew. But I enlisted as one more, whether I could be of any use to him or not. If he could write a book as fine as *The Great Gatsby* I was sure that he could write an even better one."

Hemingway and Fitzgerald each went his own way that summer, 1925. Ernest and his wife Hadley journeyed to Pamplona for the running of the bulls, Scott and Zelda to the south of France. Perkins met Fitzgerald's repeated requests for money, assuring him on Scribners' behalf that "if this puts you in a position to go straight ahead with a new novel, we are certainly mighty glad to send it." Max wanted Scott to give him some idea of what he was writing, even though he knew "it does sometimes dull the edge for the writer to do this."

Toward the end of summer Fitzgerald began his next book. It would take him five starts and seventeen versions before he could resolve it into his brutally personal work *Tender Is the Night*. As he wrote, Fitzgerald developed a number of substories, and at times, as Perkins followed Scott's progress, he could discern what appeared to be three wholly different novels.

Scott's first bulletin to Perkins about the book, written in August from Antibes, read: "*Our Type* is about several things, one of which is an intellectual murder on the Leopold-Loeb idea. Incidently it is about Zelda & me & the hysteria of last May and June in Paris. (Confidential)." Another element was a murder that followed the Leopold-Loeb case by several months, that of Dorothy Ellingson, a sixteen-year-old San Francisco girl who murdered her mother during a quarrel about the daughter's reckless living.

As usual, Fitzgerald was going to people his novel with members of the sparkling society he so admired. Drawing on his recollections of his years in Europe, Fitzgerald found that one figure stood out, a paragon who, as Fitzgerald would later remark, "had come to dictate my relations with other people when these relations were successful: how to do, what to say. How to make people at least momentarily happy." That man was Gerald Murphy, lean and elegant, with a face just this side of overbred. At their Villa America in Antibes, Murphy and his handsome wife, Sara, entertained in a manner that captivated Scott and Zelda. The Fitzgeralds had shared "many fêtes" with the Murphys.

In his first attempt at the novel, Fitzgerald gave an account of a hot-blooded young man named Francis Melarkey who is touring Europe with his dominating mother. Melarkey is taken in by the Seth Rorebacks (the Murphys), pastors of the expatriate flock on the Côte d'Azur, only to fall in love with Seth's wife, Dinah. Fitzgerald did not immediately know how he would contrive Francis Melarkey's murder of his mother, but the love triangle was clear to him. "In a certain sense my plot is not unlike Dreiser's in the American Tragedy," Fitzgerald wrote Perkins several months later from Paris. "At first this worried me but now it doesn't for our minds are so different." By then he was calling the novel *The World's Fair*.

Perkins heard little from Scott for the rest of the year except his occasional petitions for funds. "Will I ever be square?" he asked, fretting about his mounting debt to Scribners. Mindful of the steady decline in his sales since *Paradise,* Fitzgerald worried that his books might never sell again, that his newest anthology, *All the Sad Young Men,* would not reach 5,000 copies. Perkins thought the nine stories in that collection made a new and strong impression since they bridged commercialism and artistry. Thinking of "The Rich Boy" and "Winter Dreams" especially, he wrote, "They have more breadth . . . than those of earlier collections. In fact, it is remarkable that you have been able to make them so entertaining for the crowd when they have so much significance." Later he assured Scott, "Those who have believed in you can now utter another decisive 'I told you so.' "

At the year's end Scott fell into another of his "unholy depressions." Perkins was all but powerless in trying to raise his spirits because Fitzgerald's despondence was not caused by a feeling of failure as an author. "The [new] book is wonderful," he wrote Perkins; "I honestly think that when it's published I shall be the best American novelist (which isn't saying a lot) but the end seems far away." What terrified him was the prospect of growing old:

> I wish I were 22 again with only my dramatic and feverishly enjoyed miseries. You remember I used to say I wanted to die at 30—well, I'm now 29 and the prospect is still welcome. My work is the only thing that makes me happy—except to be a little tight—and for those 2 indulgences I pay a big price in mental and physical hangovers.

Perkins thought Fitzgerald's melancholy and expatriation were both curiously linked to his desperate attempts to maintain his youth. He observed Scott's struggles to hold onto it by constant travel and knew he was bound to feel dejected seeing it dimmed by his drinking. The only suggestion the editor made was that the Fitzgeralds should settle in some typical American community for a while, "not for your future as a citizen so much as for that as a writer. You'd see a new surface of life that way," he wrote Scott.

A few months later Fitzgerald announced that unless all the other Americans were first driven out of France, he would be returning to the United States. "God, how much I've learned in these two and a half years in Europe," Scott wrote Max. "It seems like a decade & I feel pretty old but I wouldn't have missed it, even its most unpleasant & painful aspects. . . . I do want to see you, Max." In Perkins's stead, Ernest Hemingway had become Scott's closest friend, the only one who could improve his mood. "He and I are very thick," Fitzgerald added.

Max wanted to establish a relationship with Hemingway as well. *Scribner's Magazine* had just received their first piece from him, "Fifty Grand," and Perkins found the man's writing "invigorating as a cold, fresh wind." To Perkins's regret the magazine did not accept the story outright but asked Hemingway to shorten it. "I wish with his very first story that we did not have to bring this up," Max wrote Scott, "[because Hemingway] is one of those whose interest is much more in producing than in publishing, and he may revolt at the idea of being asked to conform to an artificial specification in length." Hemingway never did cut the story, the equally prestigious *Atlantic Monthly* subsequently printed it, and Max feared this outcome would keep the author from ever signing any contract with Scribners. Fitzgerald sympathized with Perkins's position. "I wish Liveright would lose faith in Ernest," he wrote Max just after Christmas, 1925.

Days later, miraculously, Horace Liveright did. He cabled Hemingway: REJECTING TORRENTS OF SPRING PATIENTLY AWAITING MS SUN ALSO RISES WRITING FULLY. No sooner had the news been flashed than Fitzgerald wrote Perkins, "If he's free I'm almost sure I can get satire to you first & then if you see your way clear, you can contract for the novel *tout ensemble*."

The Torrents of Spring was a 28,000-word satire of Sherwood Anderson and his stylized, sentimental imitators. Fitzgerald loved it but said it would not be popular, and that the editors at Liveright had rejected it because their most recent work by Anderson, *Dark Laughter,* was in its tenth printing and *The Torrents of Spring* was "almost a vicious parody on him." Under the circumstances, Scott thought, Hemingway would send Perkins his other book only on the condition that he publish the satire first. Since Liveright's telegram, he said, Hemingway had intended to go straight to Scribners, but Fitzgerald thought he was wavering because of the company's persistently conservative reputation.

Word among bookmen traveled fast. Within days William Aspinwall Bradley, at Alfred Knopf, and Louis Bromfield on behalf of his publisher, Alfred Harcourt, expressed interest in Hemingway's manuscripts. Fitzgerald urged Max to act quickly. But Hemingway had no idea of double-crossing Perkins, to whom he had given his word months earlier.

By first sending the manuscript to Perkins, Hemingway told Scott, he felt he would be turning down a "sure thing" for a delay and a chance. But he was willing to take the risk because of the impression he had formed of Perkins through his letters and what Fitzgerald had told him. "Also confidence in Scribners and would like to be lined up with you," he wrote. The instant Harcourt offered an advance, Fitzgerald notified Perkins that he could get Hemingway's novel if he would promptly write without quali- fications that they would publish both the novel and the "unpromising" satire. Perkins was eager to obey Fitzgerald's direction precisely, but had to adhere to company policy on taste. He cabled Scott, PUBLISH NOVEL AT 15% AND ADVANCE IF DESIRED ALSO SATIRE UNLESS OBJECTIONABLE OTHER THAN FINANCIALLY HEMINGWAYS STORIES SPLENDID.

Max could do no better. "[There] was a fear that this satire . . . might be suppressible," he explained to Scott in a letter. "In fact, we could tell nothing about it of course in these respects and it is not the policy obviously of Scribners to publish books of certain types. For instance, if it were even Rabelaisian to any extreme degree, it might be objected to."

Max was afraid the qualification in his cable had been fatal and was ready to accept the news that he had lost Hemingway. He conceded to Scott that Harcourt was an admirable publisher, but he insisted that Hemingway would be better off in Scribners' hands "because we are absolutely true to our authors and support them loyally in the face of losses for a long time when we believe in their qualities and in them. It is that kind of a pub- lisher that Hemingway probably needs," Perkins said, "because I hardly think he could come into a large public immediately. He ought to be published by one who believes in him and is prepared to lose money for a period in enlarging his market. Although he would certainly, even without much support, get recognition through his own powers."

After several lean years of free-lancing, Hemingway saw this as the time to strike. He decided to go to New York, where he could make arrangements immediately, without weeks elapsing between each offer and counterproposal. He could personally place *The Torrents of Spring* and his novel with a new publisher and then justify his action to Horace Liveright, if the publisher chose to fight. "To hear [Hemingway] talk you'd think Liveright had broken up his home and robbed him of millions," Scott wrote Max, "—but that's because he knows nothing of publishing, except in the cucoo [sic] magazines, is very young and feels helpless so far away. You won't be able to help liking him—he's one of the nicest fellows I know." Fitzgerald's last word on the subject was an emphatic reminder to get a signed contract for *The Sun Also Rises*.

Hemingway arrived in New York on February 9, 1926. After an amicable parting with Horace Liveright and a sleepless night of indecision, he went to see Max Perkins, who offered a $1,500 advance for the first refusal rights of *The Torrents of Spring* and the unseen novel. Hemingway shook hands on it.

Perkins was extremely grateful to Fitzgerald for all his help in landing the author. "He is a most interesting chap about his bullfights and boxing," Max wrote Scott.

Scott was just as pleased that Scribners had got Hemingway. "I saw him for a day in Paris on his return," he replied, "& he thought you were great."

Hemingway returned to Austria, where by the end of March he finished work on the proofs of *The Torrents of Spring* and the draft of *The Sun Also Rises*. Then he returned to Paris and made plans to do some "fooling around with bullfighting" in the early summer. "Don't get yourself killed with all this flying and bullfighting," Max cautioned his newest author. Hemingway answered that he had no intention of letting *The Sun Also Rises* be a posthumous work.

One month later Ernest sent Max the novel and what he called a "long drooling letter." The manuscript still needed further working over, Hemingway said, but he figured Perkins would be anxious to see the pig he had bought in a poke. Hemingway supposed the editor would be so engrossed "reading the pig" that he would not be much interested in the rest of his letter, but Max was concerned with all his news, especially that about Scott Fitzgerald, with whom Hemingway's relationship had mellowed. Scott had relaxed from the eager posture he assumed when he wanted to make a new friend; Ernest, who still respected Fitzgerald's writing, no longer considered him the irrefutable elder statesman of the younger generation. In fact, Ernest was now feeling especially fatherly. He was touched by Fitzgerald's constant concern about money and had decided to alleviate it. His own meager income from European literary magazines had been supplemented in the past few years by income from the trust fund of his wife Hadley. Now he had still more money, the large sum from Scribners, and momentarily considered making some grand gestures. He spoke to Max of giving all his royalties to Fitzgerald, and even wrote Fitzgerald that he had just called in his attorney to make Scott his heir. If Fitzgerald found this tactless as well as facetious, there is no record of it.

Once Hemingway signed with Scribners, Max Perkins thereupon became the moderator in the literary friendship between Ernest and Scott. Until Fitzgerald's death in 1940, Max's office would be the clearinghouse for much of the emotion going back and forth between the two men, particularly when they wanted to communicate without risking a confrontation.

At the time Hemingway's novel reached Max, Scott was staying on the Riviera, at Juan-les-Pins, with "every prospect of a marvellous summer." Ernest was in Paris; after three weeks of continuous rain, he had had no exercise and consequently was suffering insomnia. Perkins's next letter was just the right tonic:

> The Sun Also Rises seems to me a most extraordinary performance. No one could conceive a book with more life in it. All the scenes, and particularly those when they cross the Pyrennees [sic] and come into Spain, and when they fish in that cold river, and when the bulls are sent in with the steers, and when they are fought in the arena, are of such a quality as to be like actual experience.

As a work of art the book seemed to Perkins "astonishing and the more so because it involved such an extraordinary range of experience and emotion, all brought together in the most skillful manner—the subtle ways of which are beautifully concealed—to form a complete design. I could not express my admiration too strongly."

In New York publishing circles the rumor began to circulate that Max's enthusiasm was not shared by all his colleagues. Max would not find it easy, said Charles A. Madison, an editorial executive at Henry Holt and Company, "to persuade [old Charles] Scribner to publish a book containing four-letter words and dialogue that crackled with obscenity." It was one thing to call a female dog a bitch (though the elderly man in charge of the Scribner stock room had been aghast to find exactly such a reference in The Great Gatsby), but it was quite another to refer to a woman—in this case, the heroine, Lady Brett Ashley—as one. Worried, Max brought the manuscript of The Sun Also Rises home and discussed it with Louise. He explained that not only certain words but often Hemingway's subject matter was shocking. Louise instinctively grasped the situation, clenched a fist, and told her husband, "You've got to stand up and fight for it, Max."

A few days later Scribners' board of editors convened for their monthly discussion of newly received manuscripts. Charles Scribner was seventy-two then, but his roar was as forceful as ever. Printing obscenities was to him unthinkable; keeping "dirty books" from sullying his imprint was a matter of great importance. He had been stunned by Hemingway's book. He had, however, kept his wits and, before the editorial meeting, had sought the advice of a friend, Judge Robert Grant of Boston, a successful novelist then in his seventies. The judge had been properly appalled by Hemingway's seamy language, but he had admired most of the novel. "You *must* publish the book, Charles," he had ruled. "But I hope the young man will live to regret it."

John Hall Wheelock remembered walking into the board meeting with this thought in his mind: that Judge Grant's decision notwithstanding, "Charles Scribner would no sooner allow profanity in one of his books than he would invite friends to use his parlor as a toilet room."

When the debate over *The Sun Also Rises* flared up, Max Perkins argued that the question went beyond this single book. He later wrote young Charles Scribner, who had not been present at the meeting, that he had asserted that it was "a crucial one in respect to younger writers—that we suffered by being called 'ultra-conservative' (even if unjustly and with malice) and that this would become our reputation for the present when our declination of this book should, as it would, get about."

Charles Scribner listened patiently to Perkins's determined presentation, which of course reminded him of the way Max had argued for Fitzgerald in 1919, and as he listened he slowly shook his head from side to side. Byron Dexter, a junior editor who was privy to the office gossip, later told Malcolm Cowley in confidence: "Perkins was the new idea and the younger people in the place were terrifically for him. I remember the moment of crisis. . . . Old Charles Scribner, Jr. ran the place then with a very firm hand—and no two ways about it. We knew that Perkins had to go to bat for Hemingway, and it was reported with hushed voices one evening that Charles Scribner, Jr. had turned down the book and Perkins was going to resign."

It never came to that. After the vote, Perkins walked back to his office and wrote young Scribner, "We took it—with misgivings." He admitted that his own view of the matter in regard to the house's reputation "influenced our decision largely . . . I simply thought in the end that the balance was slightly in favour of acceptance for all the worry and general misery involved."

The Torrents of Spring, the satire, was published on May 28, 1926. Max wrote Fitzgerald that it received some "praise but not always comprehension." Max himself saw as much real humor in the book as biting wit, which saved it from being "devastating." Even so, Max said, his deepest interest was in getting to *The Sun Also Rises,* the publication of which he impatiently anticipated. "That," he wrote Scott, "showed more 'genius' than I had inferred from *Torrents of Spring*, which I did not rate so very high."

That *The Sun Also Rises* differed in style and subject from any book Maxwell Perkins had ever edited—or even read—made him unusually hesitant to offer advice. From France, Scott Fitzgerald wrote to suggest that Max ask for only the absolute minimum of changes, because Hemingway was already "so discouraged about the previous reception of his work by publishers and magazine editors."

In *A Moveable Feast*, Hemingway says he did not let Fitzgerald see *The Sun Also Rises* until after the revised manuscript had been sent to Scribners. In fact, Fitzgerald did read the manuscript that spring and he sent a critique of the work to the author. The novel was "damn good," he said, once the reader got past the first fifteen pages. These pages were mostly introductory material about Lady Brett Ashley and Robert Cohn. Fitzgerald felt they were too loosely written. They displayed, he said, a "tendency to envelope [sic] or (and as it usually turns out) to embalm in mere wordiness an anecdote that casually appealed to you."

Days later, Hemingway suggested to Max that they lop off altogether those first fifteen pages. This threw Perkins into a quandary. He agreed with Hemingway that the information revealed in this opening section was also conveyed in the body of the book and therefore, from that aspect, unnecessary. But the material, he said, "is well said here . . . and a reader to whom your way of writing will be new and in many cases strange, would be helped by this beginning." Perkins yielded the decision to the author, noting, "You write like yourself only, and I shall not attempt criticism. I couldn't with confidence."

On other points, however, Max was less hesitant. The problems of *The Sun Also Rises*, he felt, had less to do with entire sections than with individual words and phrases—profanities and unacceptable characterizations which Perkins knew could result in the book's suppression and in libel suits. As for language, he wrote the author, the "majority of people are more affected by *words* than things. I'd even say that those most obtuse toward *things* are most sensitive to a sort of word. I think some words should be avoided so that we shall not divert people from the qualities of this book to the discussion of an utterly unpertinent and extrinsic matter." Max thought there were a dozen different passages in *The Sun Also Rises* that would offend most readers' sensibilities. "It would be a pretty thing," he said, "if the very significance of so original a book should be disregarded because of the howls of a lot of cheap, prurient, moronic yappers."

You probably don't appreciate this disgusting possibility [he continued] because you've been too long abroad, and out of that atmosphere. Those who breathe its stagnant vapors now attack a book, not only on grounds of eroticism, which could not hold here, but upon that of "decency," which means words.

"I am as sure of your artistic integrity as anything," Max insisted, but he urged Hemingway to reduce the obscenities so far as he rightly could.

Hemingway replied that he imagined that he and Perkins were on the same side regarding the use of language. He said he never used a word without first considering whether or not it was replaceable. He spent the next month making the final corrections on the proof, cutting every word he felt he could. By the end of August, 1926, he had dealt with all the hot spots Perkins had cited: Henry James, in a "historical" reference to his impotence, was identified only as Henry; direct references to such living writers as Joseph Hergesheimer and Hilaire Belloc were eliminated or changed; dashes were substituted for the letters in obscene words; and the Spanish fighting bulls were depicted without their "embarrassing appendages." The word *bitch* remained in reference to Lady Brett because Hemingway insisted he never used that word "ornamentally," only when necessary. If *The Sun Also Rises* was a profane book, Ernest said, well, he and Max would have to live with that and the hope that his next effort would be more "sacred." He was already thinking about the many stories he wanted to write, about war and love and the old "lucha por la vida."

Another editorial discussion concerned the book's epigraph. Hemingway wanted one that would set a theme which was already important to him, the struggles of his contemporaries for their identities during the upheaval and rootlessness after the war. In *A Moveable Feast* Hemingway tells how he came upon his epigraph. Gertrude Stein, he wrote, was having "some ignition trouble with the old Model T Ford she then drove, and the young man who worked in the garage and had served in the last year of the war had not been adept, or perhaps had not broken the priority of other vehicles, in repairing Miss Stein's Ford. Anyway he had not been *sérieux* and had been corrected severely by the *patron* of the garage after Miss Stein's protest. The *patron* had said to him, 'You are all a *génération perdue.*'" Later to Hemingway she remarked, "That's what you all are. All of you young people who served in the war. You are a lost generation."

Hemingway saw how applicable that last phrase was to his characters in *The Sun Also Rises*. He wrote Perkins that in composing the book's epigraph, he wanted to juxtapose Miss Stein's remark with a passage from Ecclesiastes, the one that begins:

> Vanity of vanities, saith the preacher. . . . One generation passeth, and another generation cometh; but the earth abideth forever. The sun also riseth, and the sun goeth down, and resteth to the place where he arose.

The epigraph made good sense to Perkins. Ecclesiastes was his favorite book of the Old Testament—he once told his daughter Peg that it "contained all the wisdom of the ancient world"—and he found the quotation perfectly apt. He readily agreed.

Even after *The Sun Also Rises* was published, in the fall of 1926, Hemingway kept mulling over the epigraph. He asked Perkins if the words "Vanity of vanities, saith the preacher" might be cut. The deletion, he felt, would emphasize his "real point" in the book, which was that the "earth abideth forever." Perkins again agreed. That relationship between the earth and its people was the strongest theme in *The Sun Also Rises,* he wrote Hemingway. "It has not been remarked upon by most reviewers," he said, "but I often doubt if the emotion itself . . . is felt by . . . people of the book-reading class. I believe it is felt by simpler people."

Max's daughter Bertha remembered the relief with which both her parents read the reviews in the Sunday book sections, especially Conrad Aiken's in the *Herald Tribune*:

> If there is better dialogue being written today I do not know where to find it. It is alive with the rhythms and idioms, and pauses and suspension and innuendoes and shorthands of living speech.

Max's colleague Roger Burlingame recorded years later that *The Sun Also Rises* "convinced editors like Maxwell Perkins that another generation, 'lost' though it might be, had found an understanding of the writing craft of which most of their elders had little enough." Referring to the increase in the novel's sales from 8,000 to 12,000 and beyond, Max wrote Ernest, "The Sun has risen . . . and is rising steadily."

The following spring Donald Friede, one of the partners of Boni & Liveright, visited Hemingway in Paris and offered him lavish advances, trying to tempt him back to their firm. Ernest told him flatly that he could not even discuss the matter as he was absolutely satisfied in Scribners' hands. He knew they had advertised *The Sun Also Rises* vigorously *before* it began to sell, when many publishers would have dropped it. Hemingway believed it was that advertising which eventually pushed its sale up to 20,000 copies. He did not, however, realize the extent of the support Perkins himself had given the book.

Irate reactions to the novel filled the Scribners mailbag almost every week, and they were delivered to Perkins. *The Sun Also Rises* was banned in Boston, and there were disgusted readers everywhere demanding, if not an apology, then at least an excuse for Scribners' pandering to the public's basest tastes. Perkins had become expert at answering hotheaded letters assailing the respectability of the house of Scribner; he was still receiving letters about that "foul-mouthed, vulgar, blustering upstart" F. Scott Fitzgerald. "Publishing is not, of course, dependent on the individual taste of the publisher," Perkins replied to one reader of Hemingway's novel. "He is under an obligation to his profession which binds him to bring out a work which in the judgment of the literary world is significant in its literary qualities and is a pertinent criticism of the civilization of the time." He added:

> There are two positions commonly taken with regard to books of this kind: one is, that vice ought never to be presented in literature as it actually is, because it is unpleasant, and the other is that the presentation of it as it is, actually, is valuable because it is, actually, repulsive and terrible, and if known to be so will be hated. But if ignored and concealed, it takes on a false glamour which is seductive.
>
> It has not yet been decided which of these positions is the right one.

While Perkins was wrestling with Hemingway's critics, Hemingway was having his own difficulties, not literary but matrimonial. He and his wife, Hadley, with whom he had had one son, were getting divorced. The situation had started, Hemingway wrote later, as all things truly wicked start, "from an innocence." In *A Moveable Feast* he describes the predicament: "An unmarried young woman becomes the temporary best friend of another young woman who is married, goes to live with the husband and wife and then unknowingly, innocently and unrelentingly sets out to marry the husband." The friend was a chic young woman from Arkansas, a fashion editor for *Vogue* in Paris, named Pauline Pfeiffer. In July, 1926, Ernest revealed to his wife that he and Pauline were in love. The dedication of *The Sun Also Rises* and the assignment of all its royalties to Hadley were the last rites of their marriage. Of her one meeting with Max Perkins

a short time later, Hadley recalled, "I got an agreeable impression that
he was somewhat flabbergasted that Ernest was trading me off for another
(however nice) partner." She also said: "I realized I had become an
adjunct to Hem, and he felt he needed something more to stimulate him.
Sometimes you get so close you have to part."

Other marriages stay together because of distance. "Louise and Max
were an odd pairing," Louise's sister Jean said. "Opposites attract, but
they never really got together on anything. Oh, they loved each other,
but look at the way Max worked hard in New York all day and couldn't
wait to get home to see his girls. And Louise—she never wanted to be
stuck in the house; and once she had her family she did everything she
could to get away from them."

In the mid-1920s Louise was becoming ever more active as a writer of
plays and pageants, produced locally, and as an actress. Max still did not
approve—of the acting in particular and probably of the theater in general. He decided that she should write stories and books and in 1925, as
an encouragement, he took one of her plays for children, *The Knave of
Hearts*, and had Scribners publish it in a large-format volume with lavish
illustrations by Maxfield Parrish, a friend of the Perkinses who lived
across the Connecticut River from Windsor. Parrish collectors consider
The Knave of Hearts among the artist's most prized works.

In 1926, finally yielding to her husband's prodding, Louise quit her
playwriting and made two attempts at prose—short stories called "For-
mula" and "Other Joys." Both sold, the one to *Harpers*, the other to
Scribner's—without Max's influence. He found it remarkable that she
should break into print so easily and encouraged her to get right to work
on a third story. All their daughters remembered his saying that if she
would stick to writing, "Mother could become another Katherine Mans-
field." To Louise that prospect did not hold a candle to an acting career.
But she wanted to please her husband.

Louise's energy came in spurts—sometimes years intervened between
stories—but her literary efforts showed a steady improvement in craftsmanship. Published under her maiden name, they became less heavy-
handed in their plotting, more subtle in their characterization. Even her
very first attempts contained perceptive observations that reflected deep,
inner passions. None of her early stories was particularly autobiographical,
but they were all about restless women—most often spinsters or widows

living in opulent surroundings (which she sharply detailed) but suffocating in their withdrawn existences.

Louise's new occupation proved to be an expensive luxury. Max explained to Fitzgerald: "Every time she gets a story under way, she feels that she is going to earn some money, and that this entitles her to be a little extravagant—so long before the story is finished, four or five times the amount of money that it could possibly bring in has been spent."

After a year in New Canaan, Louise and Max were convinced they had done well to move there, if only because of the supply of interesting company. The Perkinses continued to see the Colums as much as they did anyone. One night that year Molly came over with the first four pages of a book she was writing on the principles of literary criticism. Called *Wide Eyes and Wings,* it reflected her belief, Max told Scott Fitzgerald, "that criticism should be emotional and that literature should not be measured by fixed intellectual standards." Max added: "I admired her mind already, but I was astonished: there were surely four fresh *ideas* set forth and with absolute clarity—And I've so often argued (like so many others) that woman was incapable of grasping abstractions—But I'd gladly turn feminist with my multitude of girls." Those opening pages caused Perkins to offer to publish the work.

Max still remained closest to his earliest friend, Van Wyck Brooks. In early 1926 the strength of their bond came under pressure when Brooks stumbled into a pit of depression. He had gone deep into his writing of a life of Emerson and got stuck. Only his intimate friends knew that it was not the Emerson book but his last work of literary criticism, the celebrated *Pilgrimage of Henry James,* that had driven him to melancholia. John Hall Wheelock said, "Van Wyck was disturbed by the numerous unpardonable things he had written about James, when he knew the man could not defend himself." Later Brooks himself explained:

> I was consumed by . . . a feeling that my work had all gone wrong and that I was mistaken in all I had said or thought. . . . I was pursued especially with nightmares in which Henry James turned great luminous menacing eyes upon me. I was half aware, in connection with him, of the division within myself, and with all the bad conscience of a criminal I felt I had viewed him with something of Plato's "hard little eye of detraction." In short, in this middle of my life, I was thoroughly bedevilled. . . . I could no longer sleep. I scarcely sat down for a year, I lived in a Plutonian psychical twilight. . . . All my affections and interests fell into abeyance.

Perkins took a long walk with Van Wyck every Sunday, sometimes in the rain and fog. It was a joyless ordeal for Max as Brooks's depression turned grayer. He believed the cure for Van Wyck was to get him to finish his book on Emerson, but Brooks declared it an irremediable failure. Max read what had been committed to paper and suggested a whole new scheme to give it the structure it lacked, but Van Wyck refused to accept it. Instead, he insisted he must find some new work to do—a part-time job that would leave him time to write. Perkins believed that kind of arrangement would "suck a man under" and said, "What a shame at your age, with a foundation of reputation well laid. Set down the names of ten lesser American writers as titles for articles and I'll sell them at five hundred apiece, and the result will be a book that will outsell any you've done." Van Wyck said he could not write at command. Max thought he should learn.

The two men got no further. Max continued to walk in circles every Sunday with Van Wyck, who sank deeper into his *crise à quarante ans* and shrank from most human relations. "My world," Brooks later confessed, became that "of a house with the shades drawn and a man sitting within, a man who could not hear the knock when life drove up to the door with her merry summons."

Soon it became apparent to Perkins that something more than Henry James's countenance was haunting Van Wyck Brooks. Brooks's condition was complicated by guilt feelings involving Molly Colum. Only the innermost circle in New Canaan knew the story, which Max disclosed to Elizabeth Lemmon. Van Wyck, he wrote, was "shy and sensitive, and he always made friends with women. His wife, Eleanor, a fine, strong, honest woman, was not intellectually congenial. Molly Colum was. They were together a great deal." John Hall Wheelock later added to these observations: "The Brookses were a highly conventional and respectable couple, though Van Wyck had been highly sexed in college . . . and Molly was a most daring woman."

When Molly Colum first noticed Brooks's depression, she set out to rescue him: She tried to lure him into a love affair—"for his own good." Wheelock said: "She wanted to have an affair in the European style. She thought she could tear him away from the conflict between his respectable duty to family and his responsibility as an artist. 'He's got so much talent, but it's all being lost because of his dutiful attitude,' Molly once shouted. 'He has everything but the courage to be a real man. He has to go crazy to free himself.' "

Max believed Brooks was "utterly incapable of any actual disloyalty and so was Molly." Brooks's medical records indicate that physically the extent of his affair with Molly Colum was merely one erotic kiss. "But he did say things about Eleanor which he later felt were disloyal, and it seemed to him that he had done something unforgivable," Max wrote Elizabeth Lemmon. "Then he told Eleanor about it. She is what Louise calls possessive and she was jealous anyway of Molly's mental superiority. Whatever she did or said intensified Van Wyck's sense of guilt which sunk so deep in him as to become an obsession. It is this which seems to be at the bottom of his troubles now." The result was what Brooks, thinking of Rimbaud, called "a season in hell."

Brooks stopped seeing Perkins, and his depression intensified into a kind of insanity. It was somewhat mystifying to Max, but he followed Brooks's condition as closely as he could. In the late twenties, John Hall Wheelock, the only person Brooks was willing to meet, reported to Max that Brooks had become "frightfully ill," far beyond the professional insecurity that had throttled him years earlier. Brooks's mother told Perkins that her son spent his days pacing back and forth mumbling, "I shall never see Max again." After months in which they had disappeared from each other's lives, Perkins received a note from Eleanor asking him to take a walk with Brooks again, as he used to. Max was glad to do it, afraid only "that something will be said that will make trouble."

There was another, unspoken problem. It was the case with Max, as it was and is for so many editors, that writers became friends and friends sometimes became writers—an incestuous jumble that sometimes produced fine books and sometimes horrendous complications. Max's friendship with Brooks was now jeopardizing certain business dealings with Molly Colum. Max divulged all to Elizabeth Lemmon:

Years ago Molly offered me, as publisher, a book of criticism she was doing. We never gave her a contract. The matter was so personal a legal document seemed to me inappropriate. Jonathan Cape, an English publisher, gets an American partner and starts an American house—and the very first move they make is to get Molly under contract for this book. Before signing, she said she must speak to me. We had a funny time. It was like a melodrama burlesque on business. They actually tried to make her break a lunch engagement with me, and they delivered a cheque to her by messenger while I was with her. I argued that we could offer every advantage over them and she granted this. But there was some impediment. I could not imagine what. Finally she told me in tears. She had somehow heard that I was to go to the Brookses. If I was to be a friend of the Brookses how could I be her publisher!

"Now how can a man ever hope to understand women?" Max asked Elizabeth. "Or a woman either. Can you follow that reasoning? She did sign for us in the end; and now I'm pledged to make her write the book. Truth enough . . . in fact life grows more incomprehensible every day to me. I hope it does not to you."

It was usually in the summers, when his family was away and he was alone, that Max's world-weariness afflicted him most. But his emotions were on another cycle too. Over the years he had observed that his spirits were frailest during the first and last quarters of the moon. In 1926, knowing that Elizabeth Lemmon believed deeply in astrology, he mentioned to her that his saturnine moods seemed to recur at regular intervals, regardless of other facts, and that these intervals followed the moon.

To satisfy her own curiosity, Elizabeth drew Max's astrological chart, the accuracy of which made believers of several skeptics who knew Perkins. It showed a close conjunction of planets that signified "genius" and as many as four planets in the house of Secrecy. Saturn in the Ninth House kept him from traveling. Elizabeth had once asked Evangeline Adams, the best-known astrologer of the day, what the strongest signs for a book editor would be. She said Virgo, the sign of the critic, and Libra, the lover of beauty. Born September 20, 1884, at 7 A.M., Max was a Virgo with Libra rising.

In early July, 1926, the stars apparently fell into joyful alignment, for when Max went to Windsor he learned from Louise that Elizabeth was coming to visit in two weeks. "I don't really believe it," he wrote Elizabeth, "but I like to pretend it's true." Elizabeth was not one to leave her part of the country any more than Max was his, but she traveled by train to Vermont and had a wonderful few days with the Perkinses. She especially enjoyed the quiet times with Max, traipsing through the piney dells of Paradise. "Pasture Hill and Mount Max have a different quality now that you have been here," he wrote to her afterward. "But that is counteracted by the many other places that I see with rage that I did not somehow compel you to see, at whatever cost to my own reputation for maturity."

Later in the summer Molly Colum visited Windsor and was impressed by its abundance of colorful Yankees. "As a critic," she told Max, "I can't get over all this superb literary material going to waste." "I have always felt that way myself," Max wrote Elizabeth, "—which I know is a disgusting way for a man to view his own people and place."

At the end of the season Louise produced another of her plays in a clearing, hidden away in Paradise. It was just for the family—a crowd in itself. Max wrote Elizabeth that the performance was "incredibly beautiful—a most excellent feat of production in acting, scene, and costume; and wholly Louise's work. At the end, when the audience cried 'Author! Author!' the children were all cast down. They thought the cry was 'Awful! Awful!' "

Max applauded all his wife's artistic ventures, but during periods when she was not writing, he made it clear that he felt she was wasting her talents. As with his authors, Perkins never made demands on Louise: He simply expected her to fulfill herself. By never questioning Max's standards, by which writers rated higher than actors, Louise became trapped in a lifelong dilemma. She could either attempt an acting career and disobey her husband or she could disappoint herself by turning her back on her greater talent. She chose the latter, and in so doing lost some of his respect as well as her own self-respect. By never challenging her husband's position on that matter, she failed to show the strength he admired most in her. Each resented the other and this resentment remained throughout their marriage.

Max did not write to Louise as often as before when they were apart; when he did he still addressed her as "My own darling," repeatedly proclaimed, "I do love you so," and signed himself, "Your own Max." When they were together it was difficult just to maintain harmony. Their daughter Zippy once dramatized the kind of marriage it was by ramming her two fists together.

Max Perkins spent most of his life providing others, except for Louise, a warm shoulder and a sympathetic ear. "The most important obligation of friendship," he explained to Zippy, "is to listen." He confessed his own periodic melancholy only to Elizabeth Lemmon. Max would write her by hand, usually from one of his clubs in New York, trying to make every letter to her perfect and charming. While his letters to Louise were self-assured and hortatory, those to Elizabeth were eager to entertain—he told her of the female art director at Scribners who said to him: "It would do you good to get drunk"—and showed vulnerability. Max would apologize for the slightest discoloration in his stationery, then proceed to write a letter that was sparkling and epigrammatic or simple and sad. He opened himself to her—as much as he dared.

> There's a half long letter to you in New Canaan. I read it to the point at which it stands and found it too much an exposure of ego even for a letter, in which more egoism is admissable than in any other form of writing; and it's curious and creditable to mankind that in view of this fact, letter writing is so generally unpopular.

Elizabeth delighted in every one of his letters, was always understanding, and asked no questions. "Don't be curious," he once wrote her. "But you are not."

"That wasn't true at all," Miss Lemmon said years later. "I was as curious as anybody. I was dying to know more about him. But I never asked. I knew that if I did it would be the last I'd hear from him."

And so Max remained convinced that Elizabeth Lemmon was the one person to whom he could reveal his insecurities. "Would you be willing to send me a line to say if things are going well or ill with you?" he wrote her in October, 1926. "I had prepared myself to lose all my friends about this time; to have every man's hand against me. But the wind has now shifted a bit and favorably, which emboldens me to make this enquiry of you." All he ever really wanted to know from her was that his goddess was in her heaven.

Quietly suffering the kinds of loneliness that his authors so often felt, Max Perkins downed heavy doses of the remedy his Yankee forefathers would have prescribed—work. The results greatly benefited Scribners. Indeed, the list of writers Max had acquired for his company by 1926 was remarkable. They all looked upon Perkins as Fitzgerald had recently described him to the novelist Thomas Boyd, as "a wonder—the brains of Scribners since the old man has moved into another generation."

In the last several years, old CS had come to respect Perkins's judgment very much, but he did not always accept it. In 1925 Max read the manuscript of Bruce Barton's *The Man Nobody Knows*, a Madison Avenue interpretation of the New Testament. Roger Burlingame recalled that Perkins recognized its sales potential and took it up with Charles Scribner. "It treats Christ as a supersalesman," Max said, "a go-getter, a man with a talent for business. Of course it might sell." Scribner, with his long background of serious religious publishing, was properly shocked and insisted that it should be declined. Bobbs-Merrill accepted it, and at the start of the second book season of 1926 it was a runaway success. After seeing *The Man Nobody Knows* leading the best-seller lists month after month, the company patriarch sent for Perkins. "How about this book?" he asked. "Why haven't we got it?"

"Why, we discussed that, Mr. Scribner," Perkins replied. "I talked it all over with you a year ago, and we decided to decline it."

"You discussed it with me? You mean the manuscript came to us?"

Perkins was startled by this example of Charles Scribner's failing memory. "Why certainly, Mr. Scribner. Don't you remember that I told you it portrayed Christ as a salesman? And I added that it might sell."

The head of the company looked at Max a long time without a change of expression. With a faint twinkle in his eye, Scribner leaned forward, wagged his finger and said, "But you didn't tell me, Mr. Perkins, that it would sell four hundred thousand copies."

VII

A Man of Character

For months after the successful publication of *The Sun Also Rises*, Ernest Hemingway was distracted from his writing. Wary of rushing from one marriage directly into another, he absented himself from both the women in his life—his wife, Hadley, and Pauline Pfeiffer—and went skiing in Austria. The emotional tempest left him spent.

In February, 1927, Perkins wrote to him in Gstaad, in an attempt to start him working again. Max wanted Hemingway to put together a collection of his short stories and told him, "Your book will be among those most prominently presented by us."

The assignment took Hemingway's mind away from his problems. Days later he reported to Max that his head was "going well again." He was writing some "pretty good" stories and he was choosing the pieces he wanted in the collection, which he thought of calling *Men Without Women*. Perkins soon found fourteen stories before him to arrange, a process of bookmaking he took more seriously than did any of his authors. His general procedure was to space the strongest pieces at the beginning, middle, and end, varying the rest of the contents by alternating stories of different qualities back to back. He decided to open *Men Without Women* with Ernest's long story "The Undefeated," and to conclude with one of the shorter ones, "Now I Lay Me."

Despite the auspicious start, during most of 1927 Hemingway's mind was not on his work. He traveled for several months before and after his April marriage to Pauline. In September he told Perkins that he had started his next novel, but he did not say much more about it than that, because, he said, it seemed to him that the more books were talked about the slower they progressed.

Once back in Paris, Hemingway went on a daily six-hour writing regimen. Within a month he wrote 30,000 words. He then announced that, after four years abroad, he was moving back to the United States. He realized how badly he had "busted up" his life in recent years and was grateful to Perkins for at least keeping his professional life on an even keel. His "whole life and head and everything had a hell of a time for a while," he said, but he was slowly coming back. He intimated to Perkins how much he yearned to write a single, good novel, however long it took, just for the two of them. He was already thinking of settling in Key West, Florida, where he would make an important decision in that regard. If he could not continue with the novel he had been writing for some time—twenty-two chapters of a "modern Tom Jones" were completed—he would put it aside for another manuscript he had been working on for the last two weeks. The genesis of this second novel could be traced to two of Hemingway's other works: "A Very Short Story," which hinted at the love Ernest felt for a nurse in Milan during the war, and "In Another Country," which told of a major whose wife had just died of pneumonia in that same hospital. Borrowing the most dramatic elements from each, Hemingway had now started to tell that tale of "love and war and the old lucha por la vida" that he had mentioned to Perkins after the publication of *The Sun Also Rises*. And when he reached Florida he decided to continue with it.

In his eagerness to see Ernest's novel completed, Max investigated the possibilities of serializing it in the company magazine. He figured the money it could offer would give Hemingway an incentive to get the novel finished. He also had an ulterior motive. "Some of the younger, restive folk in the house," Roger Burlingame remembered, "seemed to feel that *Scribner's Magazine* was 'in a rut.' " Perkins was one of them, and he wanted to improve its literary quality. Hemingway could get much more money from any of the more commercial magazines, but Max said *Scribner's* longed to carry a major work by him and would pay the $10,000 that John Galsworthy and Edith Wharton received for such serializations. Hemingway replied that the substantial sum of money was just what he wanted, but that he was afraid that the magazine had not changed enough in the last two years to take a chance on this novel. He explained to Max the fate of his writing, which was to be turned down as "too something or other," and then after publication to be praised by everyone else, who would insist that *they* could have printed it. But he agreed to let *Scribner's* have first crack at the book.

In the middle of the summer of 1928, Pauline gave birth to their first child, a son named Patrick. Ernest was happy to have a second son but told Max he had hoped for a girl, so that he, like his editor, could be a father to a daughter. As soon as mother and child were strong enough to travel they went to Pauline's family in Piggott, Arkansas. Ernest went to Wyoming to fish for trout and write the ending of his novel. After reading the finished manuscript he celebrated with a gallon of wine, which halted progress for the next two days. When his hangover had passed, he reported that he never felt stronger in body or mind.

While out west, Hemingway learned from another Scribners editor that his long hours were running Perkins down. Ernest knew he contributed to his editor's work load as much as anyone and wanted to make things easier. Max represented Scribners to him, and his entire publishing future, so he wrote to urge his editor to take care of himself "for Gods sake, if for no other reason." Hemingway planned to be back in Key West that fall, and he asked Max to join a crew of fishing companions he was assembling that included John Dos Passos, a painter named Henry Strater, and another artist, Waldo Peirce, who had been a Harvard classmate of Max's. "I would give anything to do that kind of thing," Perkins replied, "but I never have done it, and I suppose I never shall now, with five children, etc. I have a vision of taking to the road at the age of sixty. The odds are about a thousand to one against it."

As Hemingway's novel neared completion, Perkins perceived an almost invisible stimulus which had crept into Ernest's work habits. The same cockiness appeared whenever his writing was going especially well. Scott Fitzgerald had become a rival whom Hemingway would thereafter pit himself against. At first he had admired Fitzgerald's talents and enjoyed his company; then he saw Scott's crippling financial troubles and how he was hobbling on with a book that he had talked about too long. There was something in Hemingway that preyed on the weaknesses of others, and for the rest of his career his letters to Max revealed a growing competition with Fitzgerald. Invariably he contrasted his own assiduousness and frugality with Fitzgerald's profligacy.

It was not only Scott's need for money that disturbed Hemingway but also the compromises he made in his writing. Hemingway was thinking of Fitzgerald's stories for the *Saturday Evening Post*, in particular, which he wrote in a most unorthodox fashion. Scott once told Ernest at the Closerie des Lilas in Paris how he wrote what he thought were good stories and then changed them for submission, knowing exactly how he must make the twists that rendered them salable to the magazines. This kind of trickery shocked Ernest, who declared he thought it was whoring. Scott agreed but explained that he "had to do it as he made his money from the magazines to have money ahead to write decent books." Hemingway said he did not believe anyone could write any way "except the very best he could write without destroying his talent." And that was not all; Fitzgerald's hijinks had also ceased to amuse him. After Hemingway had left Scott behind in Paris, his initial worry over Scott's wasted talents began to sour into impatience. He never failed to admit that he had had no more loyal friend in those days than Scott when he was sober, but he said he was afraid some of Scott's ideas about writing might rub off and sully his own pristine ideals.

Early in 1928 Ernest told Max how sorry he felt about Fitzgerald. For his own good, he said, Scott should have had his novel out at least one, preferably two years earlier. He now should just complete the work or throw it away and start a new one. He figured that Fitzgerald had fooled with it so long that he did not believe in it anymore, but dreaded giving it up. So Fitzgerald was writing stories—"slop," Hemingway called it—and using any excuses to keep from having to "bite on the nail and finish it." Hemingway said every writer had to give up on some novels to start others, even if it meant not always living up to the demands of the bamboozling critics, who, he said, had ruined every writer that read them.

Perkins held to an aspect of the same theory but viewed Fitzgerald's situation with more compassion. He believed Scott was mortgaging all his professional resources just to complete this one novel and to maintain his and Zelda's standards of luxury. Earlier that year Max had confided in a letter to Ernest, "It is true that Zelda, while very good for him, in some ways, is incredibly extravagant." Now he noted, "Zelda is so able and intelligent and isn't she also quite a strong person? that I'm surprised she doesn't face the situation better and show some sense about spending money. Most of their trouble, which may kill Scott in the end, comes from extravagance. All of his friends would have been busted long ago if they'd spent money like Scott and Zelda."

Hemingway had disliked Zelda since their first meeting in Paris, when he gazed into her "hawk's eyes" and saw a rapacious spirit. He estimated that 90 percent of Scott's problems were her fault, and said that almost every "bloody fool thing" his friend had done had been "directly or indirectly Zelda-inspired." Ernest often wondered if Scott would have been the best writer America ever had or was likely to have if he had not been married to someone who made him "waste" everything.

Perkins, on his part, saw other obstacles in Scott's career. For one, he guessed, Fitzgerald was attempting the impossible in this novel—in trying to blend the seriousness inherent in a story of matricide with the gloss of his tales of the haut monde—and might have come to feel that impossibility but been unwilling to acknowledge it. "If I could have got any response implying that this was right," Max wrote Ernest, "I would have advised him to let it go and begin another." But Scott slogged on. His earliest attempt at the novel had been in the third person. Now he tried the first. Unlike Nick Carraway of *The Great Gatsby*, the narrator of *The Melarkey Case*, as the book had come to be called, remained un-identified. The use of first person did not seem to help, and Scott soon gave it up entirely.

There was another problem Scott had been trying to hide behind his generally cheerful facade—his dread of aging. In her memoirs, written almost four decades later, Alice B. Toklas remembered Scott's saying to her companion Gertrude Stein during a visit in September, 1926: "You know I am thirty years old today and it is tragic. What is to become of me, what am I to do?"

A change of scenery seemed to be a good temporary solution. Weeks later Zelda wrote Max, "We are crazy to get back and longing to seem very changed after our 3 yrs. in centers of culture—though we have intermittently festerred with indignation and been prostrate with the beauty and ease of the Riviera. I think living here has been good for us in some obscure way I can't define. Anyway, its helped our manners and now we want to get back with French names on all our medicine bottles."

Home from Europe for the winter holidays, Fitzgerald met with Max and then left for three weeks of work at First National Pictures in Holly-wood. It was the first of several trips Fitzgerald would make to California. For Scott, the motion-picture business was a glamorous world at the end of a rainbow, where he always went looking for a pot of gold. "I hope it will be for only three weeks," Max wrote Scott. "The trouble is that you will be so valuable to the picture people that I am afraid they will offer you almost irresistible bribes. But I have known you to resist a good deal. You always seem to know what you're about."

Perkins wanted to believe as much. Partly to distract Scott's attention from the dazzling salaries flashing before him, he wrote, "I am under great pressure to tell people two things about you: —where you are, and what is to be the name of your novel." For the past several months Perkins had been considering *The World's Fair;* from what Scott told him of the book, he saw how fitting a title it was. Max said he wanted to announce it, thereby establishing "a sort of proprietorship. And I think it would help to arouse curiosity and interest in the novel too."

What Perkins wanted most for Fitzgerald was for him to return to America for good. Max thought Delaware, with the Du Ponts' feudalistic control of the area, would fascinate Fitzgerald, and so he house-hunted for him. Early in April, 1927, the Fitzgeralds moved into Ellerslie, a Greek Revival mansion outside Wilmington, which Perkins recommended. The modest rent was welcome, and the grandiose style appealed to them— too much, perhaps. Edmund Wilson, for one, believed it abetted Scott's lust for showy living. In an essay published years later in *The Shores of Light*, Wilson suggested that it was Scott's "invincible compulsion to live like a millionaire" as well as a "psychological 'block' " on the novel that "led him even more than usual to interrupt his serious work and turn out stories for the commercial magazines." Whatever the causes, Fitzgerald all but abandoned the book. At parties with the Delaware polo set or alone at Ellerslie, he caroused, several times landing in jail for disturbing the peace.

Max was ambivalent about Scott's taste for life's luxuries—his travels, his beautiful homes, his elegant clothes, and the wild life among the decadent rich in Europe and America. One part of Max—the Evarts part —could not respond, while the other—the Perkins side—participated in these sensual expressions with an intense vicariousness. Yankee Max would not allow himself the descent into voluptuousness that Scott enjoyed, but his fondness for Fitzgerald suggests that far from disapproving, he relished the free life from his vantage point of the interested, but still innocent, bystander. It was the relationship of a rather stiff but indulgent uncle— Max liked to surprise Scott with small gifts, replacing a favorite walking cane that Scott had lost or having a special leather-bound edition of *Gatsby* made up for him—to a spoiled, dashing, irresistible nephew.

For Fitzgerald, Perkins filled another role. Early in his childhood

Scott had lost respect for his parents for not making more of their lives or the dwindling fortune they inherited. In a later autobiographical sketch called "Author's House," Fitzgerald recalled his first childish love of himself—"my belief that I would never die like other people, and that I wasn't the son of my parents but a son of a king, a king who ruled the whole world." He had recently written Max, "My father is a moron and my mother is a neurotic, half insane with pathological nervous worry. Between them they haven't and never have had the brains of Calvin Coolidge." Perkins was prepared to act *in loco parentis*, and he kept sending Fitzgerald back to his novel, whose plot was becoming overworked. In June, 1927, Scott came up with a stark title distinctly different from his others—*The Boy Who Killed His Mother*—then spent months in silence and isolation trying to untangle the roots of the novel.

In the spring of 1927, Louise Perkins's seventy-one-year-old father, who had retired to a life of travel and ornithological pursuits, fell ill in London. Fearing the worst, Max and Louise sailed on the S.S. *Olympic* for England in June. She was going to look after her father, while Max would tend to business at Scribners' London office. It was the first time he had left American soil. He found the ship a deluxe prison. The meals were interminable and there was nothing to do between them. "The ocean doesn't even give a sense of immensity," he wrote Elizabeth Lemmon, "because you can clearly see the edge, equally distant in every direction. The ocean is a disc." A few days out, the ship started to roll, and Max realized for the first time the majesty of the ocean. Listening to the splash of waves outside his open porthole, he wrote his daughter Zippy, "The next time I live, I think I'll run away to sea."

Perkins had always imagined London to be a "drab, monotonous place, full of stiff, cold people," and found to his surprise that he was wrong. ("See what books have done for me!" he wrote Elizabeth.)

When Max was not doing business, he and Louise spent most of their time with her recuperating father. The Perkinses saw no more of Europe than London, except for a night and day in Sussex with John Galsworthy, after visiting his town house, where Max and Galsworthy talked books most of the time. Perkins wanted to enlist his support in widening Scott Fitzgerald's audience in England, but the cause hardly stirred Galsworthy. In fact, Max found him not at all in sympathy with contemporary literature. He spoke of *The Great Gatsby* as "a great advance," but the only books he truly seemed to admire, Max later wrote

Fitzgerald, were those "laid out on the old lines . . . and not expressive of present thought or feeling." Galsworthy told Perkins: "These writers who become writers at the start are invariably disappointments. It is much better for a man to have been something else than a writer so that he has viewed the world from a fixed position."

Mrs. Galsworthy could scarcely have been more rude. While pouring Louise's tea from the pot she had brewed, Mrs. Galsworthy said, "Of course, I know you'd prefer a teabag." When lighting the wood in the fireplace, she peered down her nose and remarked, "You are used to gas logs, of course." Louise ignored the insults, for she was much more upset by Max's behavior. At one point in the afternoon, Mrs. Galsworthy, admiring his refined manner, sputtered, "Mr. Perkins, you might be English."

"Well, I'm not," he said tersely with a stone face, bringing the conversation to dead silence.

"There we were," Louise told Max's nephew Ned Thomas years later, "Max and his damn stubborn Evarts contrariness. He ruined the whole luncheon." Later Galsworthy told a friend that Perkins was the most interesting American he had ever known.

One afternoon Max and Louise toured the House of Commons, and the Chancellor of the Exchequer, Winston Churchill, happened to be on the floor. The Members of Parliament were droning about finance, but Max found Churchill "brilliant with life." He wrote home to his daughters: "Winston Churchill, whom I someday hope to persuade to write a history of the British Empire, made a speech, and whenever he said anything the members of either party liked, they would say, 'Hear! Hear!' "

Max sent a long, detailed account of his trip to Elizabeth Lemmon. He interrupted his description of the sights for one exceptionally tender remark: "Quite often in London you see girls that are like you, more than any you ever find here. They have hair that, anyhow, reminds one of yours, though I never saw any as lovely."

Impressed as he was with his week and a half in London—"I never felt so much at home in a city in my life," he wrote Elizabeth—Max did not quite give in to enjoying himself. Louise could have happily remained all summer, but soon, leaving Mr. Saunders in good health, they headed for Southampton and sailed home.

Once the Perkinses were resettled in America, Louise and the children went to Windsor. Except for occasional visits there, Max spent the summer in his father-in-law's town house on East Forty-ninth Street where he looked after Mr. Saunders's pet parrot and monkey. It was an easy walk to Scribners.

Max wrote to Elizabeth several times that year and often sent her books. Elizabeth's study of astrology had recently got him into trouble at home, he told her, because Louise had consulted an astrologer she had recommended, who had done a chart of Max and observed that he was in a "desperate situation apparently from love."

"Oh, I know he can't be, for I see him every night," Louise said.

"But," the astrologer had persisted, "you don't know what he does in the afternoons." The fortune teller had insisted that Max was undergoing intense "anguish" and that Louise knew nothing about her husband at all.

"How do you account for all that?" Max asked Elizabeth. She flippantly replied that Max had obviously been involved in a love affair that spring. "You must know—though I know you don't rate me high—" Max wrote her back, "that I am at least incapable of that. There was simply no truth in what that lady said." The stars notwithstanding, Elizabeth said, she believed him.

The following winter Max wrote three long letters to her, which he crumpled up and never mailed. "I don't know exactly why," he tried to explain. "I felt you had transferred your interests to other planets." Indeed, whenever Elizabeth did write to him, he would stare in disbelief at her letter among his business mail. "I pushed all the others aside and read it," he told her after one note that September, though "I thought that long ago you'd forgotten us in riotous living, or even in peaceful country life."

Perkins's most frequent correspondent that year was his former English professor, Charles T. Copeland. Since 1920, Max and several other publishers had been after Copeland to write a book of reminiscences, but sloth as much as pride had kept him from "memoirizing." He thought that rendering an account of one's life was an admission that he'd been sent to pasture. Copey had years of teaching left in him and he was not prepared to relive his past now. He did, however, assemble what he called "a living book." It was a 1,700-page anthology of his favorite selections, works that he had read to his students during twenty years of teaching, called *The Copeland Reader*.

"Thus began what became one of the most extraordinary relationships between author and publisher in the history of the trade," wrote J. Donald Adams, editor of the *New York Times Book Review* and author of *Copey of Harvard.* "Perkins in his eagerness to publish the work of a man he so highly regarded, was ready to meet any reasonable demands"; but he did not realize at the outset that in matters of editorial cooperation, Copeland would exact the last pound of flesh. The files on *The Copeland Reader* (and a companion volume of Copey's favorite foreign selections called *Copeland's Translations*) take up more space in Scribners' cabinets than those concerning any other two books. As Adams explained,

> His letters dealing with textual matters, with the choice of selections, with advertising and other promotion, were incessant; his inquiries as to when there would be another printing, and of what size, were repeated and insistent. . . . No matter how querulous the communications, so often requesting a reply "by return of post," they were always answered with consideration and dispatch.

One postcard reminded Perkins that the Table of Contents "must be liberally spaced." Perkins's compliance with almost every one of Copeland's wishes went beyond blind obedience; he coddled Copey as he did no other author—certainly no anthologist. At Perkins's direction, Scribners gathered for him all the texts he needed to make up his book. Contrary to standard procedure, they also assumed the costs of all copyright permissions and undertook all correspondence and negotiations necessary in obtaining the permissions.

"But nothing was more singular in their business relations than Copeland's attitude in the matter of advances on royalties," Adams noted. Copey insisted on regarding them as loans, which, strictly speaking, they were. As a result, his biographer noted, "Copeland is probably the only author in publishing history who would accept an advance only with the stipulation that he be charged interest for this accommodation."

In another respect Copey was like every other author on Perkins's list. Over the years *The Copeland Reader* would sell tens of thousands of copies, but when it was introduced to the public, Copey complained that his book was not sufficiently advertised. He rode Max even harder after the editor agreed with him. To the end Max believed advertising was like a man pushing a stationary automobile: "If he can get it to move, the more he pushes the faster it will move and the more easily. But if he cannot get it to move, he can push till he drops dead and it will stand still."

Although he was busier than ever, Max knew that he and Louise would not be able to refuse forever the Fitzgeralds' persistent invitations to join them for a weekend at their mansion in Delaware. He told Elizabeth he was dreading it "on account of advertising, cocktails, made-up girls, cigarette smoke, and talk"—all the things he hated and was told a sophisticated New York editor ought to appreciate. But the Perkinses paid Scott and Zelda a visit in October, 1927.

Ellerslie Mansion, Max wrote Hemingway, "which is solid and high and yellow, has more quality of its own than almost any house I was ever in." It was very old (for America) and the trees around it sprawled. It had columns at the front and back, second-story verandahs, and a lawn that rolled right down to the Delaware River. On Sunday, Max rose earlier than the rest and took breakfast alone. An autumn breeze was playing at the curtains, and the sun was coming in. "It was like remembering something pleasant of a long time ago," he told Eilizabeth Lemmon. "It all belongs to the quiet past and made me feel quiet and happy."

But the master of the house was not at peace amid all that serenity and tradition. Fitzgerald was in a state of frazzled nerves. He was drinking heavily and talking nervously; his hands trembled. Max feared Scott might have a breakdown at any minute and prescribed clean living—less alcohol, a month of hard exercise, and denicotinized cigarettes called Sanos. Zelda, he was happy to see, was in good health and high spirits. "She's a girl of character," Max wrote Elizabeth, "meant for a far better life than she has led."

Later in the month, Fitzgerald came to New York to see Max. He said his novel was only 5,000 words from completion, but to Max he seemed too high-strung to get them down on paper. Scott worked for an hour in the book-lined sitting room on Scribners' fifth floor, then was seized by one of his nervous fits. He had to go out for a walk, and he insisted that Perkins join him for a drink. Unsure of the effect it would have on Scott's condition, Max warily agreed, saying, "Well, I'll go if it's just one drink." Fitzgerald snapped, "You talk to me as if I were Ring Lardner." In a moment Max was walking with him out of the building and Fitzgerald already seemed calmer. "We had a great talk over the drink," Max wrote Lardner the next day. "I am sure anyhow, that if he will finish up his novel . . . and will then take a real rest and regular exercise, he will be in good shape again."

For a year or two Fitzgerald's income had been sweetened by sales of subsidiary rights—a play of *The Great Gatsby* had a good run in New York and the book was sold to Hollywood. Then he went back to the

Saturday Evening Post for their fat checks of $3,500 per story. Most of each month for the rest of the year, he neglected his novel, against which Perkins still sent advances, to write *Post* stories. On the first day of 1928 Fitzgerald took account of his situation and wrote Perkins: "Patience yet a little while, I beseech thee and thanks eternally for the deposits." He felt bad about owing so much money but assured Max that it could be written off as a "safe investment and not as a risk" because he had been on the wagon since the middle of October and was still smoking only Sanos.

"I think we ought all to be proud of the way you climbed on the water wagon," Max wrote back. "It is enormously harder for a man who has no office hours and has control of his own time,—and it is hard enough for anybody." Max's real worry about Fitzgerald's career was the three years that had elapsed since *Gatsby* failed commercially, leaving few readers who remembered its quality and fewer who were looking forward to his next book. Then Perkins talked to another of his writers, poet and novelist Conrad Aiken, and was considerably heartened. Aiken's estimation of *Gatsby* was still as high as the day it was published. Furthermore, Aiken said, the book had grown in critical stature, for "now everybody knows anyhow what it was, and what 'Gatsby' means."

Another event that cheered Max was his publishing a promising new writer named Morley Callaghan, a Canadian. Callaghan had met Hemingway when their careers at the Toronto *Star* overlapped; then he went to Paris, where he hobnobbed with many other American expatriates, Fitzgerald among them. Max read several of Callaghan's pieces in the little European reviews and, at first, found him no more than a "hard-boiled," realistic writer. Later, after they met, Max considered him "highly intelligent and responsive." Callaghan came to New York to write a novel called *Strange Fugitive*, the story of a lumberyard foreman who tired of his married life and got drawn into bootlegging. Perkins saw the unfinished manuscript and believed it would turn out well. It was completed within months and Scribners published it that year. Yet Fitzgerald's book poked along.

In February Scott wired from Delaware: NOVEL NOT FINISHED CHRIST I WISH IT WERE.

Even in spacious Ellerslie, the Fitzgeralds now felt boxed in. In fact, Scott recognized that all the trappings of manor life he had tried to acquire were but "attempts to make up from without for being undernourished now from within. Anything to be liked, to be reassured not that I was a man of little genius, but that I was a great man of the world. At the same time I knew it was nonsense." And so it was off to Europe again. Through the spring Scott sent Perkins only requests for money. Then he wrote in June that he and his family were settled in Paris on the Rue de Vaugirard, across from the Luxembourg Gardens. He was on the "absolute wagon and working on the novel, the whole novel, and nothing but the novel," he said. "I'm coming back in August with it or on it."

Into the fourth July since *The Great Gatsby*, Fitzgerald was encouraged when James Joyce came to dinner at his home in Paris. Scott inquired if his next work—*Finnegans Wake*, already some six years in progress— was coming along. "Yes," affirmed Joyce, "I expect to finish my novel in three or four years more at the latest." And, Fitzgerald noted to Perkins, "he works eleven hours a day to my intermittent eight."

Fitzgerald did not arrive home until October. Max met him at the gangplank and found the author still tipsy from over $200 worth of wine that he had ordered during the crossing. But Scott held on tightly to his briefcase which held the "complete . . . but not the finished" manuscript of the novel. He said it was all down on paper, only parts of it had to be worked over.

Fitzgerald went back to Ellerslie, and the following month was ready to submit material. The book was not yet finished, but, Scott wrote to his editor, "I've been alone with it too long." He had a plan for passing it on in relays, by which Max would read two chapters of this final version every month as he finished with them. "It seems fine to be sending you something again," Scott wrote, mailing Max the first package that November. It was only the first quarter of the book—18,000 words—but it had been three years since Fitzgerald had last sent him manuscript. Now Fitzgerald had to mint another short story, so he could afford to patch up Chapters Three and Four, which he hoped to send at the beginning of December. He asked Perkins to hold onto any criticisms until he had received the entire book "because I want to *feel* that each part is finished and not worry about it any longer, even though I may change it enormously at the very last minute. All I want to know is if, in general, you like it . . . My God its good to see those chapters lying in an envelope!"

"I am mighty glad you have decided on this course," Perkins wrote Scott. "Now don't change your mind on this." One week later Max commented on the newly received material: "I have just finished the two chapters. About the first we fully agree. It is excellent. The second I think contains some of the best writing you have ever done—some lovely scenes and impressions briefly and beautifully conveyed. . . . I wish it might be possible to get this book out this spring, if only because it promises so much that it makes me impatient to see it completed."

While Perkins waited for the next installment of Fitzgerald's novel, he received the next mystery from one of his best-selling authors, Willard Huntington Wright, better known to hundreds of thousands of readers as S. S. Van Dine. Once a struggling art critic and magazine and newspaper editor, Wright transferred his own elegance of manner and cultivated sensibilities to his creation, a detective named Philo Vance. For months Wright had had trouble finding a publisher for his mysteries; then Perkins read several of his plot synopses, admired their intricacy, and signed him. First Max published *The Benson Murder Case*, then, *The "Canary" Murder Case*. Now, over the New Year's holiday of 1928, he stayed up till 3:30 A.M. reading *The Greene Murder Case* and thought it was magnificent. In a very few years S. S. Van Dine had become the best-known American mystery writer since Poe, and much of his success was as a result of Perkins's meticulous aid in the characterization of Philo Vance. Perkins brought to bear on his mystery writer the same keen intelligence and uncompromising standards that he lavished on Fitzgerald, Hemingway, and his other more clearly literary authors.

During his fifteen years as an editor, Max Perkins had come to be recognized at Scribners as a most valuable employee, and he had been compensated accordingly. In the past decade his salary had been doubled—to $10,000—and he was receiving liberal amounts of private stock. As important to Max, no doubt, was the fact that Charles and Arthur Scribner were letting him gradually work free of his stodgy editorial supervisor, old William Crary Brownell. After forty years at Scribners, Brownell had recently retired. Though seventy-seven, he still reported to his desk almost every day, but his productivity had waned and Perkins's was at its greatest. Max and his contemporaries now did the main share of the editorial work. One of the most active new editors was Wallace Meyer, who had worked as advertising manager in the early twenties but had left to "see the world" before settling down to a lifelong career. In 1928 Perkins coaxed him back.

That summer, while Perkins was vacationing in Windsor, Brownell died. Max wrote Mr. Scribner, "I felt pretty sick when I read of Brownell's death. He was as good a man as I ever knew." A difference in age had separated their tastes in literature, but Perkins had found that his preceptor's nineteenth-century intellect had not lessened his skill as a literary adviser. Perkins said, "If a young man worked beside [Brownell] for some years and failed to become a passable editor he simply had no capacity for the work." One of Brownell's hard and fast principles was that almost as much could be learned about an author's abilities through an interview as by reading his manuscript, since "water cannot rise above its source." Another Brownell adage that Perkins subscribed to was that the worst reason for publishing anything was that it resembled something else, that however unconscious, "an imitation is always inferior." Sometimes a second-rate manuscript was marked by some rare characteristics that made it hard for the staff to surrender it. Brownell would close the debate by saying, "We can't publish everything. Let someone else make a failure of it."

Brownell was always considerate of the authors he turned down. Whenever a book of promise had to be rejected, it was Brownell who wrote the most sympathetic letters. Perkins admired these compassionate rejections as works of art. One was so warmhearted that the author mailed his manuscript back, having written in the margin of the letter: "Then why the devil don't you publish it?"

Above all, Perkins believed, Brownell brought dignity to his work as editor-in-chief. Upon his death, Max volunteered to cut his vacation short and report back to work within the week. "Beyond that time," he wrote Charles Scribner, disingenuously explaining away his need for the remainder of his vacation, "I couldn't occupy myself; though I feel that Wheelock and Meyer are perfectly able to do anything, and that we have now as competent an editorial force as any publisher could hope for. And I believe our list will show the effect of it."

Perkins was now forty-three and fully formed as a professional editor. His style was set. Max had told Louise early in his marriage that he wanted to be "a little dwarf on the shoulder of a great general advising him what to do and what not to do, without anyone's noticing." Max instructed his "generals" in a variety of ways. Sometimes he was bold. "You have to throw yourself away when you write," he often told writers who came to him for help with their work. Sometimes, however, he was understated to the point of muteness. When an author would come to Perkins babbling tales of woe about his work or his life, Max typically sat in silence. A Scribners colleague remembered one luncheon when a writer laid all his problems out on the table; as he talked, Max ate slowly, not saying a word. Toward the end of the meal, which lasted several hours, the writer rose from the table, grabbed the editor's hand with both of his, spluttered, "Thank you, Mr. Perkins, for all your help," and bolted out the door.

Roger Burlingame recalled an occasion when a writer stood in Max's office pouring out his unhappiness. Perkins went to the window as if overcome by the burden of his sympathy, and gazed down onto Fifth Avenue. After a few moments of surveying the street, rocking slightly, he appeared ready to speak, and the writer waited in anticipation for his editor's comment on his plight. "You know," said Perkins without turning, "I can't understand why all these busy people move so slowly. The only ones who move fast are the boys on roller skates who have nothing to do. Why don't we—why doesn't everybody—wear skates?" The writer later gave Perkins credit for thoroughly distracting him from his problems.

As he approached middle age, Perkins's tendency toward eccentricity began to flourish. He maintained an embarrassed belief in phrenology— the study of character as revealed by the protuberances of the skull. A prominent nasal bone was, he felt, the sign of individuality. He did not think any man who had a small nose or a flat back to his head could be especially worthwhile. To Perkins, it was a sign of mental weakness to confess a lapse of memory. "Never admit you can't remember," he would say. "Send a bucket into your subconscious."

In his own engaging way he was becoming a fussbudget. Babies sucking on bottles disgusted him. Once, after a dinner honoring a famous beauty, he criticized her because "she had marks of her day clothes on her bare back." He believed no "real lady" would ever drink beer or use Worcestershire sauce. "In our family," he admonished his own daughters, "we say underclothes, not underwear."

When he brought books home to put on his shelves, he immediately ripped off their dust jackets and threw them away. He instinctively closed volumes he found lying open, pages down, and he winced when he observed someone licking fingers to turn pages.

He was a doodler and would ceaselessly sketch portraits of Napoleon, always in profile. He also found pleasure in dreaming up "practical" solutions to everyday problems. Among his notions were that honey ought to be packaged in transparent containers and squeezed out like toothpaste. He went so far as to suggest to a friend in advertising that they should market the product as "Tubes of Liquid Sunshine." He also thought type-

ar Mr. Perkins:

within t
ming into possession of
less you advise me to t
sent to you for consic
gazine of for books. Th
CTICUT YANKEE reversed.
ly done, but whether yc
do not know. It is bei

The next
ble, but about that,- 1

I've no
ings I send. All I want
bother to you if they a
ey be sent to someone e

My partr
e proofs of Knopf's big
Elliott Paul. Two-thir
though Knopf is saying
mes out the twenty-four

Messrs. Charles Scribner's Sons
Fifth Avenue and Forty-eighth St:
New York City.

Gentlemen:-

I hand you herewith
following chapters of Mr. Irving
" The Art of Skating

Chapter 6. School Figures

"   17. Winners of Chamj

"   18. Hockey and Speed

Will you kindly have
as possible and send to Mr. Broka
when ready?

Very

JACruikshank/W

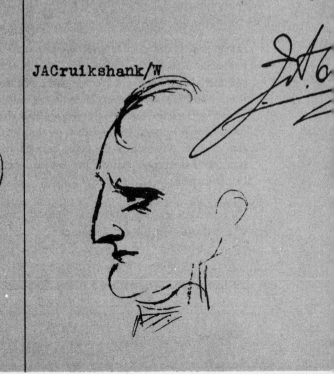

writer paper ought to come in a long, perforated roll, like bathroom tissue.

Yet Perkins had no aptitude whatever for anything mechanical. "He couldn't even drive in a screw," said one daughter. One day several people on the fifth floor of the Scribner Building went running into Max's office because they smelled smoke. They found Max totally ignoring a blaze in his wastebasket and carrying on with his work. One of old Charles Scribner's grandsons, George Schieffelin, said, "I'm sure Max had no idea how it got started and even less how to put it out."

Perkins's daughters agreed their father was all but a menace behind the wheel of a car. Peggy said: "He would drive along at a breakneck speed until he began to think about something that interested him. Then he would slow up and creep along. It infuriated him to have people pass him. He always refused to dim his lights. He said it was silly. Once we came up behind a man and woman walking together by the side of the road. He slowed up and drove very slowly behind them, trying to make us see from an artist's point of view the difference between the way a man and a woman walk. We begged him to go past, because of course the poor people were bewildered, but he wouldn't. He was too interested in the problem of how to draw the difference."

Perkins, the would-be inventor, believed the greatest inventor in the world could never compare with a great poet. The former "has made living easier, and more pleasurable so far as concerns that pleasure that comes from without," he once wrote Louise. He

> has improved—if that is improvement—our surroundings. But the poet has actually changed ourselves. The great poet has added many cubits to our spiritual stature, and we see and hear and feel things more clearly, and deeply, and broadly forever, after he has had his chance at us; and even if he has not reached us directly, we are still changed by his influence upon other people through theirs on us; so that it comes about that a whole nation is made different by the poet, through all time, as the English nation was by Shakespeare. Indeed the whole world was; and by Homer and Dante as well.

"My earliest friend Maxwell Perkins, my lifelong friend," wrote Van Wyck Brooks in his autobiography, "used to say that every man has a novel in him. The idea was not originally his,—it was, in fact, a commonplace,—but, being a man of character, he made it his; and I always felt that he might have written a first-rate novel himself if he had ranged over his own life. He was in his way a novelist born, but instead of developing this bent in himself, he devoted his intuitive powers to the development of others."

It was that civil war again—Perkins versus Evarts, Cavalier versus Roundhead. "One side appreciated the writers," Brooks observed, "the other side helped them, an ambivalence that explained why Max never became a writer himself and why he became the rock on which others leaned."

VIII

A Little Honest Help

As autumn 1928 arrived, a vivacious Frenchwoman named Madeleine Boyd, wife of literary critic Ernest Boyd and the New York agent for many European authors, came with an armful of manuscripts to see Perkins. In the course of their meeting she spoke of an extraordinary novel of great length written by a huge North Carolinian named Thomas Wolfe. Then she went on to talk about other books. When Perkins brought her back to Wolfe's *O Lost,* she seemed hesitant. "Why don't you bring it in here, Madeleine?" he said, pressing further. She finally consented upon Perkins's promise that he would read every word of it. They agreed that he could pick up the manuscript at five o'clock that afternoon. "But," Mrs. Boyd said with a smile, "you'll have to send a truck for it." At exactly five, one drove up before her apartment house. She turned the huge package over to the driver, who asked if that was one book. "Jeeesus Christ!" he said when told that it was.

"The first time I heard of Thomas Wolfe," Max wrote two decades later in an unfinished article, "I had a sense of foreboding. I who loved the man say this. Every good thing that comes is accompanied by trouble."

When *O Lost* reached Perkins, he had a lot of other work on his hands. This new manuscript of hundreds upon hundreds of pages was easy to ignore in favor of the dozens of smaller proposals and first drafts of books that crossed his desk every week. But accompanying the manuscript was a moving note for the publisher's reader in which the author explained a few of the elements of his work. It said, in part:

This book, in my estimate is from 250,000 to 380,000 words long. A book of this length from an unknown writer no doubt is rashly experimental, and shows his ignorance of the mechanics of publishing. That is true. This is my first book. . . .

But I believe it would be unfair to assume that because this is a very long book it is too long a book. . . . The book may be lacking in plot but it is not lacking in plan. The plan is rigid and densely woven. . . . It does not seem to me that the book is overwritten. Whatever comes out of it must come out block by block and not sentence by sentence. Generally I do not believe the writing to be wordy, prolix, or redundant.

I have never called this book a novel. To me it is a book such as all men may have in them. It is a book made out of my life, and it represents my vision of life to my twentieth year.

I have written all this, not to propitiate you . . . but to entreat you, if you spend the many hours necessary for a careful reading, to spend a little more time in giving me an opinion. If it is not publishable, could it be made so? . . . I need a little honest help. If you are interested enough to finish the book, won't you give it to me?

Max took up the pages and was at once enthralled by the opening, in which the hero's father, W. O. Gant, as a young boy, watched a procession of ragged Confederate troops. Then followed 100 pages about W. O.'s life, long before the birth of his son Eugene, the actual protagonist of the story. "All this was what Wolfe had heard," Max later recalled, "and had no actual association with which to reconcile it, and it was inferior to the first episode, and in fact to all the rest of the book." He then was distracted by other work and gave the manuscript to Wallace Meyer, thinking, "Here is another promising novel that probably will come to nothing."

Ten days later Meyer came in to show Perkins another extraordinary scene in that same huge manuscript, and that was enough to bring Max back to the book. He began to read it again. Soon he and Meyer were passing pages back and forth and John Hall Wheelock and the rest of the staff were grabbing whole sections at a time. When Max had finally lived up to his end of the bargain he had struck with Madeleine Boyd, he had not a shadow of a doubt about the value of the book. But he did recognize major stumbling blocks that could keep it from getting into print. He knew, for example, that so intense a work would be resented by a good many people at Scribners, for it was "very strong meat." The book would also require considerable "reorganization" and a great deal of cutting. Max realized he should not even try to get Scribners committed to it before determining what the author was like and how difficult it would be to get him to revise. But he was determined to see the book published. Remembering his battles to publish Fitzgerald and Hemingway, he was sorry for a moment that he was not a publisher on his own.

In late October, Mrs. Boyd tracked Thomas Wolfe down and sent Perkins an address in Munich where she thought he could be reached. The editor wrote the author that he did not "know whether it would be possible to work out a plan by which [the manuscript] might be worked into a form publishable by us, but I do know that, setting the practical aspects of the matter aside, it is a very remarkable thing, and that no editor could read it without being excited by it and filled with admiration by many passages in it and sections of it. . . . What we should like to know is whether you will be in New York in a fairly near future, when we can see you and discuss the manuscript."

When Wolfe received the letter, forwarded from Germany to Austria, he knew that editors from several houses had, in fact, already turned down the fictional autobiography. A few of them had nice things to say about it, but not one had expressed the vaguest interest in printing the book. "I can't tell you how good your letter has made me feel," Wolfe wrote Perkins on November 17, 1928, from Vienna. "Your words of praise have filled me with hope, and are worth more than their weight in diamonds to me." He expected to be home in America shortly before Christmas, and not having looked at his book in months, he believed he could come back with a "much fresher and more critical feeling." He admitted, "I have no right to expect others to do for me what I should do for myself, but although I am able to criticize wordiness and overabundance in others, I am not able practically to criticize it in myself.

"I want the direct criticism and advice of an older and more critical person," Wolfe continued, not quite sure whether the signature on his letter from the editor read Perkins or Peters. "I wonder if at Scribners I can find someone who is interested enough to talk over the whole huge monster with me, part by part." Wolfe was astonished he had managed to make even a connection with Charles Scribner's Sons, which "I had always thought vaguely was a solid and somewhat conservative house." He closed his letter with two hopes: first, that Perkins would be able to decipher the lightning flashes that were his script, "which is more than many people do"; and second, "that you will not forget me before I come back."

Perkins had little trouble with the first wish, none with the second. Mrs. Boyd had recently told him of Wolfe's being beaten almost to death at Munich's Oktoberfest. That event, together with the facts Perkins had gleaned from Wolfe's autobiographical work, gave him a glimpse of the pandemonium ahead. During the next few weeks, Max worried about the two "Moby Dicks" he would have to restrain—the man even more than the book.

Perkins returned to work from his New Year's holiday on Wednesday, January 2, filled with trepidation at meeting the creator of the manuscript that covered his desk. Max had been forewarned of Wolfe's unusual appearance, but he was nonetheless startled by the massiveness of the six-foot six-inch, black-haired man leaning against the jamb, filling his doorway. Years later Max recalled, "When I looked up and saw his wild hair and bright countenance, although he was so altogether different physically, I thought of Shelley. *He* was fair, but his hair was wild and his face was bright and his head disproportionately small."

Wolfe lumbered into the office and sized up the editor, finding he was not as he had pictured him. The author later wrote Margaret Roberts, his most influential schoolteacher back home in Asheville, that the man who had summoned him was not at all "Perkinsy."

[The] name sounds Midwestern, but he is a Harvard man, probably New England family, early forties, but looks younger, very elegant and gentle in dress and manner. He saw I was nervous and excited, spoke to me quietly, told me to take my coat off and sit down. He began by asking certain questions about the book and people.

Perkins talked first about a scene early in the manuscript between the hero's father—the stonecutter W. O. Gant—and the madam of the local brothel, in which she was purchasing a tombstone for one of her girls. In his eagerness Wolfe blurted, "I know you can't print that! I'll take that out at once, Mr. Perkins."

"Take it out?" Perkins exclaimed. "It's one of the greatest short stories I have ever read!"

Max proceeded to discuss different parts of the book from a stack of notes he had made, suggestions for revisions and rearrangements of scenes. Wolfe reeled off whole paragraphs he was willing to excise immediately. At each one, it seemed, Perkins interrupted him to say, "No—you must let that stay word for word—that scene's simply magnificent." Wolfe's eyes grew moist. "I was so moved and touched to think that someone at length had thought enough of my work to sweat over it in this way that I almost wept."

Out of an instinctive tendency to postpone what was difficult, not out of cunning, as Wolfe might have suspected, Perkins left the hardest point for the last. *O Lost* lacked any real form, and the only way he could see to provide that structure was by selective cutting. Specifically, Perkins thought that despite the wonderful first chapter about the hero's father as a boy, the book should begin with the father already grown in Altamont, the fictional name of Wolfe's hometown, thus framing the story within the experience and the memory of the boy Eugene. Wolfe was not yet willing, during this first editorial session, to agree to so radical a cut as the first 100 pages. But he was not put off by the suggestion. In fact, he had never been so light of heart. "It was the first time, so far as I can remember," Wolfe recorded later, "that anyone had concretely suggested to me that anything I had written was worth as much as fifteen cents."

A few days later Perkins and Wolfe met again. Tom brought notes along indicating how he proposed to set to work in shaping his novel. He agreed to deliver 100 pages of corrected manuscript every week. When he asked if he could say something positive about publication to a dear friend, a theatrical designer named Aline Bernstein, who had given his manuscript to Madeleine Boyd in the first place, Max smiled and said that he thought so, that Scribners' minds were practically made up. As Wolfe left Perkins's office, he met John Hall Wheelock. The poet–editor took him by the hand and said, "I hope you have a good place to work in. You have a big job ahead."

On January 8, 1929, Perkins wrote Wolfe that Charles Scribner's Sons had formally accepted *O Lost* for publication. Drunk with glory, Tom came in to sign the contract and receive his advance on royalties. Some years later he described in *The Story of a Novel* that euphoric moment: "I left the publisher's office that day and entered into the great swarm of men and women who passed constantly along Fifth Avenue at 48th Street, and presently I found myself at 110th Street, and from that day to this I have never known how I got there." For days he walked on air with his contract tucked in his inner breast pocket, a check for $450 (10 percent having been deducted by his literary agent) pinned to it. "There is literally no reason why I should walk around New York with these documents," he wrote Mrs. Roberts, "but in a busy crowd I will sometimes take them out, gaze tenderly at them, and kiss them passionately."

"But now," he wrote his former schoolteacher on January 12, 1929, "is the time for sanity. My debauch of happiness is over. I have made promises." He had a part-time teaching job at New York University, but revising his book took precedence over correcting his students' themes. Already he thought of quitting his job for a professional writing career. Feeling nothing less than devotion for Scribners, he wrote Perkins, "I hope this marks the beginning of a long association that they will not have cause to regret." Wolfe retired to his second-floor, rear apartment on West Fifteenth Street to face some of the problems that he and Perkins had underscored.

O Lost was a portrait of a writer in his youth, living within the mountains that encircled Asheville, North Carolina. Even before it had been edited, publishing gossip had bloated the book's length into titanic proportions. People who had seen the manuscript swore it stood several feet off the ground. In fact, it was 1,114 pages of onionskin, contained some 330,000 words, and stood five inches high. Wolfe himself realized a book that size was probably unreadable and certainly unwieldy. And so in one of his writing journals, he drafted a proposal for condensation: "First to cut out of every page every word that is not essential to the meaning of the writing. If I can find even 10 words in every page this wd. = 10,000 or more in entire mss." By the middle of January he had begun.

"When they accepted my book," Wolfe wrote his friend George W. McCoy of the Asheville *Citizen*, "the publishers told me to get busy with my little hatchet and carve off some 100,000 words." Perkins gave Wolfe some general suggestions for keeping his hero in sharp focus and let him go off alone to cut. The author put in long hours and returned a few weeks later, pleased with his new version of *O Lost*. Perkins was enthusiastic as ever about the poetic quality of the writing, but was not satisfied: For all Wolfe's work, the book was only eight pages shorter. He had made many of the deletions Perkins had suggested, but the new transitions he wrote to connect the severed portions of the narrative had swollen into thousands of words.

Wolfe told Madeleine Boyd that cutting his manuscript was a "stiff perplexing job." Practically speaking, he knew it was desirable to reduce the length of his typescript, but for hours at a time he stared at the pile of pages. "Sometimes," he wrote her, "I want to rip in blindly and slash, but unless I know *where* the result would be disastrous." Mrs. Boyd instructed Wolfe to listen to Max Perkins carefully, because, she said, "he is one of those quiet and powerful persons in the background, the sole and only excuse . . . for Scott Fitzgerald having been successful as he is." Once, sometimes twice a week, without appointment, Wolfe went to Scribners, carrying 100-page sections. If he did not appear, Perkins wrote Wolfe or simply called him up to find out why.

By spring Tom and Perkins were working every day on the revision of the book. "We are cutting out big chunks," Tom wrote his sister, Mabel Wolfe Wheaton, "and my heart bleeds to see it go, but it's die dog or eat the hatchet. Although we both hate to take so much out, we will have a shorter book and one easier to read when we finish. So, although we are losing some good stuff, we are gaining unity. This man Perkins is a fine fellow and perhaps the best publishing editor in America. I have great confidence in him and I usually yield to his judgment."

In time, rumors about the editing of *O Lost* were exaggerated as much as those about the size of the original manuscript; Perkins's evaluation of his efforts on it diminished proportionately. Ultimately he characterized his work as "a matter of reorganization." Whole chunks of the narrative were, in fact, lifted and replaced elsewhere in the book. In truth, however, the most dramatic labor done on the novel was in cutting. Ninety thousand words—enough to fill a large book—were eliminated.

As a rule every deletion was suggested by Perkins, discussed and fought over by him and Wolfe, then removed. No part of the manuscript was extracted without mutual consent; no pages were destroyed. Wolfe saved every remnant ever associated with his writing, and Perkins suggested that much of the excised material in storage might be used in some future pieces.

To create cohesion among the stories and lives which crisscrossed within *O Lost*'s hundreds of pages, Max recommended that the whole saga be "unfolded through the memories and senses of the boy, Eugene." The first and largest cut, then, was the typescript's introductory 1,377 lines. Tom finally agreed with Perkins's criticism that when he had tried to go back into the life of his father before he arrived in Asheville, events not drawn directly from Wolfe's own experience, "the reality and the poignance were diminished." So Gant's history before he arrived in Altamont was reduced to three pages and his remembrance of the Civil War to twenty-three words: "How this boy stood by the roadside near his mother's farm, and saw the dusty Rebels march past on their way to Gettysburg." For years it weighed on Max's conscience that he had persuaded Tom to cut out that first scene of the two little boys on the roadside with the battle impending, but without it, the reader was drawn right into the story.

Getting through to the end of the story, however, was more difficult. After a point Perkins had to search not for whole pages to be excised but often merely single phrases. His criterion throughout was his conviction that the interaction between Eugene and his family was the book's absolute center and that any sequences leading the reader away from this central theme had to be removed. A satirical episode about the wealthy landowners building their estates outside Asheville, for example, was deleted, as was a parody of T. S. Eliot's poetry, because the tone clashed with the pattern of the rest of the material. Cuts made because of obscenities or improprieties amounted to 524 lines.

On twenty different occasions Wolfe spoke to the reader in direct address. If the book was meant to demonstrate a growing awareness as Eugene matured into manhood, Max thought there was no place for the writer years later to make contemporary comments on the scene. They were removed.

Deletions were as difficult for Perkins to suggest as they were for Wolfe to execute. Still, he pointed out several characters he felt did not warrant as much attention as Wolfe had given them. "I remember the horror with which I realized . . . that all these people were almost completely real, that the book was literally autobiographical," Max said almost twenty years later to another of his authors, James Jones. "But Mr. Perkins, you don't understand," Tom would appeal every time Max sentenced a character to the chopping block. "I think these people are 'great' people and that they should be told about." Max agreed with Wolfe but he would have felt negligent not to argue for these deletions because he was convinced that, instead of propelling the story, the large crew of characters slowed it down. Four pages about Wolfe's mother's brother— to name but one of many examples—were reduced to: "Henry, the oldest, was now thirty."

Perkins and Wolfe made real progress with *O Lost* that April. They continued to meet whenever a section was done, and they believed the manuscript would soon be short enough for one volume. Max proposed new revisions, and Wolfe retreated to his apartment either to make further repairs or to begin new parts. With the last of Perkins's suggestions came a confession: his disapproval of the title. Neither he nor any of his colleagues especially liked *O Lost*. Tom came up with many others and

finally brought in a list. Max and John Hall Wheelock were each drawn
to a three-word phrase from Milton's *Lycidas*, the one title Wolfe had
also secretly thought the best—*Look Homeward, Angel.*

By the summer of 1929 Madeleine Boyd believed, as she would for
years to come, that "without that other genius—Max—the world would
never have heard of Tom Wolfe." At the end of July, upon reading the
revised and edited novel, she wired Max Perkins: WOLFE'S BOOK SO GOOD
THANKS TO YOU. Indeed, after witnessing the bold new kind of editorial
work Perkins was undertaking with Wolfe, Mrs. Boyd worked up the
courage to ask Max a question that had long intrigued her. "Why don't
you write yourself?" she inquired in a letter. "I have a feeling you could
write so much better than most of the people who do write." Perkins
delivered his response when they met next. She recalled, "Max just stared
at me for a long time and said, 'Because I'm an editor.'"

Once he left college, Perkins had spent his entire life working with
words. While his first professional inclination toward journalism indicated an interest in becoming a writer, he never showed signs of the
frustrated novelist in his publishing career. He vented any repressed desires to write by volunteering his ideas to authors who had the time and
temperament to devote to a single project. And he expressed himself in
his letters. During his editorial career Max dictated tens of thousands of
them, often two dozen a day, "all as if the person he was writing to was
in the room," remarked his secretary, Irma Wyckoff. "Mr. Perkins even
dictated his own punctuation"—which included a propensity for semi-
colons and for following commas and periods with dashes—"which made
his letters especially conversational. So many of his authors said that he
coud talk about literature better than any writer. That was especially true
in his letters."

Van Wyck Brooks analyzed Perkins's letters from a more scholarly
point of view and observed that "Max's epistolary style was distinctly
eighteenth century—the result of a taste I shared with him for the world
of Swift, Addison, Defoe and Pope that especially included the circle of
Dr. Johnson." One point in a Perkins letter that especially impressed
Brooks for its illustration of his friend's "writer's sensibility" was what
Max remembered of the life of Swift. It was, said Brooks,

> not the romance of Vanessa, which everyone talked of, but something a
> novelist would have observed, that Swift liked to sit in taverns on greens
> listening to the talk of teamsters and coachmen. Just so Stephen Crane had

sat by the hour in Bowery saloons, fascinated by the rhythm and tempo of living speech, and this went far to explain to me Max's intuitive understanding of the writers of his own time in his own country.

Less than a handful could understand the writer's point of view, Perkins said, while "the true artist has always insisted upon making his book what he wanted it" and should never be censored by editors or any outsider. This understanding enabled him to outline whole novels more than once that subsequently his authors executed or to suggest that in writing their books they should follow certain forms that proved to be entirely responsible for their ultimate success. Meanwhile he affirmed that "the only important things" were "loyalty, fortitude and honour" and he felt that to be "born knowing this" meant going at least a part of the way towards being "a great writer in more than the technical sense."

Though he never became a "creative" writer, Perkins came as close as he could by being a truly creative editor.

To Brooks, one of the most interesting things about Max was that "perpetual war with himself that made him in the end a 'prey to sadness.' " It was the "despairing refusal to be oneself" which really means that a man "does not give the consent of his will to his own being."

Max and Tom Wolfe spent five or six evenings together that summer. The city fascinated Wolfe, and when he was not working, he enjoyed nothing more than walking through every part of town with his editor. When they were together, Wolfe seemed to inhale an entire city block's sights, sounds, and smells. And it was on these occasions that Perkins noticed that Thomas Wolfe, like Swift or Stephen Crane, was a keen observer. "He frequented saloons, and drank there, and knew a hundred bartenders as friends," Max said; "but it was not because of the drink. He loved the live, expressive talk of natural people at a bar when their tongues are loosened a little or much and they speak in the language of life."

During his walks with Max, Tom usually talked about what he would write next. He knew unconsciously what he had to say but he was often confused about how to express it. When Wolfe became silent and the burden of conversation fell on Perkins, he used to make up ideas for books, just stories that did not amount to anything, sometimes maundering until something caught Tom's attention. Years later, Max told William B. Wisdom, a great admirer of Wolfe's work, of one particular walk when

I said to Tom that I had always thought a grand story could be written about a boy who had never seen his father, his father having left when he was a baby, or even before that, as a soldier of fortune say,—and of how this boy set out to find his father and went through a series of adventures— a picaresque kind of novel—and finally did find him in some odd situation. I just said this idly for of course such a story as I was thinking of could only be written by one of those fairy tale writers that we all publish.

But Tom ruminated on this as if it were a serious matter, then said, "I think I could use that, Max." Perkins was puzzled, because his idea was merely a superficial story of adventure, far below Tom's talents. He was even a little worried that Wolfe should consider it, until he realized the underlying truth of the idea for Wolfe, that Tom himself was "taking the search for a father in a profound sense, and that is what he was bound to write." The death of Wolfe's father in 1922, when Tom was earning his Master of Arts degree at Harvard, so traumatized the author that it took hundreds of pages in graphic detail before he wrote it out of his system. It was at the core of his writing for the next four years.

While Wolfe revised his proofs of *Look Homeward, Angel*, there were still passages that needed surgery. But he found himself constantly adding to the book, for each cut from the original body of material now appeared to him as a gaping wound that needed suturing. He was not deliberately countering his editor's advice. "I am simply not able intelligently to select between what I have left," he explained to John Hall Wheelock. "At times getting this book in shape seems to me like putting corsets on an elephant," he wrote his editors in apology for causing so much trouble. "The next one will be no bigger than a camel at the most." It was not until August 29, 1929, that everyone finished reading the final proofs.

Once the work was completed, another problem in Wolfe's life started erupting. It was the summer of 1929 when Tom first discussed with Perkins his relationship with a married woman, the celebrated scenic designer for the Neighborhood Playhouse, Aline Bernstein. (Wolfe did not mention her by name.) During the years ahead, Max would read thousands of words of description about her, for Tom transformed her into one of his fictional characters, Esther Jack.

Aline Bernstein was forty-two and Tom Wolfe was twenty-four when they met on the deck of the S.S. *Olympic* in 1925. She was a small but energetic woman, Jewish, with a fresh, ruddy, good-humored face. Tom's first impression of her was that of a "nice-looking woman" of middle age. She was settled in a passionless marriage. During their affair, Aline Bernstein supported Wolfe in every way through his struggles as an unproduced playwright and then inspired him to write his first novel. Now he found he "greatly admired but no longer loved [her] in the modern sense of the word." But she still was desperately in love with him.

Tom needed advice, and so he spoke candidly to Perkins of his almost four tender and violent years with this woman old enough to be his mother. Max thought such a matter was beyond his jurisdiction as an editor and evaded the topic on several separate occasions. Finally he said that he did not see "how the relationship could continue and that since she was so very much older, it would certainly eventually have to end." That was as far as Max would involve himself.

Shortly thereafter, Wolfe sent in his dedication for *Look Homeward, Angel*. It read "To A. B." and was followed by six lines of poetry portending farewell—John Donne's "A Valediction: Of His Name in the Window." His personal dedication of the first copy of the book to Aline Bernstein spoke of their past together, not their future. "This book was written because of her and is dedicated to her. At a time when my life seemed desolate, and when I had little faith in myself I met her. She brought me friendship, material and spiritual relief, and love such as I had never had before. I hope therefore that readers of my book will find at least part of it worthy of such a woman." Madeleine Boyd thanked Max again for all he had done for Wolfe and said Tom wanted very much to dedicate his first book to him—"but his friend Aline Bernstein who sent him to us, has first claims. So I told him I was sure you would not mind waiting for another one. I only wanted you to know by mentioning this how grateful he is, and how he understands what he owes to your kindness, patience, and understanding."

Wolfe accepted one final suggestion from Perkins by cutting from his foreword all references to his editor's assistance in shaping his book, then went home to Asheville to prepare its citizens for the publication of *Look Homeward, Angel*. "I have had a very remarkable visit down here," Tom wrote Max on a penny postcard. "The town is full of kindness and good will and rooting and boosting for the book. My family knows what it's all about, and I think is pleased about it, and also a little apprehensive."

"Although I'm aware of no book that had ever been edited so extensively up to that point," John Hall Wheelock said about *Look Home-*

ward, Angel, "Max felt that what he had done was neither more nor less than duty required." During all the time of editing the book, Wolfe expressed nothing but admiration and appreciation for Perkins's literary expertise and accepted the suggestions with grace. Wolfe believed in his writing but trusted Perkins's opinions deeply. "I have the greatest respect and liking for him," Tom wrote Madeleine Boyd that year. "My faith is too simple but I believe he can do almost everything to make a book go." Max felt uneasy about the young author's growing dependence upon him, but he understood one of Wolfe's major problems in becoming a writer, namely that he still seemed "to his family to be doing something queer,— something that really wasn't work in their opinion." As an artist, Wolfe was made to feel like a one-eyed monster. That someone should have be-friended him made him excessive in his gratitude and devotion to his protector, but blind to any dangers in their working together. "He had more respect for an editor then than later," Max once wrote John Terry, a friend of Wolfe's from Chapel Hill, in his usual understated manner.

On December 6, 1928, Perkins received a telegram from Ernest Hemingway's mother, Grace: TRY TO LOCATE ERNEST HEMINGWAY IN NEW YORK ADVISE HIM OF DEATH OF HIS FATHER TODAY ASK HIM TO COMMUNICATE WITH HOME IMMEDIATELY. Within an hour Perkins received another wire, this one from Ernest himself, who was on the Havana Special bound for Florida after a few days in New York. From Trenton he had asked Perkins to wire to the North Philadelphia Station the $100 he needed to go home again. A few days later Hemingway wrote Perkins from Oak Park that his father had shot himself, leaving a wife, six children, and "damned little money." His father was the parent Hemingway really cared about. From that day forward his relationship with Perkins deepened. Max became the solid, trustworthy older man in Hemingway's turbulent life, someone to turn to and rely on.

By the end of the year his father's affairs were put in order, and Ernest returned with one of his younger sisters to Key West, where he worked on his World War novel, revising for six to ten hours every day. By the second week of January, most of the chapters carried the author's final corrections and were being typed by his sister Sunny. Hemingway planned a short vacation out in the Gulf Stream. He invited Perkins to join him and made the offer impossible to refuse by insisting the only way Max could get hold of his manuscript would be for him to pick it up in person. Max immediately thought it might be a good idea to get

Fitzgerald to join the junket, for both their sakes, but Scott stayed behind to work on his novel.

Max met Hemingway in Florida on the first of February and spent the next eight days in Key West, a place he found full of wonders. He and Ernest started out every morning at eight and often did not get back until moonlight bathed the coconut-palmed maritime village. The sun shone every day while he and Ernest fished in the Gulf Stream. There, with the shoal refracting almost every color of the rainbow, Perkins asked, "Why don't you write about this?" Directly overhead a silly-looking, clumsy bird flapped by. "I might someday but not yet," Ernest said. "Take that pelican. I don't know yet what he is in the scheme of things here." Max had a hunch Hemingway would soon find out, for he had observed that Ernest's mind was always at work, always absorbing and creating.

Hemingway was determined that Perkins should catch a tarpon, one of the most prized species in the sea; Max, however, after exhausting struggles with barracudas, doubted his ability to land one. At the very last possible moment, on Perkins's final day in Key West, Hemingway hooked one. He instantly and insistently forced the rod into Max's hands. After staggering all over the boat for fifty desperate minutes, made more exciting by a sudden storm which sprayed them all the time and added to the tarpon's chances, Perkins and Hemingway reeled it in.

Max did not forget what he had gone to Florida for. He read Hemingway's novel, *A Farewell to Arms*, in manuscript between outings and was wild about it. He discussed serialization in *Scribner's,* though he doubted they would accept it, begrimed as it was with "dirty" words. He wired Arthur Scribner from Key West, BOOK VERY FINE BUT DIFFICULT IN SPOTS. When he returned to New York he tried to explain in a letter to Charles Scribner that "given the theme and the author, the book is [no] more difficult than was inevitable. It is Hemingway's principle both in life and literature never to flinch from facts, and it is in that sense only, that the book is difficult. It isn't at all erotic, although love is represented as having a very large physical element." Max felt constrained in specifying the troublesome areas in the book because he dictated his letter to Miss Wyckoff. But he thought the publisher's "familiarity with Hemingway's way would sufficiently supplement what I have said."

The conference between Maxwell Perkins and old Charles Scribner, when they met face-to-face, over the unprintable words in Hemingway's manuscript has become publishing legend. Malcolm Cowley's rendition of the story is generally regarded as the most reliable, for he got it from Perkins himself. When old CS got to the office, Max told Cowley, Max explained to him that there were probably three unprintable words in the manuscript. "What are they?" Mr. Scribner asked. Perkins, who seldom used a stronger phrase than "My God," and that only in moments of great distress, found that he simply couldn't speak them. "Write them, then," said Mr. Scribner. Perkins spelled out two of them on a memo pad and handed it to him. "What's the third word?" Mr. Scribner asked. Perkins hesitated. "What's the third word?" Scribner asked again, giving the pad back to him. Finally, Perkins wrote it, and Mr. Scribner glanced at the pad. "Max," he said, shaking his head, "what would Hemingway think of you if he heard that you couldn't even write that word?"

Over the years the incident was recounted in numerous apocryphal renditions. Irma Wyckoff corrected the one that held that the three questionable words were written on Max's calendar under the heading "Things to Do Today." She recalled, "Mr. Perkins did leave his desk for lunch, and halfway out the building he returned to his office to hide the list."

To his surprise, the only opposition to the manuscript that Perkins faced from the magazine staff was over those specific words. Robert Bridges, editor of *Scribner's*, thought the book was very well done, even in its portrayal of an explicit love affair between a wounded soldier and a nurse. Bridge's young heir apparent, Alfred "Fritz" Dashiell, was at least as enthusiastic and regretted that even a word would have to be altered.

At the first possible moment, Perkins informed Hemingway of the magazine's offer of $16,000, more than *Scribner's* had ever paid for first serialization rights. Max discussed the problem of those "certain words" to him in forthright terms, explaining, "I always exaggerate difficulties, partly as a matter of policy on the theory that it is better to begin by facing the worst." It was true, however, that the magazine was used as collateral reading by many schools which taught mixed classes, and *Scribner's* believed the ears of all those schoolgirls were too sensitive for the vulgarisms of Hemingway's soldiers.

Ernest replied that he did not see how any section of the manuscript could be lifted because the book was so tightly written, with each passage dependent on every other. He told Perkins that emasculation was a minor operation to perform on men, animals, and books, but its effect was great.

Perkins intended to widen Hemingway's public with *A Farewell to Arms*. His primary reason for serializing, he wrote Ernest, was "in making you understandable to a great many more people, and generally in helping you to gain complete recognition." In a letter Max reminded the author that there was a great deal of hostility to *The Sun Also Rises:*

> It was routed and driven off the field by the book's qualities and the adherence which they won. The hostility was very largely that which any new thing in art must meet, simply because it is disturbing. It shows life in a different aspect and people are more comfortable when they have got it all conventionalized and smoothed down, and everything unpleasant hidden. Hostility also partly came from those who actually did not understand the book because its method of expression was a new one . . . it was the same failure to be understood that a wholly new painter meets. People simply do not understand because they can only understand what they are accustomed to.

Perkins tried to make Hemingway realize that "if we can bring out this serial without arousing too serious objection, you will have enormously consolidated your position, and will henceforth be further beyond objectionable criticism of a kind which is very bad because it prevents so many people from looking at the thing itself on its merits."

This issue of words was no mere squabble to Hemingway but a fight for a return to the "full use of the language." He believed what they might accomplish in that direction could be of more lasting value than anything he would write. Ernest told Max that there had always been first-rate writing, then American writing. He wanted to be the writer who reversed that order. But Perkins's argument swayed him and he yielded again in blanking out the profanities.

During one of his visits to his publishers, Owen Wister, author of *The Virginian*, made a point of talking to Perkins about Hemingway's use of profanities. He objected that they were completely unnecessary and only aroused prejudice. By then Perkins realized that Hemingway did not use those words simply to exercise his literary rights, but to maintain the integrity of his style. In a letter Max told Hemingway that Wister did not seem to see

> that any circumlocutions, etc. would be inconsistent with the way you write. I tried to explain this, but I really never fully grasped how you do write, so I couldn't very well. But I pointed out as an instance that you almost never even used a simile. It is a different way of writing. I always knew it wasn't just a simple matter of not using words—that it really did mean a deviation from your style or method or whatever, to avoid them.

In March, 1929, Hemingway prepared to leave for Europe. Before boarding his ship, he dashed off a note to Max pleading with him not to give his French address to Scott Fitzgerald, who Hemingway understood was thinking of leaving for Europe as well. The last time Scott had been in Paris, he got the Hemingways locked out of one apartment and in trouble with the landlord all the time. When Ernest heard their visits were going to overlap again, it filled him with horror. He said he would meet Scott in public places, where he could walk out and leave him at any time, but he would never again let him within striking distance of his home.

The biggest hardship in Fitzgerald's life remained his unfinished novel, of which Perkins had seen only the inspiriting first quarter. "I'm sneaking away like a thief without leaving the chapters," he wrote Max early that March from Ellerslie. "There is a week's work to straighten them out and in the confusion of influenza & leaving I haven't been able to do it." Planning to work on the boat and post the manuscript from Genoa, he sent his editor a thousand thanks for his patience. "Just trust me a few months longer, Max," he pleaded. "It's been a discouraging time for me too, but I will never forget your kindness and the fact that you've never reproached me."

Perkins worried more about the author than the manuscript. Afraid that Scott was "losing his nerve," he wrote Hemingway that if Fitzgerald held on to that, "he will come out all right. And in spite of his faith in youth, he will do better in age if he will only keep out of trouble enough."

All summer, Perkins debated whether Fitzgerald ought to retreat from this present book or whether that surrender would be an irreversible setback in his career. "Do you think he ought to chuck this novel altogether, and begin another?" he asked Hemingway. After several "very bad reports" from mutual friends and but one tight-lipped message from Fitzgerald himself in which he mentioned his book as if he did not like to talk about it, Perkins wrote Scott, asking if there wasn't anything he could do for him in America. "I do not want to have you write me letters except when there is a reason because your hands are full enough," Max said.

Fitzgerald did have a reason to write Max, however; he was making progress on the novel again. That year he had written a short story, one of many for the *Saturday Evening Post,* called "The Rough Crossing." It told of a successful playwright and his wife who take a voyage to Europe to escape the Broadway crowd. Aboard ship the playwright is attracted to a beautiful brunette with ivory skin—the "pretty girl of the voyage"—and his brief infatuation rocks his marriage just as an Atlantic hurricane tosses the ocean liner. "The Rough Crossing" sent Fitzgerald in a new direction with his novel. He constructed a new love triangle, this one involving a bright young motion-picture director and his wife, Lew and Nicole Kelly. Aboard ship they meet a young woman named Rosemary who wants to break into the movies.

"I am working night and day on the novel from the new angle that I think will solve previous difficulties," Fitzgerald wrote Perkins hopefully. But this Kelly version didn't work either. Still, it was not without consequence. Many of its elements remained in Fitzgerald's imagination, where they continued to incubate. Fitzgerald went back to his Melarkey story and made one last attempt at it, then laid it to rest.

Though stymied with Scott, Max got good results with several of Scott's friends, particularly Ring Lardner, whose reputation he fought to enhance, even though Lardner's career as a journalist still seemed to deny him a position as a serious writer. While Max was assembling *And Other Stories*, Lardner's first collection in two years, the Literary Guild approached him. They wanted Perkins to bring out an omnibus of Lardner's stories, binding together those in *How to Write Short Stories*, *The Love Nest*, and the new ones already in type. More important than their $13,500 payment, which Scribners proposed dividing equally between the author and themselves, Perkins told Ring it was a highly advantageous offer because "it will put a very fine book by you in the hands of some 70,000 people to say nothing of those to whom we can sell copies through the regular trade. And so your public will be very greatly enlarged. It will also lead, we think, to a re-estimation of you as a writer of stories, etc., in all the reviewing papers, which would also be most advantageous." Perkins even got Scribners to agree to investing their $6,750 from the Literary Guild in advertising. "We have never thought that you have had the sale your books are entitled to," Max wrote Ring, "and we are going to try to get it now, and to build for the future."

Perkins dropped *And Other Stories* and started thinking about the new omnibus's title—"one of a collective sort which would emphasize the peculiarly national character of the author, or perhaps that of the people and conditions he writes about." Max submitted a list of his own suggestions to the Guild, expressing a preference for *Round Up*. "It is an American word," Max explained, "and it implies a collection—and although it might at first seem to be especially western, it is now used about almost every sort of gathering together,—even that of crooks."

During the late winter's search for a title, Lardner left for the Carib-

bean, but not as early as Max had thought. To meet their deadlines, Perkins
went ahead arranging with the Literary Guild to call the book *Round Up*
without even consulting the author. When the news finally caught up to
Lardner he wired Perkins that he preferred his own title, *Ensemble*. Max
was chagrined, but the title pages, covers, and jackets were already printed.
"I am sorry this was so," Max apologized. "We did not want to take a title
you did not fully approve, and I was stupid about your visit to Nassau."
But the Literary Guild was enthusiastic about Max's title and Scribners was
printing another 20,000 copies themselves. *Round Up* reached almost
100,000 readers.

Again Perkins asked Ring if he could not write some long story,
perhaps 40,000 words, as they had talked about for years. "Now would
be the time for it," Max urged, "with the great distribution of *Round Up*
as a background." To Perkins's regret, Lardner was still stagestruck, so
busy writing plays and vaudeville routines that he had not even considered
a novelette. "But show business is slow on financial returns," he wrote his
editor, "and maybe I'll be asking you for some advance soon."

Another of Perkins's writers, also a friend of Fitzgerald's, had been
having especially difficult times but had managed to publish, even though
he was heading for a breakdown. Edmund Wilson, overcome by disloyal-
ties and disaffection, was trying to decide whether to divorce his first wife
for another. To compound his depression, he had recently sent the manuscript of a novel, *I Thought of Daisy*, to Max Perkins and was suffering
from the blues that generally follow finishing a book.

"It is the sort of thing that has to come off completely or it is likely to
be impossible," Wilson wrote Perkins.

> I mean that, from beginning to end, I have made characters and incidents
> and situations subordinate to a set of ideas about life and literature, and
> unless the ideas are really put over, unless they are made interesting enough
> to compensate the reader for what he is missing in action and emotion, for
> what he ordinarily gets in a novel, the whole performance will fail.

Wilson had corresponded with Perkins ever since the editor had expressed interest in *The Undertaker's Garland* years earlier. Among the inde-
cisions which Max never could help Wilson resolve was what genre he
should concentrate on. *I Thought of Daisy* was his first long work of fiction, and Leon Edel, the editor of Wilson's papers and journals, noted,
"He was surprised to discover that this could be a quite different enterprise
from any other kind of writing." In the process of revising the manuscript,

Wilson began work on a series of long critical essays, which would become *Axel's Castle.* He wrote Perkins that they were "easier to do, and in the nature of a relief, from *Daisy.*" The novel sold only a few thousand copies, but its excellent reviews won him the respect of the literary crowd. Years later, Max's daughter Zippy asked her father why Wilson's novels did not have a wider public appeal. He replied, "Wilson is one of the most intellectual Americans writing, but he sounds like a smarty-pants when he writes fiction. Whenever he writes something that isn't over everybody's head, it reads as though he's writing down to the public." In another, more revealing, moment he said, "Edmund Wilson would give his eyeteeth to have half the reputation as a novelist that Scott Fitzgerald has."

Max managed to retreat for a month that summer to Windsor, where he had a splendid, practically rainless vacation. He was startled several times that August by his two oldest daughters maturing so rapidly. Bertha had once been a grave little girl behind horn-rimmed glasses; Max used to brag about her ability "to see the justice of a thing even when it was against her wishes." Zippy, the one Perkins girl who could always charm extra movie privileges out of her father, was becoming a traffic-stopping beauty. Together now the teen-agers went to dances in Windsor, Cornish, and Woodstock and stayed out until two in the morning. Max thought it insulting to wait up for them.

In the past Perkins had often left Windsor for New York to watch the impact of a particular new book he had had his hand in. This year he returned in time to preside over the publication of several. *Look Homeward, Angel* and *A Farewell to Arms* came out in September, 1929. The reaction to each work, by critics and readers, was overwhelmingly favorable.

Hemingway told Perkins to keep right on printing his novel; this was their "big shot." With the impact it was making, he guessed, they would go through 100,000 copies. Within just a few weeks *A Farewell to Arms* had sold one third that much. Ernest already had plans for the royalties from the book. He was going to establish a trust fund for his family with the earnings from the first 70,000 copies; everything beyond that was going toward the purchase of a boat.

As for Thomas Wolfe, Eugene Gant's childhood dreams of fame were coming true for his creator. Wolfe was praised as a new writer of the first rank, and he reveled in what he understood to be "the best reviews of any first novel in years." The only bad reaction to speak of was in Wolfe's hometown of Asheville, North Carolina. When the townspeople realized that they had been transformed into the citizenry of the fictional Altamont, with all their failings revealed to the nation at large, they were up in arms. One of them threatened to drag Wolfe's "big overgroan karkus" across Asheville's Pack Square. But in North Carolina, as elsewhere, the book was being bought. Scribners quickly sold some 15,000 copies.

It was a happy time for Perkins. Even the skies smiled. As October drew to a close New York basked in an Indian summer—not a hint of winter in the air. Nor was there a sign in that golden autumn of the imminent Depression and the strenuous years that lay ahead.

PART TWO

IX

Crises of Confidence

O n Thursday, October 24, 1929, the stock market crashed. "What effect that will have nobody can tell," Max Perkins wrote F. Scott Fitzgerald at the end of the month. "It may have a very bad effect on all retail business, including that of books."

When the stocks on Wall Street started nose-diving, Fitzgerald was in France, writing his novel. The stories about him all intimated that his friendships, career, and marriage were on the skids. Perkins heard one about his miskeeping the time in a boxing match between Morley Callaghan and Hemingway, which resulted in severe blows to Ernest's jaw and Scott's pride. His self-esteem dropped even further as he became aware that Hemingway was reluctant to tell Scott his whereabouts. Hemingway and Fitzgerald still exchanged letters, but they were not always friendly. In one of them Ernest called Scott a "damned fool," then exhorted him "for Christ sake" to "go on and write the novel." He warned Perkins never to trust Scott with a single word in confidence as he was absolutely incapable of keeping secrets when sober and "no more responsible than an insane man" when he was drunk.

Scott's relationships with other friends were becoming strained as well. The Murphys, for example, had wearied of his studying them for his novel. Gerald said:

> He kept asking things like what our income really was, and how I had got into Skull and Bones [a senior society at Yale], and whether Sara and I had

151

lived together before we were married. I just couldn't take seriously the idea that he was going to write about us—somehow I couldn't believe that anything would come of questions like that. But I certainly recall his peering at me with a sort of thin-lipped, supercilious scrutiny, as though he were trying to decide what made me tick. His questions irritated Sara a good deal. Usually, she would give him some ridiculous answer just to shut him up, but eventually the whole business became intolerable. In the middle of a dinner party one night, Sara had all she could take. "Scott," she said, "you think if you just ask enough questions you'll get to know what people are like but you won't. You don't really know anything at all about people." Scott practically turned green. He got up from the table and pointed his finger at her and said that nobody had ever dared say *that* to him, whereupon Sara asked if he would like her to repeat it, and she did.

The most disconcerting stories about Fitzgerald were about his marriage. Madeleine Boyd had recently visited the Fitzgeralds in Paris and told Perkins that Zelda was no longer herself and that she and Scott were constantly at each other's throats. Zelda's behavior, formerly glossed over as madcap, now struck people as weird. Its most aberrant manifestation was in her study of ballet, which she was pursuing with frenetic zeal. The hours of practice wore her down. She was underweight; her face was drawn and waxy; she was so excitable that her shrieks of anger and laughter could not always be distinguished. As Hemingway suggested in *A Moveable Feast*, she resented all the time that her husband devoted to his writing; Scott, on his part, now felt neglected because of her dancing. For Fitzgerald, after years of plummeting confidence, that was the ultimate rejection. In a letter he later addressed but never sent to Zelda, he recalled their last year together:

> You were gone now—I scarcely remember you that summer. You were simply one of all the people who disliked me or were indifferent to me. I didn't like to think of you. . . . You were going crazy and calling it genius—and I was going to ruin and calling it anything that came to hand. And I think everyone far enough away to see us outside of our glib presentations of ourselves guessed at your almost megalomaniacal selfishness and my insane indulgence in drink. Toward the end nothing much mattered. The nearest I ever came to leaving you was when you told me you [thought] I was a fairy in the Rue Palatine but now whatever you said aroused a sort of detached pity for you. . . . I wish the Beautiful and Damned had been a maturely written book because it was all true. We ruined ourselves—I have never honestly thought that we ruined each other.

The Fitzgeralds made stabs at economizing that year by living in cheaper hotels, but Scott's fiscal policy remained the same. Before the new decade was two weeks old, he asked Perkins to deposit $500 to cover his Christmas bills. His short stories had brought in $27,000 the preceding year, but his books earned only $31.77. Almost five years had passed since the publication of *The Great Gatsby*, and Scott had been advanced almost $8,000 on his next book. In response to Perkins's subtle inquiries as to when his novel would be done, Scott replied: "To begin with, because I don't mention my novel isn't because it isn't finishing up or that I'm neglecting it—but only that I'm weary of setting dates for it till the moment when it is in the Post Office Box."

His professional pride was about the only thing on which Fitzgerald kept a firm grip. "I wrote young & I wrote a lot & the pot takes longer to fill up now," he told Perkins, "but the novel, my novel, is a different matter than if I'd hurriedly finished it up a year and a half ago."

"The only thing that has ever worried me about you," Max wrote him that spring, "was the question of health. I know you have everything else, but I have often been afraid on that account, perhaps because I myself can stand so little in the way of late hours, and all that goes with them."

In the early spring of 1930 illness did step in the way. Zelda, in the frenzy of her balletomania, broke down from overwork. Fitzgerald felt incapable of writing even a letter for twenty-one days. Only after several more weeks of requests for money did he tell Max his troubles. "Zelda has been desperately ill in a sanitarium here in Switzerland with a nervous collapse," he explained. That kept Scott from his work for still more time.

While Zelda remained, in Scott's words, "sick as hell," he grew "harrassed and anxious about life." The psychiatrist who devoted almost his entire time to Zelda had become a major expense. Max inferred from Scott's letters that Zelda was on the edge of insanity if not beyond it. By summer her condition was diagnosed as schizophrenia. Because drinking was one of the images that haunted Zelda in her delirium, the doctors insisted that Scott abstain from liquor for a year; she, forever. They never actually stated that Fitzgerald's own instability and alcoholism had contributed to his wife's collapse, but Perkins had his own opinion. "Scott is blamable I know for what has come to Zelda in a sense," Max wrote Thomas Wolfe. "But he's a brave man to face the trouble as he does, always facing it squarely—no self-deceptions." In his journal Scott summarized the year: "The Crash! Zelda & America."

Even in his despair, Fitzgerald still mailed Perkins—"my most loyal and confident encourager and friend"—monthly literary reports. Since he could not claim progress on his book, he stocked his letters with publishing suggestions. He sent Max the names and works of several new authors— members of a "really new generation"—whose work he had come across in an issue of *American Caravan*. The most noteworthy, Fitzgerald said, was Erskine Caldwell, despite the "usual derivations from Hemingway and even [Morley] Callaghan." Perkins wrote to him.

Caldwell was a twenty-six-year-old Georgian who, after a short col- lege career, had worked as cotton picker, book reviewer, professional foot- ball player, lumber mill hand, and aspiring writer. He was living in Mount Vernon, Maine when Perkins asked him to submit manuscripts for con- sideration. It was the first such request Caldwell had ever received. He later recalled, "The letter touched off a three-month orgy of writing, the intensity of which had never before been reached and which I never equalled afterward."

At first Caldwell sent Max Perkins one short story every day for a week. Each was promptly declined by return mail. But Caldwell was in no mood to accept defeat. He shifted gears and each week sent two more carefully drafted stories. He had now become determined to break down the editorial resistance of *Scribner's Magazine*, but he considered Maxwell Perkins as the company's major power and sent his stories through him. As fast as each was rejected—generally for being too "anecdotal"—it was sent to one of the "little magazines"—*This Quarter*, *Pagany*, *Hound and Horn*, or *Clay*, to name a few—where it was accepted. After a month, Caldwell detected a softening in Perkins's letters of rejection. By spring Max had decided to accept one of his pieces, though he had not chosen which one. According to a chart Caldwell kept which traced the journeys of each of his stories, Perkins had five on hand from which to select.

"My immediate fear," Caldwell wrote in his memoirs, *Call It Experi- ence*, "was that he might change his mind—that the already tottering economic structure of the nation might crumble—that anything could happen before he actually printed one of my stories in the magazine." Caldwell went to work at dusk the very evening of the day he had had the good news from Perkins, and set out to supply the editor with more mate- rial to consider. Thirty-six hours later he had three new stories. These, together with three additional ones which he plucked from the stack on his table, made a total of eleven for Perkins. Instead of posting them, however, Caldwell decided to take them to New York in person. There was, after all, "the possibility of a train being wrecked, causing a serious delay in the delivery of the mail."

On the overnight bus from Portland, Maine to New York, forebodings kept Caldwell awake. "I had never seen Maxwell Perkins," he wrote, ". . . and by daybreak I was beginning to visualize him as a fearsome person who would angrily resent the intrusion and become prejudiced against my work." From eight in the morning until ten Caldwell paced the sidewalk across from the Scribner Building, trying to think of a reasonable excuse for presenting himself without appointment. Nothing convincing came to mind, but, realizing that what little courage that remained was rapidly fading, he crossed the street and entered the building, clutching his envelope of manuscripts. By the time the elevator had taken him to the editorial offices, he was so unnerved that he just gave his stories to the receptionist. He left Perkins a note that said he would be at the Manger Hotel for the next two days.

Caldwell confined himself to his hotel room all that afternoon, leaving only to grab a sandwich and some newspapers. He lay awake until past midnight, trying to summon up enough confidence to phone Scribners if Perkins failed to call before he left town. At midmorning the phone rang. The sound startled him at first, but it was so pleasing to hear, he let it ring twice before answering. "I got your new manuscripts yesterday, the ones you left at the office," Perkins said after he and Caldwell had introduced themselves to each other. "I wish you had asked for me when you were here." Caldwell recalled the rest of the conversation this way:

PERKINS: By the way, I've read all your stories on hand now, including the new ones you brought yesterday, and I don't think I need to see any more for a while.
CALDWELL: (Silence)
PERKINS: I think I wrote you some time ago that we want to publish one of your stories in *Scribner's Magazine.*
CALDWELL: I received the letter. You haven't changed your mind, have you? I mean about taking a story?
PERKINS: Changed my mind? No. Not at all. The fact is, we're all in agreement here at the office about things. I guess so much so that we've decided now to take two stories, instead of one, and run them both in the magazine at the same time. We'd like to schedule them for the June issue. One of them is called "The Mating of Marjorie" and the other one is "A Very Late Spring." They're both good northern New

England stories. There's a good feeling about them. It's something I like to find in fiction. So many writers master form and technique, but get so little feeling into their work. I think that's important.

CALDWELL: I'm sure glad you like them—both of them.

PERKINS: Now about these two stories. As I said, we want to buy them both. How much do you want for the two together? We always have to talk about money sooner or later. There's no way of getting around that, is there?

CALDWELL: Well, I don't know exactly. I mean about the money. I haven't thought much about it.

PERKINS: Would two-fifty be all right? For both of them. . . .

CALDWELL: Two-fifty? I don't know. I thought maybe I'd receive a little more than that.

PERKINS: You did? Well, what would you say to three-fifty then. That's about as much as we can pay, for both of them. In these times magazine circulation is not climbing the way it was, and we have to watch our costs. I don't think times will get any better soon, and maybe worse yet. Economic life isn't very healthy now. That's why we have to figure our costs so closely at a time like this.

CALDWELL: I guess that'll be all right. I'd thought I'd get a little more than three dollars and a half, though, for both of them.

PERKINS: Three dollars and fifty cents? Oh, no! I must have given you the wrong impression, Caldwell. Not three dollars and a half. No, I meant three hundred and fifty dollars.

CALDWELL: You did! Well, that's sure different. It sure is. Three hundred and fifty dollars is just fine.

In no time Caldwell had formulated new ambitions. The first was to get 100 short stories published.

On April 19, 1930, at the age of seventy-six, Charles Scribner died. Few of the house's authors who were flourishing when Perkins began working there were still being published. John Fox, Jr., Richard Harding Davis, and Henry James had been buried more than a decade before; John Galsworthy and Edith Wharton continued to write, but their latest novels smacked of the nineteenth century. Old CS's presence, however, lingered in the family business. His son Charles kept the name alive and his brother Arthur managed the firm. Maxwell E. Perkins was designated a company officer and was on his way toward becoming editorial director.

"After Scribner's death," Wallace Meyer observed, "Max really didn't have to defend his decisions any longer."

That year Perkins's most successful author—winning more prestige than old CS had ever dreamed he would—was Ernest Hemingway. Despite the Depression, *A Farewell to Arms* became a robust best seller, eventually reaching Number 1 on the list. Max wrote Hemingway that the Depression was "more likely to affect the general line of books—that it surely will affect—than so outstanding a book as *A Farewell*."

As a new celebrity, Hemingway became the subject of literary gossip. The most unusual stories came from the writer Robert McAlmon, whom Ernest had recommended to Perkins. At dinner Max sat dumbfounded as McAlmon slandered the man who had brought them together. He started by making nasty remarks about Hemingway's writing. Soon he was voicing the canard that Fitzgerald and Hemingway were homosexuals.

Through Fitzgerald, Hemingway himself got wind of still another story—that he was dissatisfied with his publishers and was considering others. Ernest wrote Max he did not know how to scotch these latest lies, but he assured him that he had absolutely no intention of leaving Scribners. He hoped that, if his own luck and kidneys held out long enough, Max might publish Hemingway's collected works someday. He offered to write letters proclaiming his loyalty to Perkins.

Max treasured Hemingway's letter. He confessed to him that the story had unsettled him. "One night in a nervous moment," he explained, "when the rumors were flying thick and fast, I wrote you by hand asking you if you would be willing to write a letter saying they were foundless. But then in the end, I tore up my letter because I thought it was only part of the game that we should take our own medicine." After helping put together the author's tax statement—an annual function that came easily to the former economics major—and devising a trust fund for his family, Max got Scribners to hike the author's royalty percentage on *A Farewell to Arms*, at the cost of several hundred dollars to the company, just "because we think the value of publishing for you is a great one in itself." Perkins ultimately recommended that Hemingway consider an arrangement under which Scribners would pay him a minimum annual sum on which he could absolutely count.

Ernest accepted all of Perkins's offers but the final one—he was sure he could not work under a salaried contract like that. To seal his pact with Scribners, he asked Perkins to obtain from Boni & Liveright the rights to *In Our Time*, which they had promised to sell to Scribners when Hemingway left them. When Max approached them, Horace Liveright was irate. The author was a national literary hero and he would not let the book go. "We consider Mr. Hemingway's name of value on our list," he wrote Perkins, "and in that we published his first book, we have a sentimental feeling about the matter as well." After months of Max's persistence—and the offer of a cash settlement—Scribners wrested the book away. At Hemingway's suggestion, Perkins got Edmund Wilson to write an introduction for the new Scribners edition, for Ernest believed Wilson was "the one who has understood best" what he was writing.

The book business was turning bleak that fall, and few of the season's books lasted through December. Because of four or five of Perkins's novels—including S. S. Van Dine's *The Bishop Murder Case* and Hemingway's *A Farewell to Arms* (the latter reached 70,000 copies by the dying days of the twenties)—Scribners enjoyed the palmiest year they had ever had. But Perkins knew better than to think that boded well for the future. The outlook was grim everywhere. So in that flat week between Christmas and the new year, Perkins cheered himsef up by dreaming of an excursion to the Gulf Stream.

Returning from Paris, Hemingway passed through New York in late January, 1930. He called on Perkins and seemed in fine fettle to Max, who swore he would meet him in Florida in March. Business looked so bad in February that it seemed impossible for Perkins to steal away. But, he wrote Ernest, "I have learned that the only thing to do in those cases is just to go." He arrived in Key West on March 17 and met "The Mob," a loose fraternity of Ernest's friends. Hemingway and his crew trolled to the Marquesas Keys. There Perkins hooked a kingfish weighing fifty-eight pounds, one pound heavier than the world's record. As Max reeled the fish in, the rest of the crew watched in amusement for a suggestion of a grin on his face, almost belying the nickname they had given him—"Deadpan." Throughout the expedition, Perkins was again impressed with Ernest's powers of observation, even more than with his physical strength. In recalling Key West years later, Max said: "It must require the intuition of an artist to learn quickly the geography of the ocean bottom and the ways of fish, but Hemingway learned in a year what often takes a decade or a lifetime. It was as though instinctively he projected himself into a fish—knew how a tarpon or a kingfish felt, and thought, and so what he would do."

The mariners drifted seventy miles from Key West to another group of tiny keys called the Dry Tortugas, and stayed for over two weeks instead of the four days they had planned. Only an act of God could have kept Perkins away from his office for so long a time: A norther had churned up such rough seas that they could not possibly get back to the mainland. Ernest and his Mob slept in a shed and lived off the liquor, canned goods, and supply of Bermuda onions Hemingway stowed on board before every trip, and whatever they caught. All they could do was cast plugs off the pier or venture out in the skiff for bottom fishing during lulls in the winds. They fished every day except two, when they shot at flocks of birds that the norther had driven their way. To match the rest of the marooned band, Perkins raised a beard, shorter and fairer than those of the others. Once the big blow died down and they putted safely back into port, Max glanced in a mirror. "If you'd seen me with a grizzled beard looking as tough as a pirate," Max wrote Elizabeth Lemmon afterward, "you could imagine me doing nothing unless it was murder. They said I looked like a rebel cavalry captain. I couldn't get a look at myself for two weeks and when I did I was horrified. I saw myself entirely anew and found it a shock!" He thanked Hemingway for one of the happiest times of his life.

Not long after Max's visit Hemingway left for a ranch in Montana to work on his newest book, the massive study of the Spanish bullfight that he had mentioned in his earliest correspondence with Perkins. Soon he wrote Max that he was getting no mail, had not looked at a newspaper for weeks, and was in the strongest physical shape he had been in for years. Except for indulgence in cold lager, which threatened to put a few inches on his waistline and take a few hours off his day, his habits were Spartan. He worked six days of every week, and had produced over 40,000 words within a month. And he had six more cases of beer, he told Max, which was enough for another six chapters. When Perkins sent him the proofs of the new Scribners edition of the *In Our Time* stories along with suggestions for modifications and additional selections, Ernest threw them aside and said he was working too well breaking in this new book to "flay dead horses."

Thomas Wolfe's career had been safely launched before the crash, but he felt threatened by the national calamity—all the more so because, as he later wrote of his autobiographical hero in *You Can't Go Home Again*, "in addition to the general crisis, he was caught in a personal one as well. For at this very time, he too had come to an end and a beginning. It was an end of love, though not of loving; a beginning of recognition, though not of fame."

Wolfe wanted to cut all his constricting ties to the past, but he quaked at the thought of it. He had become a pariah in Asheville, and, at last, he yearned to end his relationship with Aline Bernstein. Perkins suggested that Tom apply for a foundation grant, which might give him the security to quit his teaching job at N.Y.U. and live on his own, working abroad for a year. Mrs. Bernstein realized the implications of such independence and misconstrued Perkins's intentions. She felt that he was urging Wolfe to leave her.

Perkins wrote a letter of recommendation to the Guggenheim Foundation and Tom received a fellowship. Max further arranged a $4,500 advance in monthly installments on his new book. With the incoming royalties from *Look Homeward, Angel*, he had some $10,000 and no longer had to rely on the support of Aline Bernstein. Distraught, she tried every way she knew to make him understand her love for him, and for months Wolfe wavered in his feelings. But his love continued to diminish.

On Christmas Eve, 1929, Tom sat at a desk in the Harvard Club of New York and wrote a letter of affection to Max Perkins: "One year ago I had little hope for my work, and I did not know you. What has happened since may seem to be only a modest success to many people; but to me it is touched with strangeness and wonder. It is a miracle." He went on:

> I can no longer think of the time I wrote [*Look Homeward, Angel*], but rather of the time when you first talked to me about it, and when you worked upon it. My mind has always seen people more clearly than events or things—the name "Scribners" naturally makes a warm glow in my heart, but you are chiefly "Scribners" to me: you have done what I had ceased to believe one person could do for another—you have created liberty and hope for me.
>
> Young men sometimes believe in the existence of heroic figures stronger and wiser than themselves, to whom they can turn for an answer to all their vexation and grief. . . . You are for me such a figure: You are one of the rocks to which my life is anchored.

"I'm mighty glad you feel as you do—except for a sense of not deserving it," Perkins replied to Wolfe. "I hope anyway that there could be no serious thought of obligation between us but, as a matter of convenience of speech, I would point out that even if you really owed me a great deal, it would be cancelled by what I owe you. The whole episode, from receipt of ms., up to now was for me a most happy, interesting, and exciting one."

The recent months of contention with Aline Bernstein had pulled Wolfe apart. Some of the distress may have been rooted in a strong provincial anti-Semitism Wolfe had inherited from his mother, a tiny, tight-fisted woman with a passion for real estate. Late one night at the end of March he scratched on page 337 of his current notebook, "Went to the Public Library today—the Jews pushing in and out." He confided further to the ledger, "I find myself at the same depth of fruitless and sterile exhaustion as I had reached two years ago. I am unable to create, unable to concentrate, and I am filled with fever, with bitter and restless anger, against the world: and I am beginning to feel this against Aline. This must be the end! the end! the end!" He concluded that his only hope for survival was to leave Mrs. Bernstein for good. He would start by putting an ocean between them.

On May 10, 1930, he sailed for Europe. While the S.S. *Volendam* was at sea, Wolfe, throwing a lifeline to the mainland, wrote Perkins: "I feel like a man faced with a great test who is confident of his power to meet it, and yet thinks of it with a pounding heart and with some speculation. I am impatient to get at my book; I know it will be good if I have power to put it on paper as I have thought it out."

The "lone Wolfe," as Perkins started calling him, began wandering around France. Max sensed that Wolfe was frightened by the challenge of the second book, and so he tried to strengthen the author for the time when he would be ready to write again. "You are a born writer if there ever was one," Perkins assured him, "and have no need to worry about whether this new book will be as good as the Angel and that sort of thing. If you simply can get yourself into it, as you can, it *will* be good." Shortly after receiving Perkins's letter, Wolfe was working six to ten hours a day.

At Max's instigation, Scott Fitzgerald called Wolfe at his hotel while they were both in Paris. Tom took a single day off from his new regimen and went out to Scott's sumptuous apartment near the Bois for lunch and inordinate amounts of wine, cognac, and whiskey. Then they went to the Ritz Bar. Scott told Wolfe about Zelda's nervous breakdown and the book he was trying to complete. At first Tom found him friendly and generous, though the two argued about America. Wolfe reported back to Max, "I said we were a homesick people, and belonged to the earth and land we came from as much or more as any country I knew about—he said we were not, that we were not a country, that he had no feeling for the land he came from." Tom left Scott at the Ritz Bar, holding court before a bunch of drunk, raw Princeton boys who were making snide innuendos about Wolfe's background. But Wolfe was not put off. "I liked him," Tom wrote Perkins, "and think he has a great deal of talent, and I hope he gets that book done soon."

Fitzgerald was even more impressed by Wolfe. Back in Switzerland, where he found his wife in no condition to see him, he read *Look Homeward, Angel* in twenty consecutive hours. He wired Wolfe that he was "enormously moved and grateful," and wrote Perkins, "You have a great find in him—what he'll do is incalculable."

Wolfe reported to Perkins that he had no idea how long he would rove across Europe; he guessed it would be until he had completed the first part of his book, which he would bring back to America with him. He was almost afraid to tell Perkins that it would be a very thick volume. He did say: "You can't write the book I want to write in 200 pages." He had a grand design for a four-part book, which he was calling *The October Fair*. The book dealt with what he believed to be two of the profoundest impulses in man—"of wandering forever and the earth again." By that he meant:

> the everlasting earth, a home, a place for the heart to come to, and earthly mortal love, the love of a woman, who, it seems to me belongs to the earth and is a force that makes men wander, that makes them search, that makes them lonely, and that makes them both hate and love their loneliness.

"I hope I can do a good book for you and for myself and for the whole damn family," he wrote Perkins, adding, "Please hope and pull for me and write me when you can."

Wolfe left for Switzerland, to plan the architecture of the book, constantly seeking Perkins's comments and approval. All summer he sent a stream of scribblings to Max; they amounted to many dozens of pages, practically a book in themselves, and they detailed his ideas of the tone and attitude, the structure and character of his work.

His travels in Switzerland eventually brought him to Montreux, where he took a quiet hotel room overlooking a garden of brilliant flowers and, beyond it, Lake Geneva. He was sitting on the terrace of a casino one night when he saw Scott Fitzgerald. Scott came over for a drink and was soon leading him on a tour of Montreux's night life. During the evening Scott urged him to visit his friends Dorothy Parker and the Gerald Murphys. When Tom did not perk up at the suggestions, Fitzgerald accused him of avoiding people for fear of them. That was about the only thing Fitzgerald said that night that Wolfe agreed with. Despite his over-bearing appearance, Wolfe was by nature shy; for all his grace on paper, he was maladroit in person. "When I am with someone like Scott I feel that I am morose and sullen—and violent in my speech and movement part of the time," Tom admitted to Perkins. "Later I feel that I have repelled them."

Now Wolfe was sorry for Fitzgerald. He wondered how long Scott could last by himself with no Ritz Bar or idolatrous Princeton boys. Tom wrote Henry Volkening, a friend who had taught with him at New York University, that Fitzgerald was "sterile and impotent and alcoholic now, and unable to finish his book and I think he wanted to injure my own work." Wolfe did not consider himself very good company just then. "It would be very easy for me to start swilling liquor at present," he wrote Perkins, "but I am *not* going to do it. I am here to get work done, and in the next three months I am going to see whether I am a bum or a man. I shall not try to conceal from you the fact that at times now I have hard sledding."

Tom found inspiration in two books that summer. One was *War and Peace*, which Perkins had so often held up as the paragon of literature. "If we are going to worship anything," Tom wrote him, "let it be something like this." He noticed especially how the larger story was interwoven with the personal, particularly those episodes that were obviously from Tolstoi's own life. "This is the way a great writer uses his material, this is the way in which every good work is autobiographical, and I am not ashamed to follow this in my book." At the book's core, "much like a kernel from the beginning, but unrevealed until much later," Wolfe said, would be the idea Perkins had casually mentioned in Central Park the year before: "the idea of man's quest for his father."

Wolfe had also rediscovered the Old Testament. He appreciated it for its literary content more than the spiritual. For three days he read Perkins's favorite section, Ecclesiastes, over and over, then wrote him that it belonged "to the mightiest poetry that was ever written—and the nar-rative passages in the old testament, stories like the life of King David, Ruth and Boaz, Esther and Ahasueras, etc., make the narrative style of any modern novelist look puny." For the first part of *The October Fair*—"The Immortal Earth"—Wolfe had chosen a verse from the book of Ecclesiastes as a title page legend: "One generation passeth away, and another cometh: but the earth abideth forever." He was sorry that the same verse came just before the one Hemingway cited about the sun also rising. He guessed that people would accuse him of imitation, but it was two entirely different routes that had led them to the same point.

Wolfe was planning to celebrate his revival by catching a train to the neighboring town of Lausanne to see if there were any pretty women. "I am very lusty," he wrote Perkins; "the air, the mountains, the quiet, and the very dull, very healthy food have filled me with a vitality I was afraid I'd lost. I wish you were here and we could take a walk together."

Perkins did not address himself to the topic of lust, in his reply, but, responding to Wolfe's descriptions of his work in progress, spoke of what for Wolfe was a graver affliction—literary elephantiasis. "It sounds like a very Leviathan of a book as you describe it, now lying in the depths of your consciousness," Perkins wrote, a bit anxiously, "and I believe you are the man who can draw out such a Leviathan. So far as I can judge—by a sort of instinct—all you say of your plan and intention is right and true." Perkins warned Wolfe to be strict with himself:

> Your talent seems to me a truly great one, and that sort requires to be disciplined and curbed. Length itself is not so important as with the first book,—though there is a limit to volume. I think you'd gain the compression needed to subscribe to it, by keeping that always in your mind.

Suddenly, everything went haywire for Wolfe. Scott Fitzgerald had told a woman in Paris where he was, and she cabled the news to Aline Bernstein in America, who, in turn, began sending Wolfe letters and cables speaking of death and agony, and threatening to sail to Europe to find him. Then Wolfe's English publisher, who had been sending Wolfe the excellent English reviews of *Look Homeward, Angel*, wreaked disaster by also sending him the bad notices. They said things that Wolfe felt he could never forget. Frank Swinnerton in the London *Evening News* found the book "intolerable in his passages of ecstatic apostrophes," full of "over-excited verbosity." Gerald Gould in the *Observer* went farther to say, "I can see no reason why anybody should abstain from writing like that if he wants to write like that; I can see no reason why anybody should read the result." Wolfe found the remarks "dirty, distorted, and full of mockery." The book continued to sell, but he now considered the English edition a catastrophe.

"There is no life in this world worth living, there is no air worth breathing, there is nothing but agony and the drawing of the breath in nausea and labor, until I get the best of this tumult and sadness inside me," Wolfe wrote John Hall Wheelock. Acting as though the disapproving second wave of critics had hardened him, he said that all he wanted from the book now was money—"enough to keep me until I get things straight again."

Enraged, Wolfe could only see that *Look Homeward, Angel* had caused hate in his hometown, renewed malice among "literary tricksters in New York," and mockery and abuse in Europe. "I hoped that that book, with all its imperfections would mark a beginning," he wrote Wheelock; "instead it has marked an ending. Life is not worth the pounding I have taken both from public and private sources these last two years. But if there is some other life—and I am sure there is—I am going to have it." Thomas Clayton Wolfe, not yet thirty, announced to Scribners: "I have stopped writing and do not want ever to write again."

After Wolfe made his proclamation to Scribners, he started to compose a personal message to Maxwell Perkins: "We create the figure of our father, and we create the figure of our enemy," he wrote in a letter that he never finished. Without asking him directly, he prayed for Perkins's support against this mysterious opposition, for at least a clear statement of his position. "Send me your friendship or send me your final disbelief," Tom wrote, then stashed it away with hundreds of other pages that would not be read until after his death.

Wolfe decided to remain completely alone for some time to come. Contrary to his deepest desires, he believed he had to end the relationship with his editor. He sent Perkins from Geneva a formal note in which he asked for a financial statement and said, "I shall not write any more books and since I must begin to make other plans for the future, I should like to know how much money I will have. I want to thank you and Scribners for your kindness to me, and I shall hope someday to resume and continue a friendship which has meant a great deal to me."

"If I really believed you would be able to stand by your decision, your letter would be a great blow to me," Perkins responded on August 28, 1930. "If anyone were ever destined to write, that one is you." Notwithstanding, Perkins tallied Wolfe's royalty statement as requested and sent it. He tried to put the few negative comments from the critics in perspective, then added, "For Heaven's sake, write me again." He was unwilling to accept Wolfe's decision to quit writing; he found it impossible to believe. But as time passed without a change of heart from Wolfe, Perkins grew fearful that Wolfe had really meant what he said. Seeing ten free days before the fall book season, he went to Windsor to calm his unrest over Wolfe's silence.

Max returned from Vermont no less anxious about Thomas Wolfe than when he left. There was still no word from him. "I could not clearly make out why you had come to your decision," Perkins wrote in a second letter, "and surely you will have to change it;—but certainly there never was a man who had made more of an impression on the best judges with a single book, and at so early an age. Certainly you ought not to be affected by a few unfavorable reviews—even apart from the overwhelming number of extremely and excitedly enthusiastic reviews."

Wolfe's silence continued, but Perkins persisted, hoping that one of his letters might move him. "You know," he wrote, "it has been said before that one has to pay somehow for everything one has or gets, and I can see that among your penalties are attacks of despair, as they have been among the penalties great writers have generally had to pay for their talent." Max added, "if you do not write me some good news soon, I shall have to start out on a spying expedition myself." After four weeks of concern, Perkins received a radiogram from Freiburg, Germany: WORKING AGAIN. EXCUSE LETTER. WRITING YOU.

Two more weeks passed in silence. Waiting for the reassuring follow-up letter, Perkins wrote Wolfe again. When none came, he worried as before. "For Heaven's sake send us some word," Perkins implored. He wished Tom would come home to America but was willing to settle for a postcard. Another cabled plea from Perkins elicited no response.

On October 14, 1930, two months after he had quit as a writer, Thomas Wolfe wired Perkins from London: ESTABLISHED SMALL FLAT HERE ALONE IN HOUSE OLD WOMAN LOOKING AFTER ME SEEING NO ONE BELIEVE BOOK FINALLY COMING EXCITED TOO EARLY TO SAY LETTER FOLLOWS FAITHFULLY.

X

Mentor

Exhausted after working on his book for two solid months, Thomas Wolfe left England to ring out 1930 in Paris. He refreshed himself by gorging on food and drink, but he had not crossed the Channel to socialize. For a few days he remained alone, trying to catch up on sleep and correspondence. In an unsent draft of a letter to Perkins (a briefer version of which he mailed later) he considered the turn his writing was taking. He pondered the fact that "no one has ever written a book about America," and he came up with the intention to write one that might contain all the things every American felt but never said. "It may be grandiose and pompous for me to think I can [write it]," Wolfe said, "but for God's sake let me try."

For over a year Wolfe had been carrying in his head Perkins's idea for a book. He did not want Max to think he was giving up anything that he wanted to do, but as Wolfe explained, "I had this vast amount of material, and what you said began to give shape to it." At the same time Wolfe recalled the myth of Antaeus, the gigantic wrestler whose strength was invincible so long as he touched the earth. In a long letter which he wrote through the night back in London and did mail to Perkins, Wolfe announced that his book had a new title which was both "good and beautiful"—*The October Fair* or *Time and the River: A Vision*.

Wolfe sent Perkins a record of the book's growth, showing how the editor's passing comment in Central Park had snowballed in the author's mind to encompass not only the valley of Asheville but also the heights of Olympus. "Thank God, I have begun to create in the way I want to," he wrote Perkins, "it is more *autobiographic* than anything I ever thought of . . . but it is also completely *fictitious*." Wolfe said, "The idea that hangs over the book from first to last is that every man is searching for his father."

Already the book was immensely long, as it was bound to be, because Wolfe's mind never failed to visualize the cosmic implications of everyday occurrences. "My conviction is that a native has the whole consciousness of his people and nation in him: that he knows everything about it, every sight sound and memory of the people," he declared to Perkins. "I *know* now past any denial, that *that* is what being an American or being anything means:

> It is not a government, or the Revolutionary War, or the Monroe Doctrine, it is the ten million seconds and moments of your life—the shapes you see, the sounds you hear, the food you eat, the colour and texture of the earth you live in—I tell you *this* is what it is, and this is what homesickness is, and by God I'm the world's champion authority on the subject at present.

Wolfe crammed one of his letters that December with names that told the story of America in themselves—American states, American Indian tribes, American railways, American millionaires, American hoboes, American rivers. Tom felt that he had told Perkins too much and yet too little. But Max should not worry: "It's not anarchy, it's a perfectly unified but enormous plan," he said. "I want to come home when I know I have this thing by the well-known balls." Until then, he asked Perkins to write him if he thought all this was a good idea, without saying anything about it to anyone else. "If I've talked foolishness," he wrote, "I'd rather keep it between us."

In wishing Perkins a joyful Christmas, Wolfe said, "My own is not as happy as last year's, but by God, I believe I thrive on adversity, I am not going to be beaten because I won't be beaten—Now is the time to see what is in me." Even though Wolfe's letters did not sound happy, Perkins was delighted to receive them. There was much that he did not understand, but, he told Tom, "Every time you write about the book, I get as excited as I did when I began 'The Angel.' I wish to thunder you would come back with the ms."

By early January, 1931, Wolfe was "simply living with the book." He was determined to work on it abroad until he could write no more, which he figured would be in another six weeks; then he would return to America. "When I get back I want to see you and go to that speak-easy again," he wrote Max, "—but I'm not going to see anyone else: I mean this; otherwise, I'm done for—no parties, no going out, no literary people —nothing but obscurity and work. I shall never be a damned literary-party monkey again. I'm a poor dumb simple bloke—*but I will not fail you!*" In his flat at Number 15 Ebury Street, Wolfe thought often of Perkins. When he was feeling loneliest, he recalled when he and Max used to go to "Louis and Armand's" and have a few drinks of the strong gin they served, then ravenously tear into their thick steaks. Later they would tramp all over New York or ride the ferry to Staten Island. "To me," Tom wrote Max, "that is joy; you are a little older and more restrained but I think you had a good time, too."

Tom now had an increasing need to involve Maxwell Perkins in his life as well as his work. The two men could no longer be separated, nor did they wish to be. More and more Wolfe was becoming the son Perkins never had.

For months Wolfe had been haunted by hallucinations, until he verged on physical and mental illness. "I hear strange sounds and noises from my youth, and from America. I hear the million strange and secret sands of time," he wrote Perkins. At last Tom recognized that he needed help, and he asked Max for it. First, he wanted him to find him a quiet place near Manhattan where he could live and work in almost complete isolation for at least three months. During that period he wanted to talk to Perkins whenever Max had the time for it. Finally, Wolfe asked Perkins's help in easing one of the great agonies of his life.

> I am not asking you to cure me of my sickness, because you can't do that. I must do it myself, but I am very earnestly asking you to help me to do certain things that will make my cure easier and less painful.

For the first time, Tom described his torment over Aline Bernstein to Perkins, in almost clinical detail:

> When I was 24 years old I met a woman who was almost forty and I fell in love with her. I cannot tell you here the long and complicated story of my relations with this woman—they extended over a period of five years . . . at first I was a young fellow who had got an elegant and fashionable woman for a mistress; and I was pleased about it; then without knowing how, when, or why, I was desperately in love with the woman, then the

thought of her began to possess and dominate every moment of my life. I wanted to own, possess, and devour her; I became instantly jealous; I began to get horribly sick inside, and then all physical love and desire ended completely—but I still loved the woman. I could not endure her loving anyone else or having physical relations with anyone else, and my madness and jealousy ate at me like a poison—like all horrible sterility and barrenness.

Wolfe said he had not wanted to make this trip to Europe but had yielded to what friends wanted for her. He wrote her from the boat that took him from her, but he had not communicated with her since. During the first five months of their separation she had sent a string of messages. Snatches of them read:

DEAREST LOVE

HELP ME TOM

WHY HAVE YOU DESERTED YOUR FRIEND PAIN I BEAR TOO GREAT IMPOS-
SIBLE TO CONTINUE LIFE COMPLETELY PARTED FROM YOU

HEART HEAVY NO WORD FROM YOU LOVE ALINE

Her letters tormented Wolfe, for she sometimes signed them in her blood. Then Wolfe received another cable which read: LIFE IMPOSSIBLE NO WORD FROM YOU ARE YOU WILLING TO ACCEPT CONSEQUENCES DESPERATE. For a few days he thought he would go mad, but he neither wrote nor cabled. "Each day I would go for mail in the most horrible state of nerves, wondering if I should see some cable which carried the dreaded news," he wrote Perkins. "I longed for NO news, and I hoped for some news—but nothing came, and that was almost worse than ever." He imagined that she had killed herself and that her embittered, grief-stricken loved ones were saying nothing to him. He combed the obituaries in the American newspapers until one day he found her name—not among the death notices but on the theatrical page. He read an account of a great artistic success Aline Bernstein had scored. Later, Wolfe met a man who asked if he knew her and said that he had seen her looking radiant at a party in New York only a short time earlier.

In the final weeks of 1930 her pleas began again. There had been two months of silence during her theatrical triumph, but once her success had worn off, her pain was reborn, and again Wolfe was the cause. She wrote in despondency, "Hold out your hand to me in my hour of need.

Impossible to face New Year. I stood by you in bad years, why have you destroyed me? I love you and am faithful until death, pain I bear too great to endure." Eight or ten times she signaled in distress. Wolfe cabled back, asking if it was fair to send such messages when he was alone in a foreign land trying to write.

"You may wonder why I come to you with this," Wolfe wrote Perkins; "my answer is that if I cannot come to you with it, there is no one in the world I can come to." He tried to destroy the pain by detailing it: the pain in the pit of his stomach from the moment he awoke, the feelings of nausea and horror that he carried all day long, until he vomited from physical sickness at night. For the past three months Tom had remained in the same place and had written over 100,000 words of his book. "I am a brave man, and I like myself for what I did here," he wrote Perkins from London, "and I hope you like me too, for I honor and respect you, and believe you can help me to save myself." But Tom wanted to save more than that: His "utter and absolute belief in love and human excellence" was also at stake. "No matter what breach of faith, truth, or honesty this woman may be guilty of," Wolfe said, "I want to come out of this thing with a feeling of love and belief in her . . . [because] there is the most enormous beauty and loveliness in her yet."

"I *must* not die. But I need help—such help as a man may hope to receive from a friend," he wrote Perkins. "I turn to you because I feel health and sanity and fortitude in you. . . . [If] you understand my trouble," he wrote, "say simply that you do, and that you will try to help me." Max had once remarked that Wolfe's letters from Europe sounded "unhappy." Wolfe hoped he had at last made the reason plain.

"I'll do anything you ask of me," Perkins replied, "and any reluctance will come only from lack of confidence to do good. But I should be glad that you did feel you wanted to ask me." Perkins already looked forward to Wolfe's return and hoped he would be in New York in the summer because, he admitted, "I'm generally horribly lonely. There are people enough, but none I care really to see. I'll count on *some* of your company, anyway. . . .

"I had gathered that things were bad in some such way, but not that they were so bad as they are," Perkins continued, addressing himself to the heart of Wolfe's problem. "Heaven knows how it would go with me in such a situation, but may *you* get strength somewhere to stick it out. . . . I wish I'd been through the like of it. Then I could preach." He was certain that Tom had taken the best course in going away.

As for me, I can only feel angry with *her* [he wrote of Aline Bernstein].
She may be really fine, but there is an egotism in women beyond any
known in men, and they infuriate me. But I know I am prejudiced against
them. Did any one of them ever admit she was in the wrong about anything? I know you've been in hell. I'm no good at suffering myself and so
it's hard to encourage others to it. But I'm dead sure you've done right and
you must stand it for the sake of everything if you can.

The only consolation Perkins could offer Wolfe was in listening to his
grief; his only succor was bromidic advice about sticking to his work.
Beyond that he could do little more than write, "My great hope is some-
day to see you walk in with a ms. two or three feet thick." At the end of
February, 1931, Wolfe cabled Perkins: SAILING EUROPA THURSDAY NEED
NO HELP NOW CAN HELP MYSELF MUST WORK SIX MONTHS ALONE
BEST WISHES.

Aline Bernstein had been flirting with suicide. After reading in the
newspaper of Wolfe's return on the S. S. *Europa*, she swallowed an overdose of sleeping pills and had to be rushed to the hospital. "Apparently
to love you as I do is an insanity," she wrote Tom; "—I am having a
great fight in myself. The way I love you will never stop, but I know
now that you will no longer have me nor hold me near." Temporarily
withdrawing but not surrendering, Aline said she had one favor to ask.
She wanted to see Wolfe's new book before it was published. Mrs. Bernstein understood his method and realized that he was about to write of
the years when she entered his life. She wanted at least a voice in what
went into print. If Wolfe was reluctant to comply, she suggested allowing his Mr. Perkins to mediate.

Wolfe was busy settling into 40 Verandah Place in Brooklyn and
preparing his material to show Perkins. I MUST COME THROUGH NOW OR
EVERYTHING IS LOST, he wired Aline; HELP ME BY BEING HEALTHY AND
HAPPY AND MY DEAR FRIEND. LOVE.

Perkins saw Wolfe only a few times upon his return, and then they
talked more about his personal life than about his writing. Wolfe was
desperate. Mrs. Bernstein was doing everything in her power to persuade Tom to come back to her. "We live in a crazy world, here it is
a sin, in the eyes of ninety-nine people out of a hundred, that I love you,"
she wrote him. "But money grabbing is not such a sin." After visiting
Tom's apartment one day, she threw a $100 bill over the Brooklyn

Bridge, thinking, "If they cannot understand how I love you, here is something to appease the Gods your people worship." Max, never having had any trouble of the sort Wolfe was in, did not think he was doing him much good, but he listened patiently. Only with Elizabeth Lemmon did he even suggest the matter, obliquely at that. "I cannot bear to hear any more troubles," he wrote her. "Everyone seems to be in trouble. Nothing and no one seems any longer to be sane and healthy."

Within weeks of Wolfe's voyage home, Scott Fitzgerald's father died. Scott too, like Wolfe, had been in trouble all year, trying to find time to complete his novel, which he was calling "the encyclopedia," and to pay off his "national debt" of $10,000 to Scribners. When word of the death came he was in Gstaad trying to recover from a "shaky" time of big-money writing for the *Post*. Now he rushed back, heading for Baltimore. Perkins saw him in New York for fifteen minutes and got terribly depressed. "He is very greatly changed," Max reported to Hemingway. "He looks older, but it is more that he has lost, at least temporarily, all of the elan that was so characteristic. But he may be all the better for it because you feel at bottom he is a very real person now." Zelda was still in "mighty bad shape."

Two weeks later Perkins and Fitzgerald lunched together, just before Scott sailed back to Europe. He had seen his and Zelda's families, and Max guessed that anticipating those two visits had pained Scott greatly. But this time Perkins found him very much his old self and enjoyed being with him. "And," he wrote John Peale Bishop, "it made me think he had the resilience to stand almost anything and would come through well in the end."

"The Jazz Age is over," Fitzgerald wrote Perkins in May, 1931, from Lausanne. "If Mark Sullivan [whose fifth volume of social history for Scribners, called *Our Times*, had brought him by now from the turn of the century to the end of the World War] is going on you might tell him I claim credit for naming it & that it extended from the suppression of the riots on May Day, 1919, to the crash of the stock market in 1929—almost exactly one decade."

Perkins knew that Fitzgerald had coined that phrase and found Scott's remarks worthy of more consideration than a passing reference in a collection of history books. He believed Scott should write at least an article about it, some kind of fresh reminiscence or even an elegy that would remind the public of his influence and, at the same time, fix a point in his mind from which he could begin a new phase of his career. Perkins passed his idea on to Fritz Dashiell at the magazine, who then wrote Fitzgerald, "There is no one more qualified to sound its knell." Scott could not commit himself to the assignment, but he could not put it out of his mind.

Not until the end of August did he write to Max again. By then, Zelda had taken a turn for the better. After more than a year of psychotherapy in a sanitarium outside Geneva, and of periodic separations from Scott, her sporadic attacks of eczema and asthma, occasional irrationality and hysteria, were subdued. Her case was viewed as a "reaction to her feelings of inferiority primarily toward her husband." For several weeks, Scott and Zelda were at peace with each other and talked eagerly of going home. She was well enough to leave her Swiss doctor, and Scott wrote Max that she was even writing "some amazing stuff." Max received the article he had suggested—"Echoes of the Jazz Age"—four weeks before the *Aquitania* docked.

Fitzgerald's essay aroused much discussion, not only because of the happy memories it evoked but also because of the author's candor. That period seemed rosy and romantic to those who were young then, Fitzgerald said, "because we will never feel quite so intensely about our surroundings any more."

For some months Perkins had been less than satisfied with Erskine Caldwell's writing, feeling at times that his compact, evocative little stories carbon-copied some of Hemingway's. But he had not quite written the author off.

Following Perkins's first acceptance of his stories, Caldwell continued to write short pieces. Each was sent to *Scribner's Magazine* via Perkins. The magazine editors did not think his writing was compatible with their readership, and none of the pieces was accepted until it reached the little magazines. After several months without a *Scribner's* acceptance, Caldwell filled three suitcases with his unpublished poetry, stories, and sketches, went to a small cabin, and reread them all. The next morning he burned every page, along with his collection of rejection slips, many of which came from Perkins.

A few weeks after the bonfire Caldwell received a different kind of letter from Max Perkins. The editor had a new idea for getting Caldwell's stories across to the public. He suggested that Caldwell group enough of his strongest stories to fill a book of 300 pages—half with New England settings, the rest with Southern locales—which might be brought out after the first of the year. Once the stories were typed, Caldwell went to New York, feeling bold enough to face Perkins. He took the same rackety elevator up to the fifth floor, but this time he did not retreat. He entered Perkins's office and handed him the stories that would make up the book, *American Earth*. Caldwell recalled:

> Wearing a hat with a turned-up brim, which appeared to be at least a half a size too small for him, he sat down at his desk and slowly turned the pages of the manuscript for a quarter of an hour. No word was spoken while he sat there. At the end of that time, he got up smiling a little and moved stiffly around his office in new bright tan shoes, occasionally looking out his window at the traffic below, while he told of several incidents he recalled about life in Vermont when he was a youth.

After nearly an hour of reminiscing, sometimes seriously and often humorously, Perkins mentioned for the first time the manuscript Caldwell had brought in. All he said was that he would publish it.

American Earth came out in late April, 1931. The notices were mixed; most New York reviewers still approached Caldwell's baldly told stories as though they smelled a bad odor. The book sold fewer than 1,000 copies. In a third attempt to get Caldwell's career off the ground, at a time when publishers could ill afford taking such chances, Perkins asked Caldwell how he felt about writing a novel. Unbeknown to Max, the author had already finished a draft of one about Georgia backwoods people, *Tobacco Road*. By the summer he had revised and submitted it to Perkins.

Scribners published *Tobacco Road* in February, 1932, and it barely met Caldwell's minuscule advance against royalties. The reviews were as unenthusiastic as they had been on his first published volume, but the author dug right into another novel. *Autumn Hill* was about a family living on a back-road farm in Maine. A month after Caldwell submitted it, Perkins wrote him "that we have decided against *Autumn Hill*, personally disappointing as it is to do." Perkins was not shedding crocodile tears, as his letter went on to show:

> I believed in it, I wish to say, and still more in you; and I saw that it was given every kind of consideration. It was read by six people,—including those who necessarily consider more the business side of such questions, who in normal times would not have read it. The sales of *American Earth* and *Tobacco Road* were against it. The fact is that this depression compels

a scrutiny of manuscript from the practical point of view such as never before required, and it is very hard when confronted by the figures to resist the practical arguments. I can't tell you how sorry I am.

Perkins felt that he had no right to make suggestions about material he was rejecting, but it was a practice of his that had become habitual. In a postscript he mentioned—with some ambivalence—one or two points in the plot that he wished Caldwell would amend before submitting it to another publisher—all because "I want to see you succeed, as you ought to do."

Caldwell's literary agent was Maxim Lieber. Together they went to see Perkins in his office and had a long, friendly talk. Perkins said he hoped Caldwell would not want to find another publisher but would offer Scribners his next book, even though the option clause of their contract was now voided. The author was free to publish wherever he could, but he was willing to agree to show Perkins his next book. Before he had a chance to give his word on it, Lieber got Caldwell to leave the office with him. He liked the new novel, Lieber said; Caldwell liked it, and Max Perkins liked it. That could only mean that it was sure to find a publisher. If Scribners would not take it, they would find some house that would. Caldwell agreed.

"After knowing Max Perkins as long as I had," Caldwell remembered, "it was disturbing to think that such a decision would mean I would no longer be in a position to call upon him for help and advice." The next day, as he was walking up Fifth Avenue to the agent's office, he halted at the corner of Forty-eighth Street and looked up at the fifth-floor windows. "After a while my eyes became blurred," he recalled, "and when I finally walked away, I was thinking of how I could tell Max Lieber that I had changed my mind and did not wish him to find another publisher." Upon Caldwell's arrival at the agent's office, Lieber told him that there were only a few minutes before their appointment with Harold Guinzburg and Marshall Best at the Viking Press. Caldwell wanted to stay and explain to Lieber his most recent change of heart, but Lieber was excitedly discussing the new prospects. Within the hour Guinzburg and Best were pointing out the advantages of a Viking agreement—this over a sumptuous lunch, which they had encouraged Caldwell to order without regard to cost. He could not help silently comparing this luxurious reception with the one and only time Maxwell Perkins had bought him a meal. It was at a lunch counter. Max had ordered for each of them—

a peanut-butter-and-jelly sandwich and a glass of orange juice. The only comment Caldwell recalled Perkins's making at the time was to the effect that "in Vermont the lean and hungry countenance of man was held in fearsome respect."

Caldwell never figured out if it was the memory of the measly peanut-butter-and-jelly sandwich that turned the trick, but he was persuaded to submit his next three books to the Viking Press. They rejected *Autumn Hill* as Scribners had, but Caldwell began writing another novel set in the South—*God's Little Acre*. According to the newly signed contract, Viking had first chance to read it. By the time it was published, an adaptation of *Tobacco Road* had been written for the stage, and it began a record-breaking run of more than seven years on Broadway. Caldwell's career was to go on and on, but Scribners never published him again.

So long as he could keep his authors' minds on writing, Max Perkins believed, they could all continue their careers and get through the Depression. In a letter to Hemingway, Perkins proposed his own brand of rugged individualism: "Maybe the present discouraging state will end by improving things for those who come through."

Out in Montana, Hemingway was getting in some good writing on his bullfighting book—until November, 1930. On the evening of November 1 he was driving John Dos Passos back to Billings after ten days of hunting when the lights of an oncoming car sent Hemingway swerving into a ditch. Dos Passos climbed out of the overturned wreck unscathed. Hemingway's right upper arm was broken in such a way that it had to be slung very close to his body, bandaged tightly to keep it from jostling. Hemingway facetiously suggested to Perkins that Scribners insure him against future accidents and disease, as there would be big money in it. It might even pay better than publishing his books. Since signing with Perkins he had had anthrax, a cut right eyeball, congestion of the kidney, cut index finger, gashed forehead, torn cheek, a branch speared through his leg, and now this broken arm. On the other hand, he noted that he had never once been constipated during that same period.

Ernest made up for his latest inactivity by directing Perkins to several prize authors he might sign up. Ford Madox Ford, a former collaborator of Joseph Conrad, had met Hemingway years before in Paris, when the former edited the *transatlantic review*. He was dissatisfied with his present publisher and wished Hemingway would suggest to Max Perkins that he wanted to change. "I don't of course ask you to guarantee my selling powers or the like," Ford told Hemingway, a generation younger than himself, "but you might just mention it." Ford, for all his talent and influence, had not had a commercial success in twenty-five books. In forwarding his letter to Perkins, Hemingway enclosed an analysis of Ford's work, a cycle in which "megalomania" and success "pee-ed away" would inevitably follow his periodic good works. Hemingway estimated that Ford was due for another fine book and thought a good publisher "would hold him steady."

Perkins did not know what to do about Ford Madox Ford. He had liked the fat bear of a man since a casual meeting years earlier, and he especially liked his war novel, *No More Parades*. "But," Max wrote Ernest, "in the first place I dare say he is a man with an eye to a big advance, and it is always difficult too, to take on an older writer who has been all about and has become exacting and who having changed so often will probably change again." For Perkins, the great interest in publishing was still "to take on an author at the start or reasonably near it, and then to publish not this book and that, but the whole author." One could then afford to lose on certain books because of the gains on others.

Despite his misgivings, Perkins invited Ford in and learned of his newest plan, a three-volume *History of Our Own Time*, from 1880 to the present. Perkins thought they might be able to consummate a deal to their mutual advantage, but Ford constantly neglected the history for other projects. Scribners ended instead with only one chapter of his reminiscences, *Return to Yesterday*, which the magazine published.

With far more enthusiasm, Hemingway sent Perkins a second suggestion later in the year. The poet Archibald MacLeish, whom he had also met in Paris, was unhappy with his present publisher, Houghton Mifflin. Usually Hemingway's recommendations were out of charity toward the author, but his endorsement of MacLeish was based on great respect for him as a writer. He wrote that MacLeish was the best man Perkins could get as a poet at that time, for he had "come on steadily" while the others had stood still or retrogressed. Perkins had been "damn good" to Hemingway, and recommending MacLeish was the biggest favor he could do in return. Ernest said it would be a tragedy if Max did not sign him. After some correspondence with Perkins, and hearing a good deal more about him from both Hemingway and Fitzgerald, MacLeish said that he would let Scribners have the first refusal rights to his next book, but that it might not be done for a year or two. "I like his poetry immensely," Max wrote Ernest.

Several months later Perkins read MacLeish's long-awaited work, *Conquistador*. It was a lengthy narrative poem based on Cortez's expedition to Mexico and emphasized the love of men for adventure. Perkins thought it was magnificent. But he doubted that Scribners could capture *Conquistador* because Houghton Mifflin was taking up the gauntlet. Scribners would offer satisfactory terms, but MacLeish found it difficult to accept them on account of his relationship with Robert Linscott, his old editor. Perkins chose not to push his interest in the book or even embarrass the poet about it. Because of MacLeish's commitment to his editor he forbade Hemingway from intervening on Scribners' behalf. "I am mighty sorry to see that poem go," Perkins lamented to Hemingway, "for it is one of the kind of things that make publishing seem really worth being in." (Years later Perkins took the same honorable position with Robert Frost, who had been published by Holt. Max and Jack Wheelock lunched two or three times with the New Hampshire poet. When terms of a contract were about to be drawn up, Wheelock remembered, "Frost withdrew for fear of treating Holt shabbily. And Max felt that he could not force the issue.") Hemingway got the news about MacLeish in Piggott, Arkansas, from the poet himself, who felt bad about acting as he had. Ernest realized how little luck he had had in getting writers for Perkins, but with what he had written on his bullfight book, *Death in the Afternoon*, he vaunted that there was really "no need to get any more Hemingsteins." Ernest returned to Florida for the winter and waited for the bones in his writing arm to knit.

The 1930 congressional elections went right in every respect from Perkins's point of view—especially in regard to Prohibition. It was finally becoming a "wet" legislature, and Max hoped it would get around to repealing the Volstead Act. Among the affiliations he listed in his latest Harvard alumni report was the Association Against the Prohibition Amendment, with himself as Director. But business, he wrote Ernest, "seems to get worse and worse all the time." Max observed that "ever so many people have become so desperate that they think, or at least say, that the capitalist system is dissolving. But old Stalin thinks we shall get over it this time—and maybe one or two times more. And I hope by that time my daughters will all have married mechanics and engineers."

After a lapse of more than a year, Max received a letter from Elizabeth Lemmon. Theirs was a relationship unaffected by time. Elizabeth had been too involved with her social life in Baltimore—she had many suitors —to write; Max had his work. But they still thought about each other often. "I had written you several times," Max wrote her now, explaining, "Last July I carried a letter all addressed and stamped, in my pocket for a week; but then I tore it up."

The next day he mailed her a newsy letter, mostly about his family. Max said he was not at all upset when his eldest daughter, Bertha, an excellent student at Smith College, flunked her first midyear exam, because he understood the circumstances. She had had two days to study for it but had not put in one minute; she had taken up *Look Homeward, Angel* instead and had been able to do nothing else until she finished it. According to her, everyone at Smith was reading it, which Max thought was remarkable, because "it's far more a man's book."

In early March Max's brother-in-law Archibald Cox, to whom he was close, died, leaving seven children. The oldest, Archibald, Jr., was at Harvard considering a legal career; for a later generation he would come to symbolize certain Yankee virtues—artless decency, natural moral clarity, canniness that does not exploit advantage—that Max symbolized for those who knew him.

Max went south later in March, for what had become his annual Gulf Stream excursion. He found Ernest in good shape, except for his arm. Hemingway navigated the boat left-handed through the prow-slapping waters. With some elaborate rigging, he was able to fish, a sure sign to Max that he would be just as good as new. Perkins cruised with Hemingway and The Mob long enough to see the galley cleaned out of Ernest's supply of Bermuda onions; but he thumbed a ride back to Key West on a passing sloop, leaving for New York before they got storm-bound again.

Back in port Hemingway was soon at work again, with both arms free and a renewed determination to outwrite everyone else in the world. In fact, vying against "living merchants" had become too easy. He wrote Perkins that he preferred to outdo the dead masters. They were really the only ones who provided much competition, though he admitted that William Faulkner was "damned good when good but often unnecessary." Perkins agreed. For years Faulkner had been writing short stories and trying them on *Scribner's* with what he called "unflagging optimism" and little success. "I am quite sure that I have no feeling for short stories; that I shall never be able to write them," he admitted to the magazine staff. Faulkner seemed "crazy" to Perkins, who had just read his sensational novel *Sanctuary* and deemed it a "horrible book by a writer of great talent." Because none of Faulkner's books had commanded any kind of sale, Perkins thought this would be a good time to annex him to his list, but he did not act. John Hall Wheelock suggested that "Max didn't follow through on Faulkner just then because he was afraid of arousing Hemingway's jealousy." Hemingway had recently expressed his confidence that Thomas Wolfe would write plenty of "swell books" for Perkins, and he still believed in Fitzgerald's bedrock talent. But, Wheelock said, "in Hemingway's mind, there was no more room in Max's life for another power so threatening as William Faulkner. Hemingway's was a mighty ego, and Max knew it."

In May, Ernest went to Spain, where the newly organized Spanish Republic replaced the Carlist monarchy. Hemingway remained aloof from the political scene, working on the final chapters of his bullfight book.

That same month Douglas Southall Freeman invited the Perkinses to Richmond. This visit promised to be more social than Max's last trip there because Freeman's biography of Robert E. Lee was steadily advancing. He followed a strategy that Perkins had mapped especially for him, though it was sound advice for anyone writing in that category:

> You are not writing a study of Robert E. Lee, or a personal interpretation of him, but the first complete and perhaps the definitive, biography: a great feature of it is that it contains all the information pertinent, and that a great deal of this is new. This fact which is indisputable, must govern the character of the book. —It prevents you from any such freedom of imaginative interpretation, for instance, as Strachey allows himself. And it governs you in the matter of selecting, for you must put in everything, and not simply select what is valuable from some purely artistic or literary standpoint.

Perkins often pinpointed worthwhile themes for Freeman to develop, aspects of Lee's life which, retold, would keep the work from being strictly archival. To make the book more than a lifeless commemorative monument, Perkins reminded Freeman,

> any personal incidents or anecdotes which showed him in action, or which showed him in contrast to others, and tended to explain how he came to be so admirable and controlled, would come as a relief to the prevailing tone of the narrative.

Two more years of the most methodical writing followed, and on January 19, 1933, Freeman wired Perkins, I AM VAIN ENOUGH TO BELIEVE THAT YOU WILL REJOICE WITH ME WHEN I TELL YOU I YESTERDAY COMPLETED THE TEXT OF THE LEE. ONLY LITERARY REVISION REMAINS.

After twenty years on the project, Freeman's four-volume biography was published. It had the extraordinary distinction of being praised by the critics, winning the Pulitzer Prize for biography, and becoming a best seller. The book had taken almost two years of editing, and in December, 1934, Freeman expressed his gratitude to Perkins: "This book would never have been finished but for the encouragement I received at your hands. Many a time, when composition was lagging, a word from you prodded me on."

Freeman was already considering subjects to which he might devote the next ten years of his life. Perkins thought he could do a brilliant biography of Washington.

> It is that in his case too, you would be writing largely a military life, and whatever else may be said about the Lee, the accounts of the campaigns, and battles, are I believe, excelled by no other writer on military matters. I thought this when I first read the ms., and now we know that authorities think it. The clarity and intensity with which these campaigns are described makes most fascinating reading, and most enlightening. Of course in Washington's case, the military strategy would be much less complicated, but I do not think that the Revolutionary campaigns are even as well understood as the Civil War ones, and I think you would handle them magnificently, and that all your study of war for the Lee and previous to that, would be of great advantage to you.

Upon making his recommendation, Perkins turned Freeman over to Wallace Meyer, who had played a major role in editing the *Lee*. Freeman went on to write *Lee's Lieutenants* before getting to his seven-volume life of Washington, the final installment of which he did not live to complete.

Geographically, at this time, nothing more than the East River separated Max from Tom Wolfe, but they communicated mainly through the mail and saw each other only when Wolfe's work schedule permitted. In August, 1931, Perkins thought they should get together, at least to discuss the possible publication date of Wolfe's novel. Perkins wrote to him in Brooklyn, "You ought to make every conceivable effort to have your manuscript completely finished by the end of September. I meant to speak of this when we were last together. I hope you will come in soon and tell me what you think you can do."

"I know you are not joking and that you mean this September, and not September four, five, or fifteen years from now," Wolfe replied.

"Well, there is no remote or possible chance that I will have a completed manuscript of anything that resembles a book this September, and whether I have anything that I would be willing to show anyone next September, or any succeeding one for the next 150 years, is at present a matter of the extremest and most painful doubt to me."

Tom said he regretted destroying Perkins's belief in him almost as much as he feared failing himself. But Wolfe said he did not "care one good Goddamn of a drunken sailor's curse whether I have disappointed the world of bilge-and-hogwash writers or any of the other literary rubbish of sniffers, whiffers, and puny, poisonous apes." The only thing Wolfe cared about now was whether he had enough faith and power left that would justify his going on. He wrote to Perkins that "no one can take anything from me now that I value, they can have their cheap, nauseous, seven-day notoriety back to give to other fools, but I am perfectly content to return to the obscurity in which I passed almost thirty years of my life without any great difficulty." He had no desire to cling to his "stinking remnant of a rotten fish" of a manuscript; but, he wrote Perkins, if anyone wanted to know when he would have a new book out, he would answer without apology, "When I have finished writing one and found someone who wants to publish it."

Wolfe's most fluent channel of expression was the written word. (In fact, he stammered when he was excited.) And so, at great length, he wrote Perkins exactly what was on his mind more intimately than he could by talking to him in person. Wolfe wanted to tell Perkins finally that he was in doubt about his book but not despair. "I felt if my life and strength kept up, if my vitality moved in every page, if I followed it through to the end," he wrote Perkins, "it would be a wonderful book—

> but I doubted then that life was long enough, it seemed to me it would take ten books, that it would be the longest ever written. Then, instead of paucity, I had abundance—such abundance that my hand was palsied, my brain weary—and in addition, as I go on, I want to write about everything and say all that can be said about each particular. The vast freightage of my years of hunger, my prodigies of reading, my infinite store of memories, my hundreds of books of notes, return to drown me—sometimes I feel as if I shall compass and devour them, again be devoured by them. I had an immense book, and I wanted to say it all at once: it can't be done.

Wolfe was putting his story down like a mosaic, tile by tile. He hoped each piece would be a complete story while it made up the whole plan.

The newest section had become a big book in itself and was for the first time straight in his head to the minutest detail. He wrote Perkins, "It is a part of my whole scheme of books as a small river flows into a big one."

In getting them all published, Wolfe said he understood that he was not bound to Scribners by any sort of contract. None was offered him, nor had he taken money that was not his own. The only bond Wolfe was conscious of was one of friendship and loyalty to Max Perkins's house. He wanted to remain both Perkins's friend and author, but he believed those were honors he had to earn. He still felt so beholden to Perkins for his contribution to *Look Homeward, Angel* that he did not want to accept anything more from him until he had reimbursed him for that much. And so he said the best way to leave things between them was with the "coast clear"—without debits or entanglements. "If I ever write anything else that I think worth printing, or that your house might be interested in," he wrote Perkins, "I will bring it to you, and you can read it, accept it or reject it with the same freedom as with the first book. I ask no more from anyone."

Wolfe saw what happened to so many writers in what they were already calling "the twenties." He wanted to have nothing to do with those "nasty, ginny, drunken, jealous, fake-Bohemian little lives." He saw how the literary establishment kicked these men out, after tainting and corrupting them, and brought in another set which they called "the younger writers," among whose names Tom had seen his own included. Wolfe would not be billed like some prizefighter, he said. "The only standard I will compete against now is in me: if I can't reach it, I'll quit."

> I'm out of the game—and it is a game, a racket [Wolfe wrote Perkins]. What I do now must be for myself. I don't care who "gets ahead" of me— that game isn't worth a good goddamn: I only care if I have disappointed you, but it's very much my own funeral, too.

When Tom Wolfe was a boy, he said, he used to call someone he looked up to a "high-class gentleman." "That's the way I feel about you," he wrote Perkins. "I don't think I am one—not the way you are, by birth, by gentleness, by natural and delicate kindness. But if I have understood some of the things you have said to me, I believe you think the most living and beautiful thing on this earth is art, and that the finest and most valuable life is that of the artist. I think so, too: I don't know whether I have it in me to live that life, but if I have, then I think I would have something that would be worth your friendship."

XI

Lamentations

The most recent addition to Maxwell Perkins's list of desperate friends was Ring Lardner. At the beginning of 1931 he was laid up with what appeared to be the effects of excessive overworking, smoking, and drinking. "I guess I am paying for my past," Ring wrote Max in a short letter that was devoid of the usual wisecracks, "and I'm not averaging more than four short stories a year. None of the recent ones has been anything to boast of and I'm afraid there won't be enough decent ones to print by fall." Perkins believed Lardner had followed the "will o' the wisp of the theatre" at the expense of his real writing, though he never accused him of that. He did tell him that he wished he would take a year off from the Broadway high life to live quietly and write a novel. "Spring is not so far off now," Max wrote him, "and that always, I find, brings a man up a good many notches."

Spring came and went, and Lardner weakened. By fall, Perkins finally perceived that a recurrence of the tuberculosis that had attacked Ring years earlier was sapping his strength. For a while Ring picked up some money writing a "daily wire" for several newspapers, but it was not enough. His royalties had dwindled—*Round Up* had soared to 100,000 copies, but sales now had dropped—and his overall income had declined alarmingly. His wife, Ellis, summed up their situation for Perkins: "Ring has not been able to do any work for five months and the Lardners are pretty hard up." As the new financial administrator of the family, she asked Scribners for the $208.93 in royalties that would be due in December. Perkins had the check sent immediately, knowing it would salve the difficulties, not solve them. Apparently the only cure for Ring's condition was rest. Max knew it was hard to rest when money was such a worry. Discouraged by Ring's lack of improvement and also by what she had heard of the Fitzgeralds in recent years, Ellis Lardner asked Perkins, "Do you suppose there is anyone left in the world who is well physically, mentally, and financially?"

Six years had passed since *The Great Gatsby* was published. In the last two years Fitzgerald had hardly put pencil to paper. Certainly the major factor in his lack of progress during that time had been his wife's illness. By the fall of 1931 they had bought a Stutz car and settled into an oversized house in Montgomery, Alabama, to pick up the pieces of their lives. Scott wrote Perkins that there was, in fact, no talk of Depression in Montgomery; it seemed to have passed the city by, just as the boom did before it. After a while, however, Fitzgerald found the city's slow pace killing. The thought of each passing day dimming his fame kept him awake nights.

In November Scott packed his bags and left abruptly for Hollywood. He was gone eight weeks, working on a film treatment at Metro-Goldwyn-Mayer. In his absence, Zelda became absorbed in writing her own fiction. Scott came back to his wife and child in Alabama $6,000 ahead and full of material to write about for years to come. "At last," he wrote Perkins, "for the first time in two years and ½ I am going to spend five consecutive months on my novel." His new plan called for taking what was good in what he had already written and adding 41,000 words to it. "Don't tell Ernest or anyone," he requested of his editor; "—let them think what they want—you're the only one whose ever consistently felt faith in me anyhow."

For months Fitzgerald drafted chronological charts, lists, outlines, and character studies for the book—then called *The Drunkard's Holiday*—thinking out every detail beforehand so that this time he would not trip up once he started writing. "The novel should do this," Fitzgerald wrote at the top of his master "General Plan":

> Show a man who is a natural idealist, a spoiled priest going in for various causes to the ideas of the haute Burgoise [sic], and in his rise to the top of the social world losing his idealism, his talent and turning to drink and dissipation. Background one in which the liesure class is at their truly most brilliant & glamorous such as Murphys.

The hero, named Dick, is a psychiatrist who falls in love with one of his patients, Nicole, most of whose case history was lifted from Zelda's hospital folders. In time the story would shed the political-economic notions Fitzgerald had in mind and take on spiritual and psychological aspects. The young doctor would expend all his vitality until he would be left emotionally bankrupt, an *"homme épuisé"*; thus the novel would reflect all the inner torment Fitzgerald felt had been draining him for most of the last decade.

Shortly after Scott's arrival in Montgomery, where he began marshaling this new version of the book, Zelda's asthma and her telltale blotches of eczema reappeared. Within days her behavior retrogressed to what it had been in Switzerland. In February, 1932, Scott brought Zelda to the Henry Phipps Psychiatric Clinic of the Johns Hopkins University Hospital in Baltimore. Her mood improved once he went back to Alabama—to the point where she was able to take a major step. Ever since her ballet career had ended, writing fiction had become an effective therapy for Zelda; she felt a sense of accomplishment every time she finished a story on her own. Max knew this, but he was nevertheless surprised to receive a letter from her in March which announced: "Under separate cover, as I believe is the professional phraseology, I have mailed you my first novel." It was a full-length work entitled *Save Me the Waltz*. Zelda had written it in six weeks while at Phipps. "Scott being absorbed in his own has not seen it," she wrote Perkins, "so I am completely in the dark as to its possible merits, but naturally terribly anxious that you should like it. . . . If the thing is too wild for your purposes, might I ask what you suggest? Presuming, I realize, on your friendship to an unwarranted extent."

Perkins was perplexed. From the beginning, the manuscript had a slightly deranged quality which gave him the impression that the author had had difficulty in separating fiction from reality. Highly charged images, often with little connection to one another, crowded the prose. The plot seemed to reflect, often in a distorted fun-house-mirror style of exaggeration, Scott's early writing about their life together. *Save Me the Waltz* was the story of Alabama Beggs, a Montgomery judge's daughter who married a handsome, promising artist she met during the war; through his early triumphs, she found herself unhappy and unfulfilled and started up a ballet career. Zelda had named the artist Amory Blaine, the protagonist of *This Side of Paradise*.

Within the week Zelda wired Perkins: ACTING ON SCOTTS ADVICE WILL YOU RETURN MANUSCRIPT PHIPPS CLINIC JOHNS HOPKINS WITH

MANY THANKS REGRETS AND REGARDS. Fitzgerald had at last heard about the manuscript and wanted to read it himself before Max did. Perkins complied, writing: HAD READ ABOUT 60 PAGES WITH GREAT INTEREST VERY LIVE AND MOVING HOPE YOU WILL RETURN IT.

Perkins wrote Hemingway about the novel. "It looked as if there were a great deal that was good in it," he said, "but it seemed rather as though it somewhat dated back to the days of *The Beautiful and Damned*. And of course it would not do at all the way it was, with Amory Blaine. It would have been mighty rough on Scott. . . . I think the novel will be quite a good one when she finishes it."

Scott interrupted his own novel to confer with Zelda, then wrote Max that the entire middle section of her book would have to be "radically rewritten." The name of the artist, he said, would of course be changed. But Scott's objections, in truth, went beyond the qualities of the manuscript itself. He was furious with Zelda. It was not just that she had sent the manuscript to Perkins before showing it to him, as if going behind his back. It was also that he soon realized how much use she had made of incidents from their life together—the rich material he had been too busy to use in the last few years because he had had to write cheaper stories to pay Zelda's doctor bills.

In trying to placate Scott, Zelda all but threw herself at his feet. In a breast-beating letter she wrote, "Scott, I love you more than anything on earth and if you were offended I am miserable." She knew what she had done: "I was . . . afraid we might have touched the same material." But she explained: "Purposely I didn't [send my book to you before I mailed it to Max]—knowing that you were working on your own and honestly feeling that I had no right to interrupt you to ask for a serious opinion. Also, I know Max will not want it and I prefer to do the corrections after having his opinion. . . . So, Dear, My Own, please realize that it was not from any sense of not turning first to you—but time and other ill-regulated elements that made me so bombastic about Max."

Fitzgerald had left Alabama on March 30 to be near his wife in Baltimore. In May he reported to Max, "Zelda's novel is now good. Improved in every way. It is new. She has largely eliminated the speakeasy-nights-and-our-trip-to-Paris atmosphere. You'll like it. . . . I am too close to it to judge it but it may be even better than I think." In the middle of the month, when he mailed the manuscript to Perkins for a second reading, he noted that it had the faults and virtues of any first novel.

It is more the expression of a powerful personality, like *Look Homeward, Angel,* than the work of a finished artist like Ernest Hemingway. It should interest the many thousands in dancing. It is *about something* and absolutely new, and should sell.

At first, when Scott had feared that unrestrained congratulations might encourage the incipient egomania Zelda's doctors had observed, he had written Perkins:

> If she has a success coming she must associate it with work done in a workmanlike manner for its own sake, & part of it done fatigued and un-inspired, part of it done when even to remember the original inspiration and impetus is a psychological trick. She is not twenty-one and she is not strong, and she must not try to follow the pattern of my trail which is of course blazed distinctly on her mind.

Now he felt she deserved whatever praise Max cared to give her. She had put all her effort into the book. After first refusing to revise at all, she had reworked it completely, "changing what was a rather flashy and self-justifying 'true confessions' that wasn't worthy of her into an honest piece of work."

Perkins stashed the manuscript into his scuffed briefcase for the weekend. HAD A GRAND SUNDAY READING YOUR NOVEL THINK IT VERY UNUSUAL AND AT TIMES DEEPLY MOVING PARTICULARLY DANCING PART DELIGHTED TO PUBLISH, he wired on Monday. Later that day he wrote the author of her book, "It is alive from beginning to end." Max hoped Zelda would consider some timid suggestions, mostly stylistic matters. As in her earlier short stories, she often ran astray chasing down metaphors:

> Many of them are brilliant [Perkins wrote her], but I almost think . . . that they would be more effective if less numerous. And sometimes they seem to me to be too bold and interesting because then they have the effect of concentrating attention upon them for their own sake instead of for the illumination of the things they are meant to reveal.

Zelda was thrilled. "To catalogue my various excitements and satis-faction that you liked my book would be an old story to you," she wrote Perkins. "It seems so amazing to me that you are going to actually publish it that I feel I should warn you that it's probably a very mediocre affair that will soon be as out of date as a Nineteen Four Spalding prospectus for Lawn Tennis. My God, the ink will fade, maybe you'll discover that it doesn't make sense. It couldn't be possible that I was an author." She agreed to change any "questionable parts," but Perkins found *Save Me the Waltz*, strangely enough, virtually beyond editing. The entire manuscript was honeycombed with some of the most flowery language he had ever seen. Her similes flowed naturally if not always sensibly, sometimes dozens of them on a single page. In describing the boatloads of Americans who wandered around France in the late twenties, for example, Zelda wrote:

> They ordered Veronese pastry on lawns like lace curtains at Versailles and chicken and hazlenuts at Fountainebleau where the woods wore powdered wigs. Discs of umbrellas poured over surburban terraces with the smooth round ebullience of a Chopin waltz. They sat in the distance under the lugubrious dripping elms, elms like maps of Europe, elms frayed at the end like bits of chartreuse wool, elms heavy and bunchy as sour grapes. They ordered the weather with a continental appetite, and listened to the centaur complain about the price of hoofs.

Hardly a character, emotion, or scene was not adorned with her grandiloquence. But that was the very quality that distinguished her writing, just as it enlivened her speech. For the most part, Perkins benignly neglected the problem and chose to let it appear in public as it was, to live or die on its own.

Under her husband's eye, Zelda revised the galley proofs considerably. The book was shortened, mostly by filing down the accounts of their marital jags. During the next few months proofs were shuttled around so hectically from Perkins to the author to the typesetter, to Perkins, back to the author, and back to the typesetter—that it seemed at last that everyone, exhausted, had just quit, as if to avoid another mailing. Max thought of warning the Fitzgeralds they would have to pay for the excessive corrections, but he knew they wanted the book the way they thought it should be, regardless of cost. Ultimately, countless misspellings, unclear passages, and most of the rococo language found their way into print. Impressed with the bulk of her book once it was bound, Zelda wrote Max, "I only hope it will be as satisfactory to you as it is to me."

The Fitzgeralds' marriage worked like a seesaw. In the spring of 1932, while Zelda was high with expectations for her book, Scott was feeling low. He was torn from his past but unattached to any future. "I don't know exactly what I shall do," he wrote Perkins *de profundis*. "Five years have rolled away from me and I can't decide exactly who I am, if anyone." In his relentless search for a home that might make him feel part of a permanent and grand life, the Fitzgeralds settled into La Paix, a stolidly Victorian house on some Maryland acreage belonging to a family named Turnbull. "We have a soft shady place here that's like a paintless playhouse abandoned when the family grew up," Zelda wrote Perkins. Max hoped the peaceful surroundings would compel the Fitzgeralds to live quietly. And, he wrote Hemingway, "if Zelda can only begin to make money, and she might well do it, they ought to get into a good position where Scott can write."

That year, while Scott was still down, there was a most unusual switching of roles between editor and author, the first and last in their entire correspondence. Fitzgerald had sensed that Perkins was not quite himself, almost lethargic, heavily overburdened. "For God's sake take your vacation this winter," Scott urged. "Nobody could quite ruin the house in your absence, or would dare to take any important steps. Give them a chance to see how much they depend on you & when you come back cut off an empty head or two."

Unknown to almost everyone outside the Perkins house, Max had been greatly worried about the mysterious illness of one of his daughters, Bertha. She had been in a car accident and walked away unharmed physically, but she had then blacked out for the next eighteen hours. Max was absolutely desperate about his daughter's undiagnosed condition, which induced periodic convulsions. He disclosed the situation to Scott, who time and again volunteered to discuss the case, for he had, he said, become "such a blend of the scientific and the layman's attitude on such subjects that I could be more help than anyone you could think of." Zelda was equally solicitous. She had always been drawn toward the sickest patients in the asylums she stayed in.

"I have still got a few purgatories to get through," Max wrote Zelda that June. "But a month from now I ought to be out of some of the thickest of the woods that I have been in."

Thomas Wolfe was aware of the change in Perkins too. He believed his editor "would give his life to keep or increase virtue—to save the savable, to grow the growable, to cure the curable, to keep the good. But for the thing unsavable, for life ungrowable, for the ill incurable, he had no care. Things lost in nature hold no interest for him." If his daughter could not be cured, Wolfe believed, Perkins would not have worried

much; but circumstances being what they were, Tom observed Max growing haggard-eyed and thinner, overworking himself at the office to distract
himself from grimness at home. Wolfe himself provided Perkins with
more than enough to keep his mind on editorial problems.

Wolfe had kept very much to himself for most of the last few months.
He had left his apartment on Verandah Place, where he had produced
a tremendous volume of work, for another cycle of writing at 111 Co-
lumbia Heights, also in Brooklyn. The tools of his trade remained the
same wherever he worked: pencils, paper, floor space—and a refrigerator.
Max once told a student of Wolfe's writing how all four elements were
basic to his composition:

> Mr. Wolfe writes with a pencil, in a very large hand. He once said that he
> could write the best advertisement imaginable for the Frigidaire people
> since he found it exactly the right height to write on when standing and
> with enough space for him to handle his ms. on the top. He writes mostly
> standing in that way, and frequently strides about the room when unable
> to find the right way of expressing himself.

After Wolfe's daily stint, he gathered the papers from the floor
and had them typed. Seldom did he let anyone but the typist look at them.
Perkins told Hemingway that winter that what little he had seen of Wolfe's
latest work was "as good as it could be." Unfortunately, Tom had recurring attacks of self-doubt so wracking that he could not write. "He keeps
getting all upset, and he is so now," Max wrote Ernest at the beginning
of 1932, "and I am to have an evening with him and try to make him
think he is some good again. He is good all right."

At the end of a whiny session on January 26, 1932, Tom followed
Max to Grand Central Station and was still yammering as they boarded
the Connecticut-bound train. Wolfe needed further convincing of his
abilities, so Max had encouraged him to spend the night at his house.
But as the railroad cars lurched out of their berth, Wolfe had one of his
sudden changes of heart. He had to go back to Brooklyn, to be alone, to
write. He galloped down the aisle toward an exit door and, as the platform pulled away from him, he broad-jumped to the concrete deck. The
conductor yanked the emergency brake and Perkins rushed to aid Tom,
who lay by the track with blood streaming from his left elbow. Max accompanied him to the Grand Central emergency hospital and waited

while the arm was X-rayed and stitched. "I thank God it was my left arm rather than my right," Tom wrote his sister Mabel, "since my whole chance of living at present depends more or less on my right hand."

That same month, Perkins had to minister to Wolfe's needs again, this time as peacemaker. A communiqué from the German publishers of *Look Homeward, Angel* came into Perkins's hands, which showed that Madeleine Boyd had withheld a royalty payment from Wolfe. Tom, rightfully, was furious at this and demanded his agent meet with him and Perkins at Scribners. Before their afternoon conference, Wolfe and his editor lunched, and Tom discussed strategy. He insisted that Max be present during the showdown and that he be "unrelenting." The meeting did not, however, proceed according to plan. Several years later, Max sent an account of the afternoon to Tom's friend John Terry:

> When we reached this office, Mrs. Boyd was sitting in the little library here, turning over some papers. I went in immediately, but Tom for some reason did not. She immediately began to weep. It was at the very depth of the depression, and she was hard put to it to keep going. I couldn't help but feel sorry for her, and unfortunately at the moment when Tom entered, I was patting her on the back, and saying, "Don't cry, Madeleine, everyone is in trouble today." I suddenly became aware of Tom's presence. He was towering above us, and gave me a look of utter scorn. Mrs. Boyd then tried to explain that the failure to pay over the money was due to some confusion in bank accounts which was too complicated for either Tom or myself to understand. (She has since told me that story humorously in retrospect, and I suppose it may well be true.) But anyhow Tom was through with her. And she acknowledged the fault, if not the dishonesty, and when he said, "Don't you see, Madeleine, that this must be the end," she agreed to it.

During the meeting Tom upbraided her so bitingly that Max felt compelled to restrain him.

In all their recent times together, Perkins had tried to restore Wolfe's faith in himself, while Tom's personal and editorial needs kept Max from his family worries. That season Wolfe wrote Aline Bernstein, who was still reaching out to him, "I've got my self-confidence back . . . . which I had lost completely—and I have never worked so hard in all my life. I have been pretty close to complete ruination, but I may pull out yet." With three months of concentrated effort, Tom predicted, he could give Scribners a book of 200,000 to 300,000 words which they could publish in the fall. "But if I don't finish the book this year," he wrote Aline in an effort to keep her at arm's distance, "I'm done forever—I'll never be able to work again."

In his less sanguine moments, Perkins himself feared that just might happen to Wolfe. Maintaining every expectation of publishing Wolfe's novel that autumn, he told Wolfe as an incentive that if he had enough gumption to stick with the job and deliver the goods, Perkins would take a sabbatical half-year from his desk to motor cross-country with him in a Ford. Wolfe returned to his Frigidaire with renewed determination, eager to finish his book as much for Perkins as for himself. "He is . . . terribly tired and has had a bad year," Tom wrote Aline; "—his daughter has been having fainting spells with convulsions and no one can find out what's wrong with her. Max is a grand man, the best I ever knew, and as complete an individual as ever lived."

In anguish while the finest doctors probed for cures for Bertha's illness, Perkins wrote Hemingway about his bullfight book. "I wish that manuscript would come . . . I expect to get a lot out of it that will act as a counterbalance for things that one sees on all sides." It would be another month of labor.

Hemingway, by his own admission, had "never gone better than lately." He returned from Spain in the fall of 1931 with only the "swell last chapter" and a translation of the Spanish government's *Reglamento*, the rules governing bullfighting, remaining to be done. That, he said, would conclude "one hell of a fine book." He and Pauline settled in Kansas City and awaited the arrival of their second child. In mid-November, he announced the birth of his third son, Gregory. Max wired succinct congratulations: ENVIOUS. Hemingway wrote back that he would give out his secret for producing sons if Perkins would divulge his trick for siring daughters.

By the first of February, 1932, Max had received the manuscript of *Death in the Afternoon*. Ernest had kept his "nose to book grindstone" for a long time and so he was especially anxious to hear Perkins's reactions. "It's silly just to write you that it's a grand book—but it did do me great good just to read it," Max wrote Hemingway. "I went to bed happy for it in spite of innumerable troubles (not so bad really, I guess). The book piles upon you wonderfully, and becomes to one reading it—who at first thinks bullfighting only a small matter—immensely important." Three days later, in discussing serialization in *Scribner's*, Max noted, "It gives the impression of having grown rather than of having been planned.—

And that is the characteristic of a great book." The editorial questions Perkins foresaw were those of format. He wanted the book to be big enough in size and shape to give the illustrations a real show, but he did not want to put too high a price on it. A second problem dealt with which portions of the manuscript should be excerpted for the magazine. "It's a mean business, picking articles out of a book like this," Perkins wrote Hemingway. "But from the commercial standpoint, as we call it, it will help it."

Hemingway thought they could easily handle these matters at sea. He invited Perkins to the Tortugas, telling him "To hell with signing any goddamned contracts" unless he came. This year Hemingway's ultimatum did not work. Perkins pleaded insufficient funds and time, but it was mostly a lack of spirit. "I've got more problems on my hands now than those of all the rest of my life should add up to," he explained. His daughter was sent to Boston where he heard "they have bigger and better neurologists." Her condition remained baffling. It now was taking its toll on Louise. She collapsed trying to keep up with the girl's illness and was hospitalized herself for several weeks. "Having a hard time escaping an obsession that the Gods are sniping at me personally," he wrote Ernest. "I have a weakness for obsessions, as you've guessed. . . . But it's best to get bad luck in bunches if you can stand it." He wrapped himself in work, hating even to think about missing Key West.

That spring, after Hemingway returned from the Tortugas, Perkins talked him down from 200 illustrations to sixty-four and argued about what had come to be known as "four-letter words." Ernest agreed to comply with most state statutes by blanking out two of the letters which, Max said, "certainly does make the law what Shakespeare said it was— a fool." Hemingway was upset that the book would not be the deluxe photograph album he had imagined, but John Dos Passos raised his spirits with his remarks about *Death in the Afternoon*. It was, he said, the best writing about Spain he had ever read. At Dos Passos's suggestion, Hemingway cut several pages of philosophizing. Perkins never suggested any deletions of his own; if he had, he might have improved the book further by reducing Hemingway's literary pretentiousness.

With *Death in the Afternoon* the words *cojones* and *macho* entered the Hemingway glossary and the cult of hypermasculinity had found its spokesman. Indeed, he had become self-obsessed, and the writing lacked its former control. Perkins saw through a lot of Hemingway's posturing, but he wanted to believe that beneath it pounded the heart of a truly brave

man. He admired the manliness of Hemingway's life and his prose. Zippy
Perkins remembered her father's once explaining, "Hemingway loves to
write for those of us who will never come face to face with danger."
Just as Perkins related to Fitzgerald as uncle to a pleasure-seeking but
adored nephew, his relationship to Hemingway evoked another familial
tie. For Perkins, Hemingway was the daredevil "kid brother," forever
getting into dangerous scrapes, forever being advised and cautioned by
his "big brother." There was a rough-and-ready quality to Hemingway
that reminded Perkins of his happy boyhood, and there was an insistent
virility that Perkins could not, being a "gentleman," always express in
his own life, but of which he was jealous. Again, as with Fitzgerald,
Perkins experienced Hemingway's style, so different from his own, in a
vicarious sense. He identified with Hemingway's *machismo*, but could not
live it.

While leisurely correcting his galleys, Hemingway took a sunny room
at the Ambos Mundos Hotel in Havana. Again he urged Perkins to visit
him: Max could carry back the proofs and the pictures complete with
captions, after the two of them had discussed any problems in the book.
Max said he wished he could come down but felt it would be impossible
until July. "I am more tied down though now than ever," he wrote
Hemingway, "but also with better prospects for ultimate release."

The day before Hemingway checked out of the Ambos Mundos, he
got bathed in sweat while marlin fishing, then was showered by a sudden
cold downpour. By the time he shipped out of Cuba he had a touch of
bronchial pneumonia, which he still had not recognized. He steered across
the Florida Straits with a temperature of 102 degrees. Once at home, he
took to his bed to correct his proofs. The galleys got his blood boiling.
It was standard procedure to headline each proof sheet with the author's
last name and the title's first word. A page would be headed, accordingly,
"4 Gal 80 . . 3404 Hemingway's Death 11½–14 Scotch." Hemingway
asked Perkins if it seemed funny to him to print at the top of every sheet
"Hemingway's Death." The author did not see any humor in it. He swore
that Max should have known that he was superstitious and it was a "hell
of a damn dirty business" staring at the caption over and over again.

Perkins had not seen that line of type on the proofs. "If I had I
would have known what to do with it," he assured Hemingway, "because
you cannot tell me anything about omens. I can see more than any man
on the face of the earth, and once when things were bad and I was alone
in the car and a black cat crossed the road I actually shot around the corner.

When any of my family are in the car and that happens, I tell them not to be foolish."

For months Perkins believed his life was cursed. Several authors and colleagues suggested that he had practically sleepwalked through his work that year, preoccupied as he was over his daughter's health. Perkins had been too glum even to write Elizabeth Lemmon. That June he again explained that there were times when he started letters to her but never finished them.

> The way things have been this year I could only write gloomily and I was ashamed to do that—that I couldn't face a run of bad luck without being gloomy and cowardly about it. So I always gave up before I finished a letter.

Max's trouble was that Bertha's illness so depressed him that he could not speak cheerfully of anything that year. "At other times a number of things have always been going wrong but you could always look upon *something* that was going right," he wrote Elizabeth. "But lately, everywhere I have looked, ruin threatened." If his daughter could just recover, Max believed, that would offset every other misfortune. After more than a year of infirmity, she was showing some improvement. "Her illness filled me with cold terror," he told Elizabeth. "Then Louise was in a dreadful state, not being well anyway. And with business etc. as it was, it was a mighty bad year."

That summer Arthur H. Scribner died of a heart attack, two years after assuming the presidency of the firm. His nephew Charles succeeded him, and Maxwell Perkins was named editor-in-chief and vice-president of the company. Now there were managerial responsibilities piling on top of his regular editorial concerns—that Hemingway would do something dangerous, that Fitzgerald would not write his book, that Thomas Wolfe would require increasing expenditures of energy and emotion, or that Ring Lardner's tuberculosis and sleeplessness, caused by worry over his poverty, would worsen. "What of it?" Max asked Elizabeth Lemmon. "What is life but taking a licking?" In another letter he said:

> You know that about counting your blessings doesn't do any good to one from New England. It makes it worse. The New Englander thinks his blessings are the very things that prove he is in for a bad time because justice demands that the score shall be evened up. Some days after my father died my mother said, "I knew something was going to happen," and when I asked why she said, "Everything was going too well."—and though I was only seventeen I understood perfectly."

Max wanted to believe the world would become a better place for his
five children, if it could escape a real crash. "But," he wondered, "can
it settle in time for these girls? What can they live by—by nothing that
'the former people' did."

Louise visited Elizabeth at Welbourne for a few days of rest and
asked if she would "take care of Max" when he came down later in the
summer for what became regular appointments with his otologist at Johns
Hopkins. He knew no one in Baltimore and used to wander around Druid
Hill Park alone.

Max Perkins suffered from otosclerosis, specifically, the growth of
new bone around the footplate of the stapes in the middle ear. Noises
often rang in his left ear, sounding like the chirping of birds. Today that
tiny bone can be replaced with a synthetic one, but every three months
Perkins had to have his Eustachian tube dilated by the insertion of a medi-
cated wire so that the vibrations within his ear were more distinct. In July,
1932, Max showed up for his appointment with Dr. James Bordley. It was
too hot for him to consider asking Elizabeth to meet him afterward, but
she just appeared on Saturday at the Hotel Belvedere. That afternoon, she
drove him out to Gettysburg. "It was the hottest day I've ever felt in
my life," Elizabeth recalled forty years later, "but he climbed every monument and looked at every stone wall on the battlefield. I waited for him
in the car. When we finally got back to the city our tongues were hanging
out. Max was dying for a drink, but it was tough to find one and he said,
'This is the driest city I've ever seen.'" Later he wrote her: "They were
two of the best days I ever had . . . and I shall always be grateful to you
for them. I believe a month's vacation couldn't have done me more good.
You make everything seem right and happy. . . . Thanks ever so much
Elizabeth for being so good to me. I'll never forget it."

The next day Perkins telephoned Scott, who motored into Baltimore
and drove him out to La Paix. Max found it "really a fine sort of melancholy place," that made him want to saunter around and look at the trees.
But Scott thought they ought to settle down to gin rickeys. They drew up
chairs on a small piazza and waited for a breeze to whish through the rich
foliage. Zelda drifted outside to join them, looking well—not so pretty
as she had been, but calmer than he had ever seen her. Max found more
"reality" in her talk. But he worried about them both. Under the white
light of the summer sun, Max thought, Scott's face looked weary and
tight, skull-like. Zelda brought out some grotesque sketches she had drawn.
After lunch with the Fitzgeralds, Max drove back into town with Zelda,

who had to return to the Phipps Clinic, then hopped a plane back to New York.

"Poor old Scott," Hemingway lamented after Perkins wrote him of the battle-fatigued figures he had seen at La Paix. Ernest still thought the situation was Zelda's fault. He said Fitzgerald should have swapped her when she was "at her craziest but still salable" some five or six years back, before she was diagnosed as "nutty." He also did not think Zelda's becoming a writer was the way to bring either of them back to life. Hemingway warned Perkins that if he ever published a book by any of his wives, "I'll bloody well shoot you." Because of Zelda, he said, F. Scott Fitzgerald had become the "great tragedy of talent in our bloody generation."

"If we could only fix Scott up for a clear six months we might turn that tragedy into something else," Max wrote Ernest. "And there isn't a bad chance that Zelda might not turn out to be a writer of popular books. She has some mighty bad tricks of writing, but she is now getting over the worst of them." In fact, he hoped Zelda might prove to be Scott's ace in the hole, which he needed desperately. Perkins confided to Hemingway that Scribners had advanced Scott so much money on his novel that it was impossible to see how he could pay off his debt to Scribners even if it were a great success. As it was, they arranged for half of Zelda's royalties to be applied against Scott's debt until $5,000 had been paid back.

Max had never been concerned for Fitzgerald so much as after this last visit. "If a man gets tired and has a good alabi—and Scott has in Zelda—he's likely to accept defeat," Max wrote Elizabeth Lemmon. "They've all lost faith in him too, even Ernest. I wish it could be fixed so he could *show* them!"

Save Me the Waltz was published in October, 1932. Its sales never got moving, and only a handful of reviewers praised or even constructively criticized the book. In some respects, Perkins was responsible for the book's failure on all counts. In his distraction that year, he did not give Zelda a very strong send-off. "It is not only that her publishers have not seen fit to curb an almost ludicrous lushness of writing but they have not given the book the elementary services of a literate proofreader," said the *New York Times*.

For another year, the *Saturday Evening Post* was the Fitzgeralds' prime benefactor. It published three of Scott's stories that summer; in August he sent them a fourth. The stories contributed little to his literary reputation, but after months of inaction on his serious work, he now had enough money to proceed. "The novel now plotted and planned," he entered in his Ledger, "never more to be permanently interrupted."

In a letter to Perkins, Zelda confirmed, "Scott's novel is nearing *completion*. He's been working like a streak and people who have read it say it's wonderful." She had no firsthand opinion, because in protecting their material from the other's poaching, she wrote, "We wait now till each other's stuff is copyrighted since I try to more or less absorb his technique and the range of our experience might coincide."

In January, 1933, Scott came to New York for a three-day binge. "I was about to call you up when I completely collapsed and laid in bed for 24 hours groaning," he wrote Perkins afterward. "Without a doubt the boy is getting too old for such tricks. . . . I send you this, less to write you a *Rousseau's Confession* than to let you know why I came to town without calling you, thus violating a custom of many years standing." Back at La Paix, he vowed to go on the water wagon from the first of February until the first of April. He insisted Perkins keep that from Hemingway "because he has long convinced himself that I am an incurable alcoholic, due to the fact that we almost always meet at parties. I am his alcoholic just like Ring is mine and do not want to disillusion him, though even *Post* stories must be done in a state of sobriety." Max wrote back telling him, tactfully, that Scott had in fact called him.

Because Fitzgerald was devoting more time to his novel than before, his income that year was half what it had been in the first few years of the Depression—less than $16,000. Even after moving out of La Paix into a smaller, less expensive place in town, Scott found himself having to scrimp. He asked Perkins if Zelda had any money due on her book. "She is shy about asking," Scott wrote Max, "but she could use it to contribute to her winter outfit."

The royalties would barely clothe her. *Save Me the Waltz* sold 1,380 copies, which translated into $408.30 in earnings. After subtracting for the cost of excess corrections on the proofs, as was standard, Perkins sent Zelda her check for $120.73, noting, "The result won't be encouraging to you, and I have not liked to ask whether you were writing any more because of that fact, but I do think the last part of that book, in particular, was very fine; and if we had not been in the depths of a depression, the result would have been quite different." The only Scribners books that got any show that year were by authors who had had an earlier success —as with Galsworthy's *One More River* or James Truslow Adams's *March of Democracy*—or whose authors were celebrities, like Clarence Darrow's autobiography.

Of the sales figures on *Save Me the Waltz*, Perkins wrote Fitzgerald, "That is way above the average for a first novel in that bad year, but you are used to such big numbers that it will seem mighty bad to you." Fitzgerald took the news understandingly, especially after learning that John Dos Passos's latest book, *1919*, had sold only 9,000 copies. Scott did not see how his own book was going to cover his debt to Scribners, as Dos Passos's *U.S.A.* trilogy had kept him alive in American letters better than Fitzgerald's *Post* stories had done for him. Max wrote Fitzgerald that he did not find Dos Passos's books enthralling.

> His whole theory is that books should be sociological documents, or something approaching that. I know I never have taken one of them up without feeling that I was in for three or four hours of agony only relieved by admiration of his ability. They are fascinating but they do make you suffer like the deuce, and people cannot want to do that.

"If only this world will settle down on some kind of stable basis so that a man can attend to his own affairs," Max wrote Fitzgerald, "I think that you will soon begin to do steady and consistent work. Let the basis be anything so long as it is a basis—a relatively fixed point from which a man can view things."

Eight years had passed since *The Great Gatsby*. And yet, Max wrote Scott, "Whenever any of these new writers come up who are brilliant, I always realize that you have more talent and more skill than any of them; but circumstances have prevented you from realizing upon the fact for a long time." That summer, Max contrived a plan to get Fitzgerald out of his heavy debt to Scribners by tying in serialization of his novel in the magazine.

In late September, 1933, Fitzgerald promised a complete draft of that work by the end of October. "I will appear in person carrying the manuscript and wearing a spiked helmet," he wrote Perkins. *"Please do not have a band as I do not care for music."* Right on schedule he appeared, and a startled Perkins received the first section of what was to become *Tender Is the Night*. He immediately pronounced it "wonderfully good and new." Max timed his next visit to Dr. Bordley so that he could spend the following weekend with Fitzgerald reading the rest of the novel.

Scott kept Perkins for two solid days. Max tried to read the manuscript straight through but found it still unfinished and chaotic. Every time he got involved in a section, he found that Scott was handing him a Tom Collins, as if he were trying to make the writing go down easier. Then Scott would grab a bunch of pages to read aloud to Max. There was more work to be done, but Perkins had heard enough to tell that the book would work. When he got back to his office, he put the terms of their agreement in writing—that *Scribner's*

> agreed to serialize the new novel in four numbers beginning with the January number which appears about the 20th of December, for ten thousand dollars—six of which will be applied to reduce your indebtedness to us, and four thousand of which will be paid in cash, preferably at the rate of one thousand dollars a month as each installment is delivered.

In his Ledger, Scott marked the happiest event in years: "Max accepts book in 1st draft."

Ring Lardner was now able to work at least a few hours a day, but insomnia was getting the best of him and his income still was not enough to meet expenses. In August, 1932, Perkins sent him a royalty payment that was not due until December. It was only $222.73, but Ring said it would be a "life saver; or rather a life insurance saver." That proved worth holding onto, because in a few months he was borrowing against it.

To help Lardner scrape together a few more dollars, Perkins schemed several quick and easy ways for him to get published. Ring had written a new baseball series in the form of letters, a throwback to his *You Know Me Al*, and a new radio column in *The New Yorker*. Max suggested binding them into books. That winter Lardner's doctor ordered him to go to the desert for his health, and Lardner was obliged to borrow money he had not yet earned to pay for such a trip. "Someday I will probably realize that there is a depression," he wrote Perkins. Max sent advances in $100 increments, noting that Scribners would be willing to pay royalties almost concurrent with sales, even though a large part of their business was now done on a heavy consignment basis.

Lardner went to La Quinta, California, leaving his latest story, "Poodle," in the hands of some "poor author's agent" to peddle. It was the first story Lardner ever wrote that was not accepted by one of the first two publications to which it was offered. Within months he was back in East Hampton, critically ill and receiving no visitors. Perkins hated even to inquire.

On September 25, 1933, Ring Lardner died at forty-eight, after seven years of tuberculosis, sleeplessness, fatigue, and alcoholism. Mark Twain's sentiment in "The Two Testaments"—that "when man could endure life no longer, death came and set him free"—seemed tragically apropos.

Perkins wrote to Hemingway, who in his youth had admired Lardner:

> Ring was not, strictly speaking, a great writer. He always thought of himself as a newspaperman, anyhow. He had a sort of provincial scorn of literary people. If he had written much more, he would have been a great writer perhaps, but whatever it was that prevented him from writing more was the thing that prevented him from being a great writer. But he was a great man, and one of immense latent talent.

As a final tribute to that talent, Perkins wanted to publish a volume of Ring's material, a selection from his writing by somebody qualified to choose the most representative examples. He asked Fitzgerald whom he would suggest, barely concealing his hope that Scott himself might undertake the job. Fitzgerald said it was simply impossible for him to accept such an assignment with his own novel so near completion. He nominated Gilbert Seldes, who was both a journalist and a critic.

Within two weeks Seldes was on the project. He was particularly eager to get hold of Lardner's early material and fugitive newspaper pieces written before he got to New York. After six weeks of digging through Midwestern newspaper morgues, Seldes had the book prepared. He called it *First and Last.* Seldes's guiding principle was that "every item should be 'good Lardner.'" While the book did not include the first piece Lardner ever wrote, it did contain the last. There would be nothing more of his for his readers to enjoy, because, as Seldes pointed out, Lardner "had been ill for years and left no manuscripts. For his own fame, he did not need to."

In February, 1933, Max made a visit to Bertha in Boston and found to his great relief that she was responding to psychiatric treatment. At about the same time the doctors put Louise on a new high-protein diet that miraculously restored her health, ending a year-long worry for Max. Soon he was working again with his old vigor.

XII

The Sexes

Don't you really think, taking everything into consideration," Max Perkins once slyly asked his friend and author Struthers Burt, "that women are responsible for three fourths of the trouble in the world?"

"Far from being a misogynist," Burt said later, "Max so admired the potentialities of women that he despised what most of them did with the talents entrusted to them. He thought that as a sex they were poor stewards, that given freedom they preferred slavery, and that entirely able to fight on equal terms with candor and intellect, they fell back on easier weapons of intrigue, evasion, and sex. It was not that he hated women; he liked and admired too much the vision of what they might be." More than one aspiring female author wrote him asking if it were true that he disliked women. Max dumped all such queries into Irma Wyckoff's lap to answer in his name. "Yes, I don't like women—but I love them too," she once responded for him. When Perkins read that, he told her, "That sounds more like me than I do."

During the thirties, many women brought their books and ideas to Perkins. He always maintained his distance. "I have seen more men ruined by charm than anything else," he once told his daughter Peggy. The pretty ones unnerved him most. "I am always scared," he confided to his author James Boyd, "when confronted by a charming young woman." Whatever his trepidations, they did not repel. Women writers generally found him magnetic. They perceived his sensitivity for the kinds of stories they wanted to tell; and the fact that he was an attractive but not sexually aggressive man put them at ease. Most wrote to please him, as an expression of a "safe" affection.

Marcia Davenport, daughter of the diva Alma Gluck, worked on the staff of *The New Yorker*. In 1930, at the age of twenty-seven, she began to think about writing a biography of Mozart. Anxious for a publisher's opinion, she described the book she had in mind to Eugene Saxton of Harper & Brothers, who was as close to a rival as Max Perkins had. He said that he would look at the manuscript, if she wrote it, but could not guarantee that Harpers would publish it.

Mrs. Davenport was discouraged until a friend, the poet Phelps Putnam, said he liked the idea. "The year before, Scribners had published Putnam's first book of poetry," Marcia Davenport wrote in her memoirs, *Too Strong for Fantasy,* "and Put had become one of the writers who worshipped Maxwell Perkins. He asked Max to see me and next day I found myself in the famous cluttered, dusty office sitting beside the shabby oak desk with the slithering piles of books and the rough-rider ashtray on it; and behind it the reserved, laconic man with the sensitive face and the extraordinary eyes. Max said little. His essential quality was always to say little, but by powerful empathy for writers and for books to draw out of them what they had it in them to say and to write." No editor in New York could have had less interest in Wolfgang Amadeus Mozart than Maxwell Perkins. But he sat through Mrs. Davenport's recital of reasons for wanting to do such a book, watching her as much as he listened, then said, "Go ahead and write it. We will publish it." Perkins suggested she compose a few pages for his immediate inspection. From them, he wrote critic Alice Dixon Bond years later, "we saw . . . that she had skill, and from what we saw of her that she was unconquerable and would do what she undertook." Marcia Davenport noted in her autobiography that that was "the most editorial 'we' ever used."

After a year and a half of work Marcia Davenport submitted a manuscript to Perkins. In handing it over she noticed for the first time his peculiar habit of flipping directly to the last page. "I am sure he did not know in the beginning what this meant to me," Mrs. Davenport wrote in her memoirs, "but the fact is that when I am ready to write a book, I write the ending first." This was an extension of some childhood advice her mother had given her in practicing the piano: "Finish with a bang."

Several days later Perkins sent for Mrs. Davenport. She spent nearly two hours circling the block before she found the courage to enter the building. She was sure Perkins was going to tell her pityingly that the book was not fit to publish. It took little more than a few minutes for Max to persuade her of his great enthusiasm for it. "Of course the book may fail, it may not sell," she wrote him afterward, "—but your sympathetic attitude is the one I hoped to find (and did not dare believe I would)."

Mozart was an artistic and financial success, and it was not long before Mrs. Davenport was writing a new book, a novel.

In 1928, Max Perkins had met Nancy Hale, the bright and beautiful granddaughter of Edward Everett Hale, the author of "The Man Without a Country." Only twenty years old, she was writing for *Vogue* when a friend at the magazine asked if she wanted to be introduced to Max Perkins. They met and in May, 1931, Max saw the first quarter of a novel she was writing. By the end of the summer *The Young Die Good* was complete. Perkins suggested only minor alterations, and Scribners published it the following spring. The book had a brief life. A few years later Nancy Hale won the O. Henry Prize for one of her short stories.

A second novel made no more of a splash than her first. "I thought she could write before she had written," Perkins told Elizabeth Lemmon, who knew her, "—like you Virginians think a colt could run when he could barely stand. So I watched her and got us to publish her when she couldn't sell. Now she has a great name in the magazines, but she hasn't yet sold for us. So I want to be vindicated. I'm always in that position."

Then came a third novel. By the time the editor had seen two thirds of it, he felt it to be that vindication. And then, Max wrote Elizabeth in woe, she "began having a baby."

Through letters he tried to keep Nancy Hale—then Mrs. Charles Wertenbaker—from worrying about her work:

> Writing a novel is a very hard thing to do because it covers so long a space of time, and if you get discouraged it is not a bad sign, but a good one. If you think you are not doing it well, you are thinking the way real novelists do. I never knew one who did not feel greatly discouraged at times, and some get desperate, and I have always found that to be a good symptom.

He realized it would be several more years before she would finish her book, but he willingly waited for her.

Among the writers Max Perkins respected most was Caroline Gordon. She was the wife of Allen Tate, one of the "Agrarians," who took a stand favoring a return to the artistic heritage of the old South. Minton, Balch, and Company, later absorbed by G. P. Putnam's, had already issued Tate's biographies of Stonewall Jackson and Jefferson Davis, as well as his first major book of verse, *Mr. Pope and Other Poems*. When Tate switched to Scribners in 1932, they printed books of his poetry and essays. "From then on Max and I became very good friends," Tate said, "and he was willing to publish me even though my books didn't make any money."

In 1931, Scribners brought forth *Penhally,* Caroline Gordon's first novel. It spanned three generations on a Kentucky plantation, and Perkins thought it a beautiful piece of work, without a "false note in the whole length of it." It required little editorial attention. "Any writer worth his salt didn't get much advice from Max Perkins," she said later.

It was heartbreaking for Perkins to publish good books such as *Penhally* at a time when so few customers could be lured into a bookstore. Scribners' profits had shrunk drastically. In 1929, their big year, their net earnings had been $289,309; in 1932 they netted only $40,661. He had to inform not just Caroline Gordon but all his authors that Scribners now had to be more frugal in their advances. Throughout the Depression, Max often worked himself into dramatic soliloquies about the nation's disastrous economic conditions. Malcolm Cowley told of one writer who was especially insistent on getting an advance; Max talked to her so plaintively that as he spoke she had sad visions of standing beside him in the breadline. Afterward he invited her to the Ritz for a drink. As they went past the uniformed doorman, she laid her hand on his arm and said, "Mr. Perkins, are you sure you can afford this?"

Alice Longworth was the eldest of Theodore Roosevelt's six children. From the time she was six years old she had been surrounded by politics, and she became famous for her spontaneous and unconventional reactions to Washington life. After her father had succeeded to the White House in 1901, Miss Roosevelt's sparkling wit and impromptu pranks had made her the darling of the American public. When it was revealed that her favorite color was a particular shade of gray-blue, "Alice blue" became the last word in fashion. In 1905, when the President's pretty daughter with the pert nose and big smile accompanied her father's Secretary of War, William Howard Taft, on an inspection tour of the Orient, she was received as royalty. Also making that voyage was Nicholas Longworth, a Republican congressman from Ohio. She was fifteen years younger, but American newspapers suggested a "tropical romance" between them. The next year TR gave her away at her wedding in the East Room of the White House. As both a President's daughter and, beginning in 1915, the wife of the Speaker of the House of Representatives, Mrs. Longworth became a leader in Washington's social life. Her cluttered salon on Massachusetts Avenue, at one end of Embassy Row, was the center of Washington gossip and rumor. A pillow rested on one of her sofas with her watchword boldly needlepointed: IF YOU DON'T HAVE ANYTHING GOOD TO SAY ABOUT ANYBODY, COME SIT BE- SIDE ME.

After her husband died in 1931, Alice Longworth found herself afflicted with debts. The *Ladies' Home Journal* offered to pay Mrs. Long- worth for the serialization rights to a book of reminiscences, if she could put one together. "At first I considered the proposition as nothing less than a great disaster," she recalled. "I had never written anything in my life longer than a postcard." Scribners heard about the prospective book and offered to publish it sight unseen, largely because of the bond be- tween Scribners and Theodore Roosevelt, which dated back to the 1880s when they began publishing his accounts of the Wild West and his African safaris.

Mrs. Longworth and Perkins first met in New York City at the old Ritz-Carlton Hotel. "I felt in an instant that he was a man throttled by women," she remembered. "And in all the time we worked together, I noticed that the unique Maxwell Perkins never once looked directly at me. Instead, he talked out of the side of his mouth, like this," she said, screwing her lips to the left side of her face, "as though looking at one more woman head-on would have been too painful."

Perkins found Mrs. Longworth to be an engaging conversationalist but too reticent on paper. "I felt truly sorry for poor Max," she said, "as he tried to draw things out of me. I wasn't trying to act contrary. It was just that I regarded the writing of this book as a horrible incursion into revealing things." Perkins thought Scribners had a gold mine in her if he could get her to write candidly. During their first meeting he made enough suggestions to get her through the initial work. "Try writing it as you would talk it," he urged.

Within days, Alice Longworth was so involved in her memoirs that she was composing at the typewriter. A self-proclaimed eager beaver, she soon had produced hundreds of pages of reminiscences, which she called *Crowded Hours,* and easily met her *Ladies' Home Journal* deadlines. On paper, Mrs. Longworth's words varied from stiff attempts at being literary to pointless chatter—often in the same paragraph. She had no sense of which observations were sharp and apt and which were not. After reading the first few installments in the *Journal,* Perkins wrote Elizabeth Lemmon, "I was really cold with panic."

Perkins met with Mrs. Longworth several times more, hoping he could get her to be more relaxed and revealing. "Over and over," she recollected, "he said to me, 'Can't you say anything more interesting than Mr. Taft was there?'" Perkins examined each sentence and made suggestions for almost every scene in the first chapter of *Crowded Hours.* He cautioned her to slow down and avoid the humdrum. "Make every person a character and make every action an event," he said. Occasionally Mrs. Longworth reached a significant episode she could not remember much about. Perkins advised her not to apologize for her poor memory: "Don't tell us what you don't know; tell us what you do know." Time and again he asked her to describe people and tell how she felt about them personally. As she wrote, she imagined Perkins standing over her shoulder, asking her questions.

Within five or six months, Mrs. Longworth's writing had improved. "All those 'Maxims' finally sank in," she said. What began as a bloodless work of disconnected memories took on definition and shape and even got somewhat tart. Of Coolidge she wrote, "I do wish he did not look as if he had been weaned on a pickle." After several pages on Harding and the scandals that surrounded him, she said: "Harding was not a bad man. He was just a slob."

In late October, Perkins could honestly write Elizabeth Lemmon that "we made a silk purse out of a sow's ear with Alice Longworth's book—or she did. . . . Now it's a good book. It might have been a splendid one. But we had to build up from worse than nothing." For weeks *Crowded Hours* was the best nonfiction seller everywhere. Once its success was established, Max admitted that working with the author had been interesting, though an "almighty hard job."

Marjorie Kinnan Rawlings was a pretty, moonfaced newspaper-woman with dark brows arched high over penetrating blue eyes. She was living with her husband, Charles, in Rochester, New York, where they were both active journalists. She described her experience as a Hearst "sob sister" as a "rough school, but I wouldn't have missed it. . . . You learn a lot when you must put down what people said and how they acted in great crises in their lives. And it teaches you objectivity." But she said it was "scrappy" and she was "always in a hurry and I hate hurry." Her marriage was no more satisfying than her career. In 1928 she and her husband abandoned journalism and went off to try saving their marriage by leading a simpler life. They bought a seventy-two-acre orange grove at Cross Creek outside Hawthorn, Florida, in the heart of the scrub country, and lived there and worked 4,000 trees.

"When I came to the Creek, and knew the old grove and farmhouse at once as home," she wrote years later in her book *Cross Creek,* "there was some terror, such as one feels in the first recognition of a human love, for the joining of person to place, as of person to person, is a commitment to shared sorrow, even as to shared joy."

For the first several years she tried her hand both at farming and at writing fiction. In 1931 she sent several vignettes about the Florida hammock to *Scribner's,* telling herself if they were not accepted she would give up writing altogether. Perkins read them, and on his recommendation *Scribner's* published them as "Cracker Chidlings." They took several more stories in the following months, and Max then encouraged her to plan some major piece of writing.

That fall, Mrs. Rawlings went deep into the scrub and lived for several weeks with an old woman and her moonshiner son. She came back with zestful stories about the hand-to-mouth existence just beyond the borders of civilization. "I have voluminous notes of the intimate type, for which the most prolific imagination is no substitute," she wrote Perkins upon her return. Her mind was reeling with the thousands of mental images she had absorbed. In sorting them out she saw that moonshining would necessarily become the connecting thread of her book. She later wrote:

> These people are lawless by an anomaly. They are living an entirely natural, and very hard life, disturbing no one. Civilization has no concern with them, except to buy their excellent corn liquor and to hunt, in season, across their territory with an alarming abandon. Yet almost everything they do is illegal. And everything they do is necessary to sustain life in that place. The old clearings have been farmed out and will not "make" good crops any more. The big timber is gone. The trapping is poor. They 'shine because 'shining is the only business they know that can be carried on in the country they know, and would be unwilling to leave.

The next year Marjorie Rawlings presented her editor with the manuscript of a true-to-life novel entitled *South Moon Under*. The title was a local expression for the time of year when the people "felt" the moon under the earth.

"Marjorie had a heart as big as the Big Scrub she wrote about," Marcia Davenport said in *Too Strong for Fantasy*. "She was intensely American in the rooted, regional earthy sense that I am not. She had a rowdy, bellowing love of laughter, a passionate tenderness for animals, illimitable hospitality, she was a superb cook, and she loved to eat and drink." Max felt easy with her and always enjoyed her newsy and opinionated hand-written letters.

Like Hemingway, Mrs. Rawlings peppered her writing with off-color language. She told Perkins that her husband had read the manuscript of *South Moon Under* and suggested that all the "four-letter words" be cut, so that it might become a boys' book as well as a regular trade novel. Perkins concurred: "There is no doubt that Hemingway has sacrificed thousands in his sales by the use of what we have come to call the 'four letter words' and I do not think he need have done it. The truth is that words that are objected to have a suggestive power for the reader which is quite other than that which they have to those who use them; and therefore they are not right artistically. They should have exactly that meaning and implication which they have when uttered. But they have an altogether different one when they strike unaccustomed ears and eyes."

By the beginning of 1933 *South Moon Under* was out of Mrs. Rawlings's hands and the mild profanities were still in the book. Max Perkins submitted the novel to the Book-of-the-Month Club, and they accepted it for the spring. "I think, really, you are taking the most beautiful care of me," she wrote Perkins. "As far as I was concerned, I had washed my hands of *South Moon Under*. The book doesn't suit me at all, but I had done the best I could for the moment, and I had the feeling that it was your affliction now, not mine." When Perkins wrote again to urge her to do a new novel, she replied, "I had the guilty thought that if Scribners lost every cent they had invested in my first book, you'd never want to see me again, to say nothing of talking about another novel."

Mrs. Rawlings's forecast of success was not far off the mark. Ironically, *South Moon Under*'s biggest break hurt its sales. The book club's scheduling delayed its appearance until that very day in 1933 when President Roosevelt ordered all the banks to close for a holiday. The company sold 10,000 copies of a book that Max felt should have sold 100,000.

In the weeks that followed, Perkins and Rawlings exchanged letters full of ideas for new books. In fact, she had another novel in mind, one in which an Englishman visited the cracker country. Perkins did not especially like the sound of that one. He kept thinking about the boy Lant in *South Moon Under* and wrote:

> I was simply going to suggest that you do a book about a child in the scrub, which would be designed for what we have come to call younger readers. You remember your husband spoke of how excellent parts of *South Moon Under* were for boys. It was true. If you wrote about a child's life, either a girl or a boy, or both, it would certainly be a fine publication.

Mrs. Rawlings liked the idea but had begun her English novel and was reluctant to leave it. She was also afraid of not being able to surpass *South Moon Under*. "You do have to do what you want to do in writing," Perkins wrote her, "but if you could put off the novel (and it would be growing in your consciousness all the time) for a long enough time to do this, I think it would be the better course." He volunteered to read any fragments of the new work as she might complete them, adding, "You must not let my Yankee reticence ever make you feel that there is any [other] book in which I should be so interested."

He was in truth more interested in the juvenile, but he admitted that it could incubate in her consciousness just as well as the book about the Englishman. Over the next few years he made periodic suggestions about the book in his letters, as its theme became clearer and clearer in his own mind, and he often urged her to begin it. "A book about a boy and the life of the scrub is the thing we want. . . . It is those wonderful river trips, and the hunting, and the dogs and the guns, and the companionship of simple people who care about the same things which were included in *South Moon Under* that we are thinking about. It is all simple, not complicated—don't let anything make it complicated to you." Mrs. Rawlings read that particular letter again and again, particularly the part in which he said he already associated the unstarted work with such books as *Huckleberry Finn*, Kipling's *Kim*, David Crockett's memoirs, *Treasure Island*, and *The Hoosier School Boy*: "All of these books are primarily *for boys*. All of them are read by men, and they are the favorite books of some men. The truth is the best part of a man is a boy." "Do you realize," she asked her editor, "how calmly you sit in your office and tell me to write a *classic?*"

After the better part of a year Perkins received the manuscript for the English novel, called *Golden Apples,* the book she could not bring herself to abandon. Perkins was not impressed, but he realized she had to finish it before she could properly approach the next book. And so he helped it along to completion and uneventful publication. Marjorie Rawlings was still resisting the happy fate, the colossal success, that Max was pushing her toward.

Ernest Hemingway warned Perkins not to become so engrossed with his women writers that he would fail to see the differences between their books and his. He said *Death in the Afternoon* would sell plenty too, if it were advertised like hell; but if Perkins got "spooked" the book would naturally flop in such hard times.

The book business was in a worse state than Hemingway knew. Many of the retail bookstores, including the three largest in New York, were on the verge of closing. None would reorder even a single copy of a book without the certainty of selling it.

Death in the Afternoon was published in September, 1932, and sales started off well. The reviews were good from the publishers' standpoint, but Max knew that there were remarks in them that Ernest would hate. Critic Edward Weeks enjoyed the book, but wrote in the *Atlantic* Bookshelf, "I dislike the deliberate circumlocution of his style. I am bored as much as amused by his sexual license, and I resent his occasional pose as 'the hard guy' in literature." The *Times Literary Supplement* reviewer stated: "His prose style is irritating, his supercharged 'he-mannishness' is brutal and infuriating." Few of the reviews were that discriminating in their criticism. Most brushed the book aside as fairly unimportant. Perkins explained to Ernest that in economizing, newspapers were assigning all their reviews to their salaried staff instead of to qualified book reviewers.

Hemingway traveled from Wyoming to Key West, then joined Pauline and his three sons in Arkansas. By then, *Death in the Afternoon* had frozen at 15,000 copies. Sales began to drop off about two weeks into October, an entire month sooner than the usual seasonal decline. Perkins believed the immediate future was all a question of what happened after Thanksgiving. The presidential election was approaching, and Franklin D. Roosevelt's victory seemed inevitable. "You know it is my opinion that if Roosevelt gets elected we shall have a woman President," Max

wrote V. F. Calverton, the left-wing editor of *Modern Monthly* and author of several books for Scribners. "I have met Mrs. Roosevelt, and I
think poor easy-going Franklin is ridden with both whip and spur."
Perkins voted against Hoover.

In the middle of December, 1932, Hemingway invited Perkins to
Arkansas, where they would live for a week on a rented houseboat and
shoot ducks. All Max had to put in his duffel bag was some warm clothes.
Ernest guessed that Max's lady writers and gaggle of girls at home would
squawk at his leaving, but he thought his editor needed to get away.
He promised the sort of shooting their great-grandfathers once had, and
that if Perkins did not have the time of his life, he would wheelbarrow
him all the way back to New York.

Max met Ernest in Memphis during a cold snap, then traveled five
more hours with him, half by train, the rest by car. That first night, on
their houseboat, Max stripped down to a pair of longjohns and crawled
into bed. Early the next morning, in the pitch dark, Ernest awakened
him, and they headed up the ice-caked river and found a blind. All that
sunless morning and for five mornings afterward they crouched there in
the snow, loading and firing and watching the birds fall. In the afternoons
they tracked through forests all silvery with ice. They also went aboard
several houseboats to buy corn whiskey and to talk with men who had
lived all their lives on that river. One afternoon, at dusk, Max and Ernest
heard a terrific racket around the bend. An old-time Mississippi steamboat
with large sidewheels and two parallel funnels pouring out wood smoke
thrashed toward them. "To Hemingway this was a commonplace," Max
wrote years later to an author, Ann Chidester, "but to a Vermont Yankee
it was like going back eighty or ninety years and coming into Mark Twain's
world."

Together Max and Ernest shot a few dozen ducks, though not nearly
so many as Hemingway said they should have. Max was more interested
in the company than the game anyway. They talked a lot about what
Ernest might work on next. Max said he looked forward to the day when
Ernest would write a book about Key West and the fishing there, a work
"full of incidents about people and about weather and the way things
looked and all that." In the evenings after dinner the men warmed themselves with highballs, and Max listened while Ernest took shots at some
of his other writers.

He professed to be "simply wild" about Thomas Wolfe's writing
and said he wanted to meet the man he called Perkins's "world genius,"

though he was afraid that their conflicting natures would set them off once they met. Max and Ernest also talked a great deal about the Fitzgeralds. Ernest had picked up Zelda's novel but found it "completely and absolutely unreadable." Scott, he believed, had gone in for the cheap "Irish love of defeat, betrayal of himself." So far as Hemingway could see, only two things could make a writer of Scott Fitzgerald again: Zelda's death, "which might put a term to things in his mind"; or for his stomach to give out, so that he could never drink again. Despite Hemingway's tough talk, these nighttime hours alone with him by the fire were for Max the best part of the trip.

Once Max started to enjoy himself, he got anxious to go home. Ernest explained to Charles Scribner years later that Max had that "awful puritanical thing" that made him give up anything as soon as he had fun doing it.

Weeks after Perkins left Arkansas, Hemingway announced that he was coming to New York. Thomas Wolfe was in Brooklyn Heights, and so Max arranged for Scribners' two mightiest novelists to meet. He knew that no two writers were farther apart in style and method, but he thought Wolfe could benefit from an informal seminar with Ernest. "I brought it about," Perkins later told Wolfe's friend John Terry, "because I hoped Hem would be able to influence Tom to overcome his faults in writing, even though they were the defects of his qualities, such as his tendency to repetitions and excessive expression." Max took them to lunch at Cherio's on Fifty-third Street. At a large round table he sat between the two of them and said little. For the most part he let Hemingway hold forth on writing, and Tom sat there in rapt attention. One of the helpful tips Ernest passed on was always "to break off work when you 'are going good.'—Then you can rest easily and on the next day easily resume." "[Hemingway] *can* be blunt," Perkins wrote John Terry, "but he can also be more gentle in speech than anyone I know. He wanted to help Tom, and everything went well, except I think Tom was not in the least affected."

Hemingway continued to express admiration for Wolfe, mostly out of respect for Perkins, but he really had no patience for such "literary writers." When he was told of an author who could not get on with his work until he found the right place in which to create, Hemingway insisted there was only one place for a man to write—in his head. He thought of Tom as something like a born but undisciplined fighter: the "Primo Carnera of writers," he called him. He told Perkins that Wolfe had that quality endemic to all geniuses—he was like a great child. But such people, he wrote Perkins, were a "hell of a responsibility." Hemingway believed Wolfe had a magnificent talent and a delicate spirit, but he knew that Perkins was doing a lot of the author's thinking for him. He cautioned Perkins never to lose Tom's confidence, for the author's sake.

The June, 1933, number of the *New Republic* carried a late review of *Death in the Afternoon* by Max Eastman, an erstwhile friend of Hemingway and the author of several books for Scribners, including *The Enjoyment of Poetry*. It was an attack entitled "Bull in the Afternoon." It taunted Hemingway for "juvenile romantic gushing and sentimentalizing of simple facts." "Hemingway is a full-sized man," wrote Eastman, but he "lacks the serene confidence that he is a full-sized man.

> Most of us too delicately organized babies who grow up to be artists suffer at times from that small inward doubt. But some circumstance seems to have laid upon Hemingway a continual sense of the obligation to pour forth evidences of red-blooded masculinity. It must be obvious not only in the swing of the big shoulders and the clothes he puts on, but in the stride of his prose style and the emotions he permits to come to the surface of things.

Eastman charged that Hemingway had slung "an unconscionable quantity of bull" and helped beget a literary style "that was comparable to wearing false hair on the chest."

Hemingway, enraged, construed the review as impugning his sexual potency. He wrote a hotheaded letter to the *New Republic* asking them to "have Mr. Max Eastman elaborate his nostalgic speculations on my sexual incapacity." He let off more steam writing Perkins that if Eastman ever got a solvent publisher to print that "libel" between covers it would cost them plenty of money and Eastman would have to serve time in jail for it. Legal retaliation and financial remuneration were secondary. He swore to his editor that if he ever saw Max Eastman anywhere he would get redress in his own fashion.

Still infuriated, Hemingway admitted to Perkins that he was tempted never to publish another damned thing, because the droves of critical "swine" simply were not worth writing for. He found every phase of that "whole racket" as disgusting as vomit. Ernest insisted that every word he had written about the Spanish fighting bull was absolutely true, the result of careful observation, and he was irate that someone would pay Eastman, who knew nothing about it, to say that Hemingway wrote sentimental nonsense, as though the critic really knew what bulls were like. What they could not get over, he told Perkins, was that Ernest Hemingway was a man, that he could "beat the shit" out of any of them, and, most upsetting, that he could write.

Perkins assured Hemingway that the Eastman article could do no harm. "The reality," he said, "is in the quality of what you write and cannot be hurt by anybody, or only momentarily." Before Hemingway departed for Spain, where he and bullfighter Sidney Franklin were producing a motion picture of *Death in the Afternoon*, Max Eastman apologized in what Hemingway called a "kissass letter" for the misunderstanding between them; he denied any personal slurs in his review. Hemingway was not mollified.

Perhaps the contest between writer and critics inspired his choice of title for his new collection of stories: *Winner Take Nothing*. Hemingway sent it off to Perkins with a brief parable, whose moral was never to lose confidence in old Papa. If at the end of the first hour the fish was killing him, at the end of two hours Hemingway would always kill the fish. THINK TITLE EXCELLENT, Perkins wired, AND YOU ARE ABSOLUTELY INVULNERABLE TO EASTMAN AND OTHERS.

Another "other" appeared that summer. Gertrude Stein's memoirs, masquerading as *The Autobiography of Alice B. Toklas*, were being serialized in the *Atlantic Monthly*. In them she got in a few licks at several of her former friends. Like Max Eastman's, her criticism fused Hemingway the man with his writing. Stein stated that she and Sherwood Anderson had in effect created Hemingway and "were both a little proud and a little ashamed of the work of their minds." Then she questioned Ernest's strength and endurance. Hemingway railed at her public betrayal of him and deplored the loss of "poor old Gertrude Stein's" judgment. He told Perkins that he had always been completely loyal to Miss Stein until she practically threw him out of her house. Then she reached menopause, went "gaga," took up with a "fourth-rate lot of fairies," and her entire sense of taste went "phtt." That alleged deterioration made it easier for Ernest to tolerate some of the "fine apocryphal incidents" she invented about him. Now, he said, he only felt sorry for her, because she had written a "damned pitiful book." He resolved to write good memoirs someday because he was jealous of nobody and had a steel-trap memory.

Perkins had also been reading Gertrude Stein's articles and thought it was too bad she ever did such a book. He said it "blew her up." It showed the high priestess to be a "petty character . . . and a petty character cannot amount to much. She had this great reputation, and now she exploded it. What's more, I think there must have been contemptible malice in what she said about you," Max wrote Ernest. "And mighty female malice too, which is the worst kind. The whole show seemed to me a poor affair."

Hemingway professed indifference, but "poor old Stein's" and Max Eastman's insults blackened his mood and kindled his wrath. The Hemingways were about to embark on a voyage from Key West. The proofs of *Winner Take Nothing* had not arrived—but some of Max's suggestions had. Hemingway was furious. He said this happened to be a time when he would have appreciated a little loyalty, but if Perkins felt that Scribners regretted the few thousand dollars he had been advanced, he would be glad to return it all and call their publishing arrangement off. He told Max that would be very shortsighted, though, because contrary to what Max Eastman said, Hemingway was not "washed up." He had a good third of a novel done, better than any of the "poor twirps" that Perkins published would ever come within "100 leagues of doing."

Perkins regretted that the proofs were not delivered on time but took exception to the rest of Hemingway's comments. Two weeks later Hemingway apologized for his crabby letter. As a peace offering, he agreed not to spell out the Anglo-Saxonisms in *Winner Take Nothing*, even though he was still on the warpath against the "genteel tradition."

After a year at sixes and sevens, which included a false start on a Gulf Stream novel, Hemingway began several months of travels. He went to Cuba and Spain, both of which were in political turmoil, then arrived in Paris. There he received Perkins's first report of *Winner Take Nothing*'s progress. The anthology's initial sale was a sound 9,000 copies, and Scribners was receiving reorders by telegraph for the first time in two years. But Perkins found the reviews "absolutely enraging."

It had become open season on Ernest Hemingway. Even though the book contained finely crafted stories such as "After the Storm," "A Clean Well-Lighted Place," and "A Way You'll Never Be," many critics condemned his factual accounts as imaginary; others dismissed the imaginary ones as mere reportage. In November, 1933, Hemingway put all the maddening criticisms behind him. The voyage he had dreamed of for years—and which Perkins had repeatedly suggested wiping from his mind because of the danger—was about to become a reality. Hemingway left for the green hills of Africa.

By January, 1934, he had reached Tanganyika. After years in Europe, the Gulf Stream, and the remotest corners of America, Ernest felt he had seen a lot of the world, but this, he wrote Perkins almost upon arrival, was the most spectacular country he had ever set foot in. Africa was full of so many actual wonders that he talked of settling there.

During a hunting expedition, he came down with amebic dysentery. He would not let it keep him from the big game, so he staggered around with it for two weeks, hunting every day but two. A few days later, after passing several pints of blood, he was carried by stretcher to a bush plane and flown to Nairobi. It was a bumpy trip of 700 miles, but the snow-capped dome of Kilimanjaro reigning mightily in the distance, looking vast enough to shoulder the heavens, was an unforgettable sight. Within days Ernest rejoined his safari at the Ngorongoro Crater to hunt rhinoceros, sable antelope, and the elusive kudu. He trekked across Africa for several more weeks, in utter awe, already wondering how to get it down on paper.

In January, 1933, after Hemingway had left Perkins and Wolfe at their lunch together, Max suggested that Tom accompany him to Baltimore when he went to visit the ear doctor. Wolfe agreed to come. On the way back he told Perkins about a story he had written. It made Perkins realize that Wolfe had a whole ragbag of manuscripts at home, dozens of remnants. Max said, "For Heaven's sake bring it in, and let us publish it." There followed the usual series of procrastinations, but eventually Wolfe did turn up with about 60,000 words of his very best sort of writing. It was extremely "dithyrambic," with little dialogue and direct narrative, but the whole thing was definitely a unit.

Then Perkins had another, even more startling perception. He thought back on the other fragments he had already read from Wolfe's library of manuscripts, and he saw how they dovetailed; he realized that they could be made to complete the gigantic manuscript Wolfe was working on. After assembling the pieces in his mind, Perkins called Wolfe and said, "All you have to do is close your hand, and you have your novel."

They spent hours talking about it. Tom kept breaking loose into excursions from the main idea, but Perkins got him to promise that he would put the book together on the lines he suggested. Wolfe delivered the pages as scheduled and Perkins did not even wait for the weekend. "I have always enjoyed reading what you have done, and working in connection with it," he explained to Wolfe before tearing into the pages. "It is a thing that does not happen to publishers often."

Perkins was dead set upon getting Thomas Wolfe's book out that fall. He knew it would mean an immense amount of work through the first half of the summer, but as an Evarts, that was what he prided himself on doing.

But the flow had hardly begun. In mid-April, 1933, Wolfe appeared and dropped onto his editor's desk some 300,000 words of manuscript, considerable sections of which Max had seen before. The editor already had in hand some 150,000 words, but Perkins accepted the new pages with open arms, still believing the final version of the book was practically a reality. He was delighted to find that this new book had half a dozen chapters in it that were beyond anything in *Look Homeward, Angel*. While the manuscript was still mushrooming but getting no nearer to completion, Perkins wrote Elizabeth Lemmon, "I'm meditating a plot to get it and him off into the country for a month with me. It will be an agonizing month though." But the month never happened.

Max knew he had to get his hands on all of Wolfe's pages. He first tried to persuade Tom, who needed money, that certain portions of his material were suitable for magazine publication as long short stories, but Wolfe hesitated. Sending some of the manuscript to the printer implied finality. With John Hall Wheelock's assistance, Max made Wolfe understand that the only way he could be regarded as an author was to have material put before the public. In February, 1933, when Tom had "just $7.00 left in all the world," he pulled "No Door" out of his raw manuscript, and it appeared as a neatly spun short story in the July *Scribner's*.

Perkins had another persuasive argument. He said that he could not do a proper job on the book without seeing its largest sections beforehand. Wolfe still had, for example, a major section entitled "The Hills Beyond Pentland." Max begged:

> Why don't you give me the section . . . and let me read it, and so get familiar with that? Because when we begin to get the book ready for the printer, you will probably want me also to understand it fully all around. And it is a big book, and not easy to grasp. I wish you would give me that section and let me read it and say nothing about it.

Wolfe began to submit to Max's pressure. There was a great deal more writing to be done, but days later, Wolfe moved "The Hills Beyond Pentland" into Max's office.

A. S. Frere-Reeves of William Heinemann, Ltd., in London, Wolfe's

British publisher, was hounding Perkins regularly by mail for another book by Wolfe. He reminded Max, "We did so well with *Look Home-ward, Angel*, but marching time draws on, and the public memory is pain-fully short." Six months later he added, "I am very anxious indeed to keep Thomas Wolfe going as a property over here," and he suggested getting together a volume of Wolfe's stories, especially those which had been appearing in *Scribner's*. In the fifteen months since the spring of 1932, five had been printed, amounting to over 100,000 words. (*Scribner's* awarded one of them, "A Portrait of Bascom Hawke," $2,500 as co-winner of their short novel contest in 1932.) Max thought another, "The Web of Earth," had "perfect form for all its intricacy," despite the popular critical objection that Wolfe was incapable of giving his writing a frame-work. Perkins had said to him, "Not one word of this should be changed."

Perkins was sorry he had not arranged to publish a book of stories earlier, but both Tom and the Scribners sales department had opposed it. For various reasons, Perkins did not think one could be prepared now. There was nothing to do but wait for the author to finish writing the book. "The trouble with Tom," Perkins explained to Frere-Reeves, "is not that he does not work, for he does, like a dog. It is that everything grows and grows under his hands, and he cannot seem to control that."

Perkins told Elizabeth Lemmon that it was the completion of Scott Fitzgerald's book and the success of Alice Longworth's which fortified him enough to fight it out with Tom. He arranged his appointments so that the two of them could meet alone daily and review the material. Of late, Perkins was having to wait for more than just pages; he often had to wait for the author. Perkins knew that Tom drank heavily only when he was brooding. Aline Bernstein's continued attempts to cling to Tom and Wolfe's failure to let go of her were driving him to gin. While Max had once wished for punctuality, now he hoped that Wolfe had not gotten drunk before their meeting and that he would remember to show up . . . and if he did, that he would be sober enough to talk coherently about his writing.

On Wolfe's birthday, October 3, 1933, he wrote furiously in his note-book: "I am 33 years old and I have nothing left, but I can begin again." In that new life, he resolved, there was no place for Mrs. Bernstein. "Aline, the time for your helping me is past," he put down in the middle of an unsent letter. "There is nothing you have now that I want." With-out receiving the page on which he spelled it out, she already knew she had been thoroughly replaced, in Wolfe's mind, by the man she had grown to resent during the last five years. Tom had written: "There is just one person in the world today who believes I will ever come to anything. That person is Maxwell Perkins, but that man's belief means more to me now than anything on earth, and the knowledge that I have it far outweighs the disbelief of everyone else." Wolfe would allow himself to be possessed by Aline no longer. More resolutely than ever he wanted to possess Maxwell Perkins.

In the early summer of 1933 Bertha Perkins, who had just finished her third year at Smith College, told her father she was bringing home her fiancé, a second-year Harvard medical student named John Frothingham. Max was happy for his daughter but grouched whenever he talked about her engagement. "Here Bert was, really getting good in philosophy and history!" he wrote Elizabeth Lemmon. On the morning of the wedding Max went into his daughter's room and told her, "You don't have to go through with this, Duck. It's still not too late." Just a few hours later, he gave her away in the living room of the New Canaan house.

Soon another upheaval changed Perkins's life. Louise, who longed for the gaiety of the city, had persuaded her husband that they should move into her father's former home in Turtle Bay, at 246 East Forty-ninth Street. Max agreed to relocate chiefly for his daughters' education, because he realized that they were not getting first-rate instruction in the New Canaan schools. After all, he wrote Elizabeth, "we want to give these girls an education—so they can cook etc. for medical student husbands etc." Max had expected he would not be living in Manhattan until the winter, but Louise began the moving just a few weeks later. His new home was only a short walk to Scribners. He no longer had to make the long commutation on the 8:02 out of New Canaan (which he always caught with just seconds to spare), but he did not alter the time of his arrival at the office. It had always been nine-thirty, and nine-thirty it remained.

Max began his business day by removing his coat, but not his hat, and sitting at his desk to read correspondence, dictate letters to Miss Wyckoff, and receive callers. Upon taking his chair he instinctively dropped his right hand into his coat pocket, fished around, and withdrew one cigarette from a pack of "Lucky Strikes." (As the years passed he switched to "Camels" and eventually was smoking two packs a day.) The morning concluded with informal editorial conferences, the most important of them with Charles Scribner. Max's contemporary, Scribner was a reserved man, with neatly parted flaxen hair, who was much more aggressive when dressed in his hunting pinks in Far Hills, New Jersey, where he rode to hounds, than in the office. He ran his business with courtly kindness, in close relation to his editor-in-chief. Scribner's secretary, Betty Youngstrom, observed, "There was a mystical kind of telepathy between him and Mr. Perkins. They had an understanding that went beyond business or friendship. Neither of them had to say much and yet they always completely understood each other." At some point in the morning, one would go into the other's office, and Perkins would start describing some book being considered by the company. "Scribner was not especially literary, but he did have a feeling for what could sell," said John Hall Wheelock. "He would sit with his elbows braced into his knees, bend his head down as he listened —always looking as though he expected to be bored. No matter what Max said, Scribner nodded. If the report had been favorable, Scribner would say, 'Go ahead with the book.'"

Sometime after 12:30, usually closer to 1:00, Perkins would leave his office, walk north four and a half blocks to Fifty-third Street, and march east until he reached his favorite restaurant, Cherio's, at Number 46. Once inside the door, he would greet the proprietor, Romolo Cherio, a small, dark, and slight Italian, then descend one flight to the downstairs dining room, where to the immediate left was a round table for six. A "Reserved" sign and a special mill of cayenne pepper never left the tabletop. No one sat there except at the invitation of Maxwell Perkins. It was seldom filled, but there was always a writer or agent or daughter there to join him. The novelist Struthers Burt, who was one of Max's authors, wrote:

> He was not given to explanations. One of the most curious things I ever saw him do, and I saw him do a good many—was on a day when we had gone as usual to Cherio's for luncheon. To my surprise as we entered the downstairs dining room I saw two comely young women sitting at the forbidden table. Without a word Max brushed past and went straight to the bar, where we had the two cocktails with which we always celebrated our reunions. "There are people at my table," Max murmured out of the corner of his mouth. Then he led me back to the table and introduced me to the two trespassers. They were his oldest and next oldest daughters, two of the five Misses Perkins.

After Prohibition, Perkins always sipped a martini at lunch, sometimes two. His menu was nearly invariable. When he found a dish that pleased him, he ordered it one day after the next, until the waiters knew to bring it without having to be told. Creamed chicken was one longtime favorite, until he tasted the roast breast of guinea hen. Perkins deviated from the guinea hen only on the occasions when Cherio himself sent another entree to the table. If Max had not started eating the new dish by the time the waiter had made his rounds, it was swept away and replaced with the guinea hen.

After leaving Cherio's, Max would buy an afternoon newspaper at the corner, glance at the headlines, and tuck it under his arm as he proceeded down Madison Avenue. By two-thirty he was back in his office, reading manuscripts or seeing visitors, until sometime between four-thirty and five, when, in the days when he still commuted, he left for his last and longest conference of the day. This was "tea," usually held at the Ritz Bar, en route to Grand Central Terminal. The location allowed him to catch the 6:02 back to New Canaan, again with seconds to spare. Other commuters tended to suspect that they held the train for Perkins, but it was not true. The gateman, however, was known to look up and down the station if Perkins had not left his conference on time, and he would often wait as long as the crucial half-minute before closing the gate.

Robert Ryan, who was a newspaperman before becoming a successful actor, used to ride the same train. He recalled, "After several weeks I was intrigued by this guy. I think he always sat in the same corner seat of the train. He never took his hat off, you know. This will sound crazy, but one night I went all the way to Connecticut without taking my eyes off him. It was fascinating. The rest of the world was just a blur to him. He plopped down without even looking around, then reached into his briefcase. For the next hour he just read. I noticed that he moved his lips when he read. He always looked a little lost. I guess he was just living vicariously through some writer's work. And there I was almost doing the same thing, just watching him. I never approached the man. God, I never dared speak to him. Nobody did. Everybody noticed him, though he didn't notice us; but nobody wanted to bother him. You were afraid you might throw some poor writer's career in jeopardy."

After more than twenty years of marriage, Louise figured if living in New York could not arouse Max, it would at least provide enough cultural activity to satisfy her. And she was closer to the theater. She still dabbled with the notion of acting: She rehearsed roles and went out to audition. A producer came to the house one day to discuss a role for a woman as young as Louise looked. When he saw several nearly grown girls about, she told him, "Oh, these are my husband's children from his first marriage." Elizabeth Lemmon remembered that another producer, who had seen Louise in an amateur theatrical, had held up his production of *Rain* for six months, hoping to persuade her to play Miss Sadie Thompson. Louise could have used her husband's tacit disapproval as a reason to bow out, but instead said it was because of her daughters— "Nancy likes me to read to her at night." Afterward, Louise wailed to Elizabeth, "Oh, if the Lord had only given me one inch of backbone, I'd take the part," a remark that suggested that her own lack of confidence, more than Max, kept her from an acting career. "God," Elizabeth Lemmon said many years later, "she could have taken the part if she really wanted it. Max wouldn't have divorced her."

One evening Max, finally settled in but not happy about living in New York, was looking down to the end of the dining room from his place at the head of the table, gazing at the statue that he and Louise had bought just after their marriage.

"The old Venus looks fine," he said.

"Thank you, Max!" Louise came back, right on cue.

They quarreled often. They were each strong-willed and independent. Several times a week, she would quibble with something he had said. It would go on from there, and eventually Max, no longer listening, would flop into his armchair and start his reading for the evening.

Louise occasionally came by his office during the day. Once she found him standing at his desk-lectern, wearing his hat as he read. "Why are you wearing your hat in the office, Max?" she asked, knowing that he would not offer her the standard explanation he used on unwelcome visitors—that he was on his way out.

"Just for fun," he said sheepishly.

"If wearing an old fedora is all the fun there is around this place," she replied, "I'm sorry for you."

Max still had considerable respect for Louise's judgment in artistic matters. He seldom showed manuscripts to anyone outside the office, but he readily entrusted them to Louise. When Fitzgerald sent his new novel in, Perkins rushed home with it for Louise's opinion, hoping she would share his enthusiasm.

"Louise sometimes seems surprisingly wise," Max wrote Elizabeth Lemmon, "but about the way the world is, she knows nothing." Elizabeth saw Louise throughout the Thirties and believed as much. She said, "Louise was the vaguest human being in the world. And when it came to money, she had absolutely no understanding. One day she had no money in her purse—not a cent—only a check for $1,500." Another time, they were on a crowded train and she said, "Elizabeth, don't you just hate bonds? Daddy gave me a stock that would pay an extra dividend of $4,000. And Max is so extravagant. He spent it all on bonds. Bonds! They're just pieces of paper with railroads on it."

Louise's father had died in 1931 in the Canary Islands. Although he had left Louise and her sister a large inheritance, the Perkinses continued to live on Max's salary. Any money he did not earn he did not consider his. He said it belonged to his children's future. Max loathed managing the Saunders estate, but he toiled hard at it. Herman Scheying, who handled the Saunders-Perkins account, thought Max's philosophy toward investing was that of a hardscrabble farmer who had experienced a cold winter: "Max believed if he didn't store something away he would not have it later. He took few chances. He was shrewd." He didn't believe in buying for rises. ("I think it's immoral," he once wrote Elizabeth of the practice. "I think you ought to lose by it.") He never touched the principal, sold losing stocks early, and reinvested two thirds of his profits instead of spending them. To the amazement of Wall Streeters he knew, Max Perkins made substantial gains in the stock market during the worst months of the Depression.

Max had sleepless nights worrying about Louise's inheritance, more money than he knew what to do with. But there is, at least, one story that indicates that the task of fiscal management didn't inevitably spoil his mood. "One day," Irma Wyckoff recalled, "Mr. and Mrs. Perkins had to go downtown to a bank for some business involving her father's estate. When he returned to the office he looked at me as if he were in a dream and said, 'Miss Wyckoff, you should have seen Louise today. She bloomed like a rose in the concrete jungle of Wall Street.'"

Louise's was not the only bloom that attracted Max. He enjoyed looking at beautiful women. The Perkinses had a maid who was very pretty, and he liked to follow her with his eyes as she went around the table serving, staring straight up at her when she came near him—only to burlesque her reaction later to amuse his girls. Women, in turn, were often attracted to Max. "Mademoiselle," the governess, was forever flirting with him, to the disgust of his daughters, and there were always women at Scribners trying to get close to him ostensibly in the hope of advancing themselves. One secretary even offered to work for him for no pay, just to be near him. Struthers Burt confirmed that Max was very attractive to women, "although he behaved as if totally unaware of this and gave them no leeway."

Max cared little for the nonliterary arts—there was something almost effeminate about them, a delicacy that was at odds with his Evarts up-bringing. He did appreciate classical sculpture, and he said every young boy should have a picture of the masculine *Thinker* by Michelangelo from the Medici tombs. (Even though he had only daughters, he saw to it that there was always one in the Perkins home.) No doubt because of his bad hearing and a ringing in his ears, he showed almost no interest in music. On the few occasions when he was coerced into attending a concert, he instructed his daughters not to applaud too much, for "they might start in again." The tunes he liked most were such old favorites as "Sweet Afton" and "There Are Eyes of Blue." He saw Victor Herbert's *Babes in Toyland* over and over. John Hall Wheelock remembered how embarrassed Max was when, having let himself be dragged to a nightclub, he saw a chorus line of male dancers starting to perform; he had to shield his eyes with his hand until the men two-stepped away. No performance could de-light him more than those occasions when one of his daughters sat at the Perkinses' out-of-tune piano to accompany herself as she sang:

> *I ain't got no use for the women,*
> *Not ladies nor gals of the town.*
> *They will use a man for his money*
> *And laugh in his face when he's down.*

That was the outward Max. To Elizabeth Lemmon, whom he allowed passage partway into his soul, he confided his deeper, unsuspected feel-ings on the subject of the sexes. "Girls don't get an equal chance in this world, not by many miles," he wrote her on the question of rearing daughters. "If we are ruled by a just Deity, men will have to be women once and go through with that,—or else will have to have been women, which is what I pray."

XIII

Triumphs over Time

In the fall of 1933 Scott Fitzgerald, though still not quite finished with his novel, was already laying out its advertising campaign. Just before sending off the first installment for the magazine serialization he and Perkins had agreed upon, he wrote Max, "I should say to be careful in saying it's my first book in seven years *not to imply that it contains seven years work.* People would expect too much in bulk & scope. . . . This novel, my 4th, completes my story of the boom years. It might be wise to accentuate the fact that it does *not* deal with the depression. Don't accentuate that it deals with Americans abroad—there's been too much trash under that banner. . . . No exclamatory 'At last, the long awaited, *ect.*' That merely creates the 'Oh yeah' mood in people."

Fitzgerald took the title *Tender Is the Night* from Keats's *Ode to a Nightingale.* The story, Perkins told James Gray of the St. Paul *Dispatch*, concerned "the brilliant surface of life on the Riviera and among wealthy and futile people, through the eyes of a simple, raw, and young person." That person was Rosemary Hoyt, a young actress enamored of the attractive psychiatrist hero, Richard Diver. Fitzgerald flashed back to the beginning of Dr. Diver's relationship with his wife and former patient, Nicole, moving forward to the conflict of their lives in the Midi. "The book is truly very fine as a whole," Perkins wrote Hemingway. "It has a very tight plot. . . . It is the sort of story you can imagine Henry James writing, but of course it is written like Fitzgerald, and not James." Max said it came from deeper inside Scott than had his earlier works and that "Scott could never have written it unless he had come into contact with sanitariums, psychiatrists, etc. etc. on account of Zelda's illness." It was so complex a work, Perkins believed, that it really ought not to be chopped up and serialized. But "authors must eat and magazines must live." Perkins felt that it was his suggestion to serialize that had compelled Fitzgerald to finish the book: "He had to do it once that was agreed upon."

Scott had raced to produce the magazine excerpts in time. Now Max was anxious for him to ready the whole manuscript for publication in book form. He suggested that Fitzgerald send him pages in batches, as he finished polishing them, so that they could be set in type while he worked on the rest. The suggestion proved wise, because Scott was proceeding slowly. He was still his own most punctilious editor. He checked every sentence not just for literary perfection but for medical accuracy. When it looked as if weeks would pass before he would be satisfied, he wrote his editor, "After all, Max, I am a plodder." He rewrote the entire novel by the spring of 1934.

Once he got the complete manuscript, Perkins gave it a consecutive reading. He felt there was a lag in the beginning of the book, largely because of a sequence at the train station that was peripheral to the main story; he asked Fitzgerald to consider cutting it because "as soon as people get to Dick Diver their interest in the book, and their perception of its importance increases some thirty to forty percent."

Fitzgerald valued Perkins's advice as much as ever, but he could not see deleting the trainside incident. He maintained:

> I like the slow approach, which I think has a psychological significance affecting not only the work in question, but also having a bearing on my career in general. Is that too damn egotistical an association?

When the book went into galleys, Fitzgerald kept picking at it until the proofs were almost illegible. Scribners had another set run off, and then another. "This is an awful mess," Fitzgerald concluded, returning one set, but he could not stop. At the same time he sent Max instructions about getting review copies to the right people, suggested advertising copy, and even complained that the dust jacket, with its reds and yellows, evoked the Italian Riviera more than the Côte d'Azur's white and blue sparkle. "Oh God, it's hell to bother you with all this," Scott said, "but of course the book is my whole life now and I cannot help this perfectionist attitude." Later he said:

> I have lived so long within the circle of this book and with these characters that often it seems to me that the real world does not exist but that only these characters exist, and, however pretentious that remark sounds (and my God, that I should have to be pretentious about my work), it is an absolute fact—so much so that their glees and woes are just exactly as important to me as what happens in life.

Fitzgerald naturally needed money, but the well of advances against this book's royalties had dried up. Perkins divined a new source: He had a check drawn for $2,000 as a loan from Scribners at 5 percent, to be repaid upon the sale of the motion-picture rights to the novel.

The circulation of *Scribner's* had increased with each installment of *Tender Is the Night*. That was encouraging. But there was little direct response. The only personal acknowledgments Fitzgerald received were from a few writers and motion-picture people. "Alas," he wrote to Perkins, "I may again have written a novel for novelists with little chance of its lining anybody's pockets with gold."

Max's hopes were higher. "Unless for some reason the book is above the general public's head—for some reason I cannot see, in view of its fascination,—" he wrote back, "it ought to be more than a *sucess d'estime*."

When Fitzgerald at last decided to dedicate his novel to Gerald and Sara Murphy, his models for Dick and Nicole Diver at times during the book, he wrote Perkins, "My only regret is that the dedication isn't to you, as it should be, because Christ knows you've stuck with me on the thing through thick and thin, and it was pretty thin going for a while." By mid-March the first printing of *Tender Is the Night* was being stitched and glued.

Zelda was now spending hours each day painting and reading Scott's book. To her dismay she found it contained almost verbatim transcriptions of her own letters and her own case history posing as fiction. The effect on her was visible: The lines in her face deepened and her mouth began twitching. She had agreed to let an art dealer named Cary Ross exhibit her paintings at his Manhattan gallery, but she could not cope with the preparations. She relapsed and returned to Phipps Clinic. After she had gone a month without improvement, Scott placed her in a luxurious rest home called Craig House, two hours up the Hudson River from New York.

Scott and his daughter came to New York at the end of March for the opening of Zelda's show. Scottie stayed at the Perkins's. Zelda was released one afternoon for her exhibit and lunched with Max and Scott. Perkins did not find her well at all. Her eyes were sunken and swimming; her hair, once golden against her Riviera-bronzed skin, looked mousy. Her show was only moderately successful. Scott, curiously, was better than Max had seen him for years. Perkins wrote Hemingway:

> I believe that Scott will be completely reinstated, if not more, by his *Tender Is the Night*. He has improved it immensely by his revision—it was chaotic almost when I read it—and he has made it into a really most extraordinary piece of work. . . . Domestically things are still bad with him but about himself he feels like a new man, I could see. He has all kinds of plans now for writing—wants to begin another novel immediately.

Louise threw a dinner party that week for Scott Fitzgerald. Allen Campbell and Dorothy Parker were there, recently married after living together during the preceding year, and so was Elizabeth Lemmon. It was an odd assortment. Scott got drunk and boisterous, and Dorothy Parker became acerbic and stung everyone at the table with her sharp words. Louise tried hard to find fun in it all. Max sat stiff as a board all evening. Elizabeth looked lovely in a pale-gray Empire-style dress with a huge velvet rose in front—apart from that, he found nothing to enjoy about the evening. "He felt uncomfortable with the Allen Campbells around," Elizabeth said, "because he thought they were still living in sin." At the end of the evening Cary Ross, who had tried to outdrink Scott and had passed out, was lying on the sofa groaning. "I'm sure if we had known him under different circumstances, we'd like him," Louise commented charitably. "Oh, Louise," Dorothy Parker interjected, "you talk as if God were always listening." In the confusion of leaving New York, Fitzgerald forgot to pay the bill for his room at the Algonquin. Max took care of that.

In mid-April, 1934, *Tender Is the Night* was published. Fitzgerald was anxious for a selling trend to develop. "*The Great Gatsby* had against it its length and its purely masculine interest," he wrote to Perkins, "while this book . . . is a woman's book. I think given a decent chance, it will make its own way in so far as fiction is selling under present conditions." The reviews were prominent and some were favorable. Kind personal letters from James Branch Cabell, Carl Van Vechten, Shane Leslie, John

O'Hara, and various members of *The New Yorker* crowd fell like flower petals before Fitzgerald. Morley Callaghan, to whom Perkins had sent a copy, wrote his editor: "It's a fascinating book, an absolutely unrelenting book. . . . Scott is about the only American, at least the only one I know, who has that French classic quality of being able to note a point of character and then make a general observation with some wit, and yet make it a part of the fabric of the prose." Scott appreciated all the kind words, but waited most eagerly for the opinion of Ernest Hemingway, who had not yet rendered his verdict.

After seven months abroad, one third of which was spent in Africa, Hemingway was back in Key West. He told Perkins he hoped *Tender Is the Night* was getting good reviews, though after reading it himself, he had some opinions of his own. He thought it had the same brilliance and most of the same defects as all Fitzgerald's writing. There were the splendid cascades of prose, but there seemed to be something wrong beneath the surface, behind "the worn Christmas ornaments that are Scott's idea of literature." Ernest believed the characters suffered from juvenile, even silly, romantic notions Scott had about them as well as about himself, and so it appeared that their creator knew nothing about them emotionally. Hemingway saw that Fitzgerald had fictionalized Gerald and Sara Murphy, for example, and got the "accent of their voices, their home, their looks marvellously." But then he transmuted them into romantic figurines, not understanding what they were really about. He cast Sara into a psychopathic case, then into Zelda, back into Sara, and "finally into nothing." Similarly, Dick Diver was made to do things that happened to Scott but never could have befallen Gerald Murphy.

Perkins agreed with Hemingway's observation about Fitzgerald's fight to hang onto his youthful dreams, but believed "a great deal of the good writing he has done has come from the very fact of a sort of adolescent romanticism." Max had just seen Scott in Baltimore and discussed that very point. He explained to Hemingway:

> There are certain fundamental things about which he has the strangest, most unreal ideas. It has always been so of him. But about one of these delusions I think I made an impression. Here he is, only about 35 or 6 years old, with immense ability in writing and in a state of hopelessness. But it is useless to try to talk directly to him about it.—The only way one could make an impression would be by some oblique method, and that takes a cleverer person than I am.

Tender Is the Night became the best seller in New York for a short time, but nationally sales barely exceeded 10,000 copies, nothing near as good as those of several other novels. Hervey Allen's *Anthony Adverse*, for example, sold over 1 million copies between 1933 and 1934. Fitzgerald was even outdone by a lesser-known Perkins writer. Stark Young, after a string of unsuccessful books, produced a novel of the old South, under Max's guidance, called *So Red the Rose*. It became one of the most talked-about books of the year.

Fitzgerald's descent into debt resumed. He got Zelda "out of hock at the exorbitant clinic" in New York, and entered her into the Sheppard and Enoch Pratt Hospital outside Baltimore. She was virtually catatonic. To cover Fitzgerald's immediate needs, Perkins squeezed $600 more from Scribners as an advance on Scott's next anthology of stories. Preparing that book for publication proved more arduous than either Perkins or Fitzgerald had anticipated. Many of the stories in the new collection had been written during the final siege of his novel, and Scott had "stripped" and "bled" their strongest passages to build up anemic sections in *Tender Is the Night*. Because the novel had gone through so many revisions, Fitzgerald could not remember what was finally retained and what was not. Now he had to thumb through the novel to see which phrases had already been used. When Perkins said he saw no reason why an author could not repeat himself occasionally, as Hemingway had done, Scott accused his editor of "specious reasoning."

> Each of us has his virtues and one of mine happens to be a great sense of exactitude about my work. He might be able to afford a lapse in that line where I wouldn't be and after all I've got to be the final judge of what is appropriate in these cases. Max, to repeat for the third time, this is in no way a question of laziness. It is a question absolutely of self-preservation.

Four months later, when he was still putting in days combing the novel for sentences he had cribbed from himself, Fitzgerald wrote Perkins, "Certain people I know read my books over and over again and I can't think of anything that would more annoy or disillusion a reader than to find an author using a phrase over and over, as if his imagination were starving."

To pay off his debts, Fitzgerald went back to moonlighting for the *Saturday Evening Post*, but after a few weeks of it he collapsed and took to his bed. In his Ledger he noted: "Hard times begin for me." While he was recovering, Thomas Wolfe sent him a warm note about *Tender Is the Night*. "Thanks a hell of a lot for your letter which came at a rather sunken moment and was the more welcome," Fitzgerald replied. "I am glad to hear from our common parent, Max, that you are about to publish." As in the case of putting together Fitzgerald's anthology, that was easier said than done.

Wolfe's new agent, Elizabeth Nowell, said, "In publishing, a novel by an unknown writer is a very difficult thing to sell. The only thing more difficult is a novel by a writer who had some slight success and then, through failure to produce, has become a has-been." Since *Look Homeward, Angel*, Max Perkins's foremost interest had been Wolfe's career. But Perkins was powerless to further it until that second book reached print. For months Tom had been spinning events of his life into fiction so frantically that Perkins feared he was approaching exhaustion. Max also worried that if Wolfe continued writing, his book could never be contained within two covers. It was already four times as long as the uncut manuscript of *Look Homeward, Angel*, over ten times the length of most novels. And Wolfe was adding 50,000 words a month. For the author's welfare, Perkins was considering drastic action.

By the end of 1933 Tom's mounting tension was manifesting itself in insomnia or guilt-filled nightmares. "He can't go on like that!" Max said repeatedly to John Hall Wheelock. Max explained later in an article for *The Carolina Magazine*, "Time, his old enemy, the vastness and toughness of the material, the frequent and not always sympathetic inquiries of people about his progress toward another book, and financial pressure too—all were closing in on him." Perkins was convinced Wolfe was headed for a breakdown, fearful that he might go insane. One day, while standing in the common area central to the editorial offices, Max shook his head and announced to his colleagues, "I think I'll have to take the book away from him."

Wolfe remembered Perkins's action precisely. "In the middle of December of that year," he recorded in a short documentary book called *The Story of a Novel*, "the editor . . . who during all this tormented period had kept a quiet watch upon me, called me to his home and calmly informed me that my book was finished." Wolfe also recalled his own reaction:

> I could only look at him with stunned surprise, and finally I could only tell
> him out of the depth of my own hopelessness, that he was mistaken, that

the book was not finished, that it could never be complete, that I could write no more. He answered with the same quiet finality that the book was finished whether I knew it or not, and then he told me to go to my room and spend the next week in collecting in its proper order the manuscript which had accumulated during the last two years.

Tom obeyed. For six days he hunkered down in the middle of his apartment floor, encircled by a mountain range of manuscript. On the night of the fourteenth of December, at about half-past eleven, Wolfe arrived customarily late for his appointment with Perkins. He entered Max's southwest-corner office and unloaded a heavy bundle on his editor's desk. It was wrapped in brown paper, twice tied with string, and stood two feet high. Perkins opened it and found it packed with typescript—more than 3,000 rough-draft pages, the first part of the novel. The sheets, all different kinds of paper, were not consecutively numbered, since the sections had not been consecutively written. "God knows a lot of it is still fragmentary and broken up," Tom explained afterward in a letter to his mother, "but at any rate he can now look at it and give me an opinion on it."

"You have often said that if I ever gave you something that you could get your hands on and weigh in its entirety from beginning to end, you could pitch in and help me to get out of the woods," Wolfe wrote Perkins the following day. "Well, now here is your chance. I think a very desperate piece of work is ahead for both of us, but if you think it is worth doing and tell me to go ahead, I think there is literally nothing that I cannot accomplish. . . . I don't envy you the job before you."

In spite of all the rhythms and chants—which Perkins called "dithyrambs"—marbled throughout the manuscript, Tom noted, "I think you will find when I get through that there is plenty of narrative—or should I say when *you* get through—because I must shamefacedly confess that I need your help now more than I ever did."

Wolfe meant that literally, and Perkins knew it. Years later in his article for *The Carolina Magazine*, Perkins revealed what really lay at the heart of his task:

I, who thought Tom a man of genius, and loved him too, and could not bear to see him fail, was almost as desperate as he, so much there was to do. But the truth is that if I did him a real service—and in this I did—it was in keeping him from losing his belief in himself by believing in him. What he most needed was comradeship and understanding in a long crisis, and those things I could give him then.

Years later Max wrote John Terry: "I swore to myself that I would get it done if it killed me,—as Van Wyck Brooks once said it would when I left dinner early to come to the office to meet Tom."

Two days before Christmas, 1933, Wolfe delivered the rest of his pages. Max had seen most of them as fragments during the preceding years. For the first time he could peruse them in sequence. Wolfe left Perkins believing, as he acknowledged in *The Story of a Novel*, that once again Perkins's intuition had been right—"He had told me the truth when he said that I had finished the book.

> It was not finished in any way that was publishable or readable. It was not really a book so much as it was the skeleton of a book, but for the first time in four years, the skeleton was all there. I was like a man who is drowning and who suddenly at the last gasp of his dying efforts feels earth beneath his feet again. My spirit was borne upward by the greatest triumph it had ever known.

In reading the manuscript all together, 1 million words, Perkins discovered that it actually contained two separate cycles, both chronologically and thematically. The first, as Wolfe later came to see and articulate, "was a movement which described the period of wandering and hunger in a man's youth." This was the story which grew out of the idea that "every man is searching for his father." Its hero was Eugene Gant again, finding himself. It was called *Of Time and the River*. The other "described the period of greater certitude, and was dominated by the unity of a single passion." This was George "Monkey" Webber's story, and it still fell under the title *The October Fair*. The second part was the more finished, but the author agreed with his editor that they ought to publish the other material first, thus continuing Eugene Gant's odyssey.

Thinking the book could be published in the summer of 1934, Perkins and Wolfe began working at Scribners for two hours every afternoon, Monday through Saturday. Max inspected the material and found it wanting in two ways. Half of *Of Time and the River* was completed but needed cutting; the other half remained to be written. Each day they argued. Perkins insisted that it was an author's duty to be selective in his writing. Wolfe asserted that it was an author's primary task to illuminate a whole way of life for the reader. Once the first few hundreds of shards of manuscript were assembled, Perkins realized that it would take months of labor before it would be ready for the printer. He and Wolfe decided to work nights in the office, six times a week, from 8:30 on.

Sometimes Perkins wrote short directives right on Tom's detailed breakdown of the book: "Insert section in train" or "Conclude Leopold." Other instructions were more comprehensive:

THINGS TO BE DONE IMMEDIATELY IN FIRST REVISION

1. Make rich man in opening scene older and more middle-aged.

2. Cut out references to previous books and to success.

3. Write out fully and with all the dialogue the jail and arrest scene.

4. Use material from Man on the Wheel and Abraham Jones for first year in the city and University scenes.

5. Tell the story of love affair from beginning to end describing meeting with woman, etc.

6. Intersperse jealousy and madness scenes with more scenes of dialogue with woman.

7. Use description of the trip home and the boom town scenes out of the Man on the Wheel. You can possibly use the trip home and boom town scene to follow on to the station scene. Play up desire to go home, feelings of homesickness and unrest and then develop idea that hometown has become unfamiliar and strange to him and he sees he can no longer live there.

8. Possible ending for book with return to the city, the man in the window scenes and the passages, "some things never change."

9. On the Night Scene which precedes the station scene, write out fully with all dialogue the episodes of night including the death in the subway scene.

10. Cut out reference to daughter.

11. Complete all scenes wherever possible with dialogue.

12. Fill in memory of childhood scenes much more fully with additional stories and dialogue.

Wolfe and Perkins kept to themselves but rumors of their work swirled around New York. They became the butt of jokes at almost every literary gathering. "The man with a legitimate grievance is Maxwell Perkins, the Scribners editor," critic John Chamberlain wrote in *Books of the Times*. "They tell stories about Mr. Perkins wrestling with Thomas Wolfe for three days, catch-as-catch-can, over the attempted excision of a phrase. Trucks are popularly supposed to deliver Wolfe's manuscripts to the Scribners door." Most of the stories were manufactured; few were completely untrue.

In the spring of 1934 Wolfe had decided to let his newest typist—
who could interpret what Tom called "my most indecipherable Chinese"
—type up everything of his that was still in manuscript so that Max could
"see the whole works so far as possible." It was a necessary step. Tom
admitted to a writer–friend named Robert Raynolds, "I no longer seem
to be able to tell what's what myself." Of Perkins, he wrote Raynolds
further:

> God knows what I would do without him. I told him the other day that
> when this book comes out, he could then assert it was the only book he had
> ever written. I think he has pulled me right out of the swamp just by main
> strength and serene determination.

Perkins and Wolfe struggled through the spring. "I am cutting it
hard now, and reducing it very greatly," Max wrote Frere-Reeves in
London. "Although there will, of course, be an argument later with
Tom." Chapter by chapter—the endings of which Perkins often designated—they examined each paragraph and sentence. "Cutting had always
been the most difficult and distasteful part of writing to me," Wolfe admitted in *The Story of a Novel*. Perkins supplied the objectivity and
perspective toward the material that Wolfe lacked.

Max started with the scene on top of the bundle of Tom's pages,
which picked up where *Look Homeward, Angel* left off. Eugene Gant,
about to go beyond the hills to Harvard, stands on the platform of the
railroad station in Altamont saying good-bye to his family. The passage
ran over 30,000 words. Perkins told Wolfe it should be shrunk to 10,000.
In the *Harvard Library Bulletin*, he recorded what he told Tom: "When
you are waiting for a train to come in, there is suspense. Something is
going to happen. You must, it seemed to me, maintain that sense of
suspense and you can't to the extent of 30,000 words." Perkins marked
the material that could go and showed Wolfe, who understood. The author
himself wrote Robert Raynolds:

> I suffer agony over some of the cutting, but I realize it's got to be done.
> When something really good goes it's an awful wrench, but as you probably
> know, something really can be good and yet have no place in the scheme
> of a book.

As with *Look Homeward, Angel*, Perkins said in his article for Harvard,
"there never was any cutting that Tom did not agree to. He knew that

cutting was necessary. His whole impulse was to utter what he felt, and he had no time to revise and compress."

It was not just the number of scenes in Wolfe's book that made it so difficult to condense. Another troublesome aspect of his writing was what he later described as his attempts "to reproduce in its entirety the full flood and fabric of a scene in life itself." In one section of the book, for example, four people talked to each other for four hours without an intermission. "All were good talkers; often all talked, or tried to talk at the same time," Wolfe wrote. When he got all their thoughts expressed, he had 80,000 words—200 printed pages for a minor scene in an already enormous book. Perkins made him realize that "good as it was, it was all wrong and had to go." As usual, Tom argued, then agreed.

Hemingway invited Perkins to Key West in June, but Max would not leave New York. "I am engaged in a kind of life and death struggle with Mr. Thomas Wolfe still," he explained, "and it is likely to last through the summer." Max wrote his other author in Florida, Marjorie Kinnan Rawlings:

> If he will go on for six weeks more at the present rate, the book will be virtually done. I could even now, if I dared, send a third of it to the printer. But Tom is always threatening to go back to the early part, and if he does that, I do not know what the result will be. We might have to go through the whole struggle over again. It has become an obsession with me now, one of those things that you get to tell yourself you have got to do even if it costs your life.

Tom and Max now were working on Sunday nights as well. Sometimes Wolfe pulled a chair up to a corner of Max's desk and feverishly scribbled one of the requested connecting passages right there. Facing him from the other side of the desk, with the bulk of the manuscript before him, Max would read slowly. In his high jagged script he would make his notations. Every time he slashed a page from corner to corner, Perkins could see that Tom's eye was following his hand. Wolfe winced with pain, as though Max had gouged his skin. Perkins would glance at one of his notes, clear his throat, and speak up. "I think this section should be omitted."

After a long sulky pause Wolfe would say: "I think it's good." "I think it's good too, but you have expressed the thing already." "Not the same thing."

It was on one such night that summer when Tom, after arguing over a big deletion, looked fixedly at the rattlesnake skin hanging with Max's hat and coat and said, "Aha! The portrait of an editor!" After the laughter, Tom and Max quit for the night and went to the Chatham Walk, an open-air extension of the Chatham Hotel's bar, and talked for another hour under the stars.

Convincing Tom of the necessity of cuts was only one aspect of Perkins's task. He had allocated space for certain missing material, and now Wolfe was trying to compensate for his earlier losses by jamming verbiage into those lacunae. When they came to the point in the narrative where the hero's father died, for example, Max said that it must be written about. Because Eugene was away at Harvard at the time, he said, Tom need only record the shock of the news and Eugene's return for the funeral. Perkins figured it was a matter of 5,000 words. Tom agreed.

The next night Wolfe came in with several thousand words about the life of the doctor who attended old Gant. "This is good, Tom," Perkins said, "but what has it to do with the book? You are telling the story of Eugene, of what he saw and experienced. We can't waste time with all this that is so outside it." Tom accepted that, but the next night he brought in a long passage about Eugene's sister Helen, her thoughts while shopping in Altamont and then at night in bed when she heard the whistle of a train. "How in God's name will you get this book done this way, Tom?" Max asked. "You have wasted two days already, and instead of reducing the length and doing what is essential, you are increasing it and adding what doesn't belong here."

Tom was penitent. He did not argue back. He promised to write only what was needed. The next night he brought in thousands of words more about Gant's illness, all extraneous to what Perkins thought was wanted. Max laughed at the whole matter and said, "Really this does not seem to me to be essential to the book and we ought to get forward." But Perkins also felt that those pages were too good to let go. Gant's death scene remained in the book. It was one of the finest passages Wolfe ever wrote. During the course of the year, Wolfe estimated that he composed over a half million words of additional manuscript, of which only a small part was finally used.

"A couple of nights ago," Max wrote Hemingway in June, 1934, "I told Tom that a whole lot of fine stuff he had in simply ought to come out because it resulted in blurring a very important effect. Literally we sat here for an hour thereafter without saying a word, while Tom glowered and pondered, and fidgeted in his chair. Then, he said, 'Well, then will

you take the responsibility?' And I said, 'I have got to take the responsibility—And what's more,' I said '—I will be blamed either way.'"

Sometimes Max was at fault for the lengthening. He recalled that
wonderful scene that for five years he had regretted deleting from the
beginning of *Look Homeward, Angel*—about young Gant and his brother
watching the Confederate troops march by to Gettysburg. He saw how that
could be shoehorned into this volume as a part of old Gant's dying memories, and it was.

One night Max set aside his red pencil and took Wolfe to Lüchow's
restaurant. After a few hours there, Tom wanted to walk off the hearty
German food. He insisted that Perkins accompany him to Brooklyn Heights
to see the apartment where he had written so much of his manuscript.
Absentmindedly, Wolfe led Max to a brownstone he had vacated just a
few weeks before. When he found his door locked, he searched for his
keys, then growled something about having lost them. He led Max up
the fire escape and into the large furnished railroad flat on the top floor
of the building. Tom pointed out the refrigerator on which he had written
the book, then offered Max a chair and poured a whiskey from the bottle
sitting on the living room table. Several drinks later, the couple who lived
in the apartment walked in. Max understood the situation in an instant
and sank deeper into the chair.

After the wife ran for the police, Wolfe poured the husband a drink of
his own whiskey and was soon slathering on his charm in his honeyed drawl.
"That man hadn't read anything but Dodger box scores in twenty years,"
Perkins recounted years later, "but Tom treated him as though he were
the editor of the *Atlantic Monthly*. He asked his advice on how to write
short stories and begged for help on his next book." By the time the
police arrived the man was regaling Perkins and Wolfe with stories from
his own life. Max and Tom remained another hour. Several days later
Tom brought in 35,000 words that he wanted incorporated into *Of Time
and the River*. It was an account of their night in Brooklyn. It was not used.

Into July they worked, now searching for the book's conclusion. Max
thought they might not ever finish because what seemed to him the very
hardest part still remained—those pages about Eugene Gant's association
with Esther Jack, the character modeled after Aline Bernstein.

Max and Aline Bernstein had been aware of each other for five years,
but Perkins did not meet her until he was working on *Of Time and the
River*. Then a man introduced them in Cherio's one day. Max was so
skittish that little was said. Not long thereafter, however, Mrs. Bernstein

called Perkins for an appointment in his office. There she swore that she would do everything in her power to prevent the publication of that book if she was a character in it. Perkins had to represent Tom, and so he could not agree to any concession whatever, but he remained cordial and open-minded. When she was leaving he held out his hand. Aline swung hers behind her back, saying, "I regard you as an enemy."

The entire section that Wolfe had written about Aline Bernstein had never rung true to Perkins. He thought it was "too fresh to be written of objectively," and he dreaded the struggle he knew they would have over it. Then it occurred to him that they might just end this large volume with Eugene's first meeting Esther Jack on his return trip from Europe to America—and nothing more. By putting their story off into another book, Max knew he would not be eliminating the problem, but he could at least postpone it. *Of Time and the River* had its dramatic conclusion at last.

Until this time, Perkins's office life and homelife had been two separate zones. He and Louise socialized with a few of his authors, but she saw to it that business seldom mixed with pleasure. Thomas Wolfe was the only author in Max's life to pass freely from one sector to the other. Once the Perkinses had moved to New York, Wolfe took frequent advantage of his editor's hospitality. Even the Perkins girls, who were afraid of him, came to realize that Tom was by nature extremely gentle, though he could be ranting at the top of his lungs in an instant. They all found Wolfe terrifying to sit close to at the dinner table. In the end, the youngest proved her valor. One night, Nancy recalled, "I was sitting on Daddy's left at dinner and Wolfe was on his right. Tom was at his most horrid, cursing and raving at Daddy as though nobody else was in the room." His words hurt her so that she burst into tears and yelled at Wolfe not to talk to her father that way. Max smiled gently and calmed her with a low voice. "It's all right, Duck," he said. "Never mind. Honestly, it's all right." Perkins never apologized for Wolfe, but he did try to explain his behavior, as he did once to Wolfe himself. "Tom," he said, "you have in you ten thousand devils and an archangel."

The weather in New York turned torrid but Perkins and Wolfe kept at their work. On the seventh of July, Tom lunched with Max and Scott Fitzgerald, who had come to town from Baltimore. Fitzgerald tried to console Wolfe about the truncating of his manuscript by saying, "You never cut anything out of a book that you regret later." The next day Tom wrote Robert Raynolds, "I wonder if this is true. Anyway, I shall do all I can in what time is left to me, and then I suppose I will have to leave the

matter on the lap of the gods and Maxwell Perkins." Three days after
that, the arguments between them grew so intense that Perkins packed up
part of the manuscript and, without further discussion, sent it to the press.

Tom panicked and protested. When he came to his senses he wrote
to his friend Catherine Brett, "I suppose I have got attached to it, as one
might get attached to some great monstrous child, and I was a little terrified when I had to give it up.

> It means that the proof will start coming back within a few weeks now,
> and it also means that all I expect or want, or hope to get done must be
> done within a little more than two months. After that the die is cast.
> I think Mr. Perkins is right in feeling that I ought to submit to this neces-
> sity, and that with a book which is as long as this and which has taken as
> much time, it is possible to get a kind of obsession, so that one can per-
> fectly well work on it forever in an effort to perfect it and to get in every-
> thing he wants to get in, but I believe it is more important to get this one
> done now and to go on to other work.

Perkins had never spent so little time with his family as during the
last year. That summer, his women scattered in all directions. Louise took
a cruise, Bert was married and living in Boston, Zippy and Peggy traveled
to Struthers Burt's ranch in Wyoming, and the youngest girls, Jane and
Nancy, went to New Canaan. Zippy and Peggy came back from the West
saying they would never marry, Max wrote Elizabeth Lemmon, "because
cowboys couldn't support them and all Eastern men are as nothing beside
them." Max understood their reaction entirely:

> I never was so flattered as when a man pointed me out as Will James—
> and Bill gave a very wan smile when I told him of it. It's one reason we
> have wars: a man who wends his life with his knees crooked under a desk
> is not more than half a man, and we all know it. And Dr. Johnson said,
> when they were running down the military, "If a general walked into this
> room now we'd all be ashamed." And if a good workman, a mechanic,
> walked into a boardroom at a directors meeting, the directors would all feel
> ashamed. And if old Zimmerman, foreman at our press, a man like Adam
> Bede, in a striped apron, walked into our directors meeting we'd all feel
> ashamed. And that is true and must mean something, but what, I don't
> know.

On September 8, 1934, Max's first grandchild, Edward Perkins Frothingham, was born to Bertha and her husband. Perkins referred to the baby

with feminine pronouns for months, insisting that it was from force of habit.

Somehow Max had found time in the last few months—usually in the hours when Wolfe was overdue for his appointments—to dispatch several bulletins of his progress with Tom to Elizabeth Lemmon. A few days before he was scheduled to visit Dr. Bordley in Baltimore, he wrote her again to report that he was coming and to say he hoped she'd meet him there. "I'll pretend to myself you're not anyhow," he said, "to avoid as much disappointment as I can." On the eve of Max's departure, Elizabeth thought of making a small party of the trip by asking Tom Wolfe to accompany Perkins. She correctly guessed where Max and Tom would be that night, and paged Wolfe at the Chatham Walk. She invited them both to Welbourne. Tom gave his regrets. There was still a great deal that he wanted to do to his manuscript and time was running out. Instead, he said, he wished Elizabeth could lure Max from Baltimore to Virginia for a while. "I think he is very tired, and know that a vacation would do him a lot of good," Tom wrote the next day, adding, "He has sweated and labored and lavished untold care and patience upon this huge ms. of mine. There is no adequate way in which I can ever express my gratefulness, but I can only hope the book may have something in it which will in some measure justify his patience and care."

After his ear treatment at Johns Hopkins, Perkins visited Scott in Baltimore, and then the two of them went by train to Washington. Elizabeth met them with her car in Georgetown and drove them on to Middleburg. Max had known Elizabeth for more than a decade, but this was his first visit to Welbourne. It seemed at first exactly as he had envisioned it. But he was on edge after a few minutes. He did not want to examine the place too closely for fear that its reality might mar his idealized image. ("The haze of glamour vanishes under the sun of fact," he had written her ten years before.) He felt like a trespasser in forbidden land, and so he suggested taking in some Civil War monuments. Elizabeth agreed to drive them to Appomattox. After touring the site, Max insisted on returning to New York. Elizabeth, a little surprised she had gotten him to stay so long as he did, drove him to the Washington station. Before putting him aboard an air-cooled train, she extended an open invitation for a longer visit to him and Fitzgerald, as well as to Thomas Wolfe. "I only wanted to thank you for your great kindness in taking us to Welbourne," he wrote Elizabeth the following week. "It's as if I had drunk the milk of Paradise once and seen an enchanted place."

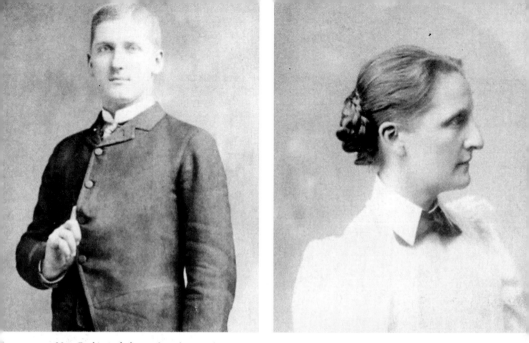

Max Perkins's father, Edward C. Perkins, a lawyer in Plainfield, New Jersey,
came from a long line of cultivated Bostonians. Max's mother,
Elizabeth Evarts Perkins, descended from stern New England clergymen and statesmen,
whom Max described as "rigorous for duty."

Max at age eight (upper right), surrounded by his brothers Edward and
Charles (left and right) and his sister Molly.

(TOP)
Max (seated at right, wearing
light suit) was not the only
member of the 1907 Harvard
Advocate staff to distinguish
himself in the world of arts
and letters. Van Wyck Brooks
(left, mustached), his best
friend, became a major essayist
and critic; another lifelong
friend, Edward Sheldon (standing
at center, light suit), wrote
a Broadway hit while at Harvard.
(By permission of the Houghton
Library, Harvard University.)

(BOTTOM, LEFT)
Louise Saunders at the age of
eighteen, four years before she
married Max. They had known
each other since dancing class
in Plainfield. To a friend she
spoke of him as "my Greek god."

(BOTTOM, RIGHT)
Louise with the Perkinses'
three oldest daughters—
(from left) Peggy, Zippy, and
Bertha. Max yearned for boys
but fathered five girls.

(RIGHT)
Max about to take a "real walk"
from the Plainfield house
with his fourth daughter, Jane.
This was his customary daughter-
carrying position—on the
shoulders, one leg down.

(ABOVE)
1916 : Max (center) on the
Mexican border with National
Guard Squadron A from Plainfield.
The squadron spent three
months trying to capture Pancho
Villa but never even glimpsed
him. Max reread the Iliad
that summer; the southwestern
plains reminded him of Troy.

"Dea incessu patuit" (And
she revealed herself to be a
goddess), Max wrote of Elizabeth
Lemmon in a letter to her
just after they met. A belle of
Baltimore and the Virginia
hunt country, she represented
ideal womanhood to Max.
(She also managed the Upperville,
Virginia, baseball team.)
For twenty-five years they
maintained a platonic love affair.

Max the young editor, about 1920, just after his discovery of F. Scott Fitzgerald and the beginning of his illustrious career at Scribners.

Authors at work : Fitzgerald (opposite top), the first of the legendary Perkins authors, steered him to two others, Ring Lardner (right), and Ernest Hemingway (opposite bottom, shown writing in Spain during the civil war). Max saw each of the three through severe personal and professional difficulties; his warmth and steadfast support meant as much to them as his editorial guidance. (Bettmann Archive; Granger Collection; © Robert Capa, John F. Kennedy Library)

(LEFT)

Thomas Wolfe with one of the three crates containing the manuscript of Of Time and the River. Wolfe's novel was the challenge of Perkins's lifetime. The massive editing job consumed two intense, often violent years, resulting first in a great success and then in a rift between author and editor. The book was dedicated to Perkins : "A great editor . . . and unshaken friend."
(Robert Disraeli Films)

Two Perkins bestsellers : Marjorie Kinnan Rawlings (top), at her Cross Creek, Florida, home; her greatest success, the Pulitzer Prize-winning novel The Yearling, was a book Perkins conceived and kept after her for years to write. James Jones (bottom), inspired by the story of Wolfe and Perkins, brought Max his own autobiographical novel, which was declined; then Perkins urged him to write From Here to Eternity. It was the last book Perkins edited. (Both photographs courtesy of Charles Scribner's Sons)

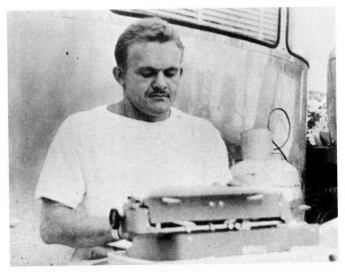

*Max was famous for one eccentricity:
wearing a hat indoors and out,
nearly all the time. The caricature
ran with Malcolm Cowley's* New Yorker
*profile of Perkins. (Illustration by
A. Birnbaum © 1994 The New Yorker
Magazine Inc. All rights reserved.)*

A meeting in Max's office between two very different Perkins authors: S.S. Van Dine (left), author of the enormously successful Philo Vance mysteries, was elegant and intellectual; Hemingway scorned "literary" writers and seldom wore a tie. At right, Charles Scribner III and Perkins. (Robert Disraeli Films)

Key West, 1935: Max, Ernest, and trophies. Hemingway tried annually to get the busy editor away from his desk for adventurous holidays. Not satisfied that this, one of his few successful attempts, was properly recorded, Hemingway took a picture himself (far right).

(OPPOSITE, TOP)
Max in the company of his wife (left) and
Aline Bernstein, who had been Thomas Wolfe's
lover and early inspiration. Both women
had resented the amount of time that Max spent
with Wolfe. (Carl Mydans, Life *magazine*
© Time Inc.)

(OPPOSITE, BOTTOM)
Max's features play through the faces of
his five beloved daughters : (from left) Peggy,
Jane, Bertha, Zippy, and Nancy.

Louise late in life. Frustrated by a prenuptial
vow she had made to Max to give up her acting
aspirations, she converted to Roman Catholicism,
which annoyed him even more than
her passion for the theater.

One of the last photographs of Maxwell Perkins. (Al Ravenna)

Thomas Wolfe wrote Miss Lemmon that Max had "talked about the place a hundred times since he was there. He says it is the finest place he ever saw. I think you almost made a Rebel out of him, and I didn't think that was possible." Fitzgerald thanked Perkins for taking him into that "novel and stimulating atmosphere" for he had been in a "hell of a rut." Even so, Max did not think his authors should avail themselves so readily of Welbourne's splendors. It was not jealousy that made him say that. He tried to explain to Elizabeth that it was professional concern, but he found it hard to get his point across because of "the ancient trouble of a woman not understanding how things are with men."

"You want to have Tom Wolfe and Scott play, and I want to have them work," he reproved Elizabeth, going on to say,

> It's enormously more for their own sake than for Scribners that I want them to do it. If the time I've given, and the neglect of other things on account of it were reckoned, it would be inconceivable that Scribners could be repaid by what Tom's book might do. But for his sake he must finish it. It's a desperate matter for him. . . . As for Scott: he's easily beguiled from work to drink. . . . There is no one I so dislike to displease as you. . . . But Elizabeth, you must forgive me about Scott and Tom. I truly know more about that than you do.

Besides, Max once told her, if she continued to invite them, she would find herself a character in their fiction. "Scott will disguise you," he said, "but Tom will write you exactly as you are."

Fitzgerald was disappointed that the sales of *Tender Is the Night* had stopped at 15,000 copies. He was selling stories regularly since its publication, but his heart was not in them. Whenever his working spirit took leave, he turned south to Virginia. He went to Middleburg, to mingle among the wealthy gentry and play to the hilt the part of the gentleman novelist. But Elizabeth knew that the water pitcher Fitzgerald emptied during the course of the afternoon was filled with straight gin. He brought along the galleys of his short-story collection, now titled *Taps at Reveille*, but would not even look at them. When Elizabeth pointed out that he had given one character two different names, he threw the galleys at her and said, "Here, you correct them."

On Perkins's next visit to Baltimore he met again with both Scott and Elizabeth. Fitzgerald was still going through a period of despair and he discussed his state of mind. "I am ashamed and felt very yellow about it afterwards," he admitted to Perkins. "But to deny that such moods come increasingly would be futile." What weighed heaviest on Max was his inability to help him. "I can't seem to," he wrote Elizabeth, "perhaps because I never had trouble comparable to what he has had. And so I can't feel what he does. Then too he and I are really friends, but he doesn't think I know much."

Years later Elizabeth wrote Louise that "Scott sobered up and tried to put on a show when Max came to Baltimore, and to this day I don't know if Max actually saw through him, but those efforts kept Scott going and Max accepted them as though they were genuine—perhaps they were, perhaps Max reached the truth in him as he did in everyone." Still later she realized that Max had been wise to Scott all along. Perkins did know how annoying Scott Fitzgerald could be, but he preferred to ignore it. One night at a display of modern Pullmans in the middle of Washington's Union Station, Scott drunkenly hurled himself onto a bed and cried with outstretched arms, "Louise, come to me!" Max looked the other way. Once while having "tea" at the Plaza, Scott, intoxicated again, poked Zippy Perkins in the arm and said, "I could take you upstairs anytime." She remembered, "Daddy gave me a look that meant we should feel sorry for Fitzgerald, but then pretended that he didn't hear what he said." Elizabeth Lemmon recalled another occasion when Perkins was not present. "Scott introduced me to Archibald MacLeish, saying, 'This *used* to be Max Perkins's girl,' implying that I was now *his* girl," Elizabeth said. "But my God, after knowing Max Perkins, how could anyone be Scott's mistress!"

Fitzgerald thought "Beth" Lemmon was "charming" and wondered "why the hell she never married." Perkins was pleased that Scott liked Elizabeth. ("Don't call her Beth," he told Fitzgerald; "the name does not suit her at all, and I have always refused to use it.") On the train home Max wrote a letter to her, which he destroyed because it seemed to make little sense. He explained later, "The trouble is that after seeing you I stay for about four days in a kind of bemused state resembling that of the knight-at-arms Keats wrote about."

In November, 1934, Fitzgerald's story "Her Last Case" appeared in the *Post*. Welbourne provided the background. Without the $3,000 the *Post* paid him for it, Scott could hardly have gotten through the year, because Charles Scribner's Sons was run differently than it had been. The house now had a half-dozen different departments, and the heads of all of them had a say in the business policy of the firm. Perkins was more sympathetic to Fitzgerald's financial situation than ever before; but, he wrote, "It is impossible to make such a one, for instance, as the head of the educational department (which by the way, does better than we do in the depression) understand it. He would think we were just crazy, having all but cleared up your indebtedness by the way we arranged for *Tender Is the Night,* to let it all pile up again. I wish to Heaven—and I know you do too—that we could work out some way. But you have had a run of mighty bad luck and have struggled against it very valiantly, and it still is true, as the feller says, that the only sure thing about luck is that it will change."

In October, 1934, Tom Wolfe grew so weary of words that he left town for a few days to visit the World's Fair in Chicago. It was his first extensive vacation after a year of work. While he was gone, Max had his whole manuscript set in type: 450,000 words in 250 galleys would appear as 900 pages of book. When Wolfe returned to New York, he learned that his editor had made an even more arbitrary decision during his absence. He was going to send the galleys back to the typesetters without waiting for the author to look at them. Perkins had seen Wolfe pore over the galleys of the first section of the book for weeks in the Scribners library without correcting them. Without an ultimatum he might hold onto them forever. Perkins told him he was going to send out twenty galleys a day, proofread by Wheelock, to be set into pages.

"You can't do it," Tom protested. "The book is not yet finished. I must have six months more on it." Perkins answered that the book was indeed finished; further, that if Wolfe took an additional six months, he would then demand another six months and six months more beyond that. He would become so obsessed with this one work that he would never get it published. Wolfe recorded the rest of Perkins's argument in *The Story of a Novel*:

> I was not, he said, a Flaubert kind of writer. I was not a perfectionist. I had twenty, thirty, almost any number of books in me, and the important thing was to get them produced and not to spend the rest of my life perfecting one book.

In his piece for the *Harvard Library Bulletin* Perkins wrote, "It is said that Tolstoi never willingly parted with the manuscript of *War and Peace*. One could imagine him working on it all through his life." So it was with Wolfe and *Of Time and the River*.

"I think I'm peculiarly cursed in almost always knowing what I ought

to do," Max wrote Elizabeth Lemmon. "If you don't know it's all right
enough; but if you do know and don't do it, that's bad." As a result, he
confided, "I've taken awful risks about that book, but I had to do it. It had
to be done, and because of the peculiar circumstances of the case I almost
know that no one else could have done it as well and finished it. You may
hear me damned for it some day but I reckoned that in from the start. I'm
mentally prepared for it but whether emotionally I don't know."

Late that fall, Wolfe resisted Elizabeth Lemmon's invitations no
longer. After Max had spoken so much about each of them to the other,
they met in Middleburg. Elizabeth adored Tom. She said, "He was a much
more natural person than Fitzgerald. Scott's inferiority complex made him
always the show-off. Tom had a more basic kind of dignity. He was completely honest." Because of Wolfe's genuine warmth and interest in everyone around, she was inclined to overlook his occasional vituperation.
She showed him around Middleburg one day, and one woman with
whom they started talking about literature thoughtlessly dropped the comment that she never remembered the name of the author of any book.
Elizabeth remembered that "Tom sulked the rest of the time we were
there; but when we left he blew up. 'W-W-Why did she h-h-have me over
if she w-w-wanted to insult me?' he bellowed."

After leaving Welbourne, he wrote Elizabeth:

> Your America is not my America and for that reason I have always loved it
> even more—there is an enormous age and sadness in Virginia—a grand
> kind of death . . . I've got to find my America somehow here in Brook-
> lyn and Manhattan, in all the fog and the swelter of the city, in subways
> and railway stations, on trains and in the Chicago Stock Yards. I'm so glad
> you let me see your wonderful place and see a little of the country and the
> kind of life you have down there.

That October, out of the clear blue, Aline Bernstein contacted Perkins.
The passing of time and the acceptance of the truth had diluted her earlier
antagonism to him but left her worn down. She knew that *Of Time and
the River* was approaching publication and that the character of Esther
Jack was now limited to the final scene. Now she told Perkins that years
earlier, when Tom went abroad on his Guggenheim Fellowship, he had
presented her with the manuscript of *Look Homeward, Angel*. Recently,
she said, she had been hospitalized and unable to work. She was going to
California to rest and was eager to give up her house in Armonk, New

York. Before leaving she wanted that manuscript, like its author, out of her life. "I want to give you the manuscript, if you care to have it," she wrote Perkins, "on the condition that you will never under any circumstances return it to Tom. If you do not want it, I will destroy it before I leave, as I do not care to have it fall into other hands than yours or mine."

Perkins offered to keep the manuscript safely at Scribners, but said, "I could never regard it as anything but yours since I know the circumstances in which it was given to you."

Aline appreciated Perkins's generosity toward both herself and Tom. Later she wrote Max, "My wound is as fresh today as the day [Tom] found it necessary to turn away from me." But she added, "I have always believed Tom to be the greatest artist writing today, and I think it is wonderful that you have been at his side all this time." She accepted Max's proposal but insisted the manuscript eventually go to the editor, "for you have done all the good things for Tom that I had hoped to do."

There was, in fact, still more that Perkins wished he had been able to do to Wolfe's new manuscript, but he realized that an editor too must eventually give up a book. He wrote Elizabeth Nowell: "The book will contain many too many adjectives, and much repetition of a sort, and too much loud pedalling. Those are faults that Tom won't dispense with as yet." Still, he maintained, it would make a great impression and be a success, and he thought the criticism on such points would drive Wolfe to sterner discipline.

All year, Ernest Hemingway had been aware that Perkins had shifted most of his attention toward Thomas Wolfe. In October, 1934, he told Max outright that he thought Wolfe's short stories were getting "quite pretensious" and that the subtitle for his novel—*A Legend of Man's Hunger*—was just plain bad. Hemingway believed the reason Perkins's "world geniuses" stalled so long was that they feared their works would be found to be "phoney" instead of being "world masterpieces." He said it was better to create books one at a time, let the critics jump on what they did not like, and have orgasms about what they did, because the author himself would know which were good.

Hemingway admitted he was getting a little "snooty" because he had just completed the project he started two seasons earlier, and he needed nobody to help him cut or finish it. Smugly he decided it was best not to speak ill any further of his "overassed and underbrained contemporaries"—but there was no feeling, he told Max, like knowing you can do the "old stuff" even though it makes you "fairly insufferable at the time to your publishers."

Hemingway had finished his "long bitch" of a work about Africa on the morning of November 13. The 70,000-word manuscript, which started as a story and kept spreading, was tentatively entitled *The Highlands of Africa*. Ernest insisted it was not a novel in form, but more like "Big Two-Hearted River" than anything else. It had a definite beginning and an end and a "hell of a lot" of action in between. Before this, Hemingway said, he had never known a book that made him see and feel Africa as it actually was. He said he had written the book absolutely truly, with no fudging of any kind, and that he was the only "bastard" just then who could do it.

Hemingway felt he had lost a large part of his following after *A Farewell to Arms*, and he wanted to win his readers back now by giving them what was really literature without being arty, leaving Perkins's "pompous guys" to blow themselves up like balloons until they burst. He supposed that 70,000 words was long for a story, but he wanted to publish it with something else in the book to give the people a "super-value." He proposed running it with his recent *Esquire* articles. Perkins objected. Whether or not Hemingway regarded this as a novel, he pointed out, it was a whole unit and considerably longer than would be necessary to make a full book. Max thought combining the story with other pieces would only distract the critics from the main work. "I hope you will publish it by itself," he stated.

Hemingway's, Fitzgerald's, and Wolfe's books were practically done, and Perkins felt he could go down to Key West to read Ernest's manuscript. "I'd like to do it mighty well," he told him. "I would like to spend an afternoon on the dock looking at those lazy turtles swimming around."

On the eve of Perkins's departure for Key West, the second week in January, only two parts of Tom Wolfe's book remained to be agreed upon. The first was a foreword, which Wolfe had written. Max urged him to drop it. He explained: "A reader is meant to enter into a novel as if it were reality and so to feel it, and a preface tends to break down that illusion, and to make him look at it in a literary way." The other part of the book to be discussed was the dedication page, which Wolfe had been drafting in the back of his mind since he had first begun the manuscript. In recent weeks John Hall Wheelock had been helping him polish it. Max knew little about it but had suspicions. Now, about to leave for Florida, he decided to speak his mind. "Nothing could give me greater pleasure or greater pride as an editor," he wrote Tom, "than that the book of the writer whom I have most greatly admired should be dedicated to me if it were sincerely done.

> But you cannot, and should not try to change your conviction that I have deformed your book, or at least prevented it from coming to perfection. It is therefore impossible for you sincerely to dedicate it to me and it ought not to be done. I know we are truly friends and have gone through much in company and this matter, for my part, can have nothing to do with that, or ever shall. But this is another matter. I would have said this sooner, but for some fear that you would misinterpret me. But the plain truth is that working on your writing, however it has turned out, for good or bad, has been the greatest pleasure, for all its pain, and the most interesting episode of my editorial life. The way in which we are presenting this book must prove our (and my) belief in it. But what I have done has destroyed your belief in it and you must not act inconsistently with that fact.

Louise accompanied Max to Key West this time, and during their eight fine days in the Gulf Stream, Max caught a whopping sailfish. On a postcard to Scott Fitzgerald from Key West, he wrote: HEMS BOOK IS ABOUT HIS OWN HUNTING IN AFRICA, BUT DIFFERENT FROM ANY OTHER HUNTING BOOK MAGICAL IN THE LAST THIRD. LOUISE TURNS OUT A GREAT FISHERMAN. MY FACE IS BURNED BLACK. BE BACK MONDAY.

When Perkins returned from his vacation he found that he had succeeded in getting Wolfe to leave out his long foreword, but he had failed to keep Wolfe from dedicating the novel to him. *Of Time and the River* was entirely in print—including Wolfe's lavish inscription. "I fought with Tom to keep it at a minimum," Wheelock said later, "to a level of propriety that would not embarrass Max altogether." The dedication read:

TO

MAXWELL EVARTS PERKINS

A great editor and a brave and honest man, who stuck to the writer of this book through times of bitter hopelessness and doubt and would not let him give in to his own despair, a work to be known as "Of Time and the River" is dedicated with the hope that all of it may be in some way worthy of the loyal devotion and the patient care which a dauntless and unshaken friend has given to each part of it, and without which none of it could have been written.

To

Maxwell Evarts Perkins
a dauntless, loyal, ~~d~~
~~a~~ ~~great editor~~, ~~and~~
~~unbroken~~ friend,
~~a loan and honest man~~ who
stuck to the writer _this_
book ~~through~~ times _bitter_
hopelessness and doubt, ~~and~~ would
not let him give in to his
own despair, a work to be known
as _Of Time And The River_ is
dedicated, with the hope that
all of it may be in some

Once Perkins saw it he wrote Wolfe, "Whatever the degree of justice in what it implied, I can think of nothing that could have made me more happy. I won't go further into what I feel about it: I'm a Yankee and cannot speak what I feel most strongly, well, but I do wish to say that I think it a most generous and noble utterance. Certainly for one who could say that of me I ought to have done all that it says I did do."

Of Time and the River sprang from the symbiotic union of two artistic forces—Wolfe's passion and Perkins's judgment. The two men had been at frequent odds, but together they both had accomplished the greatest work of their careers.

Max wrote Tom on February 8, 1935, "I swear, I believe that in truth the whole episode was a most happy one for me. I like to think we may go through another such war together."

A torn fragment in Wolfe's journals, never sent to Perkins, states: "In all my life, until I met you, I never had a friend."

PART THREE

XIV

Going Home Again

When he returned from Key West in early February, 1935, Maxwell Perkins urged Charles Scribner and Fritz Dashiell of *Scribner's* to serialize Hemingway's new book, now called *Green Hills of Africa*. It was a narrative expedition into contemporary literature almost as much as into the Serengeti plains. As with *Death in the Afternoon*, Hemingway, writing in the first person, was the guide. At conveniently located water holes in the safari, he paused to discuss writers and writing; for example, at one point he mused about Thomas Wolfe:

> Writers are forged in injustice as a sword is forged. I wondered if it would make a writer of him, give him the necessary shock to cut the over-flow of words and give him a sense of proportion, if they sent Tom Wolfe to Siberia or to the Dry Tortugas. Maybe it would and maybe it wouldn't.

Perkins wired Hemingway of *Scribner's* enthusiasm for his book but said they would need to study the manuscript further before confirming the $5,000 proposal Max had mentioned while they were fishing in the Gulf Stream. It was a question of quantity of material, not quality. A week later Perkins wired: WRITING ABOUT PRICE. WISH TO PAY $4500. WILL BEGIN MAY NUMBER. PUBLISH BOOK OCTOBER. . . .

In his letter Perkins added little to his telegram except his chagrin about the price. He knew Hemingway could get at least twice that much from any of the bigger magazines. "It is not a question of what *Green Hills* is worth intrinsically at all," Perkins explained, "but of what we can rightly pay for it and still run the magazine on as nearly sound an economic basis as the present situation allows, which is not a sound one."

By the time Hemingway received the offer he was "touchy as hell." He was more anxious about the reception of *Green Hills of Africa* than of any of his previous works, for in it he vented his aggressions not only against other writers but also against the critics who had tried to put him down in the last few years. Hemingway was laying his career on the line; and he hotheadedly interpreted Perkins's hard feelings about the money as an invitation to refuse the offer, thereby releasing *Scribner's* from purchasing it. So far as Hemingway knew, he told Max, the magazine had never run on a sound economic basis; but then, neither had Hemingway. He maintained that he had never cost a publisher anywhere any money, except Horace Liveright . . . by leaving him. Perkins avoided a flap by getting *Scribner's* to pay Hemingway the $5,000.

That spring Ernest cruised for the first time to the island of Bimini, a fisherman's paradise 175 miles northeast of Key West. Perkins withheld his editorial comments on *Green Hills of Africa* for the galleys, hoping the few months in Bimini might calm Hemingway.

At about this time Fitzgerald went off to a hotel in Hendersonville, North Carolina, for four weeks of rest. After writing for fifteen years, he was less secure than the day he started. He was flat broke and was beginning to realize he was no better a caretaker of his physical resources than of his fiscal ones. "I do not think he is especially sick," Perkins wrote Hemingway, "but just exhausted from work and alcohol." Home again in Baltimore, Fitzgerald wrote Max that he had "been on the absolute wagon for a month, not even beer or wine, and feel fine."

The news pleased Perkins, but he believed that Fitzgerald would soon suffer symptoms of withdrawal—a letdown and then a struggle. He knew Fitzgerald would need the support of all the friends that he could get, but Scott was hard put to find them just then. That year, almost simultaneously, three of his friendships with Perkins's writers deteriorated.

Months earlier Fitzgerald had openly admitted a kind of literary inferiority to Hemingway. He had written him that his respect for Ernest's artistic life was absolutely unqualified, "that save for a few of the dead and dying old men you are the only man writing fiction in America that I look up to very much." But their personal relationship had become distant, less because of Fitzgerald's envy than of Hemingway's arrogance. When Per-

kins suggested that Ernest find the time and some reason to write Fitzgerald, to brace him for "the crisis he will have to meet after a bit" from
giving up liquor, Hemingway said he could not think of a way to write
him without hurting Scott's feelings.

Several months later, however, Hemingway asked Perkins to tell Scott
that, strangely, *Tender Is the Night* kept improving every time he picked
it up. Fitzgerald was cheered by Hemingway's kind words. The book had
fallen flat, but the author still believed in it profoundly. "Things happen
all the time which make me think that it is not destined to die quite as
easily as the boys-in-a-hurry prophesied," he wrote Max. His friendship
with Hemingway, on the other hand, had been one of the "high spots of
life," but, Scott wrote Perkins, "I still believe that such things have a
mortality, perhaps in reaction to their very excessive life, and that we will
never again see very much of each other."

Fitzgerald also wanted to avoid Thomas Wolfe for a while, after
reading the advance copy of *Of Time and the River* which Perkins had
sent him. He admired Wolfe's lavish dedication, and wrote Max, "I am
sure that nothing Tom has said in his dedication could exaggerate the debt
that he owes you—and that stands for all of us who have been privileged
to be your authors." Fitzgerald thought the book went downhill from
there, but he asked Max on no account to tell Tom this, "for responding
as he does to criticism, I know it would make us life-long enemies and we
might do untold needless damage to each other."

Of Time and the River helped Fitzgerald realize "that the very excellent organization of a long book or the finest perceptions and judgment in
time of revision do not go well with liquor." A short story could be written on a bottle, Fitzgerald saw, "but for a novel you need the mental speed
that enables you to keep the whole pattern in your head and ruthlessly
sacrifice the sideshows as Ernest did in *A Farewell to Arms*. If a mind is
slowed up ever so little it lives in the individual part of a book rather than
in a book as a whole; memory is dulled." Still on the wagon and full of
sober regrets, Fitzgerald told Perkins, "I would give anything if I hadn't
had to write Part III of *Tender Is the Night* entirely on stimulant. If I had
one more crack at it cold sober I believe it might have made a great
difference."

The old friendship between Fitzgerald and Edmund Wilson had also
lapsed. They had gone in opposite directions. Antagonism had mounted
because of their respective reputations as scholar and wastrel, and it came
to a head in an argument over that very issue. "Bunny [Wilson's nick-

name] was the one who quarrelled, not Scott," Perkins wrote Hemingway years later, "and Bunny behaved, I almost thought, childish." More than ever, Perkins thought Wilson was a "remarkable chap and a man of natural integrity," who had done some magnificent writing in his last book for Scribners, *American Jitters: A Year of the Slump (1932)*. But during the next few years, Wilson's animosity toward Fitzgerald spilled over into his relationship with Perkins. Several times he came to Max for money against the earnings of future books. Once he requested the modest sum of $75; another time he asked Scribners to help him get a bank loan. "You wouldn't do anything for me on either occasion at a time when you were handing out money to Scott Fitzgerald like a drunken sailor—which he was spending like a drunken sailor," Wilson wrote Perkins years later. "Naturally you expected him to write you a novel which would make you a great deal more money than my books seemed likely to do. But, even so, the discrepancy seemed to me somewhat excessive." Wilson did not attribute this to malice. "You're the only person I ever see around there, and I've always felt I was on very good terms with you," Wilson wrote Perkins. He ascribed it to the "general apathy and moribundity into which Scribners seems to have sunk. You people haven't shown any signs of life since old man Scribner died—except when you have a paroxysm over some writer —usually very unreliable like Scott or Tom Wolfe—upon whom you squander money and attention like a besotted French king with a new favorite." Years later Wilson admitted: "I . . . was never one of his favorites," thus explaining why he left Scribners for another house in the mid-thirties. At that point he struck up a profound intellectual affair with Marxism, which threw into bolder relief for him Fitzgerald's social and historical shallowness. It would be years before Fitzgerald and the man he called his "intellectual conscience" would sit down and talk as friends again.

On several occasions, Scott had seen Elizabeth Lemmon at small parties in Baltimore. (Max envied him that. He had not been with Elizabeth for months. "I know it is my destiny to see you very seldom," he wrote her, "and I can endure it well enough even if the interval is to be years, when I know it in advance.") Max felt Elizabeth, in those brief meetings, had done Fitzgerald a lot of good. "Scott is under forty," he told her, "and if he's finished with alcohol he might do greater things than he had ever thought of. I know you had not consciously or directly influenced Scott but you were a revelation to him and did unconsciously." If Fitzgerald could stop drinking for good, Perkins believed, it would be largely because of Elizabeth Lemmon.

On the wagon longer than he had been in ages, Scott found his life "uninspiring," whereas, he believed, these should be his most productive years. "I've simply got to arrange something for the summer that will bring me to life again," he wrote Perkins, "but what it should be is by no means apparent."

For lack of a better suggestion, Max urged Scott to continue work on a novel he had begun which was set in medieval Europe—a long way from West Egg. Fitzgerald replied that the 90,000-word book would be called *Philippe, Count of Darkness.* His hero was a Frankish tough guy in armor—"It shall be the story of Ernest," Fitzgerald put down in a notebook. Then he outlined parts of it that he could sell separately to magazines. He said Perkins could have it all by the late spring of 1936. "I wish I had these great masses of mss. stored away like Wolfe and Hemingway," Fitzgerald wrote Perkins, "but this goose is beginning to be pretty thoroughly plucked, I am afraid."

In May, 1935, Fitzgerald visited Perkins in New York. A bright period in Zelda's health had proved to be just a flash, and Scott's mood the evening they were together reflected it. He was scrappy, putting Max on the spot about books Scribners was publishing. He expressed his greatest dissatisfaction over Tom Wolfe. Scott had recently read Wolfe's story "His Father's House" in the latest issue of *Modern Monthly*, published by V. F. Calverton. It embodied all Wolfe's faults and virtues and made Fitzgerald wish Tom were the sort of person with whom one could discuss his writing.

> How he can put side by side such a mess as "With chitterling tricker fast-fluttering skirrs of sound the palmy honied birderies came" and such fine phrases as "tongue-trilling chirrs, plumbellied smoothness, sweet lucidity" I don't know. He who has such infinite power of suggestion and delicacy has absolutely no right to glut people on whole meals of caviar.

Fitzgerald's unusual surliness with Perkins was provoked mostly by his own poor health. Just days before, the phantom illness he had so often blamed for his ills had materialized in a spot on his lung. The air in Wolfe country was reputedly therapeutic for tubercular conditions, and so Scott took a room at the Grove Park Inn in Asheville. The move to

North Carolina, he said, was an attempt to commute a "death sentence" his doctor had handed down if Scott were to revert to his old ways of living. Fitzgerald's return address for the next few months was "Gant's Tomb, Asheville."

"I was a good deal dismayed & probably jealous so forget all I said that night," Fitzgerald wrote Perkins after he had returned to Baltimore. "You know I've always thought there was plenty room in America for more than one good writer, & you'll admit it wasn't like me."

Perkins thought everything Fitzgerald said about Wolfe was as true as truth can be, but there was little anyone—even Perkins—could do about it. "Even if one had an utterly free hand, instead of being subject to constant abuse ([with accusations of] God damned Harvard English, grovelling at the feet of Henry James, etc.)," Perkins explained to Fitzgerald, "it would be a matter of editing inside sentences even, and that would be a dangerous business." Max thought criticism and age might make an impression and that Wolfe's writing would mature on its own. For the present, he said, "It is not that he thinks he is better than anyone else. He just does not think about the other people at all. When he reads them he is quite keen about them for a while, but [they do not seem important to him] because what he is doing seems to him momentous."

The appearance of *Of Time and the River* was the most fervently anticipated literary event of the spring season of 1935. The book had been talked about for months before the March 8 publication date. Max sent first editions to most of his friends and authors, even though he was sure some of them would never trudge through the 912-page volume. Van Wyck Brooks saw the sweat of Perkins's brow on every page, unable as he was to forget the hundreds of hours Max labored "through jungle-like nights in the middle of summer," slowly going under as he tried "to hang onto the fin of a plunging whale." Ernest Hemingway said the book was "something over 60% shit."

Wolfe believed the best way to avoid the same kind of public hysteria and private confusion that had accompanied his first book would be to leave America. He later gave his thoughts on exile in *You Can't Go Home Again*, through his character George Webber:

> When his first book had come out, wild horses could not have dragged him from New York: he had wanted to be on hand so he could be sure not to miss anything. He had waited around, and read all the reviews, and almost camped out in [his editor's] office, and had expected from day to day some

impossible fulfillment that never came. . . . So now he was gun-shy of publication dates, and he made up his mind to go away this time—as far as possible. Although he did not believe there would be an exact repetition of those earlier experiences, just the same he was prepared for the worst, and when it happened he was determined not to be there.

Wolfe booked passage on the *Ile de France*, and crated for storage everything he owned. His itinerary was as vague as his plans upon returning. On the night of March 1, the eve of Wolfe's departure, a cab pulled up to 246 East Forty-ninth Street. A man leapt out and pounded on the Perkinses' door. Max came down, not surprised to find Wolfe standing there, but astonished that he had brought a wooden packing case, five feet by two feet by a foot and a half. It contained every page of his manuscript, including the bundle of sheets they had worked over during the last five years. Tom and Max and the driver hauled it from the taxi and set it down inside the house. Then Tom asked the cabby his name. He said, "Lucky." "Lucky!" whooped Tom, pumping the man's hand. It seemed a good omen. The three had just completed a great effort together. They all stood there, smiling at one another for a moment, then they all shook hands. "Lucky" drove off, and the large packing case blocked the Perkinses' hall for days.

After Wolfe sailed, a letter from Aline Bernstein arrived for him at Scribners. Perkins wrote her back that he could do no more than hold it, because Tom had expressly forbidden him to forward any mail. He had left with the idea of taking a complete vacation for a couple of months, to be disturbed by neither personal mail nor even reviews.

As it happened, Tom himself had written Aline Bernstein a twenty-page message which he had mailed from Sandy Hook before the *Ile de France* reached the high seas. In it he told her about a copy of his book that he had left for her in Perkins's care. Then he wrote "how wonderful and great a person" Max was. Aline realized that provoking Max's hostility would kill any hope of her ever reaching Tom again. Ironically, getting through to Perkins was her last resort. In a friendly tone she now wrote Perkins a long letter, this one from Hollywood, where she was working for RKO Pictures. She really was not well enough to take the job, she wrote—"all these years of pain and sorrow about Tom have finally worn me out"—but she wanted to help her family, who had tried to help her mend the heartbreak of the last several years. Mrs. Bernstein asked Max to send her copy of Tom's book to California. "I cannot read it now," she explained, as "I am too deeply moved by anything concerning

Tom, even his name in a newspaper sends a dart of pain through me. I cannot understand his complete betrayal of me, but I have reached a place in life where all is a mystery. Forgive me, that I write you this way, but . . . I think that you and I have been closer to Tom than any other beings. I still live all my life with him, as I did the many years we were together, and now I want life no more without his friendship."

At Mrs. Bernstein's request Max returned those of her letters that were sitting at Scribners and sent her her copy of Tom's book.

It was because of her family that Aline wrote to Perkins once again. She knew about *Of Time and the River*'s conclusion, in which Eugene Gant coming home from a European journey beheld a rosy-cheeked Jewish woman older than himself. Aline realized that Wolfe was soon to write about their relationship. The next book, she feared, would expose their love affair for all the world to see. She wrote Perkins:

> I have already lived the great part of my life. But some time ago, he read [me] certain portions which he had written about my sister and my children, that must never be published . . . they have all stood by me when Tom almost wrecked my bright soul and loving heart. I will not have them traduced, no matter what means I take to prevent it. This concerns not only me, but yourself in your editorial capacity.

> Tom has often told me that you hate women, no doubt you think I am behaving like one. Well, I am. I consider it a curse to be a woman, a double curse to be a woman and an artist, but I cannot help it any more than I can help the color of my eyes. When Tom and I were first lovers, I told him it was the only time I was glad to be a woman, to complete him. I am still proud of my relation to him, in all its horror and beauty.

Wolfe had sworn that he would show Aline Bernstein *The October Fair* before any of it went to Perkins for editing. That was a long while ago, when it was to be his second book. "He has broken his word of honor to me so many times that I cannot trust him in this," she wrote Perkins. "So I appeal to you." She begged him to understand that "He cannot, he must not, I will not allow him again to betray me."

Perkins replied:

> From your earlier letter I judge that you suppose that Tom had given me reason to think of you as a "monster,"—this is the reverse of the truth, but I now begin to suspect that he must have given you to suppose that I was one. You are enough of a psychologist to know that the men who are

thought to hate women are the ones who are affected just the other way, so that they had to set up a "defense mechanism." I think women are extremely annoying, but that is because a man sees them in perspective. At any rate, nobody could fully understand that part of your letter in which you address me as an editor, but *October Fair* will not be published anyway for a year, and perhaps not as soon as that, and I cannot tell much about it until Tom returns.

On publication day of *Of Time and the River*, Perkins violated his vow of silence to Wolfe, but not in regard to Aline Bernstein. He sent a cable to the American Express office in Paris about the book: MAGNIFICENT REVIEWS SOMEWHAT CRITICAL IN WAYS EXPECTED FULL OF GREATEST PRAISE. Expecting no mail but checking for some, Wolfe received the message, then rambled along the boulevards of Paris in a reverie. Later he could remember almost nothing of the next six days. But Perkins's words were only a tantalizing morsel of the glory for which he hungered. Wolfe wired back: YOU ARE THE BEST FRIEND I HAVE. I CAN FACE BLUNT FACT BETTER THAN DAMNABLE INCERTITUDE. GIVE ME THE STRAIGHT PLAIN TRUTH. Perkins's second telegram poured it on even thicker than the first: GRAND EXCITED RECEPTION IN REVIEWS. TALKED OF EVERYWHERE AS TRULY GREAT BOOK. ALL COMPARISONS WITH GREATEST WRITERS. ENJOY YOURSELF WITH LIGHT HEART.

That same day Perkins wrote further, "Everybody outside of this house, outside the business, was amazed by the reception of *Of Time and the River*." Most of the reviews drew parallels with the venerated writers, from Dostoevski to Sinclair Lewis. "Honestly, unless you expected no degree of adverse criticism at all, because of course there was that about too great length and the sort of thing we all talked of," Perkins wrote him, "I cannot imagine why you should have any restraints upon your happiness in this vacation. If any man could rest on laurels for a bit, the man is you."

The economy in the spring of 1935 continued to worsen, the book business along with it. But Scribners soon had printed five editions of Wolfe's book, totaling 30,000 copies. Within weeks they had sold most of them, putting *Of Time and the River* in the top three on every bestseller list. By the end of the year, another 10,000 copies were printed.

The *Times, Tribune,* and *Saturday Review* gave Wolfe full front pages, and his picture was everywhere. Those who went out on Sunday afternoon to tea, as Louise did, found that even where there were no publishing people the book was excitedly talked about. Even Perkins's seventy-seven-year-old mother, who spoke of literature as "mental candy," was reading it, though her reaction was atypical. For five or six days she sat with it, emoting as much as a wooden Indian, until someone asked how she was getting on. As though she had waited a week for the question, she dropped the closed book to her lap, lifted her face and declared, "I've never read such language in my life." To one of her granddaughters she called, "Molly, go upstairs and get me a volume of Jane Austen so I can purge my mind!"

For weeks Wolfe traveled incommunicado. He had been completely worn out upon landing in Europe and in a state of nervousness over *Of Time and the River* that made even letter-writing impossible. That book, which had induced this state, now snapped him out of it. "Max, Max," Wolfe wrote his editor, "perhaps you think I hate all forms of criticism, but the sad truth is how much more critical am I, who am supposed to be utterly lacking in the critical faculty, than most of these critics are." The bulk of Wolfe's first letter home was his own reaction to *Of Time and the River*. He carried a copy of the book under his arm wherever he went but found it torture to read, save for a page or two at a time. Even then he found "at every point the deficiency of my performance compared with the whole of my intent, stares me in the face." The prickliest nettles were the countless mistakes in wording and proofreading, and the textual discrepancies. He absorbed the blame for all of them. During the first two months after publication, the staff at Scribners discovered some 200 errors, including the mysterious reappearance of Mr. Wang. Wang is the round-faced Chinese student from whom Eugene Gant borrows fifty dollars in his midnight race to old Gant's deathbed. Eugene arranges to mail the money to Wang. Wolfe wrote: "The boy never saw him again." Sixty-five pages later, however, Eugene raps on Wang's door and asks the Chinaman if a friend can spend the night on his couch.

"I fell down on that final job," Tom admitted. "The book was written and typed and rushed in to you in such frantic haste day after day that I did not even catch the errors in wording the typist made in an effort to decipher my handwriting—there are thousands of them." He listed some:

Battersea Lodge should have read Battersea Bridge
the character of my brain—the diameter of my brain
African beings—African kings
shaking his beard—shaking his head

"Max, Max, I cannot go on," Tom wrote after listing a fraction of the corrections that had to be made. He said, "We should have waited six months longer—the book, like Caesar, was from its mother's womb untimely ripped—like King Richard, brought into the world 'scarce half made up.'"

Wolfe worked at a four-part letter to Perkins for over a week. After registering his own criticism of the book, Wolfe reviewed his critics, interpreting every complaint as an attack on him personally. In response to Mark Van Doren's remark, a year before, that "The public is justified in asking Mr. Wolfe whether he can keep himself out of the picture in books to come," Tom now reminded Perkins, "You yourself told me you took one of your daughters through the Grand Central Station and showed her twenty people who might have stepped right out of the pages of Dickens, all just as true to life, but worthy of fiction." Because Burton Rascoe said that Wolfe had no evident sense of humor, Tom listed the scenes he considered comical. Reacting to Clifton Fadiman, who said it was debatable "whether he is a master of language or language a master of him," Wolfe ranted for paragraphs.

He closed Section 1 of his letter with the hope "that we have had a genuine and great success and that when I come back I will find my position enormously enhanced. If that much is true—if it is true that we have successfully surmounted the terrible, soul-shaking, heart-rending barrier of the accursed second book—I believe I can come back to work with the calm, the concentration, the collected force of my full power which I was unable to achieve in these frenzied, tormented, and soul-doubting last five years."

That spring Louise Perkins decided to tour Europe with her daughters Zippy and Peggy. When Wolfe learned of the plans in the making, he asked her to persuade Max to take a short vacation as well. "The one thing I have observed in Max in the last few years which worried me and which seemed wrong," Wolfe wrote Louise, "was a growing tenacity in the way he stuck to business—what seemed to me sometimes an unreasonable solicitude and preoccupation with affairs which might be handled by proxy or in less exhausting ways." He thought it was surely a sort of vanity, even in so modest a man as Max, to feel that a business could not run itself in his absence for a few weeks. Tom believed Max was at the "summit of his powers," that his best work was still before him. "[It] would be a tragedy," Wolfe wrote Louise, "if he in any way blunted or impaired his great faculties at this time simply because he failed to take advantage of a chance to recuperate and replenish his energies."

Perkins gave no indication that he had considered leaving his office even for a day. He wrote Elizabeth Lemmon that very month, "I'm in for a horrible summer alone here, but in a way I look forward to it. There won't be much I want to do, but still I won't have to do anything I don't want to do. Or maybe I'm fooling myself about that." He certainly would not have to go out to parties, as he and Louise had been doing many nights since moving to New York.

Before her trip, Louise Perkins had one of her paroxysms of spring cleaning. To burn off some of her energy, she weeded the bookshelves. She filled barrels with several hundred volumes, then paid a dealer $5 to haul them away. Weeks later, David Randall, the Scribners rare book authority, was walking down Second Avenue, window-shopping at the used book stores, when one display practically jumped out at him. There were dozens of books inscribed to Maxwell Perkins by Galsworthy and other eminent authors. When Max learned the facts, Randall went to buy them back, and was told the collection would cost $500. "We settled on $25," Randall recalled years later, "when I said it wasn't Mrs. Perkins, but the crazy maid who sold all the books to him. I said we'd meet him in court if he charged anything more." Max, Randall remembered, "laughed that quiet laugh of his, shaking his head back and forth, as if only *his* wife could have done such a thing."

Perkins's summer proved to be as horrible as he had anticipated. "You don't know how lonely it is here at night," he wrote Elizabeth Lemmon on June 28, 1935. "I forget about it in the day and when people ask me to do things at night I say I can't and then regret it. But I'd regret the other way too and get less work done. It's as bad here as in Baltimore when you're not there. It's worse, because there I always did have the hope that some miracle would bring you." With a Spartan spirit, Max told the maid who was supposed to look after him that all he wanted for dinner one night was cream cheese and bread. She fixed her eyes on his, then rolled them heavenward as if he had gone mad, which perversely made him request the same thing the next night. Each evening she hovered in puzzlement to watch him eat his meager meal. Stubbornly, Max ordered the entree for nights on end. "So now it's got to be bread to eternity," he wrote Elizabeth. In fact, however, he would occasionally duck out to the dining room at the Hotel Barclay, where he dined alone but had some good food.

The appearance that season of an old friend broke Perkins's loneliness. Van Wyck Brooks dropped in unannounced and seemed just as good as ever. Until recently, he had still been in the grasp of his long-lived depression. Perkins was convinced that Brooks never could have recovered if his wife, Eleanor, had not stood by him—patiently raising the family and running the house until he was back on his feet. "It was one of the best things I know of anyone's doing," Max told Elizabeth Lemmon, "and I don't believe there's a man would have been equal to the equivalent of it."

Brooks's only other stroke of good fortune in the last five years was in his professional life, and that had been the result of Perkins's devotion. For years Max had regarded Brooks's *Life of Emerson* as the log that was jamming his career. With Perkins's patient encouragement, Brooks had completed the biography in 1931. But this did not free him of his psychological torment.

Brooks still maintained he was hopeless as a writer, that nothing of his could possibly be worth printing. Perkins and Jack Wheelock both read the manuscript and repeatedly insisted that it was "quite good" and that they were eager for Scribners to print it. When Brooks explained his commitments to E. P. Dutton and Company, Max persuaded Van Wyck to let go of the manuscript, then carried it by hand to Dutton's publisher, John Macrae. At the same time, Perkins contacted Carl Van Doren at the Literary Guild and urged him to get the Guild to adopt the book as one of its selections. Dutton and the Guild both accepted *The Life of Emerson*, but Brooks refused to let it be typeset. In the spring of 1931 Max delegated Wheelock, whom he considered Van Wyck's most trusted friend, to go to Four Winds, a small, private sanitarium in Katonah, New York, and talk some sense into him.

"The boys have gone berrying," the attendant at Four Winds told Wheelock upon his arrival. Wheelock walked into the woods and found Van Wyck with an empty pail in his hand. He was all but mute and utterly remote. He stared at Wheelock as though looking right through him, but Brooks knew exactly why he had come. They walked among the brambles in silence until Wheelock pleaded, "Won't you let the Guild publish it?"

"No," Brooks snarled.

Wheelock assured him that they would not want the book if it were less than first-rate.

"Bad! Bad! Bad!" Brooks exclaimed, and Wheelock left.

Perkins himself saw Brooks during the next several months and insisted he agree to the offers. Van Wyck slowly came around and eventually asked Max to be his publisher—only if "the thing can be managed without hurting the feelings of Mr. Macrae who has been so decent to me." Perkins saw no way of managing it. In 1932 Dutton published the book. It became a critical success and solved Brooks's financial crisis. Van Wyck realized that he could earn a good living as a writer, and he recovered enough to write steadily for the next thirty years of his life. When he visited Max in the summer of 1935 he was in the middle of writing *The Flowering of New England*, his masterwork. Two years later it won the Pulitzer Prize—and was dedicated to Maxwell Evarts Perkins.

Despite the enormous success of *Of Time and the River*, Tom Wolfe experienced the same unrest that afflicted him after his first book. When he could stand the distress no longer, he suddenly thought of Germany with intense yearning. As for George Webber, in *You Can't Go Home Again*, Germany was for Wolfe the country

> after America, which he liked the best, and in which he felt most at home, and with whose people he had the most natural, instant, and instinctive sympathy and understanding. . . . And now, after the years of labor and exhaustion, the very thought of Germany meant peace to his soul, and release, and happiness, and the old magic again.

Besides Wolfe's passion for Germany, there was Germany's for him. *Look Homeward, Angel* had been translated and published there in 1933, and though Tom was not aware of it, the Germans were awaiting his return with great eagerness.

"I have heard it said that Lord Byron awoke one morning at twenty-four to find himself famous," Thomas Wolfe wrote Max Perkins on May 23, 1935. "Well, I arrived in Berlin one night, when I was thirty-four, and got up the next morning and went to the American Express and for the last two weeks at least I have been famous in Berlin." He found letters, telephone messages, and telegrams from all sorts of people— German journalists and publishers and various diplomats. For two weeks Wolfe met throngs of admirers, attended parties, and gave interviews.

But Wolfe told Max he had some "disturbing things" to tell him about Germany. Wolfe had heard the sounds of booted feet and rolling army trucks clashing with the sounds of singing, dancing, and laughter in the peaceful villages. The discord frightened him, but the nationalistic fervor got him thinking about America. It renewed a sense of pride and faith in his own country and himself. Once again in Berlin he wrote Perkins, "I feel myself welling up with energy and life again and if it is really true that I have had some luck and success at home I know I can come back now and beat all hollow anything I have ever done before, and certainly I can surprise the critics and the public who may think they have taken my measure by this time—and I think I may even have a surprise or two in store for you."

Wolfe begged Perkins not to proceed too far on the book of short stories Max had wanted to bring out, and for which Max had requested a title. "There are things I can do that will make them much better," he assured Max, "and if you will only wait on me I will do them and we will have a fine book of stories and unlike any I know of." But as Wolfe had got sidetracked in the past, now he was already living for another book about his characters the Pentlands. It was swelling and gathering in him like a thunderstorm, he told Perkins; "and I feel if there is any chance of my doing anything good before I am forty it will be this book." Tom resolved to become more withdrawn in his life than ever before. As he plunged into this new work, he also wanted to intensify his relationship with Max. "I will go down deeper in myself than I ever have before," he vowed to Perkins, insisting, "You must try to help me in every way to do this."

In the midst of his planning Wolfe received a letter from one Henry Weinberger, counselor-at-law. He represented Madeleine Boyd, who was claiming full agent's commissions for royalties on *Of Time and the River* as well as on Wolfe's future books. The action struck Wolfe like a bombshell. "This was the thing you said could not 'happen,' the thing she 'would not dare to do' because she knew she was ruined by her dishonesty," Tom wrote Perkins, remembering the scene in Perkins's office just two years earlier. "Well, she has done it, as I told you she would— because we were foolish, benevolent, soft-hearted, weak—call it what you like." Wolfe believed they should have made *the thief sign the confession of her theft* when she was weeping, sobbing, crying in abject fear at the discovery and possible consequences of her crime."

While the legal business hung in abeyance until Wolfe's return, Perkins forwarded him an invitation to be the visiting novelist at the Colorado Writers' Conference in July. The symposium offered to pay Wolfe

$250 for ten days of round-table discussions and conferences with student-authors. Hopeful that this might lure him home to complete his anthology of stories, Max asked Wolfe to cable his reply and a probable date of return. Three days later Wolfe wired: ACCEPT COLORADO OFFER RETURN EARLY JUNE, NO TITLE STORIES YET . . . WAIT FOR ME.

Max could not wait much longer. A half-year had passed since Aline Bernstein's fears regarding Wolfe's writing about her had possessed her, and she was becoming hysterical again. She impulsively visited Perkins to demand justice. Her screams could be heard through the walls of his office. The following day she was more in control of herself, but her feelings still ran high. "I wish I could have been able to show you a better side, that part of me which my friends love," Mrs. Bernstein wrote Perkins. "It is not easy for me to be hard, and I had to push myself in that direction, in order to speak to you at all of what was in my mind." She was not acting out of vengeance, she explained.

> I still love Tom and wish him no evil, what I demand is only because of my feeling for my own family, and I sincerely believe that my love for Tom, and his for me, while it lasted, is not a matter for public consumption, nor do I think that he has any right to use material that I have given him, since he has chosen to break every tie that bound us.

"I know nothing of the way the publishing business is handled," she wrote Perkins.

> I do not know if you yourself make all the decisions for your firm. If not, if there is some committee or some individual who shares the responsibility with you, I want to state my case, though I have little hope that anyone, in this vale of tears, would come to any decision contrary to his own best interests.
>
> A point is reached where one has literally to choose between good and evil. I know the complexity of duties and friendships, of all the threads that bind us to life, how complex a man's relation is to himself. Whether or not this book is published by you, or another, you are faced with your own decision, whether a family and a human being is to be destroyed or not.

Aline was more convinced than ever that Perkins had tampered with her life, that he had told Tom to break with her. Days later she wrote him again, "I trust that never again will you try to play providence."

Perkins did his best to inject some reason into this affair. He would not allow Mrs. Bernstein to assume that he had meddled with her life. He wrote:

> I do not interfere in people's private affairs. Certainly anyone who has lived for any length of time would never venture to interfere in a situation of that sort.
>
> I have every wish to do anything that would be of advantage to you in so far as I can do it rightly in view of the various obligations which I am compelled to fulfill, even if they are to my own personal disadvantage.

Mrs. Bernstein took Perkins's advice and tried appealing to Wolfe in a letter, which she sent in Perkins's care.

As near as Perkins could guess, Wolfe was due to return to America on Independence Day. For the week Wolfe was still aboard ship, Max fretted about his recent exchanges with Mrs. Bernstein. At one point she had mentioned a gun, but whether it was to be aimed at him, or Tom, or at herself Perkins did not know. "I'd much rather it was aimed at me," Max wrote Elizabeth Lemmon. "I'm so fed up on contention, and struggle with irrational people." Max first thought he should prepare Wolfe for trouble, then decided it would be easier to mind his own business and go to Windsor.

Thomas Wolfe arrived on a blazing-hot Fourth. By then Mrs. Bernstein's protestations about the publication of Tom's next book had become utterly illogical. Max believed the effect on Wolfe of this sudden tirade might be to ruin his entire future, and so he stayed in New York and went to the pier to break it to Tom gently. He found Wolfe's baggage already on the wharf and waited by it, long after everyone else had come ashore. When Tom finally disembarked, Perkins was sitting on one of the valises with his head down. Max was pondering the problem of Aline Bernstein when he heard a low Southern voice say, "Max, you look so sad. What's the matter?" Max said nothing immediately about Aline Bernstein's hysteria. They stored Tom's baggage and went to the Mayfair Yacht Club. There on the East River, with boats scudding up and down, Tom asked to hear everything that concerned him. Max then told him all about Mrs. Bernstein. Wolfe, however, did not seem to take the matter too seriously. He asked if that was all. When Max assured him it was, he said, "Well then, now we can have a good time."

They were on their way to the Lafayette Hotel when Tom stopped at Eighth Street and pointed. "There, Max, is the place where I lived in the attic and wrote *Look Homeward, Angel,*" he said. "Let's go up and see if we can get in." They climbed the stairs and knocked on the door, but there was no answer. While Tom was still rapping, Max looked out the window at the rear of the building and saw a fire escape that ascended to the open dormer of Wolfe's loft. "Well, Tom," Max said, "if you really want to see the nest where the young eaglet mewed his mighty youth, it can be done!" And so the editor-in-chief of Charles Scribner's Sons, in fedora and suit, led the way on a second expedition of breaking-and-entering. He crawled out to the fire escape, clambered up to the window and stepped in. Wolfe followed. "You could call it an attic," Perkins wrote John Terry years later in trying to reconstruct the scene, "for it was at the top of the house and there was a certain amount of slope to the upper halves of the walls, but it was magnificent—not the kind of attic you think of poets residing in at all. In fact, I would say it was the best place Tom ever did live in." Before leaving, Wolfe scrounged for a pencil, then scribbled on the wall of the vestibule: THOMAS WOLFE LIVED HERE.

After a drink at the Lafayette they crossed the East River into Brooklyn. The sun was setting, and Max and Tom went to the Saint George Hotel, where from the rooftop they looked down upon the city. It was like a spectacle about to begin. The sunlight dimmed to darkness and Manhattan came to life in a million twinkling lights.

They left Brooklyn and returned to the Lafayette for another drink, then walked uptown through the heat, with their coats slung over their shoulders. They talked all the way. Around three in the morning, they parted in a bar on the East Side, near Forty-ninth Street. At nine o'clock, Perkins, red-eyed, his head swimming, was sitting in a Pullman seat of the White Mountain Express, as the train chugged northward to Windsor.

XV

Critical Times

Perkins spent only a few days in Vermont. Tom Wolfe was back in town, and that meant legal and romantic problems in addition to editorial duties. Max felt his presence in New York was essential.

After Wolfe had been back for more than a week and still had not answered Aline Bernstein's last letter, she swallowed her pride and asked Perkins's support once again. "I am in distress," she wrote Max, "and I would be grateful if you will ask him to answer me. He must be in a great rage." Then she left another letter without an envelope for Tom, so that Max could also read it.

> I want you and Mr. Perkins to know that I will have nothing to do with the law in connection with you or your publishers, for what you may write of me or what you use of my material. This may or may not relieve your minds, I do not care. If I cannot come to a personal and human agreement with you, I may as well quit. . . . When we were together I believed that if you wrote this book about us, you would stand by me, as you often promised. Steadfast was your word. I know enough to know that I cannot command love of any sort, if what I am is not enough to hold it. Maybe I am a fool to expect honorable treatment: I had faith in you, Tom.

Thoroughly confused about how to proceed, Wolfe did nothing, not even his work. To get him thinking about his writing again, Max told him of the sacks full of mail waiting for him at Scribners. Perkins had seen the fan letters of many authors, but no one had received as many as Wolfe. His readers worshiped him and wanted to express their gratitude. Tom began coming to Scribners every day to work in the fifth-floor library, writing cordial responses to his admirers.

Perkins felt that Wolfe was adjusting to his return pretty well, though he still had not worked on the proofs of his book of short stories. Wolfe was just killing time until his writers' conference in Colorado. Max knew Tom well enough to worry that he might stretch out his upcoming travels, leaving the anthology in limbo. So almost daily, over lunch or a drink, he urged Wolfe to get on with his writing. One afternoon not long after Wolfe's arrival in America, while they were having "tea" at the Chatham Bar, Mrs. Bernstein appeared.

Aline was seated alone at a small table by the wall, with her head bowed down and her face partly covered by the brim of her hat. Perkins recognized her and pointed her out. Tom rushed over, but the bar was too public a place for a reunion like that, so he and Mrs. Bernstein and Perkins went back to Max's office. There, Wolfe tactlessly spoke of compensating Aline in dollars for all the help she had given him. He asked Max if he might see him alone for a minute and in Perkins's office he spoke of giving her some payment out of his royalties from *Of Time and the River*— the book had by then sold 40,000 copies. Mrs. Bernstein, meanwhile, was waiting in the railed-off receptionist's area by the elevator. When Tom returned to her, Aline had a vial of pills at her lips. He lunged toward her and slapped the bottle from her hands. Aline swooned into his arms. Perkins, suspecting she had already swallowed an overdose of barbiturates, rang the elevator bell for the night watchman, who directed them to a dermatologist working late in her office in the Scribner Building. The doctor counted the pills, phoned the pharmacy, and ascertained that all of them were still there. Thus began a reconciliation of sorts between Tom Wolfe and Aline Bernstein.

A few days later Aline apologized to Perkins:

> I have been on the rack for a long time, and I am taking punishment for two things I cannot help any more than the color of my eyes. I was born too soon, and I love too well. I wish I could show you what is in my heart, how I understand what you have done for Tom and how I understand your special quality. I have said things to you I should not have said for I know the road you have travelled with him.

What she could not make clear to Wolfe she explained to his editor: While Tom wanted to cancel his debts with cash, she would never accept any kind of reimbursement.

> Whatever I did for him in those early years of his work was done from the fullness of our love and my faith in him. Let me keep that, it is the one best thing in my life. There will never be a question of any claim, there surely can be no question of repayment in money.

During this time Aline Bernstein was working day and night in the theater and was tired and sleepless. From time to time she saw Wolfe, but never with much satisfaction; his mind was on other things and they were uncomfortable together. In the last week of July she collapsed and remained unconscious for three days. She had developed pleurisy. "It is awful, I am gasping for breath in an oxygen tent and the pain is awful," she wrote Wolfe when she came to. "I was never so sick but I'm going to get well, I have a lot to finish. I hope you never get pleurisy."

Wolfe went west on July 27, to the writers' conference at the University of Colorado in Boulder, and in mid-August Max received his first letter from him. "This has been, and is going to be, an extraordinary trip," he wrote Max just before leaving for Denver and points south. After all the discussions, lectures, readings, and parties, he too was exhausted.

Perkins was most concerned about Tom's anthology, now titled *From Death to Morning*. Still distressed by all the mistakes in *Of Time and the River*, Wolfe wrote Perkins, "You must not put the manuscript of a book of stories in final form until after my return to New York. If that means the book of stories will have to be deferred till next spring, then they will have to be deferred, but I will not consent this time to allow the book to be taken away from me and printed and published until I myself have had time to look at the proofs, and at any rate to talk to you about certain revisions, changes, excisions, or additions that ought to be made. I really mean this, Max." He added: "I propose rather to prepare my work in every way possible to meet and refute, if I can, some of the very grave and serious criticisms that were made about the last book."

Max had gone through the proofs and once again was impressed by them. "They show how objective you can be, and how varied you can be," he wrote to Tom. As it was, he said, the entire book would be an effective refutation to earlier adverse criticism.

As Wolfe toured the West, spending time with, among others, Edna Ferber and, in Hollywood, Dorothy Parker, Perkins kept sending him reminders about the unmarked proofs. Wolfe's only replies were postcards exclaiming about scenic wonders or relaying anecdotes. Finally, on September 1, Wolfe decided that his vacation, which had expanded to six months, enough for anyone, was over. He felt almost guilty enough, he told Max, to get back to work.

While on the road, Wolfe had mulled over his future projects. At Boulder and elsewhere the author had discussed a "book of the night" which was beginning to take hold of him. He explained to Perkins:

> I have told how much of my life has been lived by night, also the chemistry of darkness, the strange and magic thing it does to our lives, about America at night, the rivers, plains, mountains, rivers in the moon or darkness.

Wolfe believed his realization that Americans were a "nighttime people" was one of the most precious ideas he had conceived, one to which he wanted to devote a special book. At last he wanted to try writing from the outside rather than from within, to invent a universe in which he himself was not the absolute center. He wrote Perkins, "I want to assert my divine right once and for all to be the *God Almighty* of a book, to be at once the spirit to move it, the spirit behind it, never to appear, to blast forever the charges of 'autobiography' while being triumphantly and impersonally autobiographical."

"What are we to work on next?" he wrote Max as he started east. There was *The October Fair,* the "Pentland book," *The Book of the Night,* short stories. . . . Or should he respond to numerous offers to lecture? Max had plenty of time to formulate his answer, for Wolfe was still loitering. In mid-September, for example, he stopped off in Reno and was bedazzled by the town with its casinos and bars and dance halls eternally ablaze in neon.

Perkins continued to believe that the volume of short stories must come first. He had corrected the proofs as much as he dared and returned them to the press to be sent back in revised galleys. "The moment Tom gets here I am going to try to make him read them," Perkins wrote Frere-Reeves in London. "If he will not, I shall try to get them away from him and put them into pages unread." The book now contained 95,000 words, a normal amount, and Perkins was afraid only that Wolfe would want to add stories yet to be written. "I shall fight hard against this," he wrote

Frere-Reeves. "He seems to feel a certain shame at the idea of turning out a book of reasonable dimensions."

On Friday, July 25, Perkins had gone to Baltimore for an appointment with Dr. Bordley. The last time he had been in Baltimore he had made what he now considered a rash promise to Elizabeth Lemmon—to visit her home and spend the night, his first in Middleburg. She met him Saturday afternoon, and for only the second time in their thirteen-year friendship, Max went to Welbourne. Later in the day, Elizabeth drove him in her shiny new Ford coupe along the recently paved Skyline Drive, which ribboned among the peaks of the Blue Ridge Mountains. Mile after mile, Max's pouched, unblinking eyes swept the lovely vista. He looked very tired to Elizabeth. She had never pushed him to discuss his work, but this day she did gently remark that she knew almost nothing about what his job actually entailed. Max said he would tell her someday, in a letter.

Max did sleep over at Welbourne, but early the next morning he was packed and clearly ready to leave. Elizabeth persuaded him to stay long enough to meet several of her friends and relatives. Then he departed for New York. Afterward, safely distant from her most affecting presence, he wrote her:

> You really have had a wonderfully happy and good life, and have kept out of all the grime, and you always represented that to me. . . . Elizabeth, you always looked sad when you were thinking—maybe you haven't been happy in the cheap sense—you wouldn't be—but you have done good. If I survive in another life I'll remember your comings to Baltimore in all the heat and I'll thank you for them.

Perkins disliked being indebted to people, "but not to you—" he wrote Elizabeth, "which is fortunate for me because I owe you more than I ever could repay. After I have been with you I always feel again that those things that now generally seem to be an illusion really do exist. . . . As for last weekend, I'll always have it to remember and shall think about everything and everyone there with gratitude and pleasure." Max never visited Welbourne again, and its perfection never dimmed for him.

True to his word, Perkins described for Miss Lemmon a typical workday: Tuesday, July 29, 1935. As always, Max said, he began with the heap of mail waiting on his desk. "One letter," he wrote Elizabeth, "was from an agent asking us to take over a young East Side . . . author [named Henry Roth] who wrote *Call It Sleep*." Perkins had skimmed the novel and wished that he had had a chance to publish it. From its tight, eloquent opening pages describing the huddled masses on Ellis Island, Max admired Roth's penetrating recreation of a pocket of American life near "Avenyuh D" in New York City. Perkins told Elizabeth that "such a writer would make no end of trouble for me on account of his complete contempt for any conventional restraint—much worse than any one we have published. Still, I wrote encouragingly and sent for [his next] book. We are publishers after all."

Later that day, Perkins told Elizabeth, he spoke to Charles Scribner about a book on the training of bird dogs, which they decided to accept. Then he and Scribner discussed a limited edition of William Butler Yeats's works. Scribner was by nature skeptical of poetry, but Perkins thought Yeats was the most important twentieth-century poet in the English language, and contended there was a need for such a book. He reminded Scribner that they had profited from an equally unpromising set of O'Neill's plays. Scribner yielded and told Max to arrange with Macmillan for the reprint rights to the material.

Then, Max wrote, S. S. Van Dine called "to give notice" that he would bring in his newest manuscript—*The Kidnap Murder Case*—by the first of August. "Good," Perkins remarked, "but why the ultimatum?"

"Because," Van Dine replied, "you said I was not punctual after I got married." Perkins did tease people who waited so late as their forties to marry, as Wright had done. "After all that time, why bother?" he would say.

For the rest of the morning Max dictated letters. He and Scribner went to the nearby "air-cooled" Longchamps for lunch, over which Perkins told him about that wonderful road that snaked across the Blue Ridge Mountains.

Back at the office, Max managed to dictate the rest of his letters just before the tennis champion Helen Wills Moody strode in. Scribners had published her instructional book on tennis. She now launched into a volley-by-volley account of her recent match with Helen Jacobs. "Certainly she is beautiful in her way, and strong and healthy, and natural in a way you like to think is American," Max wrote Elizabeth. And, he conceded, her first book was successful. But, Perkins told Miss Lemmon, "Helen Wills can't write." He wanted to tell her "to have some children before it was too late, and forget writing." Instead he looked up the sales figures on her book and ordered a new edition. "I don't work properly on that kind of thing," Max said, meaning nonliterary works, "because it bores me."

Her appointment was followed by several others. Before the afternoon ended, Max also heard from Thomas Wolfe's lawyer. Wolfe, he reported, had burrowed into his papers and found his correspondence with Madeleine Boyd, the agent who was suing him. To Max it looked as though that would end their trouble with her. Later Wolfe asked Max to help him in every way possible to keep him from this kind of "shameful and ruinous invasion" in the future. Perkins could be counted upon to do his best. He wrote Tom, however, that such assaults were a part of life. "Like fleas to a dog, as the fellow said, they are probably good for us."

That day Perkins did not have to go off for a late-afternoon drink with anyone, so he stayed in the office and read, interrupted only by a little trouble with some advertising copy. On the whole, he told Miss Lemmon, "it was a fair day." For his evening reading he stuffed into his briefcase a narrative by an old hunter in the Southwest who had fought Apaches.

"I have much more variety in work than most people," Max once wrote Miss Lemmon, explaining how he talked himself out of taking vacations. In fact, he said, the work so suited him that he could see no reason not to do it seven days a week. "No one thinks a very good job was done with the Creation," he told Elizabeth. "It was probably rushed to get the seventh day off. That's why we don't work on it and I hate it, and all other holidays, and also nights."

In September, 1935, Louise and the two girls returned from Europe. Peggy had left behind her a European race-car driver who had proposed marriage, after knowing her less than a week, then attempted suicide because she turned him down.

In late September there was another important arrival. Tom Wolfe returned to New York. Max had been braced for a scrap with Wolfe over the proofs of the short-story collection. To his amazement, Wolfe corrected them immediately and without fuss or demand. Perkins's arguments that the book must be brought out quickly had apparently been convincing. Within a month the book was in the stores.

Wolfe now moved into a new apartment at 865 First Avenue, just two blocks toward the East River from the Perkinses' house. Soon Max was once again spending a great deal of time with him. Wolfe had already become a fixture at the Perkinses', but now, as Tom's agent, Elizabeth Nowell, observed,

he all but lived there as a member of the family—or as Perkins's son, which to all intents and purposes he was. Perkins never seemed to see enough of him, and Mrs. Perkins fed him, cared for him, listened to his problems and entertained his friends with the patience of a saint.

In the fall of 1935, Scott Fitzgerald sank into his deepest troubles yet. It began when Edwin Balmer of *Redbook* lost interest in *Philippe, the Count of Darkness* after printing the third installment. Scott fell heavily into debt, then grew ill and could not work. For weeks he languished. Perkins received only telegrams and brief requests for money. "I know that he has been sick and poor," Perkins wrote Hemingway, "but maybe this sickness is partly his old hypochondria."

That winter Fitzgerald expressed his anguish in a long article entitled "The Crack-Up." It appeared in three monthly installments in *Esquire*.

> I had a strong sudden instinct that I must be alone. . . . I saw that even my love for those closest to me was becoming only an attempt to love, that my casual relations—with an editor, a tobacco seller, the child of a friend were only what I remembered I should do from other days.

Perkins did not know what to make of Scott's article. Scheduled to see his own doctor in Baltimore, he paid a visit to Scott and found him in bed with the grippe, wheezing and gasping for air. "I saw Scott, but it did not do any good at all, maybe harm," Perkins wrote Hemingway after his house call. "It was not possible to talk to him, and I finally left him asleep, if you could call it sleep."

Oddly enough, Fitzgerald's depressing *Esquire* pieces proved to Perkins that Fitzgerald's case was not hopeless. He explained to Hemingway:

> Nobody would write those articles if they were really true. I doubt if a hopeless man will tell about it, or a man who thinks he is beaten for good. Those people I should think would not say anything at all, just as those who really intend suicide never tell anybody. So I thought that in some deep way, when he wrote those articles, Scott must have been thinking that things would be different with him. He may have lost that passion in writing which he once had, but he is such a wonderful craftsman that he could certainly make out well if he were able to control himself and be reconciled to life.

Perkins agreed with John Peale Bishop's suggestion that only returning to the Catholic Church could save Scott. "I know and always did, from his very first writing, that he has a fundamental inclination that way," Max wrote Ernest. Fitzgerald's public confession of a crisis of the spirit made Perkins guess such an announcement might be forthcoming.

Desperate for money, Fitzgerald spent the spring writing sketches for *Esquire* and a few forgettable stories for the *Post*. His income that year plummeted to $10,000, the lowest it had been since the publication of *This Side of Paradise*.

Ernest Hemingway thought the "Crack-Up" pieces were "miserable." People experienced emptiness many times in life, he said, and he thought they should come out of it fighting, not whining in public. He wrote Scott a few times to cheer him up but found him taking pride in his "shamelessness of defeat." Ever since he first met F. Scott Fitzgerald, Hemingway said, he had thought that if the man had gone to that war he always felt so bad about missing, he would have been shot for cowardice. Hemingway was convinced that Scott's troubles were self-inflicted. It was a terrible thing for Scott to love youth so much that he leapfrogged from childhood to senility without experiencing manhood.

Hemingway made one of his infrequent visits to New York that season. He was nervous about the reception of *Green Hills of Africa*, and with just cause. As fascism rose in Europe in the thirties, leftist "essayists," as many American literary critics preferred to call themselves, proclaimed that the purpose of literature was to remedy the world's social ills. They were angry that Hemingway, one of the best-known voices of America, had not joined their cause. He remained unaffiliated with any group, committed only to his writing. His reputation was in great shape, he told Perkins—André Gide, Romain Rolland, and André Malraux, he pointed out, had just invited him to an international writers' congress— but he was not deceived; the critics would have their knives out. He doubted, however, that they could kill him off for a while yet. "Papa is pretty durable," he assured Perkins.

When Perkins received the proofs of *Green Hills of Africa* from Ernest in late August, 1935, he thought everything about them was all right, except for a backhanded swipe at Gertrude Stein which Ernest had inserted. "I think it was better not to call the old girl a bitch," Perkins wrote Hemingway of the indirect reference to her. Hemingway pointed out that he had not mentioned Miss Stein by name and there was nothing that proved it was definitely she. Besides, he asked Max, what should be put in place of "bitch"? Certainly not "whore." Hemingway offered to modify the noun with "lousy" or "lesbian," but if anyone was ever a bitch, he said it was Gertrude Stein. He did not see what Perkins was fussing about, unless he thought the word would just give the critics something else to "burp about."

In *Green Hills of Africa,* Hemingway pointed out that writers who read the critics practically destroyed themselves.

> If they believe the critics when they say they are great then they must believe them when they say they are rotten and they lose confidence. At present we have two good writers who cannot write because they have lost confidence through reading critics. If they wrote, sometimes it would be good and sometimes it would be quite bad, but the good would get out. But they have read the critics and they must write masterpieces. The masterpieces the critics said they wrote. They weren't masterpieces, of course. They were just quite good books. So now they cannot write at all.

Hemingway had discussed Scott Fitzgerald and Thomas Wolfe with Perkins in almost identical phraseology.

At last he made what, for him, was a conciliatory gesture, by altering his reference to Gertrude Stein, calling her a "female." He thought that would anger her the most, and please Perkins.

Max expected a cold critical reaction to *Green Hills,* but not because of the vendetta Hemingway predicted. Max had observed enough careers to believe in their natural ebb and flow. He knew that if the critics did not have an issue at hand on which to take Hemingway to task, they would invent one. "Every writer seems to have to go through a period when the tide runs against him strongly," Perkins wrote Fitzgerald, "and at the worst it is better that it should have done this when Ernest was writing books that are in a general sense minor ones."

And indeed, the reviews of *Green Hills of Africa* were tepid. Charles Poore in the *New York Times* wrote that it was the "best-written story of big-game hunting anywhere" and that Ernest's writing was "better than ever, fuller, richer, deeper and only looking for something that can use its full powers." Edmund Wilson took what Max called a "Marxian crack" at it in the *New Republic,* calling it Hemingway's "weakest book." Wilson had been one of Hemingway's earliest admirers, but over the next few years he became one of his most outspoken critics.

Ernest took the reviews hard. It had been some six years since his successful *A Farewell to Arms.* He believed his new book was ruined by two specific flaws, both of which could have been avoided. The first, he

maintained, was that he had offended the daily critics in the book by
referring to the New York crowd as "angleworms in a bottle" and to
critics as the lice that crawl on literature; they ganged up on him for it.
But Perkins did not think there was anything either of them could have
done about that. He explained, "I knew, and I never dreamed that you
did not, that you were telling plain truths to the reviewers in *Green Hills.*
I could have warned you about that, but I did not think you wanted it,
and I do not believe you would have heeded it for an instant. Nor do I
think you should have. . . . You told the truth about them and it won't
act against you over a fairly long space of time, but only momentarily."

Hemingway's second point was about the book's advertising. Scribners'
former best-selling author John Fox, Jr. once wrote old Charles Scribner,
"A publisher is a man who is blamed if a book fails and ignored if it
proves a success." Now Hemingway beefed that Scribners was not playing up *Green Hills* enough. "Advertising," Perkins said, "is a matter
that nobody can ever speak of positively, and it would be silly to say they
might not have done wrong about it." But *Green Hills* got the same backing in advertising as Perkins's other offerings that season, including Mark
Sullivan's latest installment of *Our Times,* S. S. Van Dine's *Garden
Murder Case,* and Robert Briffault's controversial best seller, *Europa.*
After years of experience, Max found that one could not "answer unfavorable reviews by following them up two or three days later. . . . It
is stupid that this is so, but we have been convinced of it."

After two months and a piddling sale, Perkins explained the book's
failure to the author this way:

> It was mostly due to something that often happens in publishing: the pub-
> lic gets a superficial impression of what a book is and the one they got of
> this book was that it was an account of a hunting expedition to Africa,
> covering a short space of time, and was therefore a distinctly minor piece
> of work.

"I should have foreseen it," Max wrote. "The public regards you as a
novelist." Once again, as he had several times that year, he told Hemingway that he must produce a novel.

Hemingway started right in on the kind of writing the public expected from him. He wrote Perkins that it would become a short novel
or a "hell of a long story" set in the Gulf Stream. Max wished he could
get down to Key West for a while, where they might discuss it, but the

sudden temporary loss of his right-hand man prevented that. John Hall
Wheelock had to go off for a rest, and nobody could tell for how long.
"One of those mysterious breakdowns," Max confided to Hemingway.

The pressures of the last few years, working through the Depression, had imposed a strain on Wheelock. Waves of fear made him feel
ineffectual, unable to edit his authors or even complete his own book of
poetry. Max had talked a great deal with Wheelock before his going off
and guessed that "his feeling that people here think that he ought to
brace up etc. is more or less part of the illness." In fact, nobody at
Scribners did feel that way about it. Wheelock went to Stockbridge, Massachusetts, for a rest; Max assured him there was nothing for him to
worry about at Scribners. "You went at the very best time of year from
the point of view of work. So don't worry about that. I am telling you
the truth." It was a white lie. Within days he had written Elizabeth
Lemmon, "I don't see how I can do without him, but somehow I shall."

In a complete reversal of their roles of just a few years earlier, Van
Wyck Brooks visited Wheelock at Stockbridge in January, 1936. As before, Max remained the one person with whom all parties could discuss
the situation. Brooks thought their friend's condition was more critical
than anyone supposed. "The illness is invisible," he wrote Max; "I think
Jack has a feeling that the general impression is that he is somehow playing possum." Van Wyck suggested that Scribners get the manuscript of
Wheelock's poetry off to the press at once. "It will give him a strong
outside interest during the spring months, and make him feel how much
good work he has done." Perkins acted on the idea immediately.

By February, Wheelock felt strong enough to return to work. His
doctors said that he really was not well yet, and his return was mostly
experimental. "He will find it mighty hard not to get submerged in
work though," Max wrote Van Wyck. "It is impossible to prevent it
unless he does it by refusing to work except during certain hours. That is
what he ought to do, and I hope will." Perkins sat Wheelock down and
worked out a limited schedule with him. Wheelock stuck to it and was
practically as good as new when his book of poetry came out. The volume
helped him win the Bollingen Prize.

With *From Death to Morning,* Thomas Wolfe's first collection of
short stories, Wolfe began to experience the same sort of critical back-
lash that Hemingway had. The reviews complained of his flabby emo-
tionalism and lack of polish. Deep antagonisms surfaced and affected his

behavior with Perkins. On November 29, 1935, Max and Louise joined Tom for a nightcap at a restaurant called Louis and Armand's. It turned out to be a mistake because Tom was not a one-drink man, and after two or three he could become abusive. That night he got to ranting about "capitalistic injustice." He elected Max the "King Capitalist" and said insulting things about him. Wolfe came to his office at one o'clock the next day, contrite and affectionate, saying that he must get to work and that Perkins must help him decide what to work on. Max agreed to meet him the next night to discuss it—not in his house or a café but in the very middle of an East River bridge, where there would be no whiskey within half a mile.

A few weeks later, Wolfe squabbled again with Perkins. The dispute grew out of a renewal of Tom's cockeyed plan to pay Mrs. Bernstein for past favors. On a Thursday night, he demanded that Max come up with $1,050 in cash by eleven o'clock the following morning at the latest. Max said it could not be done; Tom said it had to be done. Perkins delivered the money by the appointed hour, but when he saw Wolfe again at seven that evening, he learned that Tom had snoozed the afternoon away. The wad of bills was stuffed in his pocket. Max made him promise to go directly to the Hotel Gotham, without stopping for any drinks, and lock the money in their safe until he could get to his bank on Monday. Afterward Perkins laughed over the episode.

Then came the dreadful evening when Tom showed himself at his very worst. The Countess Eleanor Palffy was an American friend of Louise and Max's. She had recently lost an eye because of a tumor that resulted when her husband, out of jealousy, struck her with the butt of a revolver. On her first day out of the hospital the Countess phoned Max to ask if she could come to dinner. Eleanor had always been interested in writers, and Louise suggested they invite Tom as well. Max knew that would be like combining glycerin and nitric acid. He pleaded against it, knowing how this woman's social attitudes, her title, and her cosmopolitan manner would infuriate Tom. Louise insisted that the evening would be fun.

Wolfe warmed up for the occasion with a good many drinks, and as Max feared, by the time he arrived he was very drunk. Hardly inside the door, he lashed out at Eleanor. The point of his tirade was that she wasn't any better than anybody else, that he was as good as any man. Tom was so sure she was a snob and therefore anti-Semitic that he even told her that his father, the stonecutter W. O. Wolfe, was a rabbi. That only fascinated her. At one point, in frustration, Tom sprang up from the dinner table, pulled off his jacket to exhibit the label, and said, "From the best tailor in London!"

Max tried to stifle Tom's vulgarity by joking as best he could, but he realized nothing short of Tom's departure would put an end to it. Then Wolfe himself, almost in tears, got up and stomped toward the front door. Perkins caught him in the hall and persuaded him to come back and be civilized. That was a mistake. Tom returned to his chair but also the same line of talk. He pounced upon Eleanor's every word, growing ever more vitriolic until, after one comment that infuriated him, he brandished his long index finger in front of her face and said, "That's as false as—as that eye."

Eleanor said it was time for her to return to the hospital. Tom volunteered to escort her there, but Perkins insisted that he was taking her back. Both men went, then stopped at Manny Wolf's for a drink over which Tom resumed his invective. Perkins finally reached his boiling point. "I for that one time in my life," he remembered ten years later, "lost my temper with him and told him off. When I do that, I always get to shouting, and it attracted a lot of attention." Max laced into him so vehemently that the barman gave out a small cheer. A few weeks later Eleanor was asked again to the Perkinses' for dinner. Max invited Tom to come in before, just to say something to make amends. "He did come very humbly, with a big bunch of roses," Perkins recalled. Tom tried to apologize and did stammer out some well-intentioned words, but it later became apparent that forever afterward he resented Max's having dragged him on the carpet that way.

All that year it was obvious to Perkins that Tom was testing him: Max's friendship, his patience, and his confidence in Wolfe's work. Once he even told Perkins that an editor at the Viking Press had read a carbon of his latest manuscript and had warned him that it must certainly not be published. Wolfe was overjoyed when Perkins responded violently to this false provocation. "I ought not to have believed this," Perkins said, "but Tom always could fool me with such statements." Max realized "Tom had a strange distrust of himself which made him apparently actually believe that no other publisher would take him, and he often intimated that he would leave us, but I think merely to observe my reaction, until the late spring of 1936."

Perkins perceived that Wolfe was seeking excuses for disputes. "I don't mean that Tom was deliberately and consciously inventing reasons for leaving us," Max wrote years later, "but the underlying reasons were working so strongly in him and yet were not consciously acknowledged, that he thought the pretexts were true reasons."

Wolfe was now working on a book that would combine *Of Time and the River*'s original preface with notes from his lectures and seminars in Boulder. It would not be fiction at all, but a short factual work, entitled *The Story of a Novel*.

Actually, *The Story of a Novel* grew from another notion that Perkins had planted in Wolfe's mind, as the author acknowledged in the book's opening lines:

> An editor, who is also a good friend of mine, told me about a year ago that he was sorry he had not kept a diary about the work that both of us were doing [on *Of Time and the River*], the whole stroke, catch, flow, stop, and ending, the ten thousand fittings, changings, triumphs, and surrenders that went into the making of a book. This editor remarked that some of it was fantastic, much incredible, all astonishing, and he was also kind enough to say that the whole experience was the most interesting he had known during the twenty-five years he had been a member of the publishing business.

Wolfe told the whole story, and a short book developed, which the *Saturday Review of Literature* offered to serialize. Perkins privately worried that Tom would embroider on his dedication to *Of Time and the River*. He felt he had received enough public exposure already. Wolfe detailed his editor's work but never mentioned Perkins by name. Max's only contribution to the editing of *The Story of a Novel* was to persuade Tom to cut out two or three paragraphs that seemed unnecessarily political and therefore "extraneous to the purpose of the book which in itself showed how his heart was wrung by the poverty and injustice that he saw all about." But, as Max had feared, everything that Tom had been unable to express about Max in his dedication of his last novel was spelled out in this book. It was as if Wolfe, by bestowing elaborate tribute upon Perkins, was attempting to pay him off, the easier to get rid of him— just as he had tried to assuage his conscience about Aline Bernstein by forcing money on her.

It now became part of Wolfe's daily routine to walk to Scribners at four-thirty and fetch his mail. It was a good excuse to break from his work, and it was important to him to observe the people at Scribners who had been part of his life for the last six years. Although his publishers did not yet know it, he was evaluating them as both business partners and future literary material.

Wolfe realized that while he had been alone most of his life, he had never been independent. He had now entered one of those periods when he had to put his house in order—sweeping aside everything and everyone he thought he could live without. Such a decision would of course first and most particularly affect Aline Bernstein and Max Perkins. And so he seized upon the book that both had had so great a role in creating, *Look Homeward, Angel.* Tom calculated that the sale of the manuscript would forever clear the debt he owed Mrs. Bernstein. During the following months, he persisted in making it an issue with Aline and sought to involve Perkins in the negotiation. That manuscript had been a present to Aline, but Wolfe now perversely wanted her to write Max that it had been given in repayment of moneys that had passed from her to the author. Aline knew that simply was not the truth. "I understood at the time you gave it to me that it came as a gift of love and friendship, a token of the feeling you had for me at the time," she wrote Tom. "I cannot regard it in any other light." Within the week, though, Tom had bullied her into writing Perkins all that he dictated. She realized, she told him, that she was a fool to let Tom persuade her, but, she explained to Wolfe in another letter, "I love you a lot."

Wolfe's meetings with Perkins became sharp-tongued and humorless. Even when Louise tried to heal the wounds by inviting Tom to the house, Wolfe continued his attacks at Turtle Bay. One evening the arguing grew so violent that the two men almost came to blows. Max soon regained his poise and retired for the evening. Tom slammed out of the door. That night Louise wrote Wolfe a note. "Listen Tom," she said, "if anyone else were as man to man as you were tonight you would fight him! You know that he is your friend—really your friend—and that he is honorable. Isn't that enough? Please don't behave that way. It is partly because I have been so horrible and disappointed him so much that I beg you not to do it."

The long hours that Max had spent with Wolfe in recent years had not helped to bring Max and Louise any closer. At heart she could only resent the attention her husband lavished upon Tom. To compensate for her hours alone, Louise still flirted with acting. She kept up a repertoire of classical roles and could perform monologues, speeches, and poems from memory. The dramatist Edward Sheldon, one of Max's Harvard friends, said Louise had "talent galore for a career on stage." One evening, at a small dinner gathering at which the Perkinses and Wolfe were present, Max and Tom embarked upon an intense discussion about literature. Eager to be a part of the conversation but seeing little chance to break in, Louise nudged her dinner partner and whispered, "Ask me to recite, ask me to recite."

Elizabeth Lemmon said, "Louise was jealous of Max; she always wanted to be the center of attention." But it is perhaps more accurate to say that Louise's personality reached out and grabbed people, while it was Max's remoteness that attracted them. Max generally kept any adverse opinions of people to himself; once when someone remarked that an author was a son of a bitch, he said, "Yes, but an unconscious one." Louise, on the other hand, had her emotions on the surface, and it was not uncommon for her to make her disdain known. Toward the end of another small party, during which she had needled Tom Wolfe all evening, Louise sat staring at her adversary. She finally said to a friend, "God, how he hates me, and how I hate him." The remark was barely audible, but Tom's ears perked up. "No, Louise," he drawled in a low voice, "I have great admiration for you." Max's hearing was too weak to pick up either comment. It was just as well. On other occasions Tom and Louise had spoken far into the night about their mutual love and respect for Max, and as they came to understand each other their rivalry faded.

To please Max and to fulfill her own creative needs, Louise returned to her writing in the mid-thirties. It delighted Max to see her report regularly to the studio she had rented on Second Avenue. She sold several new stories and poems. She had written children's plays before (an anthology of them called *Magic Lanterns* has been selling ever since it was published in 1923), but in 1936 Louise put her mind to a more challenging work. She was inspired by the fact that their next-door neighbor was Katharine Hepburn. For Miss Hepburn, Louise wrote a play in nine scenes about Pauline Bonaparte. It was an ornate costume drama with stiff dialogue and few concerns weightier than the character's jewels and gowns. Max's lifelong obsession with Napoleon no doubt drew Louise to the period, but her own research led her to a fascination with the ravishing Pauline. She found the relationship between Pauline, the most exciting woman in court, and her older brother Napoleon very like her own feelings toward Max. Like Louise, Pauline Bonaparte was "capable of quick, kitten-like rages"; she had a childlike understanding of politics and a passion for theatricals. She lived under the sway of a man whom she exalted, though he had stunted her development. In Scene Five, when Napoleon sends away Pauline's love, De Canouville, she says:

I am so tired of disappointment and unhappiness. I have only been dragged along behind Napoleon's chariot and crushed and battered by the stones. All the intensity that I have put in my life has come to nothing.

Still, as Louise was to Max, Pauline remains Napoleon's most ardent champion. "When people hate me," she says, "I am sorry and try to make them like me again. But when they hate Napoleon, I loathe them with all my heart and could kill them." Pauline's comment on her brother's abdication for the good of the country somewhat parallels Louise's feelings, especially after having seen her husband subjected to years of authors' abuse and personal sacrifices.

His soul is like a flash of lightning. . . . No matter what they do to him, they can never destroy his light. I love him now more than anyone in the world and I shall remain faithful to him until my death.

"She was a lovely-looking creature—reaching for something on her own which she never could attain, I felt—living in the shadow of a remarkable man," Katharine Hepburn said of Louise Perkins. The actress thought *Pauline* was a "charming play," with remediable flaws. But Louise's dedication to it was at best fitful, and she never solved its problems.

"Mother was a woman of great energy," her daughter Peggy said, "but she hated drudgery and was incapable of forcing herself to do it, which is probably why she didn't write more."

The two women, Louise and Katharine Hepburn, became friendly, but Miss Hepburn never got to know Max Perkins at all. "He used to walk up and down Forty-ninth Street either conversing or in happy silence with my driver . . . who was known as the 'Mayor of Forty-ninth Street,'" she recalled. "I always hoped that someday he would speak to me," Miss Hepburn wrote of Max Perkins. But he never did.

Before *The Story of a Novel* was set in print, to be published on April 29, Perkins and Wolfe at last discussed the contractual details of the book. Because the slim volume would be much shorter than normal trade books—to say nothing of normal Wolfe books—it would have to be priced lower, which made it harder for Scribners to cover its costs. Perkins, therefore, had offered Wolfe a reduced royalty on the initial printing. Tom agreed to cut his usual 15 percent to 10 percent for the first 3,000 copies. Just before publication, however, Wolfe learned that the book was to be sold for $1.50, not the $1.25 he had been led to expect. He was furious. Scribners was paying him a lower royalty, yet selling the book for more. Tom met Perkins that evening to discuss the situation. It was not long before Wolfe began one of his tirades of ugly name-calling and insulting bombast. The following morning he wrote a note of apology. "The language that I used was unjustifiable and I want to tell you that I know it was," he wrote his editor, "and ask you to forget it."

Wolfe nonetheless felt strongly about the issue. He did not wish to rake up the embers of the night before, but he had accepted the lower terms because Max said that even though Scribners was not likely to profit from so small a book, its publication was worthwhile in itself. To prove he had not been taken advantage of, Wolfe thought Perkins should restore his former royalty.

"You have been my friend for seven years now and one of the best friends that I ever had," Tom wrote Max. "I do not want to see you do this thing now which may be legally and technically all right, but is to my mind, a sharp business practice." Wolfe granted that it was probably not Perkins himself who fixed the book's price and royalties; but, he added, "I also know the way I expect and want you to act now as my friend."

Wolfe became more and more outraged and more and more adamant. "If your refusal in this matter is final and you insist on holding me to the terms of the contracts I signed for *The Story of a Novel*," Wolfe queried, "don't you think I, or anyone else on earth for that matter, would be justified henceforth and hereafter, considering my relations with you and Scribners were primarily of a business and commercial nature, and if you make use of a business advantage in this way, don't you think I would be justified in making use of a business advantage too if one came my way? Or do you think it works only one way? I don't think it does and I don't think any fair-minded person in the world would think so either . . . you cannot command the loyalty and devotion of a man on the one hand and then take a business advantage on the other."

The following day Perkins dictated that Wolfe's royalties on *The Story of a Novel* be reckoned at 15 percent from the start. The difference Wolfe would receive amounted to $225. "We certainly do not think that we should withhold that sum of money if it is going to cause so much resentment, and so much loss of time and disquiet for all of us," he wrote Tom. Perkins believed in the author's freedom to act in his own best interests, but he knew that Wolfe had blown up this incident far beyond its just proportions. "I certainly would not wish you to make what you thought was a sacrifice, on my account . . . ," he wrote Wolfe, "and I would know that whatever you did would be sincerely believed to be right by you,—and I know that you sincerely believe the contentions you make in this letter to me, to be right. I have never doubted your sincerity and never will. I wish you could have felt that way toward us."

The moment after Perkins restored the royalty of 15 percent, Wolfe said he preferred to stand by his signature on the contract. "That goes for all my other obligations as well," he wrote Max. It occurred to him now that "life is too short to quarrel this way with a friend over something that matters so little." He said he had made up his mind the day before he received word from Perkins. He had even called him up and gone around to see him, just to tell him "that all the damn contracts in the world don't mean as much to me as you friendship means." Wolfe wanted to bring his next book to life. For that, he told Perkins, "I need your friendship and support more than I ever did."

On Perkins's stroll home from work one afternoon a short time later, Tom caught up with him and said he wanted to talk. His voice sounded unusually insistent, and they turned off Forty-ninth Street at the Waldorf Hotel instead of their regular place, Manny Wolf's. Once seated at the bar, Wolfe referred to the latest criticism against him. Then he said again that he wanted to write a completely objective, unautobiographical book.

"Tom was in a desperate state," Max wrote years later of that afternoon. "It was not only what the critics said that made him wish to write objectively, but that he knew that what he had written had given great pain even to those he loved the most." He referred to Wolfe's family in Asheville.

Wolfe went on to describe the project; Perkins became excited about it. When Tom expressed doubts as to whether or not he would be able to write such a book, Perkins told him at once that there was no doubt that he should do it, that he had known for years that someday Wolfe would have to do it, and that Tom was the only person in America who could do it.

Wolfe was calling the book *The Vision of Spangler's Paul.* He got to work, and soon he was making up a story largely out of imagination. Many of the characters he started to develop had no actual models in reality. For whole chapters the style was consciously lean, so free from embellishments that it read like nothing else Wolfe had ever written. It had lost the lyrical and poetic bounty of his earlier writing, but gained compactness along with objectivity.

Tom had, in his own words, "begun to go again like a locomotive." At three o'clock one morning that spring, when Wolfe was living near the Perkinses, another of Max's neighbors, his author Nancy Hale, heard a monotonous singsong, which grew louder. She got up from bed and looked out the window of her apartment, which was on East Forty-ninth Street near Third Avenue. There was Thomas Wolfe, wearing a black slouch hat, advancing in his long mountaineer's stride, with his billowing black raincoat, chanting, "I wrote ten thousand words today— I wrote ten thousand words today."

"God knows what the result will be," Perkins wrote Elizabeth Lemmon that season, "but I suspect it will be the end of me. A worse struggle than *Of Time and the River*, unless he changes publishers first." The protagonist of Wolfe's book assumed the name Paul Spangler, then Joe Doaks, then George Spangler. Later he adopted the family name Joyner, which was dropped for Webber. With each change, Wolfe slipped into the more familiar mode, autobiography. Except for some physical characteristics, George Webber was, in fact, practically the same person as Eugene Gant, the hero of *Look Homeward, Angel* and *Of Time and the River*.

But at least Wolfe was happily engaged in a new book, and it might have seemed to Max that his troubles with Tom were behind him, except for his deep-seated Yankee fatalism which surfaced whenever things were going too well. Days later, in the April 25, 1936, issue of the *Saturday Review*, Thomas Wolfe's long-time nemesis, Bernard De Voto, justified Perkins's anxieties.

Illustrating his lead article, "Genius Is Not Enough," was a photograph of De Voto, with a Cheshire-cat grin, lowering a revolver into cocked position. It was Wolfe he was shooting at. After a few paragraphs De Voto observed that to a large extent, Wolfe's growth as a writer had remained in darkness. "Well," De Voto wrote, "*The Story of a Novel* puts an end to speculation and supplies some unexpected but very welcome light.

> The most flagrant evidence of his incompleteness is the fact that, so far, one indispensable part of the artist has existed not in Mr. Wolfe but in Maxwell Perkins. Such organizing faculty and such critical intelligence as have been applied to the book have come not from inside the artist, not from the artist's feeling for form and esthetic integrity, but from the office of Charles Scribner's Sons. For five years the artist pours out words "like burning lava from a volcano"—with little or no idea what their purpose is, which book they belong in, what the relation of part to part is, what is

organic and what irrelevant, or what emphasis or coloration in the completed work of art is being served by the job at hand. Then Mr. Perkins
decides these questions—from without, and by a process to which rumor
applied the word "assembly." But works of art cannot be assembled like a
carburetor—they must be grown like a plant, or in Mr. Wolfe's favorite
simile, like an embryo. The artist writes a hundred thousand words about
a train: Mr. Perkins decides that the train is worth only five thousand
words. But such a decision as this is properly not within Mr. Perkins's
power; it must be made by the highly conscious self-criticism of the artist
in relation to the pulse of the book itself. Worse still, the artist goes on
writing till Mr. Perkins tells him the novel is finished. . . .

Mr. Wolfe can write fiction—has written some of the finest fiction of our
day. But a great part of what he writes is not fiction at all: it is only material with which the novelist has struggled but which has defeated him.
. . . Mr. Perkins and the assembly line at Scribners can do nothing to help
him. . . .

One can only respect Mr. Wolfe for his determination to realize himself
on the highest level and to be satisfied with nothing short of greatness. But,
however useful genius may be in the writing of novels, it is not enough in
itself—it never has been enough, in any art, and it never will be. At the
very least it must be supported by an ability to impart shape to material,
simple competence in the use of tools. Until Mr. Wolfe develops more
craftsmanship, he will not be the important novelist he is now widely accepted as being. In order to be a great novelist he must also mature his
emotions till he can see more profoundly into character than he now does,
and he must learn to put a corset on his prose. Once more: his own smithy
is the only possible place for these developments—they cannot occur in the
office of any editor whom he will ever know.

In a single blow De Voto had destroyed Wolfe's pleasure of accomplishment. It was one thing for Wolfe to give Perkins his due. It was quite
another for the critics to turn his gesture against him, to make his books
seem the product of a "factory." Wolfe lashed out against De Voto to anyone who would listen, but on a deeper level the rage was probably directed
at Max. The fact that Perkins, far from seeking this public credit, had
yearned to elude it made no difference to Tom when his emotions were
running. Max had taught him, by implication, that the editor remains in
the background; now Max, thanks to De Voto, was forever to be out
front. It was something Tom could not indefinitely abide, and no one
knew this sooner or more surely than Max.

XVI

The Letter

Wolfe's *Story of a Novel* is unbearable . . . ," Marjorie Kinnan Rawlings wrote Max Perkins. The honesty, ferocity, and beauty of expression of the writer's anguish made it painful for her to read. "When a little of the torment has expended itself he will be the greatest artist America has ever produced." In the same letter, she wrote Perkins of another opinion of which she was at least as sure: "When all of us are done for, the chances are that literary history will find you the greatest—certainly the wisest—of us all."

With her last novel, *Golden Apples*, long since forgotten, Marjorie Kinnan Rawlings was finally able to give herself to the boys' book Perkins had suggested some years earlier and had tenderly encouraged ever since. In March, 1936, she holed up in an abandoned cabin to write a book for children about a boy raising a young animal in the scrub. She asked Max if he liked the title *The Fawn*. "I am glad you have the book well thought out," Perkins replied; "I think *The Fawn* is a good title, but I am not sure that it would be a wise one for it might seem too poetic, or even a little sentimental." The author agreed to reconsider it.

Mrs. Rawlings found her first attempt at the book difficult, and she often wrote Perkins for advice. She also kept harking back to the letters he had written her in 1933, especially one in which he said: "A book about a boy and the life of the scrub is the thing we want.—It is those wonderful river trips and the hunting and the dogs and guns and the companion-

ship of simple people who care about the same things which were included in *South Moon Under*." After a while, three of Perkins's points
began to sink in. The first was that her book should not be written for
a boy so much as about a boy. She also realized that her forte was not
complex plotting but stringing small episodes together. And she came
to understand that the material she handled best was the raw, regional
tales she had dug right out of the scrub swamplands, rather than anything she might derive from flights of imagination. She wrote scenes about
alligators, rattlesnakes, wolf packs, the dance of the whooping cranes,
the Northeaster of 1871, and the floods that followed.

Marjorie Rawlings wanted a bear hunt in the story, so she prowled
the countryside for someone with the appropriate experience. Finally she
met a briary old pioneer living on the Saint Johns River, a famous "bad
man" in those parts. She lived with him and his wife until she had
gathered enough of his anecdotes and hunting yarns and details of the
ways of the wilderness people to expand her cast of characters and add
some basic dramatic situations. When she returned to her homestead she
worked out the concept of the book and then wrote Perkins about it:

> It will be absolutely all told through the boy's eyes. He will be about
> twelve, and the period will not be a long one—not more than two years.
> I want it through his eyes before the age of puberty brings in any of the
> other factors to confuse the simplicity of viewpoint. It will be a book boys
> will love, and if it is done well enough otherwise, the people who liked
> *South Moon* will like it too. It is only since *Golden Apples* that I realize
> what it is about my writing that people like. I don't mean that I am writing
> *for* anyone, but now I feel free to luxuriate in the simple details that in-
> terest me, and that I have been so amazed to find interested other people—
> probably just from the element of sincerity given by my own interest and
> sympathy. . . .
>
> Now please don't write me another of those restrained "You must do it
> as seems right to you" notes. Tell me what is really in your mind.

Perkins replied:

> When I write in that do-it-as-it-seems-right-to-you way, it is because it has
> always been my conviction—and I do not see how anyone could dispute
> the rightness of it—that a book must be done according to the writer's
> conception of it as nearly as perfectly as possible, and that the publishing
> problems begin then.—That is, the publisher must not try to get a writer

to fit the book to the conditions of the trade, etc. It must be the other way around.

Perkins told Marjorie Rawlings he wanted her to rely on her own resources, but he threw in occasional suggestions. He encouraged her to write about going down a river—"because the rivers there are so good, and the journey element in a narrative is always a fine one, particularly to youth." Perkins said he knew the book would work well if she would just keep it simple and unaffected. "I would not be a bit surprised if it were the best book you have done," he declared, "and it might well be the most successful."

Like many of Perkins's writers, Mrs. Rawlings often had spells of doubt and depression. She asked him to help her through them:

> I am one of your duties, you know, Max, and you really must write me at least every couple of weeks. Sometimes a letter from you is the only thing that bucks me up. When everything else fails, I can know that it really matters to you whether or not I get a piece of work done, and how well.

He never neglected her.

Six months into the writing, Marjorie Rawlings was still hunting for a title. She sent a list of alternatives to Perkins and asked for his opinion. He did not care much for *The Flutter Mill*. Of *Juniper Island* he said: "I do not think place names are good for a book. There is not enough human suggestion in them." Of her third title he wrote, "I would think one which carried the meaning of *The Yearling* was probably right." The more he spoke of it, the better it sounded to him. He wrote her in the spring of 1937, "It seems to have a quality even more than a meaning that fits the book." It stuck.

After almost a year on the book, Mrs. Rawlings abruptly decided that what she had written was poor, and she threw out the manuscript. Perkins was shocked when she told him. There was nothing for him to do but to try to get her going again. He kept sending heartening letters, and eventually she resumed writing, more slowly but with more confidence.

In December, 1937, she sent the manuscript off to Perkins. He took days to read it, but, as he told her, that was a good sign. "The better a book is, the slower I go," he explained. "I think the last half is better than the first and that the book gets increasingly good. But the very beginning now is perfect, it seems to me, and of course the father and mother, and all about that life, and Jody's on the island, are as good as can be." He felt a few parts of the book were tainted with theatricality and romanticism and suggested that they be sacrificed in order to maintain the book's naturalism, its honest depiction of a world that was sometimes cruel and terrifying. *The Yearling* was full of very tough people, he reminded Mrs. Rawlings, "and the toughness ought to be more evident."

Marjorie Rawlings's previous books had had hard luck, but everything went right for this one. The Book-of-the-Month Club made *The Yearling* its main selection in April, 1938. In general, book sales that year were only a third of what they had been before the Depression, but *The Yearling* became a runaway best seller overnight. It also won the Pulitzer Prize.

Two years before this bonanza, in June, 1936, Marjorie Rawlings had gone game-fishing in Bimini with a friend. There she learned that Ernest Hemingway had become the hero of the most popular legends down there. The latest story concerned Hemingway's knocking a man down for calling him a big fat slob. "You can call me a slob," Hemingway had said, "but you can't call me a big fat slob." Then he struck him down. The natives of Bimini set the incident to music, and if they were sure Hemingway was not within earshot, they would sing in a calypso beat, "The big fat slob's in the harbor."

When Hemingway heard that one of Max Perkins's authors was in the same waters, he called on her. "I should have known from your affection for him that he was not a fire-spitting ogre," Marjorie wrote back to Perkins, "but I'd heard so many tales in Bimini of his going around knocking people down, that I half-expected him to announce in a loud voice that he never accepted introductions to female novelists. Instead, a most lovable, nervous and sensitive person took my hand in a big gentle paw and remarked that he was a great admirer of my work."

The day before she left, Hemingway tussled six hours and fifty minutes with a 514-pound tuna. When his *Pilar* cruised into harbor at 9:30 that night, the whole population of the island flocked to see his fish and hear his tale. "A fatuous old man with a new yacht and a young bride had arrived not long previously, announcing that tuna-fishing, of whose difficulties he had heard, was easy," Mrs. Rawlings wrote to Perkins. "So as the *Pilar* was made fast, Hemingway came swimming up from below-decks, gloriously drunk, roaring, 'Where's the son of a bitch who said it was easy.' The last anyone saw of him that night, he was standing alone on the dock where his giant tuna hung from the stays, using it for a punching bag."

In just her short stay in Bimini, Mrs. Rawlings detected an inner conflict in Hemingway. "He is so great an artist that he does not need to be ever on the defensive. He is so vast, so virile, that he does not need ever to hit anybody," Mrs. Rawlings wrote Perkins. "Yet he is constantly defending something that he, at least, must consider vulnerable." She thought the conflict might be due in part to the company he was keeping, mainly sportsmen.

> Hemingway is among these people a great deal, and they like and admire him—his personality, his sporting prowess, and his literary prestige. It seems to me that unconsciously he must value their opinion. He must be afraid of laying bare before them the agony that tears the artist. He must be afraid of lifting before them the curtain that veils the beauty that should be exposed only to reverent eyes. So, as in *Death in the Afternoon,* he writes beautifully, and then immediately turns it off with a flippant comment, or a deliberate obscenity. His sporting friends would not understand the beauty. They would roar with delight at the flippancy.

Hemingway was having what he called a *"belle époque"* that year, 1936. He had written two short stories whose background was Africa, and he was pleased with them. After he got back from Bimini, he traveled to Wyoming, where he got back to work on his new novel. All Perkins knew about the book was that the setting was the Florida Keys, Havana, and the waters between, and that Harry Morgan, the hero of two of Hemingway's *Esquire* stories, would be the central character. "I cannot give any idea of the plot," Perkins wrote the English publisher Jonathan Cape; but he imagined that the "characters will some of them be the boatmen who live by fishing and smuggling, and have a finger in the Cuban revolutions, etc. and one of the important episodes will be a hurricane. I think it sounds very fine indeed, and am looking forward to it with great impatience."

The green hills of Wyoming proved to be an adequate substitute for those of Africa. There Hemingway bagged two antelope, three grizzly bears, and 55,000 words. His plan was to complete the first draft, deposit it in a vault, and then go to Spain. Perkins worried every time Hemingway threw himself into the eye of danger—he had even told Ernest to let the grizzlies alone until he finished his book. But he knew that nothing could keep Hemingway from the Spanish Civil War. Just from what he had read in the newspaper, Perkins told him, he imagined that a magnificent tale could be written on the recent defense of the Spanish fortress, the Alcázar. "If you had been there, and got out of it safely, what a story! But I wish you would not go to Spain. . . . Anyhow, I hope you will let nothing prevent the publication of a novel in the Spring. And it should be early too." Hemingway was determined to go to the battle-front, but he was in no great hurry. He suspected the Spaniards would be fighting for a long time.

During the spring of 1936 Hemingway had resumed his bullying of Scott Fitzgerald. In several letters to Max and to Scott himself, Ernest jabbed at the now staggering Fitzgerald. He said he did not want to believe that Scott had become the "Maxie Baer" of writers, down and out; but now the man seemed so hell-bent on wallowing in his "shamelessness of defeat" that Hemingway had no choice.

In June, 1936, Fitzgerald was back in Baltimore, living in a seventh-floor apartment across the street from Johns Hopkins. Zelda, sick as ever, had been moved to Highland Hospital, a rest home near Asheville, North Carolina. Scott was still too rattled to start any major writing, but he was full of ideas for books, mostly republications of his old works. He needed money badly, but he resisted asking for it for a time. Then, in July, he addressed a plea for $1,500, this time to Charles Scribner himself, the president of the firm. Scribner sent the check, but he also sent for the company director—Max. The two of them examined Fitzgerald's account and computed that the author's debt to the company had grown to $6,000, not including this last payment. "All this is rather painful and I hope it will not give you a headache," Scribner wrote Fitzgerald in sending a detailed reckoning of all his advances. "Max and I thought it only fair, however, by you as well as ourselves to get the figures on paper, to make sure that we agreed with you."

In addition to the company loans, Fitzgerald received dozens of loans from Perkins himself. Fitzgerald never owed Perkins at any one time more than $3,000, but it was that much on several different occasions. There had been seven loans in just the past eighteen months, for a total of $1,400. Perkins once wrote Thomas Wolfe's friend John Terry that he advanced the money "because there simply was no business justification in this house running his debt up further. I wanted to enable him to keep at writing and avoid Hollywood and that sort of racket."

In mid-July Perkins went to Baltimore and saw Fitzgerald briefly.

Scott's own writing of the period is the best record of what Max found. His essay "The Crack-Up" had described Scott's deep depression of the preceding winter; now he wrote a piece for the August *Esquire*, "Afternoon of an Author," describing an upswing:

> When he woke up he felt better than he had for many weeks, a fact that became plain to him negatively—he did not feel ill. He leaned for a moment against the door frame between his bedroom and bath till he could be sure he was not dizzy. Not a bit, not even when he stooped for a slipper under the bed.

In his 1938 story "Financing Finnegan" an editor named George Jaggers, who is constantly bailing out the "perennial man of promise in American letters" with personal loans, says: "The truth is Finnegan's been in a slump, he's had blow after blow in the past few years, but now he's snapping out of it."

Into the summer of 1936, Fitzgerald rode the upswing. He lived in Baltimore or North Carolina, close to Zelda, feeling well. Then, in July, swimming in a pool near Asheville, he did a swan dive from a fifteen-foot board. Scott was in no shape for that kind of diving. He struck the water awkwardly, breaking his clavicle and pulling his left shoulder out of its socket. He was fitted into a special halter which allowed him to write but which kept him in the rigid position of a fascist salute.

While his shoulder was healing, Scott concerned himself with a new version of *Tender Is the Night* that he had urged Bennett Cerf to consider for his Modern Library. He began the labor of revision by reviewing the criticisms of the book that Perkins had made when it was first serialized two years earlier. He saw now that Max had been right when he had said that the beginning of the book lacked clarity. Fitzgerald heeded the comment this time and switched Part One, on the Riviera, and Part Two, Dick Diver's history, so that the story was presented chronologically, without flashbacks. The only other significant alteration was the omission of one sentence: Dick's saying, "I never did go in for making love to dry loins." Scott now thought it was "a strong line but definitely offensive."

As Fitzgerald turned back to already written works for new publication, he also withdrew socially. "Me caring about no one and nothing," he confessed to his Ledger.

Eight pages preceding Scott Fitzgerald's "Afternoon of an Author"

in the August *Esquire* was Hemingway's "Snows of Kilimanjaro," which
Max now saw for the first time. It was the story of a writer on safari in
Africa, who hoped to "work the fat off his soul" so that he could write
"the things that he had saved to write until he knew enough to write them
well." The protagonist thought to himself—

> . . . you said that you would write about these people; about the very
> rich; that you were really not one of them but a spy in their country; that
> you would leave it and write of it and for once it would be written by
> some one who knew what he was writing of.

There was, of course, a similarity between this writer's self-doubts and
those of Hemingway. But toward the end of the story, Ernest drew
a bead on his real target. Again writing about "the rich," he said:

> He remembered poor Scott Fitzgerald and his romantic awe of them and
> how he had started a story once that began, "The very rich are different
> from you and me." And how someone had said to Scott, Yes they have
> more money. But that was not humorous to Scott. He thought they were
> a special glamorous race and when he found they weren't it wrecked him
> just as much as any other thing that wrecked him.

Arnold Gingrich, editor of *Esquire*, later said: "That dig at Scott went
right by me. I didn't think twice about it."

Fitzgerald, though, never forgot it. In all fairness, he told Hemingway, writing from Asheville, he thought "Snows of Kilimanjaro" was
one of Hemingway's finest stories, but he felt it was written in malicious
response to his own "Crack-Up" articles. He resented Hemingway's writing about him with all the solemnity of a pallbearer. "Please lay off me
in print," he said, adding:

> If I choose to write *de profundis* sometimes it doesn't mean I want friends
> praying aloud over my corpse. No doubt you meant it kindly but it cost
> me a night's sleep. And when you incorporate [the story] in a book would
> you mind cutting my name?

As an afterthought, Fitzgerald wrote, "Riches have *never* fascinated me,
unless combined with the greatest charm or distinction."

Hemingway in turn wrote Perkins about Fitzgerald's reaction. Here
Scott had been exposing those "awful things about himself" for the last

half-year in *Esquire*, but the moment Hemingway reproved him for his alleged breakdown he got sore. For five years, Ernest said, he had not written a line about anybody he knew because he felt so sorry for them all. He finally realized that time was getting short and he was going to cease being a gent and go back to being a novelist.

Fitzgerald also wrote to Max. Hemingway, he said, had replied to his request not to use Fitzgerald's name in future printings of his fiction:

> He wrote me back a crazy letter telling me what a great Writer he was. . . . To have answered it would have been like fooling with a lit firecracker. Somehow I love that man, no matter what he says or does, but just one more crack, and I think I would have to throw my weight with the gang and lay him. No one could ever hurt him in his first two books. But he has completely lost his head and the duller he gets about it, the more he is like a punch-drunk pug fighting himself in the movies.

The exchange between Fitzgerald and Hemingway about the very rich, with Ernest trumping Scott's line, survives as one of the notable literary anecdotes from that time. But it is spurious, for, as Max Perkins well knew, the truth was otherwise. Perkins had been present when the rejoinder had been made—in a New York restaurant. Scott Fitzgerald was not there. Those present were Hemingway, Molly Colum, and Perkins, and it was Hemingway, in fact, who spoke of the rich. "I am getting to know the rich," he declared. Whereupon Molly Colum topped him, saying: "The only difference between the rich and other people is that the rich have more money." Bested by a woman, Hemingway salved his ego by expropriating the witticism, having it come from his own lips, and making Scott, once again, the victim. Perkins thought Hemingway's behavior contemptible, and told Elizabeth Lemmon as much in a letter. He did not write Hemingway to correct him, but he saw to it that Fitzgerald's name did not appear in Hemingway's next book of stories.

Hemingway's attack ended another sorry summer for Fitzgerald. In September Scott wrote to Max about all that had happened to him since his shoulder had been cast in plaster. "I had almost adapted myself to the thing when I fell in the bathroom reaching for the light, and lay on the floor until I caught a mild form of arthritis called 'Miotoosis' which popped me in the bed for five weeks more," he said. During that time, adding further to his anguish, Fitzgerald's mother died. He tried to reach her deathbed in Washington but he could not manage the trip. Similarly, he had been within a mile and a half of Zelda all summer in Asheville, but he had not been able to visit her more than a half-dozen times. Affectionate words still passed between Zelda and Scott, mostly letters revealing their love of their former love; but Zelda was now often embarked on flights of fantasy and had taken to carrying a Bible everywhere she went.

The $26,000 in cash and bonds that Scott was inheriting from his mother's estate was less than he had hoped for. He planned to use some of it to pay off his creditors and take two or three months' rest. Finally, Fitzgerald admitted to Perkins, "I haven't the vitality I had five yrs. ago." His total accomplishment for the summer was one story and two *Esquire* articles.

With this latest decline in Fitzgerald's health, Perkins thought of sending in some reserves to boost his spirits. He wrote Marjorie Rawlings, who in her search for a quiet place to get on with *The Yearling* had settled in Banner Elk, North Carolina, not far from Asheville. He thought a visit from her would do Fitzgerald a great deal of good.

The day after he wrote her, there was another disheartening development. On the occasion of F. Scott Fitzgerald's fortieth birthday the *New York Post* ran a front-page article under the headline "The Other Side of Paradise." It consisted of a long interview conducted by Michael Mok, the purpose of which was apparently to determine just how cracked up Scott Fitzgerald actually was. It gave Perkins a chill just to read it, for it seemed as if Scott were bent upon destroying himself. Mok evidently had maneuvered his way into Fitzgerald's confidence, gotten him talking, then published all Scott's comments, even those that Scott felt had been off the record. "He was trusting the reporter," Perkins wrote Hemingway, "and so was his nurse—when a man gets himself a trained nurse, it's time to despair of him—and both of them said things which the reporter must have known were not meant to go into print." Perkins got the impression of a "completely licked and very drunk person, bereft of hope, acquiescing in his ruin."

"It might easily be the last straw for Fitzgerald," Marjorie Rawlings wrote Max after reading the article. She said she was appalled that a reporter could perpetrate so cruel an article, although she was just as tempted to damn Fitzgerald without sympathy. But, she wrote Max, "I know how that state of mind creeps up on you and I have had to fight it myself." She had had her own years of stormy marriage and alcoholism, so she understood why Max wanted her to see Scott: "The man has taken a licking and . . . you know I too have been through a great deal but that I refuse to be licked."

At Perkins's insistence, Fitzgerald agreed to meet with Mrs. Rawlings, though he was sick in bed with arthritis and a high temperature the afternoon she visited him. He perked up from the moment of her arrival. "Far from being depressing," she reported to Perkins afterward, "I enjoyed him thoroughly, and I'm sure he enjoyed it as much. He was as nervous as a cat, but he had not been drinking—had had his nurse put his liquor away." At lunch they drank only sherry and a table wine, and they clinked their glasses to Max. They proceeded to talk their heads off until, at five-thirty, Fitzgerald's nurse fussed about his not resting, and Marjorie Rawlings left. Later she sent Scott a note urging him to fight depression. She closed with the admission, "If anyone knew how good my little .32 revolver has looked to me sometimes."

Max thanked Mrs. Rawlings deeply for seeing Scott. "I have known him so long, and have liked him so much," he explained, "that his welfare is very much a personal matter with me too. I would do anything to see him recover himself." But for months Fitzgerald still believed he was washed up.

Perkins asked another of his novelists who lived in North Carolina, Hamilton Basso, to run bedcheck on Scott. Under Max's supervision Basso was writing *Courthouse Square*, an autobiographical novel. (Twenty years later, Max himself would become a character in Basso's most successful book, *The View from Pompey's Head*.) For Basso the meetings with Fitzgerald were difficult, but he was eager to oblige their editor.

The root of Fitzgerald's trouble was, as usual, his empty bank account. He figured a new book would require two years' leisure and there was no way he could see to reduce his annual expenses below $18,000. Little would be left from his inheritance after he paid his debts. And after the financial failure of *Tender Is the Night*, he could not hope to be advanced any such sum as $36,000. Fitzgerald guessed that he would have to do piecework for the *Post* or go panning for gold in Hollywood again. But, Scott observed to Perkins: "Each time I have gone to Hollywood, in spite of the enormous salary, has really set me back financially and artistically.

I certainly have this one more novel, but it may have to remain among the unwritten books of this world. Such stray ideas as sending my daughter

to public school and putting my wife in a public insane asylum have been
proposed to me by intimate friends, but it would break something in me
that would shatter the very delicate pencil end of a point of view.

"My God," Fitzgerald moaned, "debt is an awful thing."

That November, Fitzgerald gave his publishers a "business justification" for any future emergency requests by transferring all his rights,
title, and interest in and to the estate of his mother to Charles Scribner's
Sons.

Perkins had become well informed on the ways authors reacted to
criticism. Hemingway, for one, usually protested too much about his indifference to assaults. Thomas Wolfe, on the other hand, had taken to
saying frighteningly little of late. Wolfe had spent months in silent torment, and Perkins was sure that images of Perkins and the Scribners "factory" assembling his books continued to plague him. Max knew that
Bernard De Voto's questions still haunted Wolfe: Was genius enough?
Had he developed as an artist? Could he write a book by himself?

At first Wolfe took De Voto's article as a challenge. Encouraged by
Perkins to continue his "objective" book, he wrote thousands of words
a day. By the summer of 1936 his anger had inflamed him into
believing he was equal to "all the De Votos in the world."

Wolfe bickered constantly with Perkins that summer, principally
about the writing he planned to do. He now talked of basing his
new set of characters on the people he had known at Charles Scribner's
Sons. "When Tom gets around to writing about all of us, *look out!*" Max
had joked for years. But now he admitted real anxiety to John Hall
Wheelock and Charles Scribner and his other associates. "Charlie reacted humorously," Perkins recalled some years later, "though I daresay
he was worried secretly. He apparently took the matter very lightly, and
as if it were amusing more than anything else. In fact, I was the only one
who was very much worried, and that was largely because I personally
had let us in for it."

Much of Tom's material was the result not of direct observation
but of inside information he had absorbed from Max after hours when
they were unwinding after long days over *Of Time and the River*. "Max
was a sturdy drinker," John Hall Wheelock said, "and though he never
spoke carelessly, he drank enough with Tom to open up and speak to
him trustingly as a man might to a son—the son Max never had." The

first transcription of this material was "Old Man Rivers," a story which Elizabeth Nowell called a "bitter portrayal of Robert Bridges," the retired editor of *Scribner's Magazine*. Another was "The Lion at Morning," which portrayed Charles Scribner II. The third was "No More Rivers," based upon editor Wallace Meyer. The last showed the working of a publishing house—James Rodney and Company, and it was the first story Tom tried on Perkins. Max read it in Elizabeth Nowell's presence; and, the agent remembered, "At first he sat bolt upright at his desk, with unusually pink cheeks and blazing eyes, and refused to discuss the story." Soon he relented enough to take Miss Nowell to the Chatham for a drink, and there he began to talk.

Perkins felt like kicking himself. "I should have *known better*," he admitted to her, "but I've told Tom all kinds of highly confidential things about the firm and about the people there." Wolfe knew, for instance, of one Scribners executive who "never was much good." There was another, more venerable company official whom Max encountered one night in the arms of his equally venerable secretary. Perkins did not object to Tom's writing about Perkins himself. But he was distressed by what Wolfe might divulge about his colleagues.

"Can't you see," he said to Miss Nowell, "if Tom writes those things up and publishes them, it'll ruin those people's lives, and it'll be *my fault*!"

Perkins persuaded Miss Nowell to request changes that would make Wallace Meyer less recognizable. Then, after a moment of thought, he blurted out: "I'll have to resign when that book is published." Suddenly realizing what he had said, Perkins insisted that she never repeat it to anyone—least of all to Tom.

Miss Nowell later said that "the idea of Perkins's resigning from Scribners was as unthinkable as that of God's resigning from heaven." But she tactlessly told her author exactly what he had said, and that set Wolfe off again. "He seems to think that while it was all right to write about those humble people down in North Carolina . . . his own friends at Scribners are a special race," Tom replied in anger. If that was Perkins's attitude, he said it was too bad, because he was going to write what he damn well pleased. He revised "No More Rivers" by making the editor a concert pianist and eliminating the inside gossip about the publishing company. But Perkins knew that Tom "brooded over this, and that it got to seem worse and worse, and anyhow it was at this time that it became perfectly evident he would leave us." Wolfe actually drafted letters to other houses earnestly asking if they wished to print his works. "At the present time, I am engaged upon the completion of a long book, and since I have no obligation, whether personal, financial, contractual, moral of any kind soever to any firm of publishers, I am writing to inquire if you are interested in this book. . . . Frankly with no disparagement of any connection I have had—I feel the need of a new beginning in my creative life," he wrote in a letter he thought of sending to Macmillan, Harpers, Viking, W. W. Norton, Little, Brown, Houghton Mifflin, Longmans-Green, Dodd, Mead, and Harcourt, Brace.

Both friends needed a respite from the other. Wolfe returned to Germany at the end of July. The towns were mobbed with visitors to the Olympic Games, but the whole country seemed wonderfully clean and cool after New York. In Berlin he saw phalanxes of soldiers goose-stepping. "We can never learn to march like these boys," Tom wrote Max on a card of *Die Wachtruppe am Brandenburger Tor,* in Berlin, "and it looks as if they're about ready to go again." He met a woman named Thea Voelcker, a divorced artist. Into just a few days they crammed a tempestuous love affair, exploding with the passion and torment that accompanied all his relationships. For weeks after leaving Berlin, Tom thought of marrying her, until he found the difficulties of bringing her to America too great to make it worthwhile. They separated as friends.

While Wolfe was away, Max went to Quebec with Louise for two quiet weeks. In September he gave his daughter Zippy in marriage to Douglas Gorsline, a handsome painter she had introduced to Max in Boston the previous year. Her four sisters were attendants. Fitzgerald and Hemingway were invited but could not attend. Thomas Wolfe had set foot on American soil just the day before, and Louise asked a mutual friend to see that he arrived at the church in New Canaan on time and properly attired. He chose his tie on the train from an assortment he had hastily stuffed in his pocket, but all was not perfection. In the quiet just after the ceremony, the guests heard his Southern voice boom, "You didn't tell me my hatband stank of sweat." At the reception Louise gushed about losing another of her babies. Max felt the same way but went around saying, "That's two down, and only three to go."

Wolfe had returned from Germany especially to vote in the 1936 presidential election, the most important, he felt, since 1860. Wolfe considered himself a "social democrat" but to get Perkins's goat often played the soapbox Communist, and he believed that Franklin Roosevelt's reforms should get the largest mandate possible. Perkins was an independent Democrat. He feared the New Deal was becoming a juggernaut which needed the restraints that only a vigorous opposition party could impose, and so, believing that FDR was certain to be reelected, he decided to vote Republican. That appalled and angered Wolfe. He called Perkins a "conservative," denouncing him as a member of the managerial class who was removed from the struggles of life because of inherited money.

The deterioration of the Wolfe-Perkins relationship became more rapid. Wolfe acknowledged he had once needed Perkins; in his novel *You Can't Go Home Again*, his protagonist, George Webber, says to his editor:

> For I was lost and was looking for someone older and wiser to show me the way, and I found you, and you took the place of my father who had died.

But Webber adds: "The road now leads off in a direction contrary to your intent."

By November, Wolfe's impulse to sever himself from his father figure had all but overwhelmed his feelings of loyalty and gratitude. That month a woman named Marjorie Dorman unwittingly became the instrument of schism.

"I always felt somewhat guilty about the Marjorie Dorman affair," Perkins confessed a decade later.

Miss Dorman had been Wolfe's landlady in Brooklyn and was the model for "Mad Maude" Whittaker in Wolfe's story "No Door." Wolfe told of Maude's intermittent insanity and of the mental illness of her father and three sisters. Though slightly unstable herself, Maude had kept her whole family going since she had been a girl. The story was first published in *Scribner's*, then in *From Death to Morning*, the collection of Wolfe short stories. Miss Dorman had come to see Perkins shortly after the story appeared in the magazine. She wanted him to read an article she had written—Max later examined it and returned it to her— and while there she took the opportunity to tell Perkins how deeply hurt she had been by what Wolfe had written.

Many months passed, and nothing more was heard from Miss Dorman. Perkins assumed that since she had not sued for libel when the piece appeared in the magazine, which was read by 300,000 people, she would not do so when the piece reappeared in a book that would be read by perhaps only 30,000. In December, 1936, however, Miss Dorman and her family filed suit. Perkins told John Terry he imagined they had sued because they were hard up and had been told they could get money from the publishers.

Since almost every word Wolfe wrote was autobiographical, nearly all his characters based closely on real people, there had always been a risk of prosecution. "I doubt if Tom thought about the matter at all," Perkins later said to John Terry, "but of course it was up to me to guard Tom from legal dangers insofar as possible."

Perkins thought Scribners could win in court. But lawsuits drove Tom frantic, and while they waited for the case to be docketed, he became so tormented that he spent his days brooding or raving. His writing came to a halt. As the Dorman family fished for a settlement, and Max fretted about the unpredictability of juries, Wolfe grew even wilder. Perkins and Charles Scribner knew that they had to free their author of this crippling worry. One day Wolfe came up to the fifth floor of Scribners and the three men stood by the window in Perkins's office overlooking Fifth Avenue. Charles Scribner explained that it would cost far more to win the suit and that the publicity of a trial might provoke libel suits from other quarters; several others had already been threatened. Wolfe agreed to a settlement, but soon he was telling everyone how angry he was with his publishers for refusing to defend him.

Toward the end of the year Wolfe spent an evening with Perkins and ranted about the injustice done him on all hands in this "blank blank country," while Germany in contrast was "white as snow." He often spoke of "dear old Adolf" and his SS, who knew what to do with thugs who picked on artists. America was the place, he said, "where honest men were all robbed and bludgeoned by scoundrels." Then, shaking his finger at Perkins, he shouted, "And now you have got me into a $125,000 libel suit!" Wolfe and Scribners finally settled with the Dormans for $3,000. The legal fees amounted to $2,000 more. According to Tom's contract, he should have borne the entire expense, but Scribners volunteered to pay half.

On November 12, 1936, Wolfe wrote the final draft of a letter he had been contemplating for many months and mailed it to Perkins:

> I think you should now write me a letter in which you explicitly state the nature of my relation with Charles Scribner's Sons. I think you ought to say that I have faithfully and honorably discharged all obligations to

Charles Scribner's Sons, whether financial, personal or contractual, and
that no further agreement or obligation of any sort exists between us.

In view of all that had happened in the preceding year, Wolfe said, the
differences of belief, the fundamental disagreements that they had discussed "so openly, so frankly, and so passionately, a thousand times, and
which have brought about this unmistakable and grievous severance," he
felt that Perkins himself should have long since written this letter that
he was now asking for.

Wolfe's letter arrived just before the monthly meeting of Scribners'
board of directors. The meeting lasted through the entire afternoon, and
so Perkins did not have time that day to respond at length. But he did
get off a handwritten note which said in part: "I never knew a soul with
whom I felt I was in such fundamentally complete agreement as you.
What's more, and what has to do with it, I know you would not ever do
an insincere thing, or anything you did not think was right."

The next day Perkins dictated a letter which said that Wolfe had
"faithfully and honorably discharged all obligations to us, and no further
agreement of any sort exists between us with respect to the future." He
went on to say:

> Our relations are simply those of a publisher who profoundly admires the
> work of an author and takes great pride in publishing whatever he may of
> that author's writings. They are not such as to give us any sort of rights,
> or anything approaching that, over the author's future work. Contrary to
> custom, we have not even an option which would give us the privilege of
> seeing first any new manuscript.

In a third, more casual, reply to Wolfe's declaration of independence,
Perkins wrote Wolfe by hand on his personal stationery to say:

> I can't express certain kinds of feelings very comfortably, but you must
> realize what my feelings are toward you. Ever since *Look Homeward, Angel*
> your work has been the foremost interest in my life, and I have never
> doubted for your future on any ground except at times, on those of your
> being able to control the vast mass of material you have accumulated and
> have to form into books. You seem to think I have tried to control you.
> I only did that when you asked my help and then I did the best I could do.
> It all seems very confusing to me, but whatever the result I hope you don't
> mean it to keep us from seeing each other, or that you won't come to our
> house.

Two days later, as requested, Scribners sent Wolfe what moneys were due. "I wish I could see you," Perkins wrote in a covering letter, "but I don't want to force myself on you."

Perkins did see Wolfe, without untoward incident. Tom came to the Perkinses' for Christmas dinner and spoke happily of his leaving for New Orleans the next day. He said nothing of a long personal letter he had written on December 15, 1936, in which he had outlined his reasons for breaking with Perkins completely. Nor did he mention a supplement to that letter, a "business" letter, which he had written on December 23. He held onto both letters for weeks, carrying them with him on his trip, and debated with himself for weeks as to whether or not he should send them. He never mailed the business letter, but, as December of 1936 passed into January of 1937, he was resolving to send the personal letter.

He was at last provoked to do so by an unfortunate misunderstanding. A lawyer named Cornelius Mitchell, who was representing Wolfe in another legal matter, wrote him in New Orleans. Tom assumed that Perkins had given Mitchell Wolfe's New Orleans address, contrary to Tom's request. Mitchell's letter reached Wolfe the day that Wolfe was to dine with a newfound friend and admirer of his writing, William B. Wisdom. Tom drank at dinner and kept drinking that evening after Wisdom left him. On January 7, the morning after, he wired Perkins, HOW DARE YOU GIVE ANYONE MY ADDRESS? and lapsed back into stupor. Two days later Tom awoke to find himself reclining in his hotel bathtub with the knee of his trousers torn and his mind still a muddle. For reasons unknown he sent another telegram to Perkins asking, WHAT IS YOUR OFFER? Perkins did not understand either message and replied, IF YOU REFER TO BOOK WE SHALL MAKE IT VERBALLY WHEN YOU RETURN AS ARRANGEMENTS WILL DEPEND ON YOUR REQUIREMENTS. He went on to say, in his wire, that he had not carelessly given out Tom's address but that when Mitchell, Wolfe's own lawyer, had told Max it was important for Wolfe to communicate with him, Max had felt the disclosure justified.

Wolfe, now sober, apologized for telegraphing as he had; in fact, he had been so drunk that, he said, he could not recall what he had wired. Seeking sympathy he wrote: "All this worry, grief, and disappointment of the last two years has almost broken me, and finally this last letter of Mitchell's was almost the last straw. I was desperately in need of rest and quiet—the letter destroyed it all, ruined all the happiness and joy

I had hoped to get from the trip—the horrible injustice of the whole thing has almost maddened me."

Mitchell's letter concerned what Wolfe called a "blackmail" threat from an autograph dealer named Murdoch Dooher, who had been involved in selling Wolfe's manuscripts and had withheld some that Wolfe had wanted back. Perkins suggested paying a settlement at whatever cost; he felt it crucial to put an end to these suits, which were having such an awful effect on Tom. Full of self-pity and self-doubt, Wolfe denounced Perkins for choosing to settle, seeing it as proof that Max wanted to weaken him. He wrote in still another letter, which he mailed with his "personal letter":

> Are you—the man I trusted and reverenced above all else in the world— trying, for some mad reason I cannot even guess, to destroy me? How am I going to interpret the events of the past two years? Don't you want me to go on? Don't you want me to write another book? Don't you hope for my life—my growth—the fulfillment of my talent? In Christ's name, what is it, then? My health is well-nigh wrecked—worry, grief, and disillusionment has almost destroyed my talent—is *this* what you wanted? And why?

At the base of all Wolfe's anger was the general belief that without Perkins, Wolfe was unpublishable—a writer manqué. Wolfe himself had given currency to that notion, by making public facts that Perkins had fought to keep private. Wolfe had written the dedication of *Of Time and the River* and the extensive sections of *The Story of a Novel* that detailed Max's contributions to strengthen the bonds between the two men, but they were having the opposite effect. They now were impelling Wolfe to strike out on his own. In his personal letter Wolfe cited the charges of the critics that Wolfe was dependent on Perkins's "technical and critical assistance" and branded them so "contemptible, so manifestly false, I have no fear whatever of their ultimate exposure."

Wolfe granted that "you gave me the most generous, the most painstaking, the most valuable help." But, he contended, "that kind of help might have been given to me by many other skilful people." It was rather the understanding of "a fellow creature whom you know and reverence not only as a person of individual genius but as a spirit of incorruptible integrity—that kind of help I do need," Wolfe admitted, "that kind of help I think I have been given, that kind of help I shall ever more hope to deserve and pray that I shall have."

Wolfe, in his letter, agreed with Perkins that in some strange way they were in "complete and fundamental" agreement with each other. It was one of the greatest ironies of their artistic marriage, because, Wolfe asked, "Were there ever two men since time began who were as completely different as you and I? Have you ever known two other people who were, in almost every respect of temperament, thinking, feeling and acting, as far apart?" Wolfe did not know exactly how to label the two extremes they represented, but he thought Maxwell Perkins was essentially the "Conservative" while he was the "Revolutionary."

In the last two months, Wolfe believed he had conceived of the highest challenge of his life, a great work of imagination. But he hardly dared speak of this work to Perkins "for fear that this thing which I cannot trifle with, which may come to a man but once in his whole life, may be killed at its inception by cold caution, by indifference, by the growing apprehension and dogmatism of your own conservatism." This hesitation of Wolfe's, this feeling of alienation from Perkins, seemed proof enough to Wolfe, he said, that there was already in effect a severance between them. If Max disagreed, Tom said, then he should "tell me what there is in the life around us on which we both agree: We don't agree in politics, we don't agree on economics, we are in entire disagreement on the present system of life around us, the way people live, the changes that should be made."

Perkins had asserted repeatedly that he wanted to publish whatever Wolfe wrote. But Tom said he doubted Max's honesty of intent:

> There are many things that I have wanted you to print which have not been published. Some of them have not been published because they were too long for magazine space, or too short for book space, or too different in their design and quality to fit under the heading of a short story, or too incomplete to be called a novel.

Without criticizing Perkins or the mechanics that made the publication of these works impractical, Wolfe said, he maintained that "some of the best writing that a man may do is writing that does not follow under the convenient but extremely limited forms of modern publication." But as the "revolutionary" Wolfe had been telling Perkins, "the way things are is not always the way, it seems to me, that things should be."

Wolfe now described the great work he had in mind. He was about to write his own equivalent of *Ulysses*, a work of enormous originality and power which would pay no heed to publishing restrictions. The first volume was already under way, entitled *The Hound of Darkness.* "Like Mr. Joyce," Tom informed Perkins, "I am going to write as I please, and this time, no one is going to cut me unless I want them to." Since the publication of *Look Homeward, Angel,* Wolfe said, he had sensed Max's hope that the years would temper the author to a "greater conservatism, a milder intensity, a more decorous moderation." To a degree, Wolfe said, this had already happened, but in yielding to this benevolent pressure, Tom said, he felt he had allowed himself to falter in his purpose—to be diverted from the destination toward which the whole impulsion of his life and talent was driving him. "Restrain my adjectives, by all means, discipline my adverbs, moderate the technical extravagances of my incondite exuberance," Wolfe wrote Perkins, "but don't derail the train, don't take the Pacific Limited and switch it down the siding towards Hogwart Junction."

Wolfe believed Perkins had become fearful about what he might write and about whom—and that these fears might cloud his editorial judgment. If this timidity persisted and were applied to everything Wolfe wrote from then on, it would strike "a deadly blow at the very vitals of my creative life." Wolfe gathered that if he wished to continue writing books for Scribners, he must henceforth submit himself "to the most rigid censorship, a censorship which would delete from all my writings any episode, any scene, any character, any reference that might seem to have any connection, however remote, with the house of Charles Scribner's Sons and its sisters and its cousins and its aunts."

This was of course a reference to the brouhaha of the previous summer about the stories Wolfe had peopled with Scribners employees. After Perkins had told Elizabeth Nowell he would have to resign if the stories were published and she had passed this on to Wolfe, Perkins had had to explain his position to Tom. Perkins was "always with the man of talent," he told him, and that rather than restrict Wolfe, he would indeed resign. Perkins's offer was probably sincere. He did not want Wolfe to start censoring himself, and he felt that by resigning from Scribners he could take upon himself the responsibility for whatever Wolfe might write about that firm.

"Well," Wolfe now wrote in his letter, "don't worry, you'll never have to." In the first place, Tom said,

> your executive and editorial functions are so special and valuable that they could not be substituted by any other person on earth. They could not be

done without by the business that employs them. It would be like having a house with the lights turned out.

Secondly, Wolfe said, he would let no man resign on his account "simply because I won't be there to be resigned about."

"Let's make an end of all this devil's business," he continued in his letter to Perkins. "Let's stand to our guns like men. Let's go ahead and try to do our work and without qualification, without fear, without apology." Wolfe said he was prepared to try to proceed with his work. "If that cannot be done any longer upon the terms that I have stated here," he wrote Perkins, "then I must either stand alone or turn to other quarters for support, if I can find it."

> What are you willing to do? . . . You yourself must now say plainly what the decision is to be, because the decision now rests with you. You can no longer have any doubt as to how I feel about these matters. I don't see how you can any longer have any doubt that difficulties of a grave and desperate nature do exist.

Finally, on January 10, Wolfe put his twenty-eight-page, handwritten letter in the post.

There is no record of how Max Perkins's face looked as he read the letter. It is known that as he perused it he made notes in the margins. He responded, over the next several days, in three separate letters.

The first was brief. Max merely wanted to state two basic principles. It was his belief, he said, that the "one important supreme object" was to advance Wolfe's work.

> Anything in furtherance of that is good and anything that impedes it is bad. What impedes it especially is not the great difficulty and pain of doing it—for you are the reverse of lazy, you work furiously—but the harassment, the torment of outside worries. When you spoke to me about the settlement, it was, and had been before, very plain that this suit was such a worry that it was impeding you in your work. It was only because of that that I gave the advice I did. I thought, then get rid of it, forget it, and clear the way for what is really important, supremely. Now this blackmail talk puts a new face on that matter altogether.

Secondly, he said, he stood ready to help if he could, whenever Tom wanted.

You asked my help on "Time and the River." I was glad and proud to give it. No understanding person could believe that it affected the book in any serious or important way—that it was much more than mechanical help. It did seem that the book was too enormous to get between covers. That was the first problem. There might be a problem in a book, such as prohibited publication of Joyce for years in this country. If you wished it, we would publish any book by you as written except for such problems as those which prohibit—some can't be avoided but I don't foresee them. Length could be dealt with by publishing in sections. Anyhow, apart from physical or legal limitations not within the possibility of change by us, we will publish anything as you write it.

That night Max read Wolfe's letter more carefully. He did not understand why Tom should have delayed its delivery for so long. "There was mighty little of it that I did not wholly accept," Perkins wrote, "and what I did not, I perfectly well understood." He thought it was "a fine writer's statement of his beliefs, as fine as any I ever saw, and though I have vanities enough, as many as most, it gave me great pleasure too— that which comes from hearing brave and sincere beliefs uttered with sincerity and nobility." Perkins took issue only with the few things he thought Wolfe had greatly misunderstood. In his attempt to explain them, Perkins said, he realized he would first have to look within his own soul. "But what a task you've put me to to search myself—in whom I'm not so very much interested any more—and give you an adequate answer," he wrote the day after receiving Tom's letter. Two days after that, on Saturday, January 16, 1937, he embraced the task and responded in full.

Perkins completely subscribed to Wolfe's credo as a writer. He said, "If it were not true that you, for instance, should write as you see, feel, and think, then a writer would be of no importance, and books merely things for amusement. And since I have always thought that there could be nothing so important as a book can be, and some are, I could not help but think as you do. But there are limitations of time, of space, and of human laws which cannot be treated as if they did not exist." Perkins thought the writer should be the one to make his book what he wanted it to be, and that if because of the law of space it must be cut, he should be the one to cut it.

"But my impression was that you asked my help, that you wanted it," he wrote Wolfe. "And it is my impression too that changes were not forced on you (you're not very forceable, Tom, nor I very forceful), but were argued over, often for hours." Unless Wolfe wanted help in the future, it would not be thrust upon him. "I believe," Perkins wrote, "the writer anyway, should always be the final judge, and I meant you to be so. I have always held to that position and have sometimes seen books hurt thereby, but at least as often helped. The book belongs to the author."

Perkins knew that Tom's memory was miraculous, but it seemed as if Tom had forgotten the way they had worked together. Wolfe had never once been overruled during all the labor on the books. ("Do you think you are clay to be moulded!" Perkins wrote in disbelief; "I never saw anyone less malleable.") There were indeed segments from the large manuscript of Wolfe's life which had been deleted, but the cutting was always for artistic reasons. (At one point during the editing of Wolfe, Perkins had said to Jack Wheelock, "Maybe it's the way Tom is. Maybe we should just publish him as he comes and in the end it will be all right.") Perkins asked Wolfe now what he had often asked himself in the past: "If we had [refrained from cutting], and the results had been bad at the moment, would you not have blamed me? Certainly I should have bitterly blamed myself." Perkins did not want the passage of time to make Wolfe "cautious or conservative" but to give him a full control over his talents.

Perkins turned to the question of whether or not they were in "fundamental agreement." "I have always instinctively felt that it was so," he explained to Wolfe, "and no one I ever knew has said more of the things that I believed than you. It was so from the moment that I began to read your first book. Nothing else, I would say, could have kept such different people together through such trials."

Perkins's concept of social change was indeed less radical than Wolfe's:

> I believe that the only thing that can prevent improvement is the ruin of violence, or of reckless finance which will end in violence. That is why Roosevelt needs an opposition, and it is the only serious defect in him. I believe that change really comes from the great deep causes too complex for contemporary men, or any others perhaps, fully to understand, and that when even great men like Lenin try to make over a whole society suddenly the end is almost sure to be bad, and that the right end, the natural one, will come from the efforts of innumerable people trying to do right.

But on this issue, too, Perkins insisted they were essentially in agreement: "It is more that I like and admire the same things [you do] and despise many of the same things, and the same people too, and think the same things important and unimportant—at least this is the way it seemed to me."

Perkins's heartfelt, reasoned reply to Wolfe's letter appeased Wolfe enough to delay his departure from Scribners. But inside Wolfe the separation had already taken place. Sometime in January, 1937, he started a letter (probably to his lawyer Cornelius Mitchell), which he never finished. "I know I am alone now," began one paragraph. "As for Mr. Perkins—" he wrote in the letter's final fragment, "he is the greatest editor [of] this generation. I revered and honored him also as the greatest man, the greatest friend, the greatest character I had ever known. Now I can only tell you that I still think he is the greatest editor of our time. As for the rest— he is an honest but a timid man. He is not a man for danger—I expect no help from . . ."

After Perkins had written to Wolfe, he put Wolfe's letter in his desk, not in the regular files. John Hall Wheelock said that Max often pulled it out during the day, trying to read between the lines. Max, he said, was hurt that Wolfe had complained of his timidity and weakness. "Tom had moved from thinking Max was a cowardly man to not a man at all," Wheelock said. "That particular letter very nearly killed Max. But he never struck back. Thomas Wolfe was the ultimate editorial challenge, part of which meant dealing with his personal temperament." One day that spring, Wheelock happened unexpectedly into Perkins's office and found him almost in tears over the letter. When Max saw Wheelock, he slipped it furtively into the drawer and carried on with business. He never shared it with anyone or asked for sympathy.

XVII

A Sad Farewell

On January 2, 1937, Hemingway wired Max that he had finished his Gulf Stream novel. Max was already excited. The book, he felt, had one great "superficial advantage in being about a region that I think nobody has ever written well about, and a very rich and colorful scene." He thought back to that first time he had sailed in those waters, eight years before, when Hemingway told him he would not be able to write about them until he understood even the pelican's role. "But you did get around to it," Max now wrote Ernest, "when you had absorbed a sense of it and knew what part everything did play in the scheme of things. So I am not more anxious for anything than to see this novel." Because Hemingway generally gave himself several weeks away from a manuscript before he reread it himself for a new perspective, it would be another few months before Max could inspect it.

Hemingway's immediate plan was to go to Spain to cover the war there as a correspondent for the North American Newspaper Alliance. His new interest in Spain came from Martha Gellhorn, the striking twenty-nine-year-old author of a novel called *What Mad Pursuit*. Hemingway had met her that winter, just a year after she had been introduced to Harry L. Hopkins, Roosevelt's Director of the Federal Emergency Relief Administration. Hopkins had assigned her to survey living conditions of people on relief in industrial areas. She wrote four sections of her report as short stories and grouped them into a book called *The*

Trouble I've Seen. Miss Gellhorn's social convictions extended beyond America. She was particularly well informed about the Spanish Civil War, and Hemingway hung upon every word she said. During a brief visit to New York, well before he was ready to relinquish his novel, he tipped Max Perkins off about the possibility of publishing Martha Gellhorn. She had, in fact, written a story called "Exiles" which she hoped might appear in *Scribner's*. Max had admired *The Trouble I've Seen*, and days later the magazine bought "Exiles."

On February 27, Perkins saw Hemingway, a friend named Evan Shipman, and bullfighter Sidney Franklin off on a liner bound for France. "I hope they won't all get into trouble over there," Max wrote Scott Fitzgerald. "They seem to be quite bloodthirsty." Martha Gellhorn joined Hemingway in Madrid one month later. After six weeks in Spain, Ernest left, picked up the manuscript of his novel in Paris, and went to Bimini to revise it. There he was reunited with his children and Pauline. A few weeks later he came to New York again to deliver a speech before the Second American Writers' Congress at Carnegie Hall. Martha sat by his side during the speeches that preceded his. Her influence perhaps explained a new political tone that his speech displayed. "Really good writers are always rewarded under almost any existing system of government that they can tolerate," he said before the writers' congress. "There is only one form of government that cannot produce good writers, and that system is fascism. For fascism is a lie told by bullies. A writer who will not lie cannot live and work under fascism."

While still in New York, Hemingway stopped off at Perkins's house. Just before he arrived, someone told him that Scott Fitzgerald was also in town. Louise Perkins, never particularly smitten by Hemingway, cared even less for him after this visit. She resented his taking her husband for granted. "Ernest Hemingway came in here," Louise later told Elizabeth Lemmon, "hardly looking at Max and barked, 'Where's the telephone? I have to talk to Scott. He's the only person in America worth talking to.'" But Ernest did find time to talk privately to Max, and to him he expressed doubts about his new novel; he was afraid it was too short to stand alone, and he suggested beefing up the book with a few short stories. He promised to deliver his manuscript to Max for his opinion by July 5.

Flying south, Hemingway had a brainstorm. He thought he might come out with something entirely new—"a living omnibus." Under the overall title *To Have and Have Not*, he wrote Max, the volume would include: *Harry Morgan*, his novel of 50,000 words; three of his latest stories; an article on the hurricane of 1935 entitled "Who Murdered the Vets?"; one of his news dispatches from Madrid; and the text of his recent public address. He said Perkins could plug the agglomeration as a "major work," and it would give the buyers their money's worth. Most of the task of its assembly would fall into Perkins's hands, it seemed, because there was going to be a lot of blood spilled in Spain during the next several months, and Hemingway wanted to be there, ringside.

It was not until a few days later that Perkins could obtain a copy of the speech. It made him hesitate about the omnibus book. "I do think that bringing in a speech just because it is one, does tend to make the book seem too miscellaneous perhaps," he wrote Hemingway. Perkins said he preferred leaving it out but would continue to weigh the merits of the potpourri.

Hemingway returned to New York the first week of July, and Perkins was able to read *Harry Morgan* for himself. He pronounced it "very good, very moving" and left most of his criticism unsaid. He was glad Hemingway had returned to writing action-packed fiction: "It is a tough story, full of violent action that ends in great sorrow," Perkins wrote Hemingway's friend Waldo Peirce. "You get to admire Harry Morgan, bad man though he is—or almost because he is." The Hemingway philosophy seemed hard as ever: "No matter how[,] a man alone ain't got no bloody fucking chance," Harry Morgan spits out before dying. But Perkins considered the characters little more than cartoons. He kept referring t⸱ Morgan as a "type." To Hemingway, Perkins maintained his silence. He had once told his daughter Jane, "When you have a suggestion for Ernest you have to catch him at the right time." Max knew that at this point Hemingway wanted unquestionable support rather than constructive criticism, and that was what he gave him.

By the end of July, Perkins had untangled most of the confusion about the book. A book of short stories had been considered, eliminating the novel entirely. But ultimately, Hemingway was persuaded to publish the novel on its own, without any short stories, under the title *To Have and Have Not*. "It is a very satisfactory book for our lists," was as enthusiastic as Perkins got in recommending the work to Jonathan Cape in England. Once it was in print, Max did mention some of his criticism to the author over "tea" at his house in New York. He wanted Hemingway only to consider some of his comments for whatever help they might be to Hemingway's future writing. But Ernest was still in no mood to take such criticism. When he had heard enough, he whacked his hand down on the coffee table and said, "Hell, let Tom Wolfe write it for you then!"

Like Perkins, practically all the reviewers found *To Have and Have Not* exciting and alive, but they too were restrained in their praise. The writing verged on self-parody. In an essay written some years afterward, Edmund Wilson said: "The heroic Hemingway legend has at this point invaded his fiction and, inflaming and inflating his symbols, has produced an implausible hybrid, half Hemingway character, half nature myth." Though Max admitted it seldom and reluctantly, that was his own view exactly.

To Have and Have Not became a national best seller in weeks. Its 25,000 copies sold placed it fourth on the lists. Perkins was surprised how popular it became, for he did not think it was nearly as important as Hemingway's earlier works. Whether it was the freshness of the material or that Hemingway had gone back to fiction, Perkins never did decide. But it did at least allow Hemingway to reclaim his championship title in American letters, which he had forfeited once *A Farewell to Arms* fell from sight.

On the eleventh of August, days before sailing back to Spain, Hemingway dropped by Scribners without calling ahead, took the elevator to the fifth floor, and roamed back to his editor's corner office. Sitting with Perkins, his back to the door, was Max Eastman. They were planning a new edition of his *Enjoyment of Poetry*. Ernest barged in and quickly realized who the other party was. Because Hemingway had often told Perkins what he would do if he ever met Eastman, because of that piece Eastman had written several years earlier, "Bull in the Afternoon," Perkins swallowed hard and thought fast. Hoping humor would work, Perkins said to Eastman, "Here's a friend of yours, Max."

Hemingway shook hands with Eastman and they swapped amenities. Then Ernest, with a broad smile, ripped open his shirt and exposed a chest which Perkins thought was hirsute enough to impress any man. Eastman laughed, and Ernest good-naturedly reached over and unbuttoned Eastman's shirt, revealing a chest as bare as a bald man's head. Everyone laughed at the contrast. Perkins got ready to expose his chest, sure that he could place second, when Hemingway truculently demanded of Eastman, "What do you mean [by] accusing me of impotence?"

Eastman denied that he had, and there were sharp words back and forth. Eastman said, "Ernest, you don't know what you are talking about.

Here, read what I said." He picked up a copy of *Art and the Life of Action* on Perkins's desk, which the editor had there for some other reason, not even remembering that it contained "Bull in the Afternoon." But instead of reading the passage Eastman pointed out, Ernest began part of another paragraph, and trailed off into muttered profanity. "Read all of it, Ernest," Eastman urged him. "You don't understand it. . . . Here, let Max read it."

Perkins saw that things were getting serious. He started to read, thinking that would somehow calm things down. But Ernest snatched the book from him and said, "No, I am going to do the reading." As he started again, his face flushed, and he turned and smacked Eastman with the open book. Eastman rushed at him. Perkins, fearful that Ernest would kill Eastman, ran around his desk to grab Hemingway from behind. As the two authors grappled, all the precariously balanced books and papers on Perkins's desk toppled off, and both men fell to the floor. Thinking he was restraining Hemingway, Perkins grabbed the man on top. But when Max looked down, there was Ernest on his back, gazing up at him, his broken glasses dangling and a naughty grin from ear to ear. Apparently he had regained his composure instantly upon striking Eastman and put up no resistance whatever when Eastman landed on top of him.

After Hemingway and Eastman parted, Perkins spoke to the crowd of employees who had gathered. All agreed to say nothing. Max Eastman, however, wrote out an account of the incident, and the next night at a dinner where there were a number of newspaper people, he read it aloud, apparently at the urging of his wife. The next day Perkins's office swarmed with journalists, and another group interviewed Ernest at the docks just before he sailed for Europe. According to the *Times*, "Mr. Hemingway explained that he had felt sorry for Mr. Eastman, for he knew he had seriously embarrassed him by slapping his face. 'The man didn't have a bit of fight. He just croaked, you know, at Max Perkins, "Who's calling on you, Ernest or me?" ' So I got out."

Perkins maintained a public position of silent neutrality, but to special friends such as Scott Fitzgerald and Elizabeth Lemmon he told all. He believed Hemingway could have annihilated Eastman if he had wanted to; but he noted that Eastman did have both Hemingway's shoulders pinned. Fitzgerald was grateful for the blow-by-blow account, because he had heard every possible version of the tussle "save that Eastman has fled to Shanghai with Pauline." Of Ernest, Scott wrote Max further:

He is living at the present in a world so entirely his own that it is impossible to help him, even if I felt close to him at the moment, which I don't. I like him so much, though, that I wince when anything happens to him.

Hemingway went off to Spain to report the "big war of movement" which he thought would liberate Madrid.

Scott Fitzgerald was on the move all that year too, but without Hemingway's sense of purpose. After passing through New York in early 1937, he wrote Perkins that he was still suffering from that "same damn lack of interest, staleness, when I have every reason to want to work if only to keep from thinking." Perkins feared Scott was losing his obsession to succeed. Max believed it stemmed from his always playing a role, and his role of late was that of "the man burned out at forty." "Now there is somebody who ought to go to Spain for the sake of seeing something totally different from what he ever did see," Perkins wrote Marjorie Rawlings. Instead, Scott retreated to Tryon, North Carolina, where he once again placed himself under medical observation.

In the spring, Fitzgerald thought of going to Hollywood. He needed all the money he could get, because after paying the most pressing debts from his share of his mother's estate, he had only a few hundred dollars left. And Hollywood promised a change of scenery. He wrote Perkins, "I have lived in tombs for years it seems to me."

Fitzgerald's agent, Harold Ober, arranged for him to work at M-G-M for $1,000 per week. Out west, Scott wrote Max that he was happier than he had been in years. Everyone was warm to him, surprised and relieved that he was not drinking, and he approached his screenwriting seriously while sticking to a strict budget. He planned to work there until he had paid all his debts and stockpiled enough security so that his "catastrophe at forty" would not recur. Scott was sorry that he was allotting Scribners only $2,500 that first year, but he also had to repay thousands of dollars to Harold Ober who, like Perkins, was an individual, and had priority over a firm. Perkins told Fitzgerald not to repay his personal loan to him any sooner than he wanted to. But Fitzgerald began to pay. Max wrote Hemingway, "My pockets are full of money from the check that comes every week. If he will only begin to dramatize himself as the man who came back now, everything may turn out rightly."

Fitzgerald wanted to hear about his fellow Scribners authors. He asked Perkins to tell him of Hemingway and Wolfe, and of whoever

was new. The best story Max had to tell was of the unusual experience
Scribners had had with Marcia Davenport's first work in five years, a
novel called *Of Lena Geyer*.

Most books succeeded from the start or never at all—sales seldom
carried them into a new year. Without good reviews, Marcia Davenport's
story of a great diva took months to run through 10,000 copies. Then, inexplicably, it caught on. It quickly sold another 10,000 and sales continued
to climb. Neither the editor nor the author considered *Of Lena Geyer* a
solid novel. When Perkins first read Mrs. Davenport's *Mozart*, it had
seemed very plain to him that she could write fiction. And now he saw
Of Lena Geyer merely as a necessary stage in her development as a novelist.
But even with Perkins's encouragement, Mrs. Davenport realized that unlike such a writer as Thomas Wolfe, as she admitted in her memoirs,
Too Strong for Fantasy, "I was driven more by the need to write what
I knew than what I was."

Marcia Davenport had met Tom Wolfe aboard ship after she had
written *Of Lena Geyer*, when he was returning to America from the
Munich Olympic Games. It was perhaps the most incongruous pairing of
any of Perkins's writers—in physical appearance, manner, and outlook.
Mrs. Davenport was small, refined, and cosmopolitan. Wolfe looked like
a wild buffalo and was loud and obtrusive. They went into the ship's bar,
and Wolfe ordered drinks and began to talk. Five hours later they were
still sitting there, and Wolfe was still talking. "The subject was himself,"
Mrs. Davenport recalled, "only and always." She could not remember
exactly what he said, "but the core of it was his intention to prove that
he was not, as he claimed the literary world believed, the creature of
Max Perkins."

"I'm going to show them I can write my books without Max. I'm
going to leave Max and get another editor. I'm going to leave Scribners,"
he told Mrs. Davenport.

"How about the dedication in your last book?" she asked, "Are you
that much of a hypocrite?" Wolfe ignored the remark and went on to
complain that Perkins had kept out of that book some of the best things
he had ever written. Over and over he repeated his need to leave Scribners,
until Marcia Davenport let him have it.

"I think you're a rat," she said. "You're ungrateful and treacherous.
That dedication was disgusting. It didn't mean devotion to Max, it was
just spilling yourself. You have no devotion and no loyalty either. Where

would you be without Max and Scribners too? You can't face the truth."
Months later, those accusations were still festering in Wolfe's mind.

After Tom had returned from New Orleans to New York and their
long letters had been exchanged, he and Perkins felt as though their friendship had been wounded. But Wolfe still walked the few blocks to the
Perkinses' house almost every day, as though everything had been patched
up. He wrote Hamilton Basso, another Perkins novelist, in April, 1937:

> Yes, Max Perkins and I are all right. I think we always were, for that
> matter. Periodically, I go out and indulge in a sixty-round, knock down
> and drag out battle with myself but I think Max understands that.

Tom continued to war with himself but believed he would pull through
in the end, having read somewhere that "no writer has ever yet been
known to hang himself as long as he had another chapter left."

The calm did not last long. Late one afternoon that April, Wolfe
telephoned Perkins to say that a friend from Chapel Hill and his wife
had arrived in town. It was Jonathan Daniels, editor of the Raleigh *News
and Observer*, who was soon to become an aide to FDR. Tom asked if
Max and Louise could join them and several others, including Noble
Cathcart, the publisher of the *Saturday Review of Literature*, for dinner.
The Perkinses accepted, and Louise immediately insisted they all assemble
at her home for cocktails. When Max welcomed Tom's guest of honor,
Daniels made a trite and tiresome remark. He said he had supposed Maxwell Perkins would have a long white beard. From then on, Perkins
found him "bumptious."

The dinner party at Cherio's began on a festive note. Wolfe was
riding high, until a woman who had accompanied the Cathcarts and had
her eyes glued on him for an hour had a jolt of recognition and burst out,
"Oh, I know who you are. I read an article about you in the *Saturday
Review*. It was by Bernard De Voto." Perkins was dismayed. He knew
immediately that she could have said nothing worse, that the De Voto
article had not lost its power to infuriate Tom.

Max watched Wolfe coil up inside, withdrawing into silence.
Then Daniels began to wonder out loud why it was that *Scribner's* was
the only magazine to publish Wolfe. He asked Perkins what was the
matter with *Scribner's* anyway, meaning somewhat facetiously that it
should be a better magazine than that. "But to Tom, with his mistrust

of his abilities," Max said later, "it seemed to mean that they showed bad judgment in publishing him." Within the next half-hour, Tom's humor turned acidic, and he needled all the guests at the table. Everyone took it lightly, but Wolfe's face blanched as it did when he drank a great deal. Max had witnessed the condition enough times to know "all of his doubts and fears were seething up to his mind. He was in a murderous state."

Then a man who was dining with a woman in the opposite corner of the restaurant zigzagged over and mumbled something at Wolfe in a friendly, drunken way. Max foresaw a melee, so he went over to tell the woman she had better keep her escort at his own table. By the time Max returned to his seat, everybody had gotten up except Wolfe. They had realized what a state things were in and slipped out the door. Tom focused all his anger on Perkins. Cherio stood by anxiously and seemed worried about what could happen. Perkins was unable to hear what Wolfe was saying, but with the six-and-a-half-foot man standing there winding up like a baseball pitcher, Max understood. "Tom," he said, "I know if that old sledgehammer landed it would do considerable damage, but it might not land." Wolfe kept staring at Max with eyes burning. Partly on Cherio's account, Max said, "Well, if we must fight, let's do it in the fresh air." As they made their way to the door, another publisher, Harrison Smith of Harcourt, Brace, walked in, shook hands, and quipped half-knowingly, "I see you are having author trouble." Perkins spoke to him for a moment, then left the restaurant. Tom was standing off the sidewalk, waiting in the street. Perkins said later he thought that "only a miracle could prevent something dreadful happening that everyone would regret." In fact, something like a miracle did occur.

Out of a neighboring restaurant emerged a group of people including a tall, handsome, black-haired young woman. She ran straight to Tom and inexplicably threw her arms around him, saying, "This is what I came to New York to see." The daughter of a prominent Richmond family, some of whom Max and Tom had met in Middleburg, she had just finished dining with Elizabeth Lemmon's sister and brother-in-law, the Holmes Morisons. She really had been eager to meet Tom. Within the next three or four minutes this Virginia country girl was cussing jocularly at Tom in the vilest language Perkins had ever heard from any woman's mouth. ("A night club hostess couldn't excel her," Max wrote Elizabeth.) The woman completely diverted Tom's attention, and both parties trooped harmoniously to Manny Wolf's.

Back in his apartment, Wolfe again tried to draft a letter to be sent to all publishers other than Scribners. He expressed his hope that he might reach someone interested enough in his writing to listen to his story and publish his future manuscripts. He described at length the schism between him and Perkins. He did not send the letter, but he became so obsessed with breaking free that he spoke of little else, even to Max's face. Finally, in exasperation, Perkins exclaimed one day, "All right then, if you *must* leave Scribners, go ahead and *leave*, but for heaven's sake, don't talk about it anymore!"

Whereupon the prodigal son decided that, for the first time in years, he would go home again. That summer he told friends and family that he had come back to Asheville—he rented a cabin in the woods—"to set a spell and think things over." One of the items that crossed his mind was his story "Chickamauga," which he had written after his spring travels. He believed it one of the best pieces he had ever done and had instructed Elizabeth Nowell to submit it to the *Saturday Evening Post*. The *Post* had rejected it, saying it did not have enough "story element." While he was in Asheville, *The American Mercury* turned it down too, and Wolfe told Miss Nowell to try several small magazines. He knew he had *Scribner's* to fall back on, but he wanted to be published elsewhere, to prove he was not entirely dependent on Charles Scribner's Sons. Wolfe hoped for an acceptance by the time he returned.

The Perkinses also left Manhattan for the summer, moving back to New Canaan, but Max often stayed in the city, working until very late. Tom's abandonment left him more forlorn than usual. He wrote Elizabeth Lemmon that August, after a year of silence, one of the most melancholy letters he had ever written. He did not specify the reason for his unhappiness, but it was no doubt the painful decline of his relationship with Wolfe.

> I, in a way, have fallen upon evil days and that's why I haven't written you. I never could write when things were going wrong. That always worried me about the children, but they seem to be made on another pattern and only write if things go badly. And as for the evil days: we all have to have them, and what the hell, if we can take them. But I want you to know how it is, why I haven't written. You were my friend and nothing pleases me more than to know that. The future be damned, I'll remember the past.

Louise Perkins had no intention of whiling away a quiet summer in New Canaan. She had been invited to join the great Shavian actress Mrs.

Patrick Campbell and a theatrical troupe in Milford, Connecticut—as Mrs. Campbell's understudy. Realizing such opportunities seldom knocked twice, especially at this stage in her unstarted career, Louise accepted. Unfortunately, the star was frustratingly healthy and Louise waited in the wings all summer. After that experience, Max wrote Tom Wolfe in a newsy letter that summer, "I think she's pretty fed up with the thespian temperament."

By the end of the season, Wolfe's "Chickamauga" ended up in the *Yale Review*, and Elizabeth Nowell successfully placed another half-dozen of his stories. Tom even received compliments from Scott Fitzgerald for his story "E" in *The New Yorker*. Scott laid out his admiration of Wolfe's writing, calling his talent "unmatchable in this or any other country." Then Scott tried to make "a good case for your necessity to cultivate an alter ego, a more conscious artist in you. . . .

> Now the more the stronger man's inner tendencies are defined, the more he can be sure they will show, the more necessity to rarefy them, to use them sparingly. The novel of selected incidents has this to be said, that the great writer like Flaubert has consciously left out the stuff that Bill or Joe (in his case Zola) will come along and say presently. He will say only the things that he alone sees. So *Madame Bovary* becomes eternal while Zola already rocks with age.

"The unexpected loquaciousness of your letter struck me all of a heap," Wolfe wrote back to Fitzgerald. "Your bouquet arrived smelling sweetly of roses but cunningly concealing several large-sized brickbats." He found Scott's case against him not far from the common criticism of the day, and he expected better. Wolfe did not see what Flaubert and Zola had to do with his writing.

"I am going into the woods for another two or three years," Wolfe wrote Fitzgerald:

> I am going to try to do the best, the most important piece of work I have ever done. I am going to have to do it alone. I am going to lose what little bit of reputation I may have gained, to have to hear and know and endure in silence again all of the doubt, the disparagement, the ridicule, the postmortems that they are so eager to read over you even before you are dead. I know what it means and so do you. We have both been through it before.

He thought he could survive it, but he would be looking for intelligent understanding from friends outside Scribners. "Go for me with the gloves off if you think I need it," he wrote Fitzgerald. "But don't De Voto me. If you do I'll call your bluff."

That fall Scribners spruced up their library on the fifth floor with a new paint job and carpeting. Perkins told everybody the place "now resembles a boudoir," but he knew that some of the women literary agents in New York would feel more comfortable there, and he seemed to be dealing with more of them every day. In fact, women were entering the profession in such rapid numbers that Max had suggested that Diarmuid Russell, the son of the Irish poet A. E. (George William Russell), and Wolfe's friend Henry Volkening, a former English instructor at N.Y.U., join forces and start their own agency before "the damned women take over the entire business." In the process of redecorating, three large packages were discovered at Scribners which contained manuscripts of Thomas Wolfe. One of them was a chunk of *The October Fair*, a novel Tom never finished. Wolfe thought that he or Scribners had lost that, but Max remembered that Tom himself had put those manuscripts in that very place. "So," Max wrote Elizabeth Nowell, "everything of Tom's that was in our hands is still in them and in fine condition!"

Except Wolfe's career. Back in New York after three months in his cabin in North Carolina, Wolfe was still reassessing his relationship with his publisher. Another potshot by Bernard De Voto, in the August 21 *Saturday Review*, criticizing both Wolfe and Melville for their "long passages of unshaped emotion," made Tom even more determined to be published elsewhere.

One late summer morning, Wolfe called several major publishing houses on the telephone, babbling to the first editor he was connected to at each place that he was Thomas Wolfe and asking if they were interested in publishing him. Some of the publishers assumed the calls were practical jokes. But Bernard Smith at Alfred A. Knopf said he would be delighted to talk to Wolfe about his publishing future. Alfred Harcourt paid a visit to Perkins and Charles Scribner and asked them if Harcourt, Brace could in fairness accept the offer Wolfe had made to him. Perkins said he "didn't think there was any other possibility," meaning that Wolfe was too great a writer to pass by. He and Scribner both assured Harcourt that they would harbor no resentment against him, for Wolfe was evidently determined to change publishers at last. Harcourt left Perkins with the impression that Wolfe would be signing with his firm. But after almost ten years of fidelity to Scribners, Wolfe wanted to revel in this new attention. He flirted with all the suitors for his hand.

A few weeks later, Robert Linscott of Houghton Mifflin met Wolfe in their New York office. In no time they were calling each other by their first names. He and Tom arranged for the safekeeping of Tom's huge trunk of manuscripts. As a business formality, Linscott gave the author a note acknowledging receipt of the trunk. That night Wolfe, lighthearted about having found himself a publisher he liked, reached into his pocket and found the receipt. It read, in part: "I hope you realize that, under the circumstances, it [the trunk] will have to be held entirely at your risk." Wolfe broke off with Houghton Mifflin that instant, raging in an unsent letter, "It seems to me that you must assume the risk, that the entire and whole responsibility of safe-guarding an author's property, once you have requested it, is yours and yours alone." He went back to playing the field.

For weeks Wolfe's family remained unaware of the separation be- tween Tom and Perkins. Max got a postcard from Julia Wolfe, who was worrying because she had not had word from her son for over a month. Max also heard similarly from Tom's brother Fred. Perkins replied that Tom was all right but that mail should now be sent in Elizabeth Nowell's care, not his at Scribners. In his letter to Fred, Perkins said: "He has also turned his back on me, and Scribners, and so I have not seen him at all, though I would very much like to." It was not long before all the stories of the separation were passed among the garrulous Wolfes. Tom con- firmed to them that he was no longer with a publisher and that the cause of his separation had its origin as far back as 1935. Wolfe now real- ized the ties between him and Scribners had not been cut cleanly. In a 5,000-word letter to Perkins, he tried to answer all the accusations he had heard attributed to his editor. "In the first place," he wrote, "I did not 'turn my back' on you and Scribners, and I think it is misleading and disingenuous for anyone to say this was the case." Secondly, he did not think it was truthful for either of them to assert he had no conception of what their separation was about. Tom believed Max knew all the reasons very clearly, for they had threshed them out hundreds of times.

"You owe me nothing, and I consider what I owe you a great deal," Wolfe said. "I don't want any acknowledgment for seeing and under- standing that you were a great editor, even when I first met you, but I did see and understand it, and later I acknowledged it in words which have been printed by your own house, and of which now there is a public record. The world would have found out anyway that you were a great editor," Tom insisted. But when people now solemnly reminded him that Perkins was great, he found it ironically amusing to reflect that he himself was the first one publicly to point out that fact. "I, as much as any man alive, was responsible for pulling the light out from underneath the bushel basket," he bragged.

"This letter," he went on, "is a sad farewell, but I hope it is for both of us a new beginning." And he added,

> I am your friend, Max, and that is why I wrote this letter—to tell you so. If I wrote so much else here that the main thing was obscured—the only damn one that matters is that I am your friend and want you to be mine— please take this last line as being what I wanted to say the whole way through.

Perkins was glad to see Wolfe's handwriting again. "I am your friend and always will be I think," he replied. What had grieved Perkins most deeply in the last few months, he said, was that in making his move Tom had maneuvered behind Max's back. All that dealing under the table had been "humiliating," Perkins said. He had written Fred truly when he said he did not understand Tom's action. In the end, Max said none of this made any difference. "I hope we may soon meet as friends," he wrote, now that they were no longer associates. In December, Perkins learned from Robert Linscott that Wolfe was ready to sign with Edward C. Aswell, an assistant to Eugene F. Saxton at Harper & Brothers.

The Christmas before, Wolfe had been with the Perkinses. This Christmas he was in Chappaqua, New York, with the Aswells and their friends, drinking champagne and exchanging emotional toasts with them.

Wolfe regarded his move to a new publisher as "one of the most fortunate and happy experiences" of his life. Harpers was giving him a large advance, but more than money had been involved. Wolfe's decision was based on a personal hunch, because he was to be associated with Ed Aswell, a fellow North Carolinian, exactly his age. "I think it's going to turn out to be a wonderful experience," Tom wrote a friend, Anne Armstrong, of Bristol, Tennessee. "I feel that the man is quiet, but very deep and true: and he thinks that I am the best writer there is. . . . However, I am still a little sad about the past." But, he asked her, "You can't go home again, can you?"

Perkins accepted Wolfe's departure with grace, for he believed in its inevitability—"I can easily imagine a biography of Tom written twenty years from now that would ascribe this action to his instinctive and manly determination to free all his bonds and stand up alone," he wrote Marjorie

Kinnan Rawlings a few months later. But Max already knew that an important part of his life was gone. At the end of the year he wrote Tom Wolfe, "I drink a lonely glass of ale every night in Manny Wolf's while waiting for the paper. . . . We really had a mighty good Christmas, but we missed you."

XVIII

By the Wind Grieved

Shortly after Christmas, 1937, Thomas Wolfe, now a Harpers author, was forced to ask Max Perkins for help. The trial involving Wolfe and Murdoch Dooher, the twenty-one-year-old manuscript agent, was impending, and Tom wrote Max to ask him to testify, "not only for personal or friendly reasons, but just because it's taking a stand in favor of the human race." Perkins was glad to oblige, especially pleased that Wolfe showed neither remorse nor anxiety in asking him to appear. By now many of the specifics of the case had become fuzzy in Perkins's mind, and on the evening of February 1 he and Tom met in the lobby of the Chelsea Hotel—where Wolfe had recently moved, at Max's suggestion—to clarify them. It was their first encounter in seven months, and it was painless.

The case involved the manuscript of *Of Time and the River*. Earlier, Dooher had successfully sold a few small items of Wolfe's—books and papers—and so Wolfe had authorized him to sell the manuscript of this novel. Dooher picked up the heap of material at Scribners and set about to collate it. As he worked he discovered that what Wolfe had given him was not the manuscript that had been published but pages cut from that book. At Wolfe's insistence he went to Scribners to work with the writer on sorting this unpublished material.

As it happened, Wolfe's English publisher, A. S. Frere-Reeves, had just arrived from London that day, and Perkins, who knew him only slightly, was to meet him at the Chatham at five that afternoon. Max thought it would be nice to have Wolfe join them briefly, and so he went into the room where Wolfe and Dooher were working and took Wolfe away "for just one drink." But Wolfe had many drinks, and Dooher was kept waiting for hours. When Wolfe returned, Dooher was angry; then Wolfe got angry and discharged him. Dooher stormed out and sent Wolfe a bill of $1,000 for services rendered—specifically, lining up a buyer and working with the material—and for loss of commissions to which he felt entitled. Dooher still had in his possession many pages of Wolfe's manuscript which he refused to return without payment. Whereupon, Wolfe began legal proceedings to recover his property. Max, in his way of bearing the brunt of responsibilities, later said: "I was to blame for Dooher's having the wrong material, and also for getting both of them into an unreasonable frame of mind."

In the meeting with Wolfe to prepare for the trial, Max remembered that Tom, just before he went to Europe in 1935, had given Perkins his written power of attorney. Max's recollection was greeted joyfully by Wolfe; he regarded it as a key to his defense, for to him it clearly indicated that Wolfe had never intended Dooher to act on his own and consummate any deal without approval—of Max, if not of Wolfe himself.

On February 8, 1938, Perkins went to Jersey City for the trial. He found Wolfe "all fidgety and frowning under the slings and arrows and all" but thought Tom gave an overwhelming impression of sincerity and dignity in the courtroom. A procession of witnesses appeared in Wolfe's defense, and soon it seemed so obvious to Max that Wolfe's case was won that he believed he would not have to testify. But he was called to the stand just the same. By the time Max had his hand on the Bible, Wolfe could hardly contain his emotion; Elizabeth Nowell observed that Wolfe was moved almost to tears, because—for the first time in public—Max was wearing a hearing aid. He had stubbornly refused to use one on any previous occasion, even though everyone he spoke with had noticed how bad his hearing had grown. But Perkins felt a kind of duty to Wolfe, an obligation to understand all the proceedings clearly, that outweighed the embarrassment and the discomfort of the clumsy contraption. He proved to be the most scrupulously honest and least cooperative witness. The lawyer asked Perkins twice if the power of attorney had been given expressly for the purpose of controlling Dooher. "I felt like a silly little prig in saying that I could not actually say so," Max recounted to John Terry. "I'm sure the lawyer despised me, as I sort of despised myself." All

Perkins could truthfully testify was that no such power had ever been given him before and thus it was evidently for that purpose.

By lunchtime Wolfe was acquitted, and Perkins, relieved that his ordeal was over, considered his morning in court "good fun." Perkins believed Wolfe's vindication had "more or less restored Tom's faith in at least one American institution." Together, they ferried back to Manhattan and lunched at Cherio's. Afterward, Max realized that there no longer remained any professional reason for his ever seeing Thomas Wolfe again.

Max wrote several of his authors about the split between himself and Tom. He insisted it was in Wolfe's best interests to leave, and so it was inevitable. Hemingway, for one, thought Perkins wrote "very chic-ly" about it all, while Wolfe had acted like an enormous baby. Ernest wondered why the man could not just write, then sneered that it must be very difficult to be a genius.

In January, Hemingway returned from the Spanish Civil War. The Loyalist offensive had hardly made a dent anywhere. In fact, for months there was so little action that Ernest had not even bothered to write dispatches for the North American Newspaper Alliance. He had taken advantage of the lulls to go back to his own work. By winter's end he had finished his first play, set in the very hotel in which he was staying, the Hotel Florida in Madrid. Once word had got out, many people in the theatrical world called Perkins. Max wrote Ernest, "I cannot imagine your writing a play that would not be a sensation and a success," though he knew nothing about it except its locale.

Back in Key West, Hemingway admitted to Perkins that he was in an "unchristly jam of every kind." He was concerned about the war in Spain but was too far from it; he was eager to cast his fresh material from Spain into fiction but was too close to it. He was also engaged in a domestic battle with Pauline, who was trying to hold on to him as his relationship with Martha Gellhorn deepened. Perkins offered aid with the problems over which he had some control. If it would help get a production together, Perkins said Scribners would publish his play right away, even though the usual procedure was to publish when the play opened. (Robert Sherwood's *The Road to Rome, Reunion in Vienna,* and *The Petrified Forest* were the most successful examples on Perkins's list.) "But this play of yours," Max assured Hemingway, "will sell without a production," if only because of the public's desire to find out the way things were in Spain.

Hemingway's yearning to get back to Spain took over. He told Max he felt like a "bloody shit" lounging in Key West when war threatened

Aragon and Madrid. Against Pauline's and Max's wishes, he returned in the middle of March, 1938. He assured his editor that he had not forgotten the collection of stories that was to come out in the fall. He promised to mail it to Max from Paris, en route to Spain, and even to add several more stories just before the book went to press.

The publication of Hemingway's play was set for the fall. Ernest had left a copy with Perkins, though he still had revisions to make—among them, he said, a probable change in the title, *The Fifth Column*. GREATLY MOVED BY PLAY. IT IS MAGNIFICENT ALL GOOD LUCK, Perkins cabled Hemingway. "And by the way," he wrote the next day, "I think that you will have a hard time beating the present title." Unaware of the Hemingways' domestic estrangement, Max wrote to Pauline. "That play," he said, "made me see plenty why Ernest had to go back to Spain." Speaking of the play as a work of literature, he said: "It shows what *To Have and Have Not* did, only more so, that Ernest has moved forward into new territory and larger territory, I guess."

Aboard ship, Hemingway wrote Perkins a long letter apologizing for having been "trying" during the last few weeks. In a funereal tone Ernest thanked Max for being so loyal to him through all the times of bad temper and "general shittiness." Max assured him that no thanks were necessary. "I think you have treated us swell. We all do. I owe you plenty," he wrote back. But Perkins could not shake a feeling of depression. The letter upset him all through the weekend because it sounded as if Hemingway did not think he would ever get back from Spain. "But I haven't much faith in premonitions," Max wrote Fitzgerald, trying to dredge up some optimism. "Very few of mine ever developed. Hem seemed very well, and I thought he was in good spirits, but I guess he wasn't. I thought I would tell you that he especially mentioned you." Fitzgerald was touched that he too had been remembered in Hemingway's "premonitory last words." He was fascinated as always by the man's "Byronic intensity."

Scott Fitzgerald had come through New York early in 1938. Max had lunched with him and an attractive thirty-year-old blonde whom Scott introduced as his "girl friend" from Hollywood. Perkins was pleased to learn she was not an actress. The "girl friend" was Sheilah Graham, an Englishwoman who wrote a column about Hollywood for the North American Newspaper Alliance. Perkins knew little more about her, except that she seemed to have a good effect on Scott. Sporting a California tan, he had not been drinking, looked wonderfully healthy, and acted lively. Fitzgerald had also paid off most of his debts—including all he owed Max—and had an even better film contract for another year, which promised to get him out of debt altogether.

Upon his return to Hollywood, Scott immediately sent Max a check, the first portion of the sum he still owed Scribners. "I'd said he would do it but nobody would believe it," Max wrote Elizabeth Lemmon, "—and sometimes I didn't either." In a letter accompanying the check, written from his hotel room at the Garden of Allah on Sunset Boulevard, Fitzgerald confessed to having gone on a binge in New York after he had left Max. He swore that this bender had lasted only three days and that he had not had a drop since. As long as he was confessing, however, he thought he should admit to one other, back in September, likewise for three days. Save for those two lapses, alcohol had not passed his lips for a year. "Isn't it awful that we reformed alcoholics have to preface everything by explaining exactly how we stand on that question," he wrote Perkins. Scott said he was working on the script for a motion picture for Joan Crawford called *Infidelity*. Perkins's steady flow of letters from New York were Fitzgerald's only evidence that he existed, albeit barely, in the literary world there.

Scott felt even more estranged that spring when Scribners' vice-president in charge of sales and promotion, Whitney Darrow, informed him that *This Side of Paradise* was officially "out of print," eighteen years after it had ignited the youth of the twenties. Fitzgerald was disappointed but not surprised. "Looking it [the novel] over," he told Max, "I think it is now one of the funniest books since 'Dorian Gray' in its utter spuriousness—and then, here and there, I find a page that is very real and living." He knew that, to the generation that had replaced his, the children of his contemporaries, the concerns of the book were remote and that escapades which were startling then would now be considered tame. "To hold them [the new generation] I would have to put in a couple of abortions to give it color," Scott said, "(and probably would if I were writing it again)." Its faults aside, he wanted to know exactly what "out of print" meant. Did it mean, he asked, that he was now free to find another publisher to reprint it? And if he did, would that have the effect of suddenly making the book valuable again to "Whitney Darrow or Darrow Whitney, or whatever his name is?"

When a book was declared out of print, it meant that the publisher, because of lack of demand for the book, had decided not to print any more copies and to let the current inventory run out; the author was in-

deed free to seek a new publisher. But, said Perkins, he had his own plan
for keeping the book alive at Scribners. "I ought not to even breathe
it to you because it will probably never turn out," he wrote the author,
"but I have a secret hope that we could some day—after a big success with
a new novel—make an omnibus book." It would combine *This Side of
Paradise, The Great Gatsby,** and *Tender Is the Night,* complete with a
lengthy introduction by the author. "Those three books," Perkins wrote,
"besides having the intrinsic qualities of permanence, represent three
distinct periods.—And nobody has written about any of those periods as
well." Perkins did not want to spoil an opportunity with the premature
publication of the three-in-one volume. He explained:

> There comes a time and it applies somewhat now to both *Paradise* and
> *Gatsby,* when the past gets a kind of romantic glamour. We have not yet
> reached that with *Tender Is the Night* and not to such a degree as we shall
> later even with *Paradise,* I think. But unless we think there never will be
> good times again—and barring a war there will be better times than ever,
> I believe—we ought to wait for them.

Perkins wished Fitzgerald would turn back to his novel about the
Dark Ages, *Philippe,* but Scott had no time for that. He said the amazing
business of movie-making had a "way of whizzing you along at a terrific
speed and then letting you wait in a dispirited half-cocked mood when
you don't feel like undertaking anything else, while it makes up its
mind." Hollywood studios were filled with a "strange conglomeration of
a few excellent overtired men making the pictures and as dismal a crowd
of fakes and hacks at the bottom as you can imagine." The consequence,
Scott said, "is that every other man is a charlatan, nobody trusts anybody
else, and an infinite amount of time is wasted from lack of confidence." It
was a peculiar stretch in Fitzgerald's career, he thought, but as he looked
around, he realized that he was not the only literary fish out of water.
"What a time you've had with your sons, Max," he wrote Perkins on
April 23, 1938, "—Ernest gone to Spain, me gone to Hollywood, Tom
Wolfe reverting to an artistic hill-billy."

As for Max himself, it was an opportunity for him to catch his second
wind and redistribute his energies. After a peaceful summer in New Canaan, the Perkinses moved back there permanently. Max hoped to keep

---

* "What a pleasure it was to publish that! It was as perfect a thing as I ever had any share
in publishing," Max wrote Scott about *Gatsby* in that same letter. "One does not seem to
get such satisfaction as that any more."

Louise in the country for good, but again she found herself with an excess of energy, a surplus that city life had used to burn off. Her passion to perform on stage had eased, but a restlessness still flickered within her. She searched for a life of her own outside the house, and soon she found it.

Early in 1938 several nuns from the local Roman Catholic parish came to the Perkinses' door to speak to their Catholic cook. Louise chatted with the sisters for a few minutes, then wrote their church a generous check. The nuns stayed to talk some more, and by the time they left, Louise had become impressed with Catholicism. She looked into it a bit further, and several weeks later she found herself in earnest conversation with the parish priest. "What means the most to you apart from people?" he asked her. Her reply came without hesitation: "Talent in the theater." The priest told her to "take that and lay it on the altar of Jesus Christ." At age fifty, Louise emerged from the wings into her new holy theater with all the vitality of an ingenue and the enthusiasm of a convert. As Elizabeth Lemmon noted, "Louise always had a passion for purple." Whether or not her motivation was truly religious, it was strong. Friends and relatives indicated that Louise's conversion had more than theatrical implications. Several people said it was her "rebellion against the family." One daughter suggested it was another stage in "Mother's lifelong struggle to be creative."

Max was not convinced by Louise's new devotion. Once, when she began one of her crusades, attempting to reform her entire household, he pointed out, "Your voice takes on a phony tone whenever you talk about the Church." When she asked for the umpteenth time, "Max, why won't you try it once?"—as though it were some new headache remedy— he responded, "And have you tried Buddha?" The harder she fought to save his soul, the harder Max resisted. It was a new version of their perennial battle—silent reserve versus unrestrained enthusiasm. Louise proselytized wherever she went, often to Max's embarrassment. She sprinkled holy water all over the house, dousing Max's pillow several times a week. With a sigh he would ask his daughters if they could not "do something" about their mother. One evening, when she was running low on reasons why Max should convert, she told him if he did not start confessing his sins and taking Communion he would burn in hell. "Thank God I'm not going to heaven—" he came back, "with all you Catholics." By June she was cloistering herself on week-long retreats. Max continued to observe his wife's interest in Catholicism with disdain, but, he told John Hall Wheelock, he did not especially want it to wear off entirely. He tired of her relentless attacks on the Protestants but saw how fulfilling the Church was for her.

Because of the intensity of their working relationships with Perkins, many of his women writers felt that they understood him better than Louise did. Too quickly concluding that his discordant marriage was the cause of his evident unhappiness, and unaware of his deep love and respect for Louise, some of them readily offered unsolicited comfort and advice, especially during Louise's period of religious fervor. Marjorie Rawlings wrote Max that year that his wife "is very sweet and a little pathetic, and I understand her. You are so much wiser than she—you must not be intolerant. The Catholic matter will probably fade away." Max may have thought that too, at first; he had once written Elizabeth Lemmon that "Louise feels things passionately but soon gets over them to a great extent, which is the best way; but that is so different from the way I do that it always frightens me." But a few weeks after his wife's introduction to the Church, Max wrote Elizabeth, "Louise is now a complete Roman Catholic; the house is full of Roman Catholic literature and now and then a nun blunders in, and I always think there may be a priest on the back stair."

With Louise completely wrapped up in church affairs, Max's correspondence with Elizabeth Lemmon picked up considerably for a while. "Whenever I get a pen into my hand I can't resist writing you," he told her in February. But a few months later he said: "I could write you about a thousand things, but I am so busy. I always supposed I worked pretty hard, but I have more to do all the time and other people like me seem to have less, and I don't understand it. I work faster too and I always was good that way. I can't make out what has happened."

One thing that had happened was the advent of a talented but time-consuming new author, an English-born woman named Janet Reback. Since childhood she had been accumulating stacks of her own unpublished manuscripts. In 1937, as she approached the age of forty, she submitted a novel to the Macmillan company and had it refused, leaving her despondent. One of Macmillan's associate editors insisted that Max Perkins at Scribners would give her work, *Dynasty of Death*, a fair reading.

From the first few pages Perkins was captivated. Charles Scribner and he had lunch while he was still reading it, and Scribner remembered Max expressing his certainty even then "that this was the first book of an author who would make her name as an outstanding novelist." Perkins wrote Nancy Hale that Mrs. Reback's novel was "a regular fine old-time novel, full of characters," covering three generations—"one of those books which is good even when it is bad."

Perkins wanted to meet the writer before accepting her manuscript because he had quite a number of changes to propose. Mrs. Reback eagerly came to New York City from her home near Rochester, but left her interview extremely embarrassed. When she tried to express herself in the presence of strangers, an old speech impediment asserted itself, and all her energies were absorbed in suppressing it. The result, she feared, was "that I appeared subnormal in intelligence, and close to imbecility." The taciturn editor, whose hearing missed much, was favorably impressed anyway.

Perkins's criticisms had largely to do with overstatement. He suggested cuts in scenes where she exposed more plot than was necessary—"because I thought they could be spared and were superfluous"—and where she was more descriptive than she had to be—"It is better they should see for themselves that he had a hard, literal, inflexible nature, than that you should tell them." Wherever she posted comments like traffic signs, directing actions and emotions ("Then May did the most heroic thing in her life"), Max suggested cutting, "for the reader will know what she is doing, and will feel it poignantly without an intervention of the writer." Max's great-grandfather used to say: "One should always leave the dinner table a little hungry." Similarly, Perkins often told writers: "It is always better to give a little less than the reader wants, than more."

Mrs. Reback was also partial to melodrama. Many of her plot developments were too fortunate and neatly arranged. This was a fault common to many of Perkins's authors, who often argued that such coincidences truly reflected reality. Mrs. Reback agreed to make the events in her novel appear somewhat less contrived and to play down the melodrama, though she insisted, "I do love a death with thunder and gestures!"

Janet Reback decided to publish her novel under a pseudonym. "Foreign names seem rather suspect in the United States at the present time," she wrote Perkins, "and Reback is rather foreign." She proposed combining the surnames of her grandparents—Taylor and Caldwell. Perkins thought highly of the idea, not so much for the reason she cited as "for the fact that a book so largely about business affairs stands a better chance under a name that might be a man's."

Taylor Caldwell "worked and stewed" over the changes her editor had suggested. "Whatever else happens," she wrote Perkins, "this book has taught me more than a college course in fiction-writing." Perkins warned her, "Editors are extremely fallible people, all of them. Don't put too much trust in them."

After extensive revision *Dynasty of Death* was published in the fall of 1938. It received a number of superior reviews by critics who had gobbled it up for the pure pleasure of it. Perkins was furious when other critics and even some pedantic editors at Scribners attacked Taylor Caldwell as a pulp writer. He had generated excitement over her book because, whatever one said about her writing, she was a wonderful storyteller. The book became a best seller, giving Charles Scribner fresh reason to believe that Perkins's judgment was exceedingly sound. Taylor Caldwell was worth the extra hours that Perkins had devoted to her book, time that probably would not have been available if Thomas Wolfe still had been on the Scribners list.

Max and Tom Wolfe had reached a parting of the ways, but Wolfe was under his usual compulsion to masticate every experience, in this case his years with Perkins. To Belinda Jelliffe, whose autobiographical novel, *For Dear Life*, Perkins had published in 1936 at Tom's suggestion, Wolfe wrote that the working relationship with his former editor was "so completely and sorrowfully over that it can never be brought to life again; and now, since I have finally won through to a strength and repose that I have never had before, it can surely serve no good purpose on the part of those who count themselves my friends—and I know you are one of these—to attempt to revive it." Wolfe dismissed all the gossip swirling around New York that said Perkins was secretly wishing for Tom's failure, which would underscore his own importance. Wolfe believed Perkins had all but performed wizardry over his manuscripts, but that those days of magic had ended. The author could now think of no more appropriate shrine to his working relationship with Maxwell Evarts Perkins than to immortalize him in fiction. So Wolfe began creating a new character, an editor. He called him Foxhall Morton Edwards, "the Fox," for short.

The Fox would figure in the book Wolfe was writing for Harpers, for Tom was thinking of concluding that book by recapitulating his own career. The recapitulation would end with an open letter entitled "A Farewell to the Fox." That last section, Wolfe wrote Elizabeth Nowell, "would be a kind of impassioned summing up of the whole book, of everything that has gone before, and a final statement of what is now. . . .

If I succeed in doing . . . 'A Farewell to the Fox' as I want to do it, it will stand most tremendously on its own legs."

In May, 1938, Wolfe told his editor, Edward Aswell, that he had reached the "same state of articulation as with *Of Time and the River* in December, 1933"—the time when Max Perkins saw the manuscript in its entirety for the first time. "What he saw, of course, was only a kind of enormous skeleton," Wolfe wrote Aswell, "but at any rate, he was able to get some kind of articulate idea of the whole." Wolfe warned Aswell that this new work would make an even bigger book than *Of Time and the River*. He guessed it would take him a year of uninterrupted work to produce the final draft.

By the end of the month, he declared himself "dog-tired" from all the writing he had done and from legal ordeals, personal upheavals, and public outcries. He needed a change of scenery and knew that the "old beaten path" was no good anymore. Wolfe was going west again, to take in America's tallest trees, largest mountains, and cleanest air. In his absence he wanted Aswell to familiarize himself with his manuscript. Tom promised him, "I will not be gone for long and will see you early in June, at any rate."

The week before he was to leave, Wolfe approached with trepidation the job of assembling his manuscript. As he arranged the material, he became less certain that he should let Aswell read it. "I know where I stand," Wolfe wrote his agent, "but it is like presenting someone with the bones of some great prehistoric animal he has never seen before— he might be bewildered." Tom wavered for days but, before he left, the manuscript went to Harpers.

Perkins occasionally lunched with Elizabeth Nowell, but now the meals were not as cheery as they used to be. Perkins's remarks were tinged by wistfulness. One afternoon in June, for example, while Wolfe was away, Max dolefully asked her about Tom and all that he was doing. Thirteen years later Miss Nowell remembered Perkins that very day as seeming "terribly old and tired and discouraged and tragic." She wrote Wolfe a complete report of the luncheon and all that was discussed. After sealing the envelope she realized that she had described their conversation in a somewhat tattling, though certainly not malicious way. "I just felt very sad that Perkins should seem so old and tragic, about Tom and about the world," she recalled. She sent the letter anyway.

By the third week of June, Tom had passed through the Midwest and was on his way to Seattle. After long battles with his conscience, he decided to extend his trip. He was enthralled with the West, but he was still tired and depressed. Miss Nowell's letter about Perkins grieved him, and Wolfe was soon brooding again, this time over the literary gossip concerning his leaving Scribners. Tom's imagination acted up and he began thinking about Perkins in a different light. He wrote his agent:

> For six years he was my friend—I thought the best one I ever had—and then a little over two years ago he turned against me—everything I have done since was bad, he had no good word for it or for me, it's about as if he were praying for my failure. . . . What is this thing in life anyway that causes people to do things like this?

When he began hearing stories about Scribners salesmen running him down all across the nation as some kind of turncoat, he believed they had "been instructed to pass around" that accusation and assumed they had taken their cue from Perkins who, "under this mask of friendship, is doing the same thing.

> It's almost as if *unconsciously,* by some kind of *wishful* desires, he wants me to come to grief, as a kind of sop to his pride and his unyielding conviction that he is right in everything—the tragic flaw in his character—that keeps him from admitting he has wronged anybody or made a mistake. That is really his great weakness, and I believe it is at the root of his failure—his growing reaction, his sense of defeat, his personal tragedy in his own life and in his family life that has been so marked in recent years.

By the time he reached Portland, Oregon, Wolfe was convinced Max Perkins stood against him and his work. "I want to sever the connection entirely. Someday, perhaps, if he is willing, I'll take it up again," he wrote to Miss Nowell, "—but meanwhile, let's not play with fire." He gave her explicit instructions: "Tell him nothing about me or what I'm doing: that's the only way, believe me, to avoid trouble." It was no longer a matter of personalities. "If I am wrong it will show in my work," he wrote Miss Nowell; "if he's wrong it's going to show in his life."

In the last two weeks of June, Wolfe traveled the entire Pacific Coast from Seattle to the Mexican border, then journeyed inland 1,000 miles, and then northwest to the Canadian border. Meanwhile Edward Aswell had journeyed through the material Wolfe had left with him. YOUR NEW BOOK IS MAGNIFICENT IN SCOPE AND DESIGN, WITH SOME OF THE BEST

WRITING YOU HAVE EVER DONE, he wired Tom in Seattle on July 1, 1938. I AM STILL ABSORBING IT, CONFIDENT THAT WHEN YOU FINISH YOU WILL HAVE WRITTEN YOUR GREATEST NOVEL SO FAR. HOPE YOU COME BACK FULL OF HEALTH AND NEW VISIONS.

The author wanted to stay in Seattle a few more weeks to work on his notes of his trip and get them typed. He described his western journal to Aswell as "a kind of tremendous kaleidoscope that I hope may succeed in recording a whole hemisphere of life and of America." Aswell replied: "Not since Whitman has anybody felt America in his blood and bones, and been able to voice the feelings the way you do."

On July 12, 1938, Dr. E. C. Ruge in Seattle sent Aswell a telegram: THOMAS WOLFE IS QUITE ILL AND CONFINED IN SANATARIUM WIRE INSTRUCTIONS AS TO FINANCE. Aswell promptly replied that Wolfe's bank account was sufficient to cover all reasonable expenses, and that the doctors should give him the best care possible. Ruge soon wired again: THOMAS WOLFE TAKEN SICK IN VANCOUVER PNEUMONIA DEVELOPED EXHAUSTED FROM STRENUOUS SIGHTSEEING HIGH BLOOD PRESSURE AND FEVER RAPID HEART AND BREATHING TERRIFIC COUGH AND TEMPERATURE 105 MONDAY NIGHT WEDNESDAY MORNING TEMPERATURE 100 SEEMS TO HAVE PASSED CRISIS MUCH BETTER KIDNEY COMPLICATION ALSO MUCH BETTER.

Miss Nowell decided she had to tell Perkins something about the illness, but in remaining vague about the condition, she worried him all the more. On July 25 Max wrote to Fred Wolfe asking him for at least a postcard about Tom. "I haven't been able to find out anything that one could depend upon," he explained, "but I know he must have been mighty sick, and maybe still is." Perkins wanted to write Tom himself, but Miss Nowell intimated that even a letter from Perkins might upset Tom's convalescence.

Fred Wolfe joined his brother in Seattle. From there he wrote to Perkins that Tom had a bad case of bronchial pneumonia. By August the doctors were indicating that Wolfe was coming around, though his strength was slow in returning. When he was well enough, Fred told him of Perkins's concern. Tom asked Fred to send Max his love and best wishes. "I guess the plain truth is old Tom just wore himself down so that he had to get sick," Max wrote Fred again, adding, "I shall wait until I hear that Tom is really recuperating and then I am going to write to him, whatever they say."

Perkins heard nothing for days, but wrote anyway. He thought

Wolfe might like to hear "some of the gossip" about New York. "As I am once more a commuter, as I was born and always should have been," he wrote Tom, "I do not get around so much. But whenever I do go to any of the old places like Cherio's or Chatham Walk or Manny Wolf's, everybody asks for you." In New Canaan, Max said, he found himself with a houseful again. Visiting grandchildren—Bertha now had a daughter and Zippy a "fierce looking" son—stayed in the empty bedrooms. Everything in business was looking up, Max said, and he thought it might stay that way for another year. Marjorie Rawlings's *The Yearling* remained Scribners' great success. Everyone at the office was just as Tom remembered except for John Hall Wheelock who, Max said, was threatening to "commit the folly" of getting married. All of Wolfe's friends there were "mighty concerned" about his illness. "But honestly, Tom," Perkins wrote in closing, "it may well be the best thing that ever happened to you, for it will give you a fresh start after a good rest."

Before mailing his letter, Perkins heard from Miss Nowell that Tom had suffered a minor setback, so instead of sending it directly he addressed it to Fred and asked him to decide whether it would do Tom good or harm. "If you think he ought not to see it for any kind of reason," Max wrote, "throw it away."

Perkins's letter stirred Wolfe. He rallied what strength he had and called out for paper and a pencil. In a wobbly hand he wrote:

Dear Max:
    I'm sneaking this against orders—but "I've got a hunch"—and I wanted to write these words to you.
    —I've made a long voyage and been to a strange country, and I've seen the dark man very close; and I don't think I was too much afraid of him, but so much of mortality still clings to me—I wanted most desperately to live and still do, and I thought about you all a 1,000 times, and wanted to see you all again, and there was the impossible anguish and regret of all the work I had not done, of all the work I had to do—and I know now I'm just a grain of dust, and I feel as if a great window had been opened on life. I did not know this before—and if I come through this, I hope to God I am a better man, and in some strange way I can't explain I know I am a deeper and wiser one—If I get on my feet and out of here, it will be months before I walk back, but if I get on my feet, I'll come back
    —Whatever happens—I had this "hunch" and wanted to write you and tell you, no matter what happens or has happened, I shall always think of you and feel about you the way it was that 4th of July day 3 yrs. ago

when you met me at the boat, and we went on top of the tall building and
all the strangeness and the glory and the power of life and of the city were
below

Yours Always
Tom

"I was most happy to get your letter," Max wrote back to Tom in Seattle on August 19, "but don't do it again. That is enough, and will always be valued. And I remember that night as a magical night, and the way the city looked. I always meant to go back there, but maybe it would be better not to, for things are never the same the second time."

The next week Fred told Perkins that perhaps Tom should not have written him. Wolfe's effort ran his fever up and set him back. Tom's condition appeared more serious than bronchial pneumonia, but he seemed to be reviving. "Let us pray together that he will," Fred wrote Max.

Hemingway had come home from Spain on Memorial Day and met Perkins at the Stork Club. Perkins found him "weary and worried but otherwise well." Hemingway flew to Key West that night. Through the summer Max deliberated about how to publish Ernest's play, *The Fifth Column*, and his short-story collection. The decision, arrived at while Max was on tenterhooks over Wolfe's failing health, was to publish it all as one book under the title *The Fifth Column and the First Forty-nine Stories*. Perkins arranged the book's contents and checked to see that Scott Fitzgerald's name had been cut from "The Snows of Kilimanjaro." He found Hemingway now identified him only as "Scott." Knowing how sensitive Fitzgerald was, he urged Ernest to use another name altogether.

Hemingway arrived in New York again on August 30 and breakfasted with Perkins at the Hotel Barclay. He agreed to change "Scott" in his story to "Julian," then asked Max what he thought about his starting a novel and several short stories about the Spanish war. He wanted to take one more look at Spain, then write in Paris, where he could work in peace but keep an eye on the fighting.

Perkins realized that the left-wing American intellectuals supporting the Loyalists kept Hemingway from doing any real work while he was in the United States. They regarded him as one of themselves now, and they kept pestering him to make public appearances. So Perkins thought well of Ernest's idea of getting out of the country.

Max had been kept informed of Scott's summer activities through

Phone East 1340

PROVIDENCE HOSPITAL
17TH AVENUE AND EAST JEFFERSON STREET
SEATTLE, WASH.

Aug 12;
1938

Dear Max:

I'm sending this against orders —
but I've got a hand "— and I wanted to
write these words to you ;

— I've made a long voyage al have to e
strange country , al I've seen the death near
very close. and I don't think I was too much
afraid ; him , but as simply mortality itself
(— leaves to me — I remember most cleography i.

By permission of the Houghton Library, Harvard University

Harold Ober. He heard Fitzgerald's plans for a new novel and praise of his screen adaptation of Erich Maria Remarque's *Three Comrades*. "I knew you would be mighty good out there, and only feared you would be too good," Max wrote him. "I still do fear that too because if you get deeply interested it will keep you from getting back to writing."

Max told Scott that he had just heard from Elizabeth Lemmon. She was moving into a house bordering the grounds of Welbourne which had once been the chapel for the estate's servants. The modest Church House would be her home for the rest of her life. "She seems very happy," Max wrote Scott, adding reflectively: "But it seems all wrong that she should be living alone."

In the late summer, Max asked both Scott and Elizabeth if they could not find the time to write to the old "lone Wolfe." Tom had run a high fever for seven weeks, and the doctors were gravely concerned. By the end of the first week of September they suspected that he had some type of brain disease, a condition more serious than they could treat in Seattle. At the urging of the hospital staff, the Wolfe family arranged to transport Tom across the continent by train to Johns Hopkins University Hospital in Baltimore, where Dr. Walter Dandy, an eminent neurosurgeon, might be able to save Tom's life.

Wolfe's trip eastward began on the night of September 6. He was wheelchaired aboard the Olympian, and a doctor gave the attending nurse, a girl from Asheville, a tube of morphine to keep him "snowed under" should the pain or any convulsions get out of control.

By September 10, Wolfe was resting at Johns Hopkins, his mind sometimes alert enough to understand what was happening to him. Dr. Dandy operated that afternoon. When he trephined Wolfe's skull, cranial fluid spurted across the room from built-up pressure. Tom's severe headache went away and for a while he thought he was cured. Dr. Dandy diagnosed Wolfe's condition as tuberculosis of the brain. The only hope for him was that instead of many tubercles, there might be just one, which could be removed in a second operation.

Fred Wolfe arrived in Baltimore at four o'clock Sunday morning and sent Perkins a telegram: PLAN OPERATING ON TOM TOMORROW MORNING FEEL YOUR PRESENCE WOULD HELP IF YOU CAME TONIGHT. As soon as Perkins got the wire, he left for Baltimore alone. Aline Bernstein wanted to go as well, but Max dissuaded her, knowing how much her presence would upset Tom's mother, who despised her. Aswell, who had been at the hospital since Saturday, went back to New York to prepare the people at Harpers for the worst. Wolfe was so heavily sedated that Perkins could not bear to see him. He never even let Wolfe know he was there but just sat quietly as one of the family, cramped in the small waiting room, anxious about the results of the operation. Tom's sister Mabel and Fred and their mother were all in a highly emotional condition. Max went up to Mabel and said, "Oh, gee, let's go somewhere and get a drink."

"We can't," she told him. "There's not a drink to be had in Baltimore. It's Election Day . . . and they close everything in Baltimore on election days." They sipped cups of coffee, waiting. After several hours, Dr. Dandy and the nurse who had been with Tom since Seattle came in. The doctor explained that he had hoped to find only one tumor, but when he uncovered Wolfe's brain he discovered "myriads."

Perkins's gentle blue eyes looked from person to person. Wolfe's mother took the news stoically. The others went to pieces. Max had never heard such wailing in his life. He tried to calm Mabel, placing his hand on her shoulder. Dr. Dandy said Tom might possibly live a month and that during that time he might return to a state of mental lucidity. All that anyone could do for him was to try to make his last days as free from pain and fear of death as possible.

Perkins saw no point in lingering and he left for home. "It was a harrowing day," Max wrote to his own mother, ". . . exactly like the scene in *Look Homeward, Angel.* They are fine people, but superhuman in their energy and the power of their emotions. But the old mother is wonderful, like a New Englander."

Three days after the operation—on September 15, 1938, eighteen days short of his thirty-eighth birthday—Thomas Wolfe died. Perkins's telegram to Fred was all that he could put into words: DEEPLY SORRY. MY FRIENDSHIP WITH TOM WAS ONE OF THE GREATEST THINGS IN MY LIFE. GIVE MY LOVE TO MABEL AND YOUR MOTHER. I ADMIRED YOU ALL SO MUCH ONE CAN SEE HOW TOM CAME BY HIS GREAT QUALITIES.

A line from *King Lear* kept drumming in Max's ear as a kind of consolation. "He hates him that would upon the rack of this tough world stretch him out longer." Perkins believed Wolfe "was on the rack almost always, and almost always would have been," for his task as a writer was Herculean, beyond even Wolfe's mighty grasp.

He was wrestling as no artist in Europe would have to do, [Perkins wrote afterward for *The Carolina Magazine*] with the material of literature—a great country not yet revealed to its own people. It was not as with English artists who revealed England to Englishmen through generations, each one accepting what was true from his predecessors, in a gradual accretion, through centuries. Tom knew to the uttermost meaning the literature of other lands and that they were not the literature of America. He knew that the light and color of America were different; that the smells and sounds, its people, and all the structure and dimensions of our continent were unlike anything before. It was with this that he was struggling, and it was that struggle alone that, in a large sense, governed all he did. How long his books may last as such, no one can say, but the trail he has blazed is now open forever. American artists will follow and widen it to express the things Americans only unconsciously know, to reveal America and Americans to Americans. That was at the heart of Tom's fierce life.

Given twenty years and perhaps just as many volumes, Perkins thought Wolfe might have achieved a proper form. But just as "he had to fit his body to the doorways, vehicles, and furniture of smaller men, so he had to fit his expression to the conventional requirements of a space and time that were as surely too small for his nature as they were for his subject." Perkins revealed his personal feelings about Tom's death only to Elizabeth Lemmon. And to her he imparted little more than: "It is hard to think that Tom wouldn't have been utterly tortured as things are in the world. It was in him to do more than he ever did, but he would have suffered all the time."

Louise and Max went down to the funeral in Asheville in K19, the same Pullman car on the express night train that Tom had written so much about. After they had arrived at their hotel, they hired a taxi and drove along the ridges of the mountains that walled in the town. Upon seeing them, Max instantly realized how great an effect they had had upon Tom's development. Perkins wrote years later: "A boy of Wolfe's imagination imprisoned there could think that what was beyond was all wonderful—different from what it was where there was not for him enough of anything." All the vast world that he had read and dreamed about lay beyond those surrounding hills. Later Max and Louise walked to the town square and asked directions from a man in front of a gas station. The man said he had known Tom when he was young, and Louise asked what Tom was like then. The man replied, "Just like it says in the book."

It was a thoroughly miserable day for Perkins. "It is probably better to be emotional on occasions like that," Max said long afterward, "but it is wholly contrary to our Yankee and Episcopalian ways." Max felt that he had to go to the Wolfe home and look at Tom's body in the coffin. Wolfe was powdered and wearing a wig to cover the wounds left by the brain surgeon. Max thanked God that the corpse did not look much like Wolfe. Fred implored him to say something to Tom, but Perkins could not bring himself to do it. He stood in rigid silence.

That same morning, Louise went to the Catholic Church to ask that a Mass be said for Tom's soul. The priest was reluctant. "Ah," he said, "they were a rowdy family." Perkins knew they could not help but be, what "with all that tremendous energy in them, and the other ingredients. They must have been somewhat of a scandal." Max told John Terry, "I am sure that Tom was very sensitive to this fact, much more than any of the others were. It affected his entire life."

But most of the town paid homage to its famous son. People jammed into the First Presbyterian Church to sing hymns and hear the eulogy, which included a passage from *Of Time and the River*. Men lining the streets to Riverside Cemetery doffed their hats as the hearse drove by. At the burial Perkins did not see much, though he was an honorary pallbearer. He stood apart from all the rest, alone, in a cluster of trees. He hated the whole business. Exactly as he had during Wolfe's lifetime, Perkins stayed in the background.

The next morning a great hurricane brushing along the Atlantic Coast blew northward, as though following Max Perkins's train back to New York. Then it raged into New England. From the forests atop Mount Ascutney down to the riverbanks of Windsor, all was ravaged. Paradise was destroyed.

PART FOUR

XIX

To Everything a Season

ithin a decade of the crash on Wall Street, warfare thundered around the world. Max Perkins's family and friends observed that he was obsessed with the war. He did not believe Neville Chamberlain's boast that the Munich agreement meant "peace for our time." "I can't help thinking about these things all the time," he wrote Hemingway in December of 1938.

This preoccupation was perhaps an example of the old Yankee manner of dealing with emotion, transforming anxiety over a personal tragedy into concern for something distant or impersonal. Thomas Wolfe's death, no doubt, had also sensitized Max to violence and destruction.

Another sign of his distress was that he again resorted to his instinctive remedy for grief: At fifty-four, aging, tiring, he enclosed himself within his job. "He came back to the office from Wolfe's funeral," Miss Wyckoff remembered, "and started working harder than before." And there was a third indication. Once he had written Miss Lemmon: "I always found *War and Peace* a help in time of trouble." Now, several times that season, John Hall Wheelock discovered Max reading from his office copy of the book.

Wolfe's will, drawn up in the spring of 1937, designated Perkins as his executor. Perkins hated to take on the responsibility; but, as he wrote his mother, "there did not seem to be any decent way of not doing it." Within days of Wolfe's burial, he could already see that the appointment was going to result in endless trouble and abuse. "The Wolfes are strange people with many magnificent qualities," he told his mother, "but full of suspicions and incapable of letting anything in their hands get out of them, even though it can be proven to be to their own advantage to do it." That tangle of duties kept Perkins so busy that he barely had time for melancholy.

Wolfe's death was followed by a profusion of articles and remembrances. *The Carolina Magazine* of the University of North Carolina asked Perkins himself to write about Wolfe, but Perkins sent his regrets. It seemed impossible for him to find the time or the emotional strength to do it. But the magazine was insistent, and so because he knew that the school had meant so much to Tom, he wired back: WILL BREAK MY NECK TO SEND YOU SEVERAL THOUSAND WORDS BEFORE OCTOBER TEN. Perkins wrote 3,000 words. At the core of his remarks was this paragraph:

> The one important thing in the universe to him was his work, and this was so simply because it was so. It was not due to ambition in the cheap sense, and it was not what is generally meant by egotism. He was under the compulsion of genius, and all the accidents of life that got in the way of its expression seemed to Tom to be outrages and insults. He knew in his mind that man was born to trouble—that everyone was beset with anxieties and thwarted by obstacles—but that this work which he was bound to do should be interfered with by trivialities, was maddening. And so was the struggle with the work itself.

For months poems, tributes, letters of sympathy, and requests for information about Thomas Wolfe poured into Perkins's office. Max responded to each one. To those who were aware of his rift with Wolfe he sent a copy of Tom's last letter, to prove the author's loyalty in his final days. No one wrote Perkins with more perception than F. Scott Fitzgerald. He said he knew "how deeply his death must have touched you, how you were so entwined with his literary career and the affection you had for him." It was all but impossible for Fitzgerald to imagine that "great pulsing vital frame" quiet at last: "There is a great hush after him." Fitzgerald was struck by the irony of Perkins's role as literary executor. He supposed that Perkins was, oddly enough, more in control of Wolfe's literary destiny now than when Tom was alive.

Wolfe's estate included the rough draft of his last novel, which was under contract to Harpers and was in their safe. It was Perkins's job, as executor, to see to its orderly publication and to arrange for the publication of other work Wolfe had left behind. He approached the crates of manuscript, which Aswell sent over to him, as though Wolfe were still his author and reviewed the material methodically. He itemized every piece of manuscript as best he could, and clipped together pages which Elizabeth Nowell might sell as magazine articles.

The most immediate consideration was the disposition of the journal which Wolfe had written during his travels in the West. At first reading, Perkins found it difficult to get a coherent impression of the 10,000 words —mostly sentence fragments—which had tumbled onto the pages. Wolfe's jottings were meant to be the raw stuff of a large, dynamic novel, but as soon as Max had the pages typed and read them again, he suggested publishing the journal as it was. He tactfully reminded Aswell and Miss Nowell that in all the editing of Wolfe's previous books, no change had ever been made without the author's approval. Since Wolfe could no longer approve changes, the material must be published as Tom had written it, with only those corrections which one could reasonably infer that Tom would have made himself. The sprawling diary of his trip through the great western national parks appeared the following summer in the *Virginia Quarterly Review*—incomplete sentences, spotty punctuation and all— under the title "A Western Journey."

As for the novel, after Max had gathered and arranged the bulk of it, he turned the 750,000 words back to Aswell. "Studying the mass of his manuscript was something like excavating the site of ancient Troy," the Harpers editor wrote of Wolfe's unpublished treasure trove. "One came upon evidences of entire civilizations buried and forgotten at different levels. Some parts of the manuscript had been written as recently as four months before he died; other parts dated back to *Look Homeward, Angel,* and had, in fact, been cut from that book; still other parts had been written in each of the intervening years." Aswell realized what Perkins had known for years, that Wolfe did not write "books" in the usual sense:

> Tom really wrote only one book, and that runs to some 4,000 printed pages comprising the total of his works. The individual titles that bear his name are only so many numbered volumes of this master book. The parts should be thought of as having been brought out separately merely for convenience.

Perkins often maintained that the whole conception of Wolfe's work was clear in the author's mind. Whether or not the labeled parts could now be assembled by someone else was open to question. Guided by Perkins's rubrics—the notations he had made as he examined the novel—Aswell discovered the "wonderful thing about the manuscript—the really incredible thing—was that once the extraneous matter was removed, once the unfinished fragments and great chunks of stuff that did not belong in the books were taken out, the parts that remained fell into place and fitted together like the pieces of a jigsaw puzzle."

At the end of the year Perkins, as executor, indicated that one mammoth novel called *The Web and the Rock* would be published by Harpers in the early summer of 1939. He also said that there seemed to be enough remnants of material for an anthology of stories, to be published still later.

Perkins found no portion of the material more curious than the long section Tom had written about Foxhall Morton Edwards. For almost 1,000 pages—in a script so sprawling and hurried that there were usually only about twenty-five words to a page—Thomas Wolfe caricatured his editor. Wolfe had always believed that the way to characterize a person was to observe him from the moment he got up in the morning, chronicling his everyday habits, no matter how trivial. In the course of this depiction, eccentricities became slightly magnified. His portrait of Perkins was a perfect example, except that it is most unlikely Wolfe ever saw him in bed or soon after arising. The author undoubtedly felt he knew his subject so well that he could safely extrapolate from what he had seen:

> The Fox asleep was a breathing portrait of guileless innocence. He slept on his right side, legs doubled up a little, hands folded together underneath the ear, his hat beside him on the pillow. Seen so, the sleeping figure of the Fox was touching—for all his five and forty years, it was so plainly boylike. By no long stretch of fancy the old hat beside him on the pillow might have been a childish toy brought to bed with him the night before—and this, in fact, it was!

Wolfe then imagined the Fox sitting up, grabbing his hat and yanking it down onto his head, swinging out of bed and heading for the shower.

> Unpajamaed now, and as God made him, save for hat, starts to get in under shower with hat on—and remembers hat, remembers it in high confusion, is forced against his will to acknowledge the unwisdom of the procedure—so snaps his fingers angrily, and, in a low, disgusted tone of acquiescence

says: "Oh well, then! *All* right!" So removes his hat, which is now jammed on so tightly that he has to take both hands and fairly wrench and tug his way out of it, hangs the battered hulk reluctantly within easy reaching distance on a hook upon the door, surveys it for a moment with an unde- cided air, as if still not willing to relinquish it—and then, still with a puzzled air steps in beneath those hissing jets of water hot enough to boil an egg.

Wolfe then had the Fox put his clothes on:

They fit him beautifully. Everything fits the Fox. He never knows what he has on. . . . His clothes just seem to grow on him: whatever he wears takes on at once the grace, the dignity, and unconscious ease of his own person.

Wolfe trailed the Fox through every step of his workday:

O, guileful Fox, how innocent in guilefulness and in innocence how full of guile, in all directions how strange-devious, in all strange-deviousness how direct! Too straight for crookedness, and for envy too serene, too fair for blind intolerance, too just and seeing and too strong for hate, too honest for base dealing, too high for low suspiciousness, too innocent for all the scheming tricks of swarming villainy—yet never had been taken in a horse trade yet!

Even his deafness was explicated:

Deaf, hell! Deaf as a Fox, *he* is! That deafness is a stall—a trick—a gag! He hears you when he wants to hear you! If it's anything he wants to hear, *he'll* hear you though you're forty yards away and talking in a whisper! He's a Fox, I tell you!

Thus Wolfe, with the instrument of his exuberant imagination, revealed the man who was the fascination of his life. It is not known how Perkins took all this at first, except that he did say to Miss Lemmon with mild annoyance that he wasn't aware that he, as Wolfe said the Fox had done, went around "sniffing scornfully." It is known that he did not ask Aswell to alter or delete any of the Foxhall Edwards material; he had passed the ultimate test of his own policy of noninterference with an author's work.

During the seven and a half months it took Harpers to assemble

Wolfe's book, Perkins tidied Tom's estate. He answered all the questions of inquisitive scholars and suggested articles to others to keep Wolfe's name alive. He haggled over medical fees and tried to take some kind of lead in directing the publishing activities without stepping on anyone's toes. After weeks of not writing to Elizabeth Lemmon because he had been so busy, Max now confessed to her, and only to her, his emotional exhaustion. He often thought of her pastoral life in the Church House in Middleburg, and in a letter in December, 1938, he told her: "I wish I could get a touch of TB and have to go to Saranac for six months and then be all right again," He said. "I'd like it if it were dull and I was bored and an afternoon seemed long. You've found the right way to live."

That same month, Willard Huntington Wright—S. S. Van Dine— came up to the fifth floor and asked Perkins to be the executor of his estate. Merely the thought of it was like salt on Max's wounds, especially as Wright was several years younger than Perkins. But Max agreed. He saw that Wright was in poor health and depressed about the world. Wright and Perkins had recently taken "tea" together, and, staring into a snifter of Courvoisier, Wright had said in a tone of resignation, "I'm so glad I've had all the brandy I've had. I've enjoyed the brandy. I only regret I didn't drink more of it."

Three months later, Wright suffered a mild heart attack. He had started to make a good recovery when another attack killed him. It seemed perfectly characteristic to Perkins that Willard Huntington Wright left, upon his death, the manuscript of a completed novel, *The Winter Murder Case*, flawless to the last comma.

Perkins continued to immerse himself in work, through the winter and into the spring of 1939. During that time the book that consumed more of his hours than any other was *Artillery of Time*, a Civil War saga about slavery and industrialism by Chard Powers Smith. As he had to so many other writers, Max had sent Smith a copy of *War and Peace*, and Smith had been inspired to try to capture the spirit of an entire nation at war. But for months he had been floundering. "It may be very good," Perkins wrote Elizabeth Lemmon, "but only long hard work will make it so. I've made trouble for a lot of writers—and for myself —by getting them to read *War and Peace*." Smith was not an important author, and it was soon clear to Perkins that his book would never be great. Yet he labored for Smith as diligently as for any of his more celebrated writers, and suffered as much for him.

The manuscript had rambled to half a million words. Perkins felt that for all that verbiage there was too little story. For weeks he studied the manuscript; then he gridded it into plots and subplots, and looked for scenes which might be developed. "I am sure he never suggested the change of a word, unless an obvious mistake," Smith recalled. "Instead, he would make shy little right angles in red pencil around the beginnings and the ends of passages, sometimes running to pages, and he would suggest diffidently that if it wouldn't be too much trouble I might consider deleting them." In detailed letters, Perkins gave his reasons. He reminded the author, for example, that his first responsibility was to tell a story and that the reader

> cannot bear to be too much interrupted, and moreover he cannot absorb all the information and description you give from the middle of page 32 on throughout the chapter. You must generalize the description of the town. . . . You must remember too that if you give the right impressions at the start, the knowledge of the reader will grow by gradual accretion as the story goes along. You try to tell far too much.

Perkins explained why Smith's elaborate description of a train ride, however interesting in itself, did not help the narrative:

> It seems to be given almost wholly to show what a railroad journey was like in those days, and does not in many respects further the actual story of the book.

And so on . . . and on. Smith, an author with an unusually serene ego, found Perkins's proposals invaluable and, with trifling exceptions, he accepted them all. Picking up from his editor's counsel, he went on to make a good many improvements of his own. Then, for Max, came eternities of the most extensive editing. At the end Perkins confided to Elizabeth Lemmon that Smith's book "almost brought me to suicide." Upon reading the proofs, however, he said, he realized "the book is magnificent and [I] feel ashamed that I should have despaired about it, or doubted the author. He never knew I did though, and he did his work wonderfully." It was an example of two qualities that distinguish the professional editor: the vision to see beyond the faults of a good book, no matter how dismaying; and the tenacity to keep working, through all discouragements, toward the book's potential.

Late in 1938 Ernest Hemingway had written Perkins from Paris

about Thomas Wolfe. It was almost the last of the condolence letters that
were still dribbling in. Hemingway said he had not written sooner because he found it never did any good to discuss "casualties." He agreed
that Wolfe's deathbed letter was a good one—Max had sent him a
copy—but said that everybody writes fond letters to loyal friends when
he thinks he is going to die. Hemingway imagined Perkins would therefore amass quite a collection, including many which he himself hoped
to send during the next fifty years.

Hemingway's *The Fifth Column and the First Forty-nine Stories*
was published in late 1938. Perkins sent Hemingway all the reviews that
were of any importance. Not many critics were as impressed with the
play as Perkins was. Edmund Wilson particularly thought very little of it.
Hemingway explained to Perkins that all the alleged revolutionaries who
were really cowards and took no part in the defense of the Spanish republic, such as Wilson, felt a natural obligation to discredit those who
had laid their lives on the line. Hemingway said that was all right with
him, though he was full of animosity toward "the poor pricks." Those
guys could still gang up to put a book down, but he told Perkins, he
would still be around and going "pretty good" after they had been super-
seded by a whole new generation of critics. When Ernest riffled through
the 600 pages of his book, he said, he knew he'd be all right as a "sort
of lasting business," even if he should die the next day.

Hemingway had been caught up in the Loyalist cause in the last few
years, but he was already viewing the revolution with his former objectivity. In this war that was ending in defeat for the Republicans, he
told Perkins, there was a "carnival of treachery and rotten-ness" on both
sides. Disillusionment had combined with his depression about the reception of his book and made it difficult to work. "Writing is a hard
business," he wrote Perkins, but, he said, nothing made him feel better. Before anything fatal happened, Hemingway said, he wanted to
assure Perkins that he thought just as much of him as Tom Wolfe ever
did—"even if I can't put it so well." Hemingway told Max he would
take a final trip to Spain before coming home to work on a novel.

By the end of 1938, Perkins's saddest year, friends could see the
toll that sorrow had taken. His hair was completely gray now, except for
the widow's peak, and his depression showed in his eyes and in his
remarks. Of Christmas and New Year's, he wrote to Fitzgerald: "Whoever called these days the Holidays must have been a master of sarcasm."

In January, 1939, Perkins went to Vermont and saw the destruction of Windsor that had been inflicted by the hurricane of the preceding fall. Almost everything he truly cared about there was devastated. Max walked among the cracked limbs and uprooted remains of Paradise. In one part a fringe of pines had stood up to the storm, and Max told his daughter Zippy that those stalwart trees would make a good central image for a poem, but he never wrote it.

Back from Spain, Hemingway again passed through New York, where he saw Perkins before going to Key West. He told Max about three long stories he wanted to write. The clearest in his mind was about an old commercial fisherman alone in his skiff fighting a swordfish for four days and nights and vanquishing it, only to have sharks finally devour it because he had been unable to boat it. If he could write that and two war stories he had in mind, Hemingway said, he would make enough money to support his family for the rest of the year and could resume work on his new novel.

Meantime Hemingway waited to hear from the people who had promised to produce *The Fifth Column*. He figured they were hedging because the play read a little like yesterday's headlines. After months of talk and no action, he regretted that he had not written *The Fifth Column* as a novel, especially now that he had a lot more to say about the war. (The play was eventually put on, and had a ten-week run.) In Key West he had recurring nightmares about the war, in which he got caught in the latest Spanish retreat. Perkins prescribed drinking a bottle of stout before going to bed. "It has made me go to sleep many a time," he wrote, "and sleep well."

Hemingway left Key West for Cuba—alone; his second marriage had broken up—and took a house that proved to be a wonderful place to work. There was no telephone and nobody could bother him. He began writing at 8:30 every morning and worked straight through until two in the afternoon. He had meant to start the three new stories he had outlined for Perkins, but got sidetracked. By spring, when Martha Gellhorn joined him, he had 15,000 words of a novel set in Spain during the civil war. He was reluctant to discuss it with Max—he thought talking about a book was bad luck. He did tell Max that, in order to be free to work on the novel, he had turned down Hollywood propositions and lecture tour engagements, and thus he might have to draw money from Scribners to keep going. If Max wanted collateral, he said, he could have it; but Ernest assured him that Scribners would not need it, because the book was going so well. Each day he would read every word over from the start, and each day he concluded that he was writing as expertly as he knew how.

Perkins told Hemingway that another of his authors, Alvah Bessie, who had fought with the Lincoln Brigade, was writing a collection of personal narratives about his experiences in Spain. Hemingway was not worried about competition. He thought Bessie was one of those "ideology boys," while Hemingway himself, as he later admitted, was not a "Catholic writer, nor a party writer . . . not even an American writer. Just a writer." He held himself to no more than 1,000 words a day. Just as the thing to do with a war was to win it, he said, the thing to do with a novel was to finish it. He felt that he had lost a great deal in the last two years, and he wanted to win with this novel.

In Cuba, Hemingway happened upon a copy of *Tender Is the Night* and read it for the third time. He told Max he was amazed how "*excellent*" much of it was. He thought if Fitzgerald had "integrated" it more carefully it would have been a fine book. As it was, Hemingway said, it read better than anything Fitzgerald had done. "Is it really over," Ernest wondered, "or will he ever write again?" He asked Perkins to include his great affection when he corresponded with Scott next, admitting that he had a very stupid, immature feeling of superiority toward Fitzgerald, like that of one little boy, tough and durable, sneering at another, talented but delicate.

At the end of 1938, Fitzgerald briefly left Hollywood to visit his daughter. Scottie, blonde and petite, was midway through her first year at Vassar College, a year behind Max's fourth daughter, Jane. Scott was going with some idea of disciplining her. He feared Scottie had been taking too much interest in dates and dances, rather as Zelda used to do. En route, Fitzgerald saw Max and asked for advice, and Max offered the simplest but soundest philosophy he knew: "Never on any account . . . allow any hostility to grow up between yourself and a child."

On his way back from Vassar, Scott called on Max again. During the first visit Perkins had been delighted to see Fitzgerald looking younger and healthier than in years and appearing quite sure of himself and of his writing. But now Scott had something on his mind. *This Side of Paradise* had gone officially out of print, and Scott was worried that his literary reputation was lapsing too. Back in California he wrote Max:

> I am still a figure to many people and the number of times I still see my
> name in *Time* and the *New Yorker* ect. make me wonder if it should be

allowed to casually disappear—when there are memorial double deckers to such fellows as Farrel and Stienbeck.

Perkins spoke to Whitney Darrow about keeping *This Side of Paradise* in print, but Darrow demonstrated that it was not economically feasible for Scribners to accommodate Perkins's wishes. And so, as Max had done with Fitzgerald's manuscript of the very same book exactly twenty years earlier, he brought it to another publisher. He urged the American Mercury House, a reprinter, to publish it in one of their very cheap editions, but they argued right off that it belonged to a bygone era. Perkins promptly spoke of the great demand for it in the libraries of Windsor, Vermont, Plainfield, New Jersey, and New Canaan, Connecticut, to name but three towns. They agreed to an edition of 25,000 copies, to be kept in active sale for only a month, but they never published it.

M-G-M also backed out of a deal with Fitzgerald. After eighteen months of farming his screenplays out to other contract writers for revision, they decided not to pick up his option. Despite the loss of a weekly paycheck, Fitzgerald regarded the pink slip as a blessing in disguise. He knew it was self-destructive to continue any longer on that "factory worker's basis." He explained to Max that the studios' attitude was, in effect: "We brought you here for your individuality but while you're here we insist that you do everything to conceal it."

> Do you know [he wrote Perkins] in that "Gone With the Wind" job I was absolutely forbidden to use any words except those of Margaret Mitchell, that is, when new phrases had to be invented one had to thumb through as if it were Scripture and check out phrases of her's which would cover the situation!

A year later he admitted to Perkins, "I just couldn't make the grade as a hack—that, like everything else, requires a certain practised excellence."

Fitzgerald was eager to get to work on several ideas and felt exhilarated to be writing again instead of just "patching." He permanently buried *Philippe* and conceived a modern novel—"One of those novels that can only be written at the moment and when one is full of the idea—as 'Tender' should have been written in its original conception, all laid on the Riviera."

Just when Perkins thought Fitzgerald was finding a new self-discipline in Los Angeles, Scott skipped town for a vacation with Zelda. He took her from Highland Hospital in Asheville, and they went on a drunken spree in Cuba. In the last few years Zelda's condition had steadied enough to allow her to take short trips to be with her mother, daughter, or husband; but it seemed that whenever she and Scott confronted each other, she regressed into madness. This time, however, it was Scott who went to pieces. His binge landed him in Doctors Hospital in New York. While Scott was bedridden, Max spent a few hours with Zelda, who seemed much improved to him. "Anyone who did not know of her trouble would not have suspected it," he wrote Hemingway, "but she looked as if she had been through plenty too."

Perkins really believed that Scott did have a novel in mind and the will to write it. Extremely secretive about the idea, Fitzgerald had only hinted of its substance to Max when he had visited him in New York. Shortly after Fitzgerald returned to Los Angeles, Charles Scribner wrote him a friendly note which suggested that Scott, having worked in Hollywood, would logically find it a vast source of material for his book. Scott wrote Perkins back in terror that "this misinformation may have been disseminated to the literary columns. If I ever gave any such impression," he told Perkins, "it is entirely false; I said that the novel was about some things that had happened to me in the last two years." The book was undeniably rooted in Hollywood, but, he insisted, it was definitely "*not* about Hollywood (and if it were it is the last impression that I want to get about)." This time Fitzgerald blocked the entire novel out, so that he would be able to drop it for a month, if he needed to earn money, and pick it up again "at the exact spot factually and emotionally" where he left off.

Weeks later Fitzgerald was bedridden again, with a touch of his recurring tuberculosis. His worries were compounded when his agent, Harold Ober, who had always been his lender of last resort, decided to bail him out no longer. Fitzgerald flew off the handle. Over the years he had borrowed heavily from Ober, but he had never welshed on him. In the last eighteen months alone, Fitzgerald had paid back to Ober his entire debt of $13,000, and enabled Ober to earn $8,000 in commissions.

Scott borrowed $600 from Scribners to tide him over and asked Perkins for the names of two or three of the best agents in New York, in case he wanted to leave Ober. Perkins recommended Carl Brandt as "an extremely shrewd, and an agreeable chap, if perhaps a little bit slick," but reminded Scott that Harold Ober was one of the most loyal friends Fitzgerald had in the world. "I hope to God you will stand by him," he wrote. Fitzgerald told Max he suspected that a tiff between Scottie and Mrs. Ober—

in which Mrs. Ober had accused Scottie of visiting them merely to use their New York house as a pied-à-terre—lay at the bottom of the matter. (It is more likely that with the slate between Ober and Fitzgerald wiped clean at last, the agent simply did not want to begin lending money to Scott all over again.) Perkins's final note on the subject was, "If there is a wife at the bottom of it, one ought to be charitable. . . . Wives have a strange effect upon their husbands at times, and husbands ought not to be held accountable."

Perkins may have been thinking of his own marriage. His fellow workers noticed that when it came to the subject of religion, his sense of humor disappeared and he could become quite caustic. Louise's conversion and Max's reaction to it had all but destroyed whatever happiness they had shared. It became easier for them to avoid each other than to try to talk, for religion dominated Louise's conversation and life. She went to church every day and spent most of Sunday there. It became increasingly common for Max to come home in the evening and find her entertaining a parlor full of priests and nuns. Max barely tolerated the situation. If forewarned of such an evening, he would usually remain in New York for the night. Not only Max but his daughters and the family's friends wearied of Louise's incessant proselytizing. If asked, Max grimly told people that she was a happier person because of her new religion. But to Marjorie Kinnan Rawlings he remarked, at the end of Louise's first year in the Church, that he looked forward to the day when she would no longer be a novice; more seasoned Catholics, he said, "do not take it nearly so hard."

In early 1939, Max's third daughter, Peggy, decided to marry Robert King, a good-looking doctor from Alliance, Ohio. Max liked him very much but found him so gentle that he was afraid Peg would dominate him. On the last Saturday of March, a few dozen guests went through twelve cases of champagne at the small private wedding in the Perkinses' New Canaan house.

As the thirties drew to a close, Perkins began to urge Charles Scribner to hire more young people. He found those entering publishing better educated in literature than he had been at their age. And he realized his editorial hunches about manuscripts were not as accurate as they once had been. When he was younger, he had been able to predict an author's brilliant future by a dramatic final page or a single catchy phrase. Sometimes he would promise to publish a writer after one witty conversation. He was always partial to reminiscences and autobiographical fiction by people he felt had lived interesting lives filled with colorful characters and dramatic events. But often, he eventually realized, these were the very people who lacked the perseverance or talent to write. Perkins gave a middling advance to one artist who was famous for his exploits and wanted to write his life story. The artist used the money to hire a succession of beautiful secretaries. "No matter what chapter from his life he set out to dictate," Malcolm Cowley related in *The New Yorker* in the early forties, "he found that the only words he could say were, 'Miss Jones, did anyone ever tell you that you were beautiful?' The book hasn't been started, but Perkins thinks the artist still has it in him, and that someday, barring accidents, he will get it out."

As did every publisher, Scribners gambled away thousands of dollars on books that never materialized, and the responsibility for every one of them weighed heavily on Max's conscience. When a manuscript came in and was unpublishable, Max felt even worse. "This is the way of it," he explained to Elizabeth Lemmon. "All my life, always, I've got myself into a jam and had to get out of it or die, all because of carelessness and folly. So I take on these books from something in the writer and my response to it. Then comes the ms. or the first part of it. I can't give it to anyone else. They would say it was rotten, or not worth labor. I have to do the work, and I do it over and over in desperation. Sometimes I'd be ashamed to show it." Now, whenever he found himself with such a problem, he took heart by remembering the fix he was in with Chard Smith's *Artillery of Time*, which turned out to be a best seller and was hailed as the "Northern *Gone With the Wind*."

For Max, who listened to so many authors' laments, his correspondence with Elizabeth was still his greatest emotional release. "I wish I could talk to you, but I never can or will," he wrote one night in June of 1939 when he could not go home because Louise was entertaining her coreligionists. Alone at the Harvard Club he thought of the times he had spent with Elizabeth. "I'm so happy to be with you," he wrote, "that I can't say anything—not that it makes any difference anyhow. I mean truly that it makes no difference. I think you've found a good life in that house, with the garden and all. I think you've been good and unbeatable always, and that it wasn't easy at all. And everything should have been easy for you by rights." Since its beginning in 1922, their exchange of letters had remained pure and private, as was their love for each other. Louise knew they wrote, but not as often as they did nor what they had to say to one another; Elizabeth sent her letters to Max's office. When one of the Perkins daughters learned of the relationship thirty years later, she smiled and said, "I'm so glad Daddy had someone to talk to."

A great source of unrest for Perkins, in the spring of 1939, was the approaching publication of Thomas Wolfe's *The Web and the Rock*. "Here I am with just as much anxiety about Tom as ever,—in fact, more," he wrote Elizabeth Lemmon. Max's primary worry was Aline Bernstein. After Wolfe's funeral, she and Perkins found themselves drawn amicably to each other on several occasions. But the book Mrs. Bernstein had for years fought so hard to suppress was about to reveal the details of her love affair with Tom. "I'm so afraid that woman may kill herself," Max confided to Miss Lemmon. "I like her and I admire her, but I can't say anything to her."

In the first 300 pages of Wolfe's posthumously published manuscript, he retraced his steps to the beginning of his life story, though he wrote not about Eugene Gant of Altamont but about George "Monk" Webber of Libya Hill. Perkins saw evidence of the fresh vitality that had invigorated Tom since they worked on *Of Time and the River*, but he was sorry Wolfe felt compelled to avoid the lyrical and autobiographical. Perkins understood Wolfe's reasons. One was:

> He knew that his family had suffered very deeply, and certain other people too, because he had used them as characters, though transmuted from their real selves by his imagination. His family never complained but they did suffer, as they knew Tom had thought of them as "great people, great characters," and had not realized the personal side of the matter. He brooded over this always, and in the end I think he thought he must find a way of using them and his friends and others under a complete disguise.

Wolfe, however, had only one story to tell. The names were changed, but when Wolfe caught up for the second time to his extraordinary shipboard meeting with Esther Jack, it was through Eugene Gant's eyes once again that the reader saw Aline Bernstein:

> From that night on, Monk was never able again to see that woman as perhaps she really was, as she must have looked to many other people, as she had even looked to him the first moment that he saw her. He was never able to see her as a matronly figure of middle age, a creature with a warm and jolly little face, a wholesome and indomitable energy for every day, a shrewd, able, and immensely talented creature of action, able to hold her own in a man's world. . . .

She became the most beautiful woman that ever lived—and not in any symbolic or idealistic sense—but with all the gazing, literal, and mad concreteness of his imagination.

For the next 600 pages every emotion and event of their love affair was recorded with unflinching intimacy. Perkins went so far as to warn some of his writers not to read *The Web and the Rock* at all, even though he thought the first half contained some of the very best stories Wolfe ever wrote. Max told Marjorie Rawlings:

> It is true that the last half of the book—the love affair—is and always was not what it ought to be. It should have been written fifteen years later maybe—And there was Tom's predicament. He had caught up to himself in time, and when he wrote about things too near, he could not make them what they should have been. It was a real predicament, and I don't know what could have come of it.

By the time *The Web and the Rock* was published, in June of 1939, Perkins finally understood what had taken Aswell so long to compile it. The manuscript Tom left behind had been so enormous that it was necessary to divide it arbitrarily into two books. Also, it was built from blocks of writing intended to be used in half a dozen different books. Wolfe's inchoate attempts at his novel *The Vision of Spangler's Paul*, for example, turned up in the first section of *The Web and the Rock*. What Tom had designated as *People of the Night*, containing the portrait of Foxhall Edwards, would be worked into the sequel of *The Web and the Rock*, which would pick up exactly where that book left off. Its final line would serve as the next volume's title: *You Can't Go Home Again.*

The threat of public exposure as the Fox made Perkins uneasy, and he admitted to friends that he was concerned about it. It was not that Wolfe had maligned Perkins in his portrait. "I just hate to be written about on any account," Max wrote Scott Fitzgerald, "and it seemed odd that with all the designs he had upon Scribners, the only part that he wrote that fits into the book—and it's pretty long—should be about me."

Harpers published *You Can't Go Home Again* in 1940, hailing it as Wolfe's "latest and maturest" work. Perkins, who had seen the manuscript earlier in sections, remained less than enthusiastic about the book, partly because it suffered from the same jerry-built construction as *The Web and the Rock*, more because it would indelibly make him "the Fox," the hero George Webber's editor. Perkins wrote Elizabeth Lemmon, "I was never

a Fox. Do you think I was? I don't mean for you to answer unless just
'Yes' for I don't think you should ever speak to me again. But I never was.
Maybe something worse, but not that. Not Machiavelli ever." Two weeks
later Max saw all those chapters in print and read them through. "I was
wrong about the Fox business," he wrote Elizabeth again. "I had shrunk
from reading it all, and the part I did read, I got the wrong impression
from I guess." Once Perkins realized the portrait was mostly sympathetic,
he wrote Fitzgerald, "In reading some of it I even thought if I really were
like that man I would be quite proud of myself." In time he told Miss
Wyckoff, "I didn't make out so bad after all."

Max's daughter Peggy remembered her father reading *You Can't Go
Home Again* and shaking with laughter at the Fox's behavior. But Max
wrote agent Henry Volkening, "I see where we will lose all our lady writers
if they read it, on account of the way he has me going around muttering
curses against the women."

Especially ironic, for it had been composed just months before Wolfe
fell ill in the Northwest, were the final lines of Thomas Wolfe's great
twin-volumed novel. It concluded a thirty-six-page open letter from
George Webber to Foxhall Edwards.

> *Dear Fox, old friend, thus we have come to the end of the road that we
> were to go together. My tale is finished—and so farewell.*
>
> *But before I go, I have just one more thing to tell you:*
>
> *Something has spoken to me in the night, burning the tapers of the
> waning year: something has spoken in the night, and told me I shall die,
> I know not where. Saying:*
>
> *"To lose the earth you know, for greater knowing: to lose the life
> you have, for greater life: to leave the friends you loved, for greater loving,
> to find a land more kind than home, more large than earth——*
>
> *——Whereon the pillars of this earth are founded, toward which the
> conscience of the world is tending—a wind is rising, and the rivers flow."*

On September 1, 1939, German troops marched into Poland and war
broke out in Europe. At the peaceful L-Bar-T Ranch in Montana, Hemingway was writing his novel about Spain. Once he received the news, Ernest
wrote Perkins that he had various commitments in regard to this war, but
none would be honored until he finished his manuscript. He was in no
hurry to get over there, because he thought there would be "war enough

for all of us from now on." With the fatalism he felt whenever he smelled battle, he wrote Max that he would certainly not expect to survive this one.

Perkins hoped that England would accept Winston Churchill as its leader at least for the duration of the war. "Maybe he might be a Fascist," Max had written Ernest in July, 1939, "but he would be good in a war." Months later Perkins heard a fascinating rumor that Churchill was writing a history of the English-speaking people. This took Perkins aback at first because it was he, almost ten years earlier, who had suggested that Churchill write such a book. During the last decade, Scribners had published what Perkins considered Churchill's "magnificent" histories of the last war and his "truly great biography" of the Duke of Marlborough, which "would have been a little better if he had not been somewhat partisan as a descendant."

When Churchill had visited America in 1931 to lecture about "this new tyranny" Soviet Russia, and the need for greater cooperation between England and the United States, Perkins and Charles Scribner had a long talk with him. Max never saw a man whom he liked better in the instant of meeting him.

> He is much more an American than an Englishman [Perkins wrote Professor Copeland]. He got up and walked around the office with his cigar sticking out from his mouth, and talking. I suggested to him then that he do a history of the British Empire. It was then that he got up and began walking about rapidly, and it seemed as if at that moment he hit upon a project—a history of the English race, which was to include us. He must truly have thought of it previously, but it was as if he took the idea from the Empire and immediately enlarged and changed it.

While Churchill was in New York thinking about Perkins's suggestion, he asked for the services of a secretary for just one day. Max offered his own. Irma Wyckoff was naturally intimidated by so awesome a presence as Churchill, but she realized what most of Perkins's authors did: "When there was work to be done, Mr. Perkins could convince you you were the only person in the world to do it." The day before she was to report for duty at the Waldorf, Perkins reminded her that Churchill dictated most of his letters from bed in the morning, and that he did not wear pajamas. And, he joshed, "He's liable to jump out at any time—without warning." But Irma Wyckoff was game and Churchill was a gentleman.

Perkins found Churchill to be one of those who "thinks very little about money but needs a great deal." And so instead of publishing in the regular fashion, by negotiating a contract, Churchill would propose a book and sell it in advance for a huge sum to an English publisher. He did just that with the scheme for the history of the English race, signing with Cassell's in London for the very considerable advance of £20,000. The English publisher then auctioned it to American houses. Scribners was on a tight budget then, and for the family-operated business to put up $30,000 or $40,000 for a book not even on paper was beyond consideration. Dodd, Mead got it. Perkins remained so ardent an admirer of Churchill that he always kept a photograph of him in his office.

Churchill would have to table his project for many years, but Hemingway did not delay his. Ernest moved from Montana to Sun Valley, a new resort village in Idaho. Soon he had over 90,000 words done on his Spanish novel, which would tell how the war there really had been. If he was ever going to bring off a "hell of a big book with all sorts of people in it," he told Max, he thought it best to get it done before going off and possibly getting killed. If Perkins would visit before the close of the gaming season, he added, Hemingway promised to paddle him down a trout-filled stream and introduce him to "very beautiful glamour girls" who were getting their divorces in Idaho. Martha Gellhorn was covering the war in Finland for *Collier's*. So Ernest, now separated from Pauline, named his bachelor suite at the Sun Valley Lodge "Hemingstein's Mixed Viceing and Diceing Establishment."

Perkins could not budge from New York until Tom Wolfe's estate had satisfied the state tax officials. Then he saw that he had to be on hand to prepare his spring list, which he hoped would include Hemingway's novel. He wrote Ernest, "I would give anything if I knew just a few of the elements in it to make a note from, and the title." In January, 1940, when Hemingway was back in Cuba, he sent Perkins the first eight pages of the book and some thirty more from the middle. In them, the protagonist, an idealistic American college professor named Robert Jordan, has gone to Spain to fight for the Republican army. His duty is to blow up a bridge of strategic importance. Perkins wired the author almost immediately: EXTREMELY IMPRESSED STOP OPENING PAGES BEAUTIFUL AND CHAPTER 8 TREMENDOUS. WILL SEND CONTRACT.

As the novel approached completion, Hemingway's generally solid work habits crumbled. Weekends, he indulged himself with friends and liquor. Every Sunday began with a hangover and a soggy note to Perkins. He hoped Max would make allowances for occasional incoherencies and would agree that it was better for him to write personal letters in that condition than "hung over" pages of the novel. Nothing really made things right for Hemingway until Martha Gellhorn arrived from Helsinki in the middle of January. His weekend binges continued, but her enthusiasm for his novel made the final pages of work on the book seem easier. After several more Sundays—"damned if they don't go fast"—Hemingway arrived at the end of his story. But he was temporarily stumped by the conclusion of this, his longest novel. Perkins said he supposed Ernest knew what the outcome was to be but did not know how to express it. "Well," Max wrote him, "endings are mighty difficult anyhow."

Meantime, Hemingway hunted for a title, as Perkins had persistently requested. The author wanted a big one, and he was not worried about "over-titling" this book. "She'll carry quite a lot," he said. Hemingway often searched for titles in anthologies of English literature. When he had delved as deep into his *Oxford Book of English Prose* as the close of John Donne's "Meditation XVII," which began "No man is an Island," he decided he had found the right one. In meeting Perkins's arbitrary deadline of April 22, Hemingway sent him the first 512 pages of the manuscript under the provisional title *For Whom the Bell Tolls*. Hemingway thought it had the "magic" that a title had to have and that the book itself might make it quotable. If it did not seem that way to Perkins, the author had some thirty others. But this, Ernest said, was the first that made the bell toll for him—unless people thought of tolls as long-distance charges and of Bell as the telephone company. ALL KNOCKED OUT, Perkins wired, THINK ABSOLUTELY MAGNIFICENT AND NEW . . . TITLE BEAUTIFUL CONGRATULATIONS.

Much of Perkins's excitement came from the fact that more than a decade had passed since Hemingway had written a big novel. More came from Hemingway's superb depiction of war. Reading *For Whom the Bell Tolls* became an actual battle experience for Perkins. He wrote the author, "It has got so these things go through my head as if I had seen them. It is truly amazing." Perkins was convinced, he told Elizabeth Lemmon, that "Hem has written his best book. That's sure."

On July 1, 1940, Hemingway wired BRIDGE ALL BLOWN. That meant he had found the way to complete *For Whom the Bell Tolls*. He hand-carried the conclusion of his book to New York and applied the finishing touches there, handing each completed section of manuscript to Perkins, who in turn sent it to the printer. Perkins told Marjorie Kinnan Rawlings that he read it with intense concentration even though most of the time

Ernest was standing behind his chair and reading it over his shoulder. When Hemingway was not in the Scribner Building, he was at the Barclay Hotel, roistering. By August the harried weeks with Hemingway in town were over.

Perkins and Hemingway, who was in Havana again, were soon working over their respective sets of the book's proofsheets. The editor's marginalia were mainly questions on points of style but there were a few substantive matters—several passages, for example, which Max and Charles Scribner thought should be toned down. Scribner found the old woman Pilar's foreboding speech about the "smell of death to come" definitely horrifying; Ernest insisted it was neither gratuitously obscene nor unpublishable. Another scene portrayed Robert Jordan masturbating on the eve of an attack; Hemingway reminded Perkins that it was the small things of that sort that made the man credible, not just a hero. In the end, Hemingway trimmed the onanism scene. Perkins assured him the "death" speech was "right as written" and the other passage as corrected.

Then Hemingway got the idea of concluding his book with an epilogue. He wrote two new chapters that recapitulated the failure of the Segovia offensive, discussing the blowing up of the bridge and Jordan's disappearance, and accounted for all the rest of the characters. He said that they read well but seemed like going back into the dressing room after the fight. "Should I put on the epilogue? Is it needed?" he wrote Perkins. Or, he wondered, would it just be rhetoric and detract from the genuine emotion on which the book originally ended? Perkins felt the first ending was tremendously effective. He decided against the epilogue, and the pages were dropped for good.

Scribners converted their bookstore that season into a Hemingway shrine, filling up all their Fifth Avenue windows with copies of the novel. "It has got all round town that this book is a truly great book," Perkins wrote the author, "and that its publication is a great event. People outside all publishing and writing circles know about it."

As Hemingway's career reached its brightest point since his association with Perkins, another of Max's publishing relationships burned out altogether. That season, twenty years after writing his renowned *Winesburg, Ohio*, Sherwood Anderson informed Perkins that he was dissatisfied with Scribners' handling of his books. "I have felt all the time Max, a curious lack of interest in what I am doing, what I propose to do," he wrote.

Anderson's career at Scribners had begun in 1933, the year Horace

Liveright died and his firm went bankrupt. Perkins had then written Anderson immediately, suggesting that Scribners become his publishers. They met in New York. Max proposed that Anderson should write either a personal novel or some continuous personal narrative, something after the fashion of Anderson's *A Story Teller's Story*. When the author returned to his farm in the hills of Troutdale, Virginia, he wrote of his decision to join Perkins's company of writers—"not because of any advance you might give me on a particular book, any amount of advertising of my books you might do, etc., but because of a genuine respect I have long had for the position of the house of Scribner's in the publishing world, and also, may I say, because I instinctively liked you, Mr. Perkins." Writing under the tentative title *I Build My House*, Anderson started his memoirs. In the same letter, Anderson spoke of his desires and expectations in working with his new editor:

> I think I should feel free to come to you from time to time and talk of plans as to a friend. I have a certain conception of what I conceive to be the right relationship between a writer and publisher, a relationship that might be, at its best, a kind of intellectual marriage. . . .

Anderson's subsequent letters, however, revealed that he was more interested in a silent partner. And in the ensuing years, he used Perkins mostly as a sounding board. In one letter he indicated his superstition against even talking about novels while he was in the middle of them.

Anderson delayed working on his memoirs, as though a book of reminiscences would be the swan song of his career. He had several other ideas for books, which he fitfully attempted. In 1934, for example, he sent his editor batches of unrelated essays to be compiled into a book. Perkins pieced some of them together, and they were published under the title *Puzzled America*. Anderson worked next on a novel, *Kit Brandon*. Scribners published it in 1936, exactly as Anderson wrote it. Then the author wandered into another project which he thought of as "a novel without a purpose, not intended to reform anyone or make any new world, just the story of a rather shy little man and his half-amusing, half-tragic adventures." He told Perkins, "Most of the time as I write I sit giggling." After approaching the novel from several angles, he set off in another direction, coming back toward Perkins's original suggestion. There were several other false starts and returns.

Anderson's years at Scribners were his most restless. Like Scott Fitzgerald, he could not fulfill the promise of his brilliant early reputation.

He peregrinated from one project to another, fiddling for seven years with the autobiographical work. By the summer of 1940, at the age of sixty-four, Anderson was suffering from dissatisfaction with his career. He blamed his publishers, specifically Max Perkins.

> As you know, Max I have come to see you from time to time, being fond of you personally, as you must know, but rarely, when I have been with you have you made any inquiry at all as to what I am up to. You have indeed Max, on such occasions shown a great deal of interest in some of your other writers and I cannot blame you if you have not been interested in my own work. But in the meantime other publishers have certainly shown interest.

When people asked Anderson if he was content with his present publisher, he said, he answered, "I would be but feel they are not much interested in me." He felt "that it would be better for me to go to some house that makes me feel they really want me."

Perkins hoped that would not be Anderson's next step. In one of the most self-abasing letters of his career, Perkins explained his behavior by saying that he did not feel Anderson needed to be watched like some novice writer. "It all came only from my feeling that you knew so very well indeed what you were about and had so much your own way of doing things," wrote the man who denied he was a fox, "that it would be almost an impertinence for me to question you, or urge you, or certainly to try to direct you. I had looked upon you for so long as a master, and as the father of so many of these other people who became notable, that I could not help talking to you about them for my own enlightenment largely."

Perkins's letter touched Anderson deeply. At the same time, he told Perkins, "I can't live by merely being thought of as a sometime master of my craft." It was Anderson's conviction that books were not bought by the American people; they were sold to them. A publisher had to "back" his books. "I had a feeling when I went to Scribners," he wrote Max, "that I might get this kind of interest. I have a suspicion that perhaps I didn't get it because Mr. Scribner thought of me as a man too old to spend money on."

A few months later Anderson, Scribner, and Perkins met in the Scribners offices. The sales ledger showed that the three Anderson books published by the house had totaled no more than 6,500 copies. The author excoriated his publishers for the puny figures. Perkins understood Anderson's disappointment, that "even if the question of money were not neces-

sarily involved, an author writes his books to have them read, and wants
to have them read by as many as possible, and ought to." But he did believe the slickest huckstering in the world could not have put those books
across.

Anderson remained adamant and went to Harcourt, Brace. Only
months later, in June, 1941, he died of peritonitis. (Harcourt, Brace later
published the memoirs he and Perkins had discussed for so many years.)
At about the same time Max was upset by the suicide of Virginia
Woolf, whom he had never met but admired. With her death, Perkins
thought, a great part of a literary era had passed away. "Writers are certainly dying like flies," Hemingway commented stonily.

In October of 1939, Scott Fitzgerald had given Perkins reason to
believe he and his career were very much alive. He wired Max: PLEASE
LUNCH IF YOU CAN WITH KENNETH LITTAUER OF COLLIERS IN RELATION
TO SERIAL OF WHICH HE HAS THE OUTLINE OBER TO BE ABSOLUTELY
EXCLUDED FROM PRESENT STATE OF NEGOTIATIONS I HAD MY LAST
DRINK LAST JUNE IF THAT MATTERS TELL LITTAUER THAT I FOOLISHLY
TURNED DOWN LITERARY GUILD OFFER FOR TENDER NIGHT LETTER ME
IF YOU CAN NOVEL OUTLINE ABSOLUTELY CONFIDENTIAL AS EVEN A
HINT OF IT WOULD BE PLAGIARIZED OUT HERE.

The hero of the novel was a motion-picture studio mogul named
Monroe Stahr. The character was based on the head of M-G-M, Irving
Thalberg, who had fascinated Fitzgerald for years. Scott assured Max
that after outlining "every scene and situation . . . I think I can write
this book as if it was a biography because I know the character of this
man." From just the outline, Perkins tried to persuade Littauer "that
no [other] human being could handle such a scheme as this one." Littauer,
naturally wary of Fitzgerald's reliability, said *Collier's* was interested but
would have to see some piece of manuscript before they could make an
offer for it.

After having been all but emotionally and financially ruined, Fitzgerald had had two strokes of good fortune: He had found happiness
with the Hollywood columnist Sheilah Graham; indeed, he was contemplating marrying her, Miss Graham later wrote, if Zelda "recovered sufficiently to live for the rest of her life with her mother or if she went so
permanently mad that she lost all contact with the real world about her."
At the same time, Fitzgerald had been selling a series of short stories to
Esquire about a Hollywood hack writer named Pat Hobby. Fitzgerald

received only $250 per *Esquire* piece, less than a tenth of what the *Post* had formerly paid him. "When you're poor," he said, "you sell things for a quarter of their value to realize quickly." The money helped keep him going. But, naturally, Fitzgerald was banking as much as ever on Perkins.

By November 20 he was ready to show Perkins the first 10,000 words of his new novel. "A lot depends on this week," he wrote Max. The material was "strong," so it was even money whether *Collier's* would take it. "Of course, if he will back me it will be a life saver," Fitzgerald wrote of Kenneth Littauer, "but I am by no means sure that I will ever be a popular writer again. This much of the book, however, should be as fair a test as any."

The editors at *Collier's* deliberated for a week before they rejected it. In an instant Perkins received a hasty telegram from Fitzgerald to rush the copy to the *Post*. Scott added: I GUESS THERE ARE NO GREAT MAGAZINE EDITORS LEFT. Perkins read the material and wired Scott: A BEAUTIFUL START, STIRRING AND NEW, CAN WIRE YOU 250 AND A THOUSAND BY JANUARY. The next day he wrote:

> I thought the book had the magic that you can put into things. The whole transcontinental business, which is so strong and new to people like me, and to most people, was marvelously suggested, and interest and curiosity about Stahr was aroused. . . . It was all admirable, or else I am no judge any more.

The $1,000 Perkins promised in his telegram was to come from a small bequest he was receiving at the end of the year from the estate of his godmother. It was "what they used to call 'velvet,' " Max wrote Scott, "and you are welcome to it if it will help with this book. I can believe that you may really get at the heart of Hollywood, and of what there is wonderful in it as well as all the rest." He instructed Fitzgerald to "push on with courage for you have a right to."

"Your offering to loan me another thousand dollars was the kindest thing I have ever heard of," Scott wrote his editor. "When Harold [Ober] withdrew from the questionable honor of being my banker I felt numb financially and I suddenly wondered what money was and where it came from. There had always seemed a little more somewhere and now there wasn't," he explained.

The *Post* then rejected Scott's novel. Perkins immediately told Scott that if he was in a desperate pinch, he could call for the loan anytime after Christmas. Fitzgerald wrote Perkins for the money on December 26.

Perkins decorated his next letter, written at the turn of the decade, making it into a New Year's card. Ever proud of his ability to draw (especially his profiles of Napoleon, which still retained a recognizable touch of self-portrait), Max sketched a man standing with a drink in his hand, smiling and saying, "Here's how!" As an afterthought, Perkins labeled the drink Coca-Cola. Fitzgerald's paranoia got the better of him and he sent Perkins a starchy response. "Beneath the surface of your letter and in the cartoon of the man with coca cola I detect a certain perturbation," he said, then hastily went on to defend himself. "What happened the first part of December or thereabouts was that I quarreled with Sheilah Graham, and then encountered a New Orleans prick . . . from *Collier's* who told me my novel was no good. . . . That was all . . . after about five heavy days in which I stayed close to home, Sheilah Graham and I were reconciled." He had not had a drop for four weeks and insisted even a jiggerful made him deathly sick.

Perkins expected no such response to his letter. "I am not a subtle fellow. I am a simple fellow," Max wrote back. "There was nothing implied by that drawing. I thought you would admire the art.—And the man was not meant to be you. It was meant to be me, and to indicate my own good resolutions. Don't read any hidden meanings into what I write or draw. I only wanted to reveal to you *another* talent." Max could not resist repeating the story to a few friends. "See what a guilty conscience will do to a man!" he wrote Struthers Burt. Fitzgerald apologized for reacting as he had done and admitted that he insisted on reading into things. He reminded Perkins of the time he accused Max of sending him Grant's memoirs to show him the life of another failure.

Fitzgerald's career dwindled to grinding out quick stories and taking on pickup screen-writing assignments. Buying his way through the weeks one day at a time, he could see no farther ahead than to the completion of this one book and getting Scottie through Vassar. "The greatest privilege," he wrote Max, "would be to be able to do work so absorbing that one could forget the trouble abroad and at hime."

During Fitzgerald's years in Hollywood he made a lot of money and mixed with the rich and famous, but he felt himself to be an outcast, a has-been that the literary world had given up on and forgotten. He told Max he imagined how odd it would be in a year or so when Scottie "assures her friends I was an author and finds that no book is procurable." Whatever the reasons for that, he knew it was no fault of Perkins's. "You (and one other man, Gerald Murphy) have been a friend through every dark time in these 5 years," Scott wrote Max, adding, "Once I believed in friendship, believed I could (if I didn't always) make people happy and it was more fun than anything. Now even that seems like a vaudevillian's cheap dream of heaven, a vast minstrel show in which one is the perpetual Bones." Scott asked his friend:

> Would the 25¢ press keep *Gatsby* in the public eye,—or *is the book unpopular*. Has it *had* its chance? Would a popular reissue in that series with a preface *not* by me but by one of its admirers—I can maybe pick one— make it a favorite with class rooms, profs, lovers of English prose—anybody. But to die—so completely and unjustly after having given so much. Even now there is little published in American fiction that doesn't slightly bare my stamp—in a *small* way I was an original.

After three years in California, Fitzgerald's illusions were shattered; it was a land of dreams imprinted on celluloid strips. Throughout his letters to Max Perkins, the Murphys, and Edmund Wilson (with whom he had renewed his friendship) ran expressions of hope and belief that he could still create despite the many fallow years behind him and the paucity of time ahead. He wrote his daughter, Scottie, that fall:

> Anyhow I am alive again—getting by that October did something—with all its strains and necessities and humiliations and struggle. I don't drink. I am not a great man but sometimes I think the impersonal and objective quality of my talent and the sacrifices of it, in pieces, to preserve its essential value has some sort of epic grandeur. Anyhow after hours I nurse myself with delusions of that sort.

Faithfully, Scott wrote Zelda, who was hospitalized again in North Carolina. In one letter that summer he broke down in a few sentences and noted ruefully:

> Twenty years ago *This Side of Paradise* was a best seller and we were settled in Westport. Ten years ago Paris was having its last great American season but we had quit the gay parade and you were gone to Switzerland. Five years ago I had my first bad stroke of illness and went to Asheville. Cards began falling for us much too early.

Never had Fitzgerald felt so removed from the life in the East that had always enthralled him. He relied on Perkins for his news about all their friends, including Hemingway and Elizabeth Lemmon: "the lovely and unembittered and sacrificed virgin, the victim of what I gradually found was the vanity of her family." Scott himself had given up all contact with her, but he could not forget what he considered some of the graceless characters around Welbourne parading as aristocrats. "And in the midst, the driven snow of Elizabeth. It was too sad to bear," he said. After years of closing his letters to Max with an "Ever yours" or "Always yours," Scott signed this once with "Love to all of you, of all generations."

Miss Lemmon had been on Perkins's mind too. He and Louise had just seen her, during one of her short visits to New York; she was showing some of the pedigreed boxers she raised. The Perkinses seemed to her more remote from each other than ever. "Louise always played the misunderstood wife," Elizabeth recalled. Once when the two women were alone, Louise had impulsively asked, "Elizabeth, if I divorce Max will you marry him?" There was never a serious question of their separating. It was just her way of venting frustrations. As for Miss Lemmon, her friends in Middleburg insist she never met a man who she felt measured up to Perkins. She never married.

Before she returned south, Elizabeth reminded Max that the astrologer Evangeline Adams said everything would go to ruin for America in late 1941 or early 1942. "I wish you hadn't told me," he wrote Elizabeth. "I can't forget it." By then Perkins felt fatalistic even about his friendship with Miss Lemmon. "Elizabeth, I don't think I'll ever see you again," he wrote her in May, 1940. "But I remember everything about every time I ever did see you and there was mighty little in my life to compare any of it to. I've always thought of you and all the time."

They did see each other again. In 1943 Elizabeth came to New York and met Max at the Ritz Bar. They sat at a small table and for the first time he started to speak about their relationship. "Oh, Elizabeth," he said, reaching toward her hand but not quite touching it. "It's hopeless."

She looked him in the eyes. "I know," she replied. That closed the last and only discussion they ever had on the subject. They continued to correspond.

In October, 1940, Perkins went to Windsor to visit his mother. Days later, Elizabeth Perkins, the last of Senator Evarts's children, died at eighty-two.

Perkins had noticed that people around New York were finally "very much alive to the war and anxious we should get prepared and should help England in all ways 'short of war' in the meantime." Hemingway, on the other hand, usually bellicose, happily isolated himself in what he called his "joint on top of a hill." His large, breezy Finca Vigía overlooked Havana Harbor. It was supposed to be a secret, but Max told Scott Fitzgerald that Martha Gellhorn was living with Ernest. "You know, I guess that Pauline and he are to be divorced, and presumably he will marry Martha Gellhorn," Max wrote Scott. "This is so well known about that you must have heard of it, but otherwise it ought to be regarded as strictly confidential." Fitzgerald thought it "odd to think of Ernest married to a really attractive woman. I think the pattern will be somewhat different than with his Pygmalion-like creations." Hemingway and Martha passed through New York in late November on their honeymoon. No sooner were they made "legal" than she headed for the Burma Road, to cover for *Collier's* the war that was marching into China. Ernest had some plan to join her in the Far East a month later.

By then, *For Whom the Bell Tolls* was published. Perkins sent complimentary copies to almost everyone he knew; everyone else in the country seemed to be buying his own. Perkins gloated at the dozens of critics who had so much crow to eat. "They should have seen that [Hemingway] was going through a confused time," Max wrote Elizabeth Lemmon, "and while he might not come out of it and go forward, he could only go forward by going through such a time." The book's sales were skyrocketing, and the Book-of-the-Month Club anticipated selling no less than a quarter of a million copies as well.

Ernest inscribed a copy of *For Whom the Bell Tolls* to Scott Fitzgerald "with affection and esteem." Fitzgerald did not think the book was all that Perkins and everyone seemed to be claiming. He confidentially told Sheilah Graham that it was "not up to [Hemingway's] standard. He wrote it for the movies." But Fitzgerald responded to Hemingway without a hint of resentment. "It's a fine novel," he said, "better than anybody else writing could do. Thanks for thinking of me and for your dedication." After picking out his favorite scenes and equating some of the paragraphs with Dostoevski's "in their undeflected intensity," Fitzgerald included his congratulations on the book's great success. "I envy you like hell and there is no irony in this," he wrote. (Years before, in his notebooks under "L" for Literary, Scott had scribbled, "I talk with the authority of failure—Ernest with the authority of success. We could never sit across the same table again.")

Fitzgerald could not afford it, but he decided to give himself entirely to his book about Hollywood. On December 13, 1940, he wrote Max that the novel was progressing rapidly. "I'm not going to stop now till I finish a draft which will be sometime after the 15th of January," he said. "However, let's pretend that it doesn't exist until it's closer to completion. We don't want it to become—'a legend before it is written' which is what I believe Wheelock said about 'Tender Is the Night.'" In a postscript Fitzgerald asked, "How much will you sell the plates of 'This Side of Paradise' for? I think it has a chance for a new life."

The printing plates of *Paradise* were theoretically the author's to take to another firm, if he would pay for their cost, approximately $1,000. Max replied: "I would hate to see the book leave us." It was where their history together had begun. Maxwell Perkins and Scott Fitzgerald had come full circle: His oldest book had expired and a new book was about to be born. The hopes of the two men rested on the novel that Fitzgerald said would be completed in draft by the middle of the next month. With Christmas but eight days away, Perkins wrote, "Well, I hope that 'some time after January 15th' will come soon."

XX

Diminutions

Toward the end of the year Scott Fitzgerald had moved into Sheilah Graham's apartment. On December 20, working there, he began Chapter Six of his novel, a crucial point in the development of his hero, Monroe Stahr. It contained a scene in which Stahr drank heavily, an early sign that the original portrait of Irving Thalberg was taking on qualities of Fitzgerald's own life. By the end of the day he was able to tell Miss Graham: "I've been able to fix it. Baby, this book will be good. It might even make enough money for us both to leave Hollywood." The next day, in her apartment, Scott Fitzgerald died of a heart attack.

It was a Saturday, and Perkins was at home. He heard the news from Harold Ober, who had been notified by Miss Graham. There is no record of his wiring Zelda, but that is what he would have done. Her letter to him, which he received a few days later, reads like a reply. In the course of it she says:

> I want to convey the height of my affections for you, and the devotion and pleasure with which [Scott] always looked forward to "getting in touch with Max." . . . Scott was courageous and faithful to myself and Scottie and he was so devoted a friend that I am sure that he will be rewarded; and will be well remembered.

Zelda wondered if the 50,000 words of his unfinished novel could somehow be published. "Scott cared so deeply about his work," she said, "and

would so have liked to reach his public again—and it would be so nice
for Scottie."

The day after Christmas, Perkins replied. It was too soon to know
exactly what Scott's financial situation was at Scribners, or what the
prospects were for publishing the novel; these matters would be looked
into right away. "Everything will be done that possibly can for Scott's
sake," Max assured her, "—and yours and Scottie's."

Zelda did not come north for the funeral. Her doctors thought it
would be too great a strain on her.

Perkins did his best to inform all Scott's friends of the services but
only a few could reach Baltimore in time. Louise and Max rode the train
from Wilmington to Baltimore with Gerald and Sara Murphy and John
Biggs, a Princeton friend of Scott's and a former Perkins novelist who
had become a federal judge on the Third Circuit bench in Philadelphia.
It was a distressing day for Perkins, especially awful because, as he told
John Peale Bishop, Fitzgerald's was one of those terrible "funeral-home"
funerals. There was no alternative because the Catholic Church would not
permit Scott—who died a nonbeliever—to be interred in the Catholic
cemetery in Rockville, alongside his father's family. At the burial in the
Rockville Union Cemetery, Mrs. Bayard Turnbull, a friend of the Fitzgeralds from their days at La Paix, near Baltimore, observed Max. "He
didn't say a word to anyone . . . ," she said later, "and then, several
times, without even paying attention to what was going on, he shook his
head, lifted it slowly, and looked at the sky."

Upon his return to New York, Max sat down to a duty he had put
off: writing to Hemingway about Fitzgerald's death. "I thought of telegraphing you about Scott but it didn't seem as if there were any use in it,"
he wrote Ernest, who was in Cuba and could be assumed not to have heard
the news. "Anyhow, he didn't suffer at all, that's one thing. It was a heart-
attack and his death was instantaneous—though he had some slight attack, as they realize now, a short time before."

Fitzgerald had borrowed heavily against his life insurance in recent
years, but, Max told Ernest, it was still worth $40,000—enough, Perkins
supposed, to get Scottie through college and pay off her father's debts.
The will, however, was confused. In his original testament Fitzgerald
had nominated Harold Ober as his executor. After their recent rift Scott
crossed out his name and penciled in Perkins's. The legality of the change
was in question, and for the moment Max was enmeshed. "I am afraid
this ends my last chance of getting to Cuba for a while," he wrote

Hemingway, "for it will take some weeks to clear up confusion in the will." In due course Perkins and Harold Ober both simply renounced their claim as executors in favor of Judge Biggs. As it turned out, for the next several years Perkins was called upon to make every decision regarding Fitzgerald's literary legacy.

Perkins then addressed himself to a handful of letters of condolence. The dearth of mourners underscored the pathos of Scott's death. Frances Kroll, Fitzgerald's secretary in Hollywood, wrote Perkins to say: "I was with him through the conception and writing of the novel and perhaps questions may come up when you read the finished manuscript." Mrs. Turnbull's son Andrew, then a junior at Princeton, also wrote Perkins. "I often heard Mr. Fitzgerald speak of you during the 18 months he spent here in 1932–1933, when I was eleven years old," he said. He told Perkins that upon Fitzgerald's death he had set down his memories of the writer for fear of forgetting them. He hoped Perkins might help him get them published, because Fitzgerald's name had become "so largely identified with a dissipated and decadent generation; and I know from personal experience that no kid could hope to find a kinder companion or truer friend this side of paradise." Perkins replied that he had read the pages with appreciation and regretted that he knew no way to help them into print. (Turnbull later became one of Fitzgerald's principal biographers.)

In early January Max wrote again to Zelda. "In a way he got caught in the public mind in the age that he gave a name to," he said, "and there are many things that he wrote that should not belong to any particular time, but to all time." It was important, however, to proceed cautiously, to produce a work that would honor Scott and demonstrate that he ought not be identified solely with the Jazz Age. The painful part, he wrote Miss Lemmon, was "that this book which might have vindicated him—for the first part of it was extremely promising—was far from finished."

While the estate was being probated, Fitzgerald's daughter, Scottie, had no income, so Perkins arranged with Judge Biggs, Gerald Murphy, and Harold Ober to loan her enough to pay her way through Vassar and provide her with a monthly allowance besides.

"I can't thank you enough for the flowers," she wrote Max, "for coming down to Baltimore, and most of all for your kindness in lending me the money to go to college. . . . If the world hasn't completely collapsed by 1944, I'll be able to repay the loan. I hope by then to have produced a novel for your inspection too." Max sent Scottie some literary advice, the same dictum he gave every college student who called on him. He stressed the importance of a liberal arts education but urged her to avoid all courses in writing. "Everyone has to find her own way of writing," he wrote Scottie, "and the source of finding it is largely out of literature."

Scottie had become conscientious in her studies, but she was talking now of dropping out of Vassar and going to work. Max knew how important it had been to Scott that she become the first in her family to earn a college diploma. In the same subtle tone he used to prod Scott on to the end of a novel, Perkins wrote Scottie at the end of her junior year, "You have practically one more year in college now, and that will go quickly, and then you will still be very young and equipped with a degree."

Zelda's financial situation was also poor, and she wrote to ask Perkins if there was any way he could send her some money so she could pay her board;—she was now living with her mother in Montgomery, Alabama. She wondered if this might be "the most auspicious time to get the book under way: if you are still in mind to publish it." She wrote:

> The book was a story of Irving Thalberg, as Scott may have told you. Those minds which so nearly control the direction of public sentiment engaged Scott deeply. He wanted to render tangible the indomitable constancy of purpose and the driving necessity to achievement and the capacity for judicious and dextrous juggling of mysterious forces that distinguished such men from others.

It was still too soon for Perkins to respond with a definite plan.

Sheilah Graham—who for appearances' sake had not attended Fitzgerald's funeral—visited Perkins in New York that January. For Max it was a great pleasure to see her, even under such circumstances. "I think she was mighty good for him, and a mighty good girl herself," Perkins wrote Hemingway after their meeting. She spoke at length about Scott's novel. Max had already begun to think that there might be parts of the incomplete manuscript that could be published separately in some fashion.

Three weeks after Fitzgerald's death Sheilah Graham sent Perkins a typed copy of the original of the unfinished work, tentatively titled *The Love of the Last Tycoon*, and many of Scott's notes. She directed Max to one memo in particular, which revealed Fitzgerald's intention to recapture his readership. This book, Scott remarked, was aimed at two different generations, two readers specifically—"for seventeen as symbolized by Scottie, and for Edmund Wilson at 45." Also enclosed was an unsent letter that Fitzgerald had written to the actress Norma Shearer, the wife of Irving Thalberg, Metro-Goldwyn-Mayer's chief officer until his death at the age of thirty-seven in 1936.

> *Dear Norma:*
> *You told me you read little because of your eyes but I think this book will interest you—and though the story is purely imaginary perhaps you could see it as an attempt to preserve something of Irving.*
> *My own impression of him shortly recorded but very dazzling in its effect on me, inspires the best part of the character of Stahr—though I have put in some things drawn from other men and inevitably, much of myself. I invented a tragic story and Irving's life was, of course, not tragic except his struggle against ill health, because no one has written a tragedy about Hollywood—(a Star is Born was a pathetic story and often beautiful story but not a tragedy) and doomed and heroic things do happen here.*

Miss Graham also found a fragment Fitzgerald had addressed to himself which was so moving in its irony that she sent it to Perkins.

> *I want to write scenes that are frightening and inimitable. I don't want to be as intelligible to my contemporaries as Ernest, who as Gertrude Stein said, is bound for the museums.*
> *I am far enough ahead to have some small immortality if I can keep well.*

At the end of January Max sent Miss Graham a progress report. He regretted that he still had not come to any definite conclusion about printing the novel. "All I know," he wrote, "is that it promised to be the most completely mature, and rich, and in a deep sense the most brilliant book he ever did. I think Stahr, though incomplete, is his best character. . . . It would break a man's heart to see what this book would have been, and that it wasn't finished."

Perkins's words brought Sheilah Graham to tears. "Please do something with it," she begged the editor. "It drives me simply crazy to remember his enthusiasm and plodding work on it and then for him to die." She agreed with Max that nobody except Scott could conceivably finish the book, but it seemed that if it were published as it was, eliminating only the most unrealized parts, which Fitzgerald himself would most likely have altered or cut anyway, there would be an important piece left to publish as "a sort of unfinished symphony."

As he had done when Ring Lardner died, Perkins consulted Gilbert Seldes, who, Max thought, had "very good practical, as well as critical judgment." Seldes read the manuscript and the next week Perkins reported to Scott's executor, John Biggs, that he and Seldes were of the same mind.

> The unfinished book is most interesting. It is a tragedy it is unfinished. It was a clear step forward. I don't say that it was better in actual writing itself, or even that it would have been, than *The Great Gatsby*. But it has the same old magic that Scott got into a sentence, or a paragraph, or a phrase. It has a kind of wisdom in it, and nobody ever penetrated beneath the surface of the movie world to any such degree. It was to have been a very remarkable book. There are 56,000 words. If they were published alone it would only be read as a curiosity and for its literary interest, because people won't read an unfinished book. But it ought somehow to be published for the sake of Scott's name. My idea was to publish *The Great Gatsby,* five or six of the best stories and then this unfinished novel.

Perkins and Seldes also agreed that Edmund Wilson, whose opinion, Max believed, Scott respected more than anyone's, was the best person to write an explanatory introduction. After disagreements and discussions—mostly about "The Crack-Up" pieces, which Wilson wanted to include—Perkins finally got Wilson to consent to all his terms. Max even persuaded him to edit the manuscript and to write a summary of the plot Fitzgerald had in mind for the remainder of the novel. The book would include *The Great Gatsby* and Scott's most enduring stories—"May Day," "The Diamond as Big as the Ritz," "The Rich Boy," "Absolution," and "Crazy Sunday"—together with the unfinished work.

Wilson first called upon Sheilah Graham, to extract every memory she had of what Scott had said about the book. He then spent months examining Fitzgerald's notes. Within a half-year of Fitzgerald's death Wilson had finished the anthology. He had done more than prove his loyalty to Fitzgerald in this, his first collaborative effort with Scott since the Princeton Triangle Club production of *The Evil Eye* in 1915. In his introduction Wilson wrote,

> *The Last Tycoon* is . . . Fitzgerald's most mature piece of work. It is marked off from his other novels by the fact that it is the first to deal seriously with any profession or business. The earlier books of Fitzgerald

had been preoccupied with debutantes and college boys, with the fast lives of the wild spenders of the twenties. . . . In going through the immense pile of drafts and notes that the author had made for this novel, one is confirmed and reinforced in one's impression that Fitzgerald will be found to stand out as one of the first-rate figures in the American writing of this period. The last pages of *The Great Gatsby* are certainly, both from the dramatic point of view and from the point of view of prose, among the very best things in the fiction of our generation. T. S. Eliot said of the book that Fitzgerald had taken the first important step that had been made in the American novel since Henry James. And certainly *The Last Tycoon,* even in its unfulfilled intention, takes its place among the books that set a standard.

While Wilson wrote, Max labored to try to revive interest in Fitzgerald. He had heard a rumor that influential people at Princeton had come to look upon Fitzgerald with disfavor; hoping to squelch that rumor, he wrote Princeton to suggest that it bring out a book to honor Scott. He had no success. Not for fifteen years would the Friends of the Library of Princeton University produce a volume of Fitzgerald's work.

Max also attempted to launch a biography of Fitzgerald; he realized that it might be considered a bit early for that, but the eclipse of Fitzgerald's reputation was alarming enough to embolden him. He urged Matthew Josephson, a former staff member of the *New Republic,* to undertake the story of a "brilliant figure of a period . . . the whole background of that strange period, with Scott very distinctly in the foreground." Josephson took up his pen but soon had to throw it down. He later explained, "I knew the story of Zelda, and planned to tell it all as the central tragedy of Scott's life. . . . I learned that she had just been released from another institution where she had been confined for a couple of years and declared entirely 'cured.' So I halted; for the time being I could not tell her story in public, though I was sure she would be back in again; and decided to wait." While he waited, Arthur Mizener, a Princetonian who was then a professor at Carleton College in Minnesota, studied Fitzgerald's career and came to know his family. His biography, *The Far Side of Paradise,* the first of several of Fitzgerald, appeared in 1951.

So much of Perkins's spring had been devoted to Fitzgerald that Ernest Hemingway felt Max was giving him short shrift. He had gone to Hong Kong to cover the Sino-Japanese War, and since he had been in the Orient, he complained, four China clippers had flown in carrying not a word from Scribners. "What the hell is the matter?" he asked Perkins. Max wrote five times in the next month, mainly about the progress of *For Whom the Bell Tolls.* Sales were fast approaching the half-million mark. Concerned about the war in Europe, Perkins wrote Hemingway that he wished he "had the temperament of Van Wyck Brooks, who surveys the world like Buddha, with complete detachment apparently— and yet he really is deeply interested. He is able to do his work and not be bothered."

Despite his friendship with Brooks, Perkins privately maintained that America's most astute critic of contemporary literature was Edmund Wilson. The assertion may have been a bit painful for Perkins to make, for after *The Last Tycoon* he was no longer Wilson's publisher. The Perkins-Wilson relationship was irreparably ruptured over Wilson's most recent collection of essays, called *The Wound and the Bow.* In one of these essays Wilson had attacked Hemingway. Wilson charged that as the quality of Hemingway's writing diminished, his craving for personal publicity increased, and that his work was now dominated by fantasies. Wilson examined Hemingway's attitude toward women, especially toward the "amoeba-like little Spanish girl Maria" in *For Whom the Bell Tolls.* "This love affair with a woman in a sleeping bag," he wrote, "lacking completely the kind of give and take that goes on between real men and women, has the all-too-perfect felicity of a youthful erotic dream."

Perkins defended Hemingway. He thought Wilson's essay on Ernest was "fascinating" but dead wrong. Word around New York was that Perkins felt Wilson was hitting below the belt and that he refused to publish anything so derogatory to Hemingway. Caroline Gordon Tate remembered hearing that Wilson and Perkins had long conferences about that particular chapter of the book.

Meanwhile, Perkins met another literary critic, Maxwell Geismar, a thirty-two-year-old professor at Sarah Lawrence College, who was conducting a study of the modern American novel. He was proposing to examine the works of a half-dozen authors between the wars, in a book called *Writers in Crisis.* At the suggestion of a mutual friend, Geismer had sent Perkins chapters he had written on Ring Lardner, Thomas Wolfe, and John Steinbeck. Perkins was delighted that a scholar was at last recognizing Lardner's talents, and he thought Geismar's piece on Wolfe was "about the best that has been written." Perkins knew that the young critic had previously written favorably about Hemingway's *The Torrents of Spring,* but, cautious now, he would not accept Geismar's book for publication until he had seen his essay on Hemingway. Perkins suggested that Geismar include William Faulkner in his book, and Geismar agreed.

Perkins's dispute with Wilson grew more intense. During one debate, he mentioned Geismar's work to Wilson. Wilson looked up Geismar and they became friendly. The two of them noted that Perkins had them both in the same spot—he was stalling about accepting their books. Wilson complained to Geismar about publishers in general and remarked that editors were not terribly busy people yet took outrageous amounts of time in making up their minds.

Then came the climax. Caroline Gordon Tate remembered hearing that, in one meeting with Perkins, Wilson shouted that "all publishers were sons of bitches." Shortly thereafter he took his book to Houghton Mifflin, and since Scribners was still delaying about Geismar's book, he was able to punish Perkins further by getting Houghton Mifflin to take that book too.

When Geismar showed Wilson his Hemingway essay, he was delighted to find that it met with approval. Geismar noted years afterward: "I hardly slept a wink all night. Wilson descended portentously and said in his slight high stammer: 'I think your essay on Hemingway . . . is better than mine.' " Geismar believed it was, for Wilson "did not get at the depth wound in Hemingway, or the complete social-historical ignorance that did him in as much." After the book was published, Ernest and Martha Gellhorn Hemingway visited the Geismars at Sarah Lawrence in Bronxville, New York. "They came in from a walk along the Bronx River," Geismar recalled, "talking as if it was a safari in deepest Africa and full of dears and darlings." Over dinner at an Italian restaurant, Hemingway, who had few kind words for any critics of his work, remarked, "You know what I liked best in that essay of yours . . . was the quotations you used. I never realized how good they were."

Perkins was unhappy about losing both books to Houghton Mifflin and brooded for years over Wilson's remark about publishers. Caroline Gordon Tate said she never saw Max again without his mentioning it, "sorrowfully rather than resentfully." Perkins continued to tout Geismar as the best of the up-and-coming literary essayists. Wilson's criticism was always somewhat personal, he said, while Geismar's "is detached and yet alive with the enthusiasm that comes from perception of talent."

"The development of American talent and literature, that was where his main interest lay," John Hall Wheelock, Perkins's closest colleague, wrote of the editor. "To the oncoming talents in countries other than his own, he was less alert." By the 1940s Wheelock had also noticed other aspects of his taste: "Quite a few crotchety prejudices and quirks of unreason, a will 'immutable and still as stone'—that was Max. . . . Science and abstract thinking interested him less than did books on controversial subjects or those based upon the application of a theory or ideas. His passion was for the rare real thing, the flash of poetic insight that lights up a character or a situation and reveals talent at work." Perkins's partiality toward novels, Wheelock said, became an almost exclusive interest; when he was attracted to a work of nonfiction, it tended to be "crack-pot." And of late, Wheelock noted, in acquiring authors and helping shape their material "Max often became contrary and contradictory. Just plain Yankee stubborn."

Frequently, now, Perkins signed up authors, then tried to pawn off on them ideas he had treasured for years. It seldom worked. While Dixon Wecter, for example, was writing a book for Scribners entitled *The Hero in America*, Max suggested he write a book Max wanted to call *The Trouble Makers*.

> It would be a historical narrative to show how intelligence, in times of crisis, is almost always overcome, and, tragically, by emotion—that the men of good-will, detachment, far-sightedness, and intellect, are overborne by the men of powerful emotions, violence and strong will.

Perkins himself saw the flaw in this premise; he acknowledged that "No progress would be made, perhaps, without the impetuous ones. They do give the impulse which makes things move, even if through destruction."

In 1942 Perkins was reading proofs of a book that did get published only because of his obstinacy. It was Alden Brooks's *Will Shakespeare and the Dyer's Hand*. For some time the book had been a mania with him. At every editorial conference Perkins brought it up and the board unanimously voted it down. "So, being a man of infinite patience," one Scribners employee recalled, "he would reintroduce his suggestion at the next conference, with the same result." What charmed Perkins about the work was that it credited Sir Edward Dyer, an editor, with Shakespeare's success. Indeed, the book had convinced Perkins that "the man Shakespeare was not the author of what we consider Shakespeare's works." Eventually the board gave in, to please Perkins. Max sent copies to many critics, hoping to rouse support. Nearly every one dismissed the work as mere speculation.

Still Perkins retained his faith in the book and his respect for it. It made him aware, he told Hemingway, "how frightfully ignorant I am in literature, where a publishing man ought not to be."

Perkins encountered less opposition and more success editing the nonfiction of James Truslow Adams, the best-selling, Pulitzer Prize-winning author of *The Founding of New England, The Epic of America,* and *The March of Democracy.* In August, 1941, Adams sent Perkins the introduction and chapter outlines for his newest work, *The American.* Along with the material came a request. Adams knew few men who personified as many of the nation's essential characteristics as did Maxwell Evarts Perkins, and so he urged Perkins to set down his observations to help make up this mural of the American character. Max did, and in writing *The American,* Adams incorporated all of his comments, often quoting him directly.

One of the more striking was on the position and influence of the American woman, which Max said had never been fully treated in any book that he knew of. "When I was a boy in Vermont," he wrote Adams, "I used to see the middle-aged and old men going to church, not with their wives, not in front of their wives, but about fifteen or twenty feet behind them." He remembered commenting on it to his mother and her saying with a laugh "that it was supposed to be the New England way." But Perkins felt it was more than that. New England women, he felt, exerted a moral leadership that was symbolized by their leadership in the march to church. Adams picked up on this point and remarked that whereas American men had regularly tried to place women on pedestals, the women had had the good sense promptly to descend, in order to get on with their work. Perkins, in fact, always respected women who were doers; he wanted them not just to stand on their own two feet but to venture out into the world. No woman writer better embodied this idea of Perkins's than Martha Gellhorn, whose books Scribners began to publish. Not only was she the consummate venturer; she was also in full control of her career and her prose. She was in that select company of Perkins's most skilled authors—those who required little help from him.

Some of the others needed a great deal. Following her success with *Dynasty of Death,* Taylor Caldwell had pulled several large manuscripts from the drawer and sent them to Perkins. He rejected them all. Not deterred, Miss Caldwell sat down and wrote a sequel to *Dynasty of Death,* called *The Eagles Gather.* She brought it down from Rochester to New

York City in person and asked Perkins for an honest appraisal of the manuscript and of her writing talent in general.

Perkins thought the sequel was weaker than *Dynasty of Death.* But Scribners published *The Eagles Gather,* and Taylor Caldwell dedicated it to Perkins. The work did not discourage him about her future in the least. "What you have chiefly," he wrote her, "is the superb talent for telling a story on a grand scale. It is a mighty rare talent." Perkins said it was just a question of finding a theme large enough for her. He urged her to try a historical novel. In a letter on October 17, 1939, he said, "I do wish now that you would begin to consider the possibility of that kind of book." She was impressed with the idea. First she came up with a title, *The Earth Is the Lord's.* A few days later, while she was thinking of distant times to explore, Genghis Khan flashed into her head. "Why Genghis Khan," she wrote to Perkins, "I simply don't know. All I know about him is that he had an engaging little trick of slaughtering whole populations, and that he overran Asia and part of Europe, and lived somewhere towards the end of the twelfth century, and was a Mongol, son of a Mongol chieftain and a white woman, and was a fine figure of a man, and was definitely NOT Kublai Khan. But fragments keep drifting into my mind, from God knows where."

Perkins generally believed in letting characters direct the plot of novels, but he instructed Miss Caldwell to think this book entirely through before setting pen to paper. He sent her all the historical information on Genghis Khan within his reach and books that described central Asia. He suggested that instead of making Genghis himself the central figure she should write a strong personal story about someone who accompanied him and suspend the novel from that.

> Sometimes a book about periods far back like that and about great epic movements, becomes too generalized, too little about a particular individual or particular individuals. That is a danger you must guard against, particularly with your imagination which tends to see things in the large.

Perkins recommended she read Sir Walter Scott and Dumas to get the hang of writing historicals.

The Earth Is the Lord's was published in 1941. Critics did not take her history seriously and the book was not a great success. But it served as the model for best-selling fictionalizations of real lives which she would write during the next four decades—Saint Paul, Cicero, and Pericles among them. With his simple intuition that Taylor Caldwell should write historical novels, Perkins had founded one of the most enduring and profitable careers in the history of book publishing, one that continued three decades after his own death.

Another successful author whom Perkins had launched during the thirties was Marjorie Kinnan Rawlings. While *The Yearling* was enjoying its two-year tenancy on the best-seller lists—with sales of 500,000 copies, and winning a Pulitzer Prize—Max was thinking about her next book. It was even clearer to him that her gift lay in describing life in the territory she knew. Her writing lost its charm and authority when she departed from it. Perkins advised her to consider a book of true stories about her Florida scrub country.

"Your suggestion about the non-fiction book is actually uncanny," she wrote back. In fact, she said, she had been thinking of doing just such a work about her home, Cross Creek, before tackling another novel. But she wasn't yet sure. At the end of the summer of 1940 Mrs. Rawlings sent Perkins several sketches she had written, for his inspection. She asked him to tell her how she saw the book. He replied on September 20 that he envisioned it as being organized around events, with the locale itself as the protagonist.

> I think that the book should be a narrative, varied somewhat by description and by reflection—to use a figure it should be a single piece of string, with knots in it, the knots being the episodes, but each connected with the other by the incidents, etc.

Max knew that generalizations would not be enough for Mrs. Rawlings. As she had done while beginning *The Yearling,* she insisted on receiving detailed directions. And so he let his letter run to 1,800 words, full of specific suggestions. He said, for example, that the opening chapter should run no more than a few pages and proposed that her little piece called "The Road" be worked into it. "Walking along that road," he pointed out, "could enable you in the most natural way to give, at the start, a conception of the neighborhood." And that was the way *Cross Creek* began.

> Cross Creek is a bend in a country road, by land, and the flowing of Lochloosa Lake into Orange Lake, by water. We are four miles west of the small village of Island River, nine miles east of a turpentine still, and on the other sides we do not count distance at all, for the two lakes and the broad marshes create an infinite space between us and the horizon. We are

five white families; "Old Boss" Brice, the Glissons, the Mackays, and the Bernie Basses; and two colored families, Henry Woodward, and the Mickenses. People in Island Grove consider us just a little biggety and more than a little queer.

Perkins offered other devices for making the episodes mesh—a cycle of the four seasons, to name one. He also told her which characters he thought should reappear and which adventures should be extended. Mrs. Rawlings followed Max's advice to the letter, and, after four drafts, written in almost two years, *Cross Creek* became another of her highly acclaimed best sellers.

Nancy Hale's was another career which had to be guided painstakingly. In her case the problem was not the prose but the author's morale. Her third novel, *The Prodigal Women,* had been interrupted by the dissolution of her second marriage and a nervous breakdown.

Perkins's compassion for troubled writers had not lessened. At about this time he wrote to one author in almost the same words he had used earlier with Thomas Wolfe and Scott Fitzgerald, advising a creative pause:

> You won't have lost time for the rest will have made you younger, so to speak. And turning things over in your mind, and reflecting upon them and all, is something that a writer ought to have to do in quiet circumstances once in a while. That is one of the troubles with writers today, that they cannot get a chance, or cannot endure to do this. Galsworthy, who never over-rated himself as a writer but was one of great note in fact, always said that the most fruitful thing for a writer to do was quiet brooding.

For Nancy Hale, Max prescribed this effective remedy. She spent months in the Southwest and at the end of 1941 returned to resume her writing. Again she reached an impasse. Perkins reacted with the calmness of one who had seen this sort of situation often enough not to be daunted by it:

> You cannot worry me about your novel. I remember so well the quality of all that I saw of it, and I know that you have a rich and sensitive mind and memory. In fact I would be much more concerned if you did not have to go through periods of despair and anxiety and dissatisfaction. It is true that a good many novelists do not, but I think the best ones truly do, and I do not see how it would be otherwise. It is awfully hard work, writing of the kind you do.

I, myself, feel certain that it will end very well indeed, if you can endure the struggle. The struggle is part of the process. There is no sign that Jane Austen had any trouble at all, but I am sure Charlotte Bronte must have had, and almost all of the really good ones, except Jane, who is good as gold, of course.

Nancy Hale overcame her block and worked straight through to the conclusion of *The Prodigal Women.*

Marcia Davenport's writing was also interrupted—in 1940, when Wendell Willkie ran for president and she and her husband joined his barnstorming team of speech-writers and policy-makers. Knowing Perkins's feelings about Roosevelt made her less ashamed about putting aside her novel. Within weeks of Willkie's trouncing, though, she was back at her story of an industrialist's family in Pittsburgh. Perkins stayed in close touch with her for the next several months while she drafted the book, sending her short notes periodically, inviting her to tea. His advice throughout remained the same: "Just get it all down on paper and then we'll see what to do with it." When she at last delivered it in 1941, the novel was amost 800,000 words long and totally disjointed. It was not until she was deep into the book, she said, that she had realized she could not find her way out. Now she was prepared to scrap it altogether.

Perkins thought *The Valley of Decision* was the most chaotic manuscript he had ever seen in his life. He brought it home night after night to puzzle over it. Once Louise, not knowing whose manuscript it was but recognizing it by the yellow paper as the same thing that Max had been working on for so many evenings and weekends, said, "Why do you put so much time on that?" Perkins replied: "Because I am a damned fool." He later told Marjorie Rawlings that he had believed it was "only worth the time because it would not do to allow Marcia to fail on this big undertaking. It might ruin her career to get beaten that way. She was so completely entangled in the underbrush of the book that she could not manage it." After weeks of slowly going through the manuscript himself, he wrote her:

I really think that the great difficulty in bringing "The Valley of Decision" into final shape is the old one of not being able to see the forest for the trees. There are such a great number of trees. We must somehow bring the underlying scheme or pattern of the book into emphasis, so that the reader will be able to see the forest in spite of the many trees. And that will mean reducing the number of trees if we can possibly manage it—though, so far, I haven't found that easy.

Several readings later, Max organized his suggestions into a series of letters, one of them thirty pages long. His approach to the material was as orderly as that of a genealogist drawing a family tree. He started at the beginning and picked out the most important story lines, those he felt should run through the entire novel; anything that weakened those strands had no business in the book. Ignoring Mrs. Davenport's divisions, he separated the novel into three major parts and told her the principal purpose of each. Then he provided an extensive chapter-by-chapter breakdown, with detailed commentary. Finally, he clarified the characters for the author, sharpening their definition in short summaries of their traits—all this for a novel he was never quite sure would prove publishable.

Later Marcia Davenport told Malcolm Cowley, "Everything Max does is directed toward the whole effect of the book. . . . He believes in your characters; they become completely real to him. . . . He can take a mess of chaos, give you the scaffold, and then you build a house on it. . . . His dish is a big, long thing full of agony and confusion." Like so many of his authors, she discovered as she returned to work that Max's comments were effective almost subliminally; he had a way of gently tossing them out as one would pebbles into a pond, making rings of meaning which enlarged until they touched the author's consciousness.

Mrs. Davenport put Perkins's letter on one side of her typewriter and the manuscript on the other, and revised her novel according to his plan. The job took five months. Perkins assumed the outcome would be perfunctory, but she surprised him. She rewrote nearly the entire book, reorganizing and tightening it with great speed and skill, and she cut the length almost in half. "She is a woman of character and determination," Perkins told Marjorie Rawlings. As for Marcia Davenport, everywhere she went she sang Max's praises, giving him full credit for his help, calling it a "case of Trilby and Svengali." Max readied the novel for publication in 1942, hardly suspecting the immense success it would attain.

The bombing of Pearl Harbor intensified Max's obsession with the war, and he read everything about it he could find. As usual, Elizabeth Lemmon was his relief. "No use to talk about the war," he wrote her on December 23, after almost a year of silence. "You have always managed to more or less stay home," he observed, "and I think that was probably the wisest and happiest thing that could be done." Max himself was becoming home-bound, office-bound, reducing his own social contacts. Even Windsor saddened him now. "I don't like to go there," he admitted, "and it is hard to see how, as memories accumulate through the generations, people can stay in one place through hundreds of years. The past would be too much with them, I should think. You want to get back there, but it can't be done. You can't go home again."

In the last few months of 1941 Perkins's correspondence with Hemingway had slackened again noticeably as well. Max had been thinking about some kind of anthology of Hemingway's shorter works, but the idea was so nebulous to him that he could not define it, he told Ernest in September, much less urge it upon him. Perkins said he had heard from the poet and novelist Robert Penn Warren, who was assembling an anthology of fiction for college use. Warren wanted to include Hemingway's "The Killers" and follow it with a study of the story. Perkins imagined the essay would be "altogether too elaborate and theoretical," but, he said to Ernest, "there is nothing better to make a writer permanent than to have him read in the schools." Hemingway agreed about the importance of having it in the classroom, "no matter how hard it is on the poor students."

As for Scott Fitzgerald's claim on posterity, Max prayed it would be strengthened by *The Last Tycoon*. It was published in November, 1941, and Max's hopes were somewhat fulfilled. A number of reviewers said the novel made it plain that Fitzgerald was something more than just a Jazz Age chronicler. The *New York Times* reviewed the book well, and Stephen Vincent Benét, writing in the *Saturday Review*, declared: "You can take off your hats now, gentlemen, and I think perhaps you had better. This is not a legend, this is a reputation—and, seen in perspective, it may well be one of the most secure reputations of our time."

To a few old friends Zelda expressed her dislike of Scott's heroine, an Englishwoman named Kathleen Moore, but said she liked the novel as a whole. "I hope the book will sell," she wrote Max, "—at least enough to repay your interest." Despite all the praise and prayers, *The Last Tycoon* sold only 3,268 copies in its first year.

For a while Hemingway was not sure if he should tell Perkins what he thought of *The Last Tycoon*. When he did, he was brutal. He said he found some very fine parts in it but felt that most of the book had a "deadness" which he thought was unbelievable coming from Fitzgerald. He likened the novel to a slab of bacon on which mold had formed. One could scrape off what was on top, but the meat still tasted like moldy bacon. Still smarting from Edmund Wilson's criticisms of his own work in *The Wound and the Bow*, Hemingway, while conceding that Wilson had done a "very credible job" in explaining, sorting, padding, and arranging, said that Scott would never have finished the work according to that "gigantic, preposterous outline" that Wilson had fabricated.

Hemingway knew that Perkins would be impressed by the novel's thrilling "stuff about riding in aeroplanes." But, he said, that was because Max had traveled so little. Fitzgerald had flown so recently that it had impressed him too, and he had managed to instill something of the "old magic" into his writing about air travel. When he wrote about the relationships between men and women, however, Scott's skill had faltered badly. Fitzgerald, he said, had thoroughly failed to understand his people and the characters had come out as very strange. Perkins, he knew, had recently written Martha Gellhorn that Hollywood had not hurt Scott. Ernest guessed perhaps it had not, but that was because he was long past being hurt before he went out there. Scott's pulse had faded out in postwar France, he said, and the rest of him "just went on dying progressively after that." For Hemingway, reading *The Last Tycoon* was like watching an old baseball pitcher with nothing left in his arm coming out and working with his intelligence for a few innings before getting batted out of the box.

Years later, in *A Moveable Feast*, Hemingway summed up Fitzgerald's career with an image that had first struck him when reading *The Last Tycoon*:

> His talent was natural as the pattern that was made by the dust on a butterfly's wings. At one time he understood it no more than the butterfly did and he did not know when it was brushed or marred. Later he became conscious of his damaged wings and of their construction and he learned to think and could not fly any more because the love of flight was gone and he could only remember when it had been effortless.

Exercising restraint, Perkins told Hemingway that he found his criticism "very interesting," then called Hemingway's attention to the intelligent and often favorable reviews Fitzgerald was getting. "I am glad we did the book," he said simply. "People did not give Scott proper credit for *Tender Is the Night*."

Ernest and Martha had been in Sun Valley, Idaho. Early in 1942 they returned to the finca in Cuba, and Max wrote that he hoped they would both be able to "work in some degree of calm." Hemingway got detoured from his short stories, however, by a man from Crown Publishing Company who asked him to write a foreword to an anthology of great writing on war, accounts from Thermopylae to Caporetto. The book was to be called *Men at War,* and to Hemingway the assignment sounded worthwhile. But he told Max he thought that the selections to be included were terrible, and so he had insisted on including other pieces.

In time, his introduction lengthened, and he became the book's anthologist. He was sorry to disappoint Perkins by not having the manuscripts for his stories in early July as he had planned, but the "damned war anthology," he kept insisting, was holding him up.

The *Men at War* book fascinated Perkins. When he saw that Crown was going about it in a slapdash way, the editor in him was dismayed. He could not refrain from offering his own advice and did so at every opportunity. He recalled for Hemingway some of his favorite war passages—from Stephen Crane, Ambrose Bierce, Winston Churchill, and Thomas Nelson Page. He urged him to include at least one excerpt from Thomas Boyd's *Through the Wheat,* and he directed him to Tolstoi's most dramatic passages. Eventually Max became annoyed that Hemingway was so involved with the anthology that he was neglecting his own short-story writing. But the result, especially Hemingway's patriotic essay at the start of the book, made him feel better. "When I read the introduction," he wrote Ernest in September, "I was mighty glad of it. I can't forget it. It raised my morale a good many points."

Perkins's morale needed raising. That April his nephew Robert Hill Cox, his sister Fanny's son, had been killed in the battle for Tunisia. Afterward Max had come across a story the young man had written and seen that he was talented; he felt sorry he had never had the chance to talk to him about it. The boy's death saddened Max enormously and continued to affect his spirits. And then, in August of 1942, Will James died. Not just a prolific Scribners author but a close friend of Max's, the cowboy who had sent him a ten-gallon hat, James was fifty—eight years younger than his editor. Another beloved author gone.

XXI

Portrait in Gray and Black

"Daddy, don't you drink too much?" Max's youngest daughter, Nancy, asked him one day in 1942.

"Churchill drinks too much," Max replied. "All great men drink too much."

There was no question that this particular great man was drinking too much. More and more often he ducked out of the office in the late morning "to buy a newspaper"—and a drink—returning calmer, face flushed. At his round table at Cherio's, Max's preprandial martinis had become doubles, and the more of them there were, the less he ate. He often dined alone, reading a newspaper from beginning to end, examining every page for war news. "Always the same from one day to another," Cherio, the proprietor, remembered. "He like quiet. He never say one word unless you speak to him. He talk very delicate, very soft, and you won't want to miss a word."

Max, in his behavior, never showed the slightest indication of heavy drinking, according to friends and colleagues, and none of his powers appeared impaired. But his appearance showed his years and the strain. Below the brim of his hat, now battered and worn and pulled even lower on his head, his face had paled. Often the blue washed from his eyes, leaving them gray. Under his eyes the circles had deepened and darkened. He frequently wore the benign grin of the deaf person who has not heard a word that has been said but wants to seem friendly and attentive. The hacking cough from a lifetime of cigarettes was growing more severe. His hands sometimes trembled visibly.

In July, 1942, Max wrote Elizabeth Lemmon: "We are having a lonely summer, Louise and I." The differences between Max and his wife had become even more pronounced. Their conversations were now shorter and their arguments keener. Louise would say anything to break Max's Yankee composure, and Max would say anything to silence Louise. His behavior was now typical of the unhappily married man. He would delay going home. First he would stop off at his regular spot, the Ritz Bar, for a few drinks. Then he often would drop in on a married daughter—Zippy, who was living in the city, or Bertha in New Canaan—and visit with her and her family. Some evenings he never got all the way home, having spent the night in an armchair; next morning he would arrive at work wearing the same rumpled shirt and suit he had worn the day before.

And he went even deeper into his work. He complained that the Scribner Building was locked on Saturdays. "A two-day weekend . . . ," he wrote a friend, "is too much." At home, reading became his only passion. If Louise suggested going out somewhere, he would reply, "I have work to do," and spend most of the night reading manuscripts. If she invited friends to the house, Max would try to excuse himself, complaining that he was "stuck" in a manuscript. Some evenings he would not descend the stairs to greet the guests.

At the office he grew irascible. He took to commenting tartly on small matters such as a colleague's departing from work a few minutes early. His humor turned mordant, sarcastic. When his devoted secretary, Miss Wyckoff, asked for her annual vacation, his retort was a cruel insult: "What would *you* need a vacation for?" Once one of his authors wrote to say that Miss Wyckoff deserved a medal for diligence and efficiency. Max called in the selfsame Miss Wyckoff and dictated his reply: "No secretary was ever treated with more indulgence and affection. And after all, though she does work hard . . . she only works five days in the week."

Sometimes Perkins sat stock-still at his desk, mooning into space. Periodically he dozed off, and Miss Wyckoff would gently close the door to ward off intruders. One afternoon while Perkins was thus disposed, one of his more obtrusive authors came by. Miss Wyckoff said Mr. Perkins was busy. Hearing no sound from within the office, the writer determined to see for himself, dragged a chair over to the door, stood on it, and looked through the transom. Miss Wyckoff scolded him indignantly: "Don't you know he doesn't get much sleep?"

Even when the door was open, Perkins was not very approachable. His customary silences were now accentuated by forbidding stares that intimidated many of his authors. "That silence could on occasion be terrifying," said John Hall Wheelock, "and when driven to desperation by some long-winded speaker, Max would sometimes puncture it with an irritable, 'Well, what about it?' which usually served to bring things to a head. He was not by any means always amiable." And yet Perkins's testiness became part of his charm.

Late in the summer of 1942 Hemingway wrote Perkins that he had an opening for a "good old Dry Tortugas man." It had been almost ten years since Ernest had been able to cajole Max into vacationing with him, and he did not succeed this time. Scribners was somewhat short-staffed— some men were in the service, some had been let go because business was not good, and some of those who remained were themselves on vacation. Max felt he had to stay in New York. "Honestly, Ernest," he wrote, "I couldn't."

With rare exceptions Perkins was seeing no one outside the office. In the last few months, however, he had renewed his friendship with Alexander Woollcott. They had been young reporters together on the *New York Times*, and when Max had gone off into publishing, Woollcott had gone on to become a famous drama critic and a flamboyant figure of his time. The two men had a mutual attachment to Vermont. Since the twenties, Woollcott had held court at his summer place on a small island in Lake Bomoseen. More recently, he had chosen to live there year-round. In January, 1943, Woollcott told Max that he was abandoning his country home. "I am sorry you have had to leave Vermont, the best place there is to be," Perkins wrote him on January 18. "I have already given it up myself because too many people have died. There are too many ghosts where I come from." Perkins told Woollcott that he wished they could turn the clock back, that their whole pack of young reporters could be together again on the seventeenth floor of the Times Building. One week after Perkins's letter arrived, Alexander Woollcott died.

Perkins for years had talked of retiring to Vermont and editing his own country gazette. He wanted to print all the news *he* saw fit to print, perhaps reaching millions of people through his writing as the paper won fame beyond its precinct, and perhaps—a daydream about which only his closest friends knew—making him a national power . . . even president. "Of course, Max never *really* wanted to be president," John Hall Wheelock said; he merely held himself in secret readiness, articulating his positions on the issues to whoever would listen, maintaining perpetual concern for his country. The notion of retiring to Vermont had evaporated. ("I had always meant to end up there," he had written Woollcott, "but I can't do it.") The concern, however, had not lessened.

As the New Deal moved farther and farther from his Jeffersonian principles, Max became greatly irritated. The purest tenets of American democracy, as he understood them, were being undermined by "that man in the White House." In February, 1943, Perkins wrote to a Mr. Raymond Thompson:

> I think these extreme New Dealers are for the most part men of the best intentions, but that if they have their way it will inevitably lead to the concentration of all capital, and all power, in the hands of a government, and that that government must then necessarily become a dictatorship, whether it will or not. And then it will rule the nation through a bureaucracy which will become, as has happened in Russia, a kind of aristocracy, a privileged class.

Perkins believed that the only hope of man lies "in the diffusion of power. If it ever gets into the hands of any single group we are done for in every way excepting conceivably a material one. Everyone might get enough to eat, etc. but he would have no freedom. But then, on the other hand, it may be that Capitalism cannot function any longer, and that we shall have to acquiesce to communism."

Perkins's politics were reflected in Scribners' forthcoming publication of *The Fifth Seal*, Mark Aldanov's staunchly anti-Soviet novel. In a concluding passage the Russian émigré author had one of his characters say:

> "Yes, of course I hate Hitler more than I hate the Bolsheviks. But if freedom and human dignity are to be defended, they must be defended honestly: against all tyrants and all corrupters."

That was just how Perkins felt. The American Communists did everything they could to scare Scribners out of publishing *The Fifth Seal*, and the book became a *cause célèbre* early in 1943. It was a strong best seller.

Publishing companies, unlike toothpaste companies, do not produce identical products year after year. Each book is a brand-new product, with individual qualities and requiring individual attention. A toothpaste company creates a market for its product and then needs only to maintain that market. A publisher must make a new market for each book—several hundred, perhaps, each year. (This hard fact of publishing life partially explains why so few books are sold—in a nation of over 200 million people, a mere 5,000 copies is an excellent sale for a first novel—and also why publishing is not an especially lucrative endeavor.) Furthermore, while the toothpaste manufacturer can forecast his sales with some accuracy, the publisher seldom can, because each book—except for those by well-established authors—is a different sales problem. Sales may be unpredictably low—or the publisher may be surprised by sudden bounty. Books contracted for years earlier and labored upon in obscurity may suddenly skyrocket. That is what happened to Scribners in 1943. *The Fifth Seal* was one in a string of no fewer than seven best sellers. In the first nine months of the year their combined sales totaled 2 million copies.

Only one of the seven was nonfiction: *Paris Underground*, a book of personal narratives about the war in Europe, by Etta Shiber. The others were all novels, a fact that led Perkins to attribute the surge of prosperity to the public's being "cut off [by the war] from their former ways of amusement." One novel was *For Whom the Bell Tolls*, which in its third year sold 150,000 copies. There was also Edmund Gilligan's *The Gaunt Woman*. And there were three others whose success was especially cheering for Perkins.

Marcia Davenport's *The Valley of Decision*, which had come out in the fall of 1942, sold 300,000 copies within twelve months and eventually reached twice that figure. She was overwhelmed by the sales and flabbergasted by the favorable press. One evening when she was at dinner with the Charles Scribners and Max, the conversation veered to Thomas Wolfe and his problems, and Max said that Tom could have advanced with his work only by leaving Scribners, as he had done. "Oh no!" Mrs. Davenport said. "He needed you as much as I do. I couldn't write a book without you."

"If that were true," Perkins replied, "you would not be worth the work that has gone into you."

Perkins believed Marcia Davenport would not discover her full talents until she revealed more of herself in her writing. He wanted to help her to overcome her resistance against writing autobiographical fiction, for he felt she was denying herself a deeper integrity and passion in her material. He kept urging her toward it and after a year or so she capitulated. In 1945 she began a novel the theme of which was drawn from her own life in Manhattan: *East Side, West Side.*

Marcia Davenport had once made Charles Scribner shudder by divulging her dearest wish: She wanted to write a book that might sell only 1,200 copies but would be called a work of art. Under Perkins's aegis, she felt that was attainable. When she talked with him, he never stressed financial results. Once, she knew, when he had listened to someone complain about the commercial emphasis of a certain publishing house, Perkins had commented: "What you mean is, those people don't love books."

Nancy Hale did not have Marcia Davenport's difficulty with personal writing. Her novel *The Prodigal Women,* published alongside *The Valley of Decision* in Scribners' colossal year of best sellers, was a crystallization of her own experience. The book did extraordinarily well. Beyond that, Perkins admired it for revealing female character so deftly. "From the very beginning," he wrote her in reply to a letter of gratitude, "I believed in you and said so, and while I don't believe that sales are in themselves a proof, they are the only proof and the irrefutable proof to a lot of people to whom I have to say things, booksellers and such. So don't thank me for any pleasure. It is I who must thank you."

Perkins disliked business dealings, but he had long since become well known as a shrewd negotiator. An overtipper in restaurants and a soft touch to any friend or stranger who needed to borrow money, he was a Yankee mule trader in business. In discussing advances and royalties with agents or authors, Max would sit in silence at his desk, poker-faced, doodling his portraits of Napoleon, while the other person stated his demands. With his words falling on Perkins's almost deaf ears, even the toughest bargainer would gradually talk himself down. Old CS's grandson George Schieffelin said, "Max would close the deal whenever his terms were reached or his drawing was completed—whichever came first."

The seventh book in Scribners' record-breaking season was *Indigo* by Christine Weston. She was introduced to Perkins in the spring of 1939 by their mutual friend Waldo Peirce. "I had been told that Perkins liked to have aspiring writers show up with enormous amounts of manuscript," Miss Weston recalled, "and mine was certainly enormous. I was very green and timid, and had no confidence that the manuscript would ever be looked at by the great man, though Waldo Peirce assured me that once Max had undertaken to read something he never failed to do so."

Perkins admired her first novel and published her second as well. Together they sold 5,000 copies. Her third novel was set in India, where
she was born and lived until she was twenty. Published in 1943, *Indigo*
attracted 230,000 buyers in just a few months.

One did not have to sell like Hemingway, Davenport, Hale, Rawlings,
Weston, or Taylor Caldwell to get Perkins's backing. In fact, his heart
went out most readily to the person who desperately desired to be a writer
but who could not produce a good book. As it happened, many such were
women, who, charmed by his manner, could not resist coming back to
Scribners again and again. One woman dropped by every Thursday for
months, always with a different hat. Perkins would take her to "tea," not
knowing how else to accommodate her persistence. When his colleagues
asked why he spent so much time with so unpromising an author, he replied, "I'm afraid she might commit suicide if I didn't." Perkins would
take her to the bar of the Chatham Hotel, where she usually became
tipsy. One afternoon she started to fall down drunk. Max knew he could
not leave her at the bar, so he led her upstairs to a room where she could
sleep it off. Once inside the room, she unzipped her dress, kicked off her
shoes, flopped on the bed, and passed out. Max placed the key beside
her and left. Not until the moment after he quietly but firmly shut the
door, automatically locking it behind him, did he discover his overcoat
was caught in the jamb. A chambermaid eventually unlocked the door,
poked her nose in, and gave Max a contemptuous stare that he never forgot.

Women: the gossip in publishing was that Perkins was as critical
of them as ever. Christine Weston, for one, had been told that Perkins
was much more relaxed with his own sex. Her view was that

> he was more at ease with one sort of person than with another. I fancy
> he felt most at home with the big noisy egotistical types like Hemingway
> and Waldo Peirce, and that he had to feel his way cautiously with the shy
> intense ones who very likely made him feel self-conscious. . . . Personally,
> I found him attractive though emotionally remote.

Max still complained about women: "Lady writers expect you to do
many things for them apart from their books," Perkins wrote Professor
Copeland in the early forties. The big novelists insisted that he host a tea
upon publication of each of their books. Another woman called Max up in
tears to say, "My cat, John Keats, is dying." Perkins offered only sympathy.
She said, "You must send a veterinary." He replied he did not know much

about animal doctors and asked if she couldn't get one in her neighborhood. "But I haven't any money," she whimpered. "Will you pay for it?" In order to get her back to work, he did.

To persuade Michael Strange, the poet and former wife of John Barrymore, to finish her book of memoirs, Max had to dine several nights alone with her just to get her to listen to his suggestions. But she planned such sumptuous dinners and was so engaging a conversationalist that the evenings generally accomplished little. Most often the two of them indulged in political and economic discussions, for she was a radical and believed in a classless society. Michael Strange was sermonizing on that very subject one night over coffee while the maid was washing the dishes; suddenly the author interrupted herself, flinging over her shoulder, "God damn it, Kate, stop rattling those dishes."

Despite his difficulties in dealing with the gender, Max found himself working with more women than he ever had before—novelists Dawn Powell, Edith Pope, Ann Chidester, and Catherine Pomeroy Stewart, all well-known names in their day. He urged Anaïs Nin to publish her diaries. Most of the women who worked with Perkins spoke of him adoringly.

One woman, who still writes, has carried the torch for Max since the thirties. She showed little ability but great desire. To her endless letters, full of grandiloquent literary ravings and amorous overtures, he responded crisply but courteously. He spoke to her in person only twice, and then for no more than fifteen minutes. "That wasn't important," she declared forty years later, "for ours was a love of the eyes. I came into his life when he was somewhat weary and he took a deep interest in my fortunes. . . . The glow of his genius left a flame in my head." Year after year she continued to write poetry and prose; none was published, except by vanity presses. Still she worked on, because of Max's "faith" in her talent. Indeed, Max's faith was more than reciprocated. "From the day I met Max and we fell in love," she confessed, "I never shared a bed with my husband again. I would not be unfaithful to Max."

In February, 1943, Perkins attended Scottie Fitzgerald's marriage. He and Harold Ober, who gave the bride away to Lt. (j.g.) Samuel Lanahan, paid for the ceremony. As Scottie walked down the aisle of the church of St. Ignatius Loyola in New York, Perkins thought she looked very much as Zelda had almost twenty-five years earlier—"not as pretty as she was," Max wrote Hemingway, "and yet she looked better than Zelda."

The bride's mother had been unable to attend the wedding, for she was patriotically employed as a machinist apprentice in Montgomery. (She soon got fired.) She wrote to thank Max for his letter detailing the beautiful ceremony. It gave play to her own remembrances of the "mica-ed attenuation of spring so many years ago when somewhat under your friendly auspices we were married," she said. A few months later she wrote Max again. "I perform a great many foolish overtures to the past," she said dreamily, "and greatly look forward to the Judgement day."

Into his sixtieth year, Max passed several fascinating, poignant days reading his correspondence with Scott Fitzgerald. Edmund Wilson wanted some of the letters for a book of Fitzgeraldiana, the centerpiece of which was "The Crack-Up." Scribners was not publishing it, because Max maintained that Scott would not have wanted those grim pieces in book form; nonetheless Perkins approved publication of the book by another house for the same reason he consented to infrequent requests to include F. Scott Fitzgerald in fiction anthologies. He wanted to do everything in his power to keep Fitzgerald's reputation alive.

Another author whose writings Perkins was rereading was Thomas Wolfe. As Christmas, 1943, approached, he wrote Wolfe's sister Mabel: "I think of Tom a great deal at this time of the year, and remember the old days when we might expect him to drop in at the office at almost any moment." At home late at night Max would pore over the same favorite passages in *Of Time and the River.*

Thomas Wolfe had been dead for five years but his literary reputation was rising steadily. Generally, Perkins observed, even a noted author faded out shortly after his death. But the reverse had happened in the case of Wolfe, and the affairs of his literary estate still took up a great deal of Perkins's time.

Aline Bernstein, who was living in Mount Kisco, New York, learned that William B. Wisdom, Wolfe's friend from New Orleans, was buying up all of Wolfe's papers. She was upset because her letters would be included. "There could be no need for it," she wrote Perkins in the middle of 1943, "and I think I am not wrong in thinking that I should have been told. It is the one thing I have ever known you to do that was lacking in rightness, or what I consider rightness to be."

The contents of her letters—the words on the pages—were hers and no one could publish them without her permission; but the documents themselves that were in Wolfe's possession upon his death belonged to his estate. Perkins explained to Mrs. Bernstein, "It was my duty to sell whatever I could for the financial advantage of the estate." Perkins was not interested in raising money so much as in making Wolfe's papers available to writers and scholars. He thought this was essential for the reputation and influence of any important writer. It was the least one could do for Thomas Wolfe, who, Perkins said, would always be read, because "there will always be a new generation of sophomores to discover and delight in him."

William B. Wisdom had been gathering Wolfe's writings for years. He planned to establish a memorial at Harvard—a collection of all the Wolfe material he could get hold of, including, he hoped, the passionate love letters between Wolfe and Mrs. Bernstein. Their sweetest and ugliest sentiments were conveyed in those letters. One of the most memorable salutations, for example, read, "My heavy-breasted, grey-haired Jewish bitch, I love the stench of your plum-colored arm-pits." In June, 1943, Aline wrote Perkins,

> I daresay I will get used to the idea of my letters to Tom being sold, but I'm not used to it yet in spite of the fact that it is legal. It is all a shock to me, but amounts to little in the scale of people's sorrow now on earth. So this is the end of it from me to you. I carry with me always though, the pain of the fact that our relationship, Tom's and mine, was never resolved during his life. Maybe it never could have been. It held so much, for so long a time, time that was magnificent, and even at the end he must have known in his heart's core, how we were to each other.

In due course Perkins asked Mrs. Bernstein to surrender her own letters from Tom for the collection. She consented, but would not give them to Wisdom—whom she suspected of profiting from the Wolfe material—for nothing. After several years of negotiating, Wisdom purchased the collection. Mrs. Bernstein demanded that every penny of the money due her go to the Federation of Jewish Philanthropies. Writing to Max about this stipulation, she said: "It will be a retaliation for all the insults to the Jews that Tom hurled at me."

That summer Perkins saw the film version of *For Whom the Bell Tolls*. He was delighted when he first heard that Gary Cooper was going to play the lead role. Perkins admired him so much that he had seen him in *Sergeant York* twice. After seeing the new film, though, Max realized the limitations of his favorite actor and the medium itself. He wrote Evan Shipman:

Of course Gary Cooper is just the way he always is—which is good, but is not Robert, nor anything like him. That is partly because all the subjective part of the story, or almost all, has got lost. Perhaps necessarily.

The only other motion picture that Perkins had ever shown any interest in was *The Charge of the Light Brigade*. He did not want to view the entire film, just the charge itself. Max made his middle daughter, Peggy, accompany him to the theater. He stationed her so that she could watch both the screen and her father, who stood in the lobby. They waited an hour and a half for the climactic moment. When she saw that Errol Flynn was about to lead the charge, Peggy signaled, Perkins advanced through the lobby, stood in the aisle, and observed the Brigade's routing. Then Max and his daughter promptly retreated.

Ernest Hemingway had been in Cuba for the better part of the last year—"doing whatever it is he is doing," Max wrote Evan Shipman. Papa was busy patrolling in his boat, searching for German submarines. This was important work, he said, and he could not write while the war was going on. Perkins wanted to give him the benefit of the doubt but knew there was more to it than that. Martha Gellhorn Hemingway had just sent Max a novel which Scribners was publishing, and she had spent the three years of their marriage traveling and writing powerful articles for *Collier's*. "When we came home from the sea," Hemingway's youngest son, Gregory, recalled of that time, "Marty thought Papa would resume his writing. But he had other plans. 'You're the writer in the family now, Marty,' he announced—and he meant it completely and whole-heartedly! . . . Marty was flattered at first, then amazed, and finally disgusted. To *help* her career was fine, but for America's foremost novelist to retire at forty-four [sic], two years after the completion of *For Whom the Bell Tolls*, was unthinkable—even for a pioneer women's libber like Marty." She wondered what had happened to the spirit in Ernest that had driven him to Spain some six years earlier. Already there were rumors that she and Ernest were estranged. While he moped around the Gulf Stream, she went to England to continue her war correspondence. In Ernest's mind, she had turned her back on him. Hemingway wrote Perkins that he was "damned lonely" and "damned anxious to write again."

Yet soon Hemingway, peevish, feeling unloved, erupted over a minor dispute concerning royalties for the reprinting of his books, and he came to believe that Charlie Scribner wanted to pick a fight with him. Hemingway said that was fine with him if Scribner thought old Papa was "insufficiently respectful" or more bother than he was worth. For a hotheaded moment, it appeared that his publishing relationship might follow the path of most of his others during the last decade. Gregory Hemingway said of his father, "He broke off with all the early friends who helped him: he split with Sherwood Anderson, he split with Gertrude Stein, he split with Scott Fitzgerald . . . now his own Papa myth was getting too big for him to handle." Even during the blossoming of Hemingway's megalomania, however, Gregory recalled, "he never broke away from Perkins." Max's unwavering decency was the reason.

Hemingway said he would stay with Scribners on one condition. He demanded that Perkins never fight with him—"because you are my most trusted friend as well as my God damned publisher." He pleaded with Perkins to realize that his inability to create was not because he had "run dry, become a rummy or a problem writer." In fact, he wanted to write so much sometimes that it was "worse than being in jail not to have the time to do it." He wished Perkins would believe that for one year he had literally not had the hours to put out a single word. He assured him that all this time he was gathering plenty to write about, so when he was ready, he would be able to invent out of what he had experienced and learned. He told Max it would take a while to "cool out," as it always did, before he could get back to his work. Perkins never expressed any disbelief to Ernest, but he told a colleague, "I'm afraid Ernest's believing his own legends about himself . . . and that he might never be able to write truly again."

By May, 1944, Hemingway realized that all his sub-chasing in the Gulf Stream was pointless. He decided to catch up with Martha and go see the war in Europe. He went to New York and visited Perkins, who found him looking well, sporting the magnificent gray beard he had raised for protection against the seafaring sun and wind. In June, as a correspondent for *Collier's*, he reported from both sides of the English Channel, covering the D-Day invasion. Then he joined the Fourth Division and for weeks was near every action it took part in. If he got back alive, Hemingway promised Max, he would write Scribners a very valuable property, having hit "very fine pay dirt on this last prospecting trip." The book, he said, would have "the sea and the air and the ground in it." Hemingway also told Perkins that his recent activity had "cured" him of his wife. It was funny, he said, how it should take one war "to start a woman in your damn heart and another to finish her."

Marcia Davenport once asked Toscanini how he endured an entire day of exhausting rehearsal. The maestro said he drew strength from the music of his composers. Max Perkins renewed himself from his authors, but Harold Stearns, James Boyd, and John Peale Bishop had recently died. He had been close to all of them. Max withdrew even more than ever. His privacy became a passion. In the early 1940s he received an increasing number of invitations to discuss publicly his role as an editor and he usually refused with a simple explanation: "An editor should strive for anonymity." Now he was fervent about being left alone.

In the fall of 1943, one of Elizabeth Lemmon's relatives thought of writing an article about Max Perkins for *Town & Country*. Perkins's first instinct was to refuse to speak to him at all, but then he saw how Poyntz Tyler's article in the small magazine might shield him from an even greater exposure. Max explained to Elizabeth that September:

> I hate to be written about at all. I wouldn't dare say that to you if it were not true, for you know too much about me. I really have that passion for anonymity that Roosevelt talks about. What's more, I think an editor *ought* to be anonymous. He should not be important, or known to be so, for the writers are the important ones in his life. But Mr. Tyler did point out what I myself had thought of—that if Town and Country had a piece, the New Yorker would not do a Profile. And a Profile has been hanging over my head like the Damoclesian sword for months. But I think it fell through.

The editors of *The New Yorker* had first proposed the idea of writing a profile on Perkins to Thomas Wolfe in the thirties. Wolfe assigned his agent, Elizabeth Nowell, to learn if Perkins would consent to such a piece. "Perkins seemed to pretend to pooh-pooh it but wouldn't flatly refuse," Miss Nowell recalled, "and Tom and I wondered if he might secretly—beneath his shyness—rather like the idea." Still trying to figure him out, she finally went to his office one day and said, "Goddamit, Mr. Perkins, do you want a *New Yorker* profile of you or not? Answer yes or no." He scowled at her reproachfully and said, "Miss Nowell, you're a Yankee too?"

"Yes," she said.

"Well then," he said, "you *ought to know better* than to ask me that."

Wolfe dropped the project, but years later the critic Malcolm Cowley picked it up, and *The New Yorker* encouraged him. Cowley believed there was no person so important in the field of contemporary literature who at the same time was so unknown as Maxwell Perkins. Just what an editor did was a mystery to those outside the book trade, and Cowley believed Perkins obscured what little there was to be seen by standing in the shadows, like some "gray-hatted eminence." Before seeking an interview with Perkins, Cowley set about collecting facts. "Perkins, I discovered, is the nearest thing to a great man now existing in the literary world," he explained to William Shawn, his editor at *The New Yorker*. "Legends are clustered round him like truffles round an oak tree in Gascony." In late 1943, after months of research—correspendence and interviews with Perkins's friends, authors, and colleagues, and much digging up of details—Cowley was ready to confront the Fox himself.

A literary figure of importance and a charming man as well, Cowley soon worked his way past Perkins's pathological self-effacement. Perkins spent some time diminishing his own accomplishments ("I don't see why they give us credit for discovering books when we merely read manuscripts.") and blustering about the obscenity of being written about; then he settled down and acquiesced to a formal interview. In fact, he submitted to several sessions.

At one point he told Cowley that the man he would most like to resemble was Major General John Aaron Rawlins. According to the *Dictionary of American Biography*, Rawlins was "the most nearly indispensable" officer of General Grant's staff. It was his job to keep Grant sober; edit his important papers and put them in final form; apply tact and persistence in order to make critical points; and often restore the general's self-confidence.

During their time together, Cowley and Perkins discussed contemporary writers. Lately, Robert Penn Warren had become of interest to Perkins; and, of course, William Faulkner had attracted his attention early on. Perkins was most enthusiastic about Faulkner's early books and had never read anything he had written since without admiration. "My only fear about him," he told Cowley, "is that he has fallen into a certain position which is not nearly as high as it should be, and once that happens to a writer, it is extremely difficult to change the public's opinion. Anyone would be proud to publish him, but I would only be afraid that we could not do enough better than his present publishers to satisfy him."

One of Faulkner's most admiring interpreters, Cowley was aware that the author had been relegated to limbo. When he sent his Mississippi friend a "New York market report" on his current standing as a literary figure, Cowley wrote, "In publishing circles your name is mud. They are all convinced that your books won't ever sell, and it's a pity, isn't it? they say, with a sort of pleased look on their faces." Faulkner had written seventeen fictional works, then all out of print, bearing the imprints of a half-dozen houses. Now Cowley advised him to find still another publisher. He thought of Scribners because of his respect for Max Perkins and what he assumed Perkins felt for Faulkner's writing. So, not long afterward, he talked to Max about the author, only to find Perkins less than eager. Perkins had long regarded the man as a virtuoso, but thinking of the author's future writing rather than his reputation, he told Cowley emphatically, "Faulkner is finished."

It was implicit in all Perkins's comments to Cowley that he had little faith in the writing of the forties and even less hope for that which would follow. "Perhaps the trouble with literature in our time," he told Cowley, "is that there aren't as many rascals as there used to be."

Cowley completed his interviews and went off. While he was writing, Perkins tended to business. One current project involved not a rascal but a delightfully mischievous author, Arthur Train. After Train's success in writing his own autobiography, Perkins had suggested that he write the definitive story of Mr. Tutt, his celebrated hero whose fictitious adventures had delighted millions of readers over the last quarter-century. The result was *Yankee Lawyer: The Autobiography of Ephraim Tutt*, with an introduction by Train. The book was "authenticated" with "photographs" of young Tutt and his portrait from the *Saturday Evening Post* in his familiar pose of his thumbs grabbing his waistcoat—a portrait which, curiously enough, bore no small resemblance to Max Perkins. Upon the publication of *Yankee Lawyer* in 1943, people who had admired Tutt's legal skill but had wondered whether or not he was imaginary, hopped onto the side of belief. Every mail delivery brought letters to the publishers from people anxious to retain Mr. Tutt's counsel. One lonely old woman propositioned him. Another woman called Scribners and was accidentally switched onto Max Perkins's private wire. For a long time she refused to accept his assurance that there was, in fact, no Ephraim Tutt. "But there must be a Mr. Tutt," she insisted, and when finally convinced, she began to sob.

Then the literary prank boomeranged. In March, 1944, a marshal from the New York Supreme Court served Arthur Train with a summons. The complainant was Lewis R. Linet, a Philadelphian, who described himself as "a lawyer given to reading, who, deceived by the jacket, title-page, illustrations and printed content of *Yankee Lawyer*, had been tricked into parting with three dollars and a half in exchange for a piece of spurious fiction." Linet sought a rebate of $1 on the purchase price, not just for himself, but for each of the 50,000 other purchasers of the book. He was also suing Charles Scribner's Sons and the author's editorial co-conspirator, Maxwell E. Perkins, for "fraud and deceit."

The story, when it broke in the press, seemed so incredible that Perkins was accused of having cooked the whole thing up as a publicity stunt. But the injunction and $50,000 rebate that Linet sought were a matter of court record. The defendants retained the best lawyer they could think of, John W. Davis, former Democratic candidate for president, ex-ambassador to England, and an admirer of Mr. Tutt for years. It was true that misinterpretations of fact were subject to suit; the question was whether or not rules for commodities applied also to books. The defense's argument was rooted in the literary tradition of apocryphal biography or historical narrative for purposes of political or literary satire. *Robinson Crusoe* and *Gulliver's Travels*, both published as bona fide accounts, were obvious examples. While the case was still pending, Arthur Train died, before seeing Mr. Tutt cleared of charges.

Another unusual project occupying Perkins late in 1943, when Mr. Cowley came to call, involved a thirty-five-year-old man from Junction City, Kansas. Joseph Stanley Pennell ("rhymes with kennel," he used to say) had completed his first novel, *The History of Rome Hanks and Kindred Matters,* just before his induction into the army. A friend had consented to handle the business of selling his manuscript, and she sent it to Scribners in early 1943. Perkins first learned of the book when he overheard two of his associates talking about it. One of them said, "Another of those damned works of genius." Some editors are put off by brilliant but idiosyncratic manuscripts and some, such as Perkins, are enticed by them. Perkins took the book home and started to read. The syntax and punctuation were unconventional, and in general the difficulties in the manuscript seemed insuperable, but Max found value. He told a friend: "An editor does not come across such talent more than five or six times in his life. And when he does, he is bound to do what he can for it."

If that declaration echoed Max's reaction to Thomas Wolfe, it was no wonder. Pennell had been inspired by Wolfe, and his book bore many similarities to Wolfe's work. First there was the clearly autobiographical nature of the story, written in keeping with Wolfe's dictum that "we are the sum of all the moments of our lives"; practically all Pennell's moments seemed to be in the book. Fork City, Kansas, Pennell's name for his hometown of Junction City, was the equivalent of Wolfe's Altamont. The prose often had the quality of blank verse, and Pennell's chapters were often introduced by sections of italicized lyrical philosophy, some of which could have passed for Wolfe's own dithyrambs; indeed, Pennell's narrator, Lee Harrington, went Eugene Gant one better and actually composed sonnets to his lady, a beautiful blonde named Christa, to whom he was recounting the story of his ancestors in hopes of impressing her, and the sonnets were inserted in the narrative. Finally, Pennell intended his novel to be the first in a trilogy, which he was calling *An American Chronicle*.

Perkins found *Rome Hanks* a complicated admixture of narrations, flipflopping between centuries, blending a contemporary love story with a retelling of the Civil War. After several days with the tricky manuscript, he wrote Pennell and admitted that he had "not yet got the hang of the book—don't know exactly what the motive is of mixing the present with the past, etc." But, he added, "I am having a grand time reading it, and I should like to tell you that a colleague here showed me that Pickett's Charge piece, and I really do not believe I ever saw a war piece that excelled it, not forgetting Tolstoi."

Perkins was excited and tantalized. Undoubtedly he sensed that *Rome Hanks* offered him the possibility of another Tom Wolfe. But he was careful not to raise Pennell's expectations too much. He had not finished the book, and he already saw problems arising. On March 29, 1943, he wrote Pennell again:

> We have all said we have got to find some way of publishing this book, and yet there are some obstacles that are very serious, and that in fact can only be got over by drastic elimination. And I don't know whether you will consent to it. Yet I do think you should publish, and I don't think any publisher could publish a good many things that are in your book.

Perkins's first objection was that the contemporary parts seemed trivial as compared to the historical passages. The reader, he said, was conscious as he read the modern story that

> it did not blend with the rest, and was not equal with it,—and that in fact while one was reading those parts, he was impatient to get back to the early America, the war and after the war.

The second difficulty with the modern tale was that most of the "obscene" material was there; Perkins felt that much of the love story could not be printed as written. And then there was Christa, the object of the hero's love poems. With her St. Louis background and blonde, leggy looks she resembled Martha Gellhorn so much that Perkins feared libel; the similarity, he said, was "unmistakable unless there has been a most amazing series of coincidences." Perkins told Pennell that nobody could print this portrait of her without being sued; and in any case, since Scribners published Miss Gellhorn, they could not defame her, whatever the law. "It does seem to me that you would have produced something masterful," Perkins wrote, "and even conceivably better than it is now, if you took out most of what is contemporary, and merely gave the Civil War and post Civil War days—the old America."

Pennell, now in California, replied that he had considered the "drastic elimination" which Perkins urged but found it hard to accept. "First," he explained, "there is the perhaps unreasonable love of one's own words, and second, there is the plan of the longer work of which *Rome Hanks* is a part." Still, Pennell wanted to weigh Max's proposals a little longer. "Life, Sir," he said, "is most strange and wonderful—and it seems extremely amazing to me that I should sit here, near some guns in California, writing this to you in New York, whom I had for some time admired as a name with certain qualifications and then as a portrait in a book by a man from North Carolina—a man who died searching for a leaf and a door."

The whole matter gnawed at Perkins. He wanted the book, but he felt he had to alter it. Experimenting, he removed all the contemporary parts of the manuscript, then gave the remainder to another Scribners editor to read. Afterward, Perkins showed the man what had been deleted. This man, Max reported to Pennell, "with much more certainty than I who am also not very confident of my judgments, believes that this book itself would be a finer one without the contemporary parts."

But, said Perkins, still not offering a contract, "you must not let me beguile you into going against your own opinion."

Pennell finally agreed to Perkins's prescription. For the better part of a year they worked together through the mail. Both compromised. Pennell worked within Perkins's boundaries but sandwiched in a few of his modern-day interludes. Christa was no longer so clearly based on Martha Gellhorn.

"What a joke if Martha picked the wrong genius!" Marjorie Rawlings wrote Max, after learning about the novel. Perkins spoke of the book to everyone, for none in years had excited him so much. He read pages aloud to friends in the evening and handed out advance copies to visitors to his office. And when *The History of Rome Hanks and Kindred Matters* was published, in the summer of 1944, it appeared that his enthusiasm was justified. The novel ran through its entire first printing overnight and commanded national attention. "Nobody is going to be so foolish as to argue that the novel is flourishing particularly these days, because it just isn't," Hamilton Basso began his review in the July 15, 1944, *New Yorker,*

> but there is evidence around . . . to suggest that those who are waiting to nail down its coffin lid might, at least for the time being, put those hammers away. . . . [*Rome Hanks* is] a book which, unless I am greatly mistaken, will cause more fuss than any first novel since Thomas Wolfe's *Look Homeward, Angel.*
>
> One thing that is bound to happen, and I will lay bets, is that Mr. Pennell, an ex-newspaperman now in the Army, is going to be hailed, by those who go in for hailing, as another Thomas Wolfe. There will be some reason for this, because Mr. Pennell, like Wolfe, commits just about every sin known to literary man, and, again like Wolfe, thinks up a few ones all his own.

Within six months of publication, *Rome Hanks* sold close to 100,000 copies.

While *Rome Hanks* was making its author's reputation, Malcolm Cowley's profile appeared in *The New Yorker* and gave Max the fame he had for so long fled. It was entitled "Unshaken Friend," a phrase from Wolfe's dedication of *Of Time and the River,* and it was published in two successive issues in April, 1944. Profiles so long they had to be published in two parts were rare for the magazine, but William Shawn had been convinced that Perkins was every bit as important as Cowley made him out to be. In the first shock of his notoriety, Max went so far as to consult a lawyer as to what means might be taken to suppress the articles, but he never carried the effort any farther. Instead, he sought to distance himself from the portrait. When asked about the articles, he told several people: "I wouldn't mind being like that fellow." The man in the profile, he said, was "a great sight better person than myself." Perkins's friends said he groused for weeks about Cowley's comment that he dressed in "shabby and inconspicuous grays." "I felt like telling him," Cowley wrote William Shawn, "that if *The New Yorker* said he dressed in shabby and inconspicuous grays, by God he dressed in shabby and inconspicuous grays."

In time Perkins concluded that he had come off rather well in the articles, and he was pleased that Cowley had often moved away from Max himself and expanded into an informative discussion of publishing. But the articles caused trouble for Perkins. It seemed for a while that every would-be writer in America had read Cowley's depiction of the loyal and compassionate editor and his gift for identifying neglected talent, and had been stirred to seek his services. The flow of manuscripts into Scribners became nearly overwhelming, and Miss Wyckoff had all she could do to fend off phone calls from strangers. And visitors. Cowley had quoted Max as saying, "One can tell as much by seeing an author as by reading the manuscript," whereupon unpublished authors began demanding to be seen.

That spring Max's friend and neighbor Hendrik Willem van Loon died. The same week, Colonel John William Thomason, the author and illustrator of such Scribners books as *Fix Bayonets* and *Jeb Stuart*, died in the Naval Hospital in San Diego at fifty-one. That summer Perkins was further grieved by the horrible progressive illness of an even closer friend, the playwright Edward Sheldon. Sheldon, whom Max had known since Harvard, had been bedridden with arthritis for fifteen years. Now the disease had rendered him deaf, dumb, and blind, and had frozen him completely rigid. He existed in a dreadful monotony of dark, silent days.

And then Perkins's own health began to deteriorate in ways that even he could not ignore. One day one of his ankles and both his hands swelled up alarmingly. The doctor told him it was probably exhaustion. Perkins said he didn't feel tired, though he realized that he wasn't reading as attentively as before. He was persuaded to take time off, and for two weeks he mainly slept.

Perkins had had a great-grandmother who used to say, "It's wicked to be sick," and he had always acted as if he believed her. Now, however, Louise was able to coerce him into having a thorough medical examination. To his own amazement the tests turned out favorably. There was nothing dreadfully wrong—just fatigue. But the doctors were distressed that Perkins seemed to be getting about one third of his nourishment from alcohol, and that he wasn't eating nearly enough.

In recent years Max had become increasingly fussy about food. He showed little interest even in his standbys—breast of guinea hen and the Ritz's house special of venison. Louise dreamed up tempting meals for the cook to prepare, but he never ate them. (The two youngest girls, Jane and Nancy, once drew up a list of foods which he would agree to eat if placed before him, and they made him sign it. It was probably the only contract he ever willfully broke.) The doctor put Perkins on vitamins and limited him to two cocktails a day; Max indulged in a third on weekends. The cocktails made him less aware of his loneliness and the passage of time. "Everything moves too fast nowadays," he told Marjorie Rawlings, "and John Barleycorn slows things up. I had always thought that if I got very old, I would take up hashish, which completely destroys the sense of time, so that you sit in eternity."

To everyone's surprise, when Max returned from his rest he said his recent exhaustion had made him resolve to take a real vacation. He decided to take more time off in October and go visit his daughter Peggy in Alliance, Ohio. Her husband had bought two saddle horses that needed exercising. "That's something I'd like to attend to," Max wrote Mrs. Rawlings, "—the first idea of a vacation that has interested me for many years." By October, however, Max was afflicted with another ailment—eczema, which spread up from an ankle over much of his body and kept him from getting around. Again doctors told him he was run-down. "I am absolutely well," Max protested, though he admitted, again to Marjorie Rawlings, "I keep getting worse, and worse, and worse." He remembered Arthur Train's once telling him, "Never change your habits." Now he swore that changing his ways for some doctor had brought on this illness. He canceled his vacation plans and went back to working, eating, and drinking as he always had, resuming the rate of four or five martinis a day.

In spring 1944 Scribners published a novel by Taylor Caldwell, *The Final Hour*, which gave a picture of the room in which Max was playing out his life. One of its characters was a gray-haired, frosty-blue-eyed descendant of New England Puritans named Cornell T. Hawkins, an editor who was seldom without his weathered hat. In depicting his office Miss Caldwell exactly described Max's own:

> Here was no pretense, no thick rugs and fine furniture to impress the vulgar. Heaps of manuscripts lay on the splintered desk, overflowing ash-trays, disorderly piles of letters, scattered pens and pencils. The floor was grimy and discolored. Chairs with squeaking legs were thrust back against the mildewed walls. Yet, out of this disorder, this untidiness and indifference to elegance, had come some of the world's finest and noblest literature. There was an air about this man, in this casual room filled with stark sunlight, of greatness and simplicity. One knew instinctively that the veriest tyro of a frightened author would be accorded the same courtesy and consideration as the most gilded and popular writers who could boast ten or twenty "large printings."

Perkins was amused by this portrayal of the editor's milieu but feared the sordid details would frighten authors away. He commissioned Miss Wyckoff to oversee a general renovation. Even after it, the office was hardly elegant, just neat enough to make Max uncomfortable. He told Malcolm Cowley, "I was lucky to get off without a carpet on the floor."

By the mid-forties, World War II dominated America's reading. In 1944, for example, seven of the nation's ten most widely read nonfiction selections were war books, from Bob Hope's amusing front-line chronicles to Ernie Pyle's war reportage. They sold by the hundreds of thousands, but publishing was also affected adversely by the war. There were shortages of paper, for example, that made it very hard to keep books in stock. To make sure there was paper for the best sellers—the books that paid the rent—Perkins had to cut back on less commercial books, and he found himself saying to some authors what he had been obliged to say to Scott Fitzgerald twenty-five years earlier regarding *The Romantic Egotist,* that Scribners could not undertake any new ventures. That hurt. Perkins was already depressed about the state of publishing. The values of the culture were changing, and works of pure literature seemed unwelcome. A new world of materialism and expediency seemed to be corrupting serious book people. "I wish all this were over, and that there would be a quiet life again," Perkins wrote Hemingway early in 1945.

> But I know there never will be, and that what seemed to be was illusory. I even thought after the other war that things would get that way, and I

thought you would, for instance, just live quietly somewhere, and fish and shoot and write.—But that became impossible, and I suppose it may always be so.

When Hemingway returned from Europe, he stopped in to see Max and then went on to the Finca Vigía in Cuba. He soon began to send Max letters stating how hard it would be now for him to write a fine book; it got tougher every time, he explained. In the old days Max would have gently exhorted Ernest to get back to his typewriter. Now he was uninspiring, indulgent. "I think you ought to take it easy . . . ," he wrote. "Get out into that old Gulf Stream where things always seem to be right—not necessarily for you yourself, but in the big way."

But if Max's vitality and hope were ebbing, his reputation was not. He was well known to everyone who wanted to write, and unpublished authors continued to think of him as a miracle worker. When turned down, some writers thumbed through *You Can't Go Home Again* to find which traits of "Foxhall Edwards" had kept Maxwell Perkins from responding to their work. The rejected often harassed him for explanations, and it was not uncommon for Perkins to spend entire days answering them.

There was one woman in particular, an aspiring author whose novel had been declined, who railed at Perkins in a number of letters, each more inflammatory than the last. She felt she had been spurned because of her politics, that her ultraliberalism, as expressed in her book, had conflicted with Max's conservative beliefs. She complained that Max was depriving her of her right to give the world her message. She attacked him as arbitrary, a man so blinded by his prejudices that he had become an irresponsible publisher. For two years she maintained a running assault on Perkins.

Max thought the woman's manuscript had some merit, despite certain serious defects in her mastery of the English language. He kept on replying, at first out of politeness, then for the sake of justice, finally in sympathy. His many letters articulated an informal credo for publishing in America and conveyed his editorial criteria.

The ideal of publishing would be a forum where all sections of humanity could have their say, whether their object was to instruct, entertain, horrify, etc. Nevertheless, there are certain rules of quality and relevance, which can only be determined by some sort of selection and this the publisher, representing humanity at large, attempts—with many mistakes—to make. Or, to put it differently, artists, saints, and the other more sentient repre-

sentatives of the human race are, as it were, on the frontiers of time—
pioneers and guides to the future. And the publisher, in the capacity mentioned, must make some sort of estimate of the importance and validity of
their reports, and there is nothing he can base this on but the abilities to
judge that God has given him.

The woman accused Perkins of being afraid to publish her work for
fear of public reprisal. But Perkins knew he was not a censor. He pointed
out that Scribners had published Ben Hecht's attack on anti-Semitism, *A
Guide for the Bedevilled,* and Beatrice and Sidney Webb's *Soviet Communism: A New Civilization.*

At one point in the debate, fed up with the woman's continuing
vituperation, Perkins stated: "Our correspondence is futile and had
better be ended." The furious author asked Perkins just who he thought
he was. Max took the question literally. "I am," he said in a letter dated
May 19, 1944, "or at least should be if I fulfilled myself, John Smith,
U.S.A." He went on to develop his view of himself in some detail:

> He is the man who doesn't know much, nor thinks that he knows much.
> He starts out with certain ambitions but he gradually accumulates obliga-
> tions as he goes along, and they continually increase. They begin with his
> inherited family, and grow with the family that results from his marriage,
> and further increase with his associates, and those whom he represents. He
> soon finds that about all he can do, and that not too well, is to fulfill those
> obligations. He knows that he is a failure, and is bound to be, because he
> is not in the confidence of God, like some, and does not know God's
> plan. He does know what he has undertaken to do, and he hopes to Heaven
> that he will manage, to some considerable extent, to do it. That's what he
> is serious about, for he can't, in view of his observation of the rest of the
> world, be very sure about himself, or think that his fate is a matter of
> moment. He can accept the kiss of death too, as long as he doesn't let
> himself in for it by his own negligence, which would mean the betrayal
> of others.
>
> John Smith, U.S.A. is always aware of the fact that he may be, and probably
> is, wrong. That is tolerance. He simply does his simple best in the world
> and hopes to God that he will never let anybody down or betray any prin-
> ciple in which he believes.

For Perkins, then, the path of aspiration that had started in Paradise had darkened before his great objectives could be reached. He knew

it, yet he carried on, maintaining a convincing impression of steadiness
even as personal disappointments and professional pressures increased.
There was no Gulf Stream for Perkins to glide off in, just a multiplying
burden of anxieties. His authors' plights, laid upon him, became more
horrific, often macabre: One wanted Perkins's counsel regarding her
daughter who was having a breakdown; another sent him glimpses from
her own traumatic childhood—true Gothic tales of being forced to dig up
a dead sister's corpse and dress her in doll's clothes. There were distant
relatives who had to borrow money or were seeking jobs, marriage problems of inlaws, women's clubs campaigning against smut in literature,
ethnic and political groups protesting certain characterizations, young
people constantly seeking advice on becoming published writers, more
family war casualties, authors whose books demonstrated that the earth
was round but that we lived inside of it, or who had written five-volume
novels entitled *God*. Through it all he kept his head while all about him
were losing theirs.

Once again, only Elizabeth Lemmon knew. In May, 1945, she sent
him several letters Tom Wolfe had written her, thinking Max might want
them for an anthology of Wolfe's letters that Scribners was compiling.
Max replied: "I myself would have written you often, except that unlike
Tom I cannot write letters when I am in despair. I have got myself into
too many things outside of my work here, and I really should have
avoided them." Perkins said his susceptibility to entanglements stemmed
from that resolution he had made on the brink of manhood, the day he
almost let Tom McClary drown—"never to refuse a responsibility."

"I did not do this formally," Max told Elizabeth, "but I know just
when I did it, half-unconsciously, and it got to be like an obsession of
General Grant's which made it impossible for him ever to retrace his
steps, and so he did get into Richmond in the end."

XXII

A Toss of the Hat

James Jones of Robinson, Illinois, enlisted in the Army Air Corps in 1939, transferred to the infantry, rose to the rank of sergeant, and was twice busted to private. He was stationed at Hickam Field in Hawaii when he discovered the writing of Thomas Wolfe. Jones found a number of parallels between his family and the fictitious Gants. "[Wolfe's] home life seemed so similar to my own and his feeling about himself so similar to mine about myself," Jones later recalled, "that I realized I had been a writer all my life without knowing it or having written. Once I made up my mind, it seemed inevitable, something that fate had directed ever since my birth." In 1944, having been awarded a Bronze Star and a Purple Heart, he was honorably discharged and set out upon his writing career.

By February, 1945, Jones, now living in New York, had a finished draft of a very Wolfean novel called *They Shall Inherit the Laughter*. The next step was obvious: He would take it himself to Charles Scribner's Sons and the legendary Maxwell E. Perkins. He marched into Scribners, carrying a string-tied Eaton Bond box containing his manuscript, and went to the fifth floor. There an elderly receptionist brought him to a halt. She told him that Mr. Perkins was not in the office but if the manuscript was left with her, it would get a proper reading. Jones said if Maxwell Perkins was not there, he would just leave with his manuscript. The woman disappeared briefly, then reported that Mr. Perkins had just returned to his office through a rear door. She took Jones back to meet him. It was not until a long time later that Jones realized there was no rear door.

The short, stocky twenty-four-year-old entered Perkins's office expecting to see the face that Wolfe had described in his portrait of Foxhall Edwards. It was quickly apparent to him that Wolfe had exaggerated. Jones found Perkins's features much more subtle—except for the smile. "That," he said years afterward, "was as sly as the Fox's."

Immediately Perkins steered the conversation to the young man's army service. They soon were deeply involved in a discussion of the war, and the novel was set aside before Jones had even described it. As their conference on military matters continued, it got late and the staff went home. At last Perkins rose, tugged his hat down over his ears, and led the author to the Ritz Bar for tea.

Perkins did not read the manuscript that night. Instead he gave it next day to two other editors at Scribners, both of whom found it thinly plotted. Perkins was about to decline it on Scribners' behalf when, impelled by his favorable impression of the author, he browsed through it himself. He found a good deal to admire. "It is a serious attempt to do a big piece of work and the author has the temperament and the emotional projection of a writer," Perkins wrote the agent Maxwell Aley, who had taken the author under his wing after Perkins had met Jones. "We do not feel however that *They Shall Inherit the Laughter* quite comes off as a novel, nor does it turn out to be anything for which we could make you an offer."

Jones, undeterred, devoted most of 1945 to reshaping the novel, then resubmitted his manuscript to Perkins the following January. "I have a number of plans I'm champing to get into action, and all of them hinge on this book," he explained to Perkins this second time around, sounding much like Fitzgerald in 1919, "whether it is accepted or rejected, whether you will consider that it needs more work (personally, I'm sure it doesn't but it's just possible my judgment may be biased) and of course the money angle, how large an advance and how soon. I'm stony broke right now." While waiting for Max's reply, he went off to hitch-hike around the country.

Perkins took as much interest in the ideas Jones described in his letter as in the revised manuscript. Among other things, Jones wanted to start another book about the peacetime army just before Pearl Harbor. The type of man he wished to portray in this second novel was somewhat like the reprehensible Flagg or Quirt in *What Price Glory?*, Maxwell Anderson's and Laurence Stallings's drama of World War I. As Jones explained: "Enlisted men spent their entire time in the army pissed off at the officers.

And in my army, regimented as it was, men like Quirt and Flagg were made officers again. That class distinction infuriated me, and that was what I wanted to fight in my book."

In February, 1946, one month after Scribners had received the revised version of *They Shall Inherit the Laughter,* Jones arrived at his hometown in Illinois. A telegram from Perkins was waiting for him at the home of friends, offering a $500 option on the newly proposed novel, with some further payment to be made after the first 50,000 words had been submitted. WISH TO COOPERATE, Perkins's wire continued, BUT HAVE MORE FAITH IN SECOND NOVEL AND HAVE FURTHER REVISION TO PROPOSE FOR LAUGHTER. Jones greeted the proposal with mixed emotions. "My vanity was hurt and I didn't want to throw the first book away after all the work I had put into it," he said. "But I knew the story of F. Scott Fitzgerald and Thomas Wolfe and how Max Perkins had taken chances and worked wonders with their first novels." After a day or two of deliberation, he telegraphed back: PLACING MYSELF IN YOUR HANDS AND AWAITING LETTER HERE . . . WIRE $500 ANY TIME.

Perkins was pleased with Jones's decision. The new novel was to be the story of a young "go his own way" private named Prewitt coming into contact with First Sergeant Milton Anthony Warden. Perkins believed that Jones had chosen to portray a "perennial character," and said: "It seemed to us from what you said, that you saw something truly important, and that you were right in your interpretation of the nature of that type of man, and that he had never been portrayed in a way to make him understandable."

Jones balked at discarding his first manuscript but finally wrote Perkins:

> I trust your judgment from past knowledge of your work and your tremendous experience with such things that I don't have. And I'm willing to ride along. . . .
>
> I think you probably know a lot more about it than I do, which is why I'm willing to lay it aside for Prewitt. As I said, I'm putting myself in your hands, not Scribners' exactly, but you personally, because I have more faith in your ability to see further and clearer than anybody I've met or heard of in the writing game.

Perkins was as eager as Jones was to present the book to the public. Max expected there would be a new postwar literary movement and he wanted to get Jones's novel published before the new writers would start appearing and begin to crowd the field with second-rate works.

> I don't know that the form of the novel will change much [Perkins wrote Jones], but the spirit and the expression will. Some sense of direction will come in young men who are real writers, almost unconsciously, and as it does, they will formulate it.

Jones had half a dozen private meetings with his editor. "Perkins had an iron control," he recalled. "From the steady way he walked, you could never tell that he was drunk." Max seemed eager to instruct him in writing, using the curriculum he had devised over his decades of experience. Perkins's first piece of advice came from Hemingway, the only survivor of his great triumvirate of the twenties: "Always stop while you are going good. Then when you resume you have the impetus of feeling that what you last did was good. Don't wait until you are baffled and stumped." During his first few months of work on the new novel, Jones found the suggestion invaluable.

Another of the editor's rules of thumb impressed him.

> I remember reading somewhere what I thought was a very true statement [Perkins wrote him], to the effect that anybody could find out if he was a writer. If he were a writer, when he tried to write, out of some particular day, he found in the effort that he could recall exactly how the light fell and how the temperature felt, and all the quality of it. Most people cannot do it. If they can do it, they may never be successful in a pecuniary sense, but that ability is at the bottom of writing, I am sure.

In July, 1946, Jones had enough pages of his novel to show, and he sent them to Perkins, who wrote back this reaction:

> I do not know whether this book will sell, and I think there will be a very hard struggle in cutting it and shaping it up, but I think it exceedingly interesting and valid. The Army is something and I don't think anyone ever approached presenting it in its reality as you have done. I think though that one reason it needs a great deal of cutting is that you explain too much. You give too much exposition. . . . When you come to revise, you must try to make the action and talk (which is a form of action) tell us all, or almost all.

For years Jones remembered the pain he felt when he read the words

"When you come to revise." He said, "They stuck like a barb in my ass." But Perkins's writing lessons were making sense. "Eventually," Jones recalled, "something happened in my head: the concept of a paragraph came to me for the first time. I realized the power I held to raise or lower a reader's emotional level by where I ended a paragraph." At the same time Jones—whose parents died while he was overseas—was becoming increasingly dependent on Perkins. "I was too modest to even think I could ever replace Tom Wolfe—you can only have a first son once," Jones said, "but I had made a father figure out of Max Perkins."

Later in 1946, Jones came up with a title for his novel: *From Here to Eternity*. He told Perkins he had taken it from the Yale "Whiffenpoof Song": "Gentlemen songsters out on a spree, damned from here to eternity . . ." Perkins liked the title very much, but as his daughters could have told Jones, having heard it read to them by their father, the phrase was a refrain from "Gentleman Rankers," one of Kipling's *Barrack-Room Ballads*.

By the end of 1946, Perkins had received over 200 pages of *From Here to Eternity*. That same winter, Perkins's physical condition resumed its deterioration. His cough had developed into gasping attacks. His hands were so palsied that he often apologized for his jagged, occasionally illegible handwriting. He was drinking more than he ever had before.

That some year Perkins took on another young man who had gone to war, Vance Bourjaily. While in the Pacific, Bourjaily had written a play and sent it home to his mother, a successful novelist. She gave the manuscript to her agent, Diarmuid Russell, who in turn sent it to Perkins. After reading the play, Perkins matter-of-factly asked Russell if "this young fellow" wanted to write a novel; then he loaded the question with a cash offer. The agent immediately cabled Bourjaily, relaying Scribners' proposal of a $750 advance for a work of prose. "At that moment," Bourjaily recalled, "I ceased to be a playwright and became a novelist."

Once stateside, Bourjaily wrote the first draft of *The End of My Life*, a novel about a young man's mental and moral disintegration during World War II, which he had deliberately left "tantalizingly unresolved." He quickly revised it and sent it to Perkins. In December, 1946, days after receiving the pages, Max summoned the author.

Max Perkins was by now a legend to every young American author with a book to write, and for the time that Bourjaily was with him, he lived up to the legend. They met at Scribners. Bourjaily found the editor behind

his desk, wearing his hat. Perkins greeted him gruffly, then, without volunteering a word about the manuscript, said, "Well, let's go eat." They went
to Cherio's, where Bourjaily encountered, as James Jones had, a new aspect
of Perkins's behavior. That most modest editor now seemed aware of his
reputation, and for almost two hours, without prompting, spoke of his
work with Fitzgerald, Hemingway, and Wolfe, automatically reciting the
suggestions he had made to them over the years. Bourjaily sat in awe.

The moment their coffee arrived, Perkins turned to the author and
said, "Now about your book—you've got to write a last chapter. You have
to tell us how it comes out. Also the girl Cindy—she's so important a character, you can't wait so long as you do to introduce her. You'll have to write
a first chapter." Within thirty seconds, Bourjaily's manuscript had been
analyzed, two major deficiencies identified, and the solutions specified. He
saw for himself that Max Perkins possessed an "infallible sense of structure," and that for Perkins the discovery of young writers and the editing
of their works were no longer challenging and exciting but, in fact, routine.
Bourjaily said "Yes sir" to both of Perkins's directives, thanked him for the
lunch, and went home to write an opening and closing for his book. It was
published the following year and auspiciously began his enduring writing
career.

One day in January, 1946, having seen little of the Connecticut
countryside since the war began, except what was visible from his commuter train, Max took the car out for a spin, even though he had no driver's
license. "It was too dark a night to see much," Perkins later wrote Hemingway, "and after a while I thought I would come back and do some work,
and so I was driving too fast, I guess. Anyhow—I came around an easy
curve and after a minute saw the shadow of a truck ahead. I don't think
there was a tail light. I thought of skidding around it but a man might have
got out. It stood right in the middle of the road. I did everything I could
with the brake, but I must have hit the truck hard because it certainly
wrecked my car, all the front of it. I got right out, and felt all right except
that to my surprise my nose bled." The two truckers towed Perkins home,
and he felt fine the next day. But the day after, he was so stiff he could
hardly hold the telephone. Just breathing was painful and coughing was
excruciating. A doctor strapped Max's cracked ribs with adhesive, but that
did little good and he resented doctors' remedies anyway. Instead Max
fashioned his own corset with cardboard and cinched it around his chest
with a belt. He wore it for weeks. One of Perkins's daughters insisted
that he no longer drink so much and then drive. Max gave up driving.

For two months he suffered from the pain, but to him suffering was thera-peutic. He applied the same reasoning in arctic weather, when he would walk out to lunch without wearing an overcoat. "Max, aren't you cold?" a concerned colleague asked one day. "Cold?" he growled. "I'm freezing!"

That summer, 1946, Louise was wrongly diagnosed as having gall-stones and underwent surgery. The doctors discovered an ulcer of the duodenum. Her health was feeble for months. Max worried about her, and Charles Scribner started worrying about him. At lunch and in their morning meetings, he could not keep his eyes off Perkins's trembling hands. "He needs a rest badly, but refuses to take a vacation," Scribner wrote Hemingway confidentially. "There does not seem to be anything he wants to do except work. I wish you could lure him away, but for heaven's sake don't tell him that I suggested such an idea."

Hemingway was in Sun Valley with his fourth wife, the former Mary Welsh. She had been a reporter for *Time* and *Life* when they met during the war. They were married within three months of his divorce from Martha Gellhorn. In his next letter to Max, Ernest praised the countryside and ex-tended an invitation to come to Sun Valley. But a short time later, Ernest mentioned Max's condition to a mutual friend, and when Perkins heard that Hemingway thought he was sick, he insisted he was not. To prove it, he worked through the summer, right past his sixty-second birthday in September, and straight through into the new year.

Six years had passed since the publication of his last novel when Ernest Hemingway began work on *The Garden of Eden*. The Hemingway scholar Carlos Baker called this unfinished novel

> an experimental compound of past and present, filled with astonishing ineptitudes and based in part upon memories of his marriages to Hadley and Pauline, with some excursions behind the scenes of his current life with Mary. For his opening chapters he chose the locale of the seaport village of Le Grau-du-Roi at the foot of the Rhône estuary. This was the place in which he had spent his honeymoon with Pauline in May, 1927. Like Ernest at that time, the hero, David Bourne, had been married only three weeks and was the author of a successful novel. His wife Catherine fiercely shared his hungers and his pleasures. He devoted his days to her fanatical desire to tan her body by lying naked on hidden beaches. Their nights were given to experiments with the transfer of sexual identities in which she assumed the name of Pete and he the name of Catherine.

Perkins knew Ernest had been working "damned hard" on the book, but nothing more. Indeed, communications from Ernest had all but ceased. Max was understanding. "It is wonderful that you correspond at all except when you have to," he wrote. "I can't imagine doing a hard day's work at writing and then begin to do letters." Perkins's own letter-writing had fallen off—more than a year had passed since his last letter to Elizabeth Lemmon—as he attended to the disappointing manuscripts that were submitted. Writing letters, he said, "require[s] thought and one does not get time to think anymore."

What Perkins did think about that year was the deaths of more friends. After years of pain, Edward Sheldon finally died. So did the Irish critic and writer, Ernest Boyd, Madeleine Boyd's husband. Even closer to home was the tragic death of one of Max's nieces, who was run down by a bus on Fifth Avenue; Max's daughters were now saying they would never stay in Windsor again because of their memories of being with their cousin there. Perkins had given up Windsor long ago for similar reasons. "I do not see how the English go on living for generation upon generation, forever in the same place," Max wrote a friend, "where so much tragedy must have accumulated."

Charles Scribner's Sons commemorated their hundredth year of "responsible publishing" in 1946 with an informal history of their house entitled *Of Making Many Books*. It was written by Roger Burlingame, whose father had been a senior editor at Scribners when Perkins joined the firm thirty-six years earlier. Burlingame described Scribners' struggle to keep its standards even though the manufacturing costs had risen 100 percent in the last six years, mostly because of increased wages. Elsewhere the refined and gentlemanly business of publishing had yielded to the modern impersonal and statistical methods of operation. Scribners was trying desperately to hold on to its established ways. It was still emphatically a family firm. As president, Charles Scribner worked in the old north office, beneath the portraits of his father and grandfather. He welcomed his visitors, authors and employees, "with a mellowness of humor," Burlingame noted, "which it has taken, perhaps, three generations of experience and renewing youth to evolve." Maxwell Perkins, as he had been for well over a decade, was in command of all editorial affairs, continuing "as he works to doodle portraits of Napoleon which with each passing year bear a more and more convincing resemblance to Maxwell Perkins." And a new generation was settling into place. Scribner's son, the fourth Charles, had taken a desk in the advertising department, and George McKay

Schieffelin, another of old CS's grandsons, was home from the navy and working again for the company. Several others had been taken on, including a young man out of Bowdoin College, Burroughs Mitchell, who would himself become a noted editor.

Some of the younger Scribners employees were worried that Max was losing his touch. Years later the fourth Charles Scribner recalled: "Max was passing up a number of obvious sure things—outstanding books— thereby missing out on good new authors." At the same time, he was taking chances on long shots by certain regular authors, so afraid of disappointing them that he could not bring himself to turn them down. Moreover, the new men at Scribners felt that Perkins did not even want to listen to them. At the editorial conferences, he hardly permitted any of the others to speak up. He himself presented all the prospective books, often in a manner which the fourth Charles Scribner described as "Pickwickian in the extreme." Scribner felt that Perkins was overloading the list with second-rate fiction, and was not alert to the country's new hunger for nonfiction.

On the other hand, Perkins's contemporary John Hall Wheelock said, "With all the considerations before him—artistic, financial and otherwise, Perkins maintained that in the long run, one would do best by publishing the best work that appeared before him. There was the soothing writing, the books that delighted; and there was the writing that instructed, written from an author's vision of reality." Throughout his career, Wheelock said, Max maintained that "it has not yet been decided which is right. Considering both, he insisted that he was simply devoted to talent." Van Wyck Brooks wrote: "If Max was to be remembered many years after he died,— remembered far better than most of the authors he worked for,—it was largely because of his sympathetic understanding and because of the standards he maintained." Perkins was certain that the immortal books addressed themselves to the literate and the masses alike. "The great books," he said, "reach both."

In 1947 Maxwell Perkins was brought one such book. It came to him through a man named Aubrey Burns, who worked for the National Conference of Christians and Jews in San Francisco. "About the middle of December [1946] an unassuming man with a British accent appeared in the NCCJ office in San Francisco," Burns remembered. It was Alan Paton, on leave from South Africa's Department of Education to make an investigative tour of prisons and reform schools around the world. Attracted by the stranger's wit and compassion, Burns insisted that Paton stay with him and his wife, Marigold, as long as he was in northern California. Paton agreed on one condition. "I have in my suitcase the manuscript of a novel," he said, "and I will come only if both of you promise to read it and tell me where it irritates you."

A few evenings later, when they were sitting around the cleared dining room table, Paton reached into his valise and brought forth a manuscript called *Cry, the Beloved Country*. It was a few hundred pages long, penned in a tight cursive. "I found it difficult to read," Burns remembered, "partly because of the handwriting, partly because of the strangeness of the names, but chiefly because it is difficult to read small script through water—tears rose up as from a mountain spring, from one phrase to another, and from one emotion to another." It took Burns only a moment to realize he was reading a work of genius. The novel was the story of a Zulu country pastor in South Africa who had come to the city and discovered that his sister had been forced into prostitution and his brother was on trial for murder. After the trial, two-thirds of the way through the book, the plot largely gave way to a revealing account of apartheid in South Africa.

The Burnses were sure that any publisher would be eager to print this manuscript. But Paton still had to revise the last half and in any case had no time. His fixed itinerary had him leaving on a freighter from Halifax, Canada, back to Cape Town. His money was running low, and he was sure no editor would read an untyped manuscript.

Marigold Burns suggested that Paton leave the manuscript for her to type so that she and her husband might submit it for Paton. Burns said he would write a letter to accompany the first five chapters, explaining that the author could not yet submit his work for publication in its entirety and that he was sending those same pages to five publishers simultaneously as a sample of the work; anyone interested in seeing the whole book had only to respond. Paton accepted the plan and departed. Burns sent out the typed manuscript to five publishers, including Max Perkins at Scribners. For Perkins, Burns wrote a special letter. Thinking of Foxhall Edwards, Burns tried to offer some sense of Paton and said, "Alan [is] a shy person, not inclined to press his own cause." Within days two houses had asked to read the conclusion of the manuscript. Scribners was one of them, and Perkins wrote that he was eager to meet the author. Responding to Burns's description of Paton as modest, Perkins said: "I am extremely shy and I believe we two could get on most comfortably together."

At 4:30 on February 7, 1947, Paton arrived at the Scribner Building in New York and found that Perkins could not have been more wrong about being comfortable to be with. The afternoon was for Paton a bizarre encounter. Paton could not tell whether Perkins was moved by the book or not. Perkins said the book was "biblical," but Paton did not know whether this was praise or just a recital of fact. Toting the manuscript, Max escorted the author to another man on the fifth floor and said, "Charles, we must take this." Only later did Paton realize that the unintroduced co-worker was, in fact, Charles Scribner himself. When Perkins asked Paton if he ever drank, the writer hesitated, wondering if a "biblical" author was expected not to. They went to a bar and had several, but the drinks did not help. Paton's confusion only multiplied. As he later reported to Aubrey Burns:

> He lifted his glass in toast, but he didn't say what the toast was. He told me all about Thomas Wolfe. He said, of course you may not make much money. We can't guarantee that the public will buy. . . . I offered him a second drink, but he paid for that too. He said, you can pay next time, but didn't say when that time would be. I thought I would give a practical turn to the conversation by saying, here's to our association, but beyond drinking, he made no other answer.

Over the last of their drinks Max said that South Africa must be a sad country. Paton asked why and, without knowing of Max's hearing defect, found it odd that Perkins did not respond. "Whether he was just being shy or whether he was in the presence of something strange, I don't know," Paton reported. The "queer party" ended brusquely when Perkins departed to catch his train home to New Canaan. Paton was left so bewildered that he asked Aubrey Burns to write Perkins and find out what he thought of the book.

Editor and author met again the following Monday morning. At that meeting Perkins told Paton, "You are not to worry because you're not going away with a contract. I don't see how Scribners could refuse it." Perkins did not appear so cryptic now, but Paton left for home with only the fuzziest assurances.

During the long voyage, Paton read and reread Thomas Wolfe's novels. Soon after arriving in Johannesburg, he received Max's critique of *Cry, the Beloved Country*. Perkins's comments on paper were surprisingly straightforward. Paton wrote Burns in April, 1947, and told him that Perkins had said the critics would disparage the story because the final third of the book, the exposition on apartheid, came as an anticlimax after the trial scene, the dramatic peak of the novel. Paton told Burns he thought Perkins was right and stood ready to revise. But the Perkins whom Paton was to experience was a very different editor from the man who had labored so patiently with Thomas Wolfe.

In May, Perkins at last sent Paton the contract for *Cry, the Beloved Country*. By then Max had come to realize that in the end

> the real protagonist is the beautiful and tragic land of South Africa, but if you come to the human hero, it is the Zulu pastor, and he is grand. One might say that the last third of the book is something of an anti-climax, but I don't think one should look at it in a conventional way. It gives an extraordinary realization of the country and of the race problem, not as a problem but as a situation. It is a sad book, but that is as it should be. So was the Iliad and so is the Bible. But as Ecclesiastes says, "The earth endureth forever."

Perkins rushed off the manuscript to the printer, then wrote Paton regretfully "that conditions here are such that everything moves very slowly. We do not work enough, that's the truth—too many holidays, and too short hours." When Paton admitted he had failed to recognize the importance of the placing of the climax and offered to cut several scenes in the last half of the book, Perkins told him, "It takes so long anyway to publish a book nowadays that I hate to do anything to slow up the progress." The book was published as written. Perkins was not as demanding of perfection as he once was. Sometimes editing took too much effort now, too much stamina.

Paton resumed his duties in his native land. He wrote Max, "You will be interested to know that you persist in my mind, and that I have a premonition that we shall meet again in the unspeakable and incommunicable prison of this earth."

Cry, the Beloved Country sold exceedingly well and was honored by the critics.

"Do not try to make the brilliant pupil a replica of yourself," Gilbert Highet wrote in *The Art of Teaching*. "If you can send him into the world with frames of reference suggested by you and tricks of craftsmanship which he could get only from you, you will have made him your pupil, as much as he will ever be, and earned a right to his permanent gratitude." Highet cited Perkins in his book as a most "admirable teacher," commenting that a number of great writers would have wasted their talents had Perkins not shown them "how to direct their Vesuvian force."

It was in the spring of 1946 that Perkins, whose teaching had been mainly by mail, allowed himself to be recruited as a classroom instructor by Kenneth D. McCormick, the young editor in Manhattan who was conducting an extension course on publishing for New York University. When he invited him to appear as a guest lecturer, McCormick said many years later, "I promised him a class of young hopefuls, and that excited him."

Storer Lunt, who had recently become president of W. W. Norton and Company, attended the lecture with his company's vice-president and treasurer, Howard Wilson. Lunt said the whole class sat spellbound, and by the end of the evening Lunt felt they believed as he did, that Perkins "was the embodiment of the perfect editor in his time."

"His discourse quietly flowed as James Joyce would write," Lunt recalled, "and I kept thinking now and again of Charles Lamb. Max Perkins was ageless."

McCormick agreed. "By the end of the evening," he said, "Perkins had made a total impact. He snowed his audience in the quietest way, without saying a word to polish his own literary reputation." Over on Broadway, just down the street, *Carousel*, *Oklahoma*, *Born Yesterday*, and *The Glass Menagerie* were playing. After the lecture, as Howard Wilson and Storer Lunt walked past the theater marquees, the one looked at the other and, speaking of Perkins, said: "That was the best show of the season." When Perkins had left to catch his train and the students had dispersed, McCormick sat alone in the empty room and thought of something Booth Tarkington had once said, shortly before he died, about how difficult it had become for him to respond to the writing in books he read. "I know all the tricks," Tarkington remarked; he had spent so many years performing them himself. "In that same way," said McCormick, "I felt that Max knew all the tricks of his trade and he had grown weary of them."

Perkins had rushed Paton, a new author, but he still could summon the old energy for his longtime authors like Marcia Davenport. During the first months of 1947, while working on *East Side, West Side*, she had seen Max several times, mostly for moral support. She told him the book "is too autobiographical fundamentally, and therefore too carefully contrived by me to offset that basic fact, from which I always shy away like a contrary horse. So I am always at war with myself about it and I have a terrible time believing in it." For the sake of discipline and honoring her word to Perkins, she continued to work on it. At a quarter past four in the morning of April 11, she finished her manuscript, and she brought it to Perkins that afternoon. She realized that he looked tired and frail and was alarmed by the marked tremor of his hands. She thought of how, fifteen years earlier, she had circled the block for two hours before she had dropped off *Mozart*. "This time," she told Max, "I am too despairing even to walk around the block. I am just sitting with my head in my hands wondering where I can get a job as a cook."

Mrs. Davenport wanted to get to Prague; she would revise her book there. Before departing, she stopped off at the Scribner Building to pick up the typescript and Max's suggestions for the revision, a 3,000-word critique full of support and advice. "I think you have written a notable book in a first draught but that it needs, as any book, to be revised," he wrote. "The revisions should be almost only a matter of emphasis, for the scheme is right. Having borne the heat of the battle, you must not fail it now."

East Side, West Side tells the life of a writer named Jessie Bourne during a crucial week in her life, when great changes occur externally and within herself. Perkins's long letter contained editorial wisdom that applied not only to Mrs. Davenport's novel but to fiction in general:

> Generalizations are no use—give one specific thing and let the action say it. . . .

> When you have people talking, you have a scene. You must interrupt with explanatory paragraphs but shorten them as much as you can. Dialogue is *action*. . . .

> You tend to explain too much. You must explain, but your tendency is to distrust your own narrative and dialogue. . . .

> You need only to intensify throughout what actually is there—and I think you would naturally do this in revision, anyhow. It is largely a matter of compression, and not so much of that really. . . .

> You can't know a book until you come to the end of it, and then all the rest must be modified to fit that.

"You make the work almost do itself," Marcia Davenport wrote Perkins from Prague. "I think if I had to struggle alone I would give up." The first week of June, less than a month after she had gone to Czechoslovakia, Perkins received ten revised chapters. THINK FIRST 121 PAGES SPLENDID IN REVISION, he cabled.

"It is so queer about this book," she wrote Max. "I have never been able to tell anything about it or whether it is a book at all, and I have to go along like a jackass in a hailstorm content that you are on the job." She asked nothing more of Max than to watch for the Book-of-the-Month Club's reaction. If for any reason they wanted to take her novel on one of their delayed-action arrangements, she said, which might cause it to come out near the publication of Ernest Hemingway's new book, she would flatly refuse. "This book is misery enough for me," she said, "without having it steamrollered by Hem."

Mrs. Davenport need not have worried. Even though he had written close to 1,000 handwritten pages of his novel, Hemingway was a long way from publication. Perkins still knew little about the book.

The better part of a decade had passed since Hemingway had published any significant work and Max had become pessimistic about Ernest's future. Astonishingly, he confided to Louise one day that spring, "Hemingway is through."

In the spring of 1947, William B. Wisdom finally presented to the Harvard College Library the last of the massive collection of Thomas Wolfe material he had been accumulating for almost ten years. It was at once apparent that the perfect person to write an introduction to the papers was Maxwell E. Perkins, Harvard, Class of 1907. Max agreed to prepare an article for the *Harvard Library Bulletin*.

Stealing odd moments to write, Perkins continued his work with James Jones, who was living in Illinois and inching ahead with *From Here to Eternity*. Max did not know the book well enough yet to visualize it as a whole, but in a letter that May, he was able to make a few observations. Jones would always remember one of them especially. If an author worried too much about plot, Max said, he might become "sort of muscle-bound," whereas he must be flexible. "A deft man may toss his hat across the office and hang it on a hook if he just naturally does it," Perkins wrote, "but he will always miss if he does it consciously. That is a ridiculous and extreme analogy, but there is something in it."

That letter, full of warmth and belief as well as good advice, meant a great deal to Jones. "It made me feel like one of his boys," he said. "That did it."

"I certainly want to come to New York," Jones wrote Perkins, "at least for a while to see you. I feel there is so much I can learn from you that will help me." Perkins never received Jones's letter.

On Thursday, June 12, 1947, Charles Scribner had lunch with Perkins. Max seemed utterly exhausted, as he had all month, full of fits and twitches. But he still refused to take time off. The following day, he had tea with Caroline Gordon Tate. They discussed her husband's forthcoming volume of collected poems and several anthologies of fiction and essays that the Tates were doing together. That evening, Perkins went home to New Canaan, his briefcase bulging with manuscripts and galley proofs for the weekend's reading. By Sunday evening he felt uncomfortable enough to complain. He was running a fever of 103, and his cough was bad. He and Louise thought it was an attack of pleurisy. Next morning, despite her protests, Max got up to go to his office. He ran his bath but was barely strong enough to unbutton his pajamas. By that afternoon Louise suspected that he had pneumonia and called an ambulance. As the attendant came upstairs with a stretcher, Perkins carefully instructed his daughter Bertha to take the two manuscripts by his bed—one of them *Cry, the Beloved Country*, the other, pages of *From Here to Eternity*—and put them in Miss Wyckoff's hands, "and no one else's." As he was being carried out of the house, he called for the cook, who for years had lovingly catered to his picky eating habits, and she hurried to see him to the door. He looked at her from the stretcher, smiled and said, as though he knew, "Good-bye, Eleanor."

"Good-bye, Mr. Perkins. You look beautiful," she assured him.

In truth his face was drawn and wan. He looked like a dying man. Shortly after he arrived at the Stamford Hospital he was found to have an advanced infection of pleurisy and pneumonia. His chest contracted in pain with every cough. Max helplessly thrashed his arms trying to rip away the smothering oxygen tent that enclosed him. "If I could only have a drink!" he kept crying out, knowing that it would loosen him up. But hospital regulations forbade cocktails.

Louise sat at her husband's side through the night. The doctors predicted Perkins's recovery, but penicillin proved powerless against his fatigue with life itself. In the early hours of the morning there seemed to be less strain to his uneven wheezing. Louise, sensing it was the end, pulled up closer to the bed and murmured his favorite lines from Shakespeare, the lament from *Cymbeline*:

Fear no more the heat o' the sun,
     Nor the furious winter's rages;
Though thy worldly task hast done,
     Home art gone, and ta'en thy wages;
Golden lads and girls all must,
As chimney-sweepers, come to dust.

Perkins used to say that he wouldn't mind being dead but dreaded the process of dying. He drifted in and out of sleep. He was as restless as Tolstoi's dying Prince Andrei, who, aware of some dreadful "thing" that was forcing its way into his room, crawled out of his bed and propped himself against the door.

> Once again *it* pushed from the outside. His last superhuman efforts were vain and both halves of the door noiselessly opened. *It* entered, and it was death . . .

At five o'clock in the morning of Tuesday, June 17, Max lurched up from his bed as though startled by something that had quietly made its way through the door and was standing, waiting, in the morning's first light. Only Louise was in the room, but he called out to two of their daughters. "Peggoty! Nancy!" Motioning toward the corner, he asked, "Who *is* that?" He fell back on the bed and died.

Although everyone at Scribners knew that Perkins had been slowly dying, his death stunned them all. "I never had a better friend," Charles Scribner wrote Hemingway. On Wednesday, the eighteenth, he assembled the company's editorial staff and divided up the responsibilities which Perkins had long shouldered. Scribner realized his greatest task was "to do all in my power in the next days to fill the void that he left in our organization." John Hall Wheelock was to assume most of Perkins's responsibilities. Fortunately, Wallace Meyer and Burroughs Mitchell, Perkins's latest choice, were there to carry on. Scribner immediately ordered more young men from the lower floors up to the fifth. The editors wrote to their newly assigned authors and did their best to comfort them. "Fortunately," Scribner told Hemingway, "the best of [them] have decided that it is now up to them to go on writing and do their best, as that would be what Max would have wished." Hemingway, who had lost several friends that year, remarked to Charles Scribner that it looked as though "our Heavenly Father was perhaps dealing off the bottom of the deck." He would honor Perkins five years later by dedicating *The Old Man and the Sea* to him.

Elizabeth Lemmon had given up astrology years earlier, because of all the disasters she had foreseen in the lives of friends and relatives. The morning after Perkins died, her sister read his obituary in the *New York Times* and rushed to the Church House. She stood in the doorway of her sister's bedroom and said nothing more than, "Oh, Beth." Elizabeth sat up and said, "Max is dead." Days later she wrote Louise. "I have known people who were considered pillars of strength and loved to be leaned on," she said, "but Max poured strength into people and made them stand on their own feet." From that time forth, she kept every letter Max had ever sent her, arranged chronologically, in a shoebox in her bedroom.

At twelve o'clock on Thursday, June 19, 1947, the funeral of Maxwell Evarts Perkins was held at St. Mark's in New Canaan. Some of the 250 mourners had to stand outside the crowded little Episcopal church. Evartses and Perkinses were there, along with Scribners and the staff, friends from New Canaan, and many others, including Stark Young, Allen and Caroline Gordon Tate, and Hamilton Basso. Chard Powers Smith said he had "never attended a funeral where so many worldly people were crying and concealing it badly." Hemingway could not be there because of family obligations. Zelda wrote Louise a letter full of comforting religious sentiments. Marcia Davenport was in Prague finishing *East Side, West Side*, which she dedicated to Perkins. Taylor Caldwell, upon hearing of Max's death, collapsed and was sent to the hospital. Max's friend for more than fifty-five years, Van Wyck Brooks, had been seriously ill himself; he had written Louise that his doctor would not allow him to attend the funeral, but, he said, "I shall be thinking of nothing else,—and I shall think of little else for a very long time." Perkins was buried that afternoon in nearby Lakeview Cemetery, as was his wish. Later, Louise had a High Mass said for him.

James Jones's letter arrived at Perkins's office almost a week after the funeral. When Max's authors had been divided among the staff, Jones had been overlooked. Not until some days later, when Wheelock wrote him, did he know that Perkins had died. Jones wrote Wheelock back, "I have had the feeling for a long time that I should come to New York, that he might die, that I should not selfishly but for writing go where he was because there was so much that I could learn from him. But as I said, life does not ever put two such things together; his time of that was with Thomas Wolfe and not with me." For days Jones kept thinking of that phrase that drew him to writing in the first place.—"O lost, and by the wind grieved, ghost." *From Here to Eternity* would not appear until 1951. Its great success was a final confirmation of Max's gift.

Buried under piles of papers on Perkins's desk was the Introduction to the Thomas Wolfe Collection that he had written for the Harvard Library and had been going over. As Tom's deathbed letter to Perkins became his last written words, so did Max's own memorial to Thomas Wolfe become the final words that he edited.

For months after Max died, Louise was adrift. Unanchored without him, she felt lonely and vulnerable. She began having difficulty falling asleep in the upstairs bedroom she had shared with Max and so had special locks installed on all the doors. She had the whole house renovated, adding a connecting apartment. During this period the Church was her support. She talked of entering a convent. Old friends got letters telling of how she prayed that her husband's soul would receive the mercy and love of God. Molly Colum wrote Van Wyck Brooks that summer: "She writes like an old nun. . . . Does Louise really believe she knew as much about God as Max did?"

Five years later, after Caribbean cruises, religious pilgrimages, and trips to Europe, Louise was still living restlessly in New Canaan. In June of 1952, her eldest daughter, Bertha, and her son-in-law agreed to move into the family house, and Louise settled into the apartment.

Now in her sixties, she developed a drinking problem. "I feel like such a hypocrite," she confessed to Elizabeth Lemmon, "going to Mass every morning and getting drunk every night."

On Sunday, February 21, 1965, firemen were summoned to the New Canaan house at 56 Park Street, where they found smoke pouring from Louise Perkins's apartment. Her cigarette had set fire to the chair in which she had been sitting. She was rushed to the Norwalk Hospital, suffering from third-degree burns and smoke asphyxiation. She died that night.

A Requiem Mass was offered for her at eleven A.M. the following Wednesday in St. Aloysius's Church. As a light snow fell, Louise Saunders Perkins was buried by her husband's side. Their stones are plainly marked with their names and dates and simple crosses at the top. They overlook a tranquil pond, smaller than the one that still mirrors Paradise, around which Max used to take their daughters when he did not have time for a real walk.

Acknowledgments

Ⅰt is too soon to measure the achievement of an editor like Maxwell Perkins. That achievement is a part of the literary history of our day here in America," John Hall Wheelock wrote in 1950 in the introduction of *Editor to Author*. When I began researching this biography in 1971, I found, to my amazement, that Perkins's career still had been neither chronicled nor evaluated and that whole aspects of his life remained shadowy even to people who had been close to him.

To avoid secondhand facts as much as possible, I have relied almost exclusively on primary source material: tens of thousands of letters Perkins wrote and received; manuscripts he edited; interviews with those who knew him. Scores of people assisted me in both the gathering and the interpretation of information about Maxwell Perkins and in transposing that information into this book. To those named below and those too numerous to list, I offer my deepest gratitude and sincerest hope that this work compensates them for the time and effort they invested.

I am deeply indebted to Louise and Max Perkins's five daughters—Mrs. John Frothingham, Elisabeth Gorsline, Mrs. Robert King, Mrs. George Owen, and Mrs. Reid Jorgensen. Each of them took me into her home and lavished information and hospitality upon me. They made no demands and imposed no restrictions. For six years they have been more than sources of material; they became sustaining friends.

Three more of Max Perkins's relatives gave generous amounts of time and information as well. His sister Mrs. Archibald Cox, his brother Edward N. Perkins, and his niece Joan Terrall supplied me with wonderful insights and anecdotes. Mrs. Terrall, above all, kept me on the track in the earliest days of research, when there seemed to be countless trails to follow.

I am equally indebted to two of Max Perkins's dearest friends, John Hall Wheelock and Elizabeth Lemmon. The eloquent Mr. Wheelock gave so much of himself, racking his brain to recall specific moments of the last ninety years, that my long interviews with him invariably ended with his head literally aching from the effort. The charming Miss Lemmon was equally generous. Her shoebox full of personal letters from Perkins—my "Aspern Papers"—were matched in value only by the innumerable hours of delightful talk she contributed to this project.

Malcolm Cowley assisted me in three important ways: His *New Yorker* profile of Perkins, "Unshaken Friend," published in 1944, was the most comprehensive account of Perkins's life to date. It proved to be a handy Baedeker during my early wanderings. Mr. Cowley also gave generously of his time, answering dozens of queries both in interviews and letters. Finally, he provided me with the comprehensive notes he made while composing "Unshaken Friend."

The greatest single collection of Perkins material is, of course, the archives of Charles Scribner's Sons, which are housed in the Princeton University Library. For permission to roam freely through the blue boxes of letters, I am grateful to Charles Scribner, Jr. In addition, he supplied me with hours of his own recollections of Perkins, assistance in reaching other people who knew him, and a desk at which to work while I raked the file cabinets on the fifth floor of the Scribner Building in New York City. I am also obliged to Burroughs Mitchell, who assisted me in the early stages of researching and writing this book. Heartfelt thanks to Irma Wyckoff Muench, Maxwell Perkins's secretary of twenty-five years and executrix of his estate, for her remembrances and many special favors.

For interviews, informative correspondence, legal permissions, supplying letters and other information pertaining to Maxwell Perkins, I am grateful to: LeBaron R. Barker, Jr., Elizabeth Cox Bigelow, Judge John Biggs, Jr., Dr. John Bordley, Vance Bourjaily, Nancy Hale Bowers, Madeleine Boyd, Carol Brandt, Prof. Matthew J. Bruccoli, Aubrey Burns, Katherine Newlin Burt, Nathaniel Burt, Erskine Caldwell, Taylor Caldwell, Melville Cane, Cass Canfield, Marguerite Cohn, Corinne Cornish, Edla Cusick, Marcia Davenport, Dr. Josephine Evarts Demarest,

Elizabeth and Prescott Evarts, Katherine Evarts, Richard C. Evarts, Anne Geismar, Martha Gellhorn, Paul Gitlin, Arnold Gingrich, Sheilah Graham, Christine Weston Griswold, Laura Guthrie Hearne, Dr. Gregory Hemingway, Mary Hemingway, Katharine Hepburn, Mary Iacovella, Reid Jorgensen, Matthew Josephson, Frances Kellogg, Dr. Robert King, Jean Lancaster, Ring Lardner, Jr., Alice Roosevelt Longworth, Storer Lunt, Archibald MacLeish, Kenneth D. McCormick, Wallace Meyer, Hadley R. Mowrer, Robert Nathan, George Owen, Alan Paton, Emily Perkins, Marjorie Morton Prince, David Randall, Diarmuid Russell, Robert Ryan, William Savage, Herman Scheying, George Schieffelin, Scottie Fitzgerald Smith, Elizabeth Streeten, H. N. Swanson, Allen Tate, Caroline Gordon Tate, Edward Thomas, Margaret Turnbull, Howard White, Edmund Wilson, and Elizabeth Youngstrom. Special thanks to Maxwell Geismar and James Jones, who often seemed to be paying back their personal debts to Max Perkins through me.

Most of my library research was done in the Rare Books and Manuscripts Room of Firestone Library at Princeton University. I am indebted to Alexander Clark, Wanda Randall, and the rest of the staff for their assistance and kindness during my months there. I received equally efficient and courteous service at the Houghton Library at Harvard University; special thanks to Rodney Dennis and Marte Shaw. Neda Westlake at the University of Pennsylvania Library and Diana Haskell at the Newberry Library also acted above and beyond the call of duty.

For access to Maxwell Perkins's transcript, records, and other information related to his years at Harvard, thanks to the Office of the Registrar, particularly Phyllis Stevens.

I am also grateful to several personal friends for their loyalty and generosity over the last seven years: Alan D. Brinkley, Ann Brinkley, Constance Congdon, Ann Douglas, George Forgie, McKinley C. McAdoo, Paul F. Mickey, Jr., and my grandparents Rose and George M. Freedman.

Ralph L. Stanley, my best friend, never lost faith in what he called *The Book;* almost singlehandedly he pulled me through the major crises. Colleen Keegan also inspired me. *The Book* is theirs as much as it is mine.

In the thirty years since Maxwell Perkins's death, much has been said about the business of publishing overtaking the art. Notwithstanding, at E. P. Dutton I found many people who still treasure literature as much as ever. I am especially grateful to Ann La Farge and Deborah Prigoff for their editorial contributions and friendship.

Thomas B. Congdon, Jr., the editor of this book, undertook a doubly awesome responsibility: He had a massive manuscript to work with, and he unavoidably risked comparison to the master of his profession. He poured his time and special talents into this book, providing unfailing support and imaginative advice—in the true Perkins spirit—from the moment he met me in 1973.

Finally, my greatest thanks to those named on the dedication page. Without the constant encouragement and counsel of Prof. Carlos Baker, my former adviser at Princeton—where my first work on Perkins emerged as a senior thesis—this book might not have been started. Without the love and support of my parents, Barbara and Richard Berg, it might never have been finished.

Los Angeles   A. SCOTT BERG
1978

Front cover illustration by A. Birnbaum
© 1944 The New Yorker Magazine, Inc.
All rights reserved.

Sources and Notes

Most of the sources cited below are part of the archives of Charles Scribner's Sons. With few exceptions, the files for Scribners' living authors are in their New York offices; the files of those deceased are in the Rare Books and Manuscripts department of the Princeton University Library. The files generally include the original manuscript letters as received and carbon copies of outgoing letters.

The Princeton Library houses most of the Fitzgeraldiana. Other important collections used in this biography include: the William B. Wisdom Collection of Thomas Wolfe's papers in Houghton Library at Harvard University; Van Wyck Brooks's letters and notebooks at the C. P. Van Pelt Library of the University of Pennsylvania; and Malcolm Cowley's notes at the Newberry Library in Chicago. Nearly all of Maxwell Perkins's letters to family and friends are in private hands.

All book citations are to the first edition, except where otherwise noted. Information obtained through interviews has been designated with an (I).

The following abbreviations have been used:

AB	Aline Bernstein	BSF	Bertha Saunders Frothingham (MP's daughter)
AMF	*A Moveable Feast* by Ernest Hemingway (New York: Scribners, 1964)	Car. Mag.	MP's article "Scribners and Tom Wolfe" (The *Carolina Maga-*
ASB	A. Scott Berg		

zine, October, 1938)

			April 1 and 8, 1944)
CS	Charles Scribner	MKR	Marjorie Kinnan
CSS	Charles Scribner's Sons		Rawlings
CU	"The Crack-Up" by	MP	Maxwell Perkins
	F. Scott Fitzgerald	NJ	Nancy Jorgensen
	(New York: New		(MP's daughter)
	Directions, 1945)	*OMMB*	*Of Making Many Books*
DSF	Douglas Southall		by Roger Burlingame
	Freeman		(New York: Scribners,
EEG	Elisabeth Evarts		1946)
	Gorsline (MP's	PK	Peggy King
	daughter)		(MP's daughter)
EH	Ernest Hemingway	RL	Ring Lardner
EL	Elizabeth Lemmon	SA	Sherwood Anderson
EN	Elizabeth Nowell	SG	Sheilah Graham
EW	Edmund Wilson	*SN*	*The Story of a Novel* by
FSF	F. Scott Fitzgerald		Thomas Wolfe (New
HLB	MP's article "Thomas		York: Scribners, 1936)
	Wolfe" (*Harvard*	TC	Taylor Caldwell
	Library Bulletin,	TW	Thomas Wolfe
	Autumn, 1947)	VWB	Van Wyck Brooks
JHW	John Hall Wheelock	VWB Auto	The one-volume edition
JJ	James Jones		of Brooks's *Scenes &*
JO	Jane Owen		*Portraits, Days of the*
	(MP's daughter)		*Phoenix,* and *From the*
JPM	John P. Marquand		*Shadow of the*
LSP	Louise Saunders Perkins		*Mountain* (New York:
MB	Madeleine Boyd		Dutton, 1965)
MC	Malcolm Cowley	*YCGHA*	*You Can't Go Home*
MC notes	The notes MC made		*Again* by Thomas
	while preparing his		Wolfe (New York:
	Profile of MP		Harpers, 1940)
	(*The New Yorker,*	ZSF	Zelda Sayre Fitzgerald

I. THE REAL THING

MP's speech: Kenneth D. McCormick to ASB (I), June 6, 1973, and June 3, 1975; Storer Lunt to ASB, June 22, 1975; BSF to ASB (I), June 1, 1975. MP had rendered in writing several of the stories and comments he related that night. In such instances I have quoted from the printed texts for the sake of reproducing his exact words: MP to TW, Jan. 16, 1937; *Car. Mag.,* p. 16.

Other comments: "as slow as an ox": EEG to ASB (I), Dec. 15, 1911; "It's so simple . . .": JO to ASB, Aug. 1, 1972. Foxhall Edwards first appears in *YCGHA,* p. 16; description: p. 42.

II. PARADISE

Scribner Building: *New York Times,* May 18, 1913, III, 7:4; JHW to ASB (I), June 5, 1975. The building was designed by Ernest Flagg, CS II's brother-in-law.

CSS profile: MC to ASB (I), May 18, 1972; JHW to ASB (I), Apr. 3, 1972; Charles A. Madison, *Book Publishing in America* (New York: McGraw-Hill, 1966), p. 94; CS II to L. W. Bangs, July 19, 1906, quoted in A. Walton Litz, "Maxwell Perkins as Critic," *Editor Author and Publisher* (Toronto: 1969), p. 98; PK to ASB (I), Mar. 28, 1972; William C. Brownell to Edith Wharton, n.d., quoted in R. W. B. Lewis, *Edith Wharton* (New York: Harper & Row, 1975), p. 133; MP to LSP, n.d.

FSF and "The Romantic Egotist": FSF, "Who's Who—and Why," *Saturday Evening Post,* Sept. 18, 1920, p. 61; Shane Leslie to CS II, May 6, 1918; *OMMB,* p. 67; MP to FSF, Aug. 19, 1918; MP to FSF, Sept. 16, 1919; MP to Alice Dixon Bond (literary editor for the Boston *Herald*), July 17, 1944.

FSF in love with ZSF: FSF, *Ledger,* p. 173; FSF to ZSF, ca. Feb. 20, 1919.

Revision and resubmission of *This Side of Paradise*: JHW to ASB (I), Oct. 20, 1971; FSF to MP, July 26, 1919; FSF to MP, Aug. 16, 1919; MP to FSF, July 28, 1919; FSF to MP, Sept. 4, 1919; FSF to MP, Aug. 16, 1919.

Acceptance of *This Side of Paradise*: JHW to ASB (I), June 5, 1975; MP to FSF, Sept. 16, 1919; FSF, "Early Success," *CU,* p. 86; FSF to MP, Sept. 18, 1919; MP to FSF, Sept. 23, 1919.

FSF making money and writing short stories: MP to FSF, Dec., 1919; FSF to MP, ca. Nov. 15, 1919; Andrew Turnbull, *Scott Fitzgerald* (New York: Scribners, 1962), p. 62; FSF to MP, ca. Jan. 10, 1920; MP to FSF, Jan. 17, 1920.

This Side of Paradise publication: MC, "Unshaken Friend," *The New Yorker,* Apr. 8, 1944, p. 30; *OMMB,* p. 68; Mizener, *Far Side of Paradise,* p. 119; *Publishers Weekly,* Apr. 17, 1920; FSF to Lorena and Philip McQuillan (his aunt and uncle), Dec. 28, 1920; H. L. Mencken, "Books More or Less Amusing," *The Smart Set,* Aug., 1920, p. 140; Mark Sullivan, *Our Times,* vol. 6 (New York: Scribners, 1935), pp. 386–87; FSF, *This Side of Paradise,* p. 304; FSF, "Early Success," *CU,* pp. 87–88; CS II to Shane Leslie, Dec. 29, 1920; *OMMB,* pp. 112, 137.

After publication: FSF to MP, Apr. 29, 1920; CS II to Shane Leslie, Dec. 29, 1920; FSF to MP, ca. June 10, 1920. Fitzgerald's other titles for *Flappers and Philosophers* were: *We Are Seven, Table d'Hote, A La Carte, Journeys and Journey's End, Bittersweet,* and *Shortcake.*

MP sending VWB's book: James Jones to ASB (I), Mar. 3, 1972; MP to FSF, June 29, 1920; FSF to MP, July 7, 1920; Robert Sklar, *F. Scott Fitzgerald:*

The Last Laocoön (New York: Oxford University Press, 1967), p. 138; FSF, *Tales of the Jazz Age,* p. ix.

Windsor: Frances E. Cox, "The Fairs," *Vermonter,* Aug., 1967, p. 24; EEG to ASB (I), Dec. 15, 1971; NJ to ASB, Aug. 26, 1974; PK to ASB (I), Mar. 28, 1972.

III. PROVENANCE

MP's ancestry: VWB Auto, pp. 30, 33, 34; *Dictionary of American Biography,* vol. III, pp. 215, 217, vol. VII, pp. 464–65; Charles Francis Adams, *Richard Henry Dana: A Biography* (Cambridge: Houghton Mifflin, 1891), p. 26; Henry Adams, *The Education of Henry Adams* (New York: Random House, Modern Library edition, 1931), pp. 249-50; Dr. Josephine Evarts Demarest to ASB (I), Mar. 20, 1972; Joan Terrall to ASB (I), Mar. 19, 1972.

MP childhood: Fanny Cox to ASB (I), May 20, 1972; Edward N. Perkins to ASB (I), May 15, 1972; MP to VWB, n.d. (ca. 1904); PK to ASB (I), Mar. 29, 1972; MP to BSF, Aug. 24, 1927; MP to EL, June 1, 1945; EEG to ASB (I), June 11, 1973.

MP at Harvard: MP, "Varied Outlooks," Harvard *Advocate,* vol. 83 (1907), p. 19; MC notes; PK to ASB (I), Mar. 27 and 29, 1972; Richard C. Evarts to ASB (I), Nov. 10, 1971; MC to ASB (I), May 18, 1972; VWB Auto, pp. 101, 103; Adams, *Education of Henry Adams,* p. 29; MP to Thomas Wisdom, Aug. 17, 1943; MP to EL, Aug. 16, 1926; Walter Lippmann, Harvard *Crimson,* Apr. 27, 1950, quoted in J. Donald Adams, *Copey of Harvard* (Boston: Houghton Mifflin, 1960), p. 101; MP to EL, Dec. 23, 1941; MP to William Lyon Phelps, Mar. 26, 1943; Gladys Brooks to ASB (I), Mar. 20, 1972; MP to Charles T. Copeland, July 20, 1920; Marjorie Morton Prince to ASB (I), Nov. 15, 1971.

Besides the Stylus, Perkins was also a member of the St. Paul's Society, the Fencing Club, the Union Club, the Signet Club, and the Hasty Pudding-Institute of 1770. MP's articles in the Harvard *Advocate* were: "On Getting Up in the Morning," vol. 80, pp. 83–85; "On Bluffing," vol. 80, pp. 127–30; "On Taking Things Easy," vol. 81, pp. 102–04; "On Girls and Gallantry," vol. 81, pp. 119–20. He also wrote a short story entitled "A Box of Cigars" for the *Advocate,* vol. 81, pp. 104–06.

MP at the *New York Times*: VWB Auto, p. 129; MP to LSP, n.d.; MP to Nicholas Murray Butler, June 26, 1946; EEG to ASB (I), Dec. 3, 1971; MP to LSP, n.d. (ca. 1909); MP, ms. of speech, prob. May 12, 1927.

LSP and courtship: LSP, "A Long Walk to Church," unpublished ms.; BSF to ASB (I), Mar. 17 and June 1, 1975; EL to ASB (I), Apr. 25, 1972, and May 23, 1975; PK to ASB (I), Mar. 27 and 28, 1972; Fanny Cox to ASB (I), Oct. 31, 1971.

MP getting job at CSS: Barrett Wendell to CS II, Dec. 13, 1909; MP to CS II, Dec. 18, 1909; Poyntz Tyler, ms. of "Puritan in Babylon" for *Town & Country*, p. 1; Edward N. Perkins to ASB (I), May 15, 1972.

MP's engagement and early marriage: MP to JO, Aug. 1, 1927; PK to ASB (I), Mar. 27 and 29, 1972; Andrew Turnbull, *Thomas Wolfe* (New York: Scribners, 1967), p. 240; EL to ASB (I), Apr. 12 and 14, 1972; Dr. Josephine Evarts Demarest to ASB (I), Mar. 20, 1972; MP to VWB, May 14, 1916.

MP's ushers at his wedding were Harvard friends Walter G. Oakman (who threw a festive bachelor dinner at the Union Club the night before), John B. Pierce, his former roommate, William Lawrence Saunders, II, a cousin of LSP; and MP's brothers Charles C. and Edward N. Perkins. LSP's bridesmaids were her sister Jean Saunders and cousin Emily Saunders, who later married MP's brother Charles. "The bride's gown," reported the Plainfield *Press*, Dec. 31, 1910, "was of white satin, trimmed with old lace worn by her grandmother. She wore a tulle veil, caught up with orange blossoms, and carried a bouquet of white orchids." MP's uncle, the Rev. Prescott Evarts of Cambridge, Mass., performed the service.

MP as a father: Joan Terrall to ASB (I), Dec. 5, 1971; MP to EEG, Sunday, Sept. 14 (prob. 1917).

IV. BRANCHING OUT

FSF, 1920–1921: EW, "Imaginary Conversations," *New Republic*, Apr. 30, 1924, pp. 249, 253; FSF, *Ledger*, p. 174; FSF to CS II, Aug. 12, 1920; FSF to MP, Dec. 2, 1920; FSF to MP, Dec. 31, 1920; FSF to MP, Feb. 13, 1921; MP to FSF, May 2, 1921; MP to FSF, Oct. 13, 1920; MP to John Galsworthy, Aug. 2, 1921; FSF to Shane Leslie, May 24, 1921; FSF to MP, Aug. 25, 1921; MP to FSF, Aug. 31, 1921; MP to FSF, Nov. 1, 1921.

The Beautiful and Damned: FSF to MP, Oct. 20, 1921; MP to FSF, Oct. 26, 1921; FSF to MP, Oct. 28, 1921; MP to FSF, Dec. 6, 1921; FSF to MP, ca. Dec. 10, 1921; MP to FSF, Dec. 12, 1921; FSF to MP, ca. Dec. 22, 1921; FSF, unpublished fragment of *The Beautiful and Damned;* FSF to MP (telegram), Dec. 23, 1921; MP to FSF (telegram), Dec. 27, 1921; MP to FSF, Dec. 27, 1921; MP to FSF, Dec. 31, 1921; FSF to MP, ca. Mar. 5, 1922; MP to FSF, Apr. 17, 1922.

Tales of the Jazz Age: MP to FSF, May 8, 1922; FSF to MP, May 11, 1922; MP to EEG, Aug. 17, 1922; MP to FSF, Jan. 6, 1922.

First stage of *The Great Gatsby*: FSF to MP, ca. June 20, 1922.

The Vegetable: FSF to MP, ca. Aug. 12, 1922; MP, "Comment on 'Frost,'" ca. Dec. 26, 1922; FSF, *Ledger*, p. 177; FSF to MP, ca. Nov. 5, 1923; MP to CS II, Dec. 21, 1923.

Brownell's comment on editing: *OMMB*, p. x.

Meeting and editing Ring Lardner: MP to RL, July 2, 1923; John Chapin Mosher, "That Sad Young Man," *The New Yorker,* Nov. 17, 1926, p. 20; EEG to ASB (I), Dec. 15, 1971; Ring Lardner, Jr., to ASB (I), Apr. 4, 1972; RL to MP, Feb. 2, 1924; MP to RL, Mar. 17, 1924; MP to RL, Mar. 24, 1924; EW, *The Twenties* (New York: Farrar, Straus and Giroux, 1975), pp. 186–87; RL, *How to Write Short Stories,* pp. 1, 143; MP to RL, June 25, 1924.

MP and John Biggs: John Biggs to ASB (I), Dec. 12, 1971.

John P. Marquand: JPM, apparently an article for Booksellers Convention, ca. 1922; Richard C. Evarts to ASB (I), Nov. 10, 1971; MP to JPM, Nov. 23, 1923; JPM to Henry Allen Moe, June 25, 1947; MP to JPM, Jan. 20, 1926; JPM to Roger Burlingame, May 28, 1925; Roger Burlingame to JPM, June 1, 1925; MP to JPM, Oct. 14, 1926; MP to JPM, Feb. 3, 1927; JPM to MP, Nov. 2, 1926.

Will James and MP's hat: Will James, quoted in Kunitz and Haycraft, eds., *The Junior Book of Authors* (1951), p. 171; also quoted in Kunitz and Haycraft, eds., *Twentieth Century Authors,* p. 717; MP to EL, Dec. 12, 1925; MP to Will James, May 22, 1931; MP, "Compleat Commuter," ms., n.d.

James Boyd: MP to CS II, Dec. 21, 1923.

Thomas Boyd: FSF to MP, Feb. 9, 1922; MP to Woodward Boyd, Mar. 30, 1922; MP to Betty Grace Boyd, Mar. 10, 1943; MP to FSF, Oct. 7, 1921; MC notes; Thomas Boyd to FSF n.d.; Thomas Boyd to FSF n.d. (ca. spring, 1923); *OMMB,* p. 320.

Arthur Train: Arthur Train, quoted in Grant Overton's *American Night's Entertainment* (New York: D. Appleton & Co., 1923), p. 100; MP to Arthur Train, Oct. 22, 1919; Arthur Train, *My Day in Court* (New York: Scribners, 1939), pp. 387, 394; FSF to MP, June 18, 1924.

MP and editing: MP to BSF, Aug. 31, 1920; Byron Dexter to MC, Mar. 2, 1943 (MC notes); MP to CS II, Feb. 26, 1924; JHW, Introduction, Maxwell Evarts Perkins, *Editor to Author: The Letters of Maxwell E. Perkins* (New York: Scribners, 1950), p. 3; Robert Nathan to ASB (I), Dec. 1, 1974.

V. A NEW HOUSE

Writing and editing *The Great Gatsby*: FSF to MP, ca. Apr. 10, 1924; MP to FSF, June 5, 1924; MP to FSF, Apr. 16, 1924; MP to FSF, Apr. 7, 1924; FSF, "My Lost City," *CU,* p. 29; MP to Galsworthy, Dec. 13, 1929; ZSF to MP, n.d. (ca. May, 1924); FSF to MP, ca. Aug. 25, 1924; FSF to MP, ca. Oct. 10, 1924; FSF to MP, Oct. 27, 1924; MP to FSF, Nov. 17, 1924; MP to FSF, Nov. 14, 1924; MP to FSF, Nov. 20, 1924; FSF to MP, ca. Dec. 1, 1924; FSF to MP, ca. Dec. 20, 1924; FSF, ms. of *The Great Gatsby,* p. 52; FSF, *The Great Gatsby,* pp. 58, 152, 161; *OMMB,* p. 68; FSF to MP, ca. Feb. 18, 1925; FSF to MP, Jan. 24, 1925; EL to ASB (I), Apr. 7, 1975; EL to ASB, Apr. 24, 1973.

MP meets Elizabeth Lemmon: EL to ASB (I), Apr. 14, 1972, Apr. 7 and

8, 1975, May 24 and 25, 1975; MP to EL, Apr. 14, 1922; LSP to EL, May 5, 1922; MP to EL, Oct. 7, 1922. Reputedly, the best dancer in Baltimore in those days was Eleanor House.

Douglas Southall Freeman: DSF to MP, Feb. 1, 1923; MP to DSF, Feb. 3, 1923; MP to EL, June 3, 1924; MP to EL, Aug. 5, 1924.

Ring Lardner: MP to FSF, Aug. 8, 1924; MP to Thomas Boyd, Aug. 15, 1924; MP to FSF, Dec. 19, 1924; RL to MP, Dec. 2, 1924; RL, "The Other Side," *What of It?*, pp. 11, 18; MP to RL, June 1, 1925; Ring Lardner, Jr., *The Lardners* (New York: Harper & Row, 1976), p. 174; RL to MP, Dec. 2, 1924; MP to RL, Mar. 16, 1925; RL to MP, Mar. 17, 1925; FSF to MP, ca. May 8, 1926; MP to FSF, Nov. 25, 1925; MP to RL, June 10, 1926; RL to MP, June 12, 1926; MP to RL, Nov. 22, 1926; RL, *The Story of a Wonderman* (New York: Scribners, 1927), p. 29; MP to RL, Jan. 10, 1927; MP to RL, Jan. 18, 1927; MP to RL, May 6, 1927; MP to RL, Aug. 29, 1924.

MP's new house: MP to FSF, Aug. 8, 1924; MP to Thomas Boyd, July 7, 1924 and Aug. 15, 1924; PK to ASB (I), Apr. 1, 1974; MP to EL, Sept. 22, 1924; MP to EL, Nov. 6, 1924; MP to EL, Dec. 13, 1924.

Birth of Nancy G. Perkins: MP to EL, Jan. 28, 1925; New Canaan *Advertiser,* May 18, 1974, p. 11; MP to EL, Jan. 28, 1925.

Social life in New Canaan: MP to FSF, Feb. 24, 1925; MP to EL, Mar. 7, 1925; MP to EL, Nov. 6, 1924; Mary Colum, *Life and the Dream* (Garden City, N.Y.: Doubleday, 1947), pp. 335–37; MP to EL, Apr. 24, 1925; MP to PK, Oct. 28, 1925; MP to PK, Oct. 7, 1926.

The Great Gatsby—prepublication: MP to EL, Mar. 7, 1925; MP to FSF, Mar. 19, 1925; MP to FSF, Mar. 25, 1925; FSF to MP (telegram), Mar. 7, 1925; FSF to MP, ca. Mar. 12, 1925; MP to FSF, Mar. 9, 1925; FSF to MP, Mar. 19, 1925; FSF to MP, Mar. 22, 1925.

Gatsby publication and reaction: FSF to MP, Apr. 10, 1925; MP to FSF, Apr. 20, 1925; FSF to MP, ca. Apr. 24, 1925; MP to FSF (telegram), Apr. 24, 1925; MP to FSF, Apr. 25, 1925; FSF to MP, Mar. 31, 1925; FSF to MP, May 1, 1925; MP to FSF, May 9, 1925; Ruth Hale, Brooklyn *Eagle,* Apr. 18, 1925; MB to ASB (I), Feb. 20, 1972; MP to EL, Apr. 24, 1925; Struthers Burt to MP, May 17, 1925; FSF to MP, ca. July 19, 1925; FSF to MP (telegram), June 1, 1925; FSF to MP, June 1, 1925; MP to FSF, June 13, 1925.

CSS's "sudden leap": MC notes.

VI. COMPANIONS

Introduction to Ernest Hemingway: MP to FSF, Feb. 24, 1925; MP to EH, Feb. 21, 1925; MP to EH, Feb. 26, 1925; EH to MP, Apr. 15, 1925; MP to EH, Apr. 28, 1925; MP to FSF, May 9, 1925; EH to Harvey Breit, Aug. 18,

1954; *AMF,* pp. 152, 175, 176; FSF to MP, ca. May 22, 1925; MP to FSF, Oct. 18, 1924; MP to EH, July 15, 1925; EH to MP, June 9, 1925.

All the Sad Young Men and the start of *Tender Is the Night*: MP to FSF, July 9, 1925; Matthew J. Bruccoli, *The Composition of Tender Is the Night* (University of Pittsburgh Press: 1963); FSF to MP, Aug. 28, 1925; FSF, "Handle With Care," *CU,* p. 79; FSF to MP, ca. Feb. 8, 1926; FSF to MP, ca. Oct. 20, 1925; MP to FSF, Oct. 12, 1925; MP to FSF, Oct. 27, 1925; FSF to MP, June 1, 1925; FSF to MP, ca. Dec. 27, 1925; MP to FSF, June 18, 1926; FSF to MP, ca. Aug. 11, 1926.

FSF-EH friendship: FSF to MP, ca. Dec. 30, 1925; MP to FSF, Jan. 13, 1926; MP to FSF, Feb. 3, 1926; FSF to MP, ca. Dec. 27, 1925; Horace Liveright to EH (cable), Dec. 30, 1925; EH to FSF, Dec. 31, 1925.

EH signs with CSS: MP to FSF, Jan. 8, 1926; MP to FSF, Jan. 13, 1926; FSF to MP, ca. Jan. 19, 1926; FSF to MP, ca. Mar. 1, 1926; MP to FSF, Mar. 4, 1926; FSF to MP, ca. Mar. 15, 1926; EH to MP, Apr. 1, 1926; MP to EH, Mar. 24, 1926.

Acceptance and editing of *The Sun Also Rises*: EH to MP, Apr. 24, 1926; EH to FSF, ca. Apr., 1926; EH to Harvey Breit, Nov. 10, 1952; FSF to MP, ca. May 10, 1926; MP to EH, May 18, 1926; Charles Madison, "Of Men and Books —Writers and Publishers," *The American Scholar,* Summer, 1966, p. 538 (adapted from Madison's then forthcoming book *Book Publishing in America*); Byron Dexter to MC, Mar. 2, 1943 (MC notes); BSF to ASB (I), June 1, 1975; JHW to ASB (I), Oct. 20, 1971; MP to CS, May 27, 1926; MP to FSF, June 18, 1926; FSF to MP, ca. June 25, 1926; *AMF,* pp. 29, 185; FSF to EH, n.d. (quoted in *Fitzgerald/Hemingway Annual: 1970,* pp. 10–13); MP to EH, July 20, 1926; MP to EH, June 29, 1926; EH to MP, July 24, 1926; EH to MP, Aug. 21, 1926; EH to MP, Dec. 7, 1926; EH to MP, Aug. 26, 1926.

Ecclesiastes as an epigraph: PK to ASB (I), Mar. 28, 1972.

The Sun Also Rises, publication and reaction: MP to EH, Oct. 30, 1926; EH to MP, Nov. 16, 1926; EH to MP, Nov. 19, 1926; MP to EH, Dec. 1, 1926; MP to EH, Nov. 26, 1926; Conrad Aiken, New York *Herald Tribune,* Oct. 31, 1926, VII:4; *OMMB,* p. 138; MP to EH, Jan. 25, 1927; EH to MP, May 27, 1927; irate reader from Atlantic City, N.J. (who shall remain anonymous) to CSS, Aug. 24, 1928; MP to another irate reader, of Sarasota, Fla., May 4, 1927.

Dissolution of EH's marriage: *AMF,* pp. 209–10; Hadley Mowrer to ASB, Nov. 26, 1971; Hadley Mowrer to ASB (I), Dec. 14, 1971. The dedication of *The Sun Also Rises* reads: "This book is for Hadley and for John Hadley Nicanor" (their son).

LSP unfulfilled; LSP writing: Jean Lancaster to ASB (I), May 22, 1971; MP to EL, June 10, 1925; EEG to ASB (I), Dec. 15, 1971; MP to Woodward Boyd, May 17, 1926; MP to EL, Aug. 21, 1925; Edward N. Thomas to ASB

(I), Apr. 9, 1972; LSP, "Other Joys," *Scribner's,* Feb., 1927, p. 135; MP to FSF, Nov. 4, 1926.

Molly Colum: MP to FSF, July 14, 1925.

VWB's breakdown: JHW to ASB (I), June 5, 1975; VWB Auto, pp. 439–41; MP to FSF, Apr. 27, 1926; MP to EL, Feb. 2, 1926; Mary Colum, *Life and the Dream,* pp. 343–44; MP to EL, Jan. 11, 1929; James Hoopes, *Van Wyck Brooks* (Amherst: Univ. of Mass. Press, 1977), pp. 170–93.

MP's marriage, and friendship with EL: MP to LSP, June 22 (ca. 1919); MP to EL, June 26, 1926; EL to ASB (I), Apr. 24, 1975; MP to EL, July 7, 1926; MP to EL, Aug. 16, 1926; MP to EL, Sept. 16, 1926; MP to EL, Sept. 10, 1926; EEG to ASB (I), Dec. 15, 1971; MP to EL, Feb. 27, 1926; MP to EL, May 6, 1926; MP to EL, June 10, 1925; MP to EL, June 26, 1926; EL to ASB (I), Apr. 25, 1972; MP to EL, Oct. 27, 1926.

MP becoming the "brains" of CSS: FSF to Thomas Boyd, n.d.; *OMMB,* p. 141; MC notes.

VII. A MAN OF CHARACTER

EH, after *The Sun Also Rises*: MP to EH, Feb. 4, 1927; EH to MP, Feb. 14, 1927; EH to MP, Feb. 19, 1927; EH to MP, Mar. 17, 1928; *OMMB,* p. 223; EH to MP, mid-Aug., 1928; EH to MP, July 23, 1928; EH to MP, ca. Aug. 15, 1928; MP to EH, Aug. 30, 1928.

EH vs. FSF: *AMF,* p. 155; EH to MP, Mar. 17, 1928; EH to MP, Apr. 21, 1928.

FSF struggling with *Tender Is the Night*: MP to EH, Apr. 27, 1928; MP to EH, Oct. 2, 1928; EH to MP, Oct. 11, 1928; ZSF to MP, n.d. (ca. Nov., 1926); Alice B. Toklas, *What Is Remembered* (New York: Holt, Rinehart and Winston, 1963), p. 117; MP to FSF, Jan. 6, 1927; MP to FSF, Jan. 20, 1927; MP to FSF, June 18, 1926; Edmund Wilson, "A Weekend at Ellerslie," *The Shores of Light* (New York: Farrar, 1952), p. 375; FSF, "Author's House," *Afternoon of an Author* (Princeton: Princeton Univ. Library, 1957), p. 185; FSF to MP, Feb. 20, 1926; MP to FSF, June 2, 1927.

Perkinses' trip to England: MP to EL, Sept. 12, 1927; MP to EEG, June 22, 1927; MP to FSF, Apr. 27, 1926; MP to James Boyd, Jr., Jan. 4, 1946; PK to ASB, Apr. 1, 1973; Edward Thomas to ASB (I), Apr. 9, 1972; VWB Auto, p. 31; MP to William Lyon Phelps, Sept. 21, 1942; MP to EEG, July 7, 1927.

MP and EL: MP to EL, Nov. 11 and 18, 1927; MP to EL, Mar. 1, 1928; MP to EL, Sept. 12, 1927.

MP and Copey's books: J. Donald Adams, *Copey of Harvard,* pp. 247–51.

MP on advertising; MP to EL, Sept. 12, 1927; MP to SA, Aug. 21, 1940.

More struggles with *Tender Is the Night*: MP to EL, Sept. 12, 1927; MP to EH, Oct. 14, 1927; MP to EL, Nov. 11, 1927; EL to ASB (I), Apr. 14, 1972;

MP to EH, Oct. 31, 1927; MP to RL, Oct. 20, 1927; FSF to MP, ca. Jan. 1, 1928; MP to FSF, Jan. 3, 1928.

Morley Callaghan: JHW to ASB (I), June 5, 1975; MP to Callaghan, Nov. 16, 1931; MP to FSF, Jan. 24, 1928; Morley Callaghan, *That Summer in Paris* (New York: Coward-McCann, 1963), pp. 58–59.

FSF delivers chapters: FSF, "Written with Zelda Gone to the Clinique," n.d., quoted in Nancy Milford, *Zelda* (New York: Harper & Row, 1970), p. 182. ZSF to Carl Van Vechten, Mar. 23, 1928; FSF to MP, ca. July 1, 1928; FSF to MP, ca. July 21, 1928; MP to EH, Oct. 24, 1928; FSF to MP, ca. Oct. 31, 1928; FSF to MP, ca. Nov. 1, 1928; MP to FSF, Nov. 5, 1928; MP to FSF, Nov. 13, 1928.

S. S. Van Dine: MP, Introduction, *The Winter Murder Case* (New York: Scribners, 1939), pp. x–xi; Harry Salpeter, "S. S. Van Dine: The Man Behind the Mask," *Outlook,* May 9, 1928, pp. 48, 77–78; Howard Haycraft, *Murder for Pleasure* (New York: Biblo and Tannen, 1951), pp. 165–68; JHW to ASB (I), June 5, 1975; MP to Willard Huntington Wright, Jan. 3, 1928; MP to Alden Brooks, Dec. 2, 1942.

MP's rise at CSS: John P. Brown to CS II, Feb. 19, 1926; Wallace Meyer to ASB (I), Apr. 1, 1972.

Death of Brownell: MP to CS II, July 26, 1928; MP, "A Companionable Colleague," *W. C. Brownell: Tributes and Appreciations* (New York: Scribners, 1929—private printing), pp. 63–65.

MP's eccentric style: JO to ASB (I), May 8, 1972; EL to ASB (I), May 23, 1975; Burroughs Mitchell to ASB (I), Oct. 1, 1970; *OMMB,* p. 7; MP to Roy Durstine, Apr. 27, 1938; PK to ASB (I), Mar. 28, 1972; George Schieffelin to ASB (I), Apr. 3, 1972; PK to ASB (I), Mar. 29, 1972; MP to LSP, Thursday (ca. 1912); MC to ASB (I), May 17, 1972; VWB Auto, pp. 5, 31.

VIII. A LITTLE HONEST HELP

MP introduced to TW: *HLB,* pp. 270–71; MB to MC, Mar. 2, 1943 (MC notes); TW, "Note for the Publisher's Reader"; MP to John Terry, Oct. 22, 1945; MP to TW, Oct. 22, 1928; TW to MP, Nov. 17, 1928; TW to Margaret Roberts, Jan. 12, 1929; *SN,* p. 11. Aline Bernstein first brought the mansucript to Boni & Liveright, and they rejected it. Then she gave it to her friend Melville Cane, attorney for Harcourt, Brace, hoping that he would recommend it to the firm; but he refused because of its size and chaotic condition. Mrs. Boyd first submitted it to the newly founded firm of Covici-Friede. They rejected it, as did Longmans, Green.

Editing *Look Homeward, Angel*: TW to MP, Jan. 9, 1929; TW, Pocket Notebook 8; TW to George W. McCoy, Aug. 17, 1929; MP to EL, Sept. 5, 1929; TW to MB, Feb. 15, 1929; TW to Margaret Roberts, Jan. 12, 1929; TW to Mabel Wolfe Wheaton, May, 1929; *HLB,* pp. 271–72; MP to John Terry, Oct. 25, 1945; *Look Homeward, Angel,* pp. 3, 4, 13; MP to JJ, May 9, 1947; MB to ASB (I), Feb. 20, 1972; MB to MP, July 29, 1929; MB to MP, ca. Dec., 1928, Francis E. Skipp, "The Editing of *Look Homeward, Angel,*" *Papers of the Bibliographical Society of America,* vol. 57, First Quarter, 1963, pp. 1–13.

MP's literary nature: Irma Wyckoff Muench to ASB (I), Feb. 18, 1972; VWB Auto, pp. 31–36.

MP and TW developing personal relationship: MP, ms. of "Thomas Wolfe," p. 3 (appeared in *Wings,* Oct., 1939); MP to John Terry, Oct. 29, 1945; MP to William B. Wisdom, June 7, 1943; *Of Time and the River,* p. 327; TW to JHW, July 23, 1929; TW to JHW, July 22, 1929.

AB: TW, *The Web and the Rock,* p. 312; *Of Time and the River,* pp. 911–12; MP to John Terry, Oct. 22, 1945; MB to MP, ca. summer, 1929.

Final editing of *Look Homeward, Angel*: JHW to TW, Aug. 29, 1929; TW to MP, Sept. 14, 1929; TW to MB, Mar. 20, 1929; MP to William B. Wisdom, June 7, 1943; MP to John Terry, Oct. 25, 1945; JHW to ASB (I), June 5, 1975.

Deepening of MP-EH friendship: MP to EL, Nov. 11, 1927; Grace Hemingway to MP, Dec. 6, 1928; EH to MP, ca. Dec. 9, 1928; EH to MP, Jan. 8, 1929; MP to FSF, Jan. 23, 1929; MP to Earl Wilson, Jan. 30, 1941; MP to CS, Feb. 14, 1929.

A Farewell to Arms: MP to Arthur Scribner, Feb. 6, 1929; MP to CS, Feb. 14, 1929; MC notes; Irma Wyckoff Muench to ASB (I), Feb. 18, 1972; MP to EH, Feb. 13, 1929; EH to MP, Feb. 16, 1929; MP to EH, Feb. 19, 1929; EH to MP, June 7, 1929; MP to EH, July 12, 1929; MP to EH, Feb. 14, 1940; EH to MP, Mar. 11, 1929.

Tension between EH and FSF: EH to MP, Apr. 3, 1929.

FSF's new approach to *Tender Is the Night*: FSF to MP, ca. Mar. 1, 1929; MP to EH, Mar. 8, 1929; MP to EH, May 28, 1929; MP to EH, May 31, 1929; FSF, "The Rough Crossing," *Saturday Evening Post,* June 8, 1929, p. 66; FSF to MP, ca. June, 1929.

RL and "Round-Up": MP to RL, June 20, 1929; MP to RL, Dec. 27, 1928; MP to RL, Mar. 20, 1929; MP to RL, Jan. 11, 1929; MP to RL, Feb. 14, 1929; "Constant Reader" (Dorothy Parker), *The New Yorker,* Apr. 27, 1929, p. 105; MP to RL, May 31, 1929; RL to MP, June 19, 1929.

EW: EW, *The Twenties,* p. 492; Leon Edel in *ibid.,* p. 246; EW to MP, June 9, 1928; EEG to ASB (I), Dec. 15, 1971.

Bertha Perkins: MP to BSF, Aug. 21, 1927.

Fall, 1929 book season: MP to EL, Sept. 5, 1929; MC notes; EH to MP, Oct. 20, 1929; *SN,* p. 19; TW, "My Record as a Writer," submitted as part of his application for a Guggenheim Fellowship, ca. Dec. 16, 1929.

IX. CRISES OF CONFIDENCE

FSF after "The Crash": MP to FSF, Oct. 30, 1929; FSF, "Written with Zelda Gone to the Clinique"; EH to FSF, Sept. 13, 1929; EH to MP, Dec. 10, 1929; Gerald Murphy, quoted in Calvin Tomkins, *Living Well Is the Best Revenge* (New York: Viking Press, 1971), p. 113; MB to ASB (I), Feb. 20, 1972; ZSF, "Autobiographical Sketch," Mar. 16, 1932 (quoted in Milford, *Zelda,* p. 160); FSF to MP, Jan. 21, 1930; FSF to MP, ca. May 1, 1930; MP to FSF, May 14, 1930; FSF to MP, ca. July, 1930; FSF to MP, ca. July 8, 1930; FSF to MP, ca. July 20, 1930; MP to FSF, Aug. 5, 1930; FSF to MP, ca. Sept. 1, 1930; MP to TW, July 30, 1930; FSF, *Ledger,* p. 184; FSF to MP, ca. May 1, 1930; FSF to MP, Jan. 21, 1930.

MP publishes Erskine Caldwell: Erskine Caldwell, *Call It Experience* (New York: Duell, 1951), pp. 76–85; MP to Erskine Caldwell, Feb. 26, 1930.

Death of CS II: Wallace Meyer to ASB (I), Apr. 1, 1972.

EH after the crash: MP to EH, Nov. 12, 1929; MP to FSF, Oct. 30, 1929; EH to MP, Dec. 10, 1929; FSF to MP, ca. Nov. 15, 1929; EH to MP, Nov. 30, 1929; MP to EH, Dec. 19, 1929; MP to EH, Dec. 10, 1929; EH to MP, Dec. 7, 1929; Horace Liveright to CSS, Dec. 31, 1929; EH to MP, Aug. 12, 1930; MP to EH, Dec. 27, 1929; EH to MP, Jan. 4, 1930; MP to FSF, Feb. 11, 1930; MP to EH, Feb. 28, 1930; MP to Earl Wilson, Jan. 30, 1941; MP to EL, Mar. 16, 1931; EH to MP, July 24, 1930; EH to MP, Aug. 12, 1930.

TW's crises: *YCGHA,* p. 324; TW to MP, Dec. 24, 1929; MP to TW, Dec. 27, 1929; TW to Mabel Wolfe Wheaton, Mar. 29, 1930; TW, "October Fair" notebook, p. 337, Mar. 30–31, 1930; TW to MP, May 17, 1930; MP to TW, June 3, 1930; TW to A. S. Frere-Reeves, June 23, 1930.

Aline Bernstein recorded the pivotal moment of Wolfe's change in allegiances in "Eugene," one of three short stories in her book *Three Blue Suits* (New York: Equinox Cooperative Press, 1933). Perkins appears as an editor named Watkins, who suggests that Eugene Lyons, a prodigious Southern writer, apply for a Guggenheim fellowship. The story unfairly implies that Watkins has meddled in Lyons's love affair with an unnamed Jewish woman. "Watkins was right," Mrs. Bernstein wrote; "this relationship bore nothing but jealousy and pain in the end." (pp. 66–67).

FSF meets TW: TW to MP, July 1, 1930; FSF to TW, Aug. 2, 1930; FSF to MP, ca. Sept. 1, 1930; MP to FSF, Sept. 10, 1930.

"The October Fair" (*Of Time and the River*): TW to MP, July 1, 1930; TW to MP, ca. July 9, 1930; TW to MP, July 17, 1930; TW to Henry Volkening, Sept., 1930; TW to MP, July 31, 1930; MP to TW, July 30, 1930.

Critical reaction to *Look Homeward, Angel*: Frank Swinnerton, London

Evening News, Aug. 8, 1930; Gerald Gould, *Observer,* Aug. 17, 1930; TW to JHW, Aug. 18, 1930.

TW quits as a writer: TW to MP, ca. Aug. 18, 1930; MP to TW, Aug. 18, and 28, 1930; MP to TW, Sept. 10, 1930; TW to MP (cable), Sept. 13, 1930; MP to TW, Sept. 27, 1930; TW to MP (cable), Oct. 14, 1930.

X. MENTOR

Early stages of *Of Time and the River:* TW to MP, Dec. 9–29, 1930; TW to MP, ca. Dec. 25, 1930; MP to TW, Dec. 23, 1930; TW to MP, Jan. 7, 1931.

TW's unrest over AB: TW to MP, Jan. 19, 1931; TW to MP, Jan. 7, 1931; AB to TW, May 12, 1930; AB to TW, n.d. (summer, 1930); AB to TW, Oct. 2, 1930; AB to TW, Oct. 14, 1930; MP to TW, Jan. 30, 1931; TW to MP, Feb. 24, 1931; AB to TW, Mar. 24, 1931; TW to AB, Mar. 29, 1931; AB to TW, n.d. (ca. Apr., 1931); MP to EL, Mar. 16, 1931.

FSF in limbo: FSF to MP, ca. Dec. 20, 1930; FSF to MP, ca. Sept. 1, 1930; RL to FSF, Jan. 22, 1930; MP to EH, Feb. 11, 1931; MP to John Peale Bishop, Feb. 25, 1931; FSF to MP, ca. May 15, 1931; Alfred S. Dashiell to FSF, May 22, 1931; Notes from Prangins (quoted in Milford, *Zelda,* p. 191).

FSF and ZSF: "Show Mr. and Mrs. F. to Number—," *CU,* p. 52; FSF, "Echoes of the Jazz Age," *CU,* p. 22.

Erskine Caldwell leaving MP: Caldwell, *Call It Experience,* pp. 88, 122–23; MP to Erskine Caldwell, June 18, 1932.

MP on "present discouraging state": MP to EH, June 11, 1931.

EH's accident: EH to MP, ca. Nov. 15, 1930.

Ford Madox Ford: Ford to EH, Sept. 20, 1930; EH to MP, Sept. 28, 1930; MP to EH, Oct. 14, 1930.

Archibald MacLeish: EH to MP, Dec. 8, 1930; MP to EH, Jan. 22, 1931; MP to EH, Nov. 25, 1931; MP to EH, Nov. 30, 1931; JHW to ASB (I), June 5, 1975; EH to MP, Dec. 9, 1931.

Hard times: *Harvard Class of 1907 Twenty-fifth Anniversary Report: 1932,* p. 517; MP to EH, Dec. 5, 1930; MP to EL, Jan. 26, 1931; MP to TW, Jan. 30, 1931; MP to EL, Jan. 27, 1931.

Death of Archibald Cox: MP to EL, Mar. 16, 1931.

MP to Key West: MP to FSF, Apr. 3, 1931; MP to FSF, May 21, 1931.

MP on Faulkner: EH to MP, Apr. 12, 1931; William Faulkner to Alfred Dashiell, ca. Dec. 20, 1928; MP to EL, Mar. 16, 1931; JHW to ASB (I), Apr. 3, 1972; EH to MP, Apr. 27, 1931.

EH writing *Death in the Afternoon:* EH to MP, Aug. 1, 1931.

Douglas Southall Freeman: MP to DSF, June 27, 1930; MP to DSF, Apr. 23, 1930; DSF to MP, Jan. 19, 1931; DSF to MP, Dec. 26, 1934; MP to DSF, Jan. 11, 1935.

MP sees unpleasantness everywhere: MP to EH, Aug. 20, 1931.

TW fed up with the writing game: MP to TW, Aug. 27, 1931; TW to MP, Aug. 29, 1931.

XI. LAMENTATIONS

RL's illness: RL to MP, Feb. 13, 1931; MP to EH, Sept. 2, 1931; MP to RL, Feb. 16, 1931; Ellis Lardner to MP, ca. Sept. 19, 1931; Ellis Lardner to MP, ca. Sept. 25, 1931.

FSF's progress on *Tender Is the Night*: FSF and ZFS, "Show Mr. and Mrs. F. to Number—": *CU*, p. 54; FSF to MP, ca. Jan. 15, 1932; FSF, "General Plan" for *Tender;* FSF to EW, Mar. 12, 1934.

ZSF and *Save Me the Waltz*: ZSF to MP, ca. Mar. 12, 1932; MP to EH, Apr. 19, 1932; ZSF to MP, Mar. 27, 1932; MP to ZSF, Mar. 28, 1932; FSF to MP, Mar. 28, 1932; ZSF to FSF, n.d. (ca. Mar. 1932) ; FSF to MP, ca. Apr. 30, 1932; FSF to MP, ca. May 14, 1932; MP to ZSF (telegram), May 16, 1932; MP to ZSF, June 25, 1932; ZSF to MP, n.d. (ca. May 19, 1932); ZSF, *Save Me the Waltz* (New York: Signet, 1968), p. 105; MP to ZSF, Aug. 2, 1933; MP to EH, Nov. 3, 1932; ZSF to MP, n.d. (ca. Oct. 22, 1932); ZSF to MP, n.d. (ca. Oct. 1, 1932); FSF to MP, ca. May 14, 1932; ZSF to MP, n.d. (ca. June 5, 1932); MP to EH, June 11, 1932.

Bertha's illness: FSF to MP, ca. Jan. 15, 1932; FSF to MP, ca. May 14, 1932; MP to ZSF, June 10, 1932; *YCGHA,* pp. 491–92.

TW's upsets: MP to Lawrence Greene, Mar. 14, 1935; MP to EH, Jan. 14, 1932; TW to Mabel Wolfe Wheaton, Jan. 27, 1932; MP to John Terry, Dec. 11, 1945; TW to AB, n.d. (spring, 1932).

Completion of *Death in the Afternoon*: MP to EH, Jan. 14, 1932; EH to MP, Nov. 12–25, 1931; MP to EH, Nov. 12, 1931; EH to MP, Jan. 21, 1932; MP to EH, Jan. 25 and Feb. 5, 1932; MP to EH, Apr. 19, 1932; EEG to ASB (I), June 11, 1973; EH to MP, May 14, 1932; MP to EH, May 24, 1932; EH to MP (telegram), June 27, 1932; EH to MP, June 28, 1932; MP to EH, July 7, 1932.

MP's life seeming cursed: MP to EL, June 15 and 26, 1932; MP to EL, July 7, 1932; MP to EL, Aug. 10, 1934. Arthur H. Scribner died on July 3, 1932.

MP's trip to Baltimore: EL to ASB (I), June 6, 1973; EL to ASB (I), Apr. 12, 1972; MP to EL, July, 1932; MP to EH, July 22, 1932.

EH comments on the Fitzgeralds: EH to MP, July 27, 1932; EH to MP, June 2, 1932; MP to EH, Aug. 1, 1932; MP to EL, Aug. 19, 1932.

Publication of *Save Me the Waltz*: "Of the Jazz Age," *New York Times,* Oct. 16, 1932.

FSF at work on *Tender Is the Night*: FSF, *Ledger,* p. 186; ZSF to MP, n.d. (ca. Oct. 1, 1932); FSF to MP, Jan. 19, 1933; MP to FSF, Jan. 27, 1933.

Sales of *Save Me the Waltz*: FSF to MP, July 27, 1933; MP to ZSF, Aug. 2, 1933; MP to FSF, Jan. 27, 1933; MP to FSF, Feb. 3, 1933; MP to FSF, Aug. 4, 1933.

FSF completing *Tender Is the Night*: FSF to MP, Sept. 25, 1933; MP to FSF, Oct. 9, 1933; MP to EH, Jan. 12, 1934 (misdated: 1933); MP to FSF, Oct. 18, 1933; FSF, *Ledger*, p. 188.

RL's last days and aftermath: RL to MP, Aug. 18, 1932; MP to RL, Aug. 17, 1932; RL to MP, Feb. 3, 1933; MP to RL, Feb. 1, 1933; RL to MP, Feb. 3, 1933; Maxwell Geismar, *Ring Lardner and the Portrait of Folly* (New York: Crowell, 1972), p. 155; MP to EH, Nov. 28, 1934; MP to FSF, Oct. 6, 1933; FSF to MP, Oct. 7, 1933; Gilbert Seldes, Preface to RL's *First and Last*, pp. v–vi.

XII. THE SEXES

MP as a "misogynist": PK to ASB (I), Mar. 28, 1972; MP to James Boyd, Dec. 1, 1924; Struthers Burt, "Catalyst for Genius," *Saturday Review of Literature*, June 9, 1951, p. 37.

Marcia Davenport: Davenport, *Too Strong for Fantasy*, pp. 137–38, 183; MP to Alice Dixon Bond, July 17, 1944; Davenport to MP, July 16, 1931; Davenport to MP, July 18, 1932; Davenport to MP, Mar. 7, 1932.

Nancy Hale: MP to EL, Jan. 22, 1938; MP to Nancy Hale, June 18, 1937.

Caroline Gordon Tate: Allen Tate to ASB, Sept. 12, 1972; MP to Caroline Gordon Tate, Jan. 16, 1932; Caroline Gordon Tate to ASB (I), Sept. 12, 1971; MP to Caroline Gordon Tate, Nov. 12, 1931.

CSS during the Depression: Charles Madison, *Book Publishing in America* (New York: McGraw-Hill, 1966), p. 216; MC notes.

Alice Roosevelt Longworth: Alice Roosevelt Longworth to ASB (I), June 5, 1973; MP to EL, Oct. 23, 1933; Longworth, *Crowded Hours*, p. 325; MP to EH, Dec. 12, 1933.

Marjorie Kinnan Rawlings: MKR to Robert van Gelder, quoted in *Twentieth Century Authors*, p. 1,150; MKR, *Cross Creek*, pp. 5, 9; MKR, quoted in *The Marjorie Kinnan Rawlings Reader*, ed. Julia Scribner Bigham (New York: Scribners, 1956), pp. ix, xi, xiii, xiv, xvi; MP to Alice Dixon Bond, July 17, 1944; Marcia Davenport, *Too Strong for Fantasy*, p. 299; MKR to MP, June 7, 1933; MP to MKR, Nov. 21, 1932; MKR, *South Moon Under*, p. 135; MKR to MP, Jan. 19, 1933; MP to EH, Jan. 20, 1942; MP to MKR, Nov. 15, 1933; MP to MKR, June 10, 1933; MKR to MP, June 12, 1933; MP to MKR, Oct. 10, 1933; MP to MKR, Feb. 1, 1934; MP to MKR, Oct. 27, 1933; MP to MKR, Mar. 5, 1934.

Reactions to *Death in the Afternoon*: MP to EH, Aug. 26, 1932; Edward Weeks, *Atlantic* Bookshelf, Nov., 1932; *Times Literary Supplement*, Dec. 8, 1932.

MP on FDR: MP to V. F. Calverton, Feb. 13, 1932.

MP duck-hunting in Arkansas: EH to MP, Dec. 7, 1932; MP to ZSF, Dec. 23, 1932; MP to MKR, Jan. 5, 1940; MP to EL, Dec. 25, 1932; MP to Ann Chidester, July 15, 1943; MP to EH, Nov. 8, 1932; MP to TW, Dec. 23, 1932; EH to MP, Nov. 15, 1932; EH to MP, Feb. 23, 1933; EH to CS, Dec. 1, 1951; MP to TW, Dec. 23, 1932.

Meeting of TW and EH: MP to James Boyd, Dec. 29, 1932; MP to John Terry, Nov. 21, 1945; MP to Earl Wilson(?), Dec. 31, 1940; EH to MP, late Jan., 1933.

"Bull in the Afternoon": Max Eastman, "Bull in the Afternoon," *New Republic,* June 7, 1933, pp. 94–96; EH to MP, June 13, 1933; MP to EH, June 16, 1933; EH to MP, ca. July 15, 1933.

"Winner Take Nothing": EH to MP, ca. July 15, 1933; MP to EH, June 12, 1933.

Gertrude Stein: Gertrude Stein, *The Autobiography of Alice B. Toklas* (New York: Harcourt, Brace, 1934), p. 265; EH to MP, July 26, 1933; MP to EH, Aug. 2, 1933; EH to MP, Aug. 10, 1933. In contrast to her remark about EH, Miss Stein writes on page 268, "She thinks Fitzgerald will be read when many of his well-known contemporaries are forgotten."

EH, under attack, goes to Africa: MP to EH, Aug. 14, 1933; EH to MP, Aug. 31, 1933; MP to EH, Nov. 6, 1933; MP to Evan Shipman, Nov. 24, 1933; EH to MP, Jan. 17, 1934.

Getting TW to surrender *Of Time and the River*: MP to EH, Feb. 10, 1933; MP to TW, Feb. 16, 1933; MP to EL, June 29, 1933; TW to Mabel Wolfe Wheaton, Feb. 9, 1933; MP to TW, Aug. 9, 1933; A. S. Frere-Reeves to MP, Feb. 27, 1933; A. S. Frere-Reeves to MP, Sept. 5, 1933; *HLB,* p. 275; *Car. Mag.,* p. 15; MP to John Terry, Dec. 11, 1945; MP to A. S. Frere-Reeves, Sept. 25, 1933; MP to EL, Oct. 23, 1933; MP to EL, May 26, 1934; TW to AB, fragment, Oct. 3, 1933; MP to CS, Apr. 18, 1933.

Bertha's marriage: MP to EL, June 29, 1933; BSF to ASB (I), Feb. 22, 1972.

Moving to NYC and MP's quotidian routine: MP to EL, June 29, 1933; Elizabeth Youngstrom to ASB (I), Apr. 4, 1972; JHW to ASB (I), June 5, 1975; Struthers Burt, *op. cit.,* pp. 8, 36, 37; MP to Ann Chidester, Apr. 20, 1944; Irma Wyckoff Muench to ASB (I), Feb. 18, 1972; MC notes; Robert Ryan to ASB (I), Jan. 13, 1973.

MP and LSP's marriage: NJ to ASB (I), Apr. 21, 1972; EL to ASB (I), Apr. 14, 1972; EL to ASB (I), June 5, 1973; PK to ASB (I), Mar. 29, 1972; JHW to ASB (I), Oct. 20, 1971; Betty Bigelow to ASB (I), Mar. 14, 1972; Irma Wyckoff Muench to ASB (I), Feb. 18, 1972; MP to EL, Aug. 22, 1935; EL to ASB (I), Apr. 12, 1972.

MP and money: Herman Scheying to ASB (I), Mar. 22, 1972; MP to EL, Oct. 23, 1933; PK to ASB (I), Mar. 28, 1972.

MP on women and the arts: MP to EL, Oct. 19, 1932; PK to ASB (I),
Mar. 29, 1972; NJ to ASB (I), Apr. 21, 1972; JHW to ASB (I), Oct. 20,
1971; PK to ASB (I), Mar. 28, 1972; MP to EL, Aug. 10, 1934 and July 7,
1932.

XIII. TRIUMPHS OVER TIME

Finishing *Tender Is the Night*: FSF to MP, Oct. 19, 1933; MP to James Gray,
Jan. 10, 1934; MP to EH, Jan. 12, 1934; FSF to MP, Mar. 4, 1934; MP to FSF,
Jan. 15, 1934; FSF to MP, Jan. 18, 1934; FSF to MP, Feb. 1, 1934; FSF to MP,
Dec. 3, 1934; FSF to MP, Jan. 13, 1934; FSF to MP, Apr. 2, 1934.

ZSF's exhibition: Matthew Josephson to ASB, Apr. 17, 1976; MP to EH,
Feb. 7, 1934; EL to ASB (I), Apr. 8, 1975.

Publication of *Tender Is the Night*: FSF to MP, Mar. 4, 1939; Morley
Callaghan to MP, Apr. 10, 1934; EH to MP, Apr. 30, 1934; MP to EH, May 3,
1934.

FSF's difficulties over "Taps at Reveille": MP to EL, May 26, 1934; FSF
to MP, May 11 and 21, 1934; FSF to MP, Aug. 24, 1934; FSF to MP, Dec. 17,
1934; FSF, *Ledger,* p. 188; FSF to TW, Apr. 2, 1934.

Delivery of *Of Time and the River* ms.: Elizabeth Nowell, *Thomas Wolfe*
(Garden City, N.Y.: Doubleday, 1960), pp. 222–23; JHW to ASB (I), Apr. 3,
1972; MP to John Terry, Dec. 18, 1945; *Car. Mag.,* p. 15; *SN,* pp. 73–76; TW to
Julia Wolfe, Dec. 15, 1933; TW to MP, Dec. 15, 1933.

Editing *Of Time and the River*: *SN,* pp. 77–83; MP to EH, Jan. 12, 1934
(misdated: 1933); MP to A. S. Frere-Reeves, Jan. 18, 1934; MP to A. S.
Frere-Reeves, Feb. 23, 1934; MP, "Outline for *Of Time and the River*" (Houghton Library call number (46 AM-7 [24m]); MP, Note [24j]; MP to John Terry,
Oct. 22, 1945; John Chamberlain, *Books of the Times,* Mar. 8, 1934; TW to
Robert Raynolds, Feb. 2, 1934; Arnold Gingrich to ASB (I), Dec. 3, 1971; TW
to EN, Feb. 2, 1934; MP to A. S. Frere-Reeves, Apr. 6, 1934; *HLB,* p. 272; TW
to Robert Raynolds, June 5, 1934; TW to EN, June 2, 1934; MP to MKR, June
14, 1934; MC notes; *Car. Mag.,* pp. 15–16; TW to Robert Raynolds, June 8,
1934; MP to Peter Monro Jack, Sept. 29, 1938; MP to EH, June 28, 1934; Poyntz
Tyler, "Puritan in Babylon," ms. of article for *Town & Country,* p. 13; MP to
EH, Nov. 28, 1934; JHW to ASB (I), June 5, 1975; Irma Wyckoff Muench
to ASB (I), Feb. 18, 1972; MP to John Terry, Oct. 29, 1945; NJ to ASB (I),
Apr. 21, 1972; MP to MKR, Oct. 18, 1935; MP to Paul Weiss, Sept. 30, 1934;
TW to Catherine Brett, July 12, 1934.

MP's family scattered: MP to EL, Aug. 10, 1934.

MP and FSF to Welbourne: MP to EL, July 16, 1934; TW to EL, July 27,
1934; EL to ASB (I), May 25, 1975; MP to EL, Mar. 7, 1925; MP to EL, July
31, 1934; TW to EL, Sept. 14, 1934; FSF to MP, July 30, 1934; EL to ASB
(I), Apr. 24, 1975; EL to ASB (I), May 24, 1975; FSF to MP, Oct. 17, 1934;

MP to EL, Oct. 15, 1934; EL to LSP, n.d. (ca. June 20, 1947); EL to ASB (I), Apr. 8, 1975; EEG to ASB (I), June 11, 1973; EL to ASB (I), Apr. 12, 1972; FSF to MP, July 30, 1934; MP to FSF, Aug. 24, 1934; MP to EL, Oct. 15, 1934.

FSF struggling over "Taps at Reveille": MP to FSF, Oct. 17, 1934.

Final editing of *Of Time and the River*: MP to FSF, Aug. 24, 1934; MP to A. S. Frere-Reeves, Sept. 5, 1934; MP to EL, Oct. 18, 1934; MP to FSF, Dec. 6, 1934; *SN*, pp. 85–86; *HLB*, p. 273; MP to EL, Oct. 16, 1934.

TW and EL: EL to ASB (I), Apr. 12, 1972; EL to ASB (I), Apr. 24, 1972; TW to EL, Nov. 8, 1934.

AB and MP over TW's ms.: AB to MP, Oct. 17, 1934; MP to AB, Oct. 22, 1934; AB to MP, Oct. 23, 1934.

End of editing of *Of Time and the River*: MP to EN, Oct. 23, 1934.

Completion of *Green Hills*: EH to MP, Oct. 3, 1934; EH to MP, Nov. 16, 1934; EH to MP, Nov. 20, 1934; MP to EH, Nov. 28, 1934; MP to FSF (postcard), Jan. 31, 1935.

Dedication of *Of Time and the River*: MP to TW, Jan. 21, 1935; JHW to ASB (I), Apr. 3, 1972; MP to TW, Feb. 8, 1935; TW, "To a Friend," torn fragment, n.d.

XIV. GOING HOME AGAIN

Acceptance of *Green Hills*: EH, *Green Hills of Africa,* p. 71; MP to EH, Feb. 4, 1935; EH to MP, ca. Feb. 7, 1935; MP to EH, Feb. 15 and 16, 1935; EH to MP, Feb. 22, 1935.

FSF on the wagon, drifts from EH: MP to EH, Feb. 5, 1935; FSF to MP, Feb. 26, 1935; FSF to EH, June 1, 1934; MP to EH, Feb. 27, 1935; EH to MP, ca. Apr. 5, 1935; FSF to MP, Apr. 15, 1935.

FSF vs. TW: FSF to MP, Feb. 26, 1935; FSF to MP, Mar. 11, 1935.

EW rift: MP to EH, May 15, 1941; MP to V. F. Calverton, Feb. 13, 1932; EW to MP, Oct. 18, 1938; EW to ASB, Apr. 11, 1972; MP to EH, Apr. 2, 1935; FSF, "Handle With Care," *CU*, p. 79. A fourth friend, Thomas Boyd, author of *Through the Wheat,* had just recently died of a brain tumor at 37.

FSF uninspired: MP to EL, Oct. 18, 1934; MP to EL, Mar. 30, 1935; FSF to MP, Apr. 15, 1935; FSF to MP, Apr. 17, 1935.

FSF, "Notebooks": *CU,* p. 177.

FSF argues with MP about TW: FSF to MP, Apr. 15, 1935; FSF, "Notebooks," *CU,* p. 178; FSF to MP, May 11, 1935; FSF to MP, ca. June 25, 1935; MP to EH, June 5, 1935; MP to FSF, Apr. 25, 1935.

Before publication of *Of Time and the River*: MP to A. S. Frere-Reeves, Jan. 16, 1935; VWB Auto, pp. 32, 571; EH to MP, Mar. 30, 1935; *YCGHA,* p. 620; *HLB,* p. 270; MP to AB, Mar. 6, 1935; AB to MP, ca. Mar. 23, 1935; MP to AB, Mar. 25, 1935; AB to MP, Mar. 31, 1935; MP to AB, Apr. 3, 1935.

Of Time and the River, publication and reactions: MP to TW, Mar. 8, 1935; TW to MP, Mar. 13, 1935; MP to TW (cablegram), Mar. 14, 1935; MP to TW, Mar. 14, 1935; PK to ASB (I), Mar. 27, 1972; Fanny Cox to ASB (I), May 20, 1972; TW to MP, Apr. 7, 1935; *Of Time and the River,* pp. 243, 308–09; Mark Van Doren, *The Nation,* Apr. 25, 1934; Burton Rascoe, New York *Herald Tribune Books,* Mar. 10, 1935; TW to MP, Apr. 4, 1935; MP to TW, Apr. 20, 1935.

MP's lonely summer of 1935: TW to LSP, Apr. 18, 1935; MP to EL, May 18, 1935; David Randall to ASB (I), Mar. 23, 1972; MP to EL, June 28, 1935.

VWB's recovery: MP to EL, Aug. 10, 1934; MP to VWB, July 6, 1931; MC to ASB (I), May 18, 1972; Lewis Mumford to Eleanor Brooks, Jan. 3, 1929; JHW to ASB (I), June 5, 1975; VWB to MP, Wednesday (ca. Oct., 1931).

TW in Germany: *YCGHA,* p. 620; TW to MP, May 23, 1935; TW to MP, May 20, 1935.

TW's return to trouble at home: AB to MP, ca. June 19, 1935; AB to MP, ca. June 12, 1935; MP to AB, June 12, 1935; MP to EL, June 28, 1935; MP to John Terry, Nov. 1, 1945.

XV. CRITICAL TIMES

TW vs. AB: MP to FSF, July 12, 1935; AB to MP, July 11, 1935; AB to TW, July 11, 1935; MP to EL, July 12, 1935; MP to John Terry, Oct. 22, 1945; AB to MP, ca. July 14, 1935; MP to AB, July 16, 1935; AB to TW, July 25, 1935.

TW's trip west: TW to MP, Aug. 12, 1935; MP to Fred Wolfe, Aug. 19, 1935; MP to TW, Aug. 30, 1935; TW to MP (postcard), Aug. 26, 1935; TW to MP, Sept. 1, 1935; TW to MP, Sept. 12, 1935; MP to A. S. Frere-Reeves, Sept. 16, 1935.

MP and EL, trip to Welbourne and description of typical day: MP to LSP, July 22, 1935; EL to ASB (I), Apr. 12, 1972; MP to EL, Aug. 15, 1936; MP to EL, July 29, 1935; Henry Roth, *Call It Sleep* (New York: Pageant Books, 1960), pp. xxv, xlv; MP to Henry Roth, Nov. 6, 1939; Henry Roth to MP, Nov. 1, 1939; TW to MP, Aug. 12, 1935; MP to TW, Aug. 20, 1935; MP to EL, Aug. 29, 1935; Irma Wyckoff Muench to ASB (I), Feb. 18, 1972.

TW back at work: TW to Mabel Wolfe Wheaton, Oct. 16, 1935; Elizabeth Nowell, *Thomas Wolfe,* p. 292.

FSF's crack-up: MP to EH, Dec. 14, 1935; EH to MP, Sept. 7, 1935; *CU,* pp. 71–72; MP to EH, Feb. 11, 1936; MP to EH, Feb. 27, 1936; EH to MP, Feb. 7, 1936.

Critical reaction to EH: EH to MP, ca. Aug. 15, 1935; MP to EH, Sept. 10, 1935; EH to MP, Sept. 7, 1935; EH, *Green Hills of Africa,* pp. 21, 23–24, 65; EH to MP, Nov. 16, 1934; EH to MP, Apr. 21, 1928; EH to MP, Apr. 8, 1933;

MP to FSF, Sept. 28, 1935; EH to MP, ca. Dec. 30, 1935; Charles Poore, *New York Times,* Oct. 27, 1935; MP to FSF, Oct. 26, 1935; MP to EH, Dec. 14, 1935; EW, *New Republic,* Dec. 11, 1935, p. 135; EW, "Hemingway: Gauge of Morale," *The Wound and the Bow* (Boston: Houghton Mifflin, 1941), p. 226; MP to EH, Dec. 20, 1935; *OMMB,* p. 39; MP to EH, Feb. 27, 1936; MP to EH, July 9, 1935; EH to MP, ca. Dec. 30, 1935.

JHW breakdown: MP to EH, Dec. 14, 1935; MP to VWB, Feb. 3, 1936; JHW to MP, Dec. 12, 1935; MP to JHW, Dec. 14, 1935; MP to EL, Nov. 30, 1935; VWB to MP, Jan. 30, 1936; MP to VWB, Feb. 3, 1936.

TW acting up: MP to EL, Nov. 30, 1935; MP to JHW, Dec. 14, 1935; MP to John Terry, Nov. 13, 1945; EEG to ASB (I), Dec. 15, 1971; MP to John Terry, Dec. 18, 1945; *SN,* p. 1; MP to John Terry, Oct. 29, 1945; AB to TW, Apr. 3, 1936; AB to TW, Jan. 21, 1936; LSP to TW, Mar. 26, 1936.

LSP vs. MP: JHW to ASB (I), Oct. 20, 1971; EL to ASB (I), Apr. 14, 1972; CS IV to ASB (I), Feb. 14, 1972; EL to ASB (I), June 6, 1973; NJ to ASB (I), Apr. 20, 1972; LSP, "Pauline Bonaparte," unpublished ms., Scenes I:6, II:12, V:16, VI:16; Katharine Hepburn to ASB, Oct. 28, 1972; PK to ASB (I), Oct. 12, 1974.

Argument over *SN*: TW to MP, Apr. 21, 1936; MP to TW, Apr. 22, 1936; TW to MP, Apr. 23, 1936.

TW's new objective book: *HLB,* pp. 274, 276; TW to Heinz Ledig, June 10, 1936; *Car. Mag.,* p. 17; MP to EL, May 29, 1936.

De Voto: Bernard De Voto, "Genius Is Not Enough," *Saturday Review of Literature,* Apr. 25, 1936, p. 3ff.

XVI. THE LETTER

MKR and *The Yearling*: MKR to MP, ca. June 1, 1936; MKR to MP, Mar. 9, 1936; MP to MKR, Mar. 26, 1936; MP to MKR, Oct. 27, 1933; *Marjorie Kinnan Rawlings Reader,* p. xvii; MP to MKR, Aug. 5, 1936; MKR to MP, ca. Jan. 31, 1937; MKR to MP, Sept. 22, 1936; MP to MKR, Sept. 24, 1936; MP to MKR, Mar. 3, 1937; MP to MKR, Dec. 13, 1937.

MKR meets EH: MKR to MP, June 18, 1936.

EH going strong on *To Have and Have Not*: EH to MP, Apr. 9, 1936; MP to Jonathan Cape, Dec. 11, 1936; EH to MP, Sept. 26, 1936; MP to EH, Oct. 1, 1936; EH to MP, Apr. 9, 1936.

FSF hitting bottom: CS to FSF, July 10, 1936; FSF, "Financing Finnegan": *The Stories of F. Scott Fitzgerald,* ed. Malcolm Cowley (New York: Scribners, 1951), pp. 449–50; MP to John Terry, Nov. 20, 1945; FSF, "Afternoon of an Author," *Afternoon of an Author,* p. 177; FSF to Bennett Cerf, Aug. 13, 1936; FSF, looseleaf page of *Ledger,* Apr., 1936.

"Snows of Kilimanjaro": EH, "Snows of Kilimanjaro," *Esquire,* Aug.,

1936, pp. 27, 195, 200; Arnold Gingrich to ASB (I), Dec. 3, 1971; FSF to EH, ca. Aug., 1936; EH to MP, July 23, 1936; FS to MP, Sept. 19, 1936; MP to EL, Aug. 15, 1936.

FSF still depressed, receives visitors: FSF to MP, Sept. 19, 1936; MP to MKR, Sept. 24, 1936; MP to EH, Oct. 1, 1936; MKR to MP, Sept. 30, 1936; MP to MKR, Oct. 7, 1936; MKR to MP, Oct. 25, 1936; MKR to FSF, ca. Oct. 25, 1936; MP to MKR, Nov. 5, 1936; Hamilton Basso to TW, Oct. 12, 1936; FSF to MP, Oct. 16, 1936; MP to FSF, Oct. 6, 1936.

TW writing about CSS: TW to Kent Roberts Greenfield, June 23, 1936; MP to John Terry, Nov. 9, 1945; Nowell, *Thomas Wolfe,* pp. 321–22; JHW to ASB (I), June 5, 1975; MP to John Terry, Dec. 18, 1945; TW to all publishers other than Scribners (unsent), July 15, 1936; TW to MP (postcard), Sept. 4, 1936; MP to SA, Sept. 14, 1937.

MP to Quebec: MP to Elizabeth Perkins (his mother), Sept. 15, 1936.

Zippy's wedding: PK to ASB (I), Mar. 29, 1972; Turnbull, *Thomas Wolfe,* p. 244; Emily Perkins to ASB (I), Apr. 8, 1972.

Disagreements between MP and TW: TW to Jonathan Daniels, Oct. 23, 1936; TW, "political note," quoted in Richard S. Kennedy and Paschal Reeves, eds., *The Notebooks of Thomas Wolfe* (Chapel Hill: University of North Carolina Press, 1970), p. 915; MP to FSF, Nov. 7, 1936; MP to John Terry, ca. Nov. 20, 1945; TW, "No Door," *From Death to Morning,* pp. 7–8; MP to John Terry, Nov. 23, 1945; MP to EH, Dec. 9, 1936; TW to Hamilton Basso, Oct. 14, 1936.

TW separating from MP: TW to MP, Nov. 12, 1936; MP to TW, Nov. 17, 1936; MP to TW, Nov. 18, 1936 (formal letter); MP to TW, Nov. 18, 1936 (personal letter); MP to TW, Nov. 20, 1936; TW to MP, Dec. 15, 1936 (personal letter); TW to MP, unsent letter, ca. Jan. 5, 1937; TW to MP (telegrams), Jan. 7 and 9, 1937; MP to TW (telegram), Jan. 9, 1937; TW to MP, Jan. 9, 1937; MP to TW, Jan. 13 and 16, 1937; MP to TW, Jan. 14, 1937; TW probably to Cornelius Mitchell, ca. Jan. 7, 1937; JHW to ASB (I), Oct. 20, 1971.

XVII. A SAD FAREWELL

EH to Spain: MP to EH, Jan. 7, 1937; MP to MKR, Jan. 28, 1937; MP to Evan Shipman, July 6, 1937.

Martha Gellhorn: MP to Gellhorn, Jan. 25, 1937; Gellhorn to MP, Jan. 23, 1937; Gellhorn to ASB (I), May 10, 1972.

Completion of *To Have and Have Not:* MP to FSF, Mar. 3, 1937; EH's speech, quoted in Henry Hart, ed., *The Writer in a Changing World* (New York: Equinox Cooperative Press, 1937), pp. 69–73; EL to ASB (I), Apr. 14, 1972; EH to MP, June 10, 1937; MP to EH, June 17, 1937; MP to Waldo

Peirce, July 6, 1937; MP to Waldo Peirce, June 24, 1937; *To Have and Have Not,* p. 225; MP to Waldo Peirce, June 28, 1937; JO to ASB (I), May 9, 1972; MP to Jonathan Cape, July 20, 1937; MP to John Terry, Nov. 21, 1945; EW, "Hemingway: Gauge of Morale," pp. 230–31; MP to EH, Nov. 10, 1937.

EH vs. Max Eastman: MP to FSF, Aug. 24, 1937; MP to EL, Aug. 28, 1937; FSF to MP, ca. Aug. 20, 1937; FSF to MP, Sept. 3, 1937; Carlos Baker, *Ernest Hemingway: A Life Story* (New York: Scribners, 1969), p. 312.

FSF's catastrophe at 40: FSF to MP, late Feb., 1937; MP to MKR, Feb. 2, 1937; MP to FSF, Mar. 3, 1937; FSF to MP, ca. May 10, 1937; FSF to MP, ca. July 15, 1937.

Marcia Davenport: *Too Strong for Fantasy,* pp. 138, 217, 223.

Widening differences between TW and MP: TW to Hamilton Basso, Apr. 28, 1937; MP to John Terry, Nov. 13, 1945; MP to EL, Aug. 19, 1937; TW to all publishers other than Scribners (unsent), ca. Mar., 1937; EN, *Thomas Wolfe,* p. 375; TW to Hamilton Basso, July 13, 1937; MP to EL, Aug. 28, 1937; MP to TW, July 16, 1937; MP to TW, Aug. 13, 1937; FSF to TW, July 19, 1937; TW to FSF, July 26, 1937.

CSS spruces up library: MP to EN, Sept. 16, 1937; Diarmuid Russell to ASB (I), May 18, 1972.

TW's final separation: TW to SA, Sept. 22, 1937; Bernard De Voto, "English '37—The Novelist and the Reader: IX," *Saturday Review of Literature,* Aug. 21, 1937, p. 8; MP to John Terry, Dec. 18, 1945; Cass Canfield, *Up and Down and Around* (New York: Harper's Magazine Press, 1971), pp. 143–44; Robert Linscott to TW, Oct. 8, 1937; Robert Linscott to TW, Oct. 22, 1937; TW to Robert Linscott, unsent, Oct. 23, 1937; MP to Fred Wolfe, Nov. 1, 1937; Fred Wolfe to MP, Nov. 3, 1937; TW to Fred Wolfe, Nov. 17, 1937; TW to MP, Nov. 19, 1937; MP to TW, Nov 20, 1937; TW to EN, Dec. 29, 1937; TW to Anne W. Armstrong, Dec. 27, 1937; MP to MKR, Feb. 9, 1938; MP to TW, Dec. 28, 1937.

XVIII. BY THE WIND GRIEVED

Dooher trial: TW to MP, Dec. 27, 1937; MP to John Terry, Jan. 3, 1946; MP to EL, Feb. 15, 1938; EN, *Thomas Wolfe,* p. 414; MP to John Terry, Nov. 9, 1945; MP to EH, Feb. 8, 1938; EH to MP, ca. Feb. 9, 1938.

The Fifth Column; EH to Spain: MP to EH, Nov. 22, 1937; EH to MP, ca. Feb. 9, 1938; MP to EH, Feb. 3, 1938; EH to MP, Mar. 15, 1938; MP to EH (cable), Apr. 6, 1938; MP to EH, Apr. 7, 1938; MP to Pauline Hemingway, Apr. 7, 1938; EH to MP, Mar. 19, 1938; MP to FSF, Apr. 8, 1938; FSF to MP, Apr. 23, 1938.

FSF in Hollywood: MP to EL, Jan. 22, 1938; FSF to MP, Mar. 4, 1938; FSF to MP, Apr. 23, 1938; MP to FSF, Mar. 9, 1938; MP to FSF, May 24, 1938.

LSP's conversion: Caroline Gordon Tate to ASB (I), Sept. 12, 1971; EL to ASB (I), Apr. 14, 1972; JHW to ASB (I), Oct. 20, 1971; BSF to ASB (I), June 5, 1975; NJ to ASB (I), Apr. 21, 1972; PK to ASB (I), Mar. 28, 1972; BSF to ASB (I), Mar. 5, 1972; MKR to MP, May 14, 1938; MP to EL, Oct. 18, 1934; MP to EL, Feb. 15, 1938; MP to EL, July 7, 1938; EEG to ASB (I), June 11, 1973; MP to EL, Aug. 23, 1938.

Taylor Caldwell: CS to TC, June 26, 1947; MP to Nancy Hale, May 6, 1938; TC to MP, Mar. 9, 1938; MP to TC, Apr. 27, 1938; MP to TC, May 16, 1938; MP to Ray Stannard Baker, Aug. 30, 1940; TC to MP, Apr. 6, 1938; MP to TC, Apr. 9, 1938; TC to MP, May 14, 1938; MP to TC, May 17, 1938.

TW and MP working apart: TW to Belinda Jelliffe, Apr. 11, 1938; TW to EN, May 3, 1938; TW to Edward Aswell, May 6, 1938; TW to Mabel Wolfe Wheaton, May 10, 1938; TW to EN, May 12, 1938; EN to William A. Jackson, Jan. 4, 1951; TW to EN, June 15, 1938; TW to EN, June 19, 1938; TW to EN, July 3, 1938; Edward Aswell to TW, July 1, 1938; TW to Edward Aswell, July 4, 1938; Edward Aswell to TW, July 6, 1938.

TW's illness: Dr. E. C. Ruge to Edward Aswell (telegram), July 12, 1938, 5:17 P.M.; Dr. E. C. Ruge to Edward Aswell (telegram), ca. July 14, 1938; MP to Fred Wolfe, July 25, 1938; Fred Wolfe to MP, Aug. 1, 1938; MP to Fred Wolfe, Aug. 3, 1938; MP to TW, Aug. 9, 1938; MP to Fred Wolfe, Aug. 10, 1938; TW to MP, Aug. 12, 1938; MP to TW, Aug. 19, 1938; Fred Wolfe to MP, Aug. 22, 1938.

EH home from Spanish war: MP to Waldo Peirce, June 2, 1938; EH to MP, June 11, 1938; EH to MP, July 12, 1938; MP to FSF, Sept. 1, 1938.

FSF doing well in Hollywood: MP to FSF, June 29, 1938.

EL's new house: MP to FSF, Sept. 1, 1938; MP to EL, Aug. 23, 1938.

TW's final days: Mabel Wolfe Wheaton, *Thomas Wolfe and His Family* (Garden City: Doubleday, 1961), pp. 289–90; Dr. George Swift to Edward Aswell, Sept. 7, 1938; Fred Wolfe to MP, Sept. 11, 1938; Mabel Wolfe Wheaton, recorded interview, Feb. 23, 1947 (Harvard); MP to John Terry, Nov. 13, 1945; MP to Paul Weiss, Sept. 30, 1940; MP to Elizabeth Perkins, Sept. 13, 1938.

TW's death and funeral: MP to Fred Wolfe, Sept. 15, 1938; MP to SA, Sept. 23, 1938; *Car. Mag.*, p. 15; *King Lear*, V:3, 315; MP to EL, Sept. 19, 1938; *HLB*, p. 276; MP to John Terry, Nov. 13, 1945.

XIX. TO EVERYTHING A SEASON

MP's reaction to TW's death: MP to EH, Nov. 10, 1938; MP to EL, Sept. 30, 1931; *War and Peace*, Book XV: Chap. 1; Irma Wyckoff Muench to ASB (I), Feb. 18, 1972; MP to Elizabeth Perkins, Oct. 14, 1938; MP to John Creedy, Sept. 28, 1938; *Car. Mag.*, p. 17; MP to EL, Dec. 12, 1938; FSF to MP, Sept.

29, 1938; MP to Paul Weiss, Sept. 30, 1940; EN to Mrs. Robert Armstrong, Oct. 17, 1938; MP to Mrs. Russell E. Vemnon, Oct. 11, 1938.

Piecing *The Web and the Rock* together: Edward C. Aswell, "A Note on Thomas Wolfe," in TW, *The Hills Beyond* (New York: Harper, 1941), p. 369.

Reading about "The Fox": MP to EH, Dec. 8, 1938; *YCGHA*, pp. 438, 439, 441, 446, 491, 493; MP to EL, Dec. 12, 1938.

S. S. Van Dine's final days and death: JHW to ASB (I), June 5, 1975; Claire Wright to MP, Apr. 26, 1939; MP, Preface to *Winter Murder Case*, p. ix.

Chard Powers Smith: Smith, "Perkins and the Elect," *The Antioch Review*, Spring, 1962, pp. 87–98; Chard Powers Smith to MP, Oct. 22, 1938; MP to EL, Dec. 12, 1938; MP to Chard Powers Smith, Oct. 5, 1938; MP to Chard Powers Smith, Nov. 14, 1938; MP to EL, June 21, 1939.

EH preparing to write: EH to MP, Oct. 28, 1939; EH to MP, Dec. 24, 1938.

MP's saddest year: MP to FSF, Dec. 30, 1938; MP to MKR, Jan. 25, 1939; EEG to ASB (I), June 11, 1973.

EH starts *For Whom the Bell Tolls*: MP to EH, Jan. 26, 1939; EH to MP, Feb. 7, 1939; MP to EH, Feb. 10, 1939; EH to MP, Mar. 25, 1939; EH to MP, May 10, 1939; MP to EH, Mar. 29, 1939; EH to MP, Dec. 8, 1939; EH to MP, ca. Jan. 13, 1940, quoted in MP to EH, Feb. 14, 1940.

EH rereads *Tender Is the Night*: EH to MP, Mar. 25, 1939.

FSF passes through NY: MP to EL, Oct. 26, 1938; MP to FSF, Jan. 18, 1939.

FSF concerned about career, begins *The Last Tycoon*: FSF to MP, Dec. 24, 1938; MP to FSF, Jan. 18, 1939; FSF to MP, Feb. 25, 1939; FSF to MP, May 20, 1940; FSF to MP, Jan. 4, 1939; MP to EH, Apr. 27, 1939; EH to MP, May 10, 1939; FSF to MP, May 22, 1939.

FSF squabble with Harold Ober: MP to FSF, July 26, 1939; FSF to Harold Ober, Aug. 2, 1939; FSF to MP, Aug. 3, 1939; MP to FSF, Aug. 9, 1939.

LSP as a Catholic: JO to ASB (I), May 8, 1972; MP to MKR, Mar. 11, 1939.

Peggy's marriage: MP to EL, Dec. 12, 1938.

MP's burdens as editor-in-chief: MP to EL, June 21, 1939; MC notes, BSF to ASB (I), Mar. 14, 1975.

The Web and the Rock: MP to EL, June 20, 1939; MP to EL, June 21, 1939; MP to Norman Schrager, July 15, 1941; TW, *The Web and the Rock*, pp. 313–14; MP to MKR, July 28, 1939; MP to EH, July 14, 1939.

YCGHA: FSF to MP, Feb. 25, 1939; MP to FSF, Feb. 27, 1939; dust jacket of *YCGHA*; MP to EL, May 4, 1940; MP to EL, May 22, 1940; Irma Wyckoff Muench to ASB (I), Feb. 18, 1972; *HLB*, p. 275; MP to Henry Volkening, Aug. 9, 1940; *YCGHA*, p. 743; EH to MP, ca. Nov., 1940.

EH upon outbreak of war: EH to MP, Sept. 3, 1939.

Churchill: MP to EH, July 29, 1939; MP to Charles T. Copeland, July 18, 1940; Irma Wyckoff Muench to ASB (I), Feb. 18, 1972; NJ to ASB (I), Apr. 21, 1972; Irma Wyckoff Muench to ASB, Sept. 14, 1974; MP to Alexander Woollcott, Oct. 9, 1940.

Writing *For Whom the Bell Tolls*: EH to MP, Oct. 27, 1939; EH to MP, Nov. 12, 1939; MP to EH, Nov. 21, 1939; MP to EH, Jan. 18 and 19, 1940; EH to MP, ca. early Feb., 1940; EH to MP, Nov. 30, 1939; EH to MP, Feb. 18, 1940; MP to EH, Mar. 12, 1940; EH to MP, Apr. 21, 1940; MP to EH, Apr. 22 and 24, 1940; MP to EL, May 4, 1940; EH to MP, July 1, 1940.

Editing *For Whom the Bell Tolls*: MP to MKR, Aug. 7, 1940; *For Whom the Bell Tolls,* p. 256; MP to EH, Aug. 28, 1940; EH to MP, Aug. 26, 1940; MP to EH, Aug. 30, 1940; MP to EH, Oct. 15, 1940.

Sherwood Anderson: MP to SA, Aug. 1, 1933; SA to MP, Aug. 10, 1933; SA to MP, 1935, quoted in *OMMB,* p. 10; SA to MP, Jan. 2, 1936; SA to MP, early Sept., 1937; SA to MP, July 25, 1938; SA to MP, ca. Sept. 12, 1938; SA to MP, June 18, 1936; SA to MP, August 9, 1940; MP to SA, Aug. 12, 1940; MP to SA, Aug. 14, 1940; SA to MP, Aug. 16, 1940; MP to SA, Nov. 20, 1940; SA to MP, Nov. 30, 1940.

Writers dying: EH to MP, Apr. 29, 1941.

Writing *The Last Tycoon*: FSF to MP, Oct. 11 and 14, 1939; MP to FSF, Oct. 16, 1939; SG, *The Real F. Scott Fitzgerald: Thirty-five Years Later* (New York: Grosset & Dunlap, 1976), p. 71; FSF to MP, Oct. 20, 1939; FSF to MP, Nov. 20 and 28, 1939; MP to FSF, Nov. 30, 1939; FSF to MP, Nov. 29, 1939; MP to FSF, Dec. 7, 1939; MP to EH, Dec. 19, 1939; FSF to MP, Dec. 26, 1939; MP to FSF, Jan. 2, 1940; MP to EH, Jan. 11, 1940; FSF to MP, ca. Jan. 6, 1940; MP to FSF, Jan. 9, 1940; MP to Struthers Burt, Jan. 9, 1940; FSF to MP, Feb. 21, 1940; FSF to MP, May 20, 1940; FSF to Scottie Fitzgerald, Oct. 31, 1939; FSF to ZSF, June 14, 1940.

MP thinking of EL: FSF to MP, May 20, 1940; EL to ASB, Feb. 15, 1973; EL to ASB (I), Apr. 24, 1972; MP to EL, May 4, 1940.

EH and Martha Gellhorn: MP to FSF, Aug. 20, 1940; EH to MP, May 10, 1939; MP to FSF, Sept. 19, 1940; FSF to MP, Oct. 14, 1940.

For Whom the Bell Tolls, publication and reaction: MP to EL, Oct. 24, 1940, EH's inscription recorded in SG, *College of One* (New York: Viking Press, 1967), p. 159; FSF to EH, Nov. 8, 1940; FSF, "Notebooks," *CU,* p. 181.

FSF plans to finish *The Last Tycoon*: FSF to MP, Dec. 13, 1940; MP to FSF, Dec. 17, 1940.

XX. DIMINUTIONS

FSF death and postmortem: SG, *The Real F. Scott Fitzgerald,* p. 214; ZSF to MP, ca. Dec. 23, 1940; MP to ZSF, Dec. 26, 1940; ZSF to MP, ca. Dec. 31,

1940; MP to John Peale Bishop, Dec. 28, 1940; Margaret Turnbull to ASB (I), July 24, 1971; MP to EH, Dec. 28, 1940; Frances Kroll to MP, Dec. 26, 1940; Andrew Turnbull to MP, Dec. 28, 1940; MP to ZSF, Jan. 3, 1941; Scottie Fitzgerald to MP, Jan. 12, 1941; MP to Scottie Fitzgerald, Jan. 15, 1941; MP to Scottie Fitzgerald, May 15, 1941; ZSF to MP, Jan. 27, 1941.

Salvaging *The Last Tycoon*: ZSF to MP, Jan. 27, 1941; MP to EH, Apr. 14, 1941; SG to MP, Jan. 1, 1941; FSF to Norma Shearer (unsent letter), n.d.; FSF, undated note to himself; MP to SG, Jan. 31, 1941; SG to MP, Feb. 4, 1941; MP to Gerald Murphy, Feb. 7, 1941; MP to John Biggs, Mar. 4, 1941; MP to Scottie Fitzgerald, Feb. 15, 1941; MP to John Biggs, Mar. 25, 1941; EW, Foreword to FSF's *The Last Tycoon,* pp. x-xi; MP to John Biggs, June 11, 1941.

MP securing FSF's reputation: MP to John Biggs, Apr. 4, 1941; Matthew Josephson to ASB, Apr. 17, 1976.

EH getting short shrift: EH to MP, ca. late Mar., 1941; MP to EH, Apr. 4, 1941; MP to EH, Apr. 22, 1941.

EW and Maxwell Geismar; disputes over EH: EW, "Hemingway: Gauge of Morale," p. 239n; EH to MP, Aug. 26, 1941; MP to William B. Wisdom, Aug. 19, 1941; MP to Maxwell Geismar, June 19, 1941; Caroline Gordon Tate to MC,n.d. (MC notes) ; Maxwell Geismar to ASB, Aug. 22, 1974.

MP and nonfiction: JHW, Introduction, *Editor to Author,* p. 7; JHW to ASB (I), June 5, 1975; MP to Dixon Wecter, May 6, 1941; MP to Dixon Wecter, Dec. 4, 1940; David Randall, *Dukedom Large Enough* (New York: Random House, 1969), p. 93; MP to EH, Aug. 13 and 21, 1942; James Truslow Adams, *The American* (New York: Scribners, 1943), p. 356; PK to ASB (I), Nov. 23, 1974; Martha Gellhorn to ASB (I), May 10, 1972.

TC and historicals: MP to TC, Oct. 17 and 26, 1939; TC to MP, Nov. 4, 1939; MP to TC, Nov. 17, 1939.

Cross Creek: MKR to MP, May 13, 1939; MP to MKR, Sept. 20, 1940; *Cross Creek,* p. 1.

MP and troubled writers: MP to "anonymous," Mar. 11, 1941; Nancy Hale to ASB, Aug. 27, 1974; MP to Nancy Hale, Feb. 20, 1940.

Valley of Decision: Davenport, *Too Strong for Fantasy,* p. 297; MP to MKR, Nov. 13, 1942; MP to Marcia Davenport, Mar. 30, 1942; MC notes.

Pearl Harbor; nebulous idea for EH: MP to EL, Dec. 23, 1941; MP to EH, Sept. 25, 1941; MP to EH, Oct. 29, 1941; EH to MP, Nov. 15, 1941.

Reaction to *The Last Tycoon*: SG to MP, Nov. 9, 1941; ZSF to MP, Oct. 31, 1941; Stephen Vincent Benét, *Saturday Review of Literature,* Dec. 6, 1941, p. 10; EH to MP, Nov. 15, 1941; *AMF,* p. 147; MP to EH, Nov. 24, 1941.

Men at War: MP to EH, Feb. 25, 1942; EH to MP, May 30, 1942; MP to Alexander Woollcott, Oct. 22, 1942; EH to MP, May 30, 1942; MP to EH, June 8, 1942; MP to EH, Sept. 4, 1942.

MP's concern with the war: MP to EL, July 21, 1943; PK to ASB (I),

Mar. 28, 1972; Corinne Cornish to ASB (I), Jan. 20, 1972; Edward Thomas to ASB (I), Apr. 9, 1972.

XXI. PORTRAIT IN GRAY AND BLACK

MP running down: NJ to ASB (I), Apr. 20, 1972; MP to EL, July 17, 1942; MP to Viola Irene Cooper, Oct. 12, 1945; MC notes; JHW to ASB (I), Oct. 20, 1971; Ann Chidester to MP, ca. Aug. 3, 1943; MP to Ann Chidester, Aug. 5, 1943; JHW, Introduction, *Editor to Author,* p. 5; Wallace Meyer to ASB (I), Apr. 1, 1972; EH to MP, Sept. 7, 1942; MP to EH, Sept. 17, 1942.

Alexander Woollcott: MP to Alexander Woollcott, Jan. 18, 1942.

MP's "newspaper" and political views: JHW to ASB (I), Oct. 20, 1971; EEG to ASB (I), Dec. 3, 1972; MP to Raymond Thompson, Feb. 18, 1943; MP to EN, Aug. 1, 1945; Mark Aldanov, *The Fifth Seal* (New York: Scribners, 1943), p. 482.

Spectacular 1943 book season: MP to EL, July 21, 1943; Marcia Davenport to MP, Oct. 20, 1942; Marcia Davenport, *Too Strong for Fantasy,* pp. 298, 309, 369; Marcia Davenport to ASB (I), Apr. 10, 1972; MP to EL, Oct. 5, 1942; MP to Nancy Hale, Oct. 21, 1942.

MP as negotiator: George Schieffelin to ASB (I), Apr. 3, 1972.

Christine Weston and other women: Christine Weston to ASB, June 31, 1972; Elizabeth Youngstrom to ASB (I), Apr. 4, 1972; MP to Charles T. Copeland, Jan. 3, 1940; Gunther Stuhlmann, Introduction, *The Diary of Anaïs Nin:* 1931–1934 (New York: Swallow Press, 1966), p. xi; Anonymous source to ASB (I), Nov. 25, 1971.

Scottie Fitzgerald's wedding, ZSF's reaction: MP to EH, Apr. 2, 1943; ZSF to MP, ca. late Feb., 1943; ZSF to MP, ca. Nov., 1944.

Publishing "The Crack-Up": MP to John Biggs, Jan. 26, 1945.

TW's reputation and letters: MP to Mabel Wolfe Wheaton, Dec. 22, 1943; AB to MP, ca. June 1, 1943 and June 7, 1943; MP to AB, June 3, 1943; David Randall, *Dukedom Large Enough* (New York: Random House, 1969), pp. 244, 248; AB to MP, ca. June 7, 1945.

MP and movies: MP to Evan Shipman, July 22, 1943; PK to ASB (I), Mar. 28, 1972.

Martha Gellhorn "turns back" on EH: MP to Evan Shipman, July 22, 1943; MP to Sidney Franklin, May 24, 1943; Dr. Gregory Hemingway, *Papa* (Boston: Houghton Mifflin, 1976), p. 90; Martha Gellhorn to ASB (I), May 10, 1972; EH to MP, ca. Aug. 1, 1943; EH to MP, June 10, 1943; Dr. Gregory Hemingway to ASB (I), Feb. 11, 1972; EH to MP, Aug. 10, 1943; Wallace Meyer to ASB (I), Apr. 1, 1972.

EH goes to war: EH to MP, Oct. 15, 1944.

MP withdrawing, craving anonymity: Marcia Davenport to ASB (I), Apr.

10, 1972; MP to M. M. Hoover, May 24, 1943; MP to R. W. Cowden, Feb. 9, 1945; MP to EL, Sept. 15, 1943.

New Yorker Profile: EN to William A. Jackson, n.d. (Houghton Library, 46am7-24v); EN to MC, Feb. 23, 1943 (MC notes); MC to William Shawn, Apr. 8, 1943; MC notes; J. H. Wilson's *The Life of John A. Rawlins,* quoted in *Dictionary of American Biography,* vol. VIII, p. 403.

Faulkner: MP to MC, Jan. 31, 1944; MC to William Faulkner, July 22, 1944; MC to ASB (I), May 18, 1972; *The Faulkner-Cowley File* (London: Chatto & Windus, 1966), p. 10n.

The Autobiography of Ephraim Tutt: Arthur Train, *Mr. Tutt Finds a Way,* pp. 9, 16, 228; *New York Times,* May 16, 1944, p. 23.

Joseph Stanley Pennell: MP to Samuel H. Watts of New Canaan, Aug. 22, 1944; *Look Homeward, Angel,* p. vii; MP to Pennell, Feb. 19, 1943; MP to Pennell, Mar. 29, 1943; MP to Pennell, Mar. 19, 1943; Pennell to MP, ca. Apr. 1, 1943; MP to Pennell, Apr. 8, 1943; MKR to MP, Oct. 11, 1944; Marguerite Cohn to ASB (I), Feb. 16, 1972; MP to Pennell, Mar. 29, 1943; Hamilton Basso, *The New Yorker,* July 15, 1944, pp. 66, 69.

New Yorker Profile published: MC, "Unshaken Friend," *The New Yorker,* April 1 and 8, 1944; MP to Esther Meyer, May 19, 1944; MP to Nancy Hale, Apr. 18, 1944; MC to William Shawn, Apr. 7, 1944; MP to MKR, Apr. 19, 1944.

MP sick: MP to EH, July 28, 1944; MP to EL, May 18, 1935; MP to MKR, June 23, 1944; MP to MKR, July 27, 1944; MP to MKR, Oct. 17, 1944; MP to EH, July 28, 1944; Carol Brandt to ASB (I), May 17, 1972.

TC describes MP's office: TC, *The Final Hour,* p. 191; MC notes.

MP indulging EH: MP to EH, Mar. 6, 1945; MP to EH, Mar. 20, 1945; EH to MP, Apr. 14, 1945; MP to EH, Apr. 19, 1945; MP to EH, June 5, 1945.

MP and infuriated reader: MP to Esther Meyer, May 25 and 31, 1944; MP to Esther Meyer, May 19, 1944.

MP coping with burdens: MP to EL, June 1, 1945.

XXII. A TOSS OF THE HAT

James Jones: JJ to ASB (I), Mar. 3, 1972; JJ, quoted in *Twentieth-Century Authors: First Supplement,* p. 581; MP to Maxwell Aley, Feb. 28, 1945; JJ to MP, Feb. 10, 1946; MP to JJ, Feb. 15, 1946; JJ to MP, Feb. 17, 1946; MP to JJ, Feb. 19, 1946; dust jacket of *From Here to Eternity;* JJ to MP, Feb. 22, 1946; MP to JJ, June 5, 1946; JJ to MP, Oct. 21, 1946; MP to JJ, Mar. 27, 1946; MP to JJ, July 30, 1946.

Vance Bourjaily: Vance Bourjaily to ASB (I), Jan. 17, 1978.

MP's accident and fatigue: MP to EH, Jan. 9, 1946; Joan Terrall to ASB

(I), Mar. 19, 1972; Burroughs Mitchell to ASB (I), Oct. 1, 1970; CS to EH, Aug. 7, 1946; EH to MP, Oct. 4, 1946, MP to EH, Oct. 3, 1946.

EH working at new novel: Carlos Baker, *Ernest Hemingway: A Life Story* (New York: Scribners, 1969), p. 454; EH to MP, Oct. 31, 1945; MP to EH, Jan. 9, 1946; MP to JJ, Nov. 19, 1946.

More deaths: MP to Katherine Newlin Burt, Dec. 2, 1946.

OMMB: *OMMB,* p. 332.

MP on selecting books: CS IV to ASB (I), Feb. 14, 1972; JHW to ASB (I), Oct. 20, 1971; VWB Auto, p. 573.

Alan Paton: Aubrey Burns to ASB, Apr. 23, 1973; MP to Alan Paton, Jan. 20, 1947; Alan Paton to Aubrey and Marigold Burns, Feb. 9, 1947; Alan Paton to Aubrey Burns, Feb. 11, 1947; Alan Paton to Aubrey Burns, Apr. 9, 1947; MP to Alan Paton, May 6 and 14, 1947; Alan Paton to MP, June 10, 1947; Alan Paton to MP, Apr. 23, 1947; Alan Paton to MP, June 10, 1947.

MP as teacher: Gilbert Highet, *The Art of Teaching* (New York: Knopf, 1950), pp. 50, 52; Kenneth McCormick to ASB (I), June 3, 1975; Storer Lunt to ASB, June 22, 1975; Kenneth McCormick to ASB (I), June 6, 1973.

East Side, West Side: Marcia Davenport to MP, Mar. 9, 1946; Marcia Davenport to MP, ca. Apr. 20, 1947; MP to Marcia Davenport, Apr. 28, 1947; Marcia Davenport to MP, May 18, 1947; MP to Marcia Davenport, June 9, 1947; Marcia Davenport to MP, June 12, 1947; Marcia Davenport to MP, May 31, 1947.

Final words on EH: MP to EH, June 5, 1947; JHW to ASB (I), Oct. 20, 1971.

Final advice to JJ: MP to JJ, May 28, 1947; JJ to ASB (I), Mar. 3, 1972; JJ to MP, June 23, 1946.

MP's final illness: BSF to ASB (I), Oct. 31, 1971; LSP to EL, July 28, 1947.

MP's death: NJ to ASB (I), Apr. 22, 1972; Jean Lancaster to ASB (I), May 22, 1972; EEG to ASB (I), June 11, 1973; LSP to VWB, July 8, 1947; Irma Wyckoff Muench to Mrs. James Boyd, June 26, 1947; *War and Peace,* Book XII:4.

Postmortem: CS to EH, June 25, 1947; EH to CS, Sept. 18, 1947; EL to ASB (I), May 24, 1975; EL to LSP, late June, 1947; Chard Powers Smith, "Perkins and the Elect," *The Antioch Review,* Spring, 1962, p. 102; VWB to LSP, June 18, 1947; JJ to CSS, ca. June 25, 1947.

LSP's final years: Mary Colum to VWB, ca. July, 1947; EL to ASB (I), Apr. 14, 1972.

Jane Perkins married George Owen, an Englishman, in 1949; Nancy Perkins married Reid Jorgensen in 1953.

Index

Grateful acknowledgment is made for permission to reprint the following: Quotations from *Editor to Author: The Letters of Maxwell E. Perkins*, edited by John Hall Wheelock; quotations from *The Letters of F. Scott Fitzgerald;* quotations from *Dear Scott/Dear Max: The Fitzgerald–Perkins Correspondence*, edited by John Kuehl and Jackson Bryer; quotations from *The Letters of Thomas Wolfe;* and brief excerpts from *Ring Around Max: The Correspondence of Ring Lardner & Maxwell Perkins*, edited by Clifford Caruthers; *Thomas Wolfe's Letters to His Mother*, edited by John Terry; *Of Making Many Books*, by Roger Burlingame; *The Great Gatsby*, by F. Scott Fitzgerald; *A Moveable Feast*, by Ernest Hemingway; *Look Homeward, Angel*, by Thomas Wolfe; *The Story of a Novel*, by Thomas Wolfe; and *Too Strong for Fantasy*, by Marcia Davenport are all used with the permission of Charles Scribner's Sons and are fully protected by copyright. Heretofore unpublished excerpts from Maxwell E. Perkins's business correspondence are also used with the permission of Charles Scribner's Sons. 900 words (ad passim) from *You Can't Go Home Again*, by Thomas Wolfe. Copyright 1934, 1937, 1938, 1939, 1940 by Maxwell Perkins as Executor; 120 words from *The Web and the Rock*, by Thomas Wolfe. Copyright 1937, 1938, 1939 by Maxwell Perkins as Executor; and 181 words from "A Note on Thomas Wolfe" in *The Hills Beyond*, by Thomas Wolfe. Copyright 1935, 1936, 1937, 1939, 1941 by Maxwell Perkins as Executor are all reprinted by permission of Harper & Row Publishers, Inc. Excerpts from the July 1, 1938 and the July 6, 1938 letters of Edward C. Aswell to Thomas Wolfe are reprinted courtesy of Harper & Row Publishers, Inc. Quotation from *Living Well Is the Best Revenge*, by Calvin Tomkins, which first appeared in *The New Yorker*, reprinted by permission of the Viking Press. Quotations from *Copey of Harvard*, by J. Donald Adams, reprinted by permission of Houghton Mifflin. Quotations from *Thomas Wolfe*, by Elizabeth Nowell, Copyright © 1960 by Doubleday & Co., Inc., reprinted by permission of the publishers. Quotations from *The Letters of Sherwood Anderson*, selected and edited by Howard Mumford Jones, reprinted by permission of Little, Brown. Quotations from *Call It Experience*, by Erskine Caldwell, reprinted by permission of McIntosh & Otis, Inc. Quotations from *Van Wyck Brooks: An Autobiography*. Copyright © 1954, 1957, 1961 by Van Wyck Brooks; © by Gladys Brooks. Reprinted by permission of the publishers, E. P. Dutton. Quotations from *The Crack-Up* by F. Scott Fitzgerald. Copyright 1931 by Charles Scribner's Sons, Copyright 1934 and 1936 by Esquire Inc., Copyright 1945 by New Directions Publishing Corporation. Reprinted by permission of New Directions Publishing Corporation. Quotations from Struthers Burt's "Catalyst for Genius" and Bernard De Voto's "Genius Is Not Enough" reprinted by permission of *The Saturday Review*. Quotations from "Unshaken Friend" are copyright 1944 by *The New Yorker;* renewal copyright 1972 by Malcolm Cowley. Portions of "Thomas Wolfe" by Maxwell E. Perkins were originally published in *Harvard Library Bulletin*. Unpublished quotations of Thomas Wolfe, permission granted by Paul Gitlin, Administrator, C. T. A. of the Estate of Thomas Wolfe. Unpublished quotations of Ernest Hemingway published with permission granted by Mary Hemingway, Executor of the Estate of Ernest Hemingway. Unpublished quotations of Maxwell E. Perkins, permission granted by Irma Wyckoff Muench, Executrix of the Estate of Maxwell E. Perkins.

A. Scott Berg graduated from Princeton University, where his senior thesis on Maxwell Perkins received the Charles William Kennedy Prize. He spent the next seven years expanding that thesis into *Max Perkins: Editor of Genius*, which became a national bestseller and won the National Book Award. The recipient of a Guggenheim Fellowship, he has also published the international bestseller *Goldwyn: A Biography*. He lives in Los Angeles.